Butterfield's Overland Mail Co. as REPORTED in Arkansas' Newspapers of 1858 - 1861

by

Bob Crossman

Revised September 2025

To learn about the STAGECOACH LAND ROUTE across Arkansas,
refer to Bob Crossman's 2025 book:
"Butterfield's Overland Mail STAGECOACH Route Across Arkansas: 1858-1861"

To learn about John Butterfield's use of STEAMBOATS
refer to Bob Crossman's 2025 book:
"Butterfield's Overland Mail Co. use of STEAMBOATS to Deliver Mail and Passengers Across Arkansas 1858-1861"

Revised September 2025
Ingram Spark Press, First Edition 2022

John Butterfield, President, Butterfield Overland Mail Co.

Revised September 2025
ISBN: 978-0-9996578-7-4 Paperback
ISBN: 978-0-9996578-8-1 Hardback

Table of Contents

Introduction

The newspapers of Arkansas did an amazing job of covering the news around **Butterfield's Overland Mail Company.** Frequently the newspaper editors would draw information from an exchange of newspapers across the country to bring to their subscribers the most accurate and comprehensive description of facts as possible.

This book greatly expands my two previous books, *"Butterfield's Overland Mail Co. STAGECOACH Trail Across Arkansas 1858-1861,"* and *"Butterfield's Overland Mail Co. use of STEAMBOATS to Deliver Mail and Passengers Across Arkansas 1858-1861."*

While in these two previous books, I only included brief excerpts from the Arkansas newspapers of 1857-1861, in this book I have let the newspaper reporters tell the story in their own words.

It has been difficult, but I have limited my interpretive comments to a brief title I have assigned each article. In this way, today's reader can immerse themselves into the world of the 19th century citizens of Arkansas. Within a handful of articles, I have added an editorial note or definitions within brackets [ ] and italic type.

While the purpose of my research of the Overland Mail Company was to satisfy my personal curiosity, hopefully this collection of my research will also expand the pool of knowledge about the Butterfield Overland National Historic Trail.

In most cases I replicated the original newspaper's capitalization, punctuation, and spelling.

Newspapers of this period did not have the ability to print photographs. I have added photographs to embellish the text.

To assist today's readers, in most instances I have capitalized and used bold type for the words: **Butterfield** or **Overland Mail**.

Bob Crossman

Military Road used by Butterfield's Overland Mail Stagecoaches
This segment is near the author's home between the Cadron Ferry (Conway) and the Anthony House Home Station (Little Rock). The photo is circa 1947. Source: Pine Mountain Americans, by Ruff Haydn, Hobson Book Press, 110 pages, January 1, 1947

1824

July 20, 1824
Old Military Road Across Arkansas
(Used by Butterfield's stagecoaches 30 years later.)

July 20, 1824, page 3
The Arkansas Gazette, Arkansas Post, Arkansas

...The Military Road from hence *[Little Rock]* to Memphis, authorized by an act passed during the late session of Congress, which will probably be completed in all next summer, will be of incalculable benefit to this place, and to the Territory in general. It will open a direct channel through

which a large portion of the emigration to the Territory will pass, and will, no doubt, tend considerably towards making this a populous and wealthy town.
[NOTE: Construction on the Military Road did not begin until 1826. In the August 22, 1826 issue of the Arkansas Gazette, we find: *"Mr. Hunt, the Contractor for the first four miles of the Military Road has commenced opening it. Messrs. Carr, Irvin, and Anderson, will commence the 60 miles contracted for by them, on the 1st of September next."]*

1827

July 3, 1827
Military Road Specifications
(in 30 years Butterfield's stagecoaches used this road)

July 3, 1827
Arkansas Gazette, Little Rock, Arkansas

The road... will be cut full sixteen feet wide *[other documents say 24 feet wide]*. The timber, brush, drift, rocks, and every species of obstruction, are to be cleared from the surface, and all holes to be filled up, so as to render the passage smooth and easy. Large sized trees much be cut off within one foot of the ground, and the stumps hollowed outwards the centre; and saplings, at no more than 3 inches. In marshes, swamps, and bogs, a causeway is to be constructed, and the whole width of the road, to be made of rails or poles, 4 inches in diameter at the small end. They must be laid compactly together, perpendicular to the line of direction, and covered with a layer of about 12 inches of solid earth in the middle, and 6 inches on the sides, of the causeway. Substantial riders of durable timber, must be pinned on each side of the causeway, in such parts of the road, as is liable to be subjected to the effects of overflow. A ditch must be dug on the sides of the causeway, 18 inches wide and 12 inches deep.

In prairie land, which is liable to be boggy in wet sea-

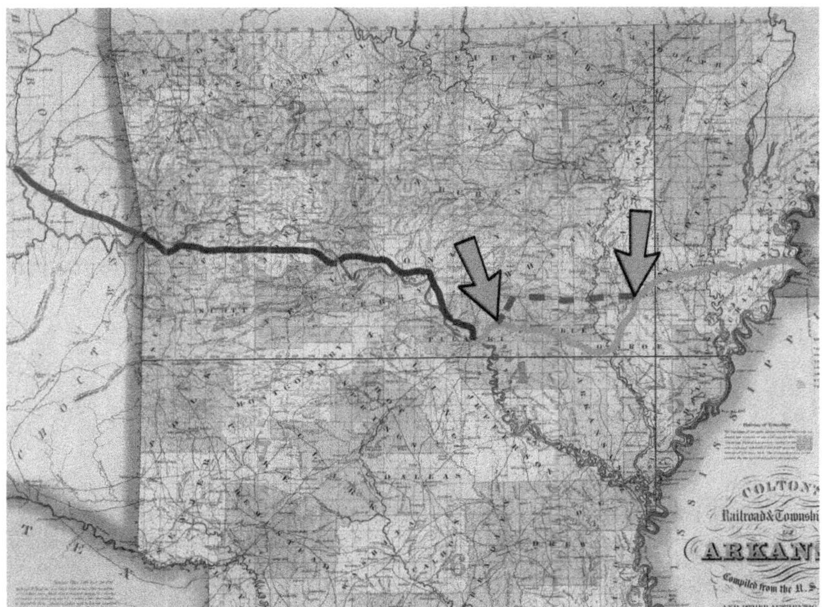

1828 Old Military Road (completed in 1839) Memphis to Fort Gibson
Butterfield used this route from Memphis to Fort Smith, with two exceptions:
he used an alternate route (shown in a dotted line between the arrows);
and Butterfield used the railroad the first 24 miles out of Memphis.

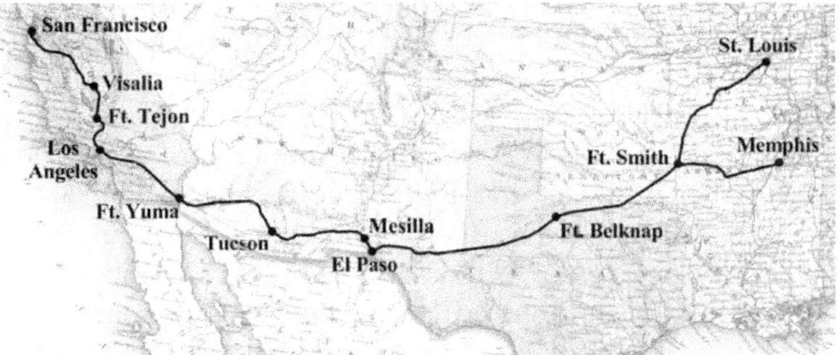

The Complete route of Butterfield's Overland Mail Company
Map from "Mails of the Westward Expansion, 1803 to 1861"
by Steven C. Walske and Richard C. Frajola

sons, a ditch of a similar kind must be dug on each side of the road, and the earth removed and thrown on the road, in such a manner as to raise it in the centre.

All hills and small elevations, on the line of the road, are to be sloped off each way, so as to permit wagons, etc. to pass with convenience.

The banks of all creeks, branches, streams and ravines, on the route, are to be dug down so as to render the ascent and descent safe and easy at all seasons of the year.

1849

July 11, 1849
Before the Butterfield Overland
It took Four Months by Wagon to Reach California

July 11, 1849
Fort Smith Weekly Herald, Fort Smith, Arkansas

From the Arkansas State Democrat, July 6, The Arkansas Route to California – It is desirable that all persons who may be contemplating an **overland** trip to California should be informed that, according to the testimony of Col. Cooke, of the U. S. Army, the route by the river Gila is A GOOD WAGON ROAD, and especially adapted for a journey during the WINTER MONTHS. The climate is mild. In the winter of '46, Col. Cooke went to California by this route and saw no snow.

The GREAT NATIONAL ROAD from Fort Smith to California, by the way of the settlements of New Mexico along the valley of the Rio Grande, and to Col. Cooke's route, had just been surveyed, opened, and put in good order, by a corps of U. S. Topographical Engineers, and a strong force of soldiers and emigrants. By this road, California can be reached from Fort Smith in about two months by pack mules, and in about four months by wagons.

Companies leaving Fort Smith, Arks., as late as October, can travel as slowly as they choose, and yet have ample time to arrive in the gold regions before the commencement of the season for digging.

The character of the country over which the Great National Road to the settlements of New Mexico is located, is such as to warrant a good supply of grass or 'range,' for the subsistence of any number of teams which may be started on this route at the time above stated; down the valley of the Rio Grande, and over Col. Cooke's route by the Gila, any amount of supplies and forage can be readily obtained.

The Arkansas River is well supplied with good steamboats capable of reaching Fort Smith at the lowest stage of water.

Old Fort Smith

The fort was built in 1838, and was used until 1871.

1850

January 8, 1850
Mail Delivery to Gold Rush '49s by Ocean Steamship to California Across the Isthmus

January 8, 1850, Tuesday, page 1

The Arkansas Banner, Little Rock, Arkansas

... it is believed they will shortly apply for the admission of California into the Union as a sovereign state...

By an act of Congress, passed August 14th, 1848, provision was made for extending Post Office and mail accommodations to California and Oregon. Exertions have been made to execute that law, but the limited provisions of the act, the inadequacy of the means to authorities, the inadaptation of our Post Office laws to the situations of that country, and the measure of compensation for services allowed by those laws, compared with the prices of labor and rent to California, renders those exertions in a great deal of ineffectual...

Complaints have been made in regard to the inefficiency of the means provided by the government of New Granada, for transporting the United States Mail across the Isthmus of Panama, pursuant to our postal convention with that Republic of March 6th, 1846. Our charge d'affaires at Bogota has been directed to make such representations to the government of New Granada, and will, it is hoped, lead to a prompt removal of this cause of complaint.

January 8, 1850
Military Road to the Pacific Needed

January 8, 1850, Tuesday, page 2
The Arkansas Banner, Little Rock, Arkansas

MILITARY ROAD TO THE PACIFIC – Among the subjects which should engage the immediate attention of Congress is the construction of a military road, by a line of military posts, to the Pacific. By military road, we mean the removal of obstructions and the erection of posts to supply aid to the emigrant travel to Oregon and California.

... these military post should be established as near to each other as one hundred miles.

In sixty days the traveller would traverse the whole distance between the Sacramento and the Missouri. In a short time we should have a telegraph line, and our people on the Pacific and those on the Atlantic would shake hands as near neighbors. – *Cincinnati Atlas*

Map 9 – Via Tehuantepec Contract Route and Via Panama Contract Route
Via Nicaragua Private Mail Route

The Old Mail Routes
Map courtesy of Richard Frajola, "The Routes" page 5

February 5, 1850
California Mail Service

February 5, 1850, Tuesday, page 2
The Arkansas Banner, Little Rock, Arkansas

THE GOLDEN ROUTE. – The *Herald* at Fort Smith publishes an extra... forcibly setting for the advantages of an **Overland** route to California, through that place *[Fort Smith]*... a route that will soon become the great thoroughfare to the gold miles of California.

THE CALIFORNIA MAIL SERVICE. – ...letters never reach their friends at the "Diggings," and from whom we seldom hear, except occasionally a complaint by private conveyance, that we never write them; while the truth is, some of us have written regularly every week since they left, last May; and prepaid the postage.

– *ONE OF THE CALIFORNIA WIDOWS*

February 15, 1850
Finding $140 Per Day in California Gold

February 15, 1850, Friday, page 2
Arkansas State Gazette and Democrat, Little Rock, Ark.

The California fever is raging in Johnson County *[Arkansas]*. Letters have been received from Capt. Rogers, who went out last spring, **Overland**, stating that he was making $140 per day, and expects to return next fall with a fortune of $100,000.

February 15, 1850
California Gold

February 15, 1850, Friday, page 2
Arkansas State Gazette and Democrat, Little Rock, Ark.

Since January 1st, 1849, there have been deposited at the mint in Philadelphia, $6,000,000 of California gold.

March 1, 1850
Wagon Train Overland to California

March 1, 1850, Friday, page 2
*Arkansas State Gazette a*nd Democrat, Little Rock, Ark.

NOTICE. – There will be a meeting, at City Hall, on Tuesday, the 5th inst., at 7 o'clock P.M. for the purpose of taking into consideration the propriety of organizing a company of emigrants to go the **Overland** trip to California, on pack mules. All those who feel interested, are invited to attend.

March 1, 1850
Overland Preferred to Ocean Steamship

March 1, 1850, Friday, page 2
*Arkansas State Gazette a*nd Democrat, Little Rock, Ark.

The experience of all the late returned emigrants is in favor of the **Overland Route**. They say that when the overlander arrives, he is fresh, vigorous, inured to exposure, and qualified to endure almost any amount of hard labor of any kind. He can do anything – drive a team, delve in the earth, work the cradle, or walk forty miles a day, and thrice on it; while the passenger by the steamers and ships, are almost totally incapacitated for the very labors which he proposes to apply himself cooped up in little vessels, ill-ventilated and badly fed – the limbs becoming stiff and indolent, instead of being lithe and elastic, as they are by exercise on the plains – the emigrant when he gets to California, is indisposed to go to work, sick, it may be, for want of bodily and mental employments, and fully prepared to be a loafer, if he was not one before he started.

We conceive, that viewing it in every possible light, the land-route must be conceded to be the cheapest and best mode by which California is to be reached; and of all the routes, we believe the Arkansas route should have the preference.

March 27, 1850
Ocean Steamship Preferred to Overland

March 27, 1850, Wednesday, page 3
Washington Telegraph, Washington, Arkansas

If you still intend going to California in the spring, allow me to persuade you to go by sea, for if you take the **Overland Route**, you will regret it a thousand times before you get through. No matter how well you fit yourself out, or what kind of a company you go with, it is impossible to have that kind of discipline observed which is necessary for your safety. Men will not believe the danger which continually encompasses them, and the first thing you know, and *always* when you least expect it, the Indians are upon you.

SECORA, RIO GRANDE, JAN. 13, 1850. – ... a party of three hundred Apaches made their appearance ... But a party of Dutch on their way to California, happening there just at that time, were induced to give up their arms, when the Indians stripped them of their clothes, robbed them of their horses, and murdered many of them in the most cruel manner imaginable.

April 2, 1850
Camp Sites On Overland Route

April 2, 1850, Tuesday, page 1
The Arkansas Banner, Little Rock, Arkansas

DISTANCES TO CAMPING PLACES ON THE **OVERLAND** ROUTE TO CALIFORNIA. – The Fort Smith *Herald* furnishes some interesting information from the journal of Mr. W. B. Bennett, who has just returned from California, who, having tried both routes, much prefers the travel by land to that by way of the Isthmus.

The *Herald* says: We publish the following for the benefit of emigrants, so that they may be enabled to know how far they will have to travel each day, and where they may find water and grass, the two essential articles for an **overland** trip. This road leaves the Rio Grande about 10 or 12 miles above Dona Ana, and is called Cook's route, thence to Cook's, *at any season of the year.*

CAMPING PLACES, DISTANCES, & C.

15 miles from the Rio Grande, Cook's wells.
3 " creek, plenty water and grass
10 " hole in the rocks, called wells – grass
22 " cold springs – plenty of grass
12 " Cow spring, plenty of grass
38 " Salt Lake, between which and Cow Spring there is good camping places on the right hand side of the road, distinctly marked.
4 " very fine springs – grass abundant
20 " Lost River, grass abundant
12 " up same, grass abundant
15 " Graham's Pass in the mountains – 4 miles south of Cook's Pass – best road by far – grass and water
10 " same
8 " deserted ranche – wild bull range – fine sport for hunters – wild bulls, antelopes and deer in abundance – good spring – range excellent – stop and recruit
20 " water brackish, wild bulls, fine sport,

range good
15 " Gnat Creek, named for the numerous quantities of these little insects
15 " another creek, name not known – good range
16 " San Padro River, plenty grass, wood and water
20 " Santa Cruz, Mexican frontier town – flour, vegetables and provisions of every kind
17 " Pedro River – fine range – tall grass, gramma grass, and wild oats. Stop here and recruit, and prepare for the Gila.

Gramma Grass *is an important, drought-resistant, short grass in the mixed prairies and throughout the Great Plains and the Southwest used as forage for domestic livestock such as sheep and cattle. It is also cherished by wild species such as mule deer, elk and bison.*

25 " down same river – deserted towns, apples, pears, peaches and quinces in abundance

The ***quince*** *is a tree that bears a deciduous pome fruit, similar in appearance to a pear, and is bright golden-yellow when mature. The raw fruit is a source of food, although some consider it too astringent to eat raw, yet it has a sweet smell.*

18	"	same river – begins to sink in the sand
35	"	water in the bed of the river – grass not so good, but plenty of it – mules fond of it.
18	"	dry creek –water in holes
10	"	same
22	"	pond water – good
35	"	pond water – good, right hand side grass .... of the best kind
10	"	water in pond – 2 miles to Gila – grass and water salty – $^1/_2$ mile from road right side, good water and grass
12	"	Hime Village – plenty of corn, wheat and fodder, which emigrants buy to feet on along the Gila and desert
40	"	desert, on the Gila – take water in casks – start in the evening and travel through in the night
4	"	plenty of grass and water down the river
18	"	Murderer's Grave – $^1/_2$ mile from river good water and grass
14	"	water – grass scare
12	"	grass, but no water – road on a ridge – very stony and rough
6	"	river – grass and water
5	"	river well, cold water, good grass
6	"	river wells
8	"	river grass and water
12	"	river grass and water
8	"	river grass on the north side of the river
18	"	river same
14	"	river same
6	"	two miles form the river plenty of grass – water in the river – last camp on the Gila – stop a few days and recruit – Umas Indians

Umas tribal representatives in Washington D.C. ca. 1890.
Back row from left: Cayuse Chief Showaway, and Palouse Chief Wolf Necklace. Front row: Umatilla Chief Peo, Walla Walla Chief Hamli, and Cayuse Young Chief Tauitau. Umas Indians, or more accurately, Umatilla are a Native American tribe who traditionally inhabited the Columbia Plateau region of the northwestern United States, along the Umatilla and Columbia rivers.

– watch your teams and provisions. Here make a raft, load with grass and muskeet beans, and float down to Colorado to cross upon.

Mesquite beans are the bean-shaped pods of mesquite trees
Commonly found in the southwestern United States. This food was once important to indigenous people in Texas. Ripe to pick when the beans will rattle in the pods. Usually ground into flour to make hotcakes.

12 " Colorado River – water and grass

15 " well – desert – 7 miles, sand deep, hard for the teams – road then becomes hard and firm – muskeet beans in abundance – gather and save
25 " well – desert, no grass or beans
12 " Camp Salvation – new river described by Col. Emory – before you get to new river water to the right – grass plenty
15 " fresh water lake –no grass, a weed the mules eat
20 " Indian Village – grass and water
20 " Indian Village – grass and water
21 " Warren's Ranche – plenty of provisions – road to Los Angelos, San Diego – water and grass
15 " Mexican Ranche
22 " San Diego

The distances, in the above, are not measured, but estimated by the time occupied in traveling.

April 5, 1850
$9,400,000 of California Gold at Mint

April 5, 1850 Friday, page 2
*Arkansas State Gazette a*nd Democrat, Little Rock, Ark.

We learn from the *Pennsylvanian*, that the whole amount of gold from California, received at the mint in Philadelphia, is about nine millions four hundred thousand dollars.

April 23, 1850
Overland Mail From Arkansas to Sante Fe Proposed in Congress

April 23, 1850, Tuesday, page 2
The Arkansas Banner, Little Rock, Arkansas

Mail from Fort Smith to Sante Fe. – On the 28th ult., Mr. Sebastian, of Arkansas, introduced a resolution in the Senate, instructing the Committee on Post Offices and Post Roads, to inquire into the expediency of establishing a semi-monthly or monthly mail between Fort Smith and Sante Fe *[New Mexico]*. If this mail route should be established, it will form one link of the chain of the internal improvements contemplated as an entering wedge for the route of a national road from the valley of the Mississippi to the Pacific.

April 26, 1850
Fort Smith to San Diego Route Expedition

April 26, 1850 Friday, page 2
Arkansas State Gazette and Democrat, Little Rock, Ark.

The Fort Smith *Herald* states that it is rumored there, that the Government intends sending out, early in June an expedition for the purpose of surveying the route from *Fort Smith to San Diego,* on the Pacific, and to select sites for the immediate establishment of *Military Posts* The *Herald* hopes that the command of this expedition will be given to Capt. Macy. The Southern Route can be traveled at all seasons, and when these Posts *[military posts with a garrison of troops in residence]*shall be established, it will become the main thoroughfare for the travel and transportation of the **mails to and from California**.

April 26, 1850
Monthly Camel Overland to California

April 26, 1850 Friday, page 2
Arkansas State Gazette and Democrat, Little Rock, Ark.

Novel Enterprise – Another Mode of Conveyance to California – Considerable of a stir was created in Baltimore a few days ago by the arrival of a herd of eleven Syrian camels at that port; and every body was wondering what on earth was to be done with such a number.

We learn from a reliable source, that Messrs. Sands & Howes, the well known enterprising circus proprietors, are about to establish an **Overland Line to California** with them, which is to leave Independence, Missouri, directed for San Francisco, early in June. These gentlemen have already, thirty-one camels in this country, and the brig Catharine, Captain Gordon, now on her passage from Algiers to New Orleans, has on board twenty-two more, making in all fifty-three, most of which have been selected with care as brood stock.

We are told that a caravan of twenty-five or more, will leave each point once a month, and continue through the year. – *N. Y. Herald*

The Arkansas route would be much preferable for making the experiment. The climate and character of the country are better suited to the habits of the Camel. It is thought they will be placed on this route.

October 18, 1850
41,261 Travel Overland to California

October 18, 1850 Friday, page 2
*Arkansas State Gazette a*nd Democrat, Little Rock, Ark.

EMIGRANTS BY THE PLAINS – The whole number of persons who passed Fort Laramie, from April 29th to the 6th of August, on their way to California, was 41,261, of whom 28,253 were men, 1,449 women, and 1,549 children. There were 307 deaths registered. As a means of emigration had 9,530 wagons, 33,816 oxen, 23,068 horses, 7,533 mules, 6,824 cows, and 1,313 sheep.

December 20, 1850
Resolution to Establish Overland Mail to California

December 20, 1850 Friday, page 3
*Arkansas State Gazette a*nd Democrat, Little Rock, Ark.

GENERAL ASSEMBLY OF ARKANSAS – RESOLUTION – ...Setting forth the advantages of the route known as Marcy's Route to California, and instructing our Senators and requesting our Representative in Congress, to recommend to Congress the establishment of a line of Military Posts on this route, and also, recommending the transportation of the **Overland Mails** by this route.

1851

January 24, 1851
Crushed Dreams of a Gold Rush '49

January 24, 1851, Friday, page 2
Arkansas State Gazette and Democrat, Little Rock, Ark.

AN EDITOR OUT OF LUCK. – The *Helena True Issue* of the 16th inst., speaks in the following flattering terms of an unlucky Editor, who thought to mend his fortunes by an **overland** trip to the land of gold, but jumped from the frying pay into the fire:

> *"T. A. Falconer, formerly Editor of the Holly Springs Gazette, who has been in California nearly two years, passed up the river a few days since, with the crown of his hat out, flat broke. Well, we suppose Tom has no money, but he has friends good and true, wherever he is known. He is worthy of them. Mr. Fillmore should appoint him to some office, if he wants honest honest men about him."*

September 19, 1851
Overland Immigration to California

September 19, 1851 Friday, page 3
Arkansas State Gazette and Democrat, Little Rock, Ark.

CALIFORNIA NEWS. – GENERAL DIGEST FROM THE ALTA CALIFORNIA OF 1ST AUG. – We give below, as usual, on the sailing of the Atlantic mail streamers, a compendium of intelligence, made up for the eastern public...

The **overland** immigration, to California is beginning to come in. The first party reached Placerville on the 17th. They represent the entire body only about a thousand strong. All in good health. Some two thousand have turned off to Oregon.

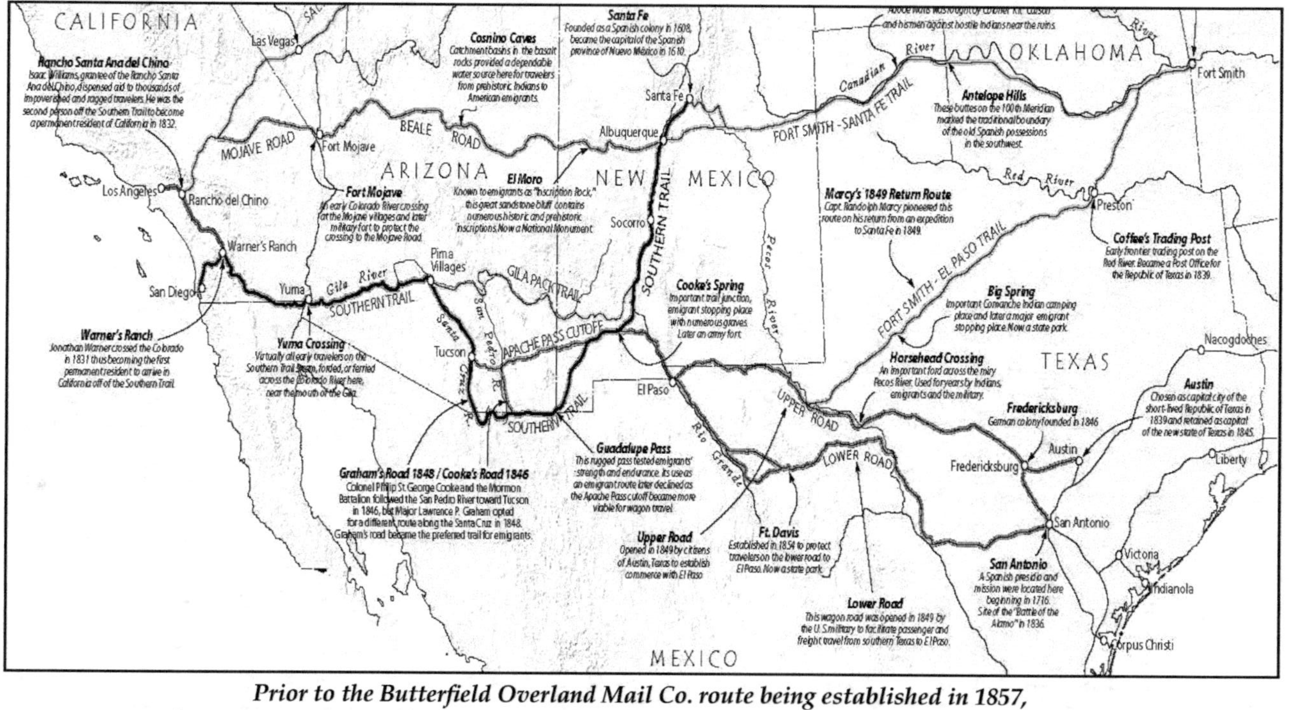

Prior to the Butterfield Overland Mail Co. route being established in 1857,
there were numerous trails already in existence as shown on the map of southwestern United States.
Source: Tom Jonas and the Southern Trails Chapter of the Oregon-California Trails Association.

Placerville, California, ca. 1849

October 31, 1851

Shameful Sporadic Mail Delivery in Arkansas

October 31, 1851, Friday, page 3

Arkansas State Gazette and Democrat, Little Rock, Ark.

Men are moving in masses all over the world, even under the reign of despotism, and bringing the public sentiment to bear upon, and in favor of the opening of roads, erecting telegraphs, and increasing mail facilities.

And shall we, Arkansans, in free America, continue for weeks at a time, deprived of all mail facilities, and be compelled to inquire of every horseman who goes through the country, to find out what is going on beyond our borders. It is a shame and disgrace to the character of any people, in this free and enlightened age, to yield to timid assent to such a state of things... It is a by-word and reproach, that business men will not come here, lest they may never hear from home again.

Early Post Office at San Francisco, 1850
"A faithful representation of the crowds daily applying at that office for letters and newspapers."

1852

February 20, 1852
Emigrants Travel Overland to California

February 20, 1852, Friday, page 2
*Arkansas State Gazette a*nd Democrat, Little Rock, Ark.

CALIFORNIA NOTICE – A meeting will be held at the Courthouse in Van Buren, on Saturday (21st inst.,) by a number of persons who intend to go to California by Overland, on Marcy's route. The object being to organize into a company and fix upon a day of departure.

November 3, 1852
Emigrant Wagon Trains to California

November 3, 1852, Wednesday, page 2
Washington Telegraph, Washington, Arkansas

THE **OVERLAND** EMIGRATION TO CALIFORNIA. – The *Sacra-*

mento Times and Transcript of Sept. 1st says:

"The latest accounts of the **overland** immigration come through a letter from Gen. Denver. On the 24th of August the General was at the Upper Relief Station, beyond the Sink of the Humboldt. He intended leaving for the Truckee on the 25th and from thence would cross over to his headquarters in Carson Valley. The scarcity of grass was beginning to be felt on the immigrant road, and, as a consequence, teams did not come through in as good a condition as those of the advance trains *[wagon trains]*. – The health of the immigrants continues good, as a general thing, although a few cases of diarrhea have occurred, in some resembling cholera, which proved fatal in a few instances. A comfortable hospital has been established on Carson River, located in a beautiful grove of trees, with excellent spring water near by, where the sick are furnished with every comfort, and supplied with sufficient means to reach California on their recovery.

The heaviest amount of the immigration has probably passed the Sink of Humboldt ere this, and it is gratifying to know that, thus far, the suffering on the much-dreaded **overland route** has been very inconsiderable. The relief furnished by California has doubtless contributed greatly to produce this happy result, and the State *[of California]* will ever have cause to be proud of the generous assistance rendered.

Of all the endeavors of the relief train *[wagon trains]*, the establishment of a water station in the midst of the great desert, to allay the parching thirst of thousands, has been the most acceptable to immigrants. – It is said that women and children frequently reach this station with their tongues parched and swollen till forced out of their mouths; and when water is furnished them, and they learn the debt due to California, their gratitude knows no bounds."

*At **Independence Rock**, in what is now Wyoming, many wagon trains on the Oregon Trail camped for the night, forming corrals. Here the original Applegate train separated into smaller parties "better suited to the narrow mountain paths and small pastures in their front."*

The Old State House as it appeared in 1871, Little Rock, Arkansas
Formerly called the Arkansas State House, it is the oldest surviving state capitol building west of the Mississippi River. Construction started in 1833 and was completed in 1842. Source: Drawn by A. Ruger. Library of Congress, Map Division.

1853

January 19, 1853
Arkansas General Assembly Proposes a Memphis to California Railroad

January 19, 1863, Wednesday, page 3

Arkansas State Gazette and Democrat, Little Rock, Ark.

ARKANSAS LEGISLATIVE PROCEEDINGS – SENATE. – *Wednesday, Jan. 5* – Mr. Clark, introduced the following preamble and resolution:

> *"WHEREAS, The great project of constructing a railroad from the Mississippi River to California, is now engaging a large share of public attention:*
>
> *AND WHEREAS, The people of the State of Arkansas feel a deep interest in the same, believing it to have been clearly proven by the surveys, reconnaissance and explorations of divers expeditions under the authority of the General Government, as well as by the experience of numerous intelligent* **overland** *emigrants, that the 'Central Route' from Memphis, through the State of Arkansas, via the river Gila, is the most eligible and least expensive;*
>
> *AND, WHEREAS, It behooves, and is expedient, and proper, that all the States in the Union, friendly to the enterprise, to meet in convention, to adopt measures for the promotion of the same:*
>
> *THEREFORE, BE IT RESOLVED, BY THE GENERAL ASSEMBLY OF THE STATE OF ARKANSAS, That their fellow-citizens, throughout the United States friendly to the construction, be, and they are hereby, invited to meet in convention, at the city of Memphis, on Monday the 6th day of May next, to consider of the best means of accomplishing the great object herein designated.*
>
> *BE IT FURTHER RESOLVED, That our fellow citizens of Arkansas be, and they are hereby, requested, and urged, to send delegates to the convention from all the counties."*

June 1, 1853
Overland Emigration to California Increasing

June 1, 1853, Wednesday, page 2

Washington Telegraph, Washington, Arkansas

The **overland** emigration from the Western States to California and Oregon, during the present season, is expected to exceed that of any previous year. It is estimated that over 100,000 head of cattle will accompany the emigrants.

September 14, 1853
Mail Route to California Through Nicaragua

September 14, 1853, Wednesday, page 2
Washington Telegraph, Washington, Arkansas

SUMMARY OF CALIFORNIA NEWS. – Accounts have been received at San Francisco from New York to the 25th of July, occupying in the transit only 25 days by the Nicaragua route. The papers speak in the highest terms of this route, it being more expeditious than via Panama from 3 to 6 days. Memorials to Congress were numerously signed to secure the transportation of the mails by the Nicaragua route.

September 14, 1853
Rufus Porter, 19th century New England Inventor, Proposes Flying to California

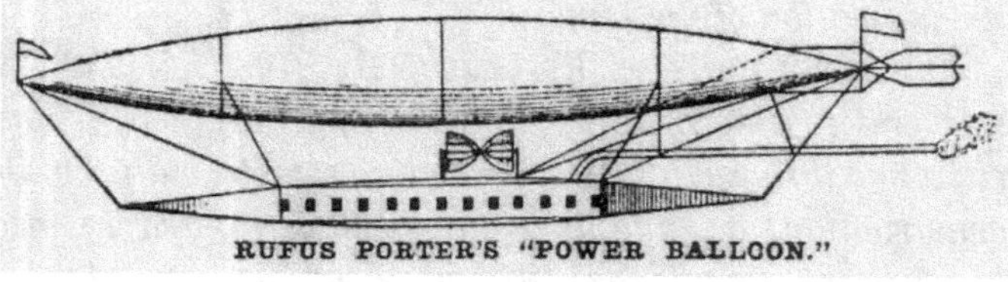

The Rufus Porter Power Balloon

September 14, 1853, Wednesday, page 1
Washington Telegraph, Washington, Arkansas

JUST THE THING – ... The Scientific American suggests that this is a splendid opportunity for Mr. Porter, with his Aeroport, *(which was to set out two years ago,* ***overland*** *and through the air, for California, a project not yet abandoned,)* to show the capabilities of his machine, and do his country some service, besides making his fortune. Traveling through the air, with a properly constructed machine, in accordance with natural laws, is probably not beyond the possibilities of the age, though Mr. Porter does not seem to have hit upon the true principles of such a machine.

1854

June 2, 1854
Westbound Overland Proposed out of Memphis to Reach Little Rock

June 2, 1854, Friday, page 2
*Arkansas State Gazette a*nd Democrat, Little Rock, Ark.

THE EASTERN MAIL – On Sunday last, intelligence was received at this place *[Little Rock, Arkansas]* that the Postmaster General had invited proposals for the carrying of a daily mail from here to Memphis by land –... There is another view of the case, that makes the carrying of the mails from Memphis through Arkansas, extremely desirable. It will connect, by stages, and make a through line, from Tennessee to Texas; connecting and placing us in speedy communication with both the east and the west – placing us in a few days drive of Austin, in Texas, and Nashville in Tennessee – two places from which we are now almost entirely cut off.

1855

January 10, 1855
Arkansas Senate Request a Mail Line from Memphis to Fort Smith

January 10, 1855, Wednesday, page 3
Washington Telegraph, Washington, Arkansas

ARKANSAS LEGISLATIVE PROCEEDINGS – SENATE. – FRIDAY, DECEMBER 29TH. – Mr. Lemoyne offered a resolution requesting our congressional delegation to procure the establishment of a mail line from Memphis to Des Arc via Lewisburg, Dardanelle and Van Buren, to Fort Smith.

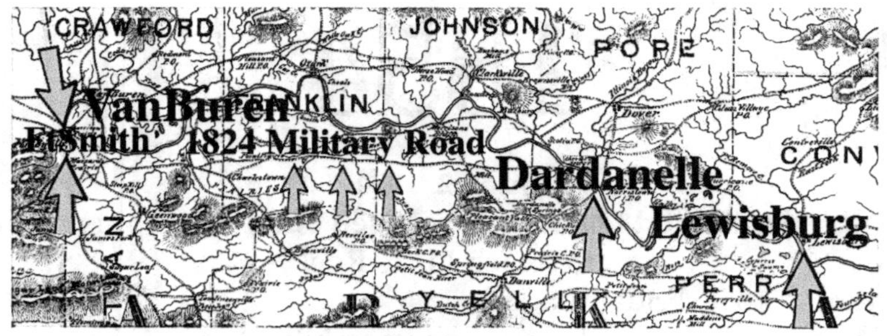

1864 Map of Arkansas
Arrows have been added to indicate location of Lewisburg, Dardanelle, Van Buren and Fort Smith. This segment of the Old Military Road would be used by Butterfield's Overland Mail from 1858 to 1860.

January 10, 1855
Weekly Mail to California Bill in Congress

January 10, 1855, Wednesday, page 3
Washington Telegraph, Washington, Arkansas

BUSINESS BEFORE CONGRESS. – The bill to provide a weekly mail to California.

January 12, 1855
Plea for Improved Mail Delivery Through Arkansas to Texas

January 12, 1855, Friday, page 2
*Arkansas State Gazette a*nd Democrat, Little Rock, Ark.

THE EASTERN MAIL. – We mentioned last week the fact that Col. McGiboney, U. S. Mail Agent, was in this place on an official tour of duty. We conversed with him on the subject of the mail facilities which are necessary in order to keep up our communication with the other States of the Union...

Some such arrangement is demanded, not only by the people of our State, but by the whole Indian country, and the military post, west, and a great portion of the State of Texas; as these countries are dependent, entirely on the Arkansas mail routes, for their mail matter. We hope our delegation in Congress, with such aid as they may, and will receive from the Texas delegation, may urge this matter on the department; and, if properly urged, there is no doubt of the success of the scheme... And justice not only to the State of Arkansas, but Texas, and the military post, and Indian country, west, demands that the department should, in accordance with the recommendation of the mail agent, and the petition of the members of the Legislature, establish a mail route from Little Rock via White River, to Napoleon, six times a week.

January 19, 1855
Transcontinental Mail Carried by Ocean Steamer

January 19, 1855, Friday, page 1
Arkansas State Gazette and Democrat, Little Rock, Ark.

ABSTRACT OF DEPARTMENT REPORTS. – POST MASTER GENERAL'S REPORT. – The Post Master General... states that the Nicaragua company have offered to carry a weekly mail between New York and California for the sum of $600,000 per annum, which he thinks is the highest rate of pay which ought to be demanded. The cost this year for a semi-monthly mail, by the Isthmus route is $757,977.03.

January 19, 1855
Overland Telegraph and Mail Route Propositions Before Congress

January 19, 1855, Friday, page 3
Arkansas State Gazette and Democrat, Little Rock, Ark.

The wild Indians and dreadful snow storms in the Rocky Mountains are serious impediments to a telegraph between the Atlantic States and California. But one will be had, somehow. Mr. Farley, of the Committee on Territories, favors the Senate bill for a *subterranean line*. He would plant the wires so far under the surface that the red man would never find or be disposed to meddle with them, or the cold and storms ever affect their working; but, like the want of the rudder in aerial navigation, a difficulty is suggested in the impracticability of discovering and repairing the breaks that must occur from time to time in this wilderness underground line.

Meanwhile there is another proposition before Congress for an **Overland Mail to California** in stage wagons and sleigh.

February 9, 1855
Lack of Daily Mail Along Mississippi River

February 9, 1855, page 4
Arkansas State Gazette and Democrat, Little Rock, Ark.

SENATE – January 22. – Mr. Jones, of Tennessee, made a violent onslaught upon the Post Master General for his neglect to furnish daily mails along the Mississippi and its tributaries, as required by the acts of Congress of 1854.

February 21, 1855
Senate Considers Mail Route from St. Louis to San Francisco

February 21, 1855, Wednesday, page 2
Washington Telegraph, Washington, Arkansas

The *Washington Star* expresses the approval of Senator Gwin's joint resolution for the establishment of a United States **mail express line from St. Louis to San Francisco**, and repudiates the idea that Congress will at present sanction any scheme for building a great Pacific Railroad. It estimates that any such project would cost the government two hundred millions of dollars before it was completed. The *Star* is considered semi-official authority.

June 15, 1855
Postal Humor
June Bugs Could Deliver Mail Better Than Current Postal Employees

June 15, 1855, Friday, page 3
Arkansas State Gazette and Democrat, Little Rock, Ark.

MR. EDITOR – ...there have been more mail failures ...than ever known previously, in the memory of man...The substance of my dream was, that the worthy Postmaster General, disgusted with mail agents, contractors, mail coaches, mail bags, and job carts, had determined, from a special regard for the people of Arkansas, to discard them altogether, and employ JUNE BUGS to discharge the duty which they had wholly failed to perform... – *H. H. Coleman*

1856

March 26, 1856
Bill in Congress for Overland Mail Route From Mississippi River to San Francisco

March 26, 1856, Wednesday, page 2
Washington Telegraph, Washington, Arkansas

FROM WASHINGTON, MARCH 12. – A bill providing for an **Overland Mail** from some point on the Mississippi to San Francisco, was referred to the Post Office Committee.
[NOTE: This article also appears in the Weekly Arkansas Gazette, March 22, 1856 page 3.]

November 16, 1856
Butterfield's Overland Stage Would Later Use This Ferry over Arkansas River at Little Rock

November 16, 1856, page 1
The True Democrat, Little Rock, Arkansas

EMIGRATION. – The number of families moving in and through the State is unprecedented. The steam ferry boat at this place *[Little Rock]*, though constantly running, cannot cross the wagons as they come, so that fifty or sixty may be seen on the opposite bank of the river.

December 2, 1856
Butterfield's Overland Stage Crossed Ferry over Arkansas River at Little Rock

December 2, 1856, page 1
The True Democrat, Little Rock, Arkansas

FERRY AND ENTERTAINMENT.

THE undersigned has got his **Ferry** in operation, two miles below Little Rock. Due and diligent attention will be given at all times to the speedy crossing of all that may wish to cross at my ferry. Doctors, and those going for them, will be crossed at any hour of the night.

Good Lots are in course of construction, on each bank of the river, for the convenience of drovers—A good supply of wood on the north bank, for the use of travelers, free of charge. Ministers of the Gospel ferried free of charge.

Living immediately on the Memphis road, I will entertain Travelers with substantial fair for them and horses, and those stopping at my house will pass the ferry free of charge.

Corn, Fodder and Oats for sale.

Oct 14 '56.-tf. JARED C. MARTIN.

Source: The True Democrat, December 2, 1856

This 1866 engraving shows wagons waiting for the ferry to cross the Arkansas River and reach Little Rock.

The ferry is shown midstream at right.

The Butterfield stages used this same ferry over 300 times to reach the Butterfield Home Station at Little Rock's Anthony House.

Illustration is from Harper's Weekly, May 26, 1866, page 328.

January 2, 1857
Snow: Why The Salt Lake Route Was Not Chosen for the Upcoming Butterfield's Overland Mail Co. Route

January 2, 1857, page 3
True Democrat, Little Rock, Arkansas

BRIGHAM YOUNG'S FLIGHT NOT CONFIRMED – By way of St. Louis we have, through the *Republican,* direct advices **overland** from Salt Lake City to the 2d of April, much later than those *via* California.

The reported flight of Brigham Young is not confirmed. He seemed still to maintain the entire confidence of the people, and was planning an excursion of exploration and pleasure to a Mormon settlement on the Salmon River, 400 miles to the north. Two hundred persons were to accompany him.

They were to leave Salt Lake City about the 20th of April or the 1st of May For some cause or other, the Mormons at San Bernardino and all the surrounding settlements had been called in to Salt Lake City...

The winter, though short, had been unusually severe, and it was computed that nine or ten feet of snow had fallen. There was about two and a half feet on the ground at one time. The weather became mild about the 1st of February. Stock of every description, however, had suffered less than during the previous winter. There was an abundance of provisions in the territory.

The parties that came through to St. Louis **with the mails** consisted of sixteen persons.

They encountered tremendous snow storms, and during the night of the 28th, six of their mules died from exposure. The southwest pass was filled to the depth of two and a half to five feet. The grass upon the route was very poor and a month later than usual, which will delay **Overland Companies to California** the coming season. No emigrants were met on the road.

The party reported two bloody battles between the Snake and Blackfeet Indians, in the first of which 27 of the latter were killed; in the second nearly a whole tribe of the former exterminated. The travelers met on the 5th a Snake Indian, who reported himself to be the lone survivor.

Difficulties with the Cheyennes has also occurred at Fort Laramie, growing out of the death of one of their number, then a prisoner. The Indians were greatly excited, and sent a party to the fort to demand the body. Col. Hoffman, in command, refused the demand, and told them to go off. The Cheyennes sent word that they were ready to fight the whites, and that they would meet them on the prairies this summer.

A report also reached the fort that the Cheyennes, alleging the loss of sixty of their warriors on the California Road, had captured and held in custody sixteen traders, and that they had despatched a party of one hundred warriors to the road, to commit depredations and avenge the loss of their tribe...

[This article was also reprinted in Little Rock's The true Democrat, in the June 02, 1857 issue on page 3.]

1857

The Story of Butterfield's Overland Mail Co. Officially begins in 1857

June 20, 1857
Bids Opened for Overland Mail to California

June 20, 1857, page 2
Arkansas State Gazette and Democrat, Little Rock, Ark.

WASHINGTON, JUNE 11. – The bids for transporting the **Overland Mail** to California have been opened. They were seven in number, varying from $400,000 to $650,000. This contest lies between St. Louis and the El Paso route.

July 7, 1857
Overland Route Will Probably Be the Southern

July 7, 1857, page 3
Arkansas True Democrat, Little Rock, Arkansas

MEMPHIS AND THE CALIFORNIA ROUTE. – The Washington correspondent of the *New York Times*, says:

> *"The **California Overland Mail** question, after undergoing thorough consideration in the Cabinet, has been referred to the Postmaster General, who is not yet prepared to pronounce a decision. The impression prevails, however, that the Southern route will be selected, commencing at Memphis, and continuing by way of Fort Smith, Donna Anna, and Fort Yuma. The object is to have the route through a country susceptible of easy settlement, and which will not be interrupted by heavy snow. Some of the bidders desire to be heard before the Postmaster General before he shall finally dispose of the question."*

July 7, 1857
Several Bid on the Overland Contract

July 7, 1857, page 2
Arkansas True Democrat, Little Rock, Arkansas

FROM WASHINGTON CITY. – *Washington D. C. June 30, 1857.* – The contract for the **Overland Mail** route to the Pacific, has not yet been awarded, though hourly looked for. The Postmaster General submitted the matter to a cabinet council on yesterday. The following are the bids received at the contract office for this service:

S. Howell and A. E. Pace; from Gaines' Landing, on the Mississippi, to San Francisco; to commence at Vicksburg, if preferred – weekly, $1,00,000 for the first year, $800,000 for the second, $700,000 for the third, and $600,000 for the fourth year.

James E. Birch; from Memphis to San Francisco – semi-

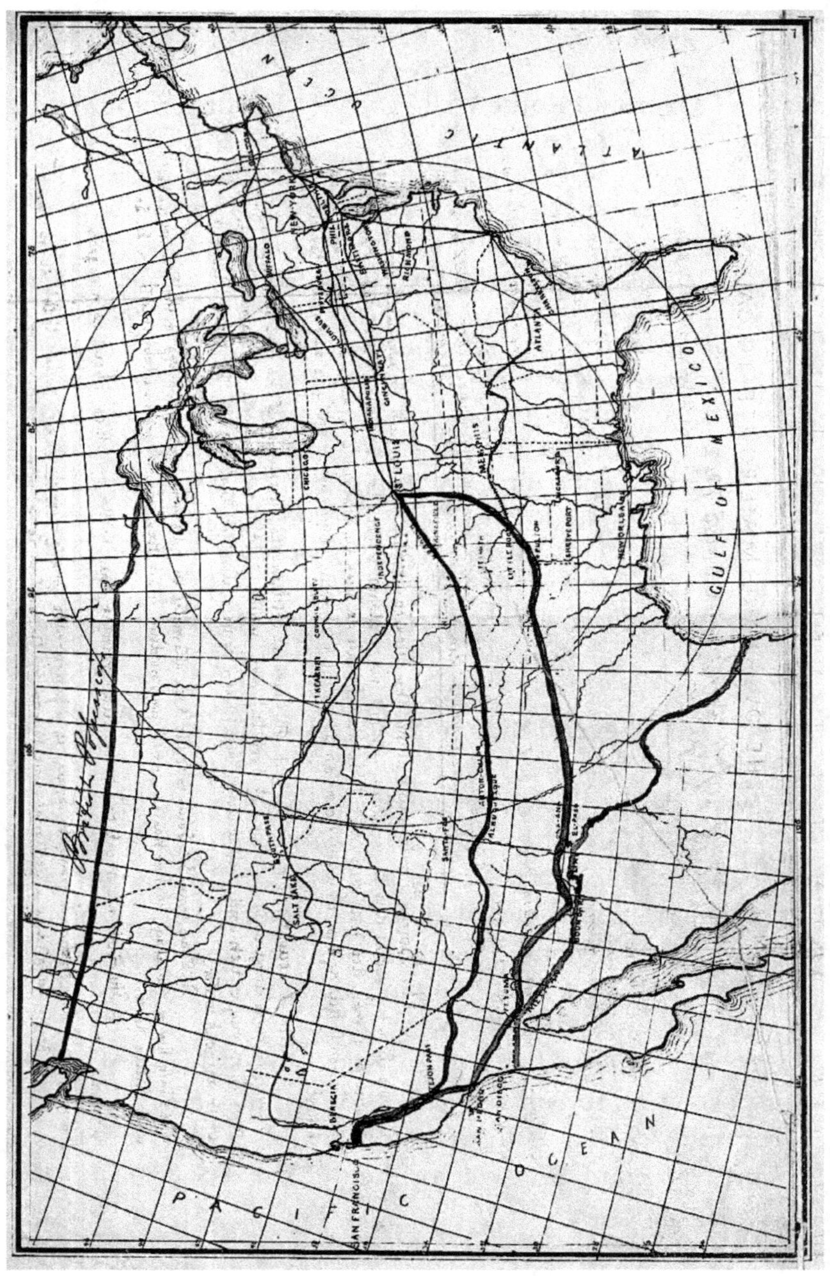
ATLANTIC OCEAN
GULF OF MEXICO
PACIFIC OCEAN
NEW YORK
BUFFALO
CHICAGO
ST. LOUIS
MEMPHIS
ATLANTA
NEW ORLEANS
SALT LAKE
SAN FRANCISCO

SKELETON MAP OF THE OVERLAND MAIL ROUTE TO CALIFORNIA

Route adopted by the Department traced in Green
Route proposed by John Butterfield and others (who were the lowest bidders) in Red.

ST. LOUIS TO SAN FRANCISCO via LITTLE ROCK, PRESTON, DONA ANA, AND SAN-PEDRO — BORDER ROUTE (GREEN) MILES 2585

ST. LOUIS TO SAN FRANCISCO, via, NEOSHO, ANTON CHICO, ALBUQUERQUE, AND TIJON PASS — 35TH PARALLEL (RED) MILES 2194

DIFFERENCE IN FAVOR OF ST. LOUIS ROUTE, FOUR DAYS TRAVEL 391 MILES.

NEW YORK TO MEMPHIS BY SOUTHERN ROUTE 1123 MILES

NEW YORK TO ST LOUIS DIRECT ROUTE 1093 MILES

NEW YORK TO SAN FRANCISCO BY MEMPHIS AND THE BORDER ROUTE 3707 MILES,

NEW YORK TO SAN FRANCISCO BY ST. LOUIS AND 35TH PARALLEL ROUTE 3287 MILES

DIFFERENCE IN FAVOR OF ST LOUIS ROUTE 420 MILES.

The Border Route passes along the Mexican Frontier through an unsettled country crossing in its way seven deserts or sandy plains viz:– Llano Estacado, 125 miles, Rio Grande to Rio Membres, 71 ms., Rio Membres to Valle de Sung 57, Valle de Sung to San Pedro 84 ms., San Pedro to Tucson 53, Tucson to Gila 79 ms., and the Colorado desert 80 ms., total 569 ms. (see pp. 79 83, 84 + 96 vol. Pac. Ro. R. R. Reports.

The St. Louis Route passes through the Cherokee Settlements, through all the best settlements of New Mexico and the Moquin villages west of Fort Defiance where supplies can always be obtained. The country most of the way is rich and well watered one plain of 40 miles, and that west of the Colorado river, to cross without water.

The Road from St. Louis to Little Rock alternates in hills and broad swamps of the St. Francis Cache and Black Rivers no stage has ever passed over it, and no direct mail Route has ever been established between St. Lo and Little Rock.

The overland mail can be carried from St Louis to Anton-Chico, about as soon as from [illegible] to Preston.

The Route proposed from St. Louis is a practicable and National Route, suited to the whole country. The Route adopted is a Sectional and Border route, suited to the views of extremists only.

This is the original map and hand-written government proposal for the Overland Mail Company contract. This map is in the New York Public Library Digital Collections. Appreciation is offered to Gerald T. Ahnert for finding this map.

weekly, $600,000.

James Glover; from Memphis or Vicksburg – semi-monthly, $300,000; weekly, $450,000; semi-weekly, $600,000.

John Butterfield, Wm. B. Dinsmore, Wm. G. Fargo, James V. P. Garner, Marcus L. Kinyon, Hamilton Spence and Alexander Holland; from St. Louis - weekly, $450,00; semi-weekly, $600,000.

David D. Mitchell, Samuel B. Churchhill, Robert Campbell, Wm. Gilpin, and others – semi-weekly, $600,000.

John Butterfield, Wm. B. Dinsmore, Wm. G. Fargo, and others; from Memphis – semi-monthly, $300,000; weekly, $450,000; semi-weekly, $595,000.

John Butterfield, and others; from St. Louis – semi-monthly, $300,000; weekly, $450,000; semi-weekly, $585,000.

James Johnson, jr. and Joseph Clark; from St. Louis – semi-monthly, $260,000; weekly, $390,000; semi-weekly, $520,000.

Wm. Hollingshead, the president of the Minnesota, Nebraska, and Pacific mail transportation company, put in a bid, but it was irregular, being after time – proposing to perform the semi-weekly service for $550,000.

John Butterfield and others, are willing to stipulate in the contract that the route indicated by them may be modified and changed to the north or south to avoid any obstacle that may be found by experience to interfere with the safe and regular transmission of the mails.

July 7, 1857
John Butterfield Awarded Contract

July 7, 1857, page 3

Arkansas True Democrat, Little Rock, Arkansas

LETTER FROM WASHINGTON. – *Washington, June 30.* – The **Overland Mail** route has been selected, beginning at St. Louis and Memphis, thence forming a junction at Little

Rock, Arkansas via Preston, to the Rio Grande, near Fort Fillmore or Donna Anna; thence along the road now constructing to Fort Yuma; thence by the best process to San Francisco.

Contract to be semi-weekly service, has been awarded to **John Butterfield**, Wm. B. Dinsmore, Wm. S. Fargo, V. H. Gardner, Maquire Kenyon, Alexander Holland of New York, and Hamilton Spencer of Illinois.

July 11, 1857
Overland Route Foreshadows Future Railroad Route
Assumption that Memphis is Terminus of Main Trunk Line

July 11, 1857, page 2

Arkansas State Gazette and Democrat, Little Rock, Ark.

The Pacific Mail Contract. – By a telegraphic dispatch, published in another column, it will be seen that the **Overland Mail Route** has been selected, beginning at St. Louis and Memphis, thence forming a junction at Little Rock, Arkansas, via Preston, to the Rio Grande, near Fort Fillmore or Donna Anna; thence by the best process to San Francisco. Contract, to be semi-weekly service, has been awarded to **John Butterfield**, Wm. B. Dinsmore, Wm. S. Fargo, V. H. Gardner, Maguire Kenion, Alexander Holland, of New York, and Hamilton Spencer, of Illinois.

This, in our opinion, settles the location of the Pacific Rail Road. Its impracticability on a Northern route, has long been known to the world. Its Northern friends are not compelled to look to the South for the only practicable rail road connection with the Pacific, over a habitable route; and the geographical position of the State of Arkansas will make it a matter of necessity that either the main trunk or a leading branch of the road must traverse her borders. We shall have more to say upon this subject; for the present, we give the following excellent article from the *Memphis Bulletin:*

THE CALIFORNIA **OVERLAND MAIL** TO START FROM MEMPHIS! – We hail, with feelings of unmingled satisfaction, the announcement made in our telegraphic dispatches, of the award of the contract for carrying the **Overland Mail** between the Mississippi River and the Pacific Coast. It is to be a semi-weekly service, and to start both from Memphis and St. Louis, the two lines converging into one at Little Rock, Arkansas.

[NOTE: Merger point was later changed to Fort Smith]

All honor to the enlightened justice which, whether it be the result of the Post Office Department, has thus done the thing which ought to have been done. It is right that St. Louis should have a branch line. It would be proper that Vicksburg or New Orleans should have another. It is especially right that Memphis should be the terminus of the main Trunk Line.

The awarding of this contract settles the question of the location of the National Pacific Rail Road. Henceforth the Memphis route is without rival; for not more surely do the "tracks of the buffalo" point to the best crossing, than will these **Overland Mail** Wagons blaze out the way for the steam locomotive. The first marks of their wheels upon the virgin soil, are but the pioneers of the driving wheels of the Iron Horse. The dream to assume the shape of reality. Hope already begins into fruition.

What a glorious prospect does this assurance of the Future, open up to our young City! – and how it should strengthen the resolve and nerve the arms of all her people to be worthy of it! Think of it! Within the life-time of thousands now living – before the boy who now runs along our streets shall have learned deeply what the battle of life is to robust manhood – Memphis, seated upon the Father of Waters, will reach out her iron arms across the Continent, and lave the fingers of her commerce in two Oceans! The dwellers from the Old World of the East, and the still Older World of the Far West, will meet and refresh themselves in her bosom. All climes and all countries of the civilized world, will pour the rich stream of their trade, travel and social intercourse, through her borders. Who can set limits to her growth, prosperity and power, if we, the moulders of her character, and the directors of her latent resources and expansive energies, are but true to the destiny that lies open to her! With a higher and better civilization, a people far elevated in the mass above the ancient Egyptians! – laved by a River richer than the Nile! Who shall say that there is not reserved for the Memphis of this era, a glory greater even than that which made the name famous among the marvels of the past!

July 14, 1857
Mail Ocean Steam Ship Route Funded

July 14, 1857, page 1

Arkansas True Democrat, Little Rock, Arkansas

BY AUTHORITY, Public Acts of the Thirty-Fourth congress of the United States, First Session.

AN ACT making Appropriations for the Transportation of the United States Mail by Ocean Steamers and otherwise, during the fiscal year ending the 30th of June, 1857.

Be it enacted, etc., That the following sums be, and the same are hereby appropriated, to be paid out of any money in the treasury not otherwise appropriated, for the year ending the 30th of June, 1857:

... For transportation of mails from Panama to California and Oregon, and back, $261,000.

... For transportation of the mails across the isthmus of Panama, $135,000.

July 14, 1857
The following proposal to carry mails by steamboat on the Arkansas River may have been part of what gave John Butterfield the failed notion that he could carry the Overland Mail across Arkansas by steamboat.

July 14, 1857, page 1
Arkansas True Democrat, Little Rock, Arkansas

PROPOSALS. Post Office Department, Contract Officer, June 20, 1857. Sir – The Postmaster General has received several letters from very respectable gentlemen, and petitions numerously signed, requesting that steamboat service be restored on the Arkansas river.

With every disposition to extend all the mail facilities in his power, and allow such mode of conveyance as the nature of the country may require, you are instructed to ascertain and report the lowest price for which you can employ steamboat service, three times a week, from Napoleon to Little Rock and back, during the term of the present contract, which ceases first July, 1858.

Give the names of the persons making the bids, the place of residence and a schedule of departures and arrivals, specifying all the intermediate offices that will be supplied.

If a proposition at a reasonable amount be received, the Postmaster General has every disposition to accept it.

In the meantime you are authorized to make up and forward the canvas bag mails for Little Rock, and points beyond in steamboats, and the letter mails for intermediate offices, not exceeding three times a week, on alternate days of those under the regular contract, at not exceeding $25 for the trip from Napoleon to Little Rock.

The accounts for this special service should be forwarded to this office at the end of each week, properly certified, that they may be submitted to the Postmaster for allowance. Very respectfully etc., etc.

WM. H. DUNDAS,
Second Ass't P. M. General
To Joseph Lemly, Postmaster, Napoleon, Arkansas
July 7 '57 – 2w.

July 21, 1857
Overland Expedition Passed Thru

July 21, 1857, page 3
Arkansas True Democrat, Little Rock, Arkansas

The expedition engaged in opening the road for the **Overland Mail** route to California passed through this place on yesterday.

July 21, 1857
Overland Route Details

July 21, 1857, page 2
Arkansas True Democrat, Little Rock, Arkansas

From Washington D.C. July 6, 1857. – **The Overland Mail**. – The **Overland Mail** route to California has been selected by the postmaster general, with the approbation of the President, and the location of that route will meet with the liveliest satisfaction from every citizen of Arkansas.

The route is as follows: Beginning at St. Louis and Memphis, on the Mississippi River, thence forming a junction at Little Rock, thence in the direction of Preston, to the Rio Grande, at the most suitable crossing of that river, near Fort Fillmore or Donna Anne, thence along the new road now being made under the direction of the Secretary of the Interior to Fort Yuma, thence by the best passes and through the best valleys for safe and expedition staging to San Francisco. The contract has been given to a company who are members of the largest express companies in the country, whose means, energy and experience, are equal to any emergency. The amount paid for semi-weekly service is $595,000 per annum.

The contract will go into operation with as little delay as possible, and will add greatly to the rapidly increasing prospects of Arkansas. The selection of this route indicates with a considerable degree of certainty the location of the route of the Pacific Railroad, and the prospects of the Cairo and Fulton Railroad are thus enhanced. The next movement after the successful operation of the **Overland Mail**, will be the establishment of a telegraph line from the Mississippi to San Francisco.

July 21, 1857
Postmaster General Congratulated

July 21, 1857, page 2
Arkansas True Democrat, Little Rock, Arkansas

THE OVERLAND MAIL TO CALIFORNIA. – The *Washington Union*, of the 1st inst., contains the following announcement:

The Postmaster General, with the approbation of the President, has selected the following route for conveying the **Overland Mail** to California, to wit: Beginning at St. Louis and Memphis...

In view of the prices bid and the supposed ability, qualifications and experience of all the parties, the Postmaster General has, also, with the approbation of the President, given the contract to **John Butterfield,** William B. Dinsmore, Wm. G. Fargo, James V. P. Gardner, Marquis S. Kinyon, Alexander Holland, of New York, and Hamilton Spencer of Illinois, at the price of $595,000 for semi-weekly service.

The *Union*, in an editorial notice of the Postmaster General's action on this subject, remarks:

"This whole subject, in all its bearings, was a matter of the greatest importance to every part of the country. Indeed, we doubt whether there will be any measure which can come before the administration for its action and decision having more important

relations to the wants, interests, and material convenience of all the States. The Postmaster General fully understood the magnitude of the measure. He has bestowed upon it the most patient and persevering labor. His examinations and investigations have been long and laborious to enable him to arrive at proper and satisfactory results. His decision being made, the President, after equal patient examination, has approved it, and it goes forth with the sanction of the administration.

The Postmaster General has, we doubt not, been most fortunate in selecting the gentlemen who are members of those powerful express companies, whose means, energy and experience are equal to any emergency, to assist him in carrying this great measure into full and successful effect. The success of the enterprise will lead to the most important consequences, looking far into the future, and bearing most emphatically upon the interests of the Atlantic and Pacific States."

July 25, 1857
Kirkbride Potts, of Potts Home Station, Was one of the 1,000's Who Went to California Seeking Fortune

Kirkbride Potts, *shown here, earned enough money selling cattle to miners in California, he was able to return the next year to build this home. It served as a Home Station on the Butterfield trail. Today, it is open for tours, and serves as the museum for Pope County, Arkansas.*

July 25, 1857

Arkansas State Gazette and Democrat, Little Rock, Ark.

LETTER FROM KIRKBRIDE POTTS, ESQ. - RED BLUFFS, CALIFORNIA, JUNE 15, 1857 - DEAR CAPTAIN:

I have no doubt you will be somewhat surprised at receiving a letter from me, situated as I am, at this time almost on the confines of the State of California, herding a little over three hundred head of cattle. I left my home, in Pope County, on the 22nd of April, 1856, expecting to have returned last winter; but not getting an offer for my stock that I thought would justify for the time, trouble, and expense, I concluded to stay one summer with them and bring them into market this coming fall or winter. They are now in fine order, and will be very fat by November, at which time I hope to meet a good market for them, and return to Arkansas by January, if possible.

The crops are very light here this year, owing to the drought in some portions of the Sacramento Valley. The wheat and barley have been dead and dry for a month. In other places, more favored by Providence, good half crops will be made. In the extreme North, about Humbolt Bay, they have had plenty of rain and have fine crops. I suppose taking California all over, good half crops will be made - sufficient probably for the present population. I see an occasional number of the *Gazette and Democrat* [an Arkansas newspaper] in this county.

Beef is down to ten cents on foot, owing to the quantity of Mexican cattle pushed into market. Last winter American beef was 12 ½ to 13 ½ on foot, and I think will bear that price again this coming winter. There is not much large America beef in the country: a few thousand head have been driven in from Oregon this spring; but it is doubtful if they get to be good beef by fall. They come in as poor as cattle driven from the States across the plains; and the grass being very short, and pretty much dried up, but few of them will be fit for market the coming fall. They come in a poor as cattle driven from the States across the plains; and the grass being very short, and pretty much dried up, but few of them will be fit for market the coming fall. I should be pleased, Captain, to hear from you.

My post office is Red Bluffs. Hoping this may meet your eyes fully restored.

I remain yours,
KIRKBRIDE POTTS.

July 25, 1857
First Survey of the Butterfield Route

July 25, 1857, -
Arkansas State Gazette and Democrat, Little Rock, Ark.

THE **PACIFIC OVERLAND ROAD PARTY** – On Wednesday last we had the pleasure of a few minutes conversation with Col. James B. Leech, who is in charge of the above company, and who is engaged in surveying a route for the purpose of carrying the **Overland Mail** from the Mississippi river to the Pacific.

The party consists of 40 wagons and 100 men, and will strike an air line from here *[Little Rock]* to Preston, Texas; from which point it will travel nearly in a westerly direction, passing a little north of Fort Belknap, 25 miles north of Fort Chadbourn, across the Pecos River at the Emigrant crossing, cross the Llano west of Cardo on the north route, and strike the Rio Grande 15 miles north of El Paso. Thence the survey will continue to Fort Yuma and San Francisco by the best and most practicable route.

We have no idea of the time it will take to survey this route, and make the road passable for mail stages; but with the force of the government and contractors to press it forward, we hope to see the work consummated at the earliest practicable day.

August 1, 1857
Route Through Hot Springs Recommended for Overland Mail to California

August 1, 1857, page 2, column 4
Arkansas State Gazette and Democrat, Little Rock, Ark.

THE CALIFORNIA OVER-LAND ROUTE – Extract of a letter from an old resident of Hot Spring county, to a citizen of this city, dated Hot Springs, July 29, 1857:

"The California road viewers left here, on Sunday morning, for Preston, via Caddo Cove. Their wagons were too heavily loaded – 1,000 to 5,000 lbs. each; 3,500 lbs. would have been load enough.

They lightened their wagons some here, by starting two more teams. They will find a good road from here to Caddo Cove; and, I am informed, they will meet with no obstructions from thence to Preston *[Texas]*.

If **Butterfield & Co.** are not influenced by interested persons, they will be sure to adopt this route *[via Hot Springs]* for their mail line to the Pacific. There is no way that a road can be got from Little Rock to Preston, that can compare at all favorably with the route by Hot Springs and Caddo Cove. There are no mountains or swamps – plenty of corn, oats and fodder – and it is better watered, by spring branches, than any road I ever traveled, and, besides, it is much the shortest route."

August 11, 1857
Overland Mail Will Result in Arizona as a State

August 11, 1857, page 2
Arkansas True Democrat, Little Rock, Arkansas

ARIZONA – The Gadsden Purchase seems to be coming into notice. Pierce's administration was abused and Gen. Gadsden was denounced, for making so worthless a purchase; but now, forsooth, the very papers that did the dirty work of slander, are the loudest in their praises of the territory. The northern newspapers teem with descriptions of Arizonia. *[Arizona]* The establishment of the **California semi-weekly mail** through that much abused territory will soon cause it to fill up with settlers, and ere long, we trust, another southern State will be knocking at the door for admission.

August 11, 1857
Southern Route Defended as Best Choice

August 11, 1857, page 2
Arkansas True Democrat, Little Rock, Arkansas

PACIFIC OVERLAND MAIL ROUTE. – *To the Editors N. Y. Daily News:* Several of the morning papers have seen fit to attack the recent decision of the Postmaster General, giving the preference to the southern route for the great **Overland California Mail.**

It is asserted boldly that no emigrant trains ever passed over the road – that the country is a desert – that it is not susceptible of early settlement – and finally, that the contract will terminate in a failure, involving great loss to the government. These statements betray so total an ignorance of the selected route, that as a matter of justice to the people who occupy the new territory through which it passes, I have hastily thrown together the facts as they exist, and as I am able to certify to them from personal observation.

In no part of it is there a distance of thirty miles without water, and it often is found at a distance of ten to fifteen, with plenty of good grazing. From Tucson, the principal town of the Gadsden purchase, (throughout the whole length of which this route runs,) to the Gila River, nineteen miles, there is in the dry season no water, and here two Artesian wells will be necessary. In the wet season there is plenty of water.

Down the Gila River to Fort Yuma, one hundred and seventy-five miles, there is plenty of water and grass. From Fort Yuma, on the Colorado River, to Carisa Creek, about one hundred miles, the route is heavy with sand, and water is found at three places in all seasons – in the wet season every few miles.

Fort Yuma (on hill in upper right) ca. 1852

According to Gerald T. Anhert, "Jaeger's camp and ferry (upper left) about five years before the camp expanded and became a Butterfield stage station. Notice the ferry floating down river. The ferry would load up on the south bank and then float about two miles down river to the opposite side. This means the Southern Overland Trail would start on the north bank of the river about two miles below Jaeger's. They would then unload and by using ropes walk along the bank hauling the ferry back up river to the camp ferry site. The hill shown lower right is now the site of the Yuma jail."

Twenty-five miles from the Fort of Colorado City, are Cook's wells, which at the expense of one thousand dollars, can be made to furnish an ample supply for any number of animals; twenty-six miles beyond are the Almo Muche wells, which can be enlarged at the same cost to any quantity desired; thirty miles further are the Indian wells, which also will yield an ample supply; twenty miles further on are the Sackett wells, which are fed from the subterranean stream and can be made to supply any desired quantity of water.

From Cerisa Creek into San Diego the route is well watered, and affords excellent grazing; the distance is one hundred and twenty-five miles, but the Supervisors of San Diego county are engaged in laying out a new road, which will shorten the distance.

The statement that no emigrant train *[wagon train]* had passed over the southern route is so totally absurd that the readers of the *Times* must have been surprised at the evident mistake. The whole southern emigration in the early days of the California excitement passed over it, amounting in some years to six or eight thousand.

***Dragoons** were considered an elite fighting force trained to fight both on horseback and on foot. By the late 1850's, the army had two regiments of dragoons, one regiment of mounted riflemen, and two regiments of light cavalry. To simplify matters, in 1861, all of the mounted regiments were redesignated or renamed cavalry, thereby ending the era of the dragoon. Image at right by H. Charles McBarron.*

Lieut. Canto, with a company of first dragoons, was sent out to the Colorado River to protect the emigration. Afterwards Major S. T. Hembyteman and Major Fitzgerald, with five companies of infantry and dragoons, were stationed at the crossing of the Colorado for the same purpose, and to chastise the Yuma Indians for the murder and robbery of emigrant trains *[wagon trains]*. Hundreds of emigrants yearly pass over it now, and during my term of service at Fort Yuma more than a hundred thousand head of sheep, besides several large droves of cattle, were driven over the entire length of the route for the California market.

Last year four companies of the first dragoons marched from El Paso to Tucson and three more companies passed over the entire route to Fort Tejon, California, with over two hundred horses and a large number of six mule teams.

At present Fort Yuma is esteemed the most important post in California, and is garrisoned by three companies to protect the emigrant trains from the attacks of the Indians.

Perry Ferry Crossing the Colorado River, Yuma, Arizona

Two ferries have heretofore found active employment in crossing emigrant trains *[wagon trains]* and cattle at the Colorado River, near Fort Yuma. They are now, by purchase at large amount, merged into one, and I have known the receipts of the Colorado ferry company to be more than $2,000 in a single day. This does not look much like an unknown and impassable route.

Already Colorado City, opposite Fort Yuma, is a place of pecuniary value *[monetary value]* and importance, and its position at the only secure crossing of the river – at the junction of the Gila River and Colorado River – at the present head of navigation of the river make it certain that it will be a large town at no distant day.

The Territory of Arizona is not only capable of attracting emigration and settlement, but is now being rapidly settled. Families, women and children are now moving from California to the new purchase – many fine claims are already located in the numerous valleys of the middle portion of the territory. Old ranches, long deserted by the Mexicans, who had not the strength or the spirit to resist Indian attacks, are being re-occupied and will this year yield large and paying crops.

Two steamers pass regular upon the Colorado River to Fort Yuma, and already an active and growing trade exists between Mexico and Tubor and Arizona and San Francisco.

In almost any issue of the San Francisco dailies, your readers may see vessels advertised for the mouth of the Colorado. The mining companies alone last year consumed about $100,000 worth of goods purchased in San Francisco, and this amount will be largely increased this year

A settlement will at once be made at every point where military protection is afforded, for the country will richly repay the industrious emigrant, be he farmer or mechanic.

Town and Valley of Mesilla, 1854.
Lithograph from drawing made by Carl Schuchard.

The Mesilla Valley already contains a respectable population, and there is no doubt but that the territory will contain at least two thousand permanent voters by the beginning of the next Congress.

The petition of the people of the new territory will, it is believed, be favorably heard by the next Congress, and a separate territorial government established. the justice of the claim, and the necessity for the legislation, is but too apparent to a resident of the territory.

The Postmaster General has shown his thorough knowledge of the country and its availability by selecting the southern route.

Town of Paso del Norte *(present day Ciudad Juarez) showing cathedral and plaza, 1854. Lithograph from drawing by Carl Schuchard.*

For years a mail has been regularly carried from San Antonio to El Paso without difficulty or danger except from Indians. At present a monthly mail is carried by government express for the troops in the Gadsden Purchase (Arizona) from El Paso to Tucson, three hundred and forty miles. It is escorted by dragoons.

Fort Yuma and San Diego have for five years been connected by a semi-monthly mail (government express) which during my two years service, at Fort Yuma was much more regular in its arrival than the New York and Washington mails have been for the past two years. – The only part of the route not opened to a mail is that from Fort Yuma to Tucson, two hundred and sixty miles, and this is almost daily travelled by the people of the territory, by emigrants, and by Mexicans. Tucson is a growing town, and will afford all the grain needed to El Paso.

The Pimas villages on the Gila River will supply grain for the route to Fort Yuma. At Fort Yuma last year a large quantity of corn was allowed to rot by the man who raised it, for want of a market. There is foraging for ten thousand animals on the river banks.

Pimos Indians

The Pima lived along the Gila, Salt, Yaqui, and Sonora Rivers. Their homes consisted of oval lodges covered in grass and mud over a superstructure of poles.

A few military posts, which would be necessary on either of the routes, will make this perfectly safe; and this immense mineral wealth in silver and copper will at once draw to Arizona a large population.

It is *the only available route* at all seasons of the year which can at once be opened.

The route through the south pass is as much closed by snow four to six months in the year as if it was barred with a gate of adamant.

During the winters of 1854 and 1855, I was in the Salt Lake Valley, and no mail from the east reached us, from November to April. The mail was carried on pack mules, and was in the charge of experienced men, who had spent their lives on the plains. If they could not get through either way with pack mules, how much less chance is there for Concord coaches?

The central route is no better. I refer to Col. Fremont, and to Lieut. Beale, upon their reputation as travelers, to state how much dependence can be placed upon the regular transmission of the semi-weekly mail, through the Cochetopee Pass, in December, January, February and March.

The route by El Paso and Fort Yuma is open the entire year. On both the other routes Artesian wells are necessary to get water at convenient distances, and this upon the southern route is therefore no extraordinary argument against it.

I may be allowed to remark that the impression so generally diffused in the eastern States that Arizona territory is a wild desert and a God-forsaken country, is entirely erroneous. It will be remembered that California was stigmatized with the same epithets, and said to produce nothing but gold. Arizona promises to command the world, not only, like California, with her gold, to produce silver enough to supply all the demands of commerce, but to show to the emigrant in search of a sweet and fruitful homestead, beautiful valleys and clear running steams, where he may cultivate two crops, with a fullness of fruit only known to the virgin soil of our western possessions.

There are other aspects to this question, such as its connection with the Pacific railroad, the acquisition of Sonora, and the repeopling of a country depopulated by the Indians, which I am tempted to touch, but my letter is already too long. I am, sir, with great regard,

Your faithful servant,
Sylvester Mowry, Lt. U.S.

August 15, 1857
Overland Route is Not Close to Hot Springs, Arkansas

August 15, 1857, Saturday, page 2
*Arkansas State Gazette a*nd Democrat, Little Rock, Ark.

Editorial Correspondence – Hot Springs. – August 12, 1857. – ... In my last letter the fact was mentioned, that the route for the Pacific **Overland Mail**, passed near this place *[Hot Springs, Arkansas]*. This was a slight mistake, induced by the fact that the party camped near where the Mount Ida road turns off. The route passes directly through the valley, crossing the Quachita River at Kerly's Ferry, thence to Caddo Cove, a distance of about 35 miles; from which place it will take as near a direct line as practicable for Preston, Texas. It is said that the country on the proposed line, between here and Red River, though somewhat undulating, is less hilly than that between Hot Springs and Little Rock. If this be the case it will be one of the very best stage roads in Arkansas.

As information is received, in regard to this survey, it shall be laid before our readers. This is the "sign" which "goes before" the great Pacific Rail Road. And, when that is completed, if it comes through our borders, we will have secured the goose which lays a golden egg each night...

Ferry and houseboat on the Ouachita River at Camden
(Ouachita County); circa 1930

August 25, 1857
Continued Interest in Route Chosen

August 25, 1857, page 2
Arkansas True Democrat, Little Rock, Arkansas

The *Washington Telegraph* has an article on the **California Overland Mail Route.** Commenting upon Lieut. Mowry's letter, it says: "This letter from one who has had every opportunity of examining the country thoroughly, shows clearly and conclusively that the Postmaster General, in giving this route the preference for the transportation of the **Overland Mail** to the Pacific, selected altogether the best and most practicable route. That it will be the route of the great Southern Pacific railroad, we think is a settled point."

The *Van Buren Intelligencer* has the following announcement: "A convention will be held at Clarksville, Johnson County, on Monday, the 14th day of September next, to devise ways and means for opening a wagon road on the 35th parallel to California, and to secure transportation of the **U. S. Overland Mail** over said road. Let every county, interested in this movement, be fully represented.

We hope this meeting will be a large one and every county in the State *[of Arkansas]* will be represented."

September 1, 1857
Continued Interest in Route Chosen

September 1, 1857, page 2
Arkansas True Democrat, Little Rock, Arkansas

FROM WASHINGTON CITY – WASHINGTON D. C., AUGUST 17, 1857 – The title to the lands belonging to the Cairo and Fulton railroad and the Memphis branch have been perfected by the General Land Office, and it is now hoped we will have good accounts from both enterprises. The location of the **Overland Mail Route** has unquestionably given these routes much prominence and favor with the public, but it is contended that of itself it is no indication the Pacific road, if built at all, will take that direction.

September 5, 1857
Waiting News From Overland Expedition

September 5, 1857, Saturday, page 2
Arkansas State Gazette and Democrat, Little Rock, Ark.

EDITORIAL CORRESPONDENCE – HOT SPRINGS. – AUGUST 25, 1857. – ... The overland train for California, which passed through Little Rock last week, has not yet arrived at this place *[Hot Springs, Arkansas]*; nor has intelligence been received of the advance *[wagon]* train which left here some weeks since to select and locate the route for the **Overland California Mail**. Soon as intelligence is received it shall be laid before our readers...

September 12, 1857
Assistant Postmaster General

September 12, 1857. Saturday, page 2
Weekly Arkansas Gazette

WASHINGTON, SEPT. 2. – Assistant Postmaster Dundas will shortly proceed to New York to make arrangements for facilitating the transportation of the **Overland Mail** to California.

1870 Bird's Eye View Map of Little Rock

September 15, 1857
Overland Mail Co. Route
Brings Bright Future for Little Rock

September 15, 1857, page 3
Arkansas True Democrat, Little Rock, Arkansas

THE CITY OF LITTLE ROCK. – *FROM THE MEMPHIS APPEAL* – As little as may have been said upon the subject, there can be no doubt but that a fair and flourishing future awaits our sister city *[of Little Rock]*.

Ere long it will be the local centre of two very important railroads, running from Cairo and Memphis. Besides this, it is the converging point of the **Overland Mail** routes to California, running from St. Louis and Memphis. These facts of themselves will make Little Rock a commercial point of no inconsiderable importance.

The City of Little Rock and its enlightened and hospitable citizens, are in every respect worthy of the high destiny that awaits them, and will be ready to receive, with welcome hands, the tide of emigrations which must inevitably contribute to populate their beautiful city, and to make it one of the most important, if not the first, trading point on the route to California, beyond the Mississippi.

Little Rock is situated on the bold and commanding bluff on the south side of the Arkansas River, and is one of the most beautiful sites for a city that could be imagined. From the edge of the bold precipitous bluff on which it is situated, there extends backward for a mile, an extended plateau, just enough undulating to admit of sufficient drain. The scenery of the river here is very picturesque, the "Big Rock" four miles above the city, presenting a fine foreground to the picture.

"Big Rock on the Arkansas River"

This steamboat is passing the landmark "big rock" which is two or three miles upstream from the "Little Rock' located on the opposite bank of the Arkansas River. Source: Harper's Weekly, May 26, 1866, page 328

BLISSVILLE, LITTLE ROCK, ARKANSAS.—[See Page 346.]

The city contains many handsome private residences and superb grounds, ornamented in the best style of landscape. The Arsenal grounds, just outside the city, present one of the most beautiful drives in the United States. Its graveled and winding roads and tastefully arranged shrubbery and shades is one of the most interesting adjuncts of the city.

Little Rock Arsenal, 1861
Source: Harper's Weekly, March 9, 1861, page 148

Main Street Little Rock, 1860-1868

There can be no doubt that when the contemplated **Overland Mail** across the continent shall be put in operation and the road is placed in traveling order, that it will carry along with it a heavy tide of trade by the way of Little Rock, which will add immensely at once to its trade. Being the first considerable point west of the Mississippi, on the two routes from St. Louis and Memphis, and situated at their junction, and being the last accessible point, by river navigation, in the direction of El Paso, its position is commanding and unequivocal, and its future prospects fixed.

But what shall we say of its destiny when trains from the Atlantic and Pacific shall meet together there and link together the eastern and western shores of the Union? What shall we predict of it when Cairo and Memphis, the northeastern and the lower Mississippi flood of travel pour over the iron roadways now in progress? We leave this to the imagination of our readers, for were we to state the reality, it would be set down as the wildest fancy. – *The Memphis Appeal*

Port of Little Rock, Arkansas River

September 15, 1857
50 Delegates Attend Overland Meeting

September 15, 1857, page 2
Arkansas True Democrat, Little Rock, Arkansas

The *Fort Smith Herald,* of the 5th, contains an account of a meeting of the citizens of Sebastian County in that city, on the Thursday previous, at which some fifty delegates were appointed to attend the convention held at Clarksville on the 14th, to take into consideration the **Overland Mail Route** to the Pacific.

September 22, 1857
Continued Interest in Route Chosen
Pacific Telegraph Hopes

September 22, 1857, page 2
Arkansas True Democrat, Little Rock, Arkansas

THE PACIFIC OVERLAND MAIL ROUTE – We are indebted to one of the secretaries, JOHN E. MANLEY, esq., for the proceedings of the convention held at Clarksville, on the 14th inst., to urge the praticability of an **Overland Mail to the Pacific**, via Fort Smith, on the 35th parallel of latitude. They were received, however, too late for insertion this week. We will publish them in full in our next issue.

For Mr. Manley's kindness in sending us these proceedings, and for many other similar valuable services, we tender him our sincere thanks. In these dull times, when it is so difficult to make up an interesting paper, such assistance as Mr. Manley frequently renders us, is highly appreciated.

FROM WASHINGTON D. C. SEPTEMBER 14, 1857 – *the Pacific Telegraph* – In the mean time on this continent another telegraphic scheme occupies the attention of the public, that of a telegraph to the Pacific. This has been agitated, but will be presented to the next Congress in a more tangible form than it has heretofore been. With the wagon roads now being opened, and the successful operations of the **Overland Mail Route**, many obstacles to the successful operation of the enterprise will be removed.

October 6, 1857
Butterfield Has Letter Held at Post Office

October 6, 1857, page 3

Arkansas True Democrat, Little Rock, Arkansas

A List of Letters remaining in the Post Office at Little Rock, Ark., on the 30th day of September, 1857; which if not taken out before the 31st day of December, 1857, will be sent to the General Post Office as dead letters. *[among a list of several hundred names...]*

Butterfield, Dinsmore & Co.

Persons calling for these letters will please say they are advertised. John E. Reardon, P. M.

October 6, 1857
Fort Smith, not Little Rock, will be the Merger Point

October 6, 1857, page 3

Arkansas True Democrat, Little Rock, Arkansas

From Washington D. C., Sept. 21, 1857 –

... Since the adoption of the **Overland Pacific Mail Route**, there has been much dissatisfaction expressed by the people and especially by capitalists in the northern and northwestern States, as all of their western railroads point to St. Louis. Before and since the adoption of the route they have vehemently protested against the route selected, so much so indeed that the Postmaster General has consented to a modification.

The branch starting at St. Louis, instead of going to Little Rock, goes further westward by way of Springfield, Mo., Fayetteville, Van Buren and Fort Smith, Ark., to Preston, Texas, where it joins the other route. This modification is well, as the north was so violently opposed to the route selected, having the power of Congress, it is said would at the next session have changed it to suit themselves, having but one starting, that of St. Louis. As it is, it will be satisfied with the change. The change will not affect the interests of the south and will give greater security to the whole route.

To Arkansas it will make but little difference as it will pass through as much of the State as before, and will certainly prove more acceptable to the west, which was disposed to grumble at the former action of the P. M. General.

This change has been effected with but little if any additional expense to the government. The contract has been agreed to and signed by the parties, goes into operation as early as practicable, and runs six years.

The first *["Jack Ass Route"]* **Overland Mail** from San Diego, Cal., has reached San Antonio, Texas, and came through without interruption.

FROM WASHINGTON, SEPT. 14 – The modifications made to the **Overland Mail Route** at the instance of Hon. John S. Phelps, but which require the assent of the contractors, are as follows: The route, starting from St. Louis, to pass not further west than Springfield, Missouri; thence by Fayetteville, Van Buren and Fort Smith, Arkansas, to Preston, Texas, intersecting at that point the route from Memphis via Little Rock, Preston and Fort Fillmore to San Francisco.

A letter received from Lt. Beale's party states that his wagon road expedition reached Albuquerque on the 9th of August en route for Forte Defiance. They will follow the Whippell trail pretty closely. the Navajas *[Navajo Indians]* were troublesome.

October 6, 1857
Overland Will Bring Prosperity

October 6, 1857, page 3
Arkansas True Democrat, Little Rock, Arkansas

SEBASTIAN COUNTY, FT. SMITH, SEPT. 27TH, 1857 – EDITOR TRUE DEMOCRAT – There is some stir about the **Overland Mail Route,** and as we all have an abiding confidence in its transit, that it must pass our flourishing town, we are in good spirits, hoping to make, in the sale of our surplus products, money enough to add to our comforts, and use our best exertions to improve the country we live in.

October 10, 1857
Local Committee Recommends a Route for the Butterfield

October 10, 1857, Saturday, page 2
Arkansas State Gazette and Democrat, Little Rock, Ark.

From the Van Buren Intelligencer

PROCEEDINGS OF THE CLARKSVILLE CONVENTION. – In answer to a call from various portions of the western counties of this State, a convention assembled at Clarksville *[Arkansas]* on the 14th inst., for the purpose of taking into consideration the establishment of an **Overland Mail** to San Francisco, California.

The convention was called to order by the Honorable W. W. Floyd, of Johnson County, upon whose motion Gen. A. G. Mayers, of Sebastian, was requested to preside over the convention, and Jordan E. Cravens, Esq., and E. Manley, Esq., of Johnson County, were appointed secretaries.

The credentials of the various delegates present were then examined, whereupon the following gentlemen appeared and took their seats:

From Sabastian County, A. G. Mayers, E. F. Clark, R. H. McConnell, J. B. Luce, B. T. Duval, Martin W. Bunch, Alexander Cahall and Thomas S. Drew.

From Crawford County, Hugh F. Thomason, John T. Humphreys.

From Franklin County, S. Boone, W. W. Mansfield, W. Shores, Richard Gaines, Wm. Steel.

From Washington County, W. D. Reagan, L. Gregg.

From Johnson County, John S. Houston, James B. Wilson, L. C. Howell, W. W. Floyd, Williams Adams, A. M. Ward, Joseph Atkins, John E. Manley, Jordan E. Cravens, Felix I. Batson, M. Rose, Jesse Mason, G. W. Paine, N. D. Griffith, Isaac W. Walton, Jacob Rogers, A. Lasater, James L. Lasater, Jos. James, T. M. Wamack, Oliver Basham, Wm. Connelly, D. Hardwick.

From Yell County, Benjamin J. Jackoway, G. W. Williams.

On motion of Mr. Thomason, the President was requested to explain the object of the convention, which he proceeded to do with great clearness and precision.

After the President had concluded his remarks, several resolutions were offered and propositions submitted by Mr. Clark, Gov. Drew, Mr. Humphreys, and others, giving rise to an animated and protracted debate which was terminated by the adoption of a resolution offered by Mr. Humphreys to refer the various matters before the convention to a committee consisting of two delegates from each county. Whereupon a committee was constituted by the appointment of J. B. Luce and B. T. Duval, of Sebastian, H. F. Thomason and J. T. Humphreys of Crawford, W. D. Regan and L. Gregg of Washington, S. Boone and W. W Mansfield of Franklin, W. W. Floyd and Wm. Adams of Johnson, G. J. Jocoway and E. W. Williams of Yell. The convention then adjourned to give the committee an opportunity of discharging its duties.

At 7 p.m. the convention re-assembled when Mr. Luce submitted, as the result of the labors of the committee, the following report:

The committee having had under consideration the matters and resolutions referred to it, beg leave to report that in regard to an **Overland Mail** route from the Mississippi River to San Francisco, the committee is satisfied from all the information within its reach that the shortest and best, is the route from Memphis, by way of the 35th parallel, following the survey made my Lieut. Whipple in 1853, to the Mohave River, and passing from thence, through the Tulare Valley to San Francisco.

In arriving at this conclusions the committee has been influenced in regard to that portion of the route lying west of the Rio Grande in part by the account of the journey of Mr. F. X. Aubrey, from California to Albuquerque, through the Telon and Zuni passes, published a few years ago, and extensively copied at the time in the Arkansas papers; but principally by the official report of Lieut. Whipple, which not only fully confirms the previous statement of Mr. Aubrey, but contains important additional facts not before known.

That part of the route lying east of the Rio Grande, is much better known not only to the committee but also to other members of the convention and to their constituents. Many of them have in person explored the country between Fort Smith and the settlements near Albuquerque; others are familiar with the route from Preston to Doma Ana, explored by Capt. Marcy and Capt. Pope. The opinion has been confidently expressed by individuals acquainted with both routes that even if Dona Ann were the western terminus, or were an essential point of transaction, it would be cheaper and better to carry the mail from Little Rock by way of Fort Smith through the Valley of the Canadian to Albuquerque, or to Isleta, and thence down the Rio Grande to Donna Ana, than to attempt to take it over the sandy deserts in that part of Texas lying between the sources of the Colorado and the Rio Grande on the route adopted by the Post Master General.

The intense cold and deep snow in the mountain passes and on the plains in higher latitudes being almost universally regarded as presenting insuperable objections to the transportation of the mail during the winter season on any of the routes North of the 35th parallel, the committee has not felt itself called upon to consider any route competing with that of the 35th except the southern route near the 32d parallel.

Whether an **Overland Mail** to the Pacific is established along the 35th parallel or not, the committee is satisfied that the government would consult its best interests in expending upon the Whipple route a portion of the money appropriated for building roads across the continent, in as much as it would thereby open the most direct communication with the public officers and troops in New Mexico, and would also attract attention to by far the most valuable portion of the public lands yet unsettled. Without referring to the rich and productive country on the waters of the western Colorado inhabited by the McQuis, the Zuni and Navajo Indians, or to the unoccupied regions on the western borders of the Choctaw and Creek territory, it is well known that there is a large body of land not secured to any Indian tribe, lying west of the 100th meridian, which is capable of sustaining a dense population. All that would be necessary to ensure its speedy settlement would be the establishment of a sufficient chain of military posts for the protection of emigrants from the depredations of the Comanche and Kioway Indians, who make it their middle camping ground in their immigrations beyond the Arkansas on the north and Red River on the south. The importance of such a chain of posts cannot be too strongly urged. The tribes in question are becoming every day more troublesome and dangerous as the buffalo disappear, and can in no other way be effectually controlled. If some such measure is not speedily adopted as a precaution against Indian hostilities, the government is likely to find the pound of cure infinitely more costly than the ounce of prevention.

The inevitable consequence of complete protection from these tribes in connection with a good wagon road, attainable at a comparatively trifling expense, would be the opening of a trade between New Mexico, and western Arkansas; such a trade has enriched central Missouri; a trade that would build up settlements along the whole extent of the road – settlements such as cannot exist on the greater portion of the road from Independence to Santa Fe, and such as cannot be made to the same extent on any other **Overland Route** to the Pacific within the United States.

In connection with such settlements, the committee has thought it advisable to suggest the propriety of urging a more thorough and complete exploration of the country already referred to, lying west of the Choctaws and Creeks, and now open to a white population, especially as it is known that the government has recently bound itself by treaty stipulations with those tribes to survey and mark their western boundaries; a duty the performance of which would an ample opportunity of furnishing desirable information to the country at large.

When the true character and advantages of this middle ground between Arkansas and New Mexico are understood and appreciated, and when the general government assumes, as sooner or later it must, the effectual control of the Upper Canadians, the question of an **Overland Mail Route** to San Francisco beyond all doubt will settle itself.

Fully appreciating the importance of the speedy construction of the Fort Smith branch of the Cairo and Fulton Rail Road, the committee has not felt itself authorized under existing circumstances to do more than express the opinion embodied in the fifth of the series of resolutions herewith presented.

It is a matter of regret that want of time precludes the possibility of furnishing more information relative to the important mater before the convention, or of adding anything to the foregoing brief expressions of the views of the committee beyond the condensed statement of their substance which they have attempted to give in the following resolutions respectfully suggesting in the last of the series the mode that appears to be the most effectual for obtaining and diffusing further information.

> *Resolved,* That this convention is satisfied from all the information within its reach that the **Overland Mail Route** near the 35th parallel, starting at Memphis and following the survey made by Lieut. Whipple in 1853, is not only the shortest and best route from the Mississippi River to San Francisco, but the only route which is practicable at all seasons of the year.
>
> *Resolved,* That the general government would consult its own best interests and the interests of the country at large by the construction of a good wagon road from Fort Smith to Albuquerque on the Rio Grande, and from thence to the crossing of the Sierra Nevada at the Tejon Pass.

Resolved, That the establishment of a chain of military post from the western settlements of the Creeks and Choctawa up the valley of the Canadian to the settlements on the Rio Grande, and from thence westward to the entrance of the Tulare valley in California, is not only necessary as a measure of sound policy in preventing Indian hostilities, but also for the development of the resources of by far the most valuable of the unsettle part of the public domain.

Resolved, That a further exploration of the country between the Arkansas and Red Rivers along the west of the 100th meridian is desirable for the purpose of calling the public attention to its resources and value.

Resolved, That a permanent committee of five persons be appointed to collect and publish information relative to the practicality and advantages of the establishment of the **Overland Mail Route** from Memphis via Fort Smith, near the 35th parallel to the Tulare Valley, and thence to San Francisco, and that such committee be requested to obtain and distribute copies of Whipple's report.

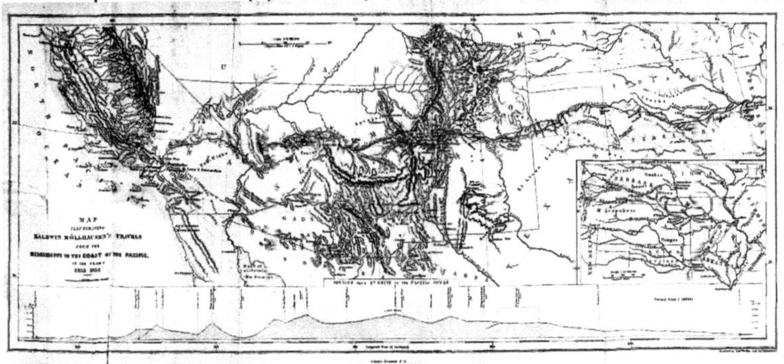

Lt. Whipple's Survey from Fort Smith to San Diego

Whipple's report, mentioned above, refers to the 13 volume 1857 government publication of Lt. A. W. Whipple's survey. It is entitled: "Reports of explorations and surveys, to ascertain the most practicable and economical route for a railroad from the Mississippi River to the Pacific Ocean. Made under the direction of the Secretary of War, in 1853-4, according to Acts of Congress of March 3, 1853, May 31, 1854, and August 5, 1854."

After reading the report and resolutions, Mr. Luce proceeded to explain at great length the reasons which had influenced the committee in arriving at its conclusions – conclusions which had met with the full concurrence of every one of its members. After he had finished, the report and resolutions were adopted without a dissenting voice.

The following resolution was then offered by ex-Gov. Drew and adopted:

> *Resolved,* That this convention views with deep concern the general apathy pervading this community in regard to the construction of the Little Rock and Fort Smith branch of the Cairo and Fulton Rail Road and while it eschews any design to take any active part in a matter pertaining exclusively to an organized company or companies, yet deems it the right of the citizens of the counties through which the road lies, to call the attention of the public to the importance of some harmonious action of the friends of each side of the Arkansas River, in view of accepting the tendered aid from abroad which has been offered in aid of the contemplated work.

The following gentlemen were then constituted members of the permanent committee of five to collect and publish information in regard to the **Overland Route** near the 35th parallel, J. B. Luce, B. T. Duval, S. F. Clark, Jesse Turner and A. G. Mayers.

A resolution was adopted requesting all papers friendly to the cause to publish the proceedings of the convention.

On motion of Mr. Humphreys the thanks of the convention were unanimously voted to the President and the secretaries for the manner in which their duties had been discharged. The convention then, at a late hour in the evening, adjourned *sine die.*

October 17, 1857
Immigrants to California

October 17, 1857, page 2

Arkansas State Gazette and Democrat, Little Rock, Ark.

California News – Overland immigrants are daily entering the State *[of California]* through the various passes of the Sierra Nevada. Many of them have, beside their ordinary household effects, more or less stock, most of which has suffered little from their long tramp across the plains. In the mountains beyond Carson Valley, the immigrants have experienced much annoyance from the depredations of Indians, who have killed or driven off stock, and, in some instances, as will be seen elsewhere, have committed murder.

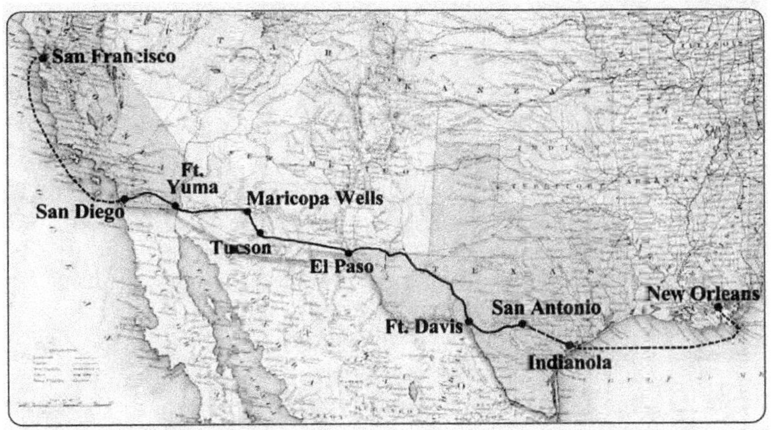

Map Showing the Entire San Diego and San Antonio "Jackass" Route
Source: Mails of the Westward Expansion,
Steven C. Walske and Richard C. Frajola, Western Cover Society

December 9, 1857
Before Butterfield
There Was The "Jack Ass" Mail Route
from San Antonio to San Diego

December 9, 1857, Wednesday
Washington Telegraph, Washington, Arkansas

Overland Pacific Mail Route – The *San Antonio Herald* states that the contractors on this route are ready to receive passengers, and that the last trip from San Antonio to San Diego was made in twenty-six days. The *Herald* says this route will soon be lined with emigrants, and dotted here and there with permanent settlers. It passes over one of the best regions in the United States, and is the shortest and the best route between the great valley of the Mississippi and the Pacific.

Drawn by Jack Ass Mail Route Passenger
*The name **"Jack Ass Mail Route"** came from the fact that on over 100 miles of this route, passengers departed the stage to ride a mule over that section.*

December 12, 1857
Kirkbride Potts Returns From Cattle Sale in California With Enough Funds to Build the Future Butterfield Potts Inn Home Station

December 12, 1857

Arkansas State Gazette and Democrat, Little Rock, Ark.

Thanks to our friend KIRKBRIDE POTTS, ESQ., of Pope County, who has just returned from California, for files of late papers. *[NOTE: Editors loved to receive copies of newspapers from other cities so they could reprint articles in their papers. In a few years this news transmittal system was replaced by the telegraph, the Associated Press (AP), then teletype, and eventually the internet.]*

December 22, 1857
More About the "Jack Ass" Mail Route That Preceded the Butterfield Overland Mail

December 22, 1857, page 3

Arkansas True Democrat, Little Rock, Arkansas

STAGING TO THE PACIFIC. – The **Overland Mail Line** now in operation form San Antonio, Texas, to San Diego, California, carries passengers through. On the sixth trip westward, four *[passengers]* were thus conveyed to San Diego. The way mails are much increased. The entire road is now stocked with four hundred animals, twenty-five coaches, and seventy five men (messengers and guards.) With this outfit they can accommodate six passengers. Further arrangements are being completed to accommodate passengers through to New Orleans by this route. The fare from San Diego to New Orleans is $200, which sum includes meals on the route. The eighth mail from San Diego was to have been dispatched on the 23d of October, with a full complement of passengers. The schedule time for the trip of this line is thirty days. *[NOTE: This article was also printed in the January 9, 1858 issue of Little Rock's Weekly Arkansas Gazette.]*

December 22, 1857
President Buchanan's State of the Union Address Commends the Overland Mail

December 22, 1857, page 3

Arkansas True Democrat, Little Rock, Arkansas

...I commend to your consideration the report of the department in relation to the establishment of the **Overland Mail Route** from the Mississippi River to San Francisco California.

The route was selected with my full concurrence as the one, in my judgement, best calculated to attain the important objects contemplated by Congress...

1858

January 5, 1858
Annual Report of the Postmaster General

January 5, 1858, page 2
Arkansas True Democrat, Little Rock, Arkansas

Annual Report of the Postmaster General. – ... The grounds of the decision of the Postmaster General in favor of the southern route between the valley of the Mississippi River and San Francisco, for the conveyance of the **Overland Mails** to California, are set forth at great length, as are also the reasons which decided the department to accept the bids of **Merrs. Butterfield & Co.** Although the route selected does not bear out the glowing descriptions given of it by some of its earlier explorers, the evidence laid before the department led to concur in the opinion of Mr. Bartlett, that is presents more advantages for a great national highway than any yet discovered to California.

January 12, 1858
Visit with Overland Superintendent

January 12, 1858
Arkansas True Democrat, Little Rock, Arkansas

We had the pleasure of a visit on yesterday form Mr. J. Glover, agent of the Pacific **Overland Mail Route,** He is upon a reconnaissance expedition to Preston. He arrived in our city on Sunday and was to have left yesterday evening. Next week we shall lay before our readers the facts we learned from him in regard to this route.

February 13, 1858
Arkansas to Send Expedition

February 13, 1858
Arkansas State Gazette and Democrat, Little Rock, Ark.

Editorial Correspondence – Fort Smith, *Feb. 6th, 1858* – Dear H. – I had hoped to be at home, or on the way thither, before this time; but, owing to unexpected delays, am still at this place *[Fort Smith]*.

My trip up on the Quapaw was a pleasant and a quick one – leaving Little Rock on Wednesday morning and arriving here on Thursday evening. Here I found great improvement since my last visit – the improvements being all the best, and the most permanent and durable character, all of the store houses large and good buildings – and some of them capacious and fine enough for any city in the Union. The country dependent on this place, as a shipping and trading point, is rich and improving as fast as the town. Business, of every kind, appears to be brisk and prosperous – and every thing promises a speedy development of the Western end of the State *[of Arkansas]*.

The Circuit Court of Crawford County met, at Van Buren, on last Monday – there was an able bar in attendance, but little business of importance. At Van Buren I had the pleasure of meeting with General H. F. Thomason, and Major W. D. Reagan – late American nominee for Congress and Presidential elector – both looking as well and as cheerful as if they had been elected, and both still firm in their belief in the cause of Americanism.

Van Buren, too has improved since my last visit – and, as at Fort Smith, the business houses and the merchants would do credit to any city. Much to the credit of both, there no longer exists the bitter spirit of rivalry, between these two frontier cities, which characterized them a few years since; for now they are working, hand in hand, for the development, progress, and advancement of the whole Western end of the State *[of Arkansas]*.

There is now a movement on foot to get the branch of the **Overland Pacific Mail** which leaves St. Louis, Missouri, to come by way of Fort Smith and up the Arkansas Valley, instead of connecting with the Memphis branch at Little Rock. To this end, an exploring expedition is to leave this place in the course of two or three weeks, for the purpose of marking out a way, finding suitable stations and camping places, and doing such other things as will tend to bring to light the true advantages of this over the other routes to the Pacific.

Delaware Indians
Kwackipahki Kamen (aka George T. Anderson) (Delaware), Wi-Ta-Pano-Xwe (aka James C. Webber) (Cherokee/Delaware/Munsee) Image taken in 1932.

This party, fitted out by the citizens of Van Buren and Fort Smith, will consist of twelve white men, and eleven Delaware Indians, commanded by Capt. John Dillard, and accompanied by Dr. Shumard, geologist, who has already made several trips over the plains.

As a citizen of Arkansas, anxious to see all of the resources of the State developed, and having no feeling in favor of one *section* of the State over another, as such, I desire to take no sides as between the rival routes to the pacific through the State until the best and the most practicable one has been discovered: when that is ascertained all should work as one man, without tiring, or stopping to rest, until it is known to the world and adopted. The citizens of this end of the State *[of Arkansas]* deserve great credit for their expenditures of labor and money to bring to light their advantages as the starting point for the **Overland Pacific Mail** and emigration; and whether they get the mail route or not, my impression is that, ere long *[ere long: before long]*, the overland emigration to the Pacific must start from this place, and make it their rendezvous preparatory to departure. And this will be of much greater importance than all of the mail routes which will ever connect the Atlantic and Pacific.

January 26, 1858
Military Road Construction in Southwest

January 26, 1858

Arkansas True Democrat, Little Rock, Arkansas

The Camels – The war department have received despatches from Lieut. Beale, formerly of the navy, superintending the construction of the military road from Fort Defiance to the Colorado, of California...

I have subjected them *[The camels]* to trials which no other animal could possibly have endured, and yet I have arrived here not only without the loss of a camel, but they are admitted by those who saw them in Texas, to be in as good condition today as when we left San Antonio...

They have traversed patiently with heavy packs, on these explorations, counties covered with the sharpest volcanic rock, and yet their feet, to this hour, have evinced no symptoms of tenderness or injury. With heavy packs they have crossed mountains, ascended and descended precipitous places, where an unloaded mule found it difficult to pass even with the assistance of the rider dismounted and carefully picking his way...

U.S. Sailors Loading Camels for Trip to Southwest USA

January 30, 1858
"Jack Ass" Overland Mail Delayed by Snow

January 30 1858, page 2

Weekly Arkansas Gazette, Little Rock, Ark.

The last San Diego overland mail arrived at San Antonio on the 10th inst., encountered very heavy snows in the gorges of the mountains, in consequence of which a portion of the matter had to be left behind.

February 27, 1858
Overland Route to California
Should be of Interest to Arkansans

February 27, 1858

Arkansas State Gazette and Democrat, Little Rock, AR

THE ARKANSAS **OVERLAND ROUTE TO CALIFORNIA**. – ITS IMPORTANCE, AND OUR DUTY. – There is, at present, a good deal of interest manifested and felt, on our western frontier, in regard to the overland travel from the Mississippi valley to California. The importance of this subject should make it a matter of deep interest to every portion of the State; for some think that the first route which is proved to be practicable for travelers, and the habitation of civilized man, during the whole of the year, will be the one over which the great Pacific railway will ultimately be built. If this be true – and who shall say that it is not! – then none will deny that every citizen of Arkansas should labor without ceasing for the consummation of so desirable, and so great, an end. But whether this be true or not, we apprehend there are few citizens of Arkansas who are not desirous that, until this great rail road be built, our State shall be, as undoubtedly she ought to be, the thoroughfare for the overland travel and trade, from the Mississippi valley to the Pacific and the country intervening.

Besides being a month earlier, the route of the thirty-fifth parallel, starting from Fort Smith, is several hundred miles shorter than the land travel over any more northern route; and, in view of the Mormon difficulties, it is fair to presume that however some emigrants might desire to travel a more northern route, none can go the Salt Lake route with safety, until rebellion is put down, and the weak arm of the law strengthened, in Utah.

The advantages of the thirty-fifth parallel, are now being tardily and unwillingly acknowledged by the leading men of Missouri; and, ere long *[ere long: before long]*, we hope and expect, to see the bulk of travel and trade from that State, to the Pacific, and the Plains, start from the frontier of our own State; for, on this route, the spring grass rises at least a month earlier than it does in Missouri, thereby affording ox-trains the means of leaving Fort Smith a month earlier than they could from any other starting point north of us – and it is now a pretty well conceded fact, that mule trains can travel on this parallel the whole year.

Premising, then, that the trade and emigration which has heretofore passe north of us, must soon seek a more southern passage over the continent, we shall offer a few suggestions to our own people, which we hope may prove useful and profitable to them.

In the first place, we would suggest, that it is not wise to attach too much importance to government aid; but let every friend of the undertaking put his shoulder to the wheel,and do his utmost to succeed on his own account. *Then,* if the government give aid, all will be *right,* and if it refuse aid; we will endeavor to *make it right* any how. And as no man is half so independent as he who has been the artificer of his own fortune, so will the success of this enterprise be more permanently valuable to the States, if it be won solely on its own worth and merit, and without the equivocal and uncertain aid of politicians. The doctrine of protection is exploded; and, in this practical day, every thing has to stand for fall – to succeed or fail – upon its own merits.

First means of success is to let the world know our advantages: the second is, after our advantages are known, to afford emigrants and travelers, who propose going our route, the facilities of reaching Fort Smith and Van Buren, as a place of rendezvous.

First, then, let all the light be given upon this subject – let all of the avenues of intelligence be opened and kept open – let every man who has information as to the advantages of our route, give it to the public – and let it be published both at home and abroad.

Second, let us establish a regular communication between the most prominent points from which overland emigrants embark, and the place for their rendezvous on our frontier.

To this end, let a weekly line of *[steamboat]* packets be put in operation, between Fort Smith and St. Louis – leaving Cairo, Memphis, Napoleon, and all other prominent points of embarkation at regular times. We have now, on this river, an abundance of first class boats to establish this line – and, after starting, it will pay better than the business in which they are, at present, engaged.

There are many reasons why a line of boats should be run from the Arkansas River to St. Louis, and why our merchants should purchase their supplies there instead of Cincinnati.

First. Missouri is our next neighbor – she is a slave-holding State, and has other interests and feelings in common with us; while Ohio is distant from us, and composed of a majority of rabid abolitionists, who would rob a southern man of her servant if taken within the limits of their State, though he might purchase a million's worth a year from their merchants, and, by his means, add yearly to the aggregate of their wealth.

Second. Taken altogether, the merchandise purchased at St. Louis, is superior in quality, and, for most things, identical in price, with Cincinnati.

Third. A steam boat can make a trip to St. Louis, and back, during a good stage of water, in about a week less time than the same boat can make a trip to Cincinnati and back – owning to the greater distance of the latter place. By this item alone, an ordinary boat would make a saving of from $700 to $1,400, by going to St. Louis instead of Cincinnati – rating her expenses at the low price of $100 to $200 a day – and this saving to the boats would, necessarily, ensure to the benefit of those who employ, and ship by, them.

Fourth. Except in extremely cold and freezing weather, which is worse on the Ohio than the Mississippi, and any boats which navigate the Arkansas River, can go to St. Louis, at any stage of the river, while it is a well known fact that Ohio, (besides its greater distance) is even a more uncertain stream for navigation, during a great portion of the year, than the Arkansas.

Looking at these advantages we can see no good reason why our merchants should not purchase such articles as they now get at Cincinnati, at the St. Louis market. This would be the commencement of a mutually profitable trade between us and our immediate neighbors, give employment to our home steam-boats, and afford overland emigrants the necessary facilities to reach their place of rendezvous on our frontier.

One thing then, and only one, would be necessary to secure the success of our route. Let our merchants, who are amply able to embark in the enterprise, establish houses in Sante Fe, and other proper points, and compete with the world for the trade of the Plains, at least in the neighborhood of, and below, the thirty-fifty parallel. Their facilities of procuring outlets, taken in connection with their advantages, of a more southern climate, will enable them to start before, and consequently reach the market earlier than, the more northern merchants who have heretofore had the monopoly of this trade.

Establish these relations between us and New Mexico, and place the Plains in a commercial dependence upon us, and we not only receive untold and almost incalculable wealth, from that source each year, but at the same time, we secure the **overland travel to the Pacific**, which all of its advantages, and make a bold and judicious, and very probably, a certain, move, towards securing the Pacific road on this line.

We have this put upon paper such thoughts as have offered to us in regard to **"The Arkansas Overland Route to California** – *Its Importance, and our Duty."* If, in the course of what we have said, we have run counter to the views of any one, we disclaim having done so in a controversial spirit. We are desirous of serving the country with which our life and our all are identified and we are unselfish in this. If any one can suggest a better plan than the one we have here briefly marked out, let him do it. Honorable success is what we want; and to achieve that we labor.

Without being wedded to our plan, if a better one be presented, as think it offers advantages over any other which we have, as yet, seen or heard of, in this – that while all other propose large expenditures of money, without any immediate return of profits, ours, to our mind, is entirely practicable, in the whole or in part, and will pay from the beginning to the end.

***Fort Chadbourne**, Texas was one of an outer ring of posts founded in the early 1850's to protect the Texas frontier from plundering Kiowa and Comanche Indians. Other forts in the ring were Forts Belknap, Phantom Hill, McKavett, and Clark. The post was built by companies A and K of the Eighth United States Infantry in 1852 and named for 2nd Lieutenant Theodore Lincoln Chadbourne who fought and was killed in the Mexican-American War in the Battle of Resaca de la Palma.*

March 2, 1858
Memphis Route Suggestions

March 2, 1858

Arkansas True Democrat, Little Rock, Arkansas

WASHINGTON D. C., FEB. 10TH, 1858. – ... From a synopsis of a report recently received from Col. J. B. Leach, superintendent of the El Paso and Fort Yuma wagon road, I take the following: He offers important suggestions, as to the proper route to be pursued by a **mail line, leaving Memphis for California**, by way of El Paso.

The greatest obstacle to the rapid transportation of the mails, is the difficulty of maintaining stations at convenient intervals, where fresh and recruited animals can be had.

It is not desirable to transport the mails by land from Memphis to Des Arc, as the country is low, swampy, and subject to overflow; whereas the White River is navigable from Memphis to Des Arc at all seasons. Commencing then at Des Arc, the road should proceed to Little Rock, then over the present mail route, via Washington to Ultima Thule; thence up the north side of Red River, crossing at Preston and following the main road traveled to Fort Belknap. From thence to Fort Cooper; thence to Fort Chadbourne; thence to Mustang Ponds; thence through Castle Mountain Pass.

March 3, 1858
Rumor of Route Changes

March 3, 1858, page 2
Washington Telegraph, Washington, Arkansas

The Washington correspondent of the *Baltimore Sun* says, "...The South should become more fully aroused to the importance of this territory *[Arizona]*, and as there are now exertions being made to change the selection of the **Overland Mail Route** to the Pacific, made by Postmaster General Brown, which passes through this territory *[of Arizona]*, our Representatives in congress should not waver in their duty, but take a bold and decided stand in favor of this route. This is a measure of more real importance to the South than all the questions of Kansas and Nicaragua combined."

March 9, 1858
Rumors in Washington D. C.

March 9, 1858
Arkansas True Democrat, Little Rock, Arkansas

WASHINGTON D. C. FEB. 22, 1858 – **THE OVERLAND MAIL ROUTE** – The **Overland Mail Route** to the Pacific is of some interest to the people of Arkansas, and every thing connected therewith demands their attention.

There is now on foot a scheme, that if successful would exclude any portion of the line from passing through the State – nothing less in short, than to change the route as located and to place its selection entirely at the option of the contractors, who have undertaken to carry the mail. Congress is now being worked upon to effect that object, but I trust and believe the scheme will fail.

The Postmaster General, in reply to the House committee on the post office, has written an able letter in reference thereto, and I send you a copy, hoping you may find room for it in your columns. I think there is no chance to ignore Memphis as one of the starting points of the route on the Mississippi River.

March 9, 1858
Letter from the Postmaster General

March 9, 1858
Arkansas True Democrat, Little Rock, Arkansas

Overland Mail Route to California – Letter of the Postmaster General to the Chairman of the Post Office Committee of the House of Representatives – *Post Office Department, February —,1858* – Sir: I have the honor to acknowledge the receipt of yours of the 26th June, 1857, enclosing House Report No. 50, and inquiring whether I have any information to communicate or recommendation to make touching the subject matter of the same. You further add, that the committee would be pleased to receive any information that may be in possession of the department, or any recommendation or suggestions which you may desire to make touching the subject of the **Overland Mail to California**, to assist them in arriving at a proper determination in the premises.

In reply, I beg leave to refer you to my elaborate report to the President on that subject, as containing my best convictions, after the most patient and laborious research, as to the proper route to be selected in order to carry out the true intent and purpose of Congress.

Whilst engaged in the investigation, I was constantly met with the suggestion, that the whole scheme was impracticable, and the natural obstacles, lying chiefly west of the Rio Grande, would render it impossible to obtain the service anticipated by Congress.

I am happy to inform your committee that, since this

route was established and the contract duly executed, all these forebodings have been dissipated, and the practicability of having a four-horse coach service, carrying passengers, with the required speed, has been fully demonstrated. The route established by Congress, from San Antonio, by El Paso, through the Gadsden Purchase or Arizona, passing Fort Yuma to San Diego, has been put in operation. Many trips, with passengers, have been made in excellent time, and with the happiest result.

Large public assemblies have been called at both ends of the line, and the most unbounded rejoicings have attested the success of the service.

The line of this San Antonio service is the same with that of the **overland mail** from the Rio Grande near El Paso to Fort Yuma, or the Colorado, and is to be discontinued between those points whenever the latter service begins. To abandon that line after it has been actually tested formally months is to abandon a certainty for an uncertainty, and to take away from the department and the public the certain assurance and positive knowledge that the service can and will be well performed on the route selected.

And what is to be substituted for this assurance which actual experiments have given? No route that Congress may prefer, or any that its committee may recommend, but the whole field is thrown open to the contractors, to go here or there, according to the suggestions of their own interest, swayed and influenced, as they may be, by large sectional or railroad combinations that may choose to appeal to their cupidity.

This department intends to intimate no combinations to have been, in fact, entered into in this case. It knows of no facts which would warrant such a charge, but the Postmaster General feels it to be his imperative duty to point out the almost certain consequences, which naturally grow out of conferring a power so vast and unbounded in the hands of a company of mere carriers, who owe no responsibility to the public, whose individual members may not even be known to the country. In this very case, if the action of the executive government is to be disaffirmed by conferring the power on **Messrs. Butterfield, Fargo & Co.**, what will be at once their condition?

The South Pass and Salt Lake route was zealously advocated, and great railroad interests and the interest of cities lying above St. Louis were invoked to sustain that route. Well, suppose these cities and railroad interests combined shall apply, not to Congress, not to your committee, not to the Executive of the United States, but to **Mr. Butterfield**, Mr. Fargo, and the rest of them, *in the exercise their discretion*, to start on the Mississippi above, or even at St. Louis, and thence by the South Pass, Salt Lake, etc. What answer would they make? Why, that the route was utterly impracticable from snow, ice, and mountains, for at least four or five months of the year.

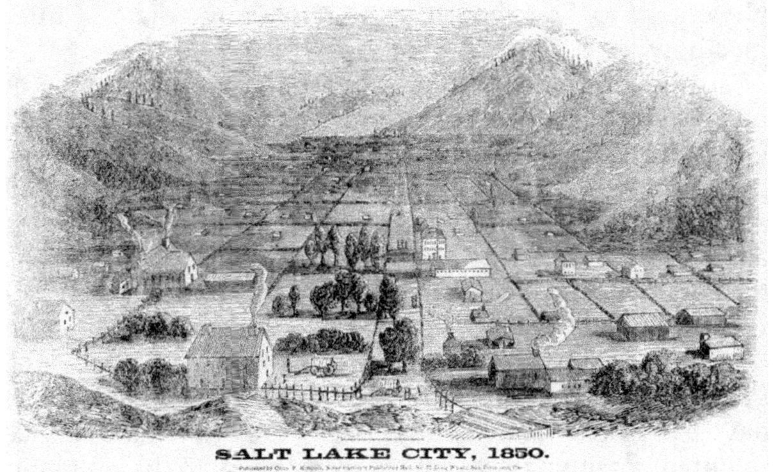

Bird's eye view of Salt Lake City, Utah, 1850,
published by Charles P. Kimball.

The reply to this may be, and according to all the laws of human nature would be, *"we know it, but we have such a large private interest vested in our railroads, town lots, etc., all along much of this route, that if you select it, we will promptly pay all the fines and forfeitures which the post office department may impose."* This might satisfy *"the bond,"* it is true, but in the meantime, for the four or five months, the public would have no mails, and the means of transportation of passengers, as well as mails, would lie entirely lost.

The department has no doubt that there are large companies and interest who might press hard on these contractors to select this Salt Lake route; and yet the positive experience of six years, as shown in pages 33 and 34 of my report, demonstrates *the utter impossibility* of conveying a mail on it for more than eight or nine months of the year. A full confirmation of all this may be found in the present condition of your army in Utah. They are embedded in the snows and ice of the Rocky Mountains. You cannot send a mule, or a horse, or a soldier, to their relief.

Although encamped within one hundred miles of the enemy, your army cannot move from its position; and from November to April you have to remain in a state of utter inactivity.

If the purpose of taking it by the Smith Pass and Salt Lake be disavowed, why is it not excluded by the bill? If St. Louis, Springfield, Neosho, Anton Chico, and Albuquerque, be the route, why not specify it as *the one* to be substituted for the one selected, leaving no room for the combinations and bids to the cupidity of contractors, under no obligations to the government or the people of the United States beyond the mere money clauses of their covenant.

Here are two routes. The one has been selected by the President, through one of his departments. The contractors have bargained, freely and willingly, to perform the service required. Positive experiments over the most difficult, and indeed, the only questionable part of the way, demonstrate beyond all *cavil*, that staged, with mails and passengers, can be, and are twice every month, conveyed in safety and comfort over it. Now, if Congress shall think this not to be the best route, why not say so itself? Why set up **Butterfield, Fargo & Co.**, not only above the President and one of his departments, but even above themselves?

There is another mode by which the propriety of this proposition may be tested by your committee. The government of the United States has a vast number of heavy contracts with steamships along our coast and steamboats along our rivers; also with railroads and stage contractors almost without number.

In every one of these the route has been established either by Congress itself or by the post office, acting under its authority. Now what would be thought of a proposition to overturn all these routes established by law, and specified in every contract, and turn the whole loose, dependent upon the selfish interest of the contractors themselves. Such a proposition would startle the whole country, and on principle would not differ in one jot or tittle from the one now under consideration.

One reflection more in this case will demonstrate beyond all disputation that this proposition is altogether wrong. By the contract made with these parties they are now bound to start at Memphis and run out to Little Rock; also, to start at St. Louis and run out, making a junction with the Memphis route either at Little Rock or Preston, in Texas, as they may choose. Other bidders stood ready to do the same service, in the same time, and for the same price, and when they lost the contract went away greatly disappointed. Now it is proposed to release **Butterfield, Fargo & Co.**, from performing the service on these two branches of the main road, and to permit them to select only *one* as may best comport with their own interest. Why, it may be well asked, this *ex post facto* easement to these particular contractors, who so many other bidders would gladly have taken the contract just as it is? If three or four hundred miles of the junction is made at Little Rock, or five or six hundred if it be by Springfield and Preston, is to be lopped off, I would think it self-evident that a pro rata deduction ought to be required in the bill proposed, which seems not at all contemplated by it in its present condition.

By reference to the 28th page of my report, it will be

seen that these contractors, and all the rest whose bids were considered regular under the advertisement and the act of Congress, expressly considered that their bids might be held and considered as extending and applying to the route selected. In proof of which, so far as the present contractors are concerned, this very line was inserted in the contract itself executed by them. On the 29th page you will discover a modification of the route, endorsed on the contract, leaving it entirely optional with them, on the conditions there expressed, to run the Missouri branch by Springfield, in Missouri, thence by Fayetteville, Van Buren, and Fort Smith, in Arkansas, making the junction at Preston, in Texas, instead of Little Rock. What the contractors may do in this respect is unknown to this department, but the option still lies open to them to do as they may choose.

This reference shows that the contractors were, in fact, *bidders ultimately for this very route,* and under any and every construction which it is possible to put on the law of Congress have no right or shadow of claim for any change or modification of their contract.

It is due to them to state that the department has no knowledge that this application is made at their instance.

Your committee having invited me to take any suggestions which I suppose might assist them in arriving at a proper determination on the subject, I avail myself of the occasion to submit a few observations in addition to those contained in my report.

If it be inquired why bidders were required in my advertisement to specify their point of starting on the Mississippi, and the prominent points by which they proposed to pass, the answer is an obvious one.

It would be otherwise impossible to judge of the *reasonableness of the price* demanded for the service. Some routes would be longer and others shorter, some more and others less expensive, some possible and others not possible; and the department not being *commanded* but only *authorized,* to establish an **overland mail** to California, could not consent in the exercise of a sound discretion, to attempt the required service over any route which, in the nature of things, could not be regularly performed.

The Postmaster General well remembers a protracted and very useful conference with the late lamented Rusk, who was as much or more the author of the measure than any body else. He had been long at the head of the post office committee in the Senate. He had resided for many years in Texas, and had traversed much of the route selected. His assurances were emphatic and frequent, that to attempt to obtain the services called for in the act of Congress over any other than the El Paso route, would prove to be a dead failure for at least three or four months of the year.

After more than one conference with Gen. Rusk, the department addressed itself to the execution of the law, with all that industry and entire exemption from personal interest and previous bias which so great a subject required. The Postmaster General refers to this report as attesting, at least, his earnest desire to collect all the facts connected with the object — the distances, the elevations, the deserts and mountains, the climate, the supplies of water, the amount of arable land, etc., on each of the prominent routes All the facts set forth in that report were drawn from the most reliable sources, and this department yet believes they are substantially correct and fully sustain the selection of route and the contract made upon it.

The Postmaster General was not selecting, nor the contractors bidding for a railroad, but for a *stage line,* to be put into operation within *twelve months,* and to be run in the short time of *twenty-five days.* But the complaints and criticism now being made relate to it as a selection of a *railroad* route to the Pacific. Estimates are made as to the relative area of country west and east of the Mississippi. But what have the number of *acres* of land — much of which is yet to be inhabited — to do with a mail stage line to be established in a single year? The desired service related to *population,* to *present correspondence,* to the immediate transportation of passengers, and not to the facilities of a railroad, which could not be completed during the entire period that this coach service was to be contracted for. What means it, then, to subject this location for one service to criticisms and argument which can have no relation but to another and different object.

Congress never ordered a railroad to laid off by this department, nor its mail to be transmitted by one, and yet the two subjects have been strangely and unnecessarily connected with each other.

The true solution of this error, however, is to be found in the supposition that the successful operation of this stage line, and the settlements made along it, many have a great influence on the future location of a railroad, if one shall be constructed, prejudicial to the interest of some railroad corporation, or injurious to the prosperity of certain rival cities that have already or may hereafter spring up on other routes than the one selected. These conflicting and rival interests now press forward with their objections to prevent the initiation of a policy which they fear may prove injurious to them. There is nothing strange, perhaps nothing wrong, in all this; and the only question presented to your committee is whether this department, acting in full and perfect harmony with the Executive, has under all the circumstances of the case, come as nearly to a fair and reasonable adjustment of these conflicting interests, as was to have been expected. Why did not Congress establish the line for both the coach service and the future railroad? Simply because they could not agree on the subject. They devolved it on the Postmaster General to do a perplexing piece of business which they themselves had tried unsuccessfully during several sessions.

He has performed the perplexing and difficult duty with a disinterestedness that challenges all complaints, but with a distrust of his ability to do it well, which will induce him to yield, with pleasure, to the superior judgment of your committee and of Congress. If he had been left to the consideration of mere geographical rights, and what was due to the present and future population of the whole country, he would have made but one terminus on the Mississippi River, and that terminus would have been Cairo, at the mouth of the Ohio.

No man can look at the map of this country without his eyes finally resting on the mouth of the Ohio as the great center of population and of commerce of the United States. The outstretching valley of that noble river, in climate, soil and production is nowhere surpassed on the habitable globe.

If Cairo had a suitable site for city, it would surpass any other inland city of this continent, or perhaps in the world. But this department had to deal with things as they are and not as it believes they will be in the glorious realizations of the future. So dealing, it saw the great railways of the north concentrating on the Mississippi at St. Louis, and those of the south concentrating on it at Memphis.

Look on the map, which I have used much in my examinations of this subject. The red lines will point you to the concentration at St. Louis; the blue ones show you the roads that approach Memphis. Cairo, lying not far from midway between them, I have regarded as the point in the future, whilst Memphis and St. Louis on opposite sides, at the present, claim equal recognition in reference to either the mail service or the construction of a railroad to the Pacific States. The act of Congress made the Mississippi the base line, on some point of which the route was to be started. Look along that base line, and see whether a larger region of country, both east and west of that river, is not accommodated by the selection of Memphis and St. Louis, with Cairo near their centre, than would have been by the selection of any other place whatever.

From all the New England States, and from every middle State, whoever desired to go over this **overland route** would most easily come to Cincinnati; from Cincinnati it is equally easy by railroad or the river to reach St. Louis,

Cairo, or Memphis, Railroads (soon to be finished) take you directly to each place. It may lie safely affirmed that the whole of these States would be as regularly accommodated by the route established as on the Albuquerque, route starting from St. Louis. It is obliged to be so, because, if you go to St. Louis, you have still to go south to Albuquerque, a point due west from Memphis. Memphis is on latitude 35 degrees, throwing away small fractions, and so is Albuquerque.— Even northern Indiana and Illinois are equally well accommodated at St. Louis or Cairo. So much for the northeastern States. When you get to the southern States, including the region about Baltimore and Washington city, the route to Memphis over the Virginia and East Tennessee road, Virginia, North and South Carolina, Georgia. Alabama, Mississippi and Louisiana, are all best accommodated at Memphis.

In short, there is no ten mile square of the territory of the United States, east of the Mississippi which is not satisfactorily provided for by the commencement at Memphis and St. Louis.

Let us consider what would have been the state of the case if I had made the terminus at either Memphis or St. Louis alone? Would the people of Louisiana, of Mississippi, Alabama. Georgia, Florida and the rest, have been at all content to have to go so far north as St. Louis? We know they would not. We have, therefore accommodated them by letting them start at Memphis, to which all their railroads have been constructed.

Now look at the other side. If Memphis had been made the sole terminus, would Iowa, Wisconsin, Minnesota, and Michigan have been satisfied? We know they would not, and, therefore, we have given them a terminus at St. Louis.

Here, then, we have two starting points, so situated, in their relation to neighboring States, as to give the highest amount of satisfaction to all. So true is this, that the St. Louis proposition itself leaves these last mentioned northwestern States entirely dependent on her, and the effort to break down Memphis as a terminus can do no good to them, whilst it does immense injustice to other portions of the southeastern and southwestern States. It would seem impossible to have made any other starting points which would have combined the interests and wishes of a greater number of both States and people to so large a degree.

The main objection, we apprehend, is not so much to the starting points as to the *direction* of the route westward from them.

The true and perhaps the only question on this part of the subject is, whether, after fixing the points of beginning on the river, I have, in going west, located the road to the best advantage to all parts of the country as far as the same was practicable; not, of course, to particular cities and States but to the whole Country at large. If it had been located through the South Pass, and in latitude 42 degrees, it would have best accommodated Minnesota, Wisconsin, and Iowa, but would have sent it through the ice and snows, away from nearly all the other States.

If it had been located bv Springfield, Neosho, and Albuquerque, it would have altogether lost the great connection by Cairo, destined at no distant day to rival, perhaps surpass in importance, either the St. Louis or the Memphis route.

It would also have lost the connection from Memphis, and with it all the States which have railroads concentrated at that point of the Mississippi.

In like manner would have been lost all connection with the Vicksburg and New Orleans road, which, under the present location, fail into it not far from Preston.

To avoid repetition on this point, I beg to refer you to the 44th page of my report, and to the map which l send you with this letter, in order to show that the road, as now located, has really combined the interest and convenience of more States than any other route that can be devised.

But it is often written and oftener said that it is absurd and unreasonable to go down so far toward the south. That

St. Louis is nearly in latitude 39 degrees, whilst Memphis is not far from latitude 35 degrees. And where is Albuquerque? In about the same latitude with Memphis. So that, by the admissions of the friends of the Albuquerque route, you cannot go west from St. Louis to San Francisco. Climate, mountains, and deserts all forbid it, and you are compelled to go southwest until you reach Albuquerque nearly due west from Memphis. This great fact is fatal, utterly fatal, to the claims of St. Louis to have this road starting out exclusively from her, and running out through her western border to Albuquerque.

The whole effort to overturn the present established route is intended to abrogate the route from Memphis altogether, and to have but one starting point, and that at St. Louis, and but one line running through that State and passing out of it into the Indian territory or into Kansas. — This is the true struggle, now being made, to abolish the Memphis route altogether, and to monopolize the starting point at St. Louis, and thence to run it off through the entire length of Missouri, east and west.

The present line gives Missouri great advantages. It gives her a terminus at her great city of which she is so justly proud. It sends the route through a most interesting portion of the State, by Springfield, for more than two hundred miles.

All this was done in the spirit of anxious desire to promote her interests, and to gratify her wishes as far as practicable. If, however, not content to be so amply accommodated, the attempt is now to be made to have but one terminus, and one road, from St. Louis by Springfield, Neosho, Albuquerque, etc., as laid down in the map filed with this bill, to the destruction of the Memphis line, it may be well to consider her claims to this exclusive possession of the route. If it is right to have but one line, as indicated by that map, to go by Albuquerque, it is not right to start at St. Louis. Albuquerque is in the same latitude with Memphis, and you ought , therefore, to start at Memphis and go direct to it, instead of starting between three or four degrees north of it. There is no escape from this argument. If you are intent on going by Albuquerque, and to have no branch to the road, such as I have given it, your terminus at St. Louis is wrong, and you are bound by every law of latitude, directness, and convenience to a large majority of the States, to start at Memphis, thence by Little Rock to Preston or Fort Smith, according to the route to be selected.

The argument has been often and earnestly pressed, that the people of the eastern, western and upper Mississippi river States, have all connection with St. Louis. If so, it may be replied: The department has done well to make St. Louis a terminus, and when there , it is everywhere admitted that they *must* still go down south three and a half degrees, and that they *must go* there from insurmountable difficulties in crossing the mountains. But the argument proceeds, that the people of the other States – southwest, south and southwest – can also go to St. Louis because there is a river and a railroad to carry them there from Memphis.

It is not equally true that persons from all the northern States, and especially those lying on the Mississippi, might also come from St. Louis to Memphis by the *same river* and the *same railroads*; and especially when it is remembered that, being at St Louis, they are compelled by physical obstacles still to come down to the latitude of *Memphis?*

Begin at St. Louis, three and one half degrees north of the proper latitude, why not come down by the railroad and river to the admitted latitude, and then start on it at once toward the point of destination?

The argument throughout is in favor of the 35th parallel route. Well, why not start on that parallel, and keep upon it by Little Rock, Fort Smith, and Albuquerque? Why start three and a half degrees north of the 35th, and thus mar and defeat its whole symmetry and proportion?

There is no solution of this strange anomaly in logic, but in the fact that unfortunately St. Louis is not where Memphis is, on the 35th parallel.

The department has not sought to compel the States lying on the upper Mississippi to come down to Memphis over this three and a half degrees, nor attempted to force the southern States *to go up* to St. Louis for a starting point to California. It has chosen to select a point of junction west of the river, and to branch the road, *sending it out to meet* the convenience of all the States north and south, at two great points at which the rivers and railroads of every section concentrate on the Mississippi.

Look again at the map. How the noble States lying along the Ohio are accommodated at Cairo. Look at the network of roads concentrating at St. Louis and Memphis, and then cast your eye at the grand junction at Fort Smith on the Arkansas. Fort Smith is the grand junction, if the route is to be sent by Albuquerque, and neither St. Louis or Memphis need be obliterated from this contract by the fiat of **Messrs. Butterfield & Company.**

This brings us down to the consideration of the true, and indeed, the only question which had been raised to the route selected. The department has made a terminus at St. Louis and Memphis, with Cairo lying nearly midway between them. The tow termini are *admitted* to be such as will accommodate the largest number of States north and south.

It is further admitted (in a letter addressed to certain citizens of Van Buren, in Arkansas, by a distinguished citizen of Missouri) that these branches should *"converge at a suitable point on the 35th parallel, in the beautiful and fertile valley of the Canadian, where, forming a common stem, the Union route proceeds west up the valley and along the 35th parallel of north latitude to Anton Chico; thence to Albuquerque, etc."*

Well, we have already permitted these contractors to start at St. Louis, to go, if they choose, by railroad to Jefferson City, and then start out their stages, and go (within a fraction) to that *very latitude* he contends for, and by that *very town of Van Buren,* whose inhabitants he was addressing, and calling on them to help him, and only a small distance below that *very beautiful and fertile valley* which he was describing. Fort Smith or Van Buren (for they are very near each other, and on opposite sides of the Arkansas River) may be, therefore, considered as a point of intersection, against which not much, if any, complaint is to be made.

It may, therefore, be fairly stated that, so far, we are agreed. All people and States who would find it most convenient to go to St. Louis may do so, and proceed on their journey to Jefferson City and Springfield to Fort Smith, on the 35th degree, (or nearly so) where they will be met by all the people from the other States, who might find it most convenient to go to Memphis on very nearly the same parallel of latitude. The only question, then, is whether this general mass, so assembled, *from all the States*, shall still go further south by the **Overland Mail Route**, or railroad, if one is to be built, or shall they go west from Fort Smith up the Canadian by Albuquerque, etc.

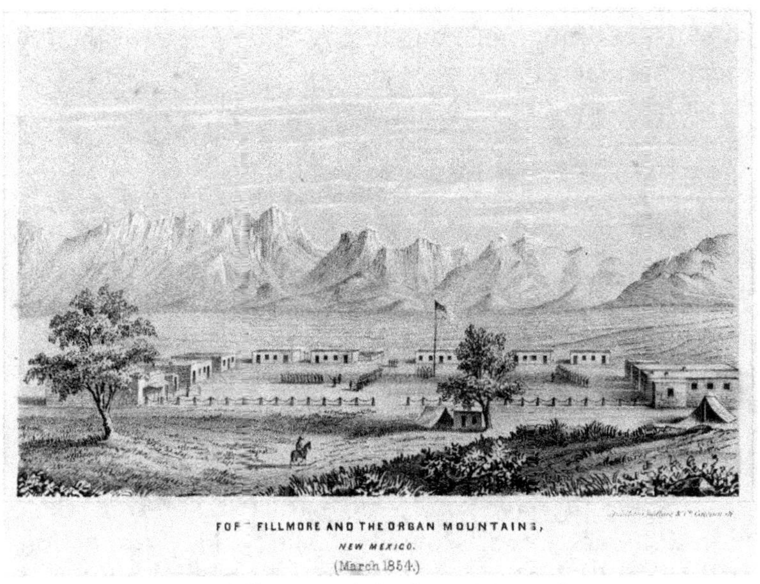

Fort Fillmore and the Organ Mountains

Fort Fillmore in March 1854, established 1851, and the Organ Mountains, south of Las Cruces. Lithograph from drawing by Carl Schuchard.

If it be wrong to go further south in the direction of Preston and Fort Fillmore, some forty miles above El Paso, then it is a wrong to all the people both north and south, for they are assembled at that point, and are entitled to go from it by the nearest and most practicable route to their place of destination.

We have now come to the precise point where any well founded controversy about the location which has been made for this route can fairly arise. Ought it to have been located from Van Buren or Fort Smith, up the Canadian, or ought it to bear still further south in the direction of Preston, in order that it may pass the Rio Grande about 40 miles above El Paso, and thence by Fort Yuma, etc., to San Francisco?

The relative advantages of these two routes, regarding Fort Smith as a great stand point, from which the subject is to be considered, is too fully discussed from page 33 to the conclusion of my report, to justify a repetition of the arguments and facts there relied upon.

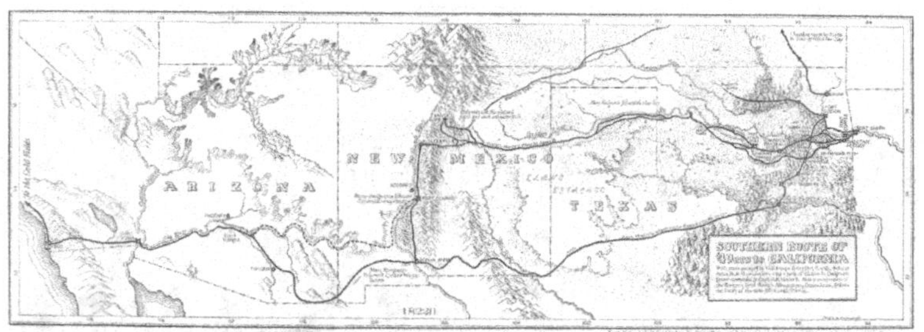

"Marcy & The Gold Seekers: The Journal of Captain R. B. Marcy,
with an Account of the Gold Rush Over the Southern Route"

I especially refer you to the extracts taken from the explorations and reports of Capt. Marcy. He was stationed at Fort Smith. He was ordered to explore both routes. The most ample preparations were furnished. He went westward by the Albuquerque route and returned by the El Paso and Preston to Fort Smith, from whence he started and the extracts furnished show a decided and palpable preference given by him to the latter route. So does Capt. Pope and Mr. A. H. Campbell, who is now at the head of the Pacific wagon road office in the Interior Department. He accompanied Capt. Whipple over the Albuquerque route and Lieu. ____ over the Fort Fillmore or El paso route as principal engineer in 1853, '54 and '55.

In relation to distances, climate, water, and pasture lands on the respective route, the department cannot but commend him to your committee, as fully competent to give every desired information. I am every day expecting his report showing the most triumphant success the state line now running semi-monthly between the Rio Grande by Fort Yuma to San Diego, which, as soon as received, shall be before your committee.

It may be proper, before closing this communication to suggest that, if the establishment of this **Overland Mail Route** is to pioneer the location of the future railroad, in my opinion it is desirable to pass from Fort Smith still south on the Preston and El Paso route. This department has nothing to do with the railroad, and has never therefore felt called to express any opinion, for or against one; but its vain and idle to pretend not to see, that it is the effort of rival railroad interests that are now sailing the line of mail stage coaches which this department has established.

The Postmaster General, is, therefore, only authorized but constrained to consider the subject, in some slight degree, in the prospect of a future railroad. In this light he ___ to the fact that the very shortest distances were to be found between existing States and the El Paso route. From the western bound out of Texas, on the Rio grande, to Fort Yuma on the western border of California – is a distance about 460 or 470 miles. On no other route the distance through the United States territory, by several hundred miles, so sh____. Four hundred and sixty or seventy miles therefore, the whole distance that the United States would be called on to make the _____ outside of existing States.

All who deny the power of the general government to make such a road only through territories as Lord Proprietor of the soil must make this route the decided preference. Especially so, when it is remembered that the value of lands to be improved by it, and to be appropriated to its construction, is notoriously as ___ not likely to be far greater than any other.

The committee can ascertain the ___ here relied on, by measuring on the map, the western boundary of Texas to the California line near Fort Yuma, and also by measuring from the western boundary of Arkansas, Missouri, west, to the California line. ___ when Kansas is admitted into the Union, the western boundary will exhibit a vastly ___ space than on the southern route. From the eastern boundary of California, at Fort Yuma by a straight line, it is one hundred and ___ miles, and by the traveled route one hundred and seventy-five miles, to San Diego, ___ Pacific. Here is a most excellent harbor, ___ terminus of a branch road there would ___ to the new State of South California a commercial emporium second only, on that coast to the city of San Francisco. The great common connection by sea between San Francisco and San Diego, with that of the railway on land, ___ make the coast of both Californians the highly favored region on this continent.

But I must forbear. This letter is, already too long, and I conclude it by expressing the confident belief that, over the route now established, and by the contract now made, service required by the act of Congress and and will be performed. The contractors and agents are now busily engaged in exploring different routes; and under the discretion powers retained by the department, to make such modifications between the main desired points as physical obstacles may render necessary, I have no doubt of complete success.

Very respectfully, your obedient servant,
Aaron V. Brown

Aaron Brown, Postmaster General

March 9, 1858
Letter from the Postmaster General

March 9, 1858, Tuesday, page 4

Arkansas True Democrat, Little Rock, Arkansas

FROM THE MEMPHIS APPEAL, FEB. 18,1858 – *Memphis and the Little Rock Railroad.*

...On the first of September the **Overland Mail** line to California will connect with this road, running four horse post coaches from its terminus, westward, which will give us daily mail to Little Rock, and this may be regarded as the beginning of the great Pacific railway which is destined some days to put us in connection with California.

We look with hope and confidence to the State of Arkansas to come forward with liberal aid to this great enterprise, which is destined to do more towards the development of her resources than any policy the State could adopt.

March 13, 1858
Memphis to Hot Springs is a More Direct Route to Preston, Texas than Memphis to Fort Smith

March 13, 1858, page 2, column 4

Arkansas State Gazette and Democrat, Little Rock, Ark.

... We wish to make a correction of a mistake made by a correspondent of the *Fort Smith Herald,* whose article was republished in the *Fort Smith Times.* This correspondent, in alluding to the agent of the **Overland Mail Company**, who came to Fort Smith, last summer, to purchase oxen, says in effect, if not in so many words, that from Des Arc to Preston, Texas, the route by Fort Smith is the nearest and the best.

The article to which we allude is well written, and in many things, correct, but we regret exceedingly that the author did not examine the map before writing it; for, by doing so, he could have seen that the route from Des Arc to Preston, by Little Rock and Hot Springs, comes nearer an air line, than almost any other road, of the same length, in the country. And as to the country over which it goes, we say, partly from our own knowledge and partly from information received from reliable men who have traveled over the whole of it, there can be no better road, of its length, made, *any where.* On the other hand, the position of Preston, on the map, is more than a degree South of Fort Smith, and a road from Des Arc by Fort Smith to Preston, must, of necessity, diverge far from a direct line...

March 16, 1858
Suggestion for Memphis Route

March 16, 1858, Tuesday, page 3

Arkansas True Democrat, Little Rock, Arkansas

VAN BUREN AND FORT SMITH ROUTE TO CALIFORNIA VIA ALBUQUERQUE. *Two hundred and twenty miles shorter than any known*

Wagon Road to California, and abounding in wood, water and grass.

The route starting from Van Buren and Fort Smith, on the Arkansas River, towns situated four miles apart on, the 35th parallel, runs west of *old Fort Arbuckle*, passing through the Choctaw nation, a country abounding in wood, water and grass, settled by friendly Indians well advanced in civilization, who devote their attention to agriculture and stock raising, a distance of two hundred miles; thence up the valley of the Canadian River, and on to Anton Chico, a distance of about five hundred miles more. This road has been traveled and marked out by Lieut. Whipple, and since sufficiently beaten to leave evident traces, so that the traveler will find no difficulty in pursuing his way over a country, extremely level and abounding in wood, water and grass except for a distance of twenty miles between the headwaters of the Canadian River and Anton Chico. From Anton Chico to Albuquerque, a distance of about seventy miles, the country is settled and subsistence abundant. From Albuquerque on by the Zuni villages, Campbell's pass, Bill Williams' fork, the Tejon pass and Tulan valley to San Francisco, the distance is 1,152 miles, making the distance on the entire route from Van Buren and Fort Smith to San Francisco 1,952 miles.

From Albuquerque through to California, Lieut. Beale declares the route unsurpassed for a wagon road, and his journey over it as a trip of pleasure, with ample supplies of wood, water and grass for the use of emigrants. This route has heretofore been unexplored west of Albuquerque, but now being made known by the exploration of Lieut. Beale, has induced the citizens of western Arkansas to fit out a train from Van Buren and Fort Smith, which left on Saturday the 27th of February, 1858, commanded by Capt Daniel R. McKisick of Benton County, Arkansas, prepared to open a good wagon road from *old Fort Arbuckle* to Albuquerque. The company consisted of men who have frequently crossed the plains to California, and we have the utmost confidence in the success of the enterprise.

Emigrants can start from here at ay time this month and until September, with entire safety as regards subsistence for their animals, and a supply of all articles required can be had here for an outfit. Horses, mules, oxen, wagons, harness, flour, bacon, etc. at reasonable prices.

This route (the 35th parallel) being the shortest to California, and as no other can be traveled safely this spring, a large emigration is expected to travel over it. Numerous enquiries are received at this place from all parts of the United States, making enquiries as the practicability of this route and the facilities for obtaining outfits. Those desirous or intending to go through overland this spring, will at all times find companies organizing which they can join. Guide books of the route will be furnished, showing the camping places and the distance apart, also the same as to water.

The company which has been sent forward will mark out the road, and indicate the best watering stations and camping places, for the information of emigrants who follow. Trains *[wagon trains]* well equipped should make the trip, allowing time for rest, in 120 days from Van Buren to California.

Van Buren Intelligencer

Fort Smith, Arkansas in 1850´s
Source: ´Le Tour du Monde´ published Paris, 1860´s

March 23, 1858
The El Paso Route for Overland Mail

March 23, 1858
Arkansas True Democrat, Little Rock, Arkansas

THE EL PASO ROUTE – We gave at the time of publication the substance of the views of the Postmaster General in favor of the southern route for the **Overland Mail** to California. It contained an able and emphatic plea for the southern route road to the Pacific as the best, and incidentally offered a strong support to the Southern Pacific road *via* El Paso.

These opinions have been combated at great length by Mr. Phelps, a representative in Congress from the State of Missouri. He has published an address to the people of Arkansas and Missouri, in favor of a more northern route, beginning at St. Louis and terminating at San Francisco *via* Albuquerque, along the 35th parallel of latitude. Mr. Phelps agrees with the Postmaster General, in dismissing the route by the Southwest Pass, as not entitled to consideration, and devotes his examination to the comparative merits of the Albuquerque and the El Paso routes, concluding the former to be the great central route, upon which all should unite.

The letter of Mr. Phelps has been answered also, at length, by Mr. Albert H. Campbell, of the road bureau at Washington City, who enters into full comparison of the route along the 35th degree of latitude, the Albuquerque route, with the El Paso route along the 32d degree, and gives solid and convincing reasons why the more southern route should be preferred.

All the routes are nearly on an equality in one respect. With a few exceptional localities, the interior of the continent to be traversed is sterile. There are oases in all, which are exaggerated in beauty by the contrast with the long arid stretches by which they are reached. But these are not of sufficient extent or value to be of any considerable weight in determining the choice of a route. The distance, and the best means of overcoming it, are the considerations, without material relief from these scattered patches of meager fertility.

The points which Mr. Campbell examined in comparison of the routes, are – the character of the surface, the length, the climate, and the supplies of water, and of timber for fuel and construction.

He speaks not only from a full acquaintance with the reports of other explorers, but from personal examination – having in 1853-54, been with Capt. Whipple's party of exploration of the Albuquerque route, and in 1854-55 with Lieut. Parke's explorations of the El Paso route and the Gila river. These were expeditions fitted out under the authority of the United States, and Mr. Campbell assisted in the examinations with a direct reference to the question of the practicability of a railroad.

The first inquiry is as to the relative amount of elevation and depression of the surface to be overcome on these two routes. the maximum points are given, with the following results:

The sum of the ascents and descents between Fort Smith and San Francisco (the upper route) is 48,521 feet. The formula of engineers makes this equivalent to an addition of 919 miles of level road – that is a locomotive can draw as much load on 3,015 miles of level road as it can on 2,196 miles of a road with these inequalities.

Along the El Paso route the ascents and descents from Fulton to San Francisco Bay amount to 38,200 feet, or an equivalent to 723 miles of level route, showing a preference of 196 miles in favor of the southern route to San Francisco. If the computation be made to the Pacific at San Diego, the difference in favor of the southern route arising from inferior grades would be 385 miles.

The next question is that of relative surface length, the distance in miles from the termini. These are necessarily inexact, and subject to corrections from future examinations. But a careful statement is given of the nearest results obtained by the several exploring parties, showing that by every computation New York is nearer to San Francisco by El Paso than by Albuquerque, and that on the most favorable estimate by the friends of the latter, the difference is so immaterial as to be of no practical importance in the selection of routes.

The subject of climate is next examined, and in this particular, the data and compilations of the Postmaster General, are reviewed and confirmed. It is established, in direct opposition to the conclusions of Mr. Phelps, that the climate on the 35th parallel, in the region of Albuquerque, and at the passes of the mountains, is sometimes intensely cold, so as to make the transit of passenger trains in mid winter, over the deserts, terribly dangerous. On the lower route the snow never lies on the plains, and the mean temperature of winter is from 14 to 24 degrees higher than on the upper route; which the extreme heat, on the supper, is quite as high as that on the lower.

The supply of water, on the two routes, is said to be nearly the same, and that of timber does not vary much; the advantages in one respect, on one line, being counterbalanced by preferences in other respects, on the other

Mr. Campbell next proceeds to quote the testimony of Lieutenant Michler, Captain Pope and Colonel A. B. Gray, scientific engineers, who have examined the country, and that of the late Senator Rusk, of Texas, who was familiar with it, to show that the line of 32 degrees forms the most natural and level line for a road; and that, thereby, the deserts to be crossed, are very much narrower than at any other points, the boundary of the cultivatable region extending several hundred miles further to the west, than on any given northern route.

The concluding pages of Mr. Campbell's letter are directed to an impeachment of the accuracy and candor of the letter of Mr. Phelps. – the charges that the letter is made up principally of 'garbled extracts from official and other sources' concerning the worst portions of the El Paso route, and the best portions of the Albuquerque route; and he retorts by copying a series of extracts from the same documents – but which Mr. Phelps suppressed – in which the Albuquerque route is made to appear barren and impracticable, and other extracts suppressed to the like manner which acknowledge the superiority of that by El Paso. He alleges, that Mr. Phelps shows entire ignorance of the country, placing mountain ranges on the southern route where there are no mountains within forty miles, and misplacing known ranges in the most confused manner.

There is something of this spirit in the whole style of opposition, which the southern road meets from northern men – who, setting out with a determination to oppose, ignore what is evident, misrepresent the plainest facts, and repulse the most clear and demonstrable plans for a great and acknowledged national want. – *New Orleans Picayane*

April 3, 1858
Fort Smith is a Beautiful Place for the Overland Route

April 3, 1858, Saturday, page 2
Arkansas State Gazette and Democrat, Little Rock, Ark.

From the Fort Smith Herald – **OVERLAND STAGE ROUTE** TO CALIFORNIA. –A HASTY VIEW OF THE UPPER ARKANSAS VALLEY – ...The city of Fort Smith, situated immediately on the Indian line, on an elevated wooded ridge, on the south bank of the Arkansas River holds a geographical position that will secure the passage by and through here of the **Overland Mail Route** from Mississippi to California, and probably may be the diverging point from whence the branches to St. Louis and Memphis will radiate; if so, and the road by Little Rock from Memphis shall pass through the valley above described, to Fort Smith. There cannot be found in the south or west a more delightful region for all classes to settle and occupy, nor one presenting more general advantages for planting, farming, or manufacturing as the surface presents a rich and lively undulating soil and bounded both north and south with the richest mountain scenery pouring out in almost every ravine fountains of living water, and in many localities chalybeate *[chalybeate - mineral spring waters containing salts of iron]* and other medicinal waters, whose curative virtues have been well tested, all which will commend it to gentleman of wealth, the invalid, and the romantic, as the future permanent seat of literary and scholastic institutions of the highest grade in the south or west.

Taking into consideration the amount and value of the lands remaining unoccupied – the probable speedy facilities that will soon be afforded by this **Overland Mail Route**, in its passage to California – the prospect of the completion of the local rail road, by the indefatigable engineer and contractors, now engaged in its construction, to say nothing of the decided advantages it holds, as a starting point for the rail road to California, together with the peculiar advantages this section of country possesses in wood, water, and coal general evenness of surface, and its latitude – no one in the habit of judging the future by the past, can successfully gainsay any of the very many superior natural advantages claimed to be possessed by this particular section of country.

None will hereafter doubt the rapid settlement and development, and as Fort Smith is a city in the woods, in the far interior of the country, approachable by the river, and soon to be by rail road, as well as by the **Overland Stage Route**, commanding already a respectable local trade, with an immense Indian money and barter trade, none other than habitual croakers *[croakers - slang for gossip]* can doubt its rapid growing importance – and, like Chicago, St, Louis, Memphis and San Francisco, will, in due season, become one of the fairest inland cities in the United States.

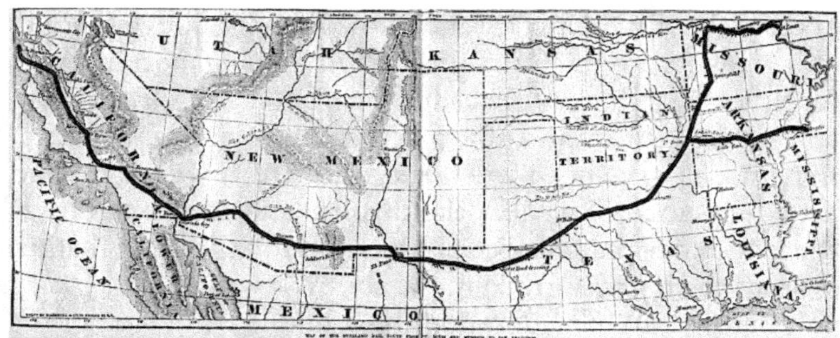

Butterfield's Overland Mail Co. southern Ox-Bow Route

April 13, 1858
Fort Smith Chosen as the Merger Point for the New Southern Butterfield Route

April 13, 1858
Arkansas True Democrat, Little Rock, Arkansas

Gallatin, Tenn., April 3d, 1858 – EDITOR TRUE DEMOCRAT – I have just returned from Washington, and am happy to inform you that the question of the route to be used by the contractors for the transportation of the **overland mail** has been settled. The contractors are satisfied with the route originally adopted by the Post Master General, and all efforts to change it have been made without their knowledge or consent.

They have obtained the permission of the Post Master General to bring the two branches together at Fort Smith, and to carry their mails and passengers on boats from Little Rock to Fort Smith – this is a very important and valuable arrangement for your city. The company will have boats built for the express purpose which will not draw more than 16 inches when loaded, and believe they can run them all the year. They have contracted for a large number of horses, mules, stages, harness, etc., and the most active preparations are being made to carry their contract into effect.

Yours truly,
JAMES GLOVER

April 16, 1858
Butterfield & Co. Selected for New Route

April 16, 1858, Friday
Arkansas Intelligencer, Van Buren, Arkansas

California Overland Mail – From the letter which we publish in another column, it will be seen that the Postmaster General has signified his consent that **Messers. Butterfield & Co.** might form the junction of the two arms of their great **Overland Mail Route** to California, from Memphis and St. Louis, at Fort Smith, instead of at Preston. This is a very important step gained for the 35th parallel route, and we have no doubt that ultimately the contractors will be permitted, to go through via Albuquerque.

The forming the junction on our frontier; will be of great advantage to Western Arkansas. It will serve to draw attention to the many advantages possessed by us, and will, undoubtedly, draw a large emigration to settle upon our cheap and fertile lands. Van Buren being the point where the route from St. Louis first strikes the Arkansas River, and where it intersects the route from Memphis and Little on the river – the Postmaster General having agreed that the contractors might carry passengers and this mails on the river to Fort Smith will be very materially benefitted, as is already apparent from the enhanced value of property.

From the Ft. Herald (Extra) of 11th Inst.

Overland Mail Junction at Fort Smith.

We received the following letter from our friend Col. James Glover, by last evening's mail, too late for our paper. We hasten to lay it before our readers it is of too much importance to the people to be suppressed

Washington, March 28, 1858

Dear Sir – I arrived here on last Monday. **Mr. Butterfield** came in last night – he is in fine health and spirits.

We called to see Gov. Brown *[Postmaster General]* last night, and I am gratified to say, we succeeded in getting his consent to make Fort Smith the connecting point of the two arms of our great route, and we also obtained his consent to run our mail and passengers on the boats from Little Rock, to your beautiful and growing city *[Fort Smith]*. This arrangement will greatly facilitate operations, and add considerably to the convenience of our passengers, beside affording great advantages to the river people.

A dispatch received last night, announces the arrival of Mr. Kenyon at New Orleans. He had charge of the expedition from the California side. Letters, also , from the party who went from St. Louis, also, from the party who went from St. Louis, give the most glowing description of their trip as far as Fort Chadbourne.

A letter from Kenyon *[Marquis L Kenyon]*, some time since, informs us that he had contracted for 400 head of mules and horses to be delivered in July.

Mr. Butterfield has contracted for a large number of coaches, wagons and harness, part of which will be shipped to California on the 10th of April.

Mr. Crocker and myself will start in a few days, to buy horses and mules, and make contracts for the delivery of grain along the route.

Thus, you see that the most active preparations are being made, for the execution of the contract.

Yours truly, James Glover

April 16, 1858

Fort Smith sends out its own expedition for the purpose of exploring the country and ascertaining the practicability of a route from Van Buren to Albuquerque

April 16, 1858, Friday, page 2

Arkansas Intelligencer, Van Buren, Arkansas

EXPLORING PARTY – The "Fort Smith and Van Buren company," exploring the **Overland Mail Route**, arrived at Fort Arbuckle on the 16th ult., all in fine health and spirits. They are about 20 in number. After resting, will start across the plains. They were at Fort Arbuckle yet, as late as the 24th

ult., arranging to cross the plains, and assembling some Delawares *[Delaware Indians]* as guides to accompany them.
– *Chickasaw Herald*

April 20, 1858
The Fort Smith and Van Buren Expedition Arrives at Fort Arbuckle

April 20, 1858, Tuesday
Arkansas True Democrat, Little Rock, Arkansas

From the *Ft. Smith Herald* ... we learn that the Fort Smith and Van Buren company exploring the **Overland Mail** route and the United States surveying party to establish the line between the State of Texas and the Choctaw and Chickasaw Nations were both at Fort Arbuckle. The Van Buren *Intelligencer* is earnestly at work to secure the **Overland Mail** route to California through that city.

April 20, 1858
Democratic Party of Crawford County Supports Overland Route on 35th Parallel

April 20, 1858
Arkansas True Democrat, Little Rock, Arkansas

Democratic Meeting – Crawford County – ... the Democratic citizens of Crawford County met in mass at the court house in Van Buren on Monday the 5th of April, 1858... Whereupon it was resolved... *[5] "Resolved, That the democracy of this country believe that the line or route, on or near the 35th parallel of latitude to California, is the shortest and most practicable route for the* ***Overland Mail*** *to San Francisco, and we hereby request our Senators and Representatives in Congress to use their influence to have the mail carried on that route."*

April 20, 1858
Democratic Party of Franklin County Supports Overland Route on 35th Parallel

April 20, 1858
Arkansas True Democrat, Little Rock, Arkansas

... the democracy of Franklin County met at the court house in the town of Ozark, on Saturday, April 3d, 1858... *[5] "Resolved, That we hereby request our delegation in Congress to use their influence in favor of ... the 35th parallel for the **Pacific Overland Mail.**"*

April 23, 1858
Butterfield Route Expedition Arrived

April 23, 1858, Friday, page 2
Arkansas Intelligencer, Van Buren, Arkansas

Overland Mail Party of Expedition – We learn from the gentlemen composing the party of expedition on the route of the California **overland mail**, who arrived in our city last Sunday, that the route they have traversed presents no very insurmountable obstacles for a wagon road, the scarcity of water on the route being the most serious.

They find a distance of about sixty miles on this side of the Rio Grande, and one of about seventy miles on the other side of the same river without water.

This difficulty, they say, must be obviated by constructing tanks. The party consisting of eight men, came thru' from San Francisco in fifty-two days, meeting with no interruption from Indians on the route.

They find the distance as measured by them to be 2,248 miles from San Francisco to Van Buren, this is somewhat a greater distance than has been estimated. The party express themselves very favorably towards the route they have traveled, but are convinced from the information they have, that the route via Albuquerque, besides being much shorter in distance, presents greater advantages in wood, water, &c. *[&c. is an abbreviation of etc., meaning et cetera, and others, or, and so forth.]*

April 23, 1858
Butterfield Stations Have Been Selected from San Francisco to Van Buren

April 23, 1858, Friday, page 2
Arkansas Intelligencer, Van Buren, Arkansas

Overland Mail Exploring Party – We had the pleasure, on Monday last of a call from Messrs. G. W. Wood, F. D. Ryther, Jesse Talcold, **John Butterfield**, Jr., J. Swortsa, T. K. Nillis, and P. C. Cole, *en route* for their homes in the State of N. Y.

These gentlemen composed a part of the company of exploration of the **Overland Mail Route** from San Francisco to this place; leaving San Francisco, California, in January, they made the trip through to Fort Smith in fifty-two days. They report the route practicable and free from Indians, having seen none on the entire route, except of a friendly character.

Messrs. Butterfield & Co., in their selection of men for this enterprise, have been extremely fortunate (if we may be permitted to form our opinion from the acquaintance we have with those, who have sojourned with us;) as to energy, tact, and qualifications, while the whole party only ranked as high privates. They each and every man were qualified to command in emergencies, as we can only say for them, had, the reveille been beaten throughout the entire State of New York, the same number and qualification could not have been selected from the muster rolls. Frank D. Ryther with his wit, humor, intelligence, sociability, captivating and gentlemanly manner possesses a *carte blanche* to travel either in a civilized or savage country, and where travel would lead, there was no necessity for a reserve. Although our acquaintance was of but a few days, we shall ever recur to it as among the pleasantest recollections of the past.

They furnished us with a statement of distances as measured by them of the road from San Francisco to Van Buren, which we publish below:

Distances traveled by ***Overland Mail***
from San Francisco to Van Buren, Arkansas.

NAMES OF PLACES			MILES
San Francisco	to	San Jose,	52
San Jose	"	San Joaquin,	120
San Joaquin	"	Visalia,	81
Visalia	"	Fort Tejon,	119

Fort Tejon	"	San Burnidino,	128
San Burnidino	"	Fort Yuma,	200
Fort Yuma	"	Pimos Villages,	182
Pimos Villages	"	Tucson,	95
Tucson	"	Messilla,	190
Mesilla (sic)	"	Franklin (Opposite El Paso),	45
From San Francisco to Franklin, total,			**1,312**
Franklin	"	Waco Tanks,	30
Waco Tanks	"	Alamos,	27
Alamos	"	Cormedas,	9
Cormedas	"	Crow Spring,	20
Crow Spring	"	Guadalupe Pass,	23
Guadalupe Pass	"	Independence Spring,	10
Independence Spring	"	Head of Delaware Creek,	17
Head of Del. Creek	"	Delaware Crossing,	23
Crossing of Del.	"	Pope's Camp,	15
Pope's Camp	"	Emigrant crossing of Rio Pecos	67
Emigrant crossing	"	First water in Sand Hills,	34
First water in Sand Hills		Second Sand Hills,	5
Second Sand Hills	"	Mustang Pond,	67
Mustang Pond	"	Colorado Springs,	25
Colorado Springs	"	Colorado River,	41
Colorado River	"	Branch of Brasos,	45
Branch of Brasos	"	Another fork of the Brasos (near Camp Cooper),	78
Branch of Brasos, (near Camp Cooper) to Belknap,			41
Belknap	"	Cotton wood spring,	13
Cottonwood spring	"	Buffalo Spring,	40
Buffalo Springs	"	Gainsville,	65
Gainsville	"	Preston,	40
Preston	"	Boggy Depot,	41
Boggy Depot	"	Scullyville,	180
Scullyville	"	Van Buren,	21
Total number of miles, San Francisco to Van Buren			**2,248**

[NOTE: The above list is also printed in the Arkansas True Democrat issue of May 4, 1858 on page 3]

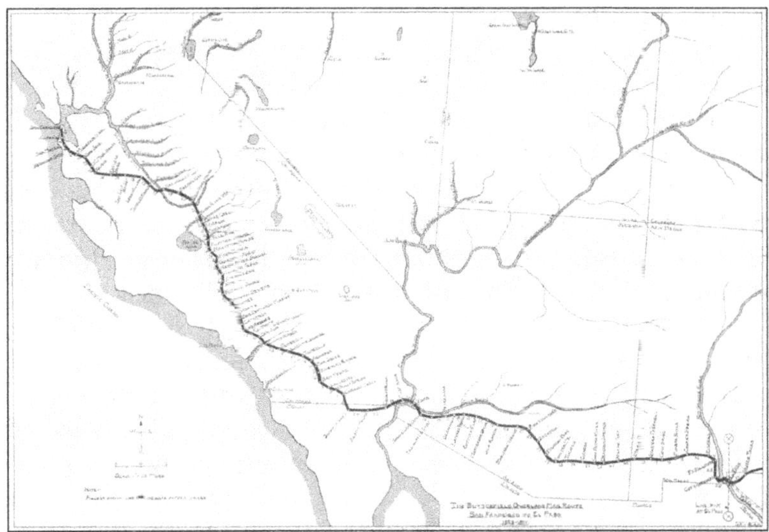

This map of the southwestern US has errors in the details, but overall it helps to visualize how stations were established every 10 to 15 miles across the 2,800 mile route.

April 23, 1858
Butterfield Survey's Report
Rebuts Rumor of Indian Hostel Intentions

April 23, 1858, Friday, page 2

Arkansas Intelligencer, Van Buren, Arkansas

"Tremendous" Excitement – 20,000 Indians in the Field – There is some exciting news afloat in regard to the hostility of wild tribes of Indians on the plains, which will probably have some effect upon the proper authorities of the government. The intelligence, we are happy to say is without foundation, excited by an expedition to Albuquerque, who were sent out by the citizens of this city and Fort Smith, for the purpose of exploring the country and ascertaining the practicability of a route from Van Buren to Albuquerque, in New Mexico, for the information of emigrants to California; went about two hundred miles and returned much frightened by the echo of some Indians, probably hunting buffalo in the southern plains.

There was a quite lengthy report published by the Fort Smith *Times* in regard to its accuracy, believing it highly necessary that the government should immediately place soldiers on the frontier for the protection of the citizens thereon. These tribes, according to report have united themselves with Brigham Young against the United States, and are determined to slay the frontier settlers and friendly Indians wherever they may find them and steal their stock.

We do not for a moment give credence to this authority, though it may be true, but having good reason to doubt its veracity, on information received by an expedition from San Francisco, sent out for the purpose of exploring the **overland mail** route across the plains, say they never saw but seven Indians of a wild nature the whole route through from San Francisco to this city. These men are reliable characters, as we think. We, therefore, pronounce the information above stated, an entire hoax and give it as a mere hypothesis.

It is quite probable that some of the wild tribes of the plains, will form alliance with the Mormons; but, even if they do, they are not going to disturb the frontier settlers and friendly Indians in the west.

Their attention will be required to defend the great city from invitation by the United States troops. We deem it highly important that government should wisely direct its attention to the approaching troubles in Utah and not to the whims of self-interest.

April 24, 1858

April 24, 1858, Saturday, page 2
*Arkansas State Gazette a*nd Democrat, Little Rock, Ark.

Overland Mail – We learn from a reliable source that the **California Overland Mail** will be in operation by the first of September and that active preparations are now being made in the way of procuring coaches, horses, & c., *[&c. is an abbreviation of etc., et cetera, meaning and others, or, and so forth.]* for the route. It is a heavy undertaking, and one which none but experienced and determined men could put into such speedy operation.

WET – The mail stage and horses, in crossing the river at Van Buren on Tuesday last, the 6th inst., by some means got into the river instead of the flat boat. All was saved, but the mail matter was considerably *damped.*

FAILED – The mail failed here on last Friday. Cause, high winds on the Arkansas River.

FAILED – On Sunday last, we had no mail either from St. Louis or Little Rock. Cause of failure unknown to us.

May 1, 1858
Expedition Sent to Set Butterfield Route

May 1, 1858, Saturday, page 2
Arkansas State Gazette and Democrat, Little Rock, Ark.

FROM THE FORT SMITH TIMES, WHOSE NEW DRESS WE HAVE HERETOFORE OMITTED TO MENTION, WE MAKE THE FOLLOWING EXTRACTS:
RETURN OF THE **OVERLAND MAIL** EXPEDITION – The expedition sent out under the auspices of the **Overland Mail Company**, which left St. Louis on the 2d of January, for the purpose of examining the route for the carriage of the **Overland Mail** from the valley of the Mississippi to the shores of the Pacific via the El Paso route returned to this city on Saturday last, having made the trip from El Paso on the Rio Grande – a distance of about nine hundred and twenty-five miles – in the unprecedented short time of twenty-five days, which we believe is the quickest trip ever made across the Plains.

At El Paso, the expedition met the Pacific party who had been waiting for them nearly a month, and a portion of the St Louis party joined the party from San Francisco and immediately sent out on their return trip. The return expedition consisted of seven men, one wagon, and thirteen animals.

The names of the gentlemen are as follows: George Wood, Jesse Talcott, and Charles P. Cole of the St. Louis party, and Frank DeRyther, S.L. Nellis, James Swart, and *[Jno. is an early abbreviation for John]* **Jno. Butterfield, Jr.** of the San

Francisco party. The route which they returned was with the Waco Tanks; the Carnudas mountains, through the Guadaloupe Pass, to the head of Deleware Creek, crossing the Rio Pecos at a new crossing recently made by Capt. Pope, of the Artezian Well Expedition thence along the east side of the Rio Pecos for a distance of sixty-five miles, to the Emigrant Crossing, where they struck Capt. Marcy's trail, proceeding to the Sand Hills, and across the *Llano Estacado,* to the Mustary Springs; thence to the Big Springs of the Colorado, the Clear Fork of the Brazos, the Rio Brazos, to Fort Belkaap, thence by the old military road to Preston, on the Red River; and from thence to this city.

The members of the expedition are highly pleased with their route, and pronounce it in all respects PERFECTLY PRACTICABLE. The only obsticle *[obstacle]* of note is the want of water on the *Llano Estacado* – a distance of sixty-five miles, but this can be easily remedied by the construction of artificial tanks. They pronounce this desert to be by no means a barren waste but is clothed with a luxuriant growth of grama grass, which with sufficient supply of water will prove practicable for staging purposes, although presenting no inducements to the agriculturist.

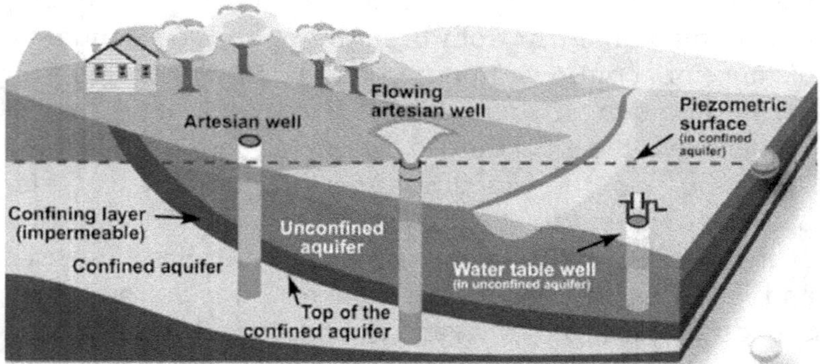

*An **artesian well** is a well that has been drilled into an aquifer in a location where the underground pressure is great enough for the water to rise inside the well. In some cases, the water is under enough pressure to rise from the aquifer to the land's surface without need of a pump.*

It can be made available for the grazing of stock, and should Capt. Pope succeed in procuring water by means of artezian wells *[artesian well]* sufficient for irrigation – which is highly probable – it can be used for agricultural purposes.

The party saw no Indians on the route, until they reached within forty miles of Camp Cooper, where they saw THREE who had been out on a buffalo hunt.

The party all expressed themselves highly pleased with the appearance of Fort Smith and the surrounding country, and seem gratified at the fact that it has been made the converging point for the routes from St. Louis and Memphis. It only remains for our citizens to bestir themselves and the city of Fort Smith, on the banks of the Arkansas, and on the most extreme western boundary of the State, will soon become one of the most populous and prosperous towns in the south and west.

...It is said that there are emigrants in the neighborhood for California. We learn that the return of the albuquerque company, has dampened their ardor a little. We would just say to them, that one of the company says he would be willing to go with only five men. There is no danger, for a company of 30 men, none in the least, as the Indians never attack a company unless they are unable to resist. Emigrants should not be frightened at a few cowardly Indians, that have nothing to fight with except bows and arrows.

It will be recollected that on last Wednesday evening an Extra was issued from this office, setting forth that 20,000 hostile Indians were in the vicinity of Fort Arbuckle. It seems that this Extra has given some dissatisfaction and created some unpleasant feelings towards us, and we would like to know why or wherein we are to blame! The report came to us, well authenticated, and we received it from an U.S. Indian agent, and a citizen of Fort Smith, whose veracity, then as now, we have no cause to suspect, but it appears that these gentlemen who brought us the news, received intelligence very much exaggerated, and gave it to us as they received it, and we are blamed for making it public. Why suppress it, if it be so? Why not in time, warn the public of danger, if any there be? Or shall we lay dormant, wait and hold out inducements to those not living here to travel this route and suppress the reports of danger, till it be heralded by some other Journal, and then, we be charged with falsity? Nay, verily, this is not a proper course to be pursued by honest men, not is it one that we should be urged to pursue.

We are pleased now, however, to be able to say that we are well informed by Captain Woods, **Paymaster of the Overland Mail Company**, that there is no danger in traveling the route, that the Indians are all friendly.

P. S. Since writing the above, the remainder of the exploring party that left here for Albuquerque have returned, believing it useless to proceed, as they met the company from California coming this way, report favorably. They confirm the report of Captain Woods, saying that they neither saw, heard of, met or apprehended any danger whatever.

May 1, 1858
Butterfield Decides to use Steamboats on Arkansas River to Deliver Overland

May 1, 1858, Saturday, page 2
Arkansas State Gazette and Democrat, Little Rock, Ark.

John B. Luck, Esq., writes to the editor of the Times, from Washington City, April 3d, as follows: **Mr. Butterfield**, and several of his associates have been here twice, during the last few weeks, endeavoring to effect a change in their contract, by procuring permission to connect at Fort Smith instead of Preston. Among other things, they propose to carry the mail from Little Rock to Fort Smith in steamboats. **Mr. Butterfield** in going down the river last January, became satisfied from observation and from the statements of pilots and others, that a class of boats could be built drawing not to exceed 12 inches, which could run up and down the river throughout the year. At any rate, he proposes, if allowed to connect at Fort Smith, to try the experiment, and he had a man employed expressly to make the necessary arrangements. This morning, Judge Sebastion told me he had a long conversation with the Postmaster General, in which the latter told him he had concluded to make the charge, that it would be better for all parties; – that passengers from California by the time they reached Fort Smith, would be glad to leave the stage and get on board of a boat, and moreover that if boats *could make regular trips*, there would be greater regularity in that mode of conveyance than by land, as high waters could not prove obstruction.

Whether we succeed is ultimately getting the mail carried by Albuquerque or not, I think you will agree with me in regarding the connection at Fort Smith, as a very important point gained, and a subject for congratulation.

Of course, you have heard, before now, of Beele's arrival, and of the very strong additional testimony he brings to the 35th parallel.

May 4, 1858
Merger Point Will be Fort Smith Instead of Preston, Texas

May 4, 1858
Arkansas True Democrat, Little Rock, Arkansas

The *Fort Smith Times* has a letter from J. B. Luce, esq., now in Washington City, in which he says that the department has consented to a change of the connection of the **Overland Mail** route so as to connect at Fort Smith instead of Preston, and to permit them to carry the mails from Little Rock to Fort Smith, all the year, in boats to be built for that purpose.

The *Times* notices the return of the Albuquerque expedition, and the **Overland Mail** expedition. The latter pronounce the route entirely practicable.

May 6, 1858
Advance Preparations

May 6, 1858
Fort Smith Times, Fort Smith, Arkansas

Latest - Mr. James Glover, of the **Overland Mail Company**, arrived here on last Saturday.

Mr. Glover is here for the purpose of making arrangements for the accommodation of the **Mail Company** & c., & c., and will we presume, in a few days be on the look our for animals, forage & c.

May 5, 1858
Exploring Party Arrives From El Paso

May 5, 1858
Fort Smith Times, Fort Smith, Arkansas

Eight of the **Overland** exploring party reached here on the 3rd. They were fourteen days coming from El Paso. They report the roads good and plenty of water except a distance of seventy-four miles across the Llano Estacado where water will have to be supplied by means of artificial tanks. [as quoted in "Butterfield Overland Mail" by Roscoe Conklin, page 217]

*Butterfield purchased a number of **water tanks** similar to this, to carry water as far as 75 miles, to fill cisterns at desert southwest stage stations.*

May 6, 1858
Advance Preparations

May 6, 1858
Fort Smith Times, Fort Smith, Arkansas

The remainder, eight in number, of the exploring party, sent out by the **Overland Mail Co.,** reached this place *[Fort Smith]* on Monday 3d. They were 41 days coming from El

Paso. They report the roads good, and plenty of water, except a distance of 74 miles across the Liano Estacado, where water will have to be supplied by means of artificial tanks. They say that the land on most of the route is excellent, and is capable of being made the best grain growing and stock raising country on the continent. They saw no Indians either as they went or returned. They left yesterday on the Fitshugh *[steamboat]*, for their respective homes in New York and Missouri. Mr. Glover, agent of the **Company**, is now here, and is daily expecting Mr. Crocker, and they will immediately commence buying stock, and employing men to send out on the plans to build stations and prepare for running the mails in September. Success to them.

May 12, 1858

The City Hotel Remodeled - Future Home Station of the Overland Mail Company

May 12, 1858
Fort Smith Times, Fort Smith, Arkansas

THE CITY HOTEL - We take pleasure in stating that this well known establishment had been thoroughly renovated, outside and inside. The Proprietor, Mr. J. K. McKenzie, showed us through the building, and we found a great change made in many of the departments, for the comfort of its guests; and nothing is more pleasing to the eye, than the Dining Room, which will compare with the best in the State; and, indeed, we doubt if there is such a comfortable and pleasant one in Arkansas anywhere. And, as to Mac, we know no better, or cleverer fellow every kept a Hotel, and this is the testimony of every one. Be sure to call at the City Hotel.

May 14, 1858

Support for 35th Parallel Route

May 14, 1858, Friday, page 2
Arkansas Intelligencer, Van Buren, Arkansas

THE FORT SMITH HERALD – The last number of the above

mentioned paper contains a leading editorial on the **Overland Mail Route** to California. The tone and spirit of which has taken us entirely by surprise. From the antecedents of that paper we did not expect it to change its position so sudden. We have seen in our time many strange and unaccountable terms and twists with editors and politicians, but the last whirl of the *Herald* for quickness of conception and rapidity of motion, beats the most expert adept in great performances.

It was but a short time since that the *Herald* said the route on the 35th parallel was the shortest and most practicable, and indeed the only one that was entirely practicable.

In this opinion we concur with the *Herald,* and we know no reason to change that opinion. But the *Herald* has discovered that the present arrangement, is as much advantage to Fort Smith as the 35th would be, and it is all right with them. They take back all they have said against the Postmaster General and he is now a mavelous *[marvelous]* proper man with that paper. We always believed Gov. Brown to be a patrioit, *[patriot]* and an officer that would honestly and faithfully discharge his duties as he understood them, but we also believed that he was laboring under a mistake as to the advantages of the 35th parallel. It was to remove if possible this error, and call the attention of the country to investigate the facts that induced us as a public journalist, to take the position we did in the matter. We thought and think yet, that the adoption of this route was the best for the country at large. The *Herald* thought or pretended to think the same. But all at once it has discovered that Mr. Phelps, of Missouri, did not think that old **John Butterfield** originated the ideas of making the connection at that place. Suppose he did; was it for the interest of Fort Smith alone or was it because **Mr. Butterfield** as the contractor who was pecuniarily interested in conveying the mail on the best route, selected it? We suppose the latter. We do not suppose that **Mr. Butterfield** knew or cared anything about Fort Smith more than he saw from the map, that it was on or near the 35th parallel, which he supposed to be the nearest and most practicable route to San Francisco.

But the *Herald* seems to be satisfied if Fort Smith is a point on the route no difference how or where the road may run. We are sorry, *Mr. Herald,* to learn that your efforts for the good of the public are confirmed to the narrow limits of your little town.

You have yet to learn it seems, *Mr. Herald,* that your place is but a small affair in the State of Arkansas, to say nothing of the United States. And if you set your gauge to measure public utility by such a standard, your compass is too small to accomplish its object.

You admit that you *"was wrong in attributing improper motives to Gov. Brown in the management of this contract because he had overlooked Fort Smith."*

Why my dear sirs, do you suppose that Gov. Brown knows or cares anything about Fort Smith? Why should he? Do you know, that in many points in this great confederacy, larger places have been built in twelve months and can and will be again. Then, why should you think that a great national thoroughfare as the **overland** route to the Pacific, would turn one-half mile out of the way to go through your town. If you suppose so, you much over rate your importance, and it may be that you are laboring under a happy delusion. But never again set up any pretensions as laboring for the public good, when you concede that your mote *[mote: tiny part]* of the public is confirmed to the pecuniary aid *[monetary aid]* of your village. It may be true that present arrangements will be as advantageous to your point, but is it to the country, and is the present route practicable? You said not, and we believed you, and give what aid we could to establish the fact. Now you acknowledge that you are satisfied as Fort Smith is made a point on the route. It is all right, Gov. Brown and every body else have done their duty. Hereafter we will understand you, and when you oppose persons or measures, we will know your motive, and give you full credit. The country will do so, and no doubt

Mr. Postmaster Brown will duly appreciate your praise, and remble *[remember]* at your censure.

May 14, 1858
Support for 35th Parallel Route

May 14, 1858, Friday, page 2
Arkansas Intelligencer, Van Buren, Arkansas
Ozark, May 13th, '58

Editor of the Intelligencer, I am somewhat astonished to see that our neighbors of Fort Smith are letting down on the 35th parallel route. If I may be allowed to form a judgement from an editorial in the last *Herald*, their only reason for at least the reasons of the *Herald's* advocacy of the 35th parallel heretofore, has been because of the benefit that would accrue to Fort Smith alone, and not because they were convinced that it was the best, nearest, and most practicable route to California. I am surprised that the *Herald* should thus acknowledge its selfish policy so openly. The editor says; *"So far as any advantage to be derived (to Fort Smith) from making this a point on the route is concerned, we derive as much benefit from it, as if it had been run on the 35th parallel, and we ought to be satisfied."*

The people ought to be satisfied? Let the route go where it will after it has reached Fort Smith, because they the people of Fort Smith will derive as much benefit, &c., *[&c. is an abbreviation of etc., et cetera, meaning and others, or, and so forth.]* as if it had been run on the 35th parallel? Very selfish all this. Is the *Herald* willing to eat its own words, to disavow all that it has heretofore said against the 32d parallel route and in favor of the 35th?

The *Herald* may rest assured that unless the 35th parallel route is established, that in less than five years from this date, Fort Smith will cease to receive any of that benefit for which the editor things *"we ought to be satisfied;"* for as soon as the railroad now in course of construction from Vicksburg to Shreveport, in Louisiana, and to Marshall, Texas, and then on in the direction of El Paso shall have been completed as far as Fort Belknap, the benefits which Fort Smith will derive from the **Overland California Mail Route** will be just none at all.

The whole article of the *Herald* appears to be a crawfishing from unjust attacks they have made upon the Postmaster General, with the idea of throwing dust in his eyes for the purpose of getting him to establish a distributing Post office at Fort Smith – the veil is so flimsy, however, that it is easily seen through as vile the following extract from the *Herald's* article:

> *"We have perhaps been wrong in attributing the Gov. Brown improper motives in this management of this great contract. We thought that he was showing great partiality to the southern and central portions of the State, to the negligence of the north and west, but we now think that his only aim has been to adopt the routes and means best calculated to insure the successful execution of the contract.*
>
> *So far as any advantage to be derived from making this a point on the route is concerned, we derive as much benefit from it, as if it had been run on the 35th parallel, and we ought to be satisfied. We owe more to Gov. Brown for increased mail facilities, than any Postmaster General we have ever had; he knows our wants, and is determined to supply them. We think this ought to be made a distributing office, and we think, if Gov. Brown will look at the number of arrivals and departures here every week – and consider the fact, that this will be the great starting office for the California mail, that he will at once make it a distributing office."*

I agree with the *Herald* that Gov. Brown had undoubtedly aimed in locating the mail route, to adopt that which he considered the most practicable. Gov. Brown has had to use his judgement in the selection of a route upon the reports of government and army officers, and we all know how one sided those reports frequently are. While we who live upon this frontier, having a more practical knowledge of the matter, and firmly fixed in our opinion, that the 35th parallel route is entirely a more practical one than the one selected, viz, the route on or near the 32d parallel. We are willing and glad to say that Gov. Brown has done more in aid of mail facilities in the west than any Postmaster General that has preceded him. He is a western man himself, and is acquainted with our wants in this regard. It would seem apparent from the whole article of the *Herald*, that if they could get a distributing office established at Fort Smith – *somebody* probably wanting very particularly the office of Postmaster – that they would be willing to give up the 35th parallel route without a further struggle, and this at a time when it's prospects are brighter than they have ever before been. I fear that I have already trespassed upon your patrons, Mr. Editor, and will close; for the whole argument of the Herald's article is, if it possesses an argument *"mole ruit sua." [Note: "mole ruit sua" is a portion of a quote from Horace, "vis consilii expers mole ruit sua" which translates: "force without wisdom collapses from its own mass."*

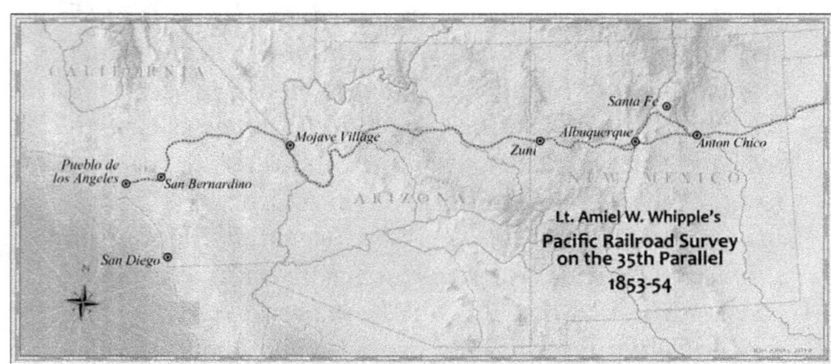

Lt. Amiel W. Whipple's Pacific Railroad Survey
on the 35th Parallel, 1853-1854

May 18, 1858
In Support of 35th Parallel Route

May 18, 1858
Arkansas True Democrat, Little Rock, Arkansas

PROCEEDINGS OF THE DEMOCRATIC CONVENTION FOR THE FIRST

Congressional District – ...instructions to our senators and request to our representatives in Congress to use all proper means to secure the adoption of the route of the 35th parallel, via Memphis, Van Buren, Fort Smith and Albuquerque, for the **Overland Mail** and Pacific railway, and to obtain a land grant for a railroad from Van Buren through north western Arkansas, in the direction of Springfield, Missouri, and a land grant for a railroad from Helena to the Iron Mountain. *[NOTE: This article was also printed in the May 21 1858 issue of the Arkansas Intelligencer.]*

May 6, 1858
Advance Preparations

May 6, 1858
Fort Smith Times, Fort Smith, Arkansas

Overland Mail – We have seen lately articles in several papers charging that the **Overland Mail Company** have no idea of attempting to carry out their contract, that they are demanding changed, & c., & c.

From the best information we can get on the subject, we are satisfied that it is all idle rumor, or rather, that is made up from the prolific brain of Washington letter writers, urged on by critics of the **Company**, who would be glad to see them fail.

We have just had a conversation with Mr. Glover, agent of the **Company**, and he says that he has received before he arrived here, a letter from **Col. Butterfield**, instructing him to arrange his plans to accompany Hawley to El Paso, and o select places for stations so as to be ready to receive stock, & c., & c. Mr Glover is expecting Messers Crocker and family every day, but , says if they do not arrive in a few days, that he will be obedient to instructions, fit out an expedition here, and proceed to El Paso, leaving men at the different points beyond Fort Belknap, that he may select, to receive and take care of stock & c., & c.

Our readers have already been appraised that the **Company** has bought a large number of coaches, a part of which have been shipped to California. We are informed that a considerable number have been shipped, and are now on their way to this place, and, also that the **Company** have bought several hundred head of horses and mules for the service.

The **Company** may practicably prefer the Albuquerque route, but as there is no prospect of there being any change made, we are satisfied that they will in good faith, and with success, carry out their contract on the route selected by the Post Master General. They have already expended too much money, and have too much at stake to fail now.

The men who have taken this great contract are made of too good a material to let anything they take hold of fail.

Butterfield says, when his teacher told him he must get a dictionary, that his father deliberately took out his pocket knife and cut out the word 'fail', and he of course does not know the meaning of the word.

May 21, 1858
Editorial Retracted

May 21, 1858

Arkansas Intelligencer, Van Buren, Arkansas

The Fort Smith Herald. –We published last week some strictures on the course of the *Herald,* in relation to the **Overland Mail** route to California. But we find, by the last issue of that paper, we were mistaken in the views of the *Herald* in relation to the 35th parallel, and we take back all we said about our contemporaries in relation to the matter, and acknowledge that we were perhaps a little too hasty in our remarks. –

We know the difficulty in editing a paper to please every body, or indeed, always to appear consistent, and the editorials are frequently gotten up in haste and without due reflection, as to the effect of the language used to express the idea intended, and thus editors are often construed to advocate a peculiar measure, when the fact they intend the reverse. Thus we suppose was the case with our neighbors of the *Herald,* when they penned the article to which we referred. And we are sorry we said anything about it. But the course of the *Herald* has been so uniformly consistent, and apparently sincere in the measures it advocated, that we were taken by surprise, in the apparent sudden change, and hastily and perhaps improperly made some remarks in relation to it, which we much regret, and hope our neighbors will excuse us, and that nothing may ever arise to mar the good feeling that has heretofore existed between us.

May 25, 1858
Support for 35th Parallel Route

May 25, 1858, page 2

Arkansas True Democrat, Little Rock, Arkansas

WHAT THE ARKANSAS PAPERS SAY – The Van Buren *Intelligencer* "pitches in" to the *Fort Smith Herald,* whom it accuses of backing down from the 35th to the 32d parallel route for the **overland mail** to California.

May 25, 1858
Artesian Well Report from Liano Estacado

May 25, 1858, page 1

Arkansas True Democrat, Little Rock, Arkansas

THE ARTESIAN WELL EXPEDITION – A correspondent of the St. Louis *Republican,* traveling with the **Overland Mail** expedition, which left Fort Chadbourne on the 26th of February, gives, in a letter dated *"Camp of the Artesian Well Expedition, Rio Pecos River, April 10,"* the following description of his visit to the camp of the expedition. The information he communicates as to the prospect of Capt. Pope's success in obtaining plentiful supplies of water on the Liano Estacado is highly gratifying, especially to all who are interested in our southern Pacific railroad enterprise.

... A full corps of mechanics and laborers are engaged in the working of the machinery used in boring the well... The bore is 2 $^{1}/_{2}$ inches in diameter, and wherever it is required, heavy copper tubing is used to protect it from being filled up with dirt. The depth now reached is one thousand and forty feet. The first water was found at a depth of two hundred and forty-four feet. Several springs have been reached since at various depths. There is an abundance of water to be obtained now at a distance of one hundred and seventy-five feet from the surface. Although large quantities of water have, several times, been pumped out from the well, the supply does not diminish, and the springs seem to be inexhaustible...

Memphis and Little Rock Railroad
This engine was used in the Little Rock Division.
Initials on the coal car: M.& L. R. R. R.
Image compliments of Mike Hood

May 28, 1858
Work Begins on Laying Railroad Track
Potts Station Among Collection Points for Ties

(NOTE: The Butterfield ended up using the first 25 miles of this track, Hopefield to Madison, starting Sept. 1858)

Wanted—35,000 Rail Road Ties.

DIVISION ENGINEERS OFFICE,
L. R. & F. S. R. R.,
Galley Creek, April 1, '58.

PROPOSALS will be received at this office until the 1st of June next, for furnishing and delivering on the line of the Little Rock and Fort Smith Railroad, 35,000 railroad ties. - Said ties to be delivered at the following points, viz:

At station 1, near the house of Mr. Tuck- sec. 31, town. 8, range 20 1,200
At station 51 .... 2,000.
At station 70, on land of Dr. Russell 2,000
At station 135, at crossing of the Dover road 1,000
At depot grounds at Russellville 2,000
A station 230 2,000
At station 260, on land of I. F. Falls 2,000
At station 300 2,000
At station 940 2,000
At station 370 1,500
At station 420, on the road crossing Neak. K. Potts 1,500
At station 460 2,000
At station 500, north of G. Sinclair's house 1,500
At station 530 1,800
At station 560, north of Slicker's house.. 1,500
At station 590, north Mr. Tarrant's house 1,500
At station 620 1,500
At station 655, north of Mr. Robinson's.. 1,500
At station 690 1,500
At Hebron depot grounds 2,500

The ties must be of the following dimensions:

Eight feet in length, not less than eight inches in thickness, hewed on two sides with a face not less than eight inches wide, one tie in every seven must have a face not less than ten inches. They must be of sound timber from post oak, cypress, walnut, or pin oak.

The ties must be delivered on or before the 1st day of September, 1858.

W. A. HAVEN,
Division Engineer.

april 9, '58–6w

Source: *Arkansas Intelligencer* (Van Buren, Arkansas, Friday, May 28, 1858, page 4

June 1, 1858
Support for 35th Parallel Route

June 1, 1858, Tuesday, page 2
Arkansas True Democrat, Little Rock, Arkansas

The *Fort Smith Herald,* has the following: The Washington correspondent of the *St. Louis Republican,* says – that the **Overland Mail Company** propose starting their mails from Memphis and St. Louis, to Fort Belknap, and from San Francisco to Fort Yuma, by the 15th of July, two months earlier than is named in their contract. We argue from this, that they have made much greater progress in their preparations, than we had supposed. All that we can say is, that we are greatly rejoiced. Come on with your apple carts, gentlemen, as soon as you please. We have a good mind to take passage on the first stage – will consult our better half about it.

June 2, 1858
Butterfield's Overland Mail to Start Soon

June 2, 1858
Fort Smith Times, Fort Smith, Arkansas

We learn from Mr. Glover that he received a letter from **Col. Butterfield,** a day or two ago, in which he says that the **Company** had obtained the consent of the P. M. General to run semi-weekly mails at the two ends of the route, and that Mr. Kenyon would go to California on the 20th, to put into operation between San Francisco and Fort Yuma, and Mr, Crocker would leave the same day for this place, and Belknap, placing stock and coaches at the stations with the view of starting the mail by the 15th of July, or the 1st of August.

June 2, 1858
Butterfield's Overland Mail to Start Soon

June 2, 1858

Fort Smith Times, Fort Smith, Arkansas

REPAIRING THE ROADS – As the **Overland Mail** will be put into operation in the course of next month, it would be well for the overseers of the roads on the line to be traveled, to go to work forthwith and repair the roads.

In this county, the roads between Fort Smith and Van Buren should, at once, be put in good order, and, also the road towards the Choctaw Agency. As far as the county line, they should also be put in good order.

There are funds in the county treasury belonging to this township, and, we hope the County Court will have the money applied to the repairing of these roads.

It is a great benefit to every citizen of this county to have the **Overland Mail** here, and for that reason, let us make good roads for their stages, and keep them up.

June 2, 1858
Butterfield's Overland Mail to Start Soon

June 2, 1858

Fort Smith Times, Fort Smith, Arkansas

We commence on our first page, this week, an article from the pen of John B. Luce, Esq., of this county, in answer to the objections of the Post Master General, for not having the **Overland Mail** carried over the 35th parallel. Since, however, Gov. Brown has settled the matter to the satisfaction of all parties, his arguments may be applied to the benefit of constructing the great national railroad to the Pacific. Every man in Arkansas should read the whole article, as it is well written and the facts systematically arranged.

June 2, 1858
Part I of John Luce's 6 Part Article
In Support of Albuquerque Route Over the El Paso

June 2, 1858

Fort Smith Times, Fort Smith, Arkansas

... Sir, The following pages were written in the fall of 1857, for the purpose of calling the attention of the people of

Arkansas to the superior advantages of the route from Fort Smith, by way of Albuquerque, for the transportation of the **Overland Mail** to San Francisco, and were left unfinished on account of unavoidable delay in procuring the material to a proper view of the subject in its full bearings.

They have been printed in their present fragmentary state, under an impression that some, at least, of the facts which they contain are not generally known, and that those facts, though collected with special reference to a route for **Mail Stages**, may prove useful in considering the selection of a route for a railroad...

OVERLAND ROUTE TO CALIFORNIA

BY J. B. LUCE, OF SEBASTIAN COUNTY

On the 1st July, 1857, it was officially announced that the Postmaster General had made a contract for the transportation of the mail from the Mississippi river, overland, in semi-weekly trips, to San Francisco; starting from two different points, Memphis and St. Louis, and proceeding by way of Little Rock, Arkansas, and Preston, Texas, to a point on the Rio Grande, near El Paso; thence to Fort Yuma, a post at the junction of the Gila and Colorado Rivers; and thence *'through the best passes and valleys, to San Francisco.'*

The act of Congress authorizing the contract required the service *'to be performed within twenty-five days for each trip,' 'with good four-horse coaches, or stage wagons, suitable for the conveyance of passengers.'*

The lowest estimate which has yet appeared of the distance from the Mississippi river to San Francisco, by the route designated in the contract, is over 2,100 miles.

The ***[Butterfield Overland]*** mail, to be delivered in the required time, must be carried more than 81 miles every 24 hours, for an average of more than three and a half miles an hour throughout the entire period of twenty-five days.

There are good reasons for believing –

1st. That owing to the peculiar character of a large portion of the country traversed by this route, this contract will never be carried into effect.

2d. That if the mail be carried **Overland** to San Francisco at all, throughout the year, in semi-weekly trips of twenty-five days each, it must be carried over or near the route known as the 35th parallel, or Albuquerque Route.

So far as the mere carrying of the mails is concerned, it is of comparatively little consequence to the public over which route it travels, as the letter communication between San Francisco and the Mississippi is likely to be, for many years, in a great degree, confined to either the Panama or the Tehuantepec steamers and their connections.

[NOTE: The Isthmus of Tehuantepec in Mexico, and also the Isthmus of Panama, are both the shortest distance overland between the Gulf of Mexico and the Pacific Ocean.]

But as an impression generally prevails that the **Overland Mail Route** is to be protected in such a manner as to encourage the settlement of regions at present exposed to Indian depredations, the whole country is interested in seeing that the effort and means of the government are so distorted and expanded as to assure the derived object; that is, such a line of settlements between the Mississippi and the Pacific as will render **overland** communication safe and convenient.

It is proposed, therefore, to state some of the facts and reasons which have led to the belief that the attempt to carry the mail in the manner indicated, by way of El Paso and Fort Yuma, will not succeed; and why, in the face of official assertions to the contrary, the Albuquerque Route is regarded as superior to that of the 32d parallel.

It must be borne in mind, in the first place, that the whole subject is comparatively new. Fifteen years ago, little was known to any but a few hunters and traders, of any part of the territory, within the present limits of the United States, lying west of the Indian settlements on the borders of Missouri and Arkansas. Everybody knew that the Rocky Mountains separated with vast prairie plains from the Pacific. Few had any clear notion of what constituted the Rocky Mountains, much less of any mountain range beyond them.

The peculiar features of the Sierra Nevada *[mountains]* were first made known to Col. Fremont, who passed along the entire length in 1842-'46, and seems to have been the first to ascertain that it exceeded the Rocky Mountains in height; that it was not at any point crossed by any river from the interior; that it ran parallel with the coast: in an average distance of a hundred, and fifty miles; and that it extended to the border of Oregon on the north and beyond the head-waters of the San Joaquin River on the south.

In the report of the same explorations, public attention was for the first time called to the fact that the vast region of country lying between the Sierra Nevada & the Rocky Mountains, now well known as the Great American Basin, had a separate system of lakes and rivers of its own, without any outlet, or any connection whatever with the waters of either the Atlantic or the Pacific – a fact which does not seem to have been completely established until after the subsequent examinations of 1845-'46. The southern limits of this basin, notwithstanding the numerous explorations and surveys recently made in that quarter, have not to this day been clearly made known.

[NOTE: The poor printing of the original page makes it difficult to distinguish between 1844 and 1841 etc. Therefore, the dates in this transcription may not be accurate.]

Before Colonel Fremont's expedition to the Rocky Mountains, in 1842, overland travel to the Pacific was confined to an occasional small emigration to Oregon. California being then a Mexican province, was only open to the few American settlers who could obtain permits or grants from the Mexican government. As late as the spring of 1844, when Fremont first visited the valleys of the Sacramento and the San Joaquin, there does not appear to have been any regular road to California from the valley of the Mississippi.

The history of the latter explorations, which formed no part of his original plan, but was a necessity to which his party was reduced by the physical structure of the country, affords a striking illustration of the best mode of approaching or leaving California.

The reader will bear in mind that these two valleys of the Sacramento and the San Joaquin, in fact, constitute one valley extending in a curved line parallel with the coast, more than 500 miles in length, and about 100 in breath – walled in on the east by the Sierra Nevada, on the west by the Coast range; the latter having an opening to the sea through the bay of San Francisco, of which the two rivers may be regarded as branches – one coming from the north, the other from the south.

Colonel Fremont, on his way homeward from the Columbia River, in the fall of 1843, had intended to cross from Klemath Lake, lat. 42 degrees 50 minutes, into the Oregon Territory, above the northern extremity of the Sierra Nevada, and over the Great Basin to the sources of the Arkansas, about 30 degrees 30 minutes. After traveling 500 miles he found himself compelled to abandon this project, and cross over the Sierra to the valley of the Sacramento.

After undergoing infinite hardship and privation he succeeded in reaching Sutter's Fort, near the confluence of the American and the Sacramento Rivers, latitude 38 degrees 31 minutes.

From this point, he says, *"our direct course was east,"* but he was *"forced by desert plains and mountain ranges, and deep snows," "south, above 500 miles of traveling, to a pass at the head of the San Joaquin River."* Meaning a pass since ascertained to be near the Tejon (pronounced Tay-hone) Pass, and not very far from the extreme southern base of the Sierra. That is to say, he was at Sutter's Fort on the Sacramento, in latitude 38 degrees 31 minutes, north of the bay of San Francisco. He wanted to travel eastward, to a point about one degree further north. To do this, he was *"forced south,"* by the Sierra Nevada, *"about 500 miles of traveling."*

This was in 1844. Since then, California has become one of the United States. Nearly everything within its limits has undergone a change, except the great physical fact which Col. Fremont has so graphically described.

To this day, the traveler seeking to leave California by land, in winter, is forced south, *"by desert plains, and mountain ranges, and deep snows,"* to the passes near the southern extremity of the San Joaquin, or, as it is now more generally called, the Tulare Valley.

Captain Stansbury, speaking of the winter of 1840-'50, in the Great Salt Lake valley, says that the snow fell constantly upon the mountains, and that *"in many of the canyons it accumulated to a depth of fifty feet, filling up the passes so rapidly that, in more than one instance, emigrants who had been belated in starting from the States, were overtaken by the storms in the mountain gorges, and forced to abandon everything, and escape on foot, leaving even their animals to suffer and perish in the snows. All communication with the world beyond was effectually cut off; and as the winter advanced, the gorges became more and more impassable, owning to the drifting of the snow into them from the projecting peaks."* (page 122, Stansbury's Report)

On the emigrant road, from the South Pass to the Salt Lake, Lieutenant Beckwith's surveying party was compelled to stop on account of a snow storm on the 7th of April 1834. On the 8th he continued encountering *"fields of snow,"* his mules *"literally rolling pitching, tumbling, and floundering through."* On the 11th, more snow than on any part of the route, the warmth of the season *"not yet sufficient to affect it;"* and on the 19th an impassable field of snow extending for several miles. (Lieutenant Beckwith's Report, 2d vol., P. R. R. R. p.12)

Everybody remembers the terrible disaster which befell Colonel Fremont in the deep snow near the Conestoga during the winter of 1848-'49. This was about latitude 38 degree.

Other evidence to the same effect could be given, but it is unnecessary. The fact that the mountain snows constitute an objection to the routes north of the 36 degree and south of 46 degree is not likely to be questioned. It is useless to consider them in connection with a contract for carrying the mail in passenger coaches **overland** to San Francisco *"in* *semi-weekly trips of twenty-five days each."*

The *"pass at the head of the San Joaquin,"* to which Col. Fremont was *"forced,"* was, as before stated, near the southern extremity of the Sierra Nevada, in latitude 35 degrees 17 minutes.

After leaving the pass, he traveled 150 miles, sometimes south, sometimes east, until he struck the Spanish trace from Los Angeles to Sante Fe. He followed this trace northwest 370 miles, from the point of intersection to the Vegas de Santa Clara and then left it, on his way north to the sources of the Arkansas, the trace bearing southeast, towards. Sante Fe.

This trace, which the Mexican caravans passed once a year from Santa Fe, with goods which they exchanged at Los Angeles for horses, does not appear to have been traveled with wagons. It was circuitous, passing more than two degrees north of a direct course, over a desert waste, to avoid the numerous lands of hostile Indians inhabiting the country a straight road would traverse. It was at that time, the first traveled approach to California, south of latitude 40 degrees, and until 1846 it seems to have been the only regularly traveled road from new Mexico to the Pacific.
[NOTE: The poor printing of the original page makes it difficult to distinguish between a "4" and a "1" or a "7" etc. Therefore, the numbers in this transcription are questionable.]

During the Mexican war, in the fall of 1816, Gen. Kearney marched, at the head of a dragoon force, from Sante Fe to San Diego, on the Pacific. Pursuing the course of the Rio Grande for some 230 miles below Sante Fe, he left it about latitude 33 degrees 3 minutes, and struck out in a westerly direction for the Gila *[River]*, which he reached in a little over a hundred miles from the Rio Grande, and followed to its mouth, near the present site of Fort Yuma, on the Colorado.

On leaving the Rio Grande, Gen. Kearney found his road impracticable for wagons. Part of his force consisted of a battalion of Mormons, under Col. Cooke. As it was desirable that the battalion should take its wagons, Col. Cooke, in search of a better road than General Kearney's mule trail, made a considerable bend to the south. Following the Rio Grande thirty miles further, he left it at a fording place, called San Diego, a little below the 33d parallel, about 260 miles from Sante Fe, and sixty seven above El Paso; and traveled southwest 150 miles to a point since ascertained to be near latitude 31 degrees 20 minutes, the south line of the Gadsden Purchase, which he skirted for eighty miles, going west to the San Pedro River. Then turning due north, he followed that river eighty miles, and again, turning west, fifty miles brought him to the town of Tucson, from which his course was ninety miles northwest to the Gila River, where he rejoined General Kearney's trail, a few miles above the Pimo villages, in latitude 33 degree 7 min and did not again leave it.

From the mouth of the Gila, the command proceeded west about a hundred miles over the Colorado desert; then northwest to the crossing of the Coast range, at Warner's Pass, and thence to San Diego.

Exterior view of Warner's ranch and stage station
Del Mendell was the agent and store owner. The house is in dilapidated condition. A skeletal wooden fence forms a perimeter around the house enclosing several trees.
Courtesy of California Historical Society
University of Southern California Digital Library

The route thus explored by Col. Cooke is substantially the same that has since been known to emigrants as the El Paso, or Dona Ana Route, and, as far as Fort Yuma, is the one over which it is proposed under the late contract to carry the ***[Butterfield Overland]* Mail** to San Francisco.

No other route to California, entering it anywhere south of the Sacramento, seems to have been generally known, even in New Mexico, in the fall of 1846, except the "Spanish Trace" to Los Angeles, already referred to as intersected by Fremont in 1844.

In the spring of 1849, a large party of emigrants, escorted by Capt. Marcy, with a command of infantry and dragoons, started from Fort Smith for California, taking the route by the Canadian River to Sante Fe. On reaching the latter place, they were informed by several of the best guides in New Mexico that it was not practicable to take wagons west from any point on the Rio Grande above San Diego, and that it would be necessary to turn south and follow Col. Cooke's route, which the emigrants accordingly did – very few of them leaving it until they reached the Pacific. The military escort returned to Fort Smith: but, in so doing, it occurred to Capt. Marcy that it would materially reduce the distance traveled by future parties from Fort Smith, if a road could be found leading directly to Col. Cooke's point of departure from the Rio Grande, nearly three degrees south of Fort Smith, instead of going first to Sante Fe, which was 300 miles out of the way. so he passed down the rio Grande to Dona Ana, a newly settled place, opposite the point where the disputed boundary line adopted by Commissioners Bartlett and Cooke leaves the Rio Grande, and about fifteen miles below San Diego, near which Col. Cooke's road leaves the river. At Dona Ana he found guides who escorted him to Preston *[Texas]*, on Red River. From Preston he came to Ft. Smith, not a little elated at the discovery that it was practicable to strike a straight course with wagons for Col. Cooke's road, south of 33 degrees. Instead of going by way of Sante

Fe, north of 35 degrees.

This is the origin of the "32d parallel route,' east of the Rio Grande, as far as Preston; and this is the road over which the ***[Butterfield Overland]* Mail** is to be carried from Preston to Fort Fillmore, which is fifteen miles below Dona Ana.

It will be observed that this return route of Capt. Marcy, and the emigrant route opened by Col. Cooke, both originated in the same cause – the impression that a route practicable for wagons, leading west from the Rio Grande, could not be found without going as far down that stream as San Diego.

The first information to the contrary that was made public, appeared in a letter from Lieut. Simpson, of the topographical engineers, to the chief of his corps, written at Sante Fe, in September, 1849, in which, after describing an expedition to the Navajo country, he expresses the belief that *"we have hit upon a middle route between the southern detour, made by Col. Cooke from Sante Fe, and the northern one, called the Spanish trail route, said to be equally as long."* After speaking of the road *"from Sante Fe to Zuni, a distance of near two hundred miles in an almost direct course to the City of the Angels,"* he added, that the guide informed him that from Zuni the road was equally practicable for wagons as far as the Colorado, and that he had very little doubt the route could be as favorably extended from the Colorado west to the Pacific.

About three months after the date of this letter of Lieut. Simpson, Capt. Ord; of the army, who had been dispatched by Gen. Riley, then stationed in California, to ascertain whether a better route could not be found for emigrants than that by the Gila, or by the Salt Lake, reported that, by leaving the San Joaquin valley, at the Tejon Pass, and proceeding, by way of the Mohave River, to the Colorado, and thence, through the settlements of the Moquis and the Zuni Indians, to Albuquerque, and from there, by way of Anton Chico, to the Canadian, the traveler could reach the Mississippi more easily than by the old routes; the only difficulty in the way arising from the fact that the route *was inhabited by hostile Indians.*

In the report of Lieut. Simpson, dated April 11, 1850, and printed by order of Congress, he again alludes to the same subject. On page 137 he states that Mr. Richard Campbell, of Sante Fe, who traveled in 1827 with pack mules from New Mexico to San Diego, by way of Zuni, found no difficulty throughout the whole distance, and that a good wagon road *"with wood, water and grass, can be found in this direction, both to San diego and the Pueblo de los Angeles."*

In the summer of 1852 an enormous letter appeared in the *New York Herald*, dated Santa Fe, July 1, 1852, stating that Capt. Joseph Walker had recently discovered a new route to the Pacific, having passed from Monterey to Albuquerque, leisurely, with pack mules in 25 days, by a route directly west, abounding in pasture and water, and as practicable for wagons and carriages as that between Sante Fe and Missouri.

In the following spring, the *Fort Smith Herald* published a letter from Col. Miles, then in command at Fort Fillmore, on the Rio Grande, (about thirty-five miles above El Paso and fifteen below Dona Ana) dated January 4, 1853, calling attention to *"the new route discovered from Albuquerque, in New Mexico, to San Francisco, in California, a journey in distance of not over twenty-five days for loaded wagons."* No particulars are given respecting this new route, but the letter deserves attention, as coming from the commanding officer at Fort Fillmore – a prominent point on the 32d parallel route.

In May, 1853, a letter was published from the celebrated Kit Carson, who accompanied Fremont over the Spanish trace in 1844, and Kearney, down the Gila, in 1816, in which he says, *"I know but one route across the continent which can be traveled winter and summer, and over a remarkably level country, and that one must cross the Rio Grande, within fifty or sixty miles from Sante Fe.*

There is no manner of doubt that the trail from Albuquerque to Zuni, along the headwaters of the streams that run into the Gila, and then crossing the big river about the Mohave and so on, is the easiest road that can be found."

About the middle of July, 1853, Lt. Whipple, of the topographical engineers, left Fort Smith, on the Arkansas River, as the head of an exploring party, to examine the route to the Pacific, by way of Albuquerque, at which place he arrived on the 3d October. Before his arrival, Mr. F. X. Aubrey came in from San Francisco, by way of the Tejon Pass, crossing the Colorado a little below the 36th parallel, and passing from thence to the Zuni village, by what line of travel does not very clearly appear. It seems to have been regarded by the Albuquerque papers at the time as bearing too far to the north.

But his account of this trip is particularly valuable, because he says: *"I set out upon this journey simply to gratify my own curiosity as to the practicability of one of the much-talked of routes for the Atlantic and Pacific railroad. Having previously traveled to Gila river route, I felt anxious to compare it with the middle route."* He had taken sheep and wagons to California by the Gila River the year before, and was about to return that way with sheep. Upon the middle route, he says: *"I encountered many hardships and dangers, and met with serious pecuniary loss, yet I say it is the best for a railroad, and would be excellent for ordinary traveling but for the Indians."*

This seems to have been the first direct confirmation of the various accounts of Lt. Simpson, Capt. Ord, Mr. Carson, and Col. Miles. It came from no secondary sources.
[*NOTE: The remainder of this paragraph is heavily over-inked and is illegible.]*

Mr. Aubrey reputation an intrepid explorer, and careful and admirable observer, was not surpassed, either in Mexico or California. Some of his trips between Sante Fe and San Francisco were made in the shortest times on record. His ride from Santa Fe to Independence, 773 miles, in five days and sixteen hours, including stoppages of every sort for sleep, meals, swimming streams, & c. – was probably never surpassed in this country or any other; the actual traveling time being four days and a half, or one hundred and seventy two miles per day, twenty miles of which he traveled on foot.

As before stated, Lt. Whipple reached Albuquerque shortly after Mr. Aubrey's arrival. But it does not appear that he followed Mr. Aubrey's trail, at least not after leaving the Zuni village. Lt. Whipple's report has not reached this quarter yet; but, on comparing the outline of it, in the first volume of the Pacific Railroad Reports, with the sketch of Mr. Aubrey's route, in the St. Louis papers, it would appear that while the latter was, in the main, south of Whipple's route, this side of the Colorado, Aubrey's point of reading that was much higher than that of Lt. Whipple, who left the Colorado (going west) near that point indicated in the papers quoted from Mr. Carters letter, the mouth of what was then supposed to be the Mohave, though ascertained to be a different stream.

1855, San Jose, California– Beaty's Hotel
Courtesy of San José Public Library, California Room

No account of Lt. Whipple's survey was published until some time in 1848. In the meanwhile another statement attributed from Mr. Aubrey, who left San Jose in California on the 6th July, 1854, with a party of 50 men, fitted out at an expense of $13,000 for the express purpose of locating a wagon road from that place (about fifty miles southeast from San Francisco) to Albuquerque, *"on the 35th parallel or as near it as practicable."* He reached the Tejon Pass in ten days from San Jose. Eight days more of travel brought him to the spot where he had crossed the Colorado the year before, which must be at least a hundred miles higher up the river than the mouth of Bill William's fork, where Whipple's route strikes the Colorado, going West.

After crossing the river, he seems to have varied materially from his course of the proceeding year. Instead of making a wide sweep to the south, he kept a mainly east course. One hundred and forty miles form the crossing, he struck Lt. Whipple's trail, which had been south of his own, followed it eight miles, and then left it to the north, still keeping an easterly course. His own trail of the year before, he did not strike, after leaving it east of the Colorado, until within thirty-five miles of Zuni. On reaching the Colorado, Chiquito, near the Moquis villages, he says in his journal, *"we have, so far, succeeded admirably in accomplishing the main object of the expedition – finding a wagon road to this place. It is clear sailing from this camp to Zuni."*

Here, then, is the testimony of a practical and thoroughly competent witness to prove the existence of *two routes*, both suitable for wagons, extending west from the Rio Grande to the Tejon Pass – both near the 35th parallel, and each one different from the line adopted by Lt. Whipple, which, judging from the accounts of it heretofore given to the public, is certainly equal to any other known route across the continent.

From the foregoing statement, it will be seen that as late as 1819, three years after Cooke's road was opened, it was not generally known that any middle route to the Pacific, between the Spanish trace to Los Angeles on the north, and Cooke's road to San Diego on the south, existed at all; and that what is now known of the middle route is chiefly derived from explorations subsequent to 1852.

This remark, however, is not applicable to that part of

the route extending east from the Rio Grande.

The road from Fort Smith to Sante Fe, by way of the Canadian River, has long been known. To say nothing of previous military explorations, it was traveled in 1833 by Mr. Josiah Gregg, author of the Commerce of the Prairies, and again in 1840 by the same gentleman, who, in each instance, had a large party with him. He has given a full account of each trip in the second volume of the work referred to.

In 1846, a party, under Capt. Leavitt followed Mr. Gregg's route as far as Sante Fe, on their way to California. The statement of Mr. Hudson, who was one of the party, appeared in the *Fort Smith Herald*, Nov. 1, 1848.

Throughout the year 1849, large numbers of emigrants passed over this route. One party was escorted by Capt. Marcy, whose report has been published, as also that of Lt. Simpson, who accompanied the escort as topographical engineer.

Finally, in 1853, it was surveyed by Lieut. Whipple. The substance of his report is given in the 1st vol. P R. R. R., *[Pacific Rail Road Reports]* pages 20, 22, and 71-78.

(TO BE CONTINUED.)

June 5, 1858

Butterfield Exploring Use of Steam Carriages?

June 5, 1858, Saturday, page 2

Arkansas Intelligencer, Van Buren, Arkansas

California Overland Mail – The Washington correspondent of the *Eagle & Enquirer*, writing from Washington City under date of May 10, says in relation to the arrangement making by **Messers. Butterfield, Fargo & Co.**, for putting the line into operation, that:

> *"The virtual defeat of the Pacific Railroad bill for the present, has caused the contractors on the* ***Overland Mail*** *route to initiate very extensive arrangements for the prosecution of their contracts. A well known engineer and machinist is now here making examinations at the Patent Office, and corresponding with the principal machinists*

through out the country, so as to enable him to adopt the best plan for a steam carriage. It is said that the contractors intend to offer a prize of $1,000 for the best paper on this subject."

Steam Powered Stagecoach
Is the above article correct? Was Butterfield actually considering the use of steam powered stagecoaches? Or was the Virots Iron Works, or others, pulling a publicity stunt to promote their Steam Carriage by implying that it merited John Butterfield's attention and consideration.

June 9, 1858
Work Party to Select and Locate Stations

June 9, 1858
Fort Smith Times, Fort Smith, Arkansas

OVERLAND MAIL COMPANY – On Sunday last, some 14 men, in the employ of the **Overland Mail Co.**, arrived here on the steamer Fitzhugh, and only await the arrival of Mr. Crocker, or **Mr. Butterfield,** to start out to select and locate stations along the route, from here to El Paso.

There is now, we trust, no doubt in the minds of many, as to the prospects of this Company carrying its contract into extraction, and that too, without loss of time. Every move leads me to convince us that the mail will start on this route true to contract time.

Mr. Crocker is looked for daily, and it may be, he will be accompanied by **Mr. Butterfield.**

June 9, 1858
Part II of John Luce's 6 Part Article
In Support of Albuquerque Route Over the El Paso

June 9, 1858
Fort Smith Times, Fort Smith, Arkansas

OVERLAND ROUTE TO CALIFORNIA

BY J. B. LUCE, OF SEBASTIAN COUNTY

[CONTINUED]

Having in view the manner in which these two routes were first brought to public notice, it is proposed next to examine the evidence in regard to their relative merits.

A glance at the prominent points of each would lead any one to think the one by way of Albuquerque was the shortest.

[NOTE: The poor printing of the original page makes it difficult to distinguish between a "4" and a "1" or a "7" etc. Therefore, the numbers in this transcription are questionable.]

Fort Smith, its eastern terminus, is in latitude 35 degree, 23 minutes, longitude 91 degree, 26 minutes.

Fulton, the terminus of the other, is in latitude 32 degree, 32 minutes, longitude 93 degree, 40 minutes.

San Francisco is in latitude 37 degrees 17 minutes, longitude 122 degrees 25 minutes.

Fulton is south 124 miles and east 59 miles from Fort Smith.

San Francisco is north 167 miles and west 1,568 miles from Fort Smith.

[NOTE: The poor printing of the original page makes it difficult to distinguish between 33 and 38 etc. Therefore, the dates in this

transcription may not be accurate.]

Fort Smith, as already stated, is in latitude 35 degree, 23 minutes. The Canadian, which skirts the road for ten degrees, runs a nearly straight course between 35 and 33 degrees. Albuquerque is in latitude 35 degree 7 minutes. The pass through the Sierra Nevada is in the same latitude 35 degrees 7 minutes. No point on the whole line is as far south as 31 degrees, or as far north as 36 degrees, until it enters the San Joaquin Valley, on the way to San Francisco.

The Fulton Road, on the other hand, first goes to Preston *[Texas]*, 140 miles west and 14 north, it then runs down to El Paso, in latitude 31 degrees 42 minutes, 137 miles south of Fulton, and 120 south of San Francisco. After winding along the 32d parallel four degrees, it runs up to the Pima villages, on the Gila, north of 33 degrees, then again goes south, to the mouth of the Gila, 32 degrees 43 minutes, when it turns to the north west, and according to the plan first submitted to the public, after crossing the Coast Range, and touching at Los Angeles, it turns due east, crosses the Coast Range the second time, and joins the Albuquerque route, near the Sierra Nevada, on its way to San Francisco.

It will thus be seen that the traveler, leaving Fulton for San Francisco, not only selects a starting point 39 miles further east and 121 miles further south from his destination than Fort Smith, but, in going to El Paso, is thrown 120 miles still further south from the point he wishes to reach, and, after all, has to turn north and strike the other route before it leaves the 35th parallel. In doing all this, he not only describes an immense curve, but has to encounter the differences in the breath of degrees of longitude between the 32d and 35th parallels of latitude, equal to two miles for each degree for about twenty degrees, or 40 miles – making an absolute difference on a straight line of 79 miles east and west, and 252 miles north and south, in favor of the Albuquerque route.

This view of the case would be taken, as a matter of course, by any one whose knowledge of the two routes was restricted to the latitude and longitude of the terminal and the principle intermediate points.

Add to that knowledge the fact that the country between Fort Smith and Albuquerque admits of a road almost mathematically straight; that Albuquerque is just halfway between Fort Smith and the pass in the Sierra Nevada, where the two routes, according to the original survey, unite on their way to San Francisco; that the road is known to be straight for two degrees west from Albuquerque; that Mr. Aubrey represents it as very direct all the way, and the conclusion will seem to be irresistible that the 35th parallel route is much the shortest.

Yet the public was informed by the Secretary of War, in the first volume Pacific Rail Road Reports, that it was 185 miles further from Fort Smith to San Francisco than it was from Fulton.

It was also stated that the distance from Ft. Smith to San Pedro, the southern terminus on the Pacific for both routes, was greater by 274 miles than it was from Fulton.

This San Pedro is the port of entry for Los Angeles, from which it lies about 25 miles from southwest. It is only approached by either road, as laid down on the map, through Los Angeles, being regarded in the ___ as a point to be reached by a ___'s road. In comparing distances, Los Angeles, therefore, may be considered the best terminus.

Los Angeles is in latitude 34 degrees 7 minutes, longitude 115 degrees 7 minutes; on an air line 1,350 miles west from Fort Smith and about 81 miles south.

As already stated, this road west takes, or ought to take, a direct course for Albuquerque; which is a little more than halfway, being in longitude 106 degrees __ ______ 12 $^1/_2$ degrees equal to 703 miles west from Fort Smith, and 18 south. From Albuquerque to Los Angeles it is west 645 and south 69 miles.

From the Rio Grande to the Pacific the road nowhere turns runs half a degree north of 35 degrees, and nowhere further south than Los Angeles, which it is 34 $^1/_2$ degrees 7 minutes.

[NOTE: The remainder of this paragraph at the bottom of the newspaper's page is heavily over-inked and is illegible.]

On the other hand, Fulton is on an air line 1,400 miles east from Los Angeles, and 37 miles south________________

The lower route, by going to El Paso, makes a bend of 150 miles south from ____ line

The upper route has no such bend.

Yet it is said that the lower route is the best by 274 miles.

It would be curious to trace all the different steps leading to such a striking contradiction of the old geometrical axiom, that a straight line is the shortest distance from one point to another. But, in the absence of Capt. Whipple's report, which thus has has not been made generally assessable, the full details of the Albuquerque route cannot be generally known. Although, however, has been published to show how ___, at least, of this difference is made up, and at all events, to show how ___ is overcome, not to say annihilated, on the El Paso route.

From the official statements, it appears that it was divided into three sections of which one,

from Fulton to El Paso is rated at............................787 miles

The next, from the Rio Grande to the

Colorado, at...578 miles

And the third, form the Colorado to

San Pedro, at ....313 miles

Making the aggregate of ....1,678 miles

given in the public abstracts.

To each of their sections an officer of the topographical corps was assigned,

The first was surveyed by Capt.Pope, from the Rio Grande, as far as Preston.

The second, by Lieut. Parks, from the Rio Grande to the Pima villages, on the Gila *[River]*.

The third, by Lieut. Williamson.

Vast ranges exist on each of the three sections, over which natural obstacles have heretofore prevented, and still prevent, travelers from pursuing a straight course. Over these sections theoretical railroad air lines have been run by the engineers. The measurement of these air lines are given to the public as the true distances, while the real distances over which the traveler would be compelled to __ are completely ignored in every abstract of the route that has thus far appeared.

For instance, in vol. 1, Pacific R. R. R., pp. 88-7, Captain Humphreys gives the distances from the mouth of the Gila to the summit of the San Gorgonio Pass, through the Coast Range, between the Colorado desert and the Pacific as 155 miles.

The tables in Lt. Williamson's report (pp. 11-2) show that the actual travel is 192 miles or 37 miles further.

From the summit of San Gorgonio Pass to San Fernando, according to Capt. Humphreys (pp. 87-8) it is 102 miles; according to Lieut. Williamson, 122. The aggregate differences between rail and wagon road lines, from the mouth of the Gila *[river]* to San Fernando, being 37 miles.

The cause of the first of these two variations is very evident. Lieut. Williamson's map shows that the shorter road is a mathematically straight line; his report shows that the line is drawn across an impracticable desert; the wagons being compelled *"to keep close"* to the *"foot hills," "as the only chance of procuring water."* – (Williamson's Report, p. 51)

Again: from the Pimo villages, on the Gila, to the Rio Grande, the distances, as stated by Capt. Humphreys, (pp. 83, 81) is 355 miles – The tables of Lieut. Parks (vol. 2, pp. 21, 24-25) show that he really traveled 444 miles – 80 further.

Again, from the Rio Grande to Preston, according to Secretary David, (p. 23) and Captain Humphreys (p. 7_) it is 640 miles.

The diary and the appendix F, attached to the report of the engineer, Capt. Pope show that he traveled 778 miles – 138 further.

It will thus be seen that in each one of the divisions of the lower route, very material differences exist between the railroad lines as furnished in the abstract, and the route actually traveled by the engineers, amounting in the aggregate to 284 miles.

The reason is why the engineer did not travel the line of survey over the Colorado desert has already been given. Between the Gila and the Rio Grande, Lt. Parke speaks of striking *"Cooke's trail,"* which, he says, is *"through this region the only route traveled by the ___ emigrants to California."* From the point at which he intersected it, his instructions required him to take a direct course to the Rio Grande. *"But,"* he adds, *"as this would involve the necessity of another ninety miles march without water,"* he *"determined to follow, for the present, the emigrant road into Mesilla."*

The most considerable of these variations is in the case of Capt. Pope, in passing from the mouth of the Delaware Creek, on the Pecos River, to the headwaters of the Colorado of Texas. The line of survey crosses the celebrated Llano Estacado, or Staked Plains.

Capt. Marcy, writing near the same spot on the Pecos, in September, 1842, says: *"Our Comanche guide informs me, this evening, that I cannot, as I desired, go directly from this point to the head of the Colorado or Brazos as no man, not even an Indian, ever undertakes to cross the Llano Estacado opposite here."* He was therefore obliged to go down the Pecos until he could with safety turn east. Capt. Pope did the same thing. He first sent a small party to explore the desired direct route across the plains to the head of the Colorado of Texas; then afterwards another small party to survey it; but he himself does not appear to have touched any part of the ____ line across the desert. He pushed completely around it, with the main body, traveling 234 miles from San Pecos to the Sulphur Springs of the Colorado, while the air line is but 123.

The sum of these variations is 281 miles, which added to 1,618, the distance in the abstract, would give 1,902 miles. To this should also be added 32 miles for the distance from Milneo, two miles above El Paso, the western terrains of Capt. Pope's survey, to Fort Fillmore, where Lt. Parke's line leaves the river – a link in the chain, omitted in the estimates and omitted in the 1st and 2d volumes of the *"Reports,"* and 20 miles additional distance from Fulton to Preston, which the report miles as 133, the true distance being 153 miles. This would increase the aggregate to 1,951 miles to San Pedro. The additional distance to San Francisco, Capt. Humphrey estimates at 421 miles, which would make the length of the line 2,372, against 2,174 which the abstract at the end of the report gives as the distance from Fort Smith to San Francisco by the Albuquerque route making the difference in favor of the latter 200 miles to San Francisco, and __ to San Pedro ___

[NOTE: The remainder of this paragraph at the bottom of the newspaper's page is heavily over-inked and is illegible.]

It must not be inferred from this forgoing statement, that the shortest and ___ from Fulton to San Francisco is 2,___ miles. What ___ ________ ______

There are parts of the wagon road of this engineers which are off from their traveled route. Capt. Pope, for instance __________________ six miles north ________ the point at which ____ survey strikes the plains.

[NOTE: Two paragraphs are illegible here.]

From _____________ 183

From Preston to Dona Ana on
the Rio Grande, by Capt. Marcy's
road, the shortest that can traveled,
it is by Marcy's measurement ....719 miles

From the Rio Grande to the Gila, Col.
Cooke's road, according to Lt. Parke,
is the only one traveled – according to
Col. Cooke himself, it is ....418 miles

From the point where Col. Cooke struck
the Gila to the mouth of that river,
according to Major Emory, it is ....193 miles

From the mouth of the Gila to San
Fernando, Lt. Williamson reports the
wagon road distance at ....314 miles

Distance from Fulton to San Fernando .... 1,827 miles
The distance to San Pedro, according to Capt. Humphreys, is the same as to San Fernando, the latter being on the direct line to San Francisco, which is reported as being beyond San Fernando 421
Making the distance from Fulton to San Francisco...2,248 miles

---

These two distances, then 1,827 to San Pedro and 2,248 miles to San Francisco, being practicable wagon routes, it would, of course, be unjust to give the other figures, 1,956 & 2,577, as representing the shortest wagon roads on the El Paso route, merely because the engineer trains had traveled that far. *Yet this is precisely what has been done with respect to the Albuquerque route.*

The distances from Fort Smith to San Pedro, and to San Francisco, were published in the abstract, on page 107, vol. 1, P. R. R., as being respectively 1,892 and 2,174 miles.

In the report of Capt Humphreys, printed with the annual report of the Secretary of War of December 3, 1855, it is stated these *"distances were measured upon trail – those now given are along the plotted ___ line."*

That is to say, the tabular statements which show 1,618 miles as the length of the El Paso line to the Pacific proceeds to place that distance in contrast with 1,892 miles as the length of the Albuquerque route, without mentioning the fact that the latter means the surveyor's wagon road, while the former refers to air lines, of which one at least, was so utterly impracticable that the principal engineer himself did not venture over it!

The engineer wagon trail of 1,892 miles, from Fort Smith to San Pedro, cannot be compared with any previous statement in print of wagon road distances, for the simple reason that the Albuquerque route is a new one, and has not the needed experience of ten years of exploration to fall back upon, but enough does exist in print to show that the distances because they clearly fall short of 1,892 miles.

The report, page 20, states that the crossing of the Rio Grande at Isleta is 854 miles from Fort Smith.

Isleta is 13 miles below Albuquerque, and was selected as a suitable place for a railroad bridge. The stage road would cross at Albuquerque, which according to Capt. Marcy, (Expedition Red River, p. _21) is 800 miles from Fort Smith.

From Albuquerque to Zuni, Lt. Simpson's measurement is 137 miles.

Mountains Near the entrance of the Canada de las Uvas
1855 image by Thomas S. Sinclair

Mr. Aubrey stated the distance from Zuni to the Canada de las Uvas, to be 682 miles.

These amounts, together, make 1,626 miles, the distance from Fort Smith to the Canada de las Uvas. This pass is described by Mr. Aubrey as the loveliest and best in the Sierra Nevada. According to Lt. Williamson, who explored it, it is the best place on the Sierra, in fact, he says, *"The line of ___ may be said to be around the end of the Sierra Nevada."* He also states that there is a good wagon road through the pass. It is fifteen miles west near the Tejon and about thirty from the Tehachapi Pass, so which the distance from Ft. Smith is said in the reports (page 22) to be 1,848 miles, 222 miles further than the distance to the Canada de las Uvas, according to Aubrey, Simpson, and Marcy.

Lt. Williamson's report, says (on page 24) that ___ from the Mohave river, the two routes through the two passes, the Canada and the Tehachapi, *"would be almost exactly the same length."* His map would seem to indicate that by one line, at least, it is much nearer to San Francisco, from the Canada, than from any of the neighboring passes.

His map, showing that coming from the Mohave a road would strike the Francisquito Pass on the Costal Range, at a point thirty miles east of the Canada. Calling it in round numbers, 1,600 miles from Fort Smith to the San Francisquito Pass, from thence to Los Angeles his table of distances gives 50 miles of wagon road; 25 miles more to San Pedro makes a total of 1,675 miles.

Thus the actual wagon road distance, if the measurements of Marcy, Simpson, Aubrey and Williamson are right, from Fort Smith to San Pedro is 1,675 miles instead of 1,892, as in the report, and to San Francisco 1,976 miles, in place of 2,171.

The figures representing the engineer's wagon trail may be correct, but unfortunately the *"report"* so far, at least, as the two lower routes are concerned, is not strictly accurate in its ___ _____ _______ ______.

[NOTE: several sentences are illegible here.}

Neither time, nor space will admit of pointing out in this report the various errors in the distances on the El Paso route; but any one who tries to find out from the reports of Secretary Davis and Capt. Humphrey ____ in 1st vol. and of Capt. Pope's in the 2d, the actual distance between Fulton and San Pedro, cannot fail to be to be struck with the numerous discrepancies, and especially with the omission, before alluded to, of the distance from Medino to Fort Fillmore (thirty-two or thirty-five miles) which does not appear

in ___
NOTE: several sentences are illegible here.}

On the Albuquerque route the error in giving wagon trail distances in place of railroad ___ has already been explained. The discrepancies, however, do not stop here. In the report – it is a rather remarkable fact that all the passes through the Sierra Nevada, which are available at all ___ are clustered together near the 35th parallel, and ____
[*NOTE: The remainder of this paragraph at the bottom of the newspaper's page is heavily over-inked and is illegible.*]
____ _______ _______ _______eight or ten miles to the north. The third is within five or six miles of Walker's Pass.

In the *National Intelligencer* of July 23, 1857, a communication appeared in vindication of the El Paso route, containing a table prepared by Capt. Humphreys, in which the distance from Fort Smith to San Pedro was stated to be 1,520 miles, and to San Francisco 2,000. The same article quotes from Capt. Whipple's own report (page 76, vol. 3, Pacific Railroad Reports), the distance as being 1,952 miles to San Francisco. The *Union* of June 16 quotes the same figures, and also 1,672 miles from Fort Smith to San Pedro.

Putting these figures in a tabular form, the distance from Fort Smith to San Pedro, according to –

Capt. Humphreys, in 1st vol. Pacific
Railroad Report, p. 107, is.............................1,882 miles
Capt. Humphreys, in his report of
November 29, 1853, is.................................1,760 miles
Capt. Humphreys, in his letter to
Union, June 18, 1857, is..............................1,820 miles
Capt. Whipple, as quoted by *Union*,
June 1_, 1857, is...1,672 miles

And from Fort Smith to San Francisco according to: Capt. Humphreys, in 1st vol. Pacific
Railroad Report, p. 107..................................2,174 miles
Capt. Humphreys, in his report of
November 29, 1853, is...................................2,025 miles

Capt. Humphreys, in his letter to
Union, June 18, 1857, is....................................2,000 miles
Capt. Whipple, as quoted by the
Union, June 18, 1837 is......................................1,952 miles

---

In each of the above tables the singular spectacle is presented of four official statements of one and the same thing; all professing to estimate from the same source (Captain Whipple) and to give an account of one and the same thing – the length of the Whipple survey – yet no two of them are alike!

One of these variations has already been explained – the substitution of wagon trail for railroad distance. The letter of Capt. Humphreys to the *Union*, from which extracts containing another variation were copied in the *Intelligencer*, may partially have given an explanation not included in the extracts. But, there still remains Capt. Humphreys third statement of November, 1853, to be reconciled with the others and with Capt. Whipple's report.

On the El Paso route the distances also change, as will presently be shown, but without affecting the general result. The only aggregate to which Capt. Humphreys seems to adhere without deviation is that of the railroad line from Fulton to San Pedro, though hardly any two sets of figures can be found in the published volumes which will produce it.

If the preceding statements are correct, the distance to San Pedro from Fulton:

By engineer trail is..1,936 miles
By wagon road..1,763 miles
By railroad line..1,613 miles

From Fort Smith:

By engineer trail is..1,872 miles
By wagon road..1,673 miles
By railroad line..1,672 miles

Being the difference:

By engineer trail is..64 miles

By wagon road .... __0 miles
By railroad line .... 59 miles

And the distance to San Francisco from Fulton
By engineer trail is .... 2,377 miles
By wagon road .... 2,200 miles
By railroad line .... 2,039 miles

And the distance to San Francisco from Fort Smith
By engineer trail is .... 2,174 miles
By wagon road .... 1,976 miles
By railroad line .... 1,952 miles
Being the difference:
By engineer trail is .... 203 miles
By wagon road .... 224 miles
By railroad line .... 87 miles

The Albuquerque route being the shortest in every case but one – the length of railroad location from Fort Smith to San Pedro.

From Fulton to Memphis it is .... 200 miles
From Ft. Smith to Memphis it is .... 307 miles
Consequently, from Memphis to San Francisco
By way of Fulton and El Paso, it is .... 2,120 miles
By way of Fort Smith and Albuquerque .... <u>2,276 miles</u>
Difference in favor of Albuquerque .... 214 miles

---

From Fulton to St. Louis it is .... 150 miles
From Fort Smith to St Louis .... 450 miles
Consequently, from St. Louis to San Francisco
By way of Little Rock, Fulton & El Paso .... 2,630 miles
By way of Ft. Smith and Albuquerque .... <u>2,376 miles</u>
Difference in favor of Albuquerque .... 256 miles

---

Or more properly, under the recent modification of the contract from St. Louis by way of Fort Smith to Preston and El Paso, it is from

St. Louis to Fort Smith .... ___ miles
Fort Smith to Preston .... 176 miles
Preston to Dura Ana.. 718 miles
Dura Ana to Fort Yuma.. 6__ miles
Fort Yuma to San Francisco .... _35 miles

[*NOTE: This concluding paragraph at the bottom of the newspaper's page has heavy water damage and is illegible.*]

June 11, 1858
The Upcoming Railroad Should Follow a Northern Route, not the Butterfield Southern Route

June 11, 1858, page 2
Arkansas Intelligencer, Van Buren, Arkansas

Washington, May 24, 1858 – To N. Paschall, Esq.: Sir – It is evident that the Central route to the Pacific Railroad, along the thirty fifth parallel of latitude, has taken a deep hold upon the public mind.

The people have come to believe that a railroad should start from a central city on the Mississippi river, St. Louis, and go thence along the valley of the beautiful Canada River, to Albuquerque, and thence to Zuni and the Tejon passes to San Francisco. This is becoming the common opinion...

But the delusion as to the value of that route is passing away. Ordering the **Overland Mail** to be conveyed over the Texas route, will undoubtedly render those heavy land purchases more tolerable, but the running of stages over it cannot redeem the route, the act will only aid in circulating knowledge of the real character of the Texas route, and will thus destroy it. A few mail contractors and their agents may possibly be made converts to the excellence of desolation, and the value of uninhabitable regions; but the mass of mankind will be found less impressible...

June 11, 1858
Active Work to Establish Stations

June 11, 1858, Friday, page 2
Arkansas Intelligencer, Van Buren, Arkansas

THE OVERLAND MAIL TO CALIFORNIA – Messrs. Frank de Ruythur, and Brainard, with some ten or twelve men in the employ of the **Overland Mail Company**, arrived on the steamer Fitzhugh, last Sunday, *en route* to Fort Fillmore, in New Mexico, for which destination they will depart in a few days.

We are indebted to Mr. de Ruythur, for the information, that the company through their agents are making active preparations for putting the line in operation at an early day; probably before their contract time in September. **Messrs. Butterfield** and Crocker are now on the line making the necessary arrangements between St. Louis and this place and will probably be here sometime next week.

June 11, 1858
Troops Headed Westward to Protect Route

June 11, 1858, page 2
Arkansas Intelligencer, Van Buren, Arkansas

THROUGH ON THE 35TH PARALLEL FROM MEMPHIS VIA VAN BUREN TO CALIFORNIA – The *True Democrat* of last week contains the following intelligence regarding a command of dragoons who are to march form Memphis through on the 35th parallel to California. The command we understand will leave Memphis about the 20th inst:

> *"We understand that Judge Sabastian has procured an order from the Secretary of War requiring Lieut. Beall, of the army, to proceed with a command of 300 dragoons from Memphis, tenn., via Little Rock, Clarksville and Van Buren to Fort Smith – and there to recruit and take the* ***Overland Route*** *along the 35th parallel to California, so that emigrants and others desiring to go to the Pacific by that route may avail themselves of the protection thus afforded. The time of starting we did not learn."*

June 16, 1858
Part III of John Luce's 6 Part Article
In Support of Albuquerque Route Over the El Paso

June 16, 1858, page 1
Fort Smith Times, Fort Smith, Arkansas

OVERLAND ROUTE TO CALIFORNIA

BY J. B. LUCE, OF SEBASTIAN COUNTY

[CONTINUED]

Other matters remain to be considered of much more importance, both to the contractors and to the public, than the saving of two or even three hundred miles.

Is the El Paso route of such a nature as to admit of semi-weekly trips in the required time!

From San Francisco, southeast, it is not likely that the difficulties would be greater than in any other quarter where the settlements are equally sparse until after crossing the Coast Range, when a desert is encountered, extending, on one road, from Carrizo Creek (near Warner's Pass) eighty miles, on another, from the foot of San Gorgonio Pass *"one hundred and sixty-four miles, by the trail"* to the Colorado. This latter is the road recommended by Capt. Humphreys, and is the one before referred to as being one hundred and ninety-two miles from Fort Yuma to the summit of the pass

Mr. Blake, geologist to the expedition which surveyed both of these lines, gives a lot of watering places on the wagon trail, which shows that there is no interval of over twenty-five miles without water. But, at page 35 of his report, he speaks of having traveled thirty-five miles (on the trail) without water, the animals showing signs of great thirst and distress, when they reached a creek in which *"the water was strongly impregnated with common salt," "a thick incrustation on the borders," "not very disagreeable to the taste, but coffee made with it was exceedingly nauseating."*

This was one of the regular watering places on the list. Another, Cook's well, is described, on page 67, as *"a hole in the clay," "only prevented from becoming a mere mud puddle by a few boards that surround the water,"* which *"is always muddy, and but a small supply in the pool. The Mesquite well (another watering place) is in a similar condition, but may be considered in better order, a barrel having been placed in it."* At the Alamo

Mocho, another watering place, *"the well is about eighteen feet deep, and contains several barrels of water."*

Exterior of the Alamo Mocho stagecoach station
Courtesy of San Diego History Center

"The country around was peculiarly dreary and desert-like. Quantities of skeletons of cattle and mules, with loose bones and skulls were lying about in confusion. Near the well were several carcasses but partly decomposed, and others completely dried up, so that the skeleton was firmly held together by the hard and firmly stretched hide. The clay surface upon which these remains were distributed was perfectly barren and overlaid by a thin coat of dry sand, which the wind drifted into little mounds and moved about with a low rustling sound."

On page 55 he says: *"The wells that have been described are on a side road, to the northward of New River, and are not relied on by emigrants, or travelers with large droves of cattle,"* their main dependence for water being upon New River and its sloughs, the Great and Little Lagoon, which on page 58, he says, *"cannot be relied upon to furnish an unfailing supply of water. It becomes filled during the season of floods, and only when the river is at its greatest height. I understand that it has not been filled during the past winter; consequently, the lagoons will soon become entirely dry, and parties of emigrants, with their teams and droves of cattle, will experience much suffering,"* & c.

The surface of the desert seems, from Mr. Blake's account, to consist of either blue clay, gravel, sand, or naked rock; little or no vegetation anywhere. After crossing the ridge, he says, *"the timber gradually disappears, the mountain sides at the foot of the slope being a mass of rugged rocks, destitute of the slightest covering of soil.* (p. 26) *The slope itself is covered with gravel, pebbles, and sand."* At another point, about half way, describing a *"fine view of the desert,"* he says, *"not a green spot in all this wide expanse was to be seen, the bald mountains near me were not only free from trees, but there was not even earth to cover the rocks."*

At another point, the rocky character of the side hill slopes *"made it necessary to descend to the hard surface of the clay."* Here their progress was impeded by a series of ravines or fissures, extending for miles across their course – twenty to thirty foot drop, with vertical sides – sometimes impassable except at their upper and lower ends.

At another point, sand hills and drifts occur, some of them fifty feet high, having their origin in a constant and powerful current of air sweeping through the pass from the Pacific, driving sand with such violence as to cut *"long parallel groves, deep enough to receive a lead pencil in the surface of the hard and homogeneous granite."* Feldspar quartz and garnet were also *"rapidly chiseled out by the sharp grains."* (p. 27)
[NOTE: The poor printing of the original page makes it difficult to distinguish between a "4" and a "1" or a "7" etc. Therefore, the numbers in this transcription are questionable.]

This powerful current of air does not prevent *"the temperature from being torrid"* (p. 29) even in November. At noon on the 20th, the mercury was at 90 degrees. (p. 35) At 3 p.m., December 5, according to Lt. Williamson, it stood at 93 degrees. (Table 16, p. 59)

Mr. Blake rates the agricultural capabilities of the desert very high; that is, *"provided it is supplied with water by irrigation,"* which he thinks can be done by constructing canals from the Colorado.
[NOTE: A large water stain across the page obscured a number of words in the paragraph below.]

In support of this opinion he speaks of 1st, a barley field

at the foot of the ___ 2d__ *growth of weeds"* thirty miles this side of the pass at the Cobulia (?) Springs, where the Indians___ vegetables; 3d, grass on ___river _____, a luxurious growth of weeds, on its lagoons, one of which is forty-five and the other fifty-five miles beyond the Colorado. With exception of an occasional mesquite tree and a little *"course grass"* on Salt Creek, he does not appear to have seen any other vegetation at all throughout the entire march of 164 miles, from the foot of the pass to the Colorado bottom at Algodones.

In the interval which must elapse before *"canals from the Colorado"* are constructed for irrigation, it does not distinctly appear how stage horses ***[of Butterfield's Overland Mail Co.]*** are to be subsisted during their semi-weekly trip of eighty miles a day over this region, exposed to a scorching sun, where the mercury sometimes stands above 90 degrees in December, where *"it is very common to find it standing at 110 degrees"* even in May and September, where the winds *"keep the air filled with clouds of fine dust,"* and where this *"fine dust occasionally obstructs the road in drifts fifty feet high."*

Aerial view of mesas in Monument Valley, on the Colorado Plateau

At Algodones, the road touches the river; thence to Fort Yuma in twelve miles. Gila to a point seven miles above the

Pima villages. On this part of the route there has been no recent survey, the information obtained while marking the Mexican boundary being probably sufficient. But Lt. Parks, who surveyed the line between the Pima villages and the Rio Grande, and who traveled up the Gila to his starting point, says: *"We moved under favorable circumstances, there having been quite a fall of rain since the last party passed, which not only laid the dust but hardened the surface of the roadway. While on the Gila* [River] *the great scarcity of grass and other forage was a constant source of anxiety, and caused much night traveling. The few patches of grass near the watering places were cropped close by the herds of stock driven to the California market, and the mesquite bean, upon which the emigrant almost solely depends for the existence of his animals, was now out of season; but by his great care and attention on the part of Lt. Stoneman, taking advantage of every bunch of cane growing at the waters edge, and the sparse tufts of a dry bunch of grass growing on the mesa at a distance from the roadside," "we succeeded in reaching the first of the Pimas and Maricopas villages, with all our animals, on the 13th of February, having just crossed a journado (literally, day's journey; applied by the Mexicans to a journey without water) of thirty-eight miles, and camped by a rain water pool, surrounded by a large area of dry brush and salt grass."* (Lt. Pare's Report, p. 6, vol. 2, P.R.R.R.)

The inference is obvious. If the [***Butterfield Overland***] Mail contractors, in any of their semi-weekly trips on the Gila should chance not to move under favorable circumstances, they might not *"succeed in reaching the first of the villages"* with all of their animals.

Major Emory, who accompanied General Kearney in 1846, gives substantially the same account of the road down the Gila. His description will be found at the close of the 2d vol. P.R.R.R. *"In leaving the mountains,"* he says, on page 8, *"we were informed that we bade adieu to grass, and our mules must henceforth subsist on willow, cottonwood, and the long green ephedra."*

Green Ephedra Viridis in Red Rock Canyon, Nevada.
Is is also known by the common names green Mormon tea, green ephedra, and Indian tea, is a species of Ephedra. It is indigenous to the Western United States

Just below the mouth of the San Pedro, near the line of the improved route lately surveyed, which Capt. Humphreys says (in his report of November 29, 1855) *"passes along the cultivable valleys instead of bare journadas." [jornadas: a days journey without water]* the *"hills were bare of vegetation,"* and the Gila flows through a wide plain *"four-fifth"* of which *"was destitute of vegetation,"* the reason, according to Professor Frazer, being a *"deficiency in organic matters."* (p. 7)

An exception to the general sterility of this region is found in the strip occupied by the Pimo and Maricopa Indians, which Mr. Bartlett says is *"twenty miles in length by four in breadth."*

Creosote Plant
The creosote plant is a prominent species in the Mojave, Sonoran, and Chihuahuan Deserts of western North America

After leaving these settlements, Major Emory speaks of long distances over plains *"of granite sand," "no growth except the Larrea Mexicana" (creosote plant)* on one occasion camping *"in a dust hole,"* where *"there was not a sprig of grass or a drop of water; and during the whole night our poor mules kept up a pitiful cry for both. There was nothing but the offensive larreas, which even mules will not touch when so hungry as to eat with avidity* [Avidity: extreme eagerness or enthusiasm] *the dry twigs of all other shrubs and trees."* (p. 12)

The next day, *"it appears that we shall meet with no more grass from this spot to the settlements, estimated to be three hundred miles distant."* (p. 13)

At other points, the plains are described as *"dreary beyond description."* Near the junction of the Gila and Colorado *"the hills and mountains appeared entirely destitute of vegetation, and on the plains could be seen, only at long intervals, a few stunted tuffs of larrea Mexicana and wild wormwood, a terminlia cana."* (p. 15)

Coming towards the Rio Grande, from the Gila to Tucson, about eighty miles, (ninety by the 'stage' road) Lt. Parks describes another desert, camping twice without water or grass, and little or no vegetation besides the grass wood, the mesquite tree, and the wild sage, which now and then occur, finding at only one point *"abundance of grass and wood."* The little water he found was from the rain in holes.

Col. Cooke's emigrant road passed through Tucson, to the Gila. After leaving Tucson, coming this way, Lt. Parks left the emigrant trace, and explored another route, which although at first adopted, and recommended to the public as part of the shortest and best route to the Pacific, has since been abandoned for a subsequent exploration – no doubt judiciously – for Lt. Parks, not withstanding occasional falls of rain, had to camp frequently without water; in one instance going three days from one watering place to another, passing over on the way a considerable area without a particle of vegetation, *"it being the perfection of sterility,"* (p. 2). The last hundred miles *"for consideration of water,"* he was on *"Cooke's trail"* the road usually traveled. From Cooke's Spring he came to the Rio Grande, fifty miles, without water, still on the emigrant trace, the line of survey having been previously abandoned because it involved *"another 90 miles without water."*

[NOTE: A sevier water mark made several phrases in the next three lines of type illegible.]

The distance he actually traveled was 410 miles. The location distance for a railroad was 355, on which he found but one permanent watering places, _____ __ _____ limited supply

The report of the last survey has not been published. An abstract of it by Captain Humphreys appears in part II President Message, 1856-'57, pp. 206-7-8.

The improvements on the former route consists in avoiding the Tucson stretch by running up the Gila to the San Pedro, and following the latter stream and one of its branches. Twenty-three miles of distance is saved. but the scarcity of water still continues on some parts of the route. Capt. Humphreys says *"the longest distance between the points which can be supplied with certainty from permanent water, is fifty-one miles."* Other stations are found ranging from ten to thirty-five miles apart. But several of these stations have to be supplied by conduits, in one instance twelve miles, in another twenty-one miles long. (pp. 206 ad 208)

Until these conduits are made it is quite evident that the ***[Butterfield Overland]* Mail** contractors, unable to go far off the road to water their horses, will continue to travel the old emigrant road.

"Whether water can be found," says Lt. Parke, *"so these plains...* [bottom edge of paper is missing]
... owing to the geological structure of the country. This experiment I consider worthy of attention, not only on account of its great and all-important bearing upon the question of locating a line for a railroad over this country, where there are intervals of fifty and seventy miles between permanent waters, but also if successful, on account of the relief rendered to various parties crossing during the dry season, whose sole and great anxiety now is, when entering upon these jornadas, [jornadas: a days journey without water] to get their animals through to the next water." (Parks Rep. 2d vol., P.R.R.R, p. 19)

In regard to this route, Mr. Aubrey says in his journal, published in the St. Louis *Intelligencer* in November, 1853: *"The Gila route proper, passing in part through Sonora, (this was before the Gadsden Purchase) is objectionable on several accounts besides its situation. In the first place, there is no timber upon the plains, nor upon the volcanic mountains that are along the way. A considerable part of the route, too, lies over a country destitute of vegetation, which, when dry, is a white powder, resembling flour, in which the feet of men and animals sink several inches. This same clay, when wet, is the most treacherous of quagmires. Some parts of the road are also very sandy. Don Ambrosio Armijo, who took sheep to California last year, lost as many as several hundred among the sand-hills west of the Colorado, by sinking in the sand and being run over by those behind."*

It will be remembered that Mr. Aubrey has himself taken sheep and wagons by the Gila route the preceding year, and was about to return that way.

Lieut. Parke's line terminates on the Rio Grande. The remainder of the route was surveyed by Captain Pope. His line commences at Molino, two miles above El Paso. In his estimate he divides it into three sections. One from the Rio Grande to the Pecos, 160 miles; one across the Staked Plains, 125 miles; and the third, from the Staked Plains to Preston, where his survey terminated, 352 miles.

At the outset of his report, Captain Pope says, *"I have carefully avoided embarrassing the subject with a narrative of the daily incidents of the expedition."* He adds that the *"diary, (kept by Mr. John H. Byrns, composer) although it contains much that is irrelevant and uninteresting, will, nevertheless, serve a useful purpose in filling up details."* No one can entertain a doubt of the truth of this last statement, after reading the *"report"* and the *"diary."* The latter serves the *"useful purpose"* of giving a much clearer idea of what the road really is, than can possible be gleaned from the report.

The *"wagon train – eight wagons, with six mules each"* started from Dona Ana, sixty miles above El Paso; and taking Captain Mercy's road, the same that the [***Butterfield Overland***] Mail stage will travel, intersected the line of survey at the Hueco, or Waco Tanks, sixty-four miles from Dona Ana, and thirty from El Paso.

Of this part of the road the *"report"* says nothing. The diary states that the *[wagon]* trains encountered deep and heavy ridges of sand, so deep in one part of the road that *"one hundred and twenty-five fanegas (a fanegas is a hundred pounds) of corn"* had to be taken out of the wagons and left on the prairie. Notwithstanding their loads were lightened, their teams were from before sunrise *"until nearly eleven o'clock, p. m."* travelling seventeen miles, about sixteen hours, including two hours rest at noon.

The Waco Tanks are natural cisterns or cavities in the rocks, on the sides of the Waco mountains. They are supplied with rain water from the mountains, and they constitute one of the principal watering places on the road between the Pecos and the Rio grande; it being thirty-eight miles to the next water, west, towards Dona Ana, and twenty-five to the next, on the road east.

The extent of the supply is best indicated by the diary. The *[wagon]* train having camped six miles west of the tanks, *"all the animals were immediately driven to water. As they had now been seventy-two hours without it, they quickly exhausted the tanks on the west side of the mountain; that upon the east, however, afforded an ample supply."* This was on the 16th February. On the 19th, the water in the other tank was *"rapidly diminishing,"* on the 20th, it was *"nearly exhausted;"* on the 21st, *"the water will not hold out longer than tomorrow."*

One of the tanks is estimated to contain 500 gallons, the other 1,500. The rainy season generally occurs once a year.

Cornados Mountains

Similar tanks are found on the *"Cornados"* mountains, thirty-three miles farther, constituting another regular watering place. They are, nine miles west from the Cottonwood Springs, and twenty-nine from the next water, towards the Pecos, the Ole del Cuervo, or Crow Springs, two sulphurous lakes, containing, in the language of at least one traveller, the late Judge C. B. Brown, whose journal was published, *"dirty, filthy water, not fit for man nor beast."*

[NOTE: A large water stain cuts across nine lines of the newspapers type and obliterates words underneath.]

Between the Waco tanks and the wagon train camped

three times without either wood or water, and twice with water but no wood. Sometimes as the road was ___ and sometimes for _____, but on whole this section of the road is infinitely preferable to the section west of the Rio Grande, and to the first section east of the Pecos.

It has already been stated that when Captain Mercy desired to cross the Staked Plains from the mouth of Delaware Creek, on the Pecos, to the source of the Colorado, his Comanche guide informed him that no man, not even an Indian, ever ventured across from that point.

Delaware River

The Delaware River is an intermittent stream that rises in the Guadalupe Mountains 2 miles north of Guadalupe Peak, and flows into the Pecos River in New Mexico.

[NOTE: A deep crease in the newspaper obscured several words in the following paragraph.]

Captain Pope, however, determined to send one of his assistants with a party to ascertain whether the journey was practicable. The party consisted of *"thirteen persons, having two light wagons, with eight mules each; rations for ten days, six bags of water and eight sacks of corn; the number of mules was __ six of the party being mounted."* They traveled five days before they found any water, then came to a *"small pond of water, each, but where ___mules had __."* The next day they reached ___ springs of the Colorado. For fifteen miles the road was good ___ that it was sandy until a short time ___ reaching water. The face of the country seems to have presented a *"perfect __ of tall reddish grass, interspersed with hills of sand."* Captain Pope says, *"although the sand packs readily into a hard surface, the passage over it is, for the first time with loaded wagons, and* [NOTE: The bottom of the page is missing.]

... they were compelled to leave their wagons. The distance travelled was estimated by one at 130, by another at 142 miles. The *"air line"* for a railroad is 125 miles. *[Air line: means 'as the bird flies,' and of course is not referring to air planes.]* In every statement that has yet appeared this hundred and twenty-five miles is included in the distance to be travelled by the ***[Butterfield Overland]*** **Mail Stages**, under the late contract.

Of course Captain Pope did not think of exposing his command to the dangers of such a passage. He moved down the Pecos ninety-six miles to *"the emigrant crossing,"* finding in the main a tolerable good road, indifferent grass, and no wood, relying for fuel upon the brush and roots of the dwarf mesquite.

Thirty miles from the crossing, he reached the first water, in the *"Sand Hills,"* which extend *"fifty miles from north to south, and fifteen east to west. They consist of white drift sand, thrown up into innumerable conical mounds, totally destitute of all vegetation. One would suppose that this region of sand is the last place where water could be found; yet, however incredible it appears, there is an abundance of water in three hills, contained in basins of the finest sand.*

Our camp was about a quarter of a mile from the water. The animals were driven up to water, sinking to their knees in sand."

Five miles further the next day, over a deep sandy road, very trying to the animals, brought them to the next watering place in the *"Hills,"* which, *"from the great quantity of fragments of abandoned wagons, has been evidently a general camping ground."* (p. 70)

After leaving this place, the party travelled for three days without water, a distance of 67 miles, to the Mustang Springs.

The character of the road across the sand hills is thus summed up in the diary: *"From the Pecos River to the level prairie east of the Sand Hills the road passes through about thirty miles of the heaviest sand. It is the worst road to be found in New Mexico, on the Rio Grande, or, indeed, anywhere else. It cannot be too strongly urged upon emigrant parties never to attempt travelling by this route except in the rainy season – from August to the middle of October – as the distance without water from the Sand Hills to the first permanent water to the eastward is sixty-seven miles, thirteen of which (immediately to the eastward of the hills) are through sand so deep and heavy as to be absolutely impassable for heavy-laden teams. With animals perfectly fresh and lightly-loaded wagons it requires all our exertions to overcome the difficulties of this dreadful road. It is also to be observed that our animals were in fine order, with eight and ten mules to each wagon."* (p. 71)

The Mustang Springs, the first permanent water to the eastward, are described forming *"several lakes, or large pools, which are, highly saline. The one at which we camped the most easterly, is less salty than the others, and is by far the best for us. It is slightly sulphurous, but not very unpalatable."*

After leaving the Mustang Springs, no more water was found before reaching the Big Springs of the Colorado – twenty-two miles – two days' travel. At the Big Springs Captain Pope left the Marcy Road, and changing his course, crossed over in a northwesterly direction to the Sulphur Springs of the Colorado, the point his exploring party had reached, and through which the location line runs.

At the Big Springs, if the present contract is ever carried into effect ***[by Butterfield's Overland Mail Co.]*** the stage road over the Staked Plains will terminate. From this point back to the Pecos, a distance, by Captain Pope's measurement, of 124 miles, the diary does not mention a single stick of timber. The sole dependence for fuel seems to have been upon the roots of the dwarf mesquite, and even this substitute is often described as difficult to collect. The grass was sometimes good, sometimes *"poor and scanty,"* (p. 70) sometimes *"poor, and full of weeds."* (p. 71)

This account of the road given by the diary does not correspond with that given by Captain Marcy, who found water between the Mustang Springs and the Sand Hills at intervals ranging from ten to twenty-five miles, and does not describe the sand as presenting any serious obstruction for more than eight or ten miles. But the difference is easily explained. Captain Marcy travelled over it during the rainy season. He crossed the Pecos on the 21st of September, 1849, and reached the Big Springs on the 3d October. His notes of the weather show that it rained on five different days between the 6th and the 20th September, and on four different days between the 21st and 27th September.

Three months later, in the same season, Lieut. Michler, of the topographical engineers, travelled over the same road, and encountered heavy rains on the __ of the Brazos, but found no water between the Mustang Springs and the Sand Hills – sixty-seven miles by his estimate. He speaks of the crossing the Sand Hills with his wagons as a difficult _____ does not distinctly state the distance leaving it doubtful whether it was two miles or fourteen.

[NOTE: Water stains and over-inking makes the next six lines illegible.]

On the other hand, Mr. A. R. Gray of Mexican boundary memory, ___ _____ __ disposed to exaggerate the difficulties encountered on any part of this route, says in his *"Survey of Southern Pacific Railroad on 32d Parallel"* p. 15: *"I well understand the terrible consequences to a party attempting the passage of these hills a hot summer day. It would be attended with almost certain disaster to a* [wagon] *train. A road over the plain __ the Mustang Springs west for one hundred fifteen miles, even without water, ___ be far better after it is beaten down __ found the springs a series if small __ of sulphurous and bitter taste ___ distance sixty-three miles to the___ and rates the breadth of the hills ___ where he crossed them in January ___ at ten miles.* [NOTE: a crease in the paper obscured the missing words in the above paragraph.]

Discrepancies in the statements of the distance traveled through heavy sand, like the different accounts of finding water, are doubtless owning to a difference in the season – the sand packing closer and presenting a firmer surface to the wagon wheels after heavy rains than it would during a dry time, such as the diary described on page 79: *"For nearly the first time since we left Dona Ana we are free from dust and sand. No one can truly appreciate this luxury but those who have scattered the clouds of sand by which the traveller in blinded, choked, and finally overwhelmed, on the blanks of the Rio Grande, and throughout nearly every portion of this county. We appear to be getting rid of this frightful nuisance."* This was April 7, 1834, at the Sulphur ___

[NOTE: The bottom of the page is missing.]

Captain Pope s survey terminates, bringing him, by his location line, 294 miles from the Rio Grande. the extracts that have been given are descriptive of what would be the stage route, under the late contract ***[of Butterfield's Overland Mail Co.]*** from Dona Ana to the Big Springs of the Colorado, 425 miles by Captain Pope's measurement: the difference of 131 miles between the two lines being the difference between the impracticable air line over the desert, and the practicable wagon road over the Sand Hills.

Between the Staked Plains and Preston, 252 miles by location line, 368 by wagon road, the party camped frequently without water, and frequently had to use water not fit to drink. But the facilities for obtaining it were so much greater, and the road generally was so much better adapted to the wants of travellers than it had been, that their difficulties may be said to have erased at the Sulphur Springs.

Whether the country thus described by Mr. Blake, Major Emory, Lieutenant Parks, and Mr. Byrne, between the Coast Range and the Colorado of Texas, more than nine hundred miles by the shortest air lines which it has entered into the heart of any engineer to conceive – more than eleven hundred by any road which any engineer has yet been able to travel, will admit of stage coaches ***[of Butterfield's Overland Mail Co.]*** during the next six years, making regular trips over eighty miles every twenty=four hours, remains to be seen. (TO BE CONTINUED)

June 19, 1858
John Butterfield Arrived in Fort Smith

June 19, 1858
Fort Smith Herald, Fort Smith, Arkansas

Messrs. **J. Butterfield**, H. Crocker, Wm Buckley, Wm. Fox and Jos. B. Nichols, and others of the **Overland Mail Company**, arrived here on Thursday evening last. **Col. John Butterfield** looks hale and hearty, after his long and tiresome trip "over the mountains."*[NOTE: This article was also printed in the June 26, 1858 issue of the Weekly Arkansas Gazette, page 2.]*

June 22, 1858
Did Butterfield Really Issue Scrip?

June 22, 1858, page 2
Arkansas True Democrat, Little Rock, Arkansas
NEWS ITEMS, – **Butterfield's Overland Mail Company** to California, have issued scrip, which is current in several localities.

Scrip is a type of money issued by an organization. ***The scrip shown above, was issued by a different Overland Mail Co.*** *No example of Butterfield's Overland Mail scrip has survived. In fact, it may have never existed.*

June 22, 1858
Congressmen Attempts to Delete Memphis from the Overland Route

June 22, 1858, page 2

Arkansas True Democrat, Little Rock, Arkansas

THE PACIFIC RAILROAD – ... So, also, when the bill making appropriations for the post office department was before the House, Blair, the freesoil member from Mo., moved to amend the bill by a provision to the effect that the **overland mail** route to California should be exclusively started from St. Louis. The motion to amend was lost.

June 23, 1858
Part IV of John Luce's 6 Part Article Arguments in Favor of the Albuquerque Route

June 23, 1858, page 1

Fort Smith Times, Fort Smith, Arkansas

OVERLAND ROUTE TO CALIFORNIA

BY J. B. LUCE, OF SEBASTIAN COUNTY

The Wagon road along the 35th parallel cannot be traced in the same manner, for the reasons already stated, that the report of the only engineer who has surveyed it, Lieut. Whipple, cannot as yet be reached by persons not at the seat of government; but enough of its contents have been made public to show that it gives a highly favorable account of the road.

Mr. Secretary Davis, who reported in favor of the El Paso route as the shortest and cheapest to the Pacific and to San Francisco, in the same report concedes to the route near the 35th parallel certain important advantages. He gives, in a very few words, a clear idea of its prominent characteristics. Its *"general features,"* he says, *"are the extension west and east of the interlocking tributaries of the Mississippi, the Rio Grande, and the Colorado of the west. It would appear to possess, also, a greater yearly amount of rain than the region immediately north and south of it, and, as a consequence, a better supply of fuel and timber."* (1st Vol. P. R. R. p. 20)

Again, on page 21: *"The principal characteristics of this route, in comparison with others, are, probably, its passing through or near more numerous cultivable areas, its more abundant natural supply of water as far west as the Colorado, and the greater frequency and extent of forest growth on the route between the Rio Grande and the Colorado. These two latter characteristics entail a third, however: of unfavorable nature – the large sum of ascents and descents."*

The difference in *"the extension of interlocking tributaries"* east of the Rio Grande, between El Paso and Albuquerque routes, is striking.

On the Albuquerque route, from the waters of the Pecos, a branch of the Rio Grande, to the waters of the Canadian, which runs through the Arkansas into the Mississippi, the distance is *only thirteen miles.*

On the El Paso route, from the waters of the same river Pecos to the waters of the Colorado of Texas, the next stream on the road, the distance is one hundred and fourteen miles.

On the same route, going west from the head of Delaware creek, which runs into the Pecos, to the first water of the Rio Grande, at El Paso, it is one hundred and thirty-two miles

On the Albuquerque route, from the Pecos itself to the first water of the Rio Grande, it is but forty-three miles on Captain Marcy's wagon road.

The same marked difference occurs west of the Rio Grande.

The railroad map, published with Secretary Davis' report, shows that Lieut. Whipple skirted a succession of watercourses all the way from Albuquerque to the very foot of the Coast Range, in California; while the engineers on the lower route, as the extracts from their reports have shown, found the watercourses separated by wide intervals, consisting of desert plains – the first of them beginning in sight of the Rio Grande, and the last of them ending on the mountains which look down on the Pacific.

So, too, respecting the supply of wood and water west of the Rio Grande. The advantages of the Whipple route have already been stated in the language of Secretary Davis.

Mr. Aubrey says of the route he explored in 1853, which, from the Colorado east, was south of but near Lieut. Whipple's: *"The existence of so many mountains along the way must be considered, in reference to railroads, as a very fortunate circumstance, instead of a disadvantage, as it is the mountains alone which furnish the timber and never-failing water. The plains are only deserts and baron spots."*

"The plateau or table lands must, of course, furnish the track upon which the road is to be laid, but the mountains adjacent must furnish the timber to make it, and the water for the use of men and animals employed in its construction."

In 1854 he crossed the Colorado at the same point, but travelled north instead of south of the Whipple route nearly all the way to the Zuni village.

He left the Colorado on the 1st August, and travelled from ten to thirty-five miles a day. He seems to have found plenty of grass and water all the way. On the 4th, 5th, 6th and 7th August he speaks of finding timber in abundance. On the 8th, *"after travelling ten miles, we struck heavy and thick timber of pine, cedar, and pinion, where we were detained hours without being able to get through it, and it is barely possible to pass it on foot."*

On the 9th he says: *"The whole of this country is well supplied with grass in great abundance, and we saw timber enough today to make a thousand miles of railroad: the trees are from one to four feet in diameter, and from one hundred to two hundred and fifty feet high. There are mountains north and south of us, covered with timber."*

On the 10th he says: *"The country today was level, and well supplied with timber and grass."*

[NOTE: A heavy watermark obliterated several words in the following paragraph.]

On corresponding portions of the 32d parallel route,

Lieut Parks says: *"The plains are destitute of trees of any description, and the mountains have a general appearance of sterility and ___, yielding in he concealed Rio ____ valleys a meagre growth of cedar and dwarf evergreen oak."* (page 18)

From the Pimo village to the Colorado, (along the Gila ____) Capt. Humphreys says: *"Water and fuel for working parties are sufficient though no grass. Logs may be driven down the Gila* [River] *from the Mogoyen Mountain* [probably meant Mogollon Mountain] *at its source: from the Pinal Liano, and down the San Francisco and Salinas Rivers, from the pine forest on the former, and the mountains at the sources of the latter."* Captain Humphreys candidly adds: *"It may be found more economical to receive all the supplies of lumber needed from the western portion of the road, either from the San Bernardino Mountains and pass, or from the harbors of San Pedro or San Diego."*

Panorama of San Bernardino Peak,
a subsidiary peak of Mount San Gorgonio

On the one road, timber enough is seen in one day to build a thousand miles of railroad. On the other *"it maybe found more economical"* to bring it 500 miles, over overland from the Pacific ocean!

No account has yet reached the public of any traveller failing to find wood or water in sufficient quantity between Fort Smith and the Rio Grande, along the Canadian River.

Mr. Greig describes his first trip in April, May and June, 1839, with loaded wagons, as *"emphatically a pioneer trip."* There was neither road nor trail to follow. He had no guide. His sole dependence was upon the compass and the sextant. Yet he met with no material difficulty, and did not suffer for either food or water. (Com. Pra., vol. 2, pp. 29, 21, 61. 62)

Exterior of the ruins of a Butterfield Stagecoach station
Courtesy of San Diego History Center

Returning with a guide, in February, March and April, 1840, he found a better road, and at the end of the trip speaks of the Canadian route, generally, as *"affording, throughout the journey, very agreeable camping places."*(ib., p. 155)
[NOTE: The poor printing of the original page makes it difficult to distinguish between a "4" and a "1" or a "7" etc. Therefore, the numbers in this transcription are questionable.]

Mr. Hodson, whose account was published in the *Fort Smith Herald,* of November 1, 1848, started to go to California, to the spring of 1846, with the unfortunate Captain Leavitt, who was killed by the Indians west of the Rio Grande. The party had no guide but Mr. Greig's book and map. They went through to Sante Fe, without any difficulty, in thirty-one days, and found good camping places every night, with plenty of wood, water and grass.

Captain Marcy travelled for several hundred miles over a different road from Mr. Greig. He camped once or twice without water, and two or three times without food, but says that, with a better knowledge of the road, he might have so arranged his travel as to secure both every night. The first camp without water was on the 16th of June, 624 miles from Fort Smith. The same day he passed an ox team that had averaged thirty miles a day with a loaded wagon; *"and notwithstanding they made a drive of thirty-eight miles yesterday, their team looked well."* (p. 186) For so long a distance he *"never passed over a country where wagons could move along with as much ease and facility, without the expenditure of any labor in making a road, as upon this route."* His trip was made in April, May and June, 1849.

In the ensuing fall, Mr. T. W. Lane, with a party of emigrants, travelled Captain Marcy's road as far as the Tu-cum-carri hills, 650 miles from Fort Smith, and then turning off to the southwest, struck the Rio Grande at Socorro, sixty or seventy miles below Albuquerque. In a letter dated Socorro, February 22, 1850, published in the *Fort Smith Herald,* of June 29, 1850, he says: *"The road from Fort Smith to Socorro, for the same distance, I have no doubt is equal to any in the United States, if not better. For wood, water, and grass, there is no necessity for making camp on the entire route without a sufficiency of these articles so essential to the emigrant."*

After leaving Captain Marcy's road at the Tu-cum-carri hills, he *"set out without a trace or mark of any description, and followed the course to the Rio Grande, finding a splendid pass through the mountains; an ordinary team could pull forty hundred pounds over every foot of it."*

The Albuquerque paper, *"El Amigo del Pais,"* of 20th October, 1853, speaking of the arrival at that place of Lieut. Whipple's party from Fort Smith, mentions that the surveying party found water at every encampment; and that, except in one instance, the intervals without water *never exceeded ten miles.*

The same paper gives an abstract of Lieut. Whipple's route, which is confirmed by the Pacific Railroad map, published by Secretary Davis, showing that Lieut. Whipple varied materially from the track of both Greig and Marcy.

The *Washington Union*, of June 16, 1857, quotes the following passage from p. 132 of Lieut. Whipple's report, in volume 3d, Pacific Railroad Reports: *"The first 650 miles, from the eastern border of the Choctaw territory to the river Pecos, possesses in the valley of the Canadian, a natural highway that established beyond question the superior advantage of this belt of country over any other that can be selected between the same degrees of longitude, within the limits of our territory. The Canadian seems formed by nature for the special object in view. In general course of the distance alluded to is nearly east. Its mean inclination is but nine feet to the mile; thus enabling us almost imperceptibly to attain the summit of the lofty table lands of New Mexico. Expensive embankments are entirely avoided; and notwithstanding the numerous affluents that fertilize and enrich the adjacent country, few bridges are required, as most of the water courses sink beneath the surface as they approach the great valley. Upon the eastern portion valuable coal mines exist, and vast forests of oak may furnish an unfailing supply of timber and fuel."*

"If the fertile valleys were thrown open to settlers, and an outlet secured for the products of the soil, this region would form the nucleus of new States, and the roving tribes of Indians that now occupy it would give place to a flourishing population. It is believed that in climate, as well as in soil, this country far surpasses that of Kansas."

The reader will observe that here are five different lines of road indicated between Fort Smith and the Rio Grande, along the Canadian:

1st Mr. Greig's outward trip.

2d. His return trip, which between the 99th and the 104th meridians, was south of his outward trip.

3d. Capt. Marcy's outward route, which for the first 250 miles, did not touch either of Mr. Greig's.

4th. Mr. Lanes's which struck the Rio Grande just above 24 degrees.

5th. Lieut. Whipple's which at various points differed from all the others.

On no one of these five possible routes is there any account of suffering at any season of the year – from February in one year, when Greig left Sante Fe, to February in another, when Lane reached Socorro – for the want of wood, water or grass; and every one of the five lines has been represented as affording a good natural road.

Between Preston and El Paso, accounts are given of two lines of road.

On one line there is a stretch of 125 miles through ___ from one watering place to another.

On the other, and only alternative line, at certain seasons, sixty-seven miles have to be travelled without water, and of these sixty-seven, thirteen are covered with sand so deep as to be almost impassable.

Long distances on other parts of the road are wholly dependent upon supplies of rain water in a region where the rainy season sometimes fails to occur.

In regard to the general superiority of the Canadian route, Colonel Miles, in the letter previously quoted, after speaking of the new route from Albuquerque to San Francisco, and of the *"good water, plenty of wood, and fine grazing"* along the Canadian, says: *"The mail route, monthly or semi-monthly, should be made between Fort Smith and Albuquerque in mail stages, instead of to Dona Ana, which is near 200 miles too far south."*

Col. Miles was then (4th January, 1853,) in command at Fort Fillmore, which is 15 miles below Dona Ana.

Another officer – who was well acquainted with the Canadian route, and whose opinions in matters relating to overland travel across the continent will be appreciated not only by all who know him personally, but also by all who have read the narrative of his explorations in Mr. Washington Irving's *"Rocky Mountain"* – Col. B. L. Boonerville, on the 30th April, 1848, writes to the *Gazette and Democrat,* at Little Rock, in regard to it, that *"it is, without exception, the prettiest country for a long road I ever saw, and leads directly to Santa Fe; possessed as many advantages over any other yet known, that it is a matter of surprise it has so long been overlooked."*

Again, on the 23d October, 1848, he writes to the editor of the *Fort Smith Herald* that it *"possess advantages not found elsewhere, the Canadian River affording quantities of sweet cotton-wood, rushes, and winter grass, enables parties of size to travel it at all seasons, even when the prairies are burnt; the Canadian bottoms are always safe."*

V.

If the official statements respecting the two routes near the 35th and near the 32d parallels are true, the question naturally presents itself, why was the latter selected in preference to the former.

The principal reasons assigned by Mr. Secretary Davis and by Capt. Humphreys, in the report of February 27, 1855, are –

1st. That it is the shortest.

2d. That it is the most level, and therefore, the cheapest, for a railroad, the nature of the ground being such as in a great measure to obviate the necessity of grading, or of costly preparation for road-beds, contrasting favorably in this respect with *the apparently rough and broken character of the country through which most of the Albuquerque route lies.* – (1st vol. P. R. R. pp. 29, 30, p. 106)

Since the date of the report it has been ascertained that the statements of distances and elevations on the Albuquerque route were incorrect. The corrected distance given by Capt. Humphreys, in his letter, has already been stated. In the same letter in appears that the height of the pass through the Sierra Madre, the first mountain range west of the Rio Grande, is 6,952 feet, instead of 7,750, as marked on the profile first published. Capt. Humphreys also says *"the elevations of several of the passes have been materially reduced"* on further examination of the barometrical observations.

The profile first published, therefore, exaggerated both the distance and the elevations on the Albuquerque route, precisely the points in which it was alleged to be inferior to the El Paso route, and which furnished the reasons for preferring the latter.

Facts and figures have already been given to show that the latter is not the shortest to San Francisco, from any point, either by wagon road, railroad line or engineer's trail.

It will be seen that even by the profile first published, for no other has reached this section, the advantage in grading was not considerable.

One of the most striking facts on the Whipple survey is, that it attains a great elevation very gradually and leaves it gradually.

Without a single grade exceeding 53 feet in 700 miles, it reaches a height of 4,700 feet above the sea, and nowhere for the next 600 miles descends below that height. When it does descend, the slopes are gentle.

The greatest elevation on the first profile was the summit of Campbell's Pass, through the Sierra Madra, 7,750 feet (since ascertained to be 5,952 feet) exceeding by 2,033 feet the highest point on the other route – the Guadalupe Peak, 5,717 feet. The profile makes the distance to Campbell's Pass 970 miles, and 270 more to the summit of the pass through the San Francisco mountains, the elevation of which is marked 7,472 feet, the two being designated as the two highest points on the entire line. The next highest points are east of the Rio Grande; no elevation on the line west of the San Francisco Pass being within a thousand feet of its height – that is, as given on the profile.

From Fort Smith to a point 30 miles beyond the summit of the pass, the distance is stated to be 1,278 miles. In that distance, which includes nearly all the most prominent elevations, the highest grade is 82 feet per mile.

For the first 700 miles the highest grade is 52 feet.

The highest grade within a hundred miles of Campbell's Pass is 40 feet.

Its summit is attained on one side with an average grade of 23 feet for 93 miles, the maximum being 25 feet. The descent on the other has an average trade of 19 feet for 137 miles and of six feet for 75 miles.

[NOTE: A large dark water stain obscures several words in the following paragraph.]

A grade of 47 feet for the next 57 miles scales the summit of the San Francisco ___. The descending grade s for __ miles is 19, 7, 69 and 24 feet. this ____ ____ ___ the point before referred to as 1,278 miles from Ft. Smith ___ on the profile, longitude 112 degrees 1_ minutes.

In all this distance no tunnels are required, and there are only four grades exceeding 62 feet, the length of all four being 48 miles; one of 00 feet for 0 miles; of 60 feet for 14 miles; 80 feet, 10 miles; and 82 feet for 13 miles.

These are the highest grades indicated in crossing the Rocky Mountains and the Sierra Madre, the highest mountains on the line from Fort Smith to the Pacific, upon a profile on which the elevations *are admitted to be exaggerated.*

Now, bearing in mind that the chief advantage claimed for the El Paso route is that its surface is more level, compare these grades with some on a corresponding portion of the lower route, from Fulton to the Pimos villages, longitude 111 degrees 41 minutes, not so far west as the point referred to on the other lines.

The distance marked at 1,175 miles. The number of miles graded at 60 feet and over 125; of which 48 have grades from 60 to 70 feet; 20 between 70 and 80; 11 miles are graded at 80 feet; 34 have grades between 90 and 100; 17 have a grade of 108 feet; and 5 of 123 feet to the mile.

The work required to produce some of the more favorable grades (45 feet and under) was of such a character that Captain Humphrey's suggests the use of temporary surface grades for six miles, ranging form 94 to 194 feet to the mile.

In another place, where grades of *"90 feet or less"* are obtained by *tunnelling, "we may use temporarily the surface grades,"* which, for seven miles, are 104, 123, 150 and 240 feet to the mile.

As far as the 112th meridian the principal ascents and descents upon one route are found in 40 miles, with grades ranging from 60 feet to 82; upon the other in 125 miles, with grades ranging from 60 feet to 123 – 46 miles of the latter having grades of over 90 feet, and 23 miles over 100 feet to the mile, without including the *"temporary surface grades."*

West of 112 degrees of longitude the grades are more favorable upon the lower route, and less so upon the upper, although the latter has but four exceeding 90 feet, the heaviest being 101. The length of all four is 107 miles.

Corresponding portions of the other route have grades of 127 and 133 feet, though for very short distances.

Going to San Francisco by the line first recommended to Congress, the El Paso route meets the other at the foot of the Sierra Nevada with 195 miles of heavy grading against 169; being an excess of 26 miles in length and of *fourteen hundred feet* in ascents and descents – that is, in the grades which exceed 55 feet.

1,691 miles (as marked on the profile) of the Albuquerque route are of grades under 55 feet; that is, all but 201 miles of the entire line to San Pedro.

952 miles are of grades less than 36 feet, and 600 miles less than 20 feet.

In these lower grades the El Paso route has the advantage: and the excess of the elevations which constitute the great objection to the other route is made up principally of grades less than 55 feet.

Sixty feet to the mile is at the rate of three inches in twenty-two feet. Three men out of five might spend their lives on floors of steeper grade, without knowing they were not level. – this is the unscientific view of the matter. – The scientific is given by Capt. Humphreys. He says, on page 90, that the Baltimore and Ohio railroad has a grade of 117 feet per mile for 17 miles; and that a locomotive can draw a train of 200 passengers with baggage, *"in the worst conditions of the rails, upon a grade of 221 feet per mile."* He also quotes three pages from the report of an able American engineer, to show that grades exceeding 100 feet are admirable; but as the statements in favor of high grades are made especially in connection with the El Paso route, one might suppose they were not applicable to the other, but for a note at the foot of the table of distances, elevations, & c., on all the different routes, on page 107, stating that, *"with the amount of work estimated for the roads in this report, the equated lengths corresponding to the sum of assents and descents, has had little practical value. With a full equipment and heavy freight business the sum of ascents and descents become important."*

In other words, when the population of the prairies and the mountains on the Albuquerque route, on the one hand, or the Staked Plains and the Colorado desert on the El Paso route, becomes dense enough to swell the business of a road up to the point of the Baltimore and Ohio, or the New York Central, then the difference between their ascents and descents becomes important, and not till then.

(TO BE CONTINUED)

June 23, 1858
Advance Preparations
The Eight Division Superintendents Assigned

June 23, 1858

Fort Smith Times, Fort Smith, Arkansas

MOVEMENTS OF THE OVERLAND MAIL COMPANY –

Mr. Buckley, agent for the **Overland Mail company**, from El Paso to Tucson, left here yesterday. with a number of men to build stations, & c. He also takes wagons and teams, camp utensils, tools and provisions to supply the stations. In a few days, they will send on their coaches, additional wagons, harness, and everything necessary, to stock the entire route to El Paso. Coaches and harness have already been shipped to California to stock the route from San Francisco to El Paso.

Mr. Crocker, assisted by Mr. Fox, has charge of the route from St. Louis and Memphis to Red River. Mr. Bates has charge of the route from Red River to Chadburn. Mr. Glover from Fort Chadburn to El Paso. Messers. Buckley and Hawley from El Paso to fort Yuma. Kenyon from Fort Yuma to San Francisco.

Thus all the divisions of this great contract, have been placed in the hands of energetic men, and the public have an assurance that it will be successfully carried out. Hurrah for **Butterfield!!**

June 23, 1858
Preparations for the Overland

June 23, 1858
Fort Smith Times, Fort Smith, Arkansas

We learn from Mr. Glover, of the **Overland Mail Company**, who has just returned from Tennessee, that he read an order in some of the papers, stating that Col. Fauntleroy is to proceed to California, by the way of Fort Smith, Fort Arbuckle, and Albuquerque. Mr. Glover saw Col. Fauntleroy in Memphis as his passed through.

June 23, 1858
Advance Preparations

June 23, 1858
Fort Smith Times, Fort Smith, Arkansas

Overland Mail – **Messers. Butterfield** and Crocker, **Overland Mail** contractors, with several men, arrived here on Thursday last. They are now making preparations to put the line in operation, and from the movements of these men – our friends, who have appeared to be incredulous about the starting of this mail, may now, feel assured that the work is progressing rapidly, and will soon be in operation. From what we have seen of these gentlemen, we would say, they are the very men to manage such a gigantic undertaking.

June 29, 1858
Postmaster Prefers Southern Route

June 29, 1858, page 2
Arkansas True Democrat, Little Rock, Arkansas

News Items – A late number of the Memphis Bulletin has this notice of the **Overland California Mail**:

Intelligence from Washington City has been received here to the effect that Postmaster General Brown's requisition on **Messrs. Butterfield & Co.**, the contractors for the **Overland Mail** to California, had been acquiesced in by those gentlemen. The Postmaster General's requisition was that the contractors should adopt the southern route, making Memphis the eastern terminus of the line. We also understand that the mail will leave this city for the first time over this route on the 1st day of July, instead of September, as before announced.

June 30, 1858
Advance Preparations

June 30, 1858
Fort Smith Times, Fort Smith, Arkansas

Messers. Glover & Bates, superintendents for **Overland Mail Co.,** started two wagons and teams, and thirteen men, for their respective Divisions on Monday evening. As soon as the Lady Walton *[steamboat]*, which is expected every moment, arrives, they will follow on, taking with them four coaches, twenty men, and 20 mules.

With the movements of **Messers. Butterfield & Co.,** before us, who will now doubt the determination of this **Company** to perform their contract, and that too, true to time –success to **Messers. Butterfield & Co.** [as quoted in "Butterfield Overland Mail" by Roscoe Conklin, page 217-8]

June 30, 1858
Part VI of John Luce's 6 Part Article
Arguments in Favor of the Albuquerque Route

June 30, 1858, page 1
Fort Smith Times, Fort Smith, Arkansas

Overland Route to California

by J. B. Luce, of Sebastian County

Details concerning the inclination of grades for railroads may seem out of place in discussing the merits of stage routes. They are given, however, not only to show exactly what it is that constitutes the alleged inferiority in this respect in the El Paso route, but also, what sort of elevations

[Butterfield's Overland] mail coaches would be compelled to ascent.

The publications in defence of the selection made by the Postmaster General, of course, do not allude to railroad grades, nor is there any attempt made in them to prove that the El Paso route is the shortest.

The most prominent among them is an article in the *National Intelligencer* of 25th July last, *"prepared by a gentleman connected with the Post Office Department,""explanatory and defensive"* of the course adopted by the Postmaster General. The grounds specially put forth for preferring the El Paso to the Albuquerque route are twofold: First, the difference in climate. Second, the alleged inferiority of the country over which is passes.

As to climate, the writer begins by giving an exaggerated statement of the difference in the mean elevation of the two routes at certain points, making it 2,800 or 3,000 feet – at least 1,000 feet beyond the mark. He then speaks of the difference in elevation as *very important in a climatological point of view,"* which he illustrates by presenting *"the following chilling facts,"* taken from meteorological records kept at Fort Defiance and Albuquerque, too long to be copied in full. The substance is, that during five winters, from December 1852 to March 1857, the mercury ranged at Fort Defiance from 49 degrees to 65 degrees above zero in its highest readings, and in its lowest, from 13 degrees above to 25 degrees below zero. This last reading is for December 1855, and is probably erroneous, for the writer afterwards says that on the 25th December, 1855, it was 32 degrees below zero at the hospital, not the coldest part of the garrison; that men on detached service had their hands and feet badly frozen, & c. & c.

The facts are sufficiently chilling. But the important fact to be ascertained is not the degree of cold, but the quantity of snow. Intense cold rarely operates as an obstruction to travel in the United States, particularly where the temperature is regular, which, in justice to Fort Defiance, must be conceded to be the case at that post: not so cold, indeed, as in the instance just specifies, for the winter of 1855-'56 is described as the severest known for many years. If *cold weather* were the only obstacle, there would probably be no difficulty in carrying the mail by way of Salt Lake. The principal obstruction on that route is the snow, falling, according to Captain Stansbury, *"constantly upon the mountains,"* accumulating in the canyons *"to the depth of fifty feet,"* cutting off *"all communication with the world beyond,"* and that *"so rapidly"* as to force emigrants *"to abandon their wagons and escape on foot," "leaving their animals to perish."* The question is not whether it was cold enough to freeze one's feet and hands on one particular day in a long series of years, a day on which the ***[Butterfield's Overland]*** mail stage might stop, if need be, till the cold abated; but whether there was danger at the same time, or at any other time, of the stage being blocked up by snow, of the driver being compelled to abandon it, or communication with the world beyond being cut off, or without proceeding to such extremities, if there was snow enough to put a stop to travel, or materially retard it.

The statements about snow are–

1. That at Fort Defiance, in December, 1851, there was *"eighteen inches snow."*

2. That during the severe winter referred to, of 1855-'56, *"those Indians who live habitually to the north of Fort Defiance, were obliged to abandon that portion of the country and move south, with their flocks and herds, in quest of grazing, on account of the depth of snow, which in the mountains, at whose base the fort is situated, has over two feet in depth in march, 1856."*

It is believed that *"eighteen inches"* or even *"two feet"* of snow, would not present an insuperable obstacle to the progress of ***[Butterfield's Overland Mail Co.'s]*** stage sleighs.

The Indians *"north of Fort Defiance,"* who moved *"south with their flocks and herds in quest of grazing on account of the depth of snow,"* evidently did not find the snow deep enough to prevent locomotion.

But suppose they did; must the stage go *"north of Fort Defiance?"* or must it climb the *"mountains at whose base the fort is situated,"* and where the deep snow is found?

By no means. Fort Defiance is not on the Albuquerque route. Lieut. Whipple's survey, after leaving a point on the Canadian, beyond the Choctaw line, is nowhere so far north as Fort Defiance; nor is the route to San Francisco, until after it becomes identical with the El Paso route. Campbell's Pass, through the Sierra Madre, is the point on the survey nearest Fort Defiance, which, according to the writer in the *Intelligencer,* is *"twenty miles north of Campbell's Pass in latitude, and from three hundred to five hundred feet higher."*

"Campbell's Pass" is one of the highest elevations on Lieut. Whipple's line, and is further north than any other other point on the survey west of the Rio Grande. This extreme point of elevation and north latitude, is from three to five hundred feet lower, and twenty miles further south, than Fort defiance, yet the record of that post are cited against the Albuquerque route without any allowance for the *"difference in elevation in a climatological point of view."*

Extracts are given in the same article from the record kept at Albuquerque for various winters from 1849 to 1857, including three embraced in the returns for Fort Defiance. On comparing the records of the two places for these three winters, it appears that the weather is uniformly milder at Albuquerque: the difference in its favor being in no case less than seven degrees and a half. The coldest weather indicated is in January, 1850, when the mercury stood at twelve below zero. In December, 1850, it was five, and in January, 1857, four degrees below zero. The mean temperature of winter is stated to be thirty seven degrees, which is warmer than it is at Washington, Cincinnati, Louisville, or St. Louis: about the same as the average temperature at Richmond, and within two and a half degrees of the average at Nashville and Knoxville, in Tennessee.

It is also stated that the Rio Grande was frozen over at Albuquerque during the winter of 1855-'5, strong enough *"to bear a horse and carts,"* and again in December, 1856, *"so as to be passable from 7th to 25th."*

This is about all that is said of Albuquerque: not one word about snow.

[NOTE: The poor printing of the original page makes it difficult to distinguish between a "4" and a "1" or a "7" etc. Therefore, the numbers in this transcription are questionable.]

The next paragraph contains the only remaining facts alleged against the climate.

"On the 24th December, 1853," the writer adds, *"Capt. Whipple experienced snow storms and weather sufficiently cold to contract the mercury 3 1/2 degrees below zero, near the San Francisco mountains, and still further west. In the Aztec Pass, to 2 1/2 degrees below zero, where he experienced another snow storm – so much for the climate of winter on the Albuquerque route."*

Captain Whipple himself evidently did not regard either the snow storms or the cold weather as insurmountable of objections, for he says in his report (as extracted in the *Union,*) *"One of the most important advantages claimed for this route is the pleasant and salubrious climate of the region through which it passes..."*

"The mountain ranges that are crossed are not blocked up in winter by ice and snow sufficient to interrupt travel. From July to January, and for the whole year, this line may be traversed in safety..."

"Upon the parallel of the 35th degree snow cannot prove an obstruction to a railway."

If there ever was a doubt of this last fact, the *"gentleman connected with the Post Office Department"* has removed it.

The law authorizing the **Overland Route** was passed on the 3d March: the Postmaster General made his contract on the 30th of June. During the intervening four months, according to his defender, *"with his accustomed industry and perseverance, he was collecting all the data pertaining to the proposed routes;"* doing this at the seat of government where *"all the data"* could be found without difficulty. *"Data"* conclusive to his mind against the climate of the Albuquerque route are laid before the public and show —– what?

Why, 1. That it is sometimes very cold above the route, at Fort Defiance;

2. That on the route, at Albuquerque, it is not any colder than it is at more than half the post towns in the United States;

3. That it sometimes snows on the San Francisco mountains; and,

4. That the snow north of Fort Defiance is sometimes deep enough to prevent Indian cattle from grazing.

The friends of the Albuquerque route are certainly under obligations to the Postmaster General and his apologetic friend for establishing so incontestably the fact stated by Capt. Whipple that *"upon the parallel of the 35th degrees, snow cannot prove an obstruction."*

There are certain other facts *"Important in a climatological point of view,"* which are not chilling, and which seem to have escaped the attention of the Postmaster General.

On page 106 of vol. 1, Pacific Railroad Reports, Captain Humphreys, in summing up its advantages, speaks of the *"mild winters and temperate summers"* of the El Paso route, *"except that portion on the Gila and Colorado desert, where, for 350 miles, labor in the open air must be suspended for three months of the year."* He does not say why, but the reason appears in the report of the geologist, Mr. Blake, whose statement that the mercury stood at ninety degrees on the 20th November has already been quoted, as also Lieut. Williamson's report of ninety-three degrees on the 5th December. Mr Blake gives, on page 40, a table extracted from a meteorological register, *"carefully kept by Mr. Milhan, United States Army,"* at Fort Yuma, on the Colorado, directly opposite the mouth of the Gila.

This table gives the highest and lowest readings of the thermometer, and its monthly mean or average for nineteen successive months commencing in May, 1852, and ending with November, 1853. The statements for May, June, July, August, September and October, 1852 and 1853 are subjoined.

At Fort Yuma –

Highest temperature in 1852:, May 108 degrees, June 106 degrees, July 106 degrees, August 108 degrees, September 105 degrees, and October 98 degrees.

Highest temperatures in 1853: May 99 degrees, June 116 degrees, July 111 degrees, August 110 degrees, September 110 degrees, October 100 degrees.

Lowest temperature in 1852: May 52 degrees. June 65 degrees, July 70 degrees, August 70 degrees, September 60 degrees, and October 50 degrees.

Lowest temperature in 1853: May 52 degrees, June 61 degrees, July 76 degrees, August 76 degrees, September 69 degrees, October 50 degrees.

Monthly mean or average, 1852: May 81 degrees, June 91 degrees, July 93 degrees, August 92 degrees, September 81 degrees, October 73 degrees.

Monthly mean or average, 1853: May 77 degrees, June 89 degrees, July 95 degrees, August 92 degrees, September 89 degrees, October 79 degrees.

The Patent Office reports for 1853, and for 1855, contain minute and carefully collected details respecting the climate and temperature of various other countries, as compared with the United States. No other part of the globe shows as high a monthly average in the returns quoted as Fort Yuma, with the single exception of Cawnpore, in India, which surpasses in the summer heat Benares, Calcutta, Madre, or any other locality cited, Fort Yuma only excepted.

This monthly average at Cawnpore for May is 96 degrees, June 91 degrees July 87 degrees, August 87 degrees, September 83 degrees, October 79 degrees; exceeding Fort Yuma in May, June and October; falling short of it in July, August, and September.

After Fort Yuma, the highest monthly report for the United States is 88 degrees at Galveston, Texas. 6 degrees below Fort Yuma.

The highest average at Key West is 83 degrees, at

Charleston 81 degrees, 3; Savanah 80 degrees, 6; New Orleans 80 degrees, 4; St. Louis 78 degrees 4; Philadelphia 75 degrees, 2; and New York 74 degrees. 9.

The highest average heat known for any one month at New York and Philadelphia is lower than the lowest reading of the thermometer at Fort Yuma throughout the months of July and August, 1853.

The highest temperature reported at any other place in the United States is at Ft. Graham, in Texas, where the mercury reached 106 degrees in August, 1851 – eight degrees below the highest reading at Fort Yuma.

The highest reported at any other place is 102 degrees at Richmond, Virginia. The highest at Washington, Philadelphia, and Baltimore is 100 degrees. The highest at New Orleans and at Charleston, is 91 degrees; at St. Louis, 97 degrees; Key West, 89 degrees.

The average heat at Fort Yuma throughout the month of July, 1853, was higher than the highest known range of the mercury at Augustine, Key West, New Orleans, or Charleston.

It may possibly be inferred from the foregoing statements that Fort Yuma is the hottest place in the Unites States. It is not.

On the El Paso route, east of the Rio Grande, at Capt. Pope's crossing of the Pecos River, on the 16th March 1854, the diary of his expedition, on page 64, reports the mercury as *"rising to 97 degrees fahrenheit in the shade."*

The highest temperature at Fort Yuma in March 1853, was 92 degrees – five degrees less.

On the same route, near the same place, on four successive days in May, 1856, the mercury stood at 113 degrees in the shade – higher than any temperature reported at Fort Yuma in May, July, August or September.

At the same point on the Pecos, in June, 1856, it stood, in the shade, on the 1st at 110 degrees, 2d, 113 degrees, 3rd 112 degrees, 4th 113 degrees, 5th 115 degrees, and 6th 118 degrees.

The last, 118 degrees, is two degrees higher than the highest reported temperature at Fort Yuma.

The average readings of these temperatures, in the shade, during the ten successive days, is 113 degrees, being higher than any reported at Fort Yuma, except one of 116 degrees for June, 1853.

These quotations are from a record kept by Dr. G. G. Shumard, the geologist who accompanied Capt. Pope while boring for water to supply his air line over the Staked Planes, along a route where, according to Capt. Pope, *"the extremes of heat and cold are absolutely unknown!"* The reader will be curious to know where Capt. Pope ever found it more extremely hot.

If labor in the open air must be suspended for three months in the year on the Gila and Colorado deserts, near Fort Yuma, for 350 miles, on account of heat, a fortiori *[fortiori: based on a conclusion for which there is stronger evidence than for a previously accepted one]* it must be suspended on the Staked Plains, where the heat is greater.

If *"chilling facts"* have not been as yet presented, it is not because they are wanting on this route.

The reader has heard the word *"norther,"* and doubtless knows what it means. If he does not Mr A. B. Gray, a stauncher advocate of the 32d parallel than Capt, Humphreys himself, can tell him.

On page 13 of this *"Survey of Southern Pacific Railroad,"* he says: *"The evening we reached Mustang Springs (22d January, 1854 on Capt. Marcy's road and Capt. Pope's wagon trail) it suddenly turned cold and blew a severe norther, making it exceedingly unpleasant. If encountered on the plains, without shelter from timber or hills, these peculiar gales are often destructive to animals. They are not frequent, however, and seldom last over a day in this region. Parties with heavy cargo on their mules, encamping after a hard days march have been caught at night by northers, and many of the fatigues and stiffened animals perished before morning. January, in this latitude, is the month of northers, ourselves experiencing three in succession; but I took the precau-*

tion, when overtaken by them without cover, to travel, whether night or day. Facing their keen blasts for seventeen miles at a time was severe on men, with their long frosted beards, from the condensation of their breath; but I was aware that our safety depended upon it, and thus prevented extreme suffering and the loss of a single animal. This was the first time we know the Staked Plains attempted to be crossed by a party in the depth of winter."

Mr. Gray errs in speaking of January exclusively as the *"month of northers."* Between the 4th and 16th December, 1849, Lt. Michler's party on the same road, near the *"Double Mountain fork of the Brazos," "suffered most severely from cold northers, heavy rains, and terrible sleets, Our mules had already become very weak, in consequence of living upon grass alone – the latter having lost most of its nourishment from the killing frosts which night after night lay upon the ground. The cold affected the rest, and nine of our animals were either frozen to death or left so stiff with cold as to be unable to be moved."* (Senate Ex. Doc., No. 64, 1st session 31st Congress, p. 36)

On the 13th October, 1842, Capt. Marcy, on the same road, one hundred and forty miles northeast of the Mustang Springs, says, *"The cold norther has had an effect upon our poor animals which I did not anticipate. Many failed before we reached camp; five gave out and died during the day. Three more have already died since we reached camp."*

On the 14th he describes *"a most terrific storm"* of the night before. *"The wind blew a perfect tempest from the north."* Twenty-five more mules perished; the whole number destroyed by the norther of the 13th October and the following night being thirty-three. (ib. p. 212, 213)

No one ever heard of a *"norther"* on the Albuquerque route.

Lt. Whipple says: *"there is no long series of parched plains rendering the summer heat intolerable; nor do those dreaded winds termed 'northers' reach this latitude."* (Part 2, vol. 3, P. R. R. R. p. 43, as quoted by the *"__on."*

It is objected that *"Capt, Whipple has thrown a little too much of the ___ __ ___in his picture."* Not a particle of evidence is adduced in support of this allegation. Still nothing is more probable. He had just spent two years in the lower route. The *"long series of parched plains,"* the *"intolerable heat,"* and the *"dreaded northers,"* which he did not find on the 35th parallel, were evidently fresh in his recollection and night render the contrast more strikingly favorable than the facts would strictly warrant.

It is also objected that *"from the Vegas de Santa Clara to the Mohave River is perhaps the worst desert road on the face of the globe. – that whole distance is blanched with the ghastly skulls and scattered bones of hapless beasts, that have perished for the want of water and from excessive heat. Even human skulls have been seen along this road."* All this is true, as the reader may see on referring to Freemont's Expedition of 1843-'44, p. 270, where he will also learn that the Vegas de Santa clara is in latitude 37 degrees 28 minutes; that the desert does not commence until after leaving the river going north (p. 261); that is becomes more repulsive (p. 264) as it extends north, the worst part (p. 256) occurring 150 miles beyond the Mohave River.

Capt. Whipple's line approaches the Mohave from the southwest, and skirts the south bank of the river, until long after the road from the desert strikes it on the north bank. It is thus seen that the region spoken of is not on the route.

An objection likely to have more weight than any other is, that Capt. Marcy, on his outward trip 1849, *"thought the Albuquerque route an excellent one, and could not be surpassed;"* but on his return by way of Dona Ana and Preston, to Fort Smith, *"was convinced of the superiority of that route to the Canadian."*

So he was, but why? Because, to see his own words:

1. He was assured *"that there was no point upon the Rio Grande, north of San Diego, from which wagons could pass through the extensive ranges of mountains lying west of that river,"* and that it would be necessary to take Col. Cooke's route to the head of the Gila should emigrants go to Sante Fe, therefore, they have to travel three hundred miles down

the river to reach this point, whereas our return route leaves this road almost directly at the placer.

2. *"The roads from Fort Smith and Independence to Sante Fe being over eight hundred miles, and the distance down the Rio Grande three hundred more over a very sandy road, makes these routes longer than the southern route from Fort Smith by two hundred miles.*

3. *"As there is no grass upon this route at all seasons of the year, it can be travelled at any time. It is true that the old grama grass dries up early in the spring, but it appears to cure like hay, and does not lose its nutritious properties."*

4. *"As San Diego on the Rio Grande, the mouth of the Gila, and San Diego on the Pacific are all very nearly on the same parallel of latitude. (32 degrees 45 minutes 54 seconds) our southern route would form a direct line of communication with Cooke's road from the United States through to the Pacific, and probably shorter, by several hundred miles, than any other."* (Marcy's Rep. Sen. F.x. doc 64, 31st Congress, 1st session, pp. 224 and 225.)

These are the reasons he assigns for the preference, and the only reasons. It will be seen that they are all, except the one relating to grass, based upon the supposition that travelers to California, by way of the Canadian, were compelled to take Col. Cooke's route, which could not be reached without travelling down the Rio Grande 300 miles, *"over a very sandy road," traversing on the way the well known 'Jornada del Muerto' or 'journey of death,' a stretch of 77 miles without water.*

When it was demonstrated four years afterwards, by the explorations of Aubrey and Whipple, that there was a point north of San Diego from which wagons could pass through the mountains west; that it was not necessary to take Col. Cooke's route, and consequently not necessary to travel *"down the Rio Grande 300 miles, over a very sandy road,"* these reasons of course, fell to the ground – all but the one relating to grass, which the experience already referred to, of persons travelling up the Canadian at all seasons, has shown to have no weight as against that route. [TO BE CONTINUED]

July 3, 1858
Stations Being Establish
Supervisors Selected

July 3, 1858
Arkansas State Gazette and Democrat, Little Rock, Ark.

MOVEMENTS OF THE **OVERLAND MAIL COMPANY** – Mr. Buckley, agent for the **Overland Mail Company**, from El Paso to Tucson, left here yesterday, with a number of men to build stations & c. *[&c. is an abbreviation of etc., et cetera, meaning and others, or, and so forth.]* He, also, takes wagons and teams, camp utensils, tools and provisions to supply the stations. In a few days, they will send on their coaches, additional wagons, harness, and everything else necessary to stock the entire route to El Paso. Coaches and harness have already been shipped to California to stock the route from San Francisco to El Paso.

Mr. Crocker, assisted by Mr. Fox, has charge of the route from St. Louis and Memphis to Red River.

Mr. Bates has charge of the route from Red River to Fort Chadburn.

Mr. Glover form Fort Chadburn to El Paso.

Messrs. Buckley and Hawley from El Paso to Fort Yuma.

Kenyon from Fort Yuma to San Francisco.

Thus all the divisions of this great contract, have been placed in the hands of energetic men, and the public have an assurance that it will be successfully carried out. Hurrah for **Butterfield** ! !

July 3, 1858
John Butterfield Arrives in Fort Smith

July 3, 1858, Saturday, page 2
Arkansas State Gazette and Democrat, Little Rock, Ark.

OVERLAND MAIL – Messrs. Butterfield and Crocker, **Overland Mail** contractors, with several men, arrived here on Thursday last. They are now making preparations to put the line in operation and from the movements of these men – our friends, who have appeared to be incredulous about the starting of this mail, may now, feel assured that the work is progressing rapidly, and will soon be in operation. From what we have seen of these gentlemen, we would say, they are the very men to manage such a gigantic undertaking.

– Fort Smith Times

July 7, 1858
Stages Distributed

July 7, 1858
Fort Smith Times, Fort Smith, Arkansas

Overland Mail Movements. - Messrs. Glover and Bates left here on Thursday morning with four stages of the Overland Mail Company, built expressly for this route. Mr. Bates superintends the route from Preston/Colbert's Ferry and Mr. Glover from Chadbourne to El Paso.

Only six of their stages reached here on the :Lady Walton" (steamboat) and there remain about sixty more to come, which are expected daily.

Messrs. Butterfield, Crocker and Cox left here on Thursday evening last, having in charge one stage for the road between here and St. Louis. Mr. Butterfield goes home, and Messrs. Crocker and Cox are at work on their respective divisions putting in stock...

A company under charge of Mr. Talcott will leave here in a few days to work on the road in the Choctaw nation, So the work goes bravely on. Hurrah for Butterfield again!
[as quoted in "Butterfield Overland Mail" by Roscoe Conklin, page 218]

July 7, 1858
Part VI of John Luce's 6 Part Article
In Support of Albuquerque Route Over the El Paso

July 7, 1858, page 1
Fort Smith Times, Fort Smith, Arkansas

Overland Route to California

BY J. B. LUCE, OF SEBASTIAN COUNTY

Those objections disposed of, the remaining conclusions to which his accustomed industry and perseverance lead the Postmaster General as stated in the *Intelligencer*, are –

First. That the El Paso route passes through a greater range of cultivable country, well timbered and well watered, east of the Rio Grande.

Second. That west of that river to the Pacific it compares favorably with the Albuquerque route in almost every important particular.

Third. That the uncultivable region, admitted to exist on both routes, is 230 miles wider on the route near the 35th parallel than the other.

In support of the first of these propositions, an extract from Capt. Pope's report describes *"the great deserts"* as commencing about the 97th meridian, and extending west from that meridian, without interruption, between the 49th and the 34th parallel, being varied below the latter by the projection of a broad belt of fertile, well watered, and well timbered country for 312 miles, between the 32d and 34th parallels, to within less than 300 miles of the Rio Grande, *"like a vast peninsula into the parched and treeless waste."* *[NOTE: The poor printing of the original page makes it difficult to distinguish between a "4" and a "1" or a "7" etc. Therefore, the numbers in this transcription are questionable.]*

In other words, that there is a fine farming country, with good timber and plenty of water, as far west as 102 degrees 20 minutes – west of the Mustang Springs – between 32 degrees and 34 degrees. While north of 31 degrees and west of 97 degrees, that is west of Fort Arbuckle and north of the main Red River as far up as the 49th parallel, including the whole Canadian country from a point east of the Cross timbers, and twenty-two miles east of Chouteau's Traveling House, in a *"parched and treeless waste."*

The reader in western Arkansas will think it incredible that such a statement should emanate from an official source. He will find it on page 5 of Capt. Pope's Report, 2d vol. P. R. R. R.

Capt. Marcy is next quoted as describing the 99th meridian as *"an immense natural barrier beyond which agriculturists should not pass,"* the country west being *"one ocean of barren prairie, with but here and there a feeble stream, and a few solitary trees."*

Finally the vindication of the Postmaster General closes with the statement of Captain Humphrey's, in a letter to the *"Union"* dated 18th July last, that the uncultivable country beginning on both routes.

By the route of the 32d parallel

To the summit of Warner's Pass
(through the Coast Range) 1,100 miles

To the summit of San Gorgonia Pass
(through the Coast Range) 1,218 miles

By the route of the 35th parallel

To the summit of the Cajon Pass
(through the Coast Range) 1,400 miles

To the summit of the Tahechaypa Pass
(through the Sierra Nevada) 1,450 miles

Thus the distance across the uncultivable region is, on the route of the 32d parallel 230 miles shorter than on the route of the 35th parallel.

Capt. Marcy's description is taken from the report of his expedition in 1842 to Sante Fe where we was sent to escort a party of emigrants, and to find a good road; not to explore a country. The road being the main point, of course he sought it where alone he could expect to find it, on the ridges; indeed, he seems never to have left them when he could help it. On the 30th May, when about seventeen miles from the 100th meridian, he says, *"our road was upon the dividing ridge all day, very firm and smooth, but somewhat circuitous, following the windings of the 'Divide.' This has generally been very direct, and for the two hundred miles we have travelled upon it I have never seen a better natural road. The country upon each end falling off towards the Canadian and Washita leaves the crest perfectly dry at all seasons, There are numberless small branches rising near the road which are skirted with timber and grass, thereby giving the traveler an opportunity to encamp at almost any time he feels disposed."* (p. 150) After reaching Sante Fe, he says, on page 191, that his course was *"altogether upon the south side of the Canadian, and generally upon the ridges dividing the tributaries of that river from those of Red River and the Washita."* Subsequent exploration shows that the head of the north fork of Red River is near the Canadian, in longitude 101 degrees 55 minutes. Up to that point, at least 165 miles west of the 95th meridian, he travelled almost exclusively on dividing ridges. Because he did not see, while on those ridges, good soil or timber to any considerable extent, it does not necessarily follow that they do not exist west of the 99th meridian.

The country on the north fork of the Canadian has never been explored. It has always been represented by the Indians that the rich soil well known to exist on its lower borders extends all the way to its head waters, which are far beyond the 100th meridian.

South of the Canadian, the question of soil and timber is not left to conjecture. Captain Marcy has himself refuted his own statement that west of __ degrees it is an ocean of barren prairie, with here and there a feeble stream and a few solitary trees.

His exploration of the Red River of Louisiana, in 1852, was confined exclusively to those waters of Red River which drain the Wichita Mountains, and the country west and northwest of them.

These mountains extend from about 99 degrees 16 minutes to a short distance beyond the hundredth degree, the boundary of Texas. Their southern extremity is several miles north of 31 degrees 30 minutes. Their eastern extremity is fifteen miles west of the 90th meridian.

Of the country about these mountains Capt. Marcy says, on page 80, that he has never visited any that *"possessed greater natural local advantages for agriculture"*

On page 96, he says: *"At almost any point throughout the*

Wichita mountains, all the requisites for building and sustaining a military post are found in great profusion. The quality of the timber, soil, and water are all far superior to that near the posts upon the Brazos."

He repeatedly mentions overcup oak, pecan, black walnut, ash and hackberry timber, besides any quantity of post oak and of cottonwood. At one camp alone there were 8,000 acres of woodland (post oak with some black walnut) within six miles. This was in longitude 99 degrees 37 minutes, latitude 34 degrees 45 minutes, within 18 miles of the 35th parallel.

He travelled some twenty-five or thirty miles along and west of the hundredth meridian, which was ascertained and marked by Captain McClellan of the engineer corps, who accompanied the expedition, being the line which separates the country open to settlement by whites from the Indian Territory. In so doing he ascended the valley of Otter Creek, a *"one bold running stream,"* with *"several thousand acres of rich alluvial land with timber in abundance. The timber – pecan, black walnut, white ash, hackberry, cottonwood, & c. extends from the mouth of the creek to its sources, some twenty miles."* (pp. 15, 16)

Eight miles northwest from Otter he crossed Elk Creek, *"a bold running stream of good water,"* valley two miles wide, dense vegetation, timber of same description but not so abundant nor of as good quality. (p. 21)

He also observed the same description of timber at a distance, upon a creek on the opposite side of the river, near latitude 35 degrees 20 minutes, and longitude 100 degrees 30 minutes. (p. 26)

Not far from Elk Creek he found in one grove four or five hundred acres of post oak *"large tall and straight."* (p. 23)

Near the 101st degree in latitude 35 degrees 24 minutes he crossed another bold running stream, called from the good quality of its water. Sweetwater Creek, which he ascended. In a northwesterly direction, thirty miles. Its banks were fringed with large cottonwoods. Its *"soil a reddish loam, and quite productive."* Near the headwaters, about longitude 101 degrees 15 minutes, he found a colony of beavers, and a beaver dam built of cottonwoods *"fifteen inches in diameter,"* floated down the stream to their position. (p. 37)

Eleven miles west from the Sweetwater he found another *"very beautiful stream of good spring water,"* valley a mile wide, excellent grass, *"heavy growth of young cottonwood," – A "winter rest for large members of the prairie Indians."* (p. 58)

During the next ten miles he found several branches of good water and a *"large grove of cottonwood," "included with a brush lean-to by the Indians."*

Native American Lean-to
A native American Lean-to was generally a temporary, make-shift shelter that was quick to erect using raw materials that were readily available in the location.

Camping on the north fork of Red River, he says, *"I have never seen so much timber at any other place upon the plains in this longitude as you find here,"* (p. 40) His northwestern most camp was *"in a grove of large cottonwood trees upon the north bank of the river,"* ascertained by *"several observations" to be in longitude 101 degrees 55 minutes, and latitude 35 degrees 55 minutes."* (p. 41) These calculations were tested by travelling to a point on the Canadian twenty-five miles distant, ascertained by Lt. Simpson in 1810 to be near 101 degrees 45 minutes, and latitude 35 degrees 54 minutes. The soil near this latter point was *"a dark brown loam, covered with a heavy coating of wild rye and mesquite."* The timber, *"wild china, hackberry, willow, and cottonwood,"* the latter sometimes of *"enormous size;" one measured near the Canadian "was nineteen and a half feet in circumference at five feet above the ground."* – (p. 40)

On leaving the North Fork to go south to the main Red River, he says, *"I have travelled over a route on the plains west of the Cross Timbers, where water, grass, and wood were as good and abundant as upon the one over which our explorations have led us.."*(p. 41)

Statements of this kind are reiterated several times, and on page 95, the establishment of a military post is recommended near the western extremity of the Wichita Mountains, which, as before remarked, cross the 100th meridian.

There is no known obstacle to prevent the traveller from going, if he choose, directly from Fort Smith, near the Wichita mountains, to the valley of the Sweetwater, and thence to the Canadian by a route quite as direct, if not more so, than the Marcy route of 1819.

The reader, therefore, forming his own conclusions respecting the sagacity of the prairie Indians, the instincts of the beaver, and the habits of the overcup oak and the black walnut, will judge for himself how far Captain Humphreys is warranted in *"assuming the arid district to begin on the Albuquerque route"* at the 99th meridian.

But say that it does commence at that, meridian on both routes, and that his distances are correct to the Pacific slope, is it right for that interval of space to put both routes in the same category?

Is it right to ignore the fact that the Albuquerque route for 200 miles passes through the center of a population of 60,000 souls?

The first settlement, going west in N. Mexico,on Lt. Whipple's line, is Anton Chico, on the Pecos, 70 miles east of the Rio Grande. This town had 500 inhabitants, who *"raise corn, wheat, onions, beans and peas."*

Fifteen miles further Capt. Marcy found a *"beautiful little town on the Pecos, called Questa."* From a high cliff he could see the valley up and down the river for several miles, *"a magnificent carpet of cultivated fields of wheat, corn, and other grains was spread out directly beneath me, with the beautiful little river winding quietly and gracefully through the center."* (Sen. Ex. Doc. __, 31st congress 1st session, p. 190)

The various descriptions of the lower part of the same river, *"near the 32d parallel,"* are pretty well embodied in the following account, on degrees 45 and 47 of the same volume by Capt. Fremont of the quartermaster's department United States army, who followed its course from Delaware Creek 175 miles, viz.

"The Pecos is a remarkable stream, narrow and deep, extremely crooked in its course and rapid in its current. Its waters are turbid and better, and carry, in both mechanical mixture and chemical solution, more impurities than perhaps any other river in the south. Its banks are steep, and in a course of two hundred and forty miles there are but few places where an animal can approach them for water in safety. Not a tree or bush marks its course and one may stand on its banks and not know that the stream is near. The only inhabitants of it waters are catfish. and the antelope and wolf alone visit its dreary, silent and desolate shores. It is avoided even by the Indians."

Forty-three miles beyond *Questa,* on a creek which runs into the Rio Grande, Capt. Marcy found another town, Galiateo, where there was a large encampment of emigrants, laying in supplies of provisions, & c., for their outward journey to California.

There are three towns, therefore, on the road from Fort Smith before reaching either Sante Fe or Albuquerque.

On the lower route there is no settlement whatever between the waters of the Brazos and the banks of the Rio Grande.

Of seven counties into which the Mexican province of New Mexico was divided, five, containing by the census of 1850, a population of 39,607, are north of Bernalillo, the county in which Albuquerque is situated, and which has 7,751 inhabitants. Isleta, the point at which the Whipple has crosses the Rio Grande is the southernmost town in the same country. The remaining county, Valencia, had a population of 11,147, chiefly in towns, none of which are more than sixty miles south from Isleta, the lowest being at least one hundred miles above Fort Fillmore, the point near which the lower routes leaves the Rio Grande, going west. El Paso, it will be remembered, is not in New Mexico, and not in the United States, being a little south of the south line of the Gladston Purchase. Dona Ana and the settlements in the Mesilla valley were not in any organized county when the census was taken. Nearly the whole population of the old province of New Mexico, therefore, is either near or north of the line of the Whipple survey.

It has been frequently asserted that the finest portion of the valley of the Rio Grande is near the 32d parallel. Mr. Greig, who is pretty good authority, says that no part of New Mexico equals the valley of Taos, north of Sante Fe, *"in amenity of soil, richness of produce, and beauty of appearance."*

The Mexican settlements, however, extend beyond the Rio Grande. Due west from Albuquerque there are at least half a dozen villages within fifty miles.

According to Lt. Simpson, 45 miles west from Albuquerque, is the p___ __ Indian village of Laquna, and not far from Laquna the pueblo of Acoma. The former has a population of 800, and it on the San Jose, the valley of which, for the distance of fourteen miles beyond Laquna, *"is cultivated in corn and melons, the luxuriance of their growth attesting the good quality of the soil. I also noticed at different points a number of circular places upon the ground where wheat had been trodden out by the horses." (p. 129)* Near the same pueblo he saw 2,000 sheep in one flock, and speaks of the cattle as being numerous, *"on account of the good pasturage in the vicinity."*

Twenty-two miles beyond Laguna, Lieut. Simpson's route, course, for *"six miles, was directly across the valley of the*

Gailo," "one of the richest I have seen, its soil being a rich black loam."

Ninety miles from Luguna, and 135 miles directly west of Albuquerque, in the pueblo of Zuni, a village, according to Lt. Simpson, of 1,200 inhabitants, having *"large herds of sheep and horses, and extensively cultivating the soil."* According to Capt. Bulgreaves (p. 6) they had 10,000 acres in corn in 1852.

Governor Calhoun, in a report to the Commissioner of Indian Affairs, in October, 1849, describes the country between Zuni and Laguna as *"beautiful and rich in its extensive valleys, highlands and lowlands affording superior grazing, the purest and most delightful water, excellent pine timber." & c. & c.*

Zuni Pueblo, 1850 illustration

Compare the foregoing accounts with the following extracts from the *National Intelligencer* of Sept. 28, 1851, describing the country in the direction of Senora on Cooke's route, the only one at present practicable from the Rio Grande to the Gila River, *"portions of the valley of the Rio Mimbres might be cultivated to the extent of half a mile in breadth; but, with this exception, there is not an acre of land from the Rio Grande to the San Pedro (223 miles) acceptable of cultivation. But it must be understood that even in the valley of the Membres, as everywhere else in this region, nothing can be done in the way of cultivation but by means _____ __ or channels of irrigation. The whole area for one hundred miles south of the range of mountains about twelve miles south of the Copper mines is a barren, desert waste, without a single tree or bush, with but three or four springs of water, and destitute of all grass, save the parched and dry mesquite, some three or four inches high."* Further south, from Yuma, in Chihuahua, westward to Promteral, in Sonora, a strip bordering Cooke's route for about a hundred miles on the south, the intermediate distance *"is occupied with a continual series of high hills and mountains, without wood, or water, except at long intervals, and then the famished traveller may only find a few drops of water trickling from the mountainside. Hence it is, that in that region there is nothing to sustain life, and it can be occupied by man."*

This account is taken from the official reports of Mr. John B. Barlett, who was employed at the time as a commissioner to ascertain the Mexican Boundary, and who has sense written a letter to favor of the lower route, referred to in the defence of the Postmaster General's selection.

Another witness referred to in the same article is Lieut. Simpson, who says on page 138 of his report. *"By references to the map it will readily be seen that a route from Sante Fe to the Pueblo de los Angeles, is the direction suggested, running as it would intermediate between the southern detour of Cooke's route and the 'northern detour' of the Spanish Trail route, or, in other words, as direct __ _____ would not only be ____ ______ ____ much as three hundred miles, than either of these routes but ___ing by the pueblos of Laguna and Zuni, and possibly of the Maquis, situated still further westward, would furnish supplies of substance and repairs of outfit, for certainly the first two hundred if not three hundred miles of the way – ______ certainly not to be disregarded."*

They certainly are disregarded on the El Paso route, for, after leaving the Rio Grande the first settlement going west is at the Pimo villages, 355 miles by railroad line, 418 by Cooke's route. The next is at Fort Yuma on the Colorado, more than 600 miles from the Rio Grande.

On the Albuquerque route after leaving Zuni, 135 miles west of the Rio Grande, the next available settlements appear to be at the villages of the Moquis Indians, who according to Captain Bitgraves, had more than 10,000 acres planted in corn in 1852. By Mr. Aubrey's measurement, their villages are 163 miles beyond Zuni. Governor Merriweather reports then being 300 miles west of Sante Fe.

Near the Colorado, Mr. Aubrey found several Indian *"rancherios"* with crops of watermelons, pumpkins, corn, & c.

This was in 1851. His line of travel in the proceeding year was south of his route in 1854, and south of Lieut. Whipple's. Of his first route he says, *"A large portion of the trail over which I passed, say some 283 miles west from the Rio Grande, is,for the most part, admirably adapted to farming and stock raising."*

With what propriety, then, can the whole country along the 35th parallel, between the 99th meridian and the coast range, be condemned as *"uncultivatable regions."*

Neither Mr. Aubrey, nor Governor Calhoun, nor Lieut. Simpson, in any of their descriptions say one word about irrigation of artesian wells. Nobody has ever hinted or suggested the necessity of resorting to any such means to supply the wants of either farmers or travelers on the Canadian.

With what degree of justice, then, can the country along the 35th parallel be classed with a country which is neither inhabited nor cultivated, and which cannot be until water is first obtained by artificial means?

Nobody doubts that along the Whipple line vast tracts exist on both sides the Rio Grande that are now and always will be unfit for cultivation. But no one will pretend that the lands which feed the 60,000 New Mexicans, and the innumerable Indians between the Zuni village and the Sierra Nevado, are *"uncultivable;"* and all other testimony, official and unofficial, thus far published, proves incontestably that the uncultivable tracts are neither so numerous nor so extensive on the Albuquerque as they are on the El Paso route.

This is substantially conceded by Secretary Davis, who says on page 21 of his report: *"The principle characteristics of this route in comparison with others are, probably, its passing through or near more numerous cultivable areas, in more abundant natural supply of water as far west as the Colorado, and the greater frequency and extent of forest growth on the route between the Colorado and the Rio Grande."*

Before dismissing Captain Humphrey's opinions of the relative merits of the two routes, the reader is requested to notice particularly what that officer says of the supply of water on the lower route.

On page 80 of the first volume Pacific Railroad Reports and elsewhere in the same volume, are statements respecting the ability of railroad trains to carry sufficient supplies of water over spaces of one hundred and twenty-five miles.

The space particularly referred to on page 80, requiring water to be carried that distance for the use of ___gifice and passengers, is on the line selected by the Postmaster General for the **[Butterfield Overland] mail stages** over the Staked Plains.

Speaking of the same space on page 79, Captain Humphreys states: *"That its geological formation is such as to render the success of artesian wells in obtaining large supplies of water is certain."*

On page 60 he estimates the cost of these wells at $1,000 per mile, allowing one well, for every ten miles at *"$10,000 each well which is double that of an excessive estimate of the cost of a series of these wells."*

Full accounts will be found among the documents printed with the President's Message for 1855 and for 1856, of the unsuccessful attempts of a party under Captain Pope to obtain water at three different points; two of them on the line before referred to over the Staked Plains, the third on Lieut. Parke's line, west of the Rio Grande. These attempts commenced in May, 1855, and were continued until late in August, 1856. Early is the first season, *"in the opinion of*

Captain Pope, the practicability of constructing artesian wells on the Liano Estacado had been fully established." The practicability of getting water out of them seems to have been a very different affair, for after spending fifteen months time and over $60,000 in money, Captain Pope was compelled to stop without bringing any water to the surface beyond a small quantity for chemical analysis: all the water used by the party having been brought in carts fourteen miles from the Pecos River.

No images exist of this 1850 ***water drilling*** *effort. However it may nad been similar to the 1890 efforts of Hart and Co. drilling a well on Cliff Table in Custer County, Nebraska. Note the use of horses to turn the drill in the lower center of image.*

The reason assigned for stopping in August, 1850, at the depth of 361 feet was for the want of boring rods, all the boring material, including the *"ash tent poles of the party and command'* being exhausted and *"the country not affording supplies of suitable wood!"*

If this state of affairs had occurred on the Albuquerque route, the conclusion would have been that it would be cheaper to let travellers carry water from the Pecos in carts, as Captain Pope's party had done, than to go on boring at such expensive rates in a country which could not supply wood enough for boring rods the kind of tent-poles, the three failures having cost $20,000 apiece, which, according to Captain Humphreys, is *"four times as much as an excessive estimate"* of the cost of series of these wells, meaning, it is to be presumed, wells which supply water.

Being however, on the shortest and cheapest route to the Pacific and San Francisco, the expense was not regarded as a sufficient objection! Captain Pope was ordered to resume his labors, and to continue them until he succeeded in bringing water to the surface.

With each ____ staring him in the face, the correspondent of the *National Intelligencer* complains of the charge, that the selection of the El Paso route was a foregone conclusion.

The Postmaster General ar______ __ ____formed industry and perseverance to very little purpose, if he failed to discover that it was a foregone conclusion long before he had anything to do with it.

In a report made by the Senate Committee on Foreign Relations, in August, 1852, upon the Mexican boundary line adopted by Commissioners Bartlett and Conde, the confident belief is expressed *"that the most practicable route for a railroad across to the Pacific in this part of our territory will be found down the valley of the Gila, or the depressions near it; and explorations,so far, have clearly indicated that if the path or route is taken north of the town of Puma, the more difficult and impracticable the country is presented by reasons of its mountainous character."*

Mr. Bartlett having surrendered our claim to the country near the town of Paso (El Paso) a strip running west 170 miles, it was bought back again eighteen months after the date of the report above referred to, with another strip further south, 31 degrees 20 minutes, being the line for three degrees longitude, along the trail of Col. Cooke's wagon road, by the Gadsden Purchase for $10,000,000.

*The **Gadsden Purchase** is a 29,670-square-mile region of present-day southern Arizona and southwestern New Mexico that the United States acquired from Mexico by the Treaty of Mesilla, which took effect on June 8, 1854. The purchase included lands south of the Gila River and west of the Rio Grande where the U.S. wanted to build a transcontinental railroad along a deep southern route, which the Southern Pacific Railroad later completed in 1881–1883.*

Every nook and corner of the country extending west from El Paso has been explored. Scarcely a year has passed since Gen. Kearney's expedition, in 1815, without the pr_____ of an experienced party on some portion of the 35th parallel route. Commissioners were employed for several years in ascertaining and defining the boundaries under the treaty of Guadalupe Hidalgo and the Gadsden Purchase.

In November, 1853, before the latter treaty was concluded, Secretary Davis writes to Lieut. Parks that *"the great emigrant trail known as Cooke's route, having been sufficiently explored will not receive your attention."*

In the same letter he says: *"As the whole country between the Gila and the Rio Brovo (Rio Grande) embraced in the parallels of latitude 62 degrees and 31 degrees, has been well covered with astronomical observations, it will probably not be necessary for you to impede your progress in checking the run of your work by elaborate astronomical observations."*

To this ample lack of information, on hand in November, 1853, covering the space between the Rio Grande and the mouth of the Gila, there has been added:

1st. Lieutenant Park's survey in 1854.

2nd The labors of the Mexican boundary survey, which Capt. Humphreys says in February 1855 *"are now in progress."*

3rd An additional exploration by Lieutenant Parks in 1855: the one which resulted in improving the *"shortest and best route"* by the discovery of another *"shorter and better"* upon which water could be obtained through conduits 12 miles and 21 miles long.

Besides these three surveys, there have been since November, 1853, three other surveys on the El Paso route:

1. Captain Pope;s east of the Rio Grande.
2. Lieutenant Williamson's, west of the Colorado.
3. Lieut. Parke's on the Pacific, ____, Los Angeles and San Jose, in California; and as already stated, Capt. Pope has been pretty steadily employed since May, 1855, in boring for water.

On the other hand, on the Albuquerque route, there has been one exploration, and only one – that of Lieut. Whipple.

The result of that exploration was reported in February, 1855, as comparing favorably with the El Paso route in every respect, except its greater length, greater elevations, and excessive cost.

In November, 1853, it was stated that a more careful examination has resulted in reducing the distance 100 miles, the elevation very materially – at one point alone 800 feet – and the cost from $175,000,000 down to $64,000,000.

It was also reported at the same time that there was a strong probability of improving the route still further by shortening distance and avoiding costly construction.

After such extremely favorable indication one would expect, as a matter of course, to hear from the next annual report whether there had been any further reduction in the distances or the estimated cost: whether its faults in these particulars had been so far obviated as to place it on a level with *"the shortest and cheapest route."*

If any such expectation existed, it was disappointed. In the report for 1856, a sort of parenthesis of exactly eighteen words, inserted between the accounts of two new explorations on the El Paso route, informed the reader that while Lieut. Parke was on his way form one point on that route to another *"the Mohave River and basin were explored and found to have no connection with the Colorado River and basin."*

These word, uttered in a style usually applied to arctic discoveries, *"geographically interesting, but practically unimportant,"* are all that relate to the Albuquerque route in the report for 1856, and contains all the information contained since the Whipple survey in 1853.

Without attempting at present to bring the forgoing paper to a conclusion, the writer deems it proper to state, that when it was written he knew nothing of Lieut. Beale's late expedition from New Mexico to California, and had not seen either of the volumes containing Captain Whipple's Report. Of course, he could not avail himself at the time of the overwhelming array of evidence in favor of the route near the 35th parallel, so carefully collected by Captain Whipple, or the corroborating and still stronger testimony supplied by Lieutenant Beale.

July 14, 1858
Butterfield's Route Through Arkansas Will Encourage Rail and Telegraph Lines To be Established

July 14, 1858, Wednesday, page 2
Arkansas True Democrat, Little Rock, Arkansas

FROM THE *FORT SMITH HERALD* we learn that the **Overland Mail Company** have received and put horses and stages on the line. By this time, we presume, a person can go to California by stages. It seems to us that the importance of this movement has never been fully understood. It must, necessarily, induce stations, taverns, shops, and settlements all along the route, and tend, in no small degree, to the rapid settlement of the country. Communication will have to be kept up with Memphis, and boats built for the purpose, kept upon the Arkansas, at all seasons. The fact of this route being in operation ought to give a new impetus to the Little Rock and Fort Smith branch railroad. Will not a telegraph line be established? The capital of our young and thriving State should, by all means, be in communication with the rest of the world, and it is time that this enterprise was set on foot.

July 14, 1858
Butterfield Agrees to Southern Route
Memphis is the Eastern Terminus

July 14, 1858, page 1
Arkansas True Democrat, Little Rock, Arkansas

Butterfield and Co., who contracted for the **Overland Mail** to California last year, and have been petitioning Congress to locate over what is known as the central route, have now acquiesced in the urgent and persistent requisition of the Postmaster General to adopt the southern route, with Memphis as the eastern terminus. They will start on the first of July. *[NOTE: **The Overland Mail** actually started mid-September.]*

July 17, 1858
Stagecoaches Arrive, More to Come

July 17, 1858
Arkansas State Gazette and Democrat, Little Rock, Ark.

Overland Mail Movement – Messrs. Glover and Bates, left here on Thursday morning last with four stages of the **Overland Mail Company,** built expressly for this route. Mr. Bates superintends the road from Preston to Fort Chadburn, and Mr. Glover, from Fort Chadburn to El Paso. Only six of these stages reached here on the Lady Walton and there remains about sixty more to come, which are expected daily.

Messrs. Butterfield, Crocker and Fox, left here on Thursday evening last, having in charge one stage for the road between here and St. Louis. **Mr. Butterfield** goes home, and Messrs. Crocker and Fox, are at work on their respective divisions, putting on stock & c. *[&c. is an abbreviation of etc., et cetera, meaning and others, or, and so forth.]*

A company, under charge of Mr. Talcoft, will leave here in a few days, to work the road in the Choctaw Nation. So the work goes gravely on. We throw up our old hat and say – "Hurrah for **Butterfield** again."

The article below is about this former Governor of Arkansas. Thomas Stevenson Drew (August 25, 1802 – January 1879) was the third Governor of the U.S. state of Arkansas.

July 21, 1858

Ex Governor Fails to Endorse Southern Route for the Upcoming Butterfield Overland Mail

July 21, 1858, page 1

Arkansas True Democrat, Little Rock, Arkansas

Ex-Gov. Drew in Hempstead County – Washington, July 10, 1858 – Today Ex-Gov. Tho's S. Drew, the self-constituted, disorganizing candidate for Congress, addressed the people here agreeable to this appointment... The failure of the Camden convention to adopt just such a platform as the Batesville convention did, to express an opinion upon the proper route for the **Overland Mail to California** and the Pacific Railroad... were in the ex-Gov.'s lucid (?) mind, all sufficient reasons for disregarding the action of said convention, and treating the whole proceedings and distinguished nominee as bogus...

July 28, 1858
Butterfield's Future Sub-Contractor is Already Operating a Route from Memphis to Fort Smith

July 28, 1858
Fort Smith Times, Fort Smith, Arkansas

REESIDE & Co. - On Thursday evening, the 15th inst., some excitement was manifested of the arrival of the Des Arc mail, direct from that place, conveyed in a vehicle called "Fort Smith," which, by the by, in our humble opinion, surpasses any thing of the kind that Arkansas has been accustomed to. And now that this route has been put into operation, we suggest to those living along the road to keep it in good order as many advantages are to be gained thereby. Mr. Reeside, accompanied by Mr. Curry, came with the mail and spent several days here, during which time, he secured to himself many friends, by his gentlemanly and social spirit always manifest He likes Fort Smith very much, and says he intends to settle here *after a while.*

Through tickets can be had on this line, in No. 1 four-horse coaches, to Memphis and New Orleans Mr. J. K. McKenzie, proprietor of the City Hotel, is the Agent.

July 28, 1858
Preparations for the Overland

July 28, 1858
Fort Smith Times, Fort Smith, Arkansas

It will be seen by the following from the Joaquin *Republican* of June 2nd, that **Butterfield & Co.**, are in earnest about making arrangements for running their overland route.

THE OVERLAND STAGES - THE preparations for placing these stages upon the Overland route have commenced in earnest, and the first mail across the country will be dispatched on the 15th of September, though the stages will probably commence running from San Francisco a month earlier. The route from San Francisco will be down the San Jose Valley, through Pacheco's Pass, down the Tulare Valley, through Tejon Pass, and via San Bernardine to Fort Yuma, and thence in the Atlantic States.

Mr. Kenyon, a brother of Mr. Martin Kenyon, of the firm of **Butterfield & Co.** have been in this vicinity recently, and has engaged in purchasing horses for the use of the company, for which 2,400 will be required. He has already obtained three hundred, of which thirty-six were purchased of Mr. Paige, of this city, being the horses formerly used by the opposition line between Stockton and Sonora, and twenty-two from Messrs. Fisher & Co., stage proprietors in this city. A large number were obtained from Mr. John White, at the Elk Horn Ranch. We understand that Messrs. Fisher & Co., are authorized to purchase eight hundred of the number required for the concern. We congratulate our citizens upon the commencement of this great and useful enterprise.

July 28, 1858
False Report that Overland is Postponed Until October 1st

July 28, 1858
Washington Telegraph, Washington, Arkansas

POSTPONEMENT OF THE **OVERLAND MAIL** – The time of the departure of the **Overland Mail** to California has been postponed to the 1st of October.

July 28, 1858
James Glover, Butterfield Superintendent, Gives Details on the Upcoming Butterfield Route

July 28, 1858, Wednesday, page 3

Arkansas True Democrat, Little Rock, Arkansas

From the Gallatin (Tennessee) *Examiner* – LETTER ON THE ***OVERLAND MAIL ROUTE*** – *Gallatin, June 12, 1858* – COL. T. BOYERS*: Sir* – I am in receipt of your note of the 9th, asking for information on the nature of the contract entered into by the **Overland Mail Company** with the Postmaster General, the services to be rendered, the pay they receive, and as much of the details of their plans of operation as I may see proper to communicate.

The company is composed of the principal business men of the American Express Co., all of them men of great energy and fine business talent and habits. They contracted to carry the mails semi-weekly from Memphis and St. Louis to San Francisco, to go through in twenty-five days – mails to be carried in four horse coaches, suitable for the conveyance of passengers and the security of the mails. Their contract is for six years, to commence on the 16th of September next, and they are to receive six hundred thousand dollars annually for their services, to be paid quarterly.

The company have obtained the consent of the Postmaster General to start their mails from St. Louis and Memphis, on the 17th of July, to run as far as Fort Belknap, Texas, and from San Francisco to Fort Yuma, on the Pacific side – mails to be carried twice a month, and the gap can be filled, so as to commence through service by the 1st of October.

It will require 1,200 horses to stock the road. They have already about 900 head of horses and mules, and all their coaches and harness – and their agents are now actively engaged in getting them on the route.

Through the settlements, say from St. Louis and Memphis to Fort Belknap, Texas, on the end of this route, and from San Francisco to Fort Yuma, 1,000 miles, there are but few settlements, and it will cost very heavily to transport provender *[dry food, such as hay or oats, for livestock]* in wagons; they will depend a great deal on grazing, and as mules will do better on short feed than horses, they will be necessary though there is but little doubt, that in two years there will be a chain of settlements along the entire route; hundreds of families have settled on the route through Texas, since the exploring parties passed through in January and February.

Through the unsettled country, the company will have to erect stations every 12 or 16 miles for their own convenience; at each of these stations there will be a smith's shop, wood and harness shops, and a post office, and at some of them there will be stores to trade with the Indians, and to supply persons in the employ of the company, and emigrants thus forming the nucleus of a settlement.

As to your suggestion of the danger of the stations being broken up, and the mails robbed by Indians, I would say that I do not apprehend much difficulty as the government will place a regiment of cavalry on the route, who will be continually moving from one station to another, and will thus prevent any marauding bands getting near the line, before they are discovered.

As regards the practicability of the route, I have little or no doubt, as it has been fully explored by competent men sent out by the company, and they report very favorably of it; indeed stages have been run from San Antonio, Texas to San Diego, regularly since last July, and they have never been interrupted.

Their route is the same as the **Overland Mail Company**, from El Paso to Fort Yuma, and will be discontinued after the 1st of October.

The company will build a telegraph line from St. Louis and Memphis via Fort Smith to San Francisco, which will prove a great convenience both to them and the country. I have been and am still of the opinion that the government ought to build it. *[referring to the telegraph line]*

According to the original contract, the company agreed to bring these two branches together at Little Rock, but on examination of the road from St. Louis to that point, it was found to be bad, the company procured the consent of the Postmaster General to select Ft. Smith as the point of connection, that being considered a better point, and they also procured his consent to carry their mails and passengers from Little Rock to Fort Smith in boats.

The distance from St. Louis to San Francisco, is 2,300 miles.

I have, I believe, given you all the information that is necessary relative to this stupendous undertaking, and I will only add that it is in the hands of men who know no such word as fail, and that there is not the shadow of a doubt but they will carry it out successfully, and that they will have more applications for passage than they can accommodate. Yours Truly, JAMES GLOVER

August 4, 1858
Survey Expedition Making Headway

August 4, 1858
Washington Telegraph, Washington, Arkansas

We learn from Mr. Nichols, agent of the **Overland Mail Company** at this place *[Fort Smith]*, that the company under charge of Mr. Talcott, working tho road from here to Preston, are making fine headway, and that ere long the road will be in splendid order for traveling. We also learn from the same source that Mr. Crocker is looked for hourly. - *Ft. Smith Times, July 21*

[NOTE: In the late summer of 1858, John Butterfield & Co. began to realize that the Arkansas River water levels might not rise enough to use his steamboat, the Jennie Whipple, from Fort Smith to Memphis.

As Butterfield hastily searched for an alternative, John T. Chidester had been running a newspaper advertisement (displayed on the following page) all summer, promoting his Chidester stage lines across Arkansas. Also, 'Chit' already had a postal contract to carry regular U.S. Mail from Fort Smith to Memphis by stagecoach three times a week.

No doubt, this combination, along with positive word of mouth concerning the reliability of the Chidester stage lines were all a part of influencing Butterfield & Co.'s choice to sign a sub-contract with John T. Chidester to carry the Overland Mail and passengers from Fort Smith to Memphis, beginning September 16, 1858. Within 12 months, Butterfield ended this sub-contract and stocked the Memphis to Fort Smith trail with his own stock and employees.]

To the Traveling Public.

GREAT WESTERN
Four Horse Stage Coach Line.

ARRIVES AND DEPARTS DAILY.

CHIDESTER, REESIDE & CO., PROPRIETORS.

THIS LINE OF COACHES runs daily from Washington, Ark's, to Gaines' Landing on the Mississippi river, reaching both points every day at noon, and making the trip through in

FORTY-EIGHT HOURS.

This line passes through the following county seats; Camden, Ouachita county; Hampton, Calhoun county; Warren, Bradley county, and Monticello, Drew county.

It connects each day at Gaines' Landing with the regular **Steam Packets**, both ascending and descending the Mississippi river, so that passengers may not be delayed at that point. It also connects each day at Camden, with the daily stage line of Messrs. Stuart & Co., running from Camden to Hot Springs.—And it is decidedly the shortest and most commodious stage route from all the south-western counties of Arkansas, and the upper, eastern and north-western counties of Texas, to the Mississippi river.

The Plank road through the Mississippi bottom to Gaines' Landing, is now undergoing repairs, and the proprietors of this line have made arrangements for the repair and placing the bridging in good order; so that the only serious difficulty in the road, (crossing the Mississippi bottom) will be in a great degree obviated.

The proprietors have placed upon this line an excellent lot of stage coaches—most of them entirely new and of the best quality, and also, most excellent teams—having taken great pains in the purchase of the same. They are determined to spare no pains to accommodate travelers, and afford a safe and rapid passage along the line, and it is, therefore, with confidence that they invite the patronage of the public.

CHIDESTER, REESIDE & CO.,
PROPRIETORS.

July 21, 1858. 29-tf

Source: Washington Telegraph, August 4, 1858 Washington, AR

August 13, 1858
Telegraph Line Needed
Along the Butterfield Route

August 13, 1858, Friday, page 2
Arkansas Intelligencer, Van Buren, Arkansas

...The establishment of a telegraph line from Memphis to California is, every day, becoming more and more, a matter of necessity.

A line from Memphis to Van Buren and Fort Smith via Little Rock will pay. In fact when we take into account the trade of the Arkansas River above this point, amounts to millions of dollars worth of goods are carried up every year, and the products of the up country carried down, that the present means of communication are slow and uncertain; it is evident that a line could be supported by the mercantile interests alone. In addition to this the newspaper press could well afford to pay a handsome sum toward its erection. Both here, and at Van Buren and Fort Smith, with a telegraph line in operation, a daily, or at least tri-weekly newspaper, would become a necessity. It has been supposed that in view of the establishment of the **Overland Mail Route**, the construction of a wagon road to the Pacific and the government interests along the route, that one would be built by the government, but this is uncertain, and if it would pay government, it will pay individual enterprise.

We would be glad to see this subject agitated, as it is a matter of importance and is fast becoming one of necessity.

[The above article was earlier printed in the August 4, 1858 issue of the Arkansas True Democrat, page 2.]

August 13 (?), 1858
John Butterfield Praised

Summer, 1858 - perhaps Aug 13, 1858
Fort Smith Times, Fort Smith, Arkansas

John Butterfield who was the man who routed the Overland stage... he had gained a reputation with the traveling public as an expert driver, a keen judge of horses, and a safe man with the whip, and for his skill in managing refractory horses.

A steamboat had arrived at the wharf with several of the large Concord coaches that were to be used on the line, and a number of the **Overland** employees were on hand with teams to get them off of the boat and up town.

A team was hitched to a coach that had been rolled on the wharf. The horses were fractious and balked at their heavy load. Several drivers, skilled men in their line of occupation, attempted to get the team to pull the coach up the bank, but failed to move the unwilling animals. Finally, **John Butterfield**, who was standing with sightseers nearby, climbed to the seat, took the reins in his hands and gave the word to the horses to move, and move they did and pulled the coach up the steep bank without hesitancy. The moment he took the reins the refractory beasts recognized the hand of a master. [as quoted in "Butterfield Overland Mail" by R. Conklin, page 218-9]

August 13, 1858
Stagecoaches, Horses and Mules

August 13, 1858, Friday, page 2
Arkansas Intelligencer, Van Buren, Arkansas

THE **OVERLAND MAIL** – A large number of horses, mules and stages, belonging to **Butterfield & Co.**, contractors for carrying the **Overland Mail to California**, passed through this place on Monday last to make their stands on the Albuquerque route.

August 15, 1858
Eight Coaches Delivered

August 15, 1858
Fort Smith Times, Fort Smith, Arkansas

Captain C. Hanley, of the **Overland Mail Company**, arrived in the city on the 8th with twenty-five men bound for El Paso. They took with them eight coaches, and forty men with which to stock part of the line. We learn that some 200 mules and horses have been sent by the company to Fort Belknap [not Fort Breckenridge] to furnish Messrs. Bates' and Glover's departments. [as quoted in "Butterfield Overland Mail" by Roscoe Conklin, page 218]

August 21, 1858
8 Stagecoaches, 40 Mules and 25 Men Arrive

August 21, 1858, Saturday, page 2
Arkansas State Gazette and Democrat, Little Rock, Ark.

HOME NEWS – **OVERLAND MAIL COMPANY** – Captain G. Hauley, of the **Overland Mail Company**, arrived in this city *[Fort Smith]* on the 8th inst., with twenty-five men, bound for El Paso. They have with them, eight coaches, and forty mules, with which to stock a part of the line. We learn that some 200 mules and horses have been sent by this **Company** to Fort Belknap, to furnish Messers. Bates and Glover's department of the line. The fact is, the movements of **Messers. Butterfield & Co.**, are such now, as to warrant the conviction that this route will be put into operation in due season.

We learn from an authentic source, that mail service is about to be ordered on the 35th parallel route, form Fort Smith to Albuquerque. This, at once, establishes the fact that the 35th parallel route is known to be a good one, and that our Senators have not been asleep, but have been on the alert for the benefit of their constituents. - *Fort Smith Times, Aug. 15th*

August 28, 1858
Butterfield Overland to Commence

August 28, 1858, Saturday, page 3
Arkansas State Gazette and Democrat, Little Rock, Ark.

WASHINGTON, AUGUST 19 – The **Butterfield Company** will commence carrying the Pacific **Overland Mail** the 5th of September.

August 28, 1858

Butterfield Overland to Commence

August 28, 1858, Saturday, page 2, column 6

Arkansas State Gazette and Democrat, Little Rock, Ark.

THE OVERLAND MAIL – The party now engaged in establishing stands and stocking the route through Texas, was at Balknap on the 16th ult. They have adopted the wise precaution of stocking the line through that state with Texas horses. The line from St. Louis to Preston has been stocked with Missouri horses and mules.

September 1, 1858

Captain Hawley, of the Overland Mail co., Left for El Paso

September 1, 1858

Arkansas True Democrat, Little Rock, Arkansas

From the *Fort Smith Times,* we have this information concerning the **Overland Mail Company:**

Capt. Hawley, of the **Overland Mail Company,** with his party fully equipped, left here on the 12th for El Paso, They all left in fine health and spirits. May they so continue, and may nothing occur to mar for a moment, the pleasure and success of the party.

[The above article was also printed in the Aug. 28, 1858 issue of the Weekly Arkansas Gazette, page two.]

September 4, 1858

Ability to "Survive" Overland Round Trip Promoted as a Measure of Good Health as a Result of the Searcy Sulphur Springs

September 4, 1858

Arkansas State Gazette and Democrat, Little Rock, Ark.

SEARCY SPRINGS, WHITE CO., ARKS, AUG. 29 – MESSRS. DANLEY & HOLTZMAN – *GENTLEMEN:* I have, been attending these Springs several days with my family. We find the Sulphur water here excellent. Indeed it is superior to any I have ever seen in the State, or elsewhere, and unlikely any other Sulphur water. It is very cool and pleasant to drink, whilst all other Sulphur water, used for its medical properties, is offensive both to the taste and smell. This water acts as a gentle aperient *[medicine chiefly used to relieve constipation]*, having a fine effect on the liver. It also acts finely on the Kidneys.

In fact its curative properties cannot be beaten for such diseases as Liver complaint, Rheumatism, Dyspepsia, and indigestion.

Many years ago I knew an old gentleman who was sorely afflicted with a most hopeless case of Dyspepsia, and after trying for years the best medical aid that could be procured in the country, he sold all his possessions and moved to these Springs. When he came here his condition was such that his stomach would reject everything, even the most innocent part of a chicken. After remaining here for two years his health was perfectly restored, and although he was 70 years of age, he afterwards went the **Overland Route to California** and came back in perfect health, performing the trip as well as any of the young men in his company – this Spring affords water enough for one thousand people, who use it daily. It is used by all for cooking, drinking, washing, and for stock, and affords an abundance for all those purposes.

I was here four years ago, since which time the whole country has improved 100 per cent.

There is more of the best quality of upland in White County than any other county in the State; and the farmers in this portion of the county will compare with those of any other portion of the State, indeed they are far in advance of any I have seen except on the Arkansas and Mississippi rivers.

There is to be an agricultural fair here in October just a few days before the fair at Des Arc, which if you wish to see a nice exhibition of everything that pertains to agriculture you should attend.

In point of trade Searcy is quite an extensive place, there being as many as eight substantial mercantile houses here. There are also a Tavern; our landlord is your old friend *John W. Bond*, who keeps without any exception the best house in the State. -D.

September 11, 1858
Butterfield Visits St. Louis

September 11, 1858, Saturday, page 2
Arkansas State Gazette and Democrat, Little Rock, Ark.

From the St. Louis Republican, 31st. ult – **Overland Mail to California** – We were pleased yesterday to meet with **Mr. Butterfield**, one of the active partners in the contract for carrying the **Overland Mail** between the Mississippi river (Memphis and St. Louis being the two points,) and San Francisco, California. He is here *[St. Louis]* to complete his arrangements for putting the contract into operation by the 15th of September. For this purpose the line has been stocked with horses, coaches, drivers and everything necessary to enable the Company to perform the contract with fidelity. The mail is to be carried in twenty-five days, and when the South west Branch of the Pacific Rail Road is completed to the western boundary of this State, it will be done in much less time. The route from Memphis and that from St. Louis connects at Fort Smith, Arkansas, and we have no fears of being able to attract our portion of the trade and travel on this route from the start. All success, we say, to the enterprise of **Messers. Butterfield and Co.** in this undertaking.

Aaron V. Brown

Source: The Miriam and Ira D. Wallach Division of Art, Prints and Photographs: Print Collection, The New York Public Library. " Honorable Aaron V. Brown Ex-Governor of Tennessee" New York Public Library Digital Collections. Accessed February 12, 2022.

September 15, 1858

Letter from Postmaster General to City of Memphis

September 15, 1858, Wednesday, page 4
Arkansas True Democrat, Little Rock, Arkansas

Postmaster General Brown on Post Office Affairs – Postmaster General Brown has declined a jubilee dinner tendered to him by the citizens of Memphis, but writes an interesting letter on post office affairs in reference to the invitation:

"I am here in your beautiful and prosperous city, on a rapid visit to Arkansas, where my private affairs require my attention. Nothing could give me greater pleasure than to partake of a public dinner, tendered to me by personal and political friends at Memphis, but the necessity of my return to Washington at the earliest possible moment deprives me of the gratification of accepting your said invitation.

Any testimonial from my fellow citizens indicating their approval of the manner in which I have discharged my public duties is always agreeable, but this one from the people of Memphis is peculiarly gratifying to me.

The apparent conflict of interest between your city and St. Louis in establishing the great **overland mail route to California**, seemed to preclude the possibility of arranging that route in a manner at once most beneficial to the country and satisfactory to the two cities whose interests would be most materially affected there by. But I was happily enabled to accomplish these objects by making both places termini of the route, thus conferring equal benefits on them and giving postal and traveling faculties to all parts of our extensive country. The cities and States lying on both sides of the Mississippi can scarcely be dissatisfied with the arrangement lately made for opening a free communication with California, and of developing the resources, mineral and agricultural, of that vast and interesting country which lies between the Atlantic and Pacific oceans.

The route from New Orleans by Tehuauntepec, *[NOTE: the Isthmus of Tehuantepec in Mexico, is the shortest distance between the Gulf of Mexico and the Pacific Ocean.]* and from the same great city by San Antonio and **overland** to San Diego, give to Louisiana and Texas all they can desire.

The route from Memphis and St. Louis, meeting at Fort

Smith, confer on Tennessee, Arkansas and southwestern Missouri, most important advantages.

The route from Independence to Sante Fe, and thence to California, and the one from Hannibal and Saint Joseph's through the South Pass to Salt Lake City and to Sacramento, furnish very great facilities to all parts of Missouri, and incidentally to the northwestern States, which will be easily and promptly reached by branches from the great route.

I trust Memphis will also be greatly benefited by the system of express mails which has been recently organized. Under that system mails are sent from the great cities on the Atlantic to those on the Mississippi River, in what, at one period, would have been considered an incredible short space of time. From Boston, Philadelphia, Baltimore and Washington, they are sent to Cincinnati, St. Louis and Chicago, under the care of agents, who travel with them nearly the entire route, giving their receipt for them at starting and taking one on delivery, all of which receipts are forthwith forwarded to the department. In this way we are now enabled, whenever a robbery is committed or a failure takes place, to know exactly in whose hands the same occurred. By these means depredations are often prevented, and the arrival of the mails secured with as much certainty as that of passengers. To these through agents I have distinctly announced, that if passengers are permitted to go ahead of the mails I will certainly remove them – for there is no reason why one should go faster than another.

The arrangements for mail service on the Mississippi River will, I hope, prove eminently satisfactory to the towns and settlements on its borders. By letting the routes in sections or subdivisions, a daily mail is furnished by river, as heretofore, from Memphis to New Orleans, and greater speed and certainty are secured in its transmission and delivery.

In addition to this, the department has contracted for the transportation of the great Cairo and New Orleans mail by the railroad from Columbus, Kentucky, by the Grand

Junction, Canton, etc., to New Orleans, Natchez, Vicksburg, Napoleon, Helena, and the cities above Memphis, will find their communication with the great emporium of the west greatly facilitated by the increased rapidity in the transmission of the mails on this route.

You are pleased to refer in complimentary terms to my connection with the present administration as one of the constitutional advisers of the President. Although my services as a member of the cabinet have not been conspicuous, your kind approval leads me to hope that they may have been to some extent useful and satisfactory to the country.

I hope that you will excuse the length of this communication, which I have extended beyond my original intention, in the hasty review I have made of the various subjects connected with the administration of the post office department, which I thought might be interesting to you, as they concern the prosperity of your city. – Aaron V. Brown

September 18, 1858
Overland Mail Begins

September 18, 1858, Saturday

Arkansas State Gazette and Democrat, Little Rock, Ark.

The **Overland Mail** — On the fifteenth of the present month the company according to contract, commences their operations. We understand that the company have the route completely equipped and are ready for business. We are further advised that the service will be made with ease: that the company have worked upon the road along the route and improved it very much, where the road was nearly utterly impassable in some places have made it a good road, by zealousness and energy. These gentle men, **Messers. Butterfield & Co.** doubtless deserve much praise and encomiums *[encomium: a speech or piece of writing that highly praises someone or something]* for their never tiring efforts and endeavors to to execute the functions of their undertaking on the route.

Fort Smith, Ark., Sept. 15th, 1858.

DEAR SIR:

In view of the fact that the first mail by the Overland Route from California, will arrrive at this place on the 13th of October next, the citizens of Fort Smith and the surrounding country, have determined to celebrate that event. We would, therefore, be glad to have you visit us on the occasion.

You are aware that Fort Smith is the point where the St. Louis and Memphis branches of the Overland Mail route form a junction.

Hoping that you may regard the occasion sufficiently National in its character to induce you to honor us with your presence, and that it may be both convenient and consistent with your engagements to do so,

We remain, very respectfully, your obedient servants.

J. J. WALTON, *Mayor*,
F. WOLFE,
GEORGE MORLEY,
B. T. DUVAL,
M. SPARKS,
JAMES BATERSBY,
DR. J. H. T. MAIN,
R. P. PULLIAM,
JOSEPH BENNETT,
JOHN ROGERS,
G. S. BIRNIE,
HENRY BECKEL,
S. L. GRIFFITH,
DR. N. SPRING,
THO'S VERNON,
A. G. MAYERS,
JOHN F. WHEELER, *Committee of Invitation.*

To

Invitation to September 15, 1858 celebration to be held at Fort Smith
when the first Overland stage was expected to arrive.
Source: Image courtesy of the Arkansas State Archives

This **Overland Mail** is an undertaking of much and fearful responsibilities, as it is running most of the way through an uninhabited portion of the country, there being but little advantages of either water or grass, and through an almost endless desert called Llano Estacado, *[see note below]* the heat of which is almost unendurable by man or beast; thus we deem it a fearful undertaking involved upon the contractors. But the perfection of this route at all events will be of much importance to the larger portion of the country at a future day, and it is to be hoped by the people of the west that it will be successfully carried into operation. It will, we think, be the fore runner of the great national Pacific rail road to California.

Since the above was put in type one of the coaches passed through this city on Thursday last, on its first trip, with three passengers. This coach was drawn by four fine able looking horses, well calculated, we think to stand the hardships that are about to be involved upon them. The coach was a well built concern, adapted to carrying passengers and to stand the rough roads over which it has to travel.

[Note: The Llano Estacado, commonly known as the Staked Plains, is a region in the Southwestern United States that encompasses parts of eastern New Mexico and northwestern Texas.]

Comanchero Traders on the Llano Estacado

September 22, 1858
Fort Smith Greets First Overland

September 22, 1858
Fort Smith Times, Fort Smith, Arkansas

Our citizens, always on the *qui vive [qui vive: on the alert or lookout]* for something good, were not lacking in the display of their readiness to perform good deeds on Saturday night last. They were fully represented by a party of young men who, prepared in two four-horse coaches, accompanied by a band of music, left town about half-past 10 o'clock that night for the purpose of meeting and escorting the Memphis branch of the **Overland Mail** into the city. Some three or four miles out we met it coming in at a 2:40 gait, and after making our turn and picking ourselves up, we succeeded in taking the lead of Reeside & Company's stage with the **Overland Mail** from Memphis, via Des Arc, from which place they traveled to this point in less than forty hours, the quickest time hitherto known in Arkansas.

[NOTE: On this final leg of the trip from Memphis, "2:40 gait" mentioned above refers to a horse traveling at a rather fast two beat rhythm, completing a mile in 2 minutes 40 seconds. This is about 22 miles an hour. Typical top speed for the stagecoach on a good road was 12 miles an hour.]

This done, the escort was informed by an express, that the St. Louis stage was about a mile from the city, when all, accompanied by the band and the Des Arc stage, started to meet this branch also and did so on the outer edge of the city, escorting it also to the City Hotel.

Fort Smith's John Rogers' City Hotel

While the mail was being made ready, a general salute in honor of the event was fired from the canon of the city by a party stationed for the purpose, after which the mail for California was started, amidst the cheering and rejoicing of a large number of our citizens, who soon afterward adjourned to champagne at Everle's where all spent a pleasant time till broad daylight, answering the first salute by a volley of 'popping corks' from sparkling Catawba. Each one felt well satisfied that he had done his part.

September 22, 1858
Wagon Road Expedition

September 22, 1858, Wednesday, page 3
Arkansas True Democrat, Little Rock, Arkansas

FROM WASHINGTON. WASHINGTON D. C. AUGUST 31, 1858 – THE ATLANTIC TELEGRAPH – ... The wagon road expedition under Lieut. Beale will start form Fort Smith about the 15th of September. It has been delayed somewhat on account of the absence of the secretary of war during the month of July.

It is to be supposed that the croakers *[croakers: people who gossip]* about Fort Smith who sneered upon the receipt of the news that the appropriation has passed for that purpose, now think it is *"a fixed fact."* But there is no telling what will satisfy the people of Fort Smith and Van Buren, favored as they are, and have been by the general government and through the efforts of members of the delegation whom they now abuse.

With the immense Indian appropriations paid there through the southern superintendency; the **Pacific Overland Mail**, the wagon road that is to be opened by Lieut. Beale, and the bill, which has passed the Senate, and it is believed at the next session will become a law, placing the U. S. District Court as an independent district, they forsooth are dissatisfied with our present Senators, and wish to send a man from that vicinity to attend to the interests of that section!...

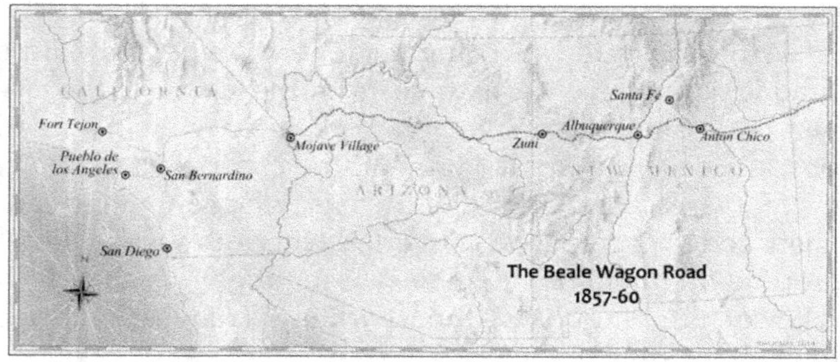

In 1857, Lieutenant Edward Fitzgerald Beale was assigned the job of building a wagon road across New Mexico and Arizona near the 35th parallel. Beale had had many years' experience in the west, first with the U.S. Navy in California, then with Kit Carson and John C. Fremont, and later, on government business and explorations in Arizona, New Mexico, Colorado, Nevada, Utah, and California.

Beale's road roughly followed Lt. Amiel Whipple's trail west across Arizona through the Flagstaff area and then headed west and a little north through Peach Springs and Truxton Wash (named for Beale's son), thence through the Kingman area and on to the Colorado River.

Source: Southwest Explorations

September 25, 1858
Overland Mail Departs Memphis

September 25, 1858, Saturday, page 2

Arkansas State Gazette and Democrat, Little Rock, Ark.

Almost every day brings to light some new move, and one nearer to completion on the part of the **Overland Mail Company** of their great undertaking. Coaches, animals, and men, are daily being dispatched to the different stations along the line, which is now almost complete. **Mr. Butterfield** and the Company, at whose head he stands, as well as the Agents thereof, deserve great credit at the hands of the public, for their energy in the carrying into execution, in season, their great contract.

September 25, 1858
Overland Mail Departs Memphis

September 25, 1858
Arkansas State Gazette and Democrat, Little Rock, Ark.

THE GREAT **OVERLAND MAIL** – The **Overland California United States Mail** left Memphis on Thursday morning last. It is brought by the Memphis and Little Rock Rail Road to within twelve miles of Madison, on St. Francis river, thence by light vehicles to Des Arc —
thence by Messrs. Chidester, Reeside & Co.'s line of four horse U. S. Mail coaches to Fort Smith, where it meets the St. Louis mail.

Train Tresles
Much of the railroad track across the "great Swamp" between Hopefield and Madison was elevated on trestles. No period photo exist of this stretch of track, however this particular image of similar trestle is near Rogers, Arkansas.

The White River at Des Arc.
When water levels were favorable, the Overland traveled by steamboat from Memphis to Des Arc. When the Overland came from Memphis by train and stagecoach, they used a ferry to cross the White River at Des Arc. The ferry was run by Erwin, by Frith & Vader, and by William H. Harvey.

Messrs. Chidester, Reeside & Co., are sub-contractors under **Butterfield & Co.,** from Memphis to Fort Smith; the whole then proceeds over the plains to El Paso and California.

R. M. Brimmer. Esq., of the firm of Chidester, Reeside. & Co., who came with the **California Overland Mail**, early yesterday morning has our thanks for Memphis papers of Thursday. This, arrangement places Des Are within fourteen hours of Memphis. We are now "close neighbors" to the Bluff City. – *Des Arc Citizen.*

September 25, 1858
Overland Mail Departs Memphis

September 25, 1858
Arkansas State Gazette and Democrat, Little Rock, Ark.
Overland Mail —

Thursday last was the day on which the **Overland Mail** should have left St, Louis and Memphis, and San Francisco for this place. We expect the stage in this evening, from

Memphis, and the one from St. Louis on Sunday morning. We look forward to the period as one of the greatest events in our history. Our citizens will make some public demonstration on their arrival from Memphis and St. Louis, but a general "turn out" is expected when they arrive from San Francisco, Cal., which will be about the 10th or 13th of October next. – *Fort Smith Times*

September 29, 1858
Passenger on First Overland out of Memphis

September 29, 1858, Wednesday, page 2
Arkansas True Democrat, Little Rock, Arkansas

The *Citizen* pays the following deserved compliment:

"Col. B. C. Harley, U.S. mail agent for the State of Arkansas, spent several days in our town during the past week. He left yesterday morning in the coach carrying the first **Overland Mail** from the MIssissippi valley, bound for Fort Smith. We have known the Colonel near eighteen years. He is a gentleman of tried integrity, energy and determination, well suited for the responsible position he occupies under the general government. We explained to him the disadvantages of the White river valley labors under in reference to the reception of mail matter from the Mississippi river, and have assurances that he will use his best endeavor to have this evil corrected. *So mote it be."*

September 29, 1858
Work Crew on California Wagon Road

September 29, 1858, Wednesday, page 3
Arkansas True Democrat, Little Rock, Arkansas

The Van Buren *Intelligencer* has the following items in connection with the overland expedition:

"Last Saturday a train of twenty government wagons passed through this place for the purpose of joining Lieut. Beale's expedition to cut out a wagon road for the **Overland Mail,** from Fort Smith to California. An Escort Necessary – It was at first thought that the party under

Lieut. Beale, about to start for the purpose of constructing a wagon road from Fort Smith to the Colorado of the west, would be strong enough to defend itself from hostile Indians, but the government had received such alarming accounts of the outrages committed by the comanches as to induce it to send a considerable escort for the protection of the expedition. They are already at Fort Smith."

Garrison Avenue in Fort Smith, circa 1881

The First Butterfield Overland Mail Run in 1858

In 1858 the Pacific Railroad from St. Louis arrived at Tipton, Missouri and John Butterfield personally carried the first mail bag, boarding an Overland Stagecoach headed thru Fort Smith and on to San Francisco. Painted by Frank Nuderscher (1880 – 1959 for the Missouri Pacific Museum.

September 29, 1858
Overland Now Operating

September 29, 1858, Wednesday, page 2
Arkansas True Democrat, Little Rock, Arkansas

From the Fort Smith Times – **Overland Mail** – This mail line, went into operation on Thursday last. The two mails from Memphis and St. Louis, left the respective post offices, simultaneously, at 8 o'clock A.M., on Thursday morning last and arrived here on Sunday morning at 2 o'clock – the line from Memphis coming in about 120 minutes ahead of the line from St. Louis.

Our citizens were on the lookout for their arrival, and when it was announced the stages had arrived, the news was sent for the slumbering world, by the roar of cannon. The town appeared to be alive to the importance of this great enterprize which is to instigate a new era in the affairs of Arkansas.

One senior came home, with his better half, on the first trip of the stages from St. Louis, and he describes the travel as rapid and far ahead of all the mail facilities he has ever known in the stage line.

The coach left the Pacific railroad depot, at Tipton, at 10 minutes past six, and drove to the first station, where the host had illuminated his houses, and the trees that surrounded his residence, which produced a very imposing and pleasing effect. An ample supper had been prepared by the host, and a crowd of persons, who had assembled there to see the first stage leave for California, and a few gentlemen, who had gone out on the stage from St. Louis, to witness the departure of the mail for that far off region, sat down to and partook of the supper which had been set by the host, and as soon as supper was over, the old **Land Admiral, John Butterfield**, cracked his whip, and the passengers were soon in their places, and he started the coach, travelling all the way to Fort Smith at the rate of 7 miles per hour; and one Senior says, he was then able, for the first time, to comprehend what mail facilities in reality meant, when compared to the speed now used by our mail stages, which generally average about 3 $^{1}/_{2}$ miles to the hour.

The stage from St. Louis was filled with passengers, and had a large amount of baggage, and we learn that the stage was also well crowded from Memphis. The trip was made from Memphis and St. Louis in two days and 18 hours – the quickest trip ever made in Arkansas.

The whole line is in admirable order, and the teams are in good condition, and every man engaged in any way, was in his place, and prompt in the discharge of his duty, and seemed to partake of the spirit of the enterprise, which in extent, labor and difficulties, far exceed the laying of the Atlantic cable.

Here is an extent of 2,500 miles, the greater portion of which is over the plains, where there are no settlements, roamed by the wild Indian and the buffalo, stations have been built, and stock and men have been placed to carry on this greatest and most magnificent enterprise of the age – carrying the **Overland Mail** from the Atlantic to the Pacific Ocean.

It is the determination of the company to put the mail through in less than 25 days, the time allowed by the contract, and we have no doubt but it will be effected when such men as **Mr. John Butterfield**, and Mr. Hugh Crocker, have management of the matter — with them there is no such word as fail.

Mr. Ormsby of the *N.Y. Herald*, was the first through passenger on the **Overland Stage**, and proceeded on immediately to San Francisco. We hope he may have a safe journey, though we know it to be a fatiguing one.

***Waterman Lily Ormsby, Jr.**, reporter for the New York Herald, was the only through passenger on the first Overland Mail Co. stagecoach all the way from St. Louis to San Francisco.*

October 2, 1858
Slightly Different Than the Above Article

October 2, 1858, page 3
Arkansas State Gazette and Democrat, Little Rock, Ark.

The stage from St. Louis was filled with passengers, and had a large amount of baggage, and we learn that the stage was also well crowded from Memphis. The trip was made from Memphis and St. Louis in two days and 18 hours — the quickest trip ever made in Arkansas.

The whole line is in admirable order, and the teams are in good condition, and every man engaged in any way, was in his place, and prompt in the discharge of his duty, and seemed to partake of the spirit of the enterprise, which in extent, labor and difficulties far exceed the laying of the Atlantic cable. Here is an extent of 2500 miles, the greater portion of which is ever the plains, where there are no settlements roamed by the wide Indian and the Buffalo, stations have been built, and stock and men have placed to carry on this greatest and most magnificent enterprise of the age — carry the **overland mail** from the Atlantic to the Pacific Ocean.

It is the determination of the company to put the mail through in less than 25 days, the time allowed by the contract, and we have no doubt but it will be effected when such men as **Mr. John Butterfield**, and Mr. Hugh Crocker, have management of the matter — with them there is no such word as fail.

Mr. Ormsby of the *N.Y. Herald,* was the first through passenger on the **Overland Stage**, and proceeded on immediately to San Francisco. We hope he may have a safe journey, though we know it to be a fatiguing one.

We have information from a very reliable source — and in fact are requested to say to the public — that all of the petty difficulties heretofore existing among the Choctaw people are fully and amicably settled; that the leaders of the two parties that were, are now on terms of unity on all matters of difference between them. We are pleased to be able to make this announcement, for we anticipate for the Choctaw Nation a bright and growing future; the beginning of which is not far distant. They are going ahead daily and in many respects, are up with their neighbors and brothers of the States around them, and we say speed the time when the Territory now known as the Choctaw Nation will claim for itself immediate kin with the Territories and States of this great and growing Confederacy. – *Fort Smith Times.*

Choctaw Village near the Chefuncte, *by Francois Bernard, 1869*

October 2, 1858

Overland Route Starts at Hopefield, Arkansas

October 2, 1858, Saturday, page 2

Arkansas State Gazette and Democrat, Little Rock, Ark.

THE **OVERLAND MAIL** – HO ! FOR CALIFORNIA ! – Today at 6 o'clock the first mail over the **Overland Mail Route** to California, will leave Hopefield opposite to this city. It will be carried over the Memphis and Little Rock Rail Road a distance of twenty four miles, and from thence in stages to Fort Smith, where the Branch Line unites with it, and thence to San Francisco by the schedule appended below:

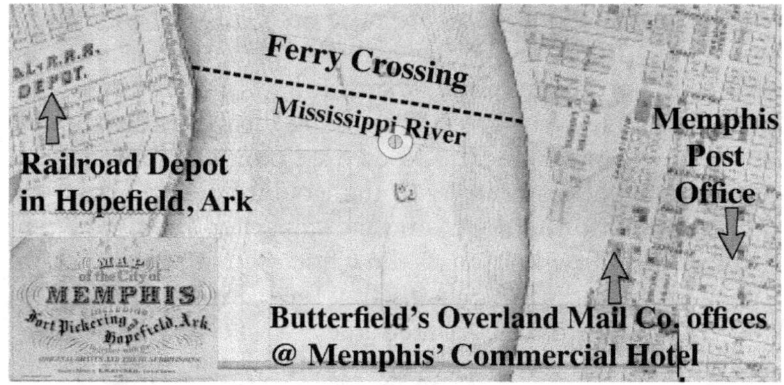

Twice a week, at the exact hour the ***Overland Mail*** *left St. Louis, it also left Memphis, crossing the Mississippi River by ferry to Hopefield, then on thru Fort Smith to arrive in San Francisco. This is an 1858 map of Memphis, Tennessee by E. W. Rucker showing location of the Commercial Hotel where the* ***Butterfield Overland Mail Co.*** *offices were located, and the location of the railroad depot in Hopefield, Arkansas. The location of the ferry shown here is from a map of Memphis printed in the May 14, 1862 issue of the New York Times. A historical marker on northeast corner of Jefferson and 3rd marks the Post Office's 1862 location.*

GOING WEST

Leave	Days	Miles
St. Louis, Mo. and Memphis, Tenn.	Mon & Thurs	___
P. R. R. Terminus, Mo.	Mon & Thurs	160
Springfield, Mo.	Wed & Sat	143
Fayetteville, Mo.	Thurs & Sun	100
Fort Smith, Ark.	Fri & Mon	65
Sherman, Texas.	Sun & Wed	205
Ft. Belknap, Texas	Mon & Thurs	146 1/2
Ft. Chadburn, Texas.	Tues & Fri	136
Pacos River.	Thurs & Sun	165
El Paso.	Sat & Tues	248 1/2
Soldier's Farewell.	Sun & Wed	150
Tucson, Arizona	Tues & Fri	184 1/2
Gila River, Arizona.	Wed & Sat	141
Fort Yuma, Cal.	Fri & Mon	135
San Bernardino, Cal.	Sat & Tues	200

Ft. Tejon (via Los Ang.) .... Mon & Thurs 150

Visatia (via Los Angeles)........ Tues & Fri..................... 127

Frebaugh's Ferry. .... Wed & Sat 82

Arrive at San Francisco. .... Thurs & Sun................ 163

GOING EAST

San Francisco, Cal. . ... Mon & Thurs .... ____

Firebaugh Ferry, Cal. . ... Tues & Fri..................... 165

Visalia, Cal. .... Wed & Sat 82

Fort Tejon (via L Angeles)...... Thurs & Sun................ 127

San Bernardino, do. .... Fri & Mon..................... 150

Fort Yuma, do. .... Sun & Wed.................. 200

Gila River, Arizona. .... Mon & Thur................ 135

Tucson, Arizona. .... Wed & Sat 141

Soldier's Farewell. .... Thurs & Sun........... 184 1/2

El Paso River. .... Sat & Tues 150

Pecos River, Texas. .... Mon & Thur........ ... 218 1/2

Fort Chadbourn, Texas. .... Wed & Sat 165

Fort Belknap, Texas. .... Thur & Sun 123

Sherman, Texas. .... Fri & Mon........... ... 146 1/2

Fort Smith, Ark. .... Sun & Wed.................. 205

Fayetteville, Mo. .... Mon & Thur.................. 65

Springfield, Mo. .... Tues & Fri..................... 100

P. R. R. terminus, Mo. .... Wed & Sat 143

Arrive at St. Louis, Mo.

and Memphis, Tenn. . ... Thurs & Sun................ 160

The rates of charges is, for through passage $200, and for the intermediate points between Fort Smith and Fort Yuma, not less than ten cents per mile. Messrs. Chidester & Co., who are the sub-contractors under **Butterfield & Co.**, between Memphis and Fort Smith, will make an early publication of the local rates through Arkansas.

This is the *first* step, taken in the grandest march of the age, the Pacific Rail Road. The train which takes the mail this morning across "Lost Swamp," a distance of twenty four miles, is a part of it – a link in the great chain which American enterprise and industry are ceaselessly forging – an enterprise which will never flag, and an industry which will not weary, until the two edges of the continent are bound together with "hooks of steel." Within seventy or eighty days more this chain will be lengthened out to the St. Francis River, thus spanning and bridging its first greatest obstacle – the dreaded "Mississippi Bottom Swamp." The worst is now over, and with the full and well organized force employed, the track-laying goes on at the rate of two miles per week. From the St. Francis to Little Rock, thence to Fulton, thence to marshall, Texas, thence to El Paso, and so onward to the shores of the Pacific, is but a work of time, which will be accomplished before our carrier-boys shall have gathered upon their faces the heard of manhood. We live in an age of miracles, in which credulity itself is reproached by facts for its want of sufficient faith. – *Memphis Bulletin*

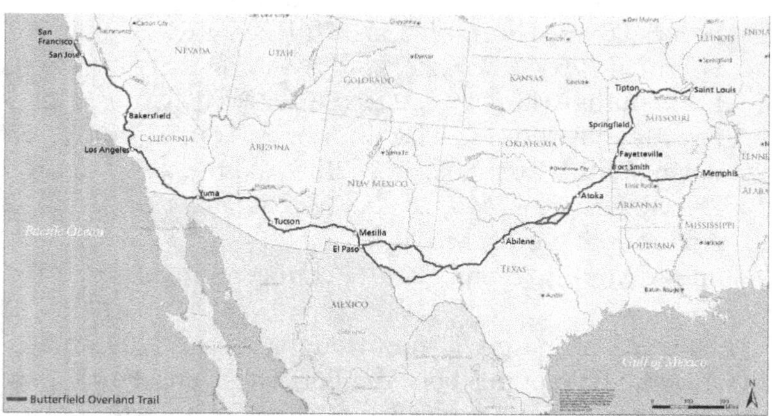

Butterfield Overland and National Historic Trail
Source: Special Resource Study, National Parks Service

October 2, 1858
Problems with the Memphis Route

October 2, 1858, Saturday, page 2
Arkansas State Gazette and Democrat, Little Rock, Ark.

THE **OVERLAND MAIL TO CALIFORNIA** – There have been

great rejoicings, at Fort Smith, over the first arrival of the **California Overland Mail** at that place. It appears that the first arrival of the St. Louis and the Memphis branches of that mail at Fort Smith were in fifteen minutes of each other. We had hoped to see if the citizens of Little Rock could get up a slight *enthusi* on the arrival of the Memphis branch of the same mail; but we have been disappointed.

The contrast is for carrying the mail, in stages, from St. Louis to Fort Smith, and from Memphis via Little Rock to Fort Smith — thence to California. We are informed that the contract has been complied with from St. Louis to Fort Smith, and the road stocked with stages — making better time than stages have ever made in the State. We regret that the contract has not been complied with on the route from Memphis, via Little Rock, to Fort Smith.

Overland Mail - The Start from Fort Smith for the Pacific Coast
First Coach Driven by John Butterfield, Jr.
Source: Frank Leslie's Illustrated Newspaper, Oct. 23, 1858

We are informed that the mail leaves Memphis on the Rail Road — that is well as far as that road goes. But we are further informed that, at the end of the Memphis rail road, there are no stages to receive the mail as provided in the contract, and that, instead of stage service, the mail is there put on horseback and carried to Des Arc. From Des Arc we are informed that Messrs. Reeside & Co., contractors on the Des Arc and Fort Smith route, carry the mail, in their stages, as far as Atlanta in Prairie county, where it is put in a buggy, or on a horse, and brought to the bank of the river opposite this place, brought across to the Post Office, and then returned, by the same conveyance, to Atlanta, where it is again put in the stages of Messrs. Reeside & Co., and sent on to Fort Smith.

However well the contractors may have done their duty on the route from St. Louis to Fort Smith, and however much credit they may be entitled to for *doing nothing but their simple duty* on that line, we regret to record the fact they have wholly failed to do their duty on the line from Memphis, via Little Rock to Fort Smith. They carry the mail from the other side of the St. Francis to Des Arc without stages, and they contracted to carry it in stages. Then they carry it from Atlanta to Little Rock and back to the same place in buggies or on horse back, or as best way they may. The only staging done on the route, is done by Messrs. Reeside & Co., who are contractors to carry the mail from Des Arc to Fort Smith.

That we may not be misunderstood, and that we may do injustice to no one, will state wherein the contractors for the **overland mail** have failed to comply with their contract on the route from Memphis, via Little Rock, to Fort Smith.

First — They have sub let their contract to Messrs. Reeside & Co., who are already contractors on the route from Des Arc to Fort Smith, and whose duties on their own contract are paramount to, and must take precedence of, any other duty or service.

Second — They have detained the mails by supplying this post office with their branch horse or buggy line from Atlanta, as the Des Arc and Fort Smith line can not lay over at Atlanta until this branch mail goes to Little Rock and returns — and this detention must be two days to each mail, and may be three days

Third — They have failed to furnish facilities for passengers from Memphis, via Little Rock, by failing to comply with their contract to carry the mail in *stages* over the whole of that route — there being no stages run by them from the other side of the St. Francis river to Des Arc, nor from Atlanta to Little Rock.

Fourth — They have reduced the grade of service on the line — a thing which they have no right to do — the contract being for *stages* over the whole route; whereas, it is carried on *horseback* from the other side of the St. Francis to Des Arc, and on horse back, or in a buggy, from Atlanta to Little Rock and back.

Fifth — They have violated their contract to carry the mail in stages from Memphis via Little Rock to Fort Smith, by failing to bring the mail via Little Rock at all — this office being furnished by a branch line from Atlanta, which detains the mail matter, sent by it, at least two days longer than it should be detained between Des Arc and Fort Smith.

Neither Memphis, nor Des Arc, nor Little Rock, nor any part of the country from Memphis to Fort Smith, can be compensated for the failure of this **Overland** California company to do their duty, by the fact that they may perform it well between St. Louis and Fort Smith. The St. Louis route is, so to speak, the Northern, and the Memphis, the Southern branch of the route — and while we do not object to the contractors doing their whole duty on the Northern, we shall insist on their asking at least a respectable *pretense* of doing their duty on the Southern branch. This is a matter in which Fort Smith has an equal interest with the balance of the State; for if it is given out that Southern men are not to have their portion of the benefits of this route they will seek a route of their own, and this may pass entirely South of the State of Arkansas; and if this be done, then the days of Fort Smith as starting point for the Pacific mail, are numbered, for Northern travel will seek a more Northern route.

We have written this article in no captious *[captious: tendency to raise petty objections]* or fault finding spirit; for, whom properly considered, we think it will be found to contain matter of far greater importance to our people than the mere fact of the compliance or non-compliance of a mail contractor with his contracts and the law; but even that is just and a thing which every one having any interest in the country has a right to insist upon and content for.

October 6, 1858
Overland Mail Schedule

October 6, 1858

Arkansas True Democrat, Little Rock, Arkansas

Opening of the **Overland Mail** Line to San Francisco – Subjoined we publish an interesting document which forms a fitting accompaniment to the great event which we have just been engaging in celebrating. It is nothing less than the time tables of the **Overland Mail Company** which opens the new wagon route from St. Louis and Memphis to San Francisco on the 16th of the present month. Next to the establishment of telegraphic communication with Europe, an **Overland Mail** connection with our Pacific territories may be considered as one of the most important forerunners of the great changes which the existing relations of the world are about to undergo. It is the pioneer of the telegraph and of the railroad lines which are destined to bring all the members of this vast confederation into closer union and communication with each other, to consolidate our national resources, multiply and strengthen our defenses, and provide new channels for the trade of the Union and of the world. In the meanwhile, through the agency of the **Overland Mail Route**, new sections of the country will be opened up, mail and passengers facilities afforded to communities situated in proximity to the line, and a means of safe internal communication with our distant States and territories secured in the event of war.

To those who dread the sea passage to California, or who enjoying traveling through comparatively wild and unexplored regions, the new route will offer great attractions. Sea Sickness, Isthmus Fever and ship wreck inconveniences, but too frequently encountered on the ocean line, may now all be avoided, Having said this much in favor of the advantages of the new route, we will now give its programe:

GOING WEST

Leave	Days	Hours	Distance Place to Place Miles
St. Louis, Mo. and Memphis, Tenn.	Mon & Thurs	8:00 A.M.	----
P. R. R. terminus, Mo.	Mon & Thurs	6:00 P.M.	160
Springfield, Mo.	Wed & Sat	7:45 P.M.	143
Fayetteville, Mo.	Thurs & Sun	10:15 A.M.	100
Fort Smith, Ark.	Fri & Mon	8:30 A.M.	65
Sherman, Texas.	Sun & Wed	12:30 A.M.	205
Ft. Belknap, Texas	Mon & Thurs	9:00 A.M.	146 1/2
Ft. Chadburn, Texas.	Tues & Fri	8:15 P.M.	136
Pacos River.	Thurs & Sun	8:45 A.M.	165
El Paso.	Sat & Tues	11:00 A.M.	248 1/2
Soldier's Farewell.	Sun & Wed	8:30 P.M.	150
Tucson, Arizona.	Tues & Fri	1:30 P.M.	184 1/2
Gila River, Arizona.	Wed & Sat	9:00 P.M.	141
Fort Yuma, Cal.	Fri & Mon	3:00 A.M.	135
San Bernardino, Cal.	Sat & Tues	11:00 P.M.	200
Ft. Tejon (via Los Ang.)	Mon & Thurs	7:30 A.M.	150
Visatia (via Los Angeles)	Tues & Fri	11:20 A.M.	127
Frebaugh's Ferry.	Wed & Sat	5:30 A.M.	82
Arrive at San Francisco.	Thurs & Sun	8:39 A.M.	163

GOING EAST

Leave	Days	Hours	Distance Place to Place Miles
San Francisco, Cal.	Mon & Thurs	8:00 A.M.	----
Firebaugh Ferry, C.	Tues & Fri	11:00 A.M.	165
Visalia, Cal.	Wed & Sat	5:00 A.M.	82
Fort Tejon (via L Angeles)	Thurs & Sun	9:00 A.M.	127

San Bernardino, do.	Fri & Mon	5:30 P.M.	150
Fort Yuma, do.	Sun & Wed	1:30 P.M.	200
Gila River, Arizona.	Mon & Thur	7:30 P.M.	135
Tucson, Arizona.	Wed & Sat	3:00 A.M.	141
Soldier's Farewell.	Thurs & Sun	8:00 P.M.	184 1/2
El Paso River.	Sat & Tues	5:30 A.M.	150
Pecos River, Texas.	Mon & Thur	12:45 P.M.	248 1/2
Fort Chadbourn, TX.	Wed & Sat	1:15 A.M.	165
Fort Belknap, Texas.	Thur & Sun	7:30 A.M.	136
Sherman, Texas.	Fri & Mon	4:00 P.M.	146 1/2
Fort Smith, Ark.	Sun & Wed	1:00 P.M.	225
Fayetteville, Mo.	Mon & Thur	6:15 A.M.	65
Springfield, Mo.	Tues & Fri	8:45 A.M.	100
P. R. R. terminus, Mo.	Wed & Sat	10:30 P.M.	143
Arrive at St. Louis, Mo and Memphis, Tenn.	Thurs & Sun		160

The rates of fare for the present will be as follows: Between the Pacific railroad terminus and San Francisco, and between Memphis and San Francisco, either way, through tickets, $200. Local fares between Fort Smith and Fort Yuma not less than ten cents per mile for the distance traveled. Between Fort Yuma and San Francisco, and between Fort Smith and the railroad terminus, the rates will be published by the superintendents of those divisions.

The meals and provisions for passengers are at their own expense, and over and above the regular fare. It is intended, however, by the company, to have suitable meals at proper places and at moderate cost prepared for passengers as soon as they can complete their arrangements.

Forty pounds of baggage will be allowed to each passenger; but the company will not at present transport any through extra baggage, freight, or parcels.

We are glad to see that the most stringent provisions are made against delays, frauds, favoritism or incivility, by the agents and employees of the company. Thus conducted, the route cannot fail to give general satisfaction to the public.
– *New York Herald*

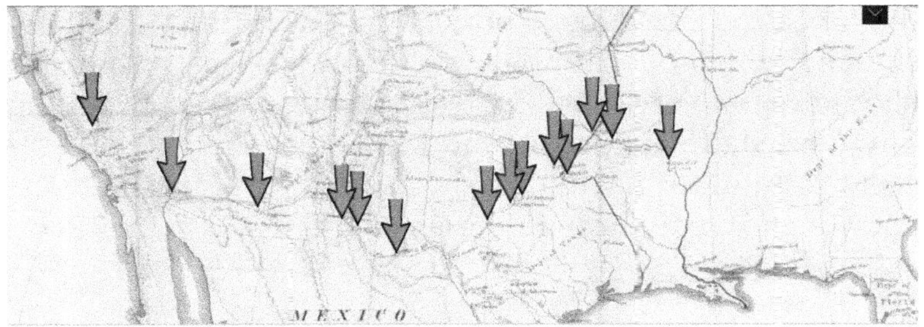

"Military Map of the United States prepared in the Office of the Quarter Master General U.S.A. November 1857"

Arrows have been added to mark military bases mentioned in the various articles in this collection. From right to left: Little Rock Arsenal, Fort Smith, Fort Gibson, Fort Washita, Fort Arbuckle, Fort Belknap, Camp Cooper, Fort Chadbourne, Fort Davis, Fort Bliss, Fort Fillmore, Fort Buchannan, Fort Yuma, and Fort Tejon.

October 6, 1858
Indian Raids
Armed Escort Proposed for each Overland Stage

October 6, 1858, Wednesday, page 3
Arkansas True Democrat, Little Rock, Arkansas

From the Fort Smith Times – A letter was received at this place on Saturday morning last, by Mr. Crocker, superintendent of the **Overland Mail**, from Mr. Bates, agent of the company, dated Sherman, Texas, Sept. 12, '58, in which he says, that he had just arrived from Fort Belknap, and that the Indians, had one week before in the settlements near Gainsville, as Mr. B. was going to Belknap, and 4 miles from where he was, met a party of whites going to their neighbors, killed two of them and wounded two others, also stole and drove off about 50 head of stock belonging to the settlers.

The whites had become so alarmed, that they were moving off leaving their homes. One of the stations of the **Overland Mail Company** had been broken up by their leaving. The Indians have stolen horses, and committed other depredations within four miles of Belknap.

We fear, that if the government does not adopt prompt

and effective measures to protect the **Overland Mail**, these Indians will prove troublesome to the company, and we should regret very much to hear of the Indians committing any depredations upon it; and to prevent this the government should, for a while at any rate, furnish an armed escort for each mail through Indian country.

[NOTE: This article was also printed in the October 9, 1858 issue of the Arkansas State Gazette and Democrat.]

October 9, 1858
Wagon Road Ready from El Paso to Fort Yuma

October 9, 1858, Saturday, page 2
Arkansas State Gazette and Democrat, Little Rock, Ark.

El Paso and Fort Yuma Wagon Road – For the information of Senator Sebastian and others who may know nothing of that work on the road from El Paso to Fort Yuma, we are now able to state that the road is complete and Colonel Leach, who has had charge of the work, pronounces it in a "passable condition – abounding with fine grading, and affording a sufficiency of water." The distances from El Paso, via the *Pimos* Villages, to Fort Yuma, according to Lieut. Parke's surveying in 1853-4, is 382 miles – more than one half of which, he states, is a smooth road, resembling a macadamized *[macadamized: a type of road construction, pioneered by Scottish engineer John Loudon McAdam around 1820, composed of a compacted subgrade of crushed granite, covered by a surface of light stone to absorb wear and tear and shed water to the drainage ditches.]* and almost equal to a plank road. This is the road which has been pronounced by skillful engineers to be "indeed highly favorable" for a post road, and to whence reports.... *[print over inked and illegible]*

October 9, 1858
Prepare to Celebrate!

October 9, 1858
Arkansas State Gazette and Democrat, Little Rock, Ark.

Notice – The Citizens of Sabastian county are requested to meet at Greenwood on Saturday, 9th Oct. 1858, at 10 o'clock, A. M. to make arrangements to unite in the celebration of the arrival of the **Overland Mail Stage** at Fort Smith from California. The farmers and citizens generally are earnestly requested to turn out on said day. The 18th of October is the day fixed for the celebration.

October 13, 1858
Arrival of the First Stage from San Francisco

October 13, 1858

Arkansas True Democrat, Little Rock, Arkansas

The **Overland Mail** arrived here yesterday morning, half past 7 o'clock, being 21 days from San Francisco, and having four through passengers from that city.

The Anvil Battery was brought forth by the young men of our city, and 350 rounds were fired, in honor of the event, and while the Anvils were playing in full tide, Lts. Steen and Bell, of the Fort, brought out two six pounders, and a detachment of U. S. troops, and fired 32 rounds, which caused the valley of the Arkansas to reverberate with the joyful news of the *safe arrival of the first* ***overland mail*** *from California.*

Three cheers for Hon. A. V. Brown, P. M. General; three cheers for **John Butterfield**, and the **Overland Mail Company.**

[NOTE: This article was also printed in the Oct. 16, 1858 issue of the Arkansas State Gazette and Democrat, page two.]

October 13, 1858
Passengers on the Memphis Route

October 13, 1858

Arkansas True Democrat, Little Rock, Arkansas

Maj. Hicken and Mr. Eberle, of this city, for whose safety so much interest was felt, on the arrival of the news of the loss of the Austria *[see photo of the SS Austria below],* arrived here this morning in the Memphis branch of the **Overland Mail,** well and hearty, without the smell of fire on their garments. We congratulate them and their friends on their safe arrival and welcome them home.

[NOTE: This article was also printed in the Oct. 16, 1858 issue of the Arkansas State Gazette and Democrat, page two.]

SS Austria
Source: www.norwayheritage.com

Sinking of the SS Austria
Source: The Deutsches Historisches Museum

The SS Austria was a steamship of the Hamburg America Line which sank on September 13, 1858, in one of the worst transatlantic maritime disasters of the nineteenth century, claiming the lives of 449 passengers and crew.

October 15, 1858
First Overland Arrives at Fort Smith

October 15, 1858
Fort Smith Times, Fort Smith, Arkansas

CELEBRATION OF THE ARRIVAL OF THE FIRST **OVERLAND MAIL** FROM CALIFORNIA AT FORT SMITH, ARKANSAS, ON THE 13TH AND 14TH INST. – FORT SMITH, ARK., OCTOBER 15, 1858

The celebration took place or rather commenced on the morning of the 13th, and was continued until the morning of the 15th. At 9 o'clock A.M. a national salute was fired by the U.S. troops at this place, under the command of Lieut. Stein, and shortly after the procession was formed on Washington Street, headed by two companies of U.S. Infantry, commanded by Lieut. Stein and Bell, gentlemen who have the escort for Lieut. Beall's Wagon Road Expedition, then came the Hook and Ladder Company in uniform; the Odd Fellows in full regalia; the mechanics – every department of which was represented – by platforms on wagons; with their tools & c., *[&c. is an abbreviation of etc., et cetera, meaning and others, or, and so forth.]* at work, with banners spread forth to the breeze, declaring the different occupations, and each one wearing a badge of his profession; then followed the farmers, on horseback, with an appropriate banner, and then came the orator of the day, Mr. John B. Luce, Honorable John Phelps of your state, the Town Council, and the Rev. Messrs. Pearce and Van Horne, seated in an **Overland Mail** Coach.

The procession reached around two or three squares, and was the largest, longest and most imposing one ever seen in any place in Arkansas. After marching through the principal streets of our young city, the procession proceeded to a grove, where preparations had been previously made for its reception, with platforms and seats. The procession was preceded by a band of music, composed of young men of the city.

The multitude being seated, the band played a very animated tune, and then the blessings of God was invoked in an appropriate manner by the Rev. Mr. Van Horne, of Fayetteville, after which the orator of the day, Mr. Luce, was introduced by our worthy Mayor, Mr. Walton, who acted throughout the day as master of ceremonies. Mr. Luce made an able speech, giving a detailed history of the progress of matters in Arkansas, the history and description of the various routes proposed for the Pacific Railroad & c. *[&c. is an abbreviation of etc., et cetera, meaning and others, or, and so forth.]* After Mr. Luce concluded, the Honorable Mr. Phelps was loudly and repeatedly called for, to address the assembly. He arose and gave a very animated and eloquent speech of an hour in length. After Mr. Phelps concluded, dinner was served by Mr. S. M. Ellis, in the form of a barbecue.

I said before, all passed off in good order, and the only drawback to the whole affair was the lack of the presence of the **Old Land Admiral, John Butterfield,** who had gone to your city with the first mail from San Francisco, and who was expected every moment, and all eyes were turned up the road, looking anxiously for him to make his appearance. A sight of the multitude and the procession in its movements would have made his heart leap for joy, for the old man – he will excuse me, I know, when I apply that appellation, as his head is now white, but his ardor and energy unabated – is one that can fully appreciate such a manifestation of the feelings of the people of this state upon the accomplishment of such a magnificent and stupendous enterprise – unequalled in any stage of the world – as the successful carrying of the **overland mail** 2,700 miles in twenty-four days, from San Francisco to St. Louis, through his instrumentality. However, he ***[Butterfield** Sr.]* did not arrive until eight o'clock in the evening; and along with him came **John Butterfield, Jr.**, a true scion of the old tree, full of energy and go-ahead-attentiveness having witnessed it fully in the first trip of the **overland mail**, which started from your city on the 16th ultimo *[of last month]*. He did not leave the seat of the driver from Tipton till the stage reached Springfield.

On the morning of the 14th, the stage from San Francisco arrived, with Mr. Bates, Superintendent on the route from Red River to Fort Chadburn, having been detained a little on its time by rains and heavy roads. These obstacles, though trifling, will soon be overcome.

All the machinery is new, and it will take some time to make all the joints work with ease. In the twinkling of an eye, almost, the stages for Memphis and St. Louis were whizzing away with the second **overland mail** from San Francisco. Just think of it! Two mails a week from California! It is like a dream.

I omitted to mention above that although **Mr. Butterfield** was not present on the 13th, yet the next man to him was here – Mr. Hugh Crooker, Superintendent of the O. & M. Company. He witnessed with great pleasure and satisfaction the procession, and listened attentively to the speeches, and was much gratified. He is a man of few words, but in his business he is in the proper place, and is capable of doing all that can possibly be required of him.

The supper was a grand affair, prepared by Mr. J. K. McKenzie, of the City Hotel. When the doors were thrown open the crowd was amazed at its appearance, so fine and so brilliant. At the head, and above the table, was a painting, executed by Mr. Syndall, of the Wagon Road Expedition, representing the Mountains of the Desert and California in the distance, with a faithful picture of the **Overland Mail Stage**, horses and driver, at full speed.

This was a sight that none of the company were prepared to see, and it was as pleasing as it was beautiful and unexpected. A large cake in the precise shape of the mail bags, endorsed **Overland Mail**, San Francisco, in gilt letters, was on the table, which when cut open had in its center a letter, post marked San Francisco, stamped in exact imitation, was taken out, directed to **Mr. John Butterfield**, President **Overland Mail Company**, Fort Smith.

Engraving Actually Drawn in 1858 in Fort Smith "The Overland Mail – The start from Fort Smith, Arkansas for the Pacific Coast – First coach driven by John Butterfield Jr." This illustration appeared in Frank Leslie's Illustrated Newspaper, Vol. VI, Oct. 23, 1858, pages 325-328. Lithograph, hand colored.

The only existing image of a Butterfield used stagecoach:

"In September 1858, Commemorating the First Trip of the Overland Mail"
This image was re-discovered by Gerald T. Ahnert in December 2023
in *The Post Standard,* April 24, 1904, page 12.
This daguerreotype was taken on the first day of the Overland's operation in front of Charles E. Butterfield's residence in Fayetteville, Arkansas.

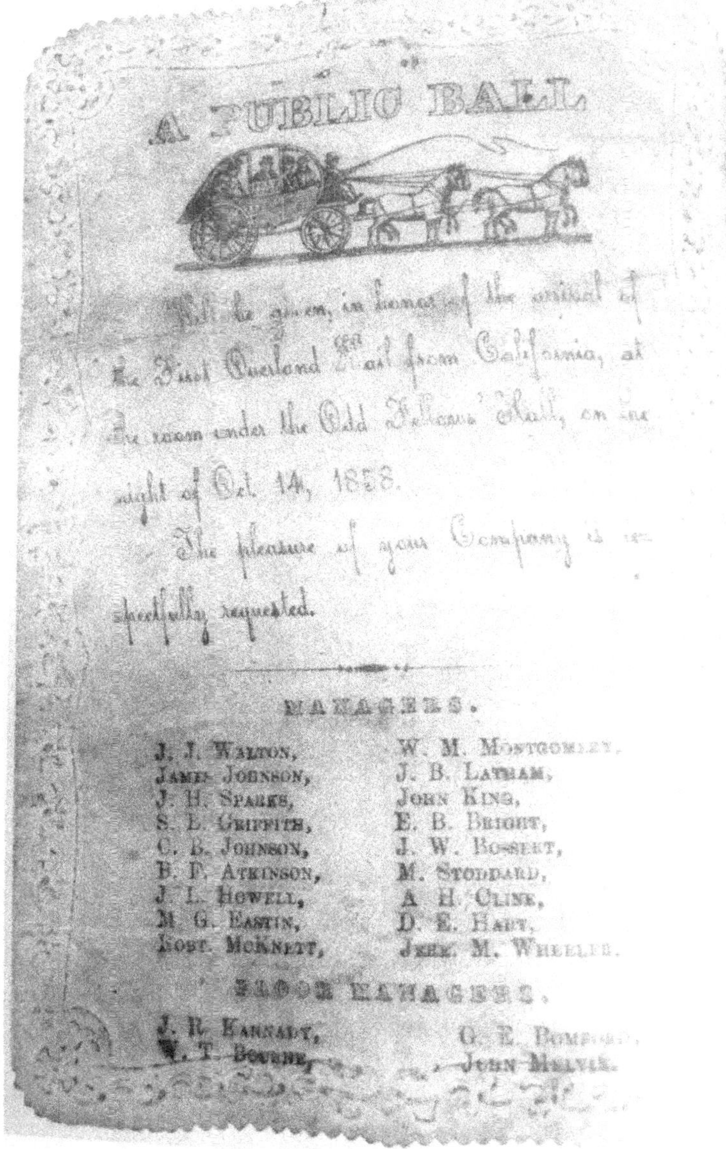

A PUBLIC BALL

Will be given, in honor of the arrival of the First Overland Mail from California, at the room under the Odd Fellows' Hall, on the night of Oct. 14, 1858.

The pleasure of your Company is respectfully requested.

MANAGERS.

J. J. Walton,	W. M. Montgomery,
James Johnson,	J. B. Latham,
J. H. Sparks,	John King,
S. L. Griffith,	E. B. Bright,
C. B. Johnson,	J. W. Bossert,
B. F. Atkinson,	M. Stoddard,
J. L. Howell,	A. H. Cline,
M. G. Eastin,	D. E. Hart,
Robt. McKnett,	Jere. M. Wheeler.

FLOOR MANAGERS.

J. R. Kannady,	G. E. Bomf[illegible],
W. T. Bourne,	John Melvin.

"A Public Ball will be given in honor of the arrival of the First ***Overland Mail*** *from California at the room under the Odd Fellows Hall, on the night of Oct. 14, 1858. The pleasure of your Company is respectfully requested."*

One of the Fort Smith buildings standing at the time of Butterfield was the "Old Fort." This postcard contains misinformation. It states the fort was built in 1830, when it was actually built in 1838. It says it was destroyed during the Civil War. Again, this is not true. The fort was used until 1871.

October 16, 1858
Celebration When Overland Arrived

October 16, 1858

Arkansas State Gazette and Democrat, Little Rock, Ark.

Arrival of the **Overland Mail** — The **Overland Mail** arrived here yesterday morning half past 7 o'clock, being 21 days from San Francisco, and having, four through passengers from that city!.

The Anvil Battery was brought forth by the Young Men of our city, and 350 rounds were fired, in honor of the event, and while the Anvils were playing in full tide, Lts. Steen and Bell, of the Fort, brought out two six pounders, and a detachment of U.S. Troops, and fired 32 rounds, which caused the valley of the Arkansas to reverberate with the joyful news of the Safe Arrival of the first **Overland Mail** from California.

Three Cheer, for Hon. A. V. Brown P. M. General; three cheers for **John Butterfield**, and his **Overland Mail Com-**

pany.

Maj. Hicken and Mr. Eberle, of this city, for whose safety so much interest was felt, on the arrival of the news of the loss of the Austria, arrived here this morning in the Memphis branch of the **Overland Mail**, well and hearty, without the smell of fire on their garments. We congratulate them and their friends on their safe arrival and welcome them home. – *Fort Smith Times*

{NOTE: A shorter version of this article was printed in the October 13, 1858 issue of the Arkansas True Democrat.]

October 23, 1858
Celebrating the Overland Arrival

Oct 23 1858, Saturday, page 2

Arkansas State Gazette and Democrat, Little Rock, Ark.

First Arrival of the **Overland Mail** Stage — The Celebration on the 18th inst. — Hoping that some of our correspondents would have favored us with a description of the celebration, we have deferred making the attempt ourselves, until the last moment. Occupying a place in the procession ourself, it is impossible for us to do justice to all and hence if anything should be omitted, we hope no one will condemn.

The morning was bright, and beautiful, and auspicious — it seemed as if the day was made for the occasion At daylight all the bells in the city were rung, rousing the inhabitants and reminding them of the joyful event to be celebrated. At nine o'clock the military fired a salute of 32 guns, when the procession formed in front of the City Hotel — the soldiers stationed at this post, commanded by Sts. Steen and Bell, preceded by a brass band in front, next the Odd Fellows in full regalia, the Hook and Ladder Company, the Mechanics and last though not least, the farmers of Sebastian, followed by a host of strangers and citizens.

The mechanics with praise worthy seal and energy, had platforms erected upon wagons and while the procession moved onward worked at their trades.

Upon one platform we noticed our venerable friend F. H. Wolfe, with manner, moulds & c, *[&c. is an abbreviation of etc., et cetera, meaning and others, or, and so forth.]* engaged in making work in his line of Gold and Silver Smith, and his son, Geo. Wolf, binding books. The platform was tastefully decorated with flags and banners bearing appropriate mottoes. Following him was a blacksmith's forge with artisans at work – an incident occurred which gave them an opportunity to show their speed and skill, one of the wagons broke down which was soon mended by them.

There were carpenters and house joiners, wheel rights, wagon makers and cabinet makers all carrying on their trades during the progress of the procession. Young America was aptly illustrated by a young person with his one horse wagon, containing the sign and tools of his father.

One of the most unique and striking representations was the butcher's wagon representing a market stall surmounted with beef, sheep, hams, and containing beef steaks and sausages.

A very large number of the farmers of the county joined in the procession carrying a banner with the inscription, *"we feed the hungry"* an apt and comfortable motto, giving assurance of thrift and plenty.

After forming, the procession marching under the command of the Chief Marshal, and his assistants, to the soul stirring music of the bands through the principal streets of the city and then to a beautiful grove in the suburbs, where a stand was erected for the orator of the day. We omitted to notice in the proper place the brass band composed of our citizens, it compares favorable with any.

We regret our inability to do full justice to the procession and the various branches of art and industry represented. No town in the Union can show a greater number of intelligent and industrious mechanics than Fort Smith.

The banners and flags with their appropriate mottoes and the large concourse thronging in every street in the city showed that the general heart was alive to the greatness of the achievement which had called them together.

On arriving at the grove the mayor accompanied by the orator of the day, J.B. Luce, Esq., and distinguished guests ascended the platform. Mayor Walton then stated to the audience that the occasion of the assemblage was to celebrate the arrival of the first **overland mail** stage at this place from California. He announced that the first stage arrived here on the 7th last, only TWENTY ONE DAYS out from San Francisco. He, in behalf of the citizens of Fort Smith and Sebastian county, tendered a warm and cordial welcome to the strangers present and invited them to partake freely of our hospitalities. He then read the letters received by the committee on invitation — we were surprised to hear none from our delegation in Congress. Surely this is an event of sufficient importance to our State to deserve from them at least a passing notice. We cannot remember all from whom letters had been received, there was one from the Hon. J. B. Floyd, Secretary of War.

After the Mayor finished reading the letters he introduced Mr. Luce who addressed the crowd upon the various routes to the Pacific, their characteristics, & c., *[&c. is an abbreviation of etc., et cetera, meaning and others, or, and so forth.]* and congratulated the country upon the success of the **Overland Mail**.

He reviewed the origin and progress of rail roads in England and this country. We cannot do justice to his speech and as we understand it will be published, we will conclude by saying that the large assemblage listened with attention, and not withstanding there were not seats good order was preserved. His speech was king and contained a large fund of useful and interesting information and will repay a careful perusal.

After Mr. Luce concluded Mayor Walton introduced the Hon. John S. Phelps, of Missouri, who addressed the audience in an able and eloquent speech. he reviewed the merits of the various proposed routes to the Pacific and proved the immense superiority of the 35th parallel over all others. He exhorted the people of Arkansas to push forward their own internal improvements and thereby secure the main trunk through our state. He alluded to his efforts to procure the transportation of the mail on the 35th parallel, and his agency in obtaining a modification of the contract, in order that the junction should be made west of Little Rock. The interest of his constituents are identified in the establishment of this route and as a faithful representative he has devoted his best energies to its accomplishment. Mr. Phelps sustained his great reputation as an orator, and has added by his visit and speech here, a host to his long list of admirers in this State.

We trust that we may have him frequently with us. We admire him for his devotion to the interests of his constituents and will ever remember that in the discharge of his duty to them, we owe the junction of the **Overland Mail** at this place. Under the influence of this junction, we hope to see Fort Smith increase in wealth and population until she will be second to no city in the Mississippi valley. In our day of prosperity we will remember, with gratitude, over debt to Hon. John S. Phelps.

At the conclusion of the speaking the company partook of a sumptuous barbecue prepared for the occasion. We will add that a large number of ladies were present and enlivened the scene by their beauty. Unable to do them full justice we will dismiss the subject by challenging the world to produce a greater display of beauty than those Arkansas ladies whose presence lent a charm to the scene of Wednesday.

The number of persons present at this celebration is variously estimated at from five to seven thousand, the largest concourse ever assembled in this State, on any similar occasion.

In the complete and triumphant success of the vast enterprise of transporting the mails from the Mississippi to the Pacific, a distance of 2,700 miles, partly over an uninhabited desert, we witness another triumph of American energy and grains.

The stage is but the precursor of the car *[railroad train car]* and ere long the Golden State, once so distant — involved from her sister States, will be but a few days journey from the center of the Union.

California, enthroned upon the Pacific, as a princess with her robes gorgeously inlaid with gold, will no longer sit in solitary grandeur, but a bevy of younger sisters will grow up to the east, under the quickening influences of the rail road, to rival her charms, and challenge her to a generous rivalry. In all this we are the finger of destiny pointing unerringly to the greatness and glory of our own State.

In conclusion we will state, that it is with pride and pleasure that we can say that no unpleasant or unbecoming incident occurred, to mar the harmony of the occasion. Every thing was conducted in good order, and all enjoyed themselves to the top of their bent. *Fort Smith Herald*

October 27, 1858
Passenger List on Overland Stage

October 27, 1858, page 2
Arkansas True Democrat, Little Rock, Arkansas

Overland Mail – We received the San Francisco *Herald* of the date of September 21st, some days since. Letters and papers to and from California can now be sent and received in three or four weeks.

Departure of **Overland Mail** – Passengers for the East by Overland – The following named gentlemen left this morning for the Atlantic States, by the **overland mail** route, (**Butterfield & Co.**). The coach took its departure at one o'clock this morning (before our going to press,) the cause being to go through Pacheo Pass *[Pacheco Pass]* before dark, which place they will reach this afternoon:

NAMES OF PASSENGERS

1. Lewis Lope, for Memphis, Tennessee
2. George W. Fidler, for Memphis, Tennessee
3. Samuel Gay, for St. Louis, Missouri

4. Virgin Oden, for St. Louis, Missouri
5. Jefferson Lake, for Memphis, Tennessee
6. William H. Hilton, for St. Louis, Missouri
7. William Rose, for Los Angeles
8. Joseph Wales, for Los Angeles

The next stage for Memphis, leaves Friday, 25th inst.; for Los Angeles, Wednesday, 23d instant. The regular trips for Memphis from this city take place for the future, without fail, on Mondays and Fridays. An additional stage for Los Angeles leaves every Wednesday.

"The Stagecoach Journey"
Painting by Morgan Weistling, 17"x 28" limited to 50 prints
Image reproduced here by permission of Morgan Weistling, Nov. 17, 2021.
Morgan Weisling's amazing art is available at
legacygallery.com/portfolio/morgan-weistling/

October 27, 1858
Overland Arrives in Fort Smith

October 27, 1858, page 3
Arkansas True Democrat, Little Rock, Arkansas

The *Fort Smith Times* is filled with an account of the **Overland Mail** celebration at that place on the 13th inst.

The procession was quite a large one, composed of the military, the different tradesmen, on platforms, engaged in their respective callings, different benevolent societies, farmers, citizens and others. The speakers were John B. Luce, esq., and Hon. John S. Phelps, of Mo. A barbecue followed and at night a ball and supper. Truly, "western interests" appear to be flourishing.

The following paragraph is startling to us if we remember that Fort Smith is 170 miles west of us or a good two days and nights journey:

> QUICKEST TIME ON RECORD: – *"Mr. Asa Bennett of this city, arrived here by the* ***Overland Mail Stage****, on Saturday last, only four days and a half running time from Boston to this place. This time cannot be beat, and to use Mr. Bennett's own language,* ***Butterfield*** *teams make better time than any other with which he has ever travelled."*

If Mr. Bennett could reach Fort Smith from Boston in four days and a half running time and bring the editor of the *Times* a Buffalo paper only five days old, we had better get our mails by way of Fort Smith. If such facilities are enjoyed by the city of neglected western interests, we should begin to hope that other parts of the State may be neglected in the same manner.

October 27, 1858
Letter from President Buchanan

October 27, 1858, page 3

Arkansas True Democrat, Little Rock, Arkansas

John Butterfield, President of the **Overland Mail Company**, having announced to the President the successful passage over the route, received the following dispatch in reply:

Washington City, Oct. 9th, 1858

JOHN BUTTERFIELD, PRESIDENT ***OVERLAND MAIL CO.****:*

Sir: Your dispatch has been received. I cordially congratulate you on the result. It is a glorious triumph for civilization and the Union. Settlements will follow the course of the road, and the east and west will be bound together by a chain of living Americans which can never be broken.

– *James Buchanan*

President James Buchannan

October 30, 1858
Wagon Road Improvement Expedition

October 30, 1858, page 3

Arkansas State Gazette and Democrat, Little Rock, Ark.

From the Van Buren Inteligencer – We learn from the Fort Smith Times of the 20th inst., that Lieut. E. F. Beale, principal of the wagon road expedition, arrived at Fort Smith on

Saturday last, accompanied by Messrs. H. B. Edwards, J. M. Beel, R. E. Floyd, Capt. W. Noland, and W. A. Tucker. The expedition will leave in about five days.

Beal's Wagon Road Expedition, 1857

In 1857, President James Buchanan appointed Beale to survey and build a 1,000-mile wagon road from Fort Defiance, Arizona to the Colorado River. During this time, the U.S. Army was conducting an "experiment" utilizing camels in the desert. Beale's Wagon Road was a trail that began at Fort Smith, Arkansas, and continued through the New Mexico and Arizona Territories into southern California. The modest but serviceable road ran for 1,240 miles from Arkansas, to the Colorado River. Edward Fitzgerald "Ned" Beale was a military officer, frontiersman, and explorer, who is best known for having blazed Beale's Wagon Road in the late 1850s.

November 3, 1858
Robbery Attempt Thwarted by OMC Employee

[Note: This is not an Arkansas newspaper, but it concerns a robbery attempt at Des Arc, Arkansas, and the article originally appeared in the *Fort Smith Times*.]
November 3, 1858, page 2
Appeal-Democrat, Marysville, California

ATTEMPT TO ROB THE OVERLAND MAIL - On the last trip of Reeside & Co's stage from Memphis to Fort Smith, says the *Fort Smith Times* of October 6th, containing the **Overland**

Mail for California, a short way out from Des Arc, the stage was approached by three men, armed, who demanded of the driver to stop and deliver the mail.

The driver, however, had company, and was not thus easily to be forced into measures. The messenger of the **Overland Mail Company** spoke out, and with pistol in hand, manifesting a determination to fight, induced the robbers to leave. 'Tis no wonder the Indians on the planes give trouble to the Mail Company, when it is done at home.

November 3, 1858
Overland Stage Arrived

November 3, 1858, page 3
Arkansas True Democrat, Little Rock, Arkansas

Overland Mail News – *St. Louis, October 27.* –The great **Overland Mail**, from San Francisco, arrived here last night with letters of the 1st, and no San Francisco papers.

This stagecoach in the Otero Museum, La Junta, Colorado was made by J. S. & E.A. Abbot of Concord, New Hampshire, who manufactured the Butterfield stagecoaches.

From among Abbot's product line, John Butterfield chose the "Mail Stage Coach" and the "Australian Wagon." Butterfield had the Australian Wagon modified to suit his wishes, and named it a "Celerity" wagon (which means 'swiftness of speed').

November 3, 1858
Landscape of the Western Overland Stage Route

November 3, 1858, page 3

Arkansas True Democrat, Little Rock, Arkansas

From the Mariposa (Cal.) Gazette – **OVERLAND** STAGES – Stages 3 and 10, of the **Overland Stage Company**, arrived in Stockton, on Thursday, and will be dispatched forthwith upon the road. The *Republican* says they used large Concord built, covered spring wagons, capable of carrying fourteen persons comfortably and were manufactured by Messrs. J. S. Abbot.

As the ship in which are fifty ___ and two hundred sets of harness arrived, though over two hundred of these coaches were purchased in San Francisco. The first stage for Memphis, Tennessee, will be dispatched on the 15th of September, and from Los Angeles probably a month after.

The *Republican*, speaking further of this company and the route, says:

> *"This route will present to the traveler a most extensive view of California. It passes through the counties of __, Joaquin, Stanislaus, Merced, Fresno, Tu___, Keru, Los Angeles, San Bernardino, and San Diego. Some portions of this immense county's mining land, but far the greater portion of an agricultural character, the products of which are of every variety, embracing the wheat and barley of the north, and the ___ bountiful vineyard fields of the south. A traveler from this city will have an opportunity to see the immense Tulare country, with ___ lake. He rides through the famous ___ and visits Los Angeles and the ___ about it. From thence to the ___ of San Gabriel, through El ___far-famed Mormon county of San ___, one of the finest in the State. [California]*
>
> *Of this latter place he passes across to Fort ___ on the Colorado River, which is the ____ line between California and New Mexico. From Fort Yumas he proceeds ___ New Mexico, on his way to the east."*

November 6, 1858

Wagon Road Improvement Expedition Departs

November 6, 1858, page 2

Arkansas State Gazette and Democrat, Little Rock, Ark.

Departure of the Wagon Road Expedition – Today the expedition for opening a wagon road from Fort Smith to California, under the Superintendency of Lt. Beale, takes its departure. The company when together including the Military escort will amount to about 200 men, and there will be a train of 35 wagons, &c.

The escort will consist of 150 U. S. Troops under the command of Lt. Steen.

The following is a list of the names of the officers belonging to Lt. Beale's expedition to wit:

Lieut. F. P. Beale, Superintendent
H. B. Edwards, 1st Assistant
J. M. Bell, Secretary and Assistant
W. P. Floyd, Surgeon and Physician
J. R. Crump, Engineer and Astronomer
Capt. W. H. Noland, Asst. Physician

The names of the officers of the escort:

Lt. Steen, Commander
Lt. Bell, A. A. Q. M. and A. A. G. S.
Dr. Duval, Surgeon
Thos. Rector and John Young, wagon masters
C. A. Birnie, Sutler

November 10, 1858

Postmaster Responds to Memphis Route Problems

November 10, 1858, page 2

Arkansas True Democrat, Little Rock, Arkansas

Overland Mail – W. H. Dundas, first Assistant Postmaster General, says the *Memphis Eagle,* has written a letter to **John Butterfield & Co.**, contractors on this route, notifying them that the same grade of service must be employed between Memphis and Fort Smith that is between St. Louis and Fort Smith.

The truth is that the mail should reach Memphis, and through Memphis, Washington City, several days sooner than via St. Louis; Memphis being much nearer Fort Smith than the former place:

To ***John Butterfield & Co.*** *Washington City, Oct. 25, 1858*

"Sir: Reports and complaints have reached this department relative to defects in the performance of the ***overland route*** *to California, between Memphis and Fort Smith. It appears to have been done in a manner quite inferior to the part between St. Louis and the latter place, with the omission of Little Rock, on some of the trips, if not all, from the main service. It is stated also that your company have sub-let the portion of the route, referred to, to other parties.*

The Postmaster General directs me to inform you that he regards these things as entirely at variance with the understanding he had with your company, as well as with the stipulations of the contract; further, that he cannot countenance any inferiority in the grade of efficiency of the service between Memphis and Fort Smith, or the transfer of any portion of the route contracted for, to other persons, considering it important that the whole of it should be under the superintendence of the company. W. H. Dundas

[Note: The Weekly Arkansas Gazette also reprinted this letter, as seen farther below, on Nov. 13, 1858.]

November 10, 1858
Troops to Protect the Overland Route

November 10, 1858, page 3

Arkansas True Democrat, Little Rock, Arkansas

OVERLAND MAIL. - *Washington, Tuesday, Nov. 2*- The U. S. Government promises **Mr. Butterfield**, the president of the California **Overland** route, U. S. forces to protect this route.

Mr. Butterfield left this afternoon for Memphis, Little Rock and Fort Smith to ascertain whether the mail route cannot be greatly improved.

ANOTHER AVENUE OF TRAVEL TO BE OPENED – We learn from

Mr. Bates, superintendent of the **Overland Mail** from Red River to Chadburn, that there is a stage line from Austin to McKinney, Texas, running two or three times a week, and, that it is but thirty miles from McKinney to Sherman, through which the **Overland Mail** runs. Now if a stage line could be put in operation between the two latter named places, then there would be a stage connection with Austin, and a large amount of travel would come through Arkansas to the western and eastern States.

Let us have the connection, Mr. Brown."

HOTELS, LIVERY STABLES, &C.

JACKSON HOUSE,

AND STAGE OFFICE,

Des Arc, Arkansas.

M. M. ERWIN, Proprietor.

HAVING purchased this large and commodious public house, and erected additional buildings, the proprietor respectfully informs his friends, and the public generally, that he is prepared to accommodate all who may favor him with their patronage.

His Table

is supplied with the best the country affords, and the proprietor pledges himself to spare no pains or expense to promote the comfort of his guests.

The Rates of Charges are as follows:

Board and Lodging per month	$20 00
Board without Lodging per month	15 00
Board per day	1 50
Single meal—Dinner	50
Single meal—Breakfast or Supper	50
Supper, Lodging and Breakfast	1 00
Lodging	25

The stage office of CHIDESTER, REESIDE & Co.'s line of four-horse post-coaches, from Des Arc to Fort Smith, has been permanently located at the Jackson House.

oct2-tf

Source: Des Arc Citizen, November 13, 1858, page 4

November 13, 1858
Memphis Route Complaints

November 13, 1858, page 2

Arkansas State Gazette and Democrat, Little Rock, Ark.

THE **OVERLAND MAIL** – Some weeks since we called attention to the fact that the contractors were failing and neglecting to do their duty in carrying the **Overland Mail** from Memphis to Fort Smith. That failure was also reported to the Department by the Postmaster at this place, and the mail agent, Col. Harley also reported the same fact, and, with this report, sent our article to the Department, as covering the whole ground of complaint. The Department has given indications of action on this subject sooner than we had expected – for which we award due praise.

The services, or rather, the lack of service on this route is now the same that was when complaint was first made. It remains to be seen whether or not the Department will go beyond mere words in this matter. Below is the letter to the contractors: *Washington City, Oct. 25, 1858*

*To **John Butterfield & Co.***

*"Sir: Reports and complaints have reached this department relative to defects in the performance of the **overland route** to California, between Memphis and Fort Smith. It appears to have been done in a manner quite inferior to the part between St. Louis and the latter place, with the omission of Little Rock, on some of the trips, if not all, from the main service. It is stated also that your company have sub-let the portion of the route, referred to, to other parties.*

The Postmaster General directs me to inform you that he regards these things as entirely at variance with the understanding he had with your company, as well as with the stipulations of the contract; further, that he cannot countenance any inferiority in the grade of efficiency of the service between Memphis and Fort Smith, or the transfer of any portion of the route contracted for, to other persons, considering it important that the whole of it should be under the superintendence of the company.W. H. Dundas

[Note: The True Democrat also reprinted this letter, as seen above, on Nov. 10, 1858.]

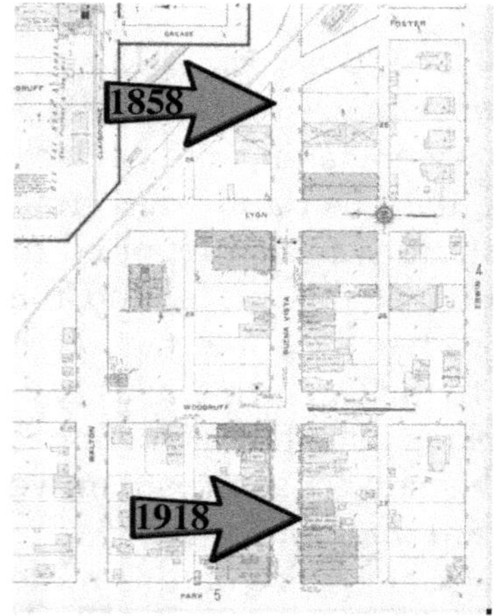

Some time before 1918, the Des Arc Hotel relocated two blocks west, from the corner of Foster Street, to 330 Buena Vista Street, as shown on this 1918 Sanborn Fire Insurance Company map of Des Arc. *Image courtesy of the Library of Congress.*

[Note this research of Brian J. Deaton corrects the location of the Jackson House that was given in this book's 2022 first edition.]

November 20, 1858
Little Rock Should be Added To Butterfield Route

November 20, 1858, Saturday
Weekly Arkansas Gazette,], Arkansas

The undersigned, citizens and later members of the Grand Jury of Pulaski county, desire, before separating for their respective homes, to call the attention of the citizens of this county, members of the legislature and their fellow citizens of this State generally to the importance of a direct communication with the cities upon the western shores of this continent.

It will be within the recollection of our citizens that a semi-weekly "**overland mai**l" was determined upon, by the general government, the initial, or starting points being St. Louis, Mo., and Memphis, Tenn.; concentrating and uniting in this city. This point was adopted by the P.M. General, after a careful and diligent inquiry into all the proposed routes and schemes submitted for that purpose; showing alike the wisdom and sagacity *[sagacity: keen and farsighted judgment]* of that officer, in making this selection. The contract, after much inquiry and competition, was awarded to **Butterfield & Co.**, for a series of years. This contract is now in part in operation – we say in part, because it is not performed as intended, and carried out as it should be.

We have no California mail connected with this city – none at all. The correspondence of the officers of the General Government goes by the circuitous route of St. Louis, instead of upon a direct line by way of Little Rock and Memphis. The contract is sub let, the mails are put in other conveyance from Memphis to Fort Smith, no regular line runs from Memphis to this point as the contract requires it should be.

Private speculation appears to have prostrated a great national enterprise; lukewarmness, if not an entire indifference appears to have taken possession of our public guardians. Instead of Little Rock being the central starting point, as originally intended, she is entirely omitted, thrown in the shade and cast aside.

We desire respectfully but earnestly to call the attention of our Senators and Representatives in Congress to this important subject, fully assured that they will use their best exertions to remedy so glaring an inconsistency as in now attempted to be practiced upon the general government and our citizens in particular.

Had the citizens of this portion of the State *[Arkansas]* been as commendably industrious in season and out of season as our neighbors of Fort Smith, a very different state of affairs would now be found to exist.

Look at the map of the United States, and every intelligent person will at once observe that the first decision of the P.M. General was right and proper; every departure from that decision was a step in the wrong direction. The Memphis and Little Rock Rail Road will, we feel assured, soon be completed to this point, hence, here is another reason, if one were wanting, why this point should be fixed and immovable in the great scheme of a direct communication with the Pacific Ocean – but why argue a position that is self-evident and convincing to all.

The undersigned would respectively ask the publication of the above in our city papers, and those friendly to our views in Memphis and elsewhere.

LITTLE ROCK, *Nov. 8th, 1858*

JOHN WASSELL	S. G. PARKER
G. MCPHERSON	JOSEPH FENNO
GEO. B. KING	WM. F. POPE
JNO. E. REARDON	JAMES WILSON
G. D. BECKHAM	W. W. MORROW
W. V. HUTT	J. ASH
E. C. GALLOWAY	J. M. GILES
JNO. G. FLETCHER	BEN F. DANLEY

November 20, 1858
Memphis Route
Slower than St. Louis Route

November 20, 1858 , Saturday, page 2
*Arkansas State Gazette a*nd Democrat, Little Rock, Ark.

THE **OVERLAND MAIL** - ANOTHER FAILURE! – The **Overland Mail** reached Memphis late on Tuesday night, bringing dates from San Francisco of the 11th. This is four and a half days behind schedule time, and about five days behind the St. Louis mail, which got in *six hours ahead of schedule time.* Of course, all the contents of this mail have been anticipated by the arrival at St. Louis.

How long is Memphis to be thus imposed on by the Sub-Contractor between this *[Memphis]* and Fort Smith! Practically, the **Overland Mail** to *Memphis*, is utterly worthless; as its advices are invariably anticipated by the prompter delivery of that at St. Louis. Unless matters can be mended, it would be better to abolish it entirely, and thus save to the Government the money paid for a service which ought to be, but is not rendered. *{Memphis Bulletin 11th}*

November 20, 1858
Butterfield's Letter to the Little Rock Postmaster

November, 20, 1858, Saturday
Arkansas State Gazette and Democrat, Little Rock, Ark.

NEW YORK, NOV. 3, 1858 – T. J. CHURCHHILL, ESQ., *Postmaster at Little Rock, Arkn.:*

Dear Sir – Your favor of Oct. 19, with a copy of your report, reached me here within a few days, and for which please receive my thanks.

I had heard from other sources in regard to the services on the Memphis Branch, and have just been on to Washington City, and have arranged with Gov. Brown to have the services performed in a satisfactory manner and according to contract, as soon as it is possible for me to go there and attend to it.

I hope before long to make it a popular line with the citizens of Little Rock, and of Arkansas generally.

Respectfully, your obedient serv't,

JOHN BUTTERFIELD, *President*
Overland Mail Co.

November 20, 1858
Overland Stage Arrived
Passenger List

November, 20, 1858, Saturday, page 3
Des Arc Citizen, Des Arc, Arkansas

FROM CALIFORNIA BY **OVERLAND MAIL** – We are indebted to Ed. S. Mowry, Esq., who came a passenger by the **Overland Mail**, for an extra of the San Francisco *Alta California*; of the 25th Oct., from which we make the following extracts:

Since the departure of the **Overland Mail** of the 22nd *[from San Francisco]*, the storm which was then raging, has been followed by another, which commenced at sundown on the evening of the 23rd, and continued during the greater part of the night. During no previous year since the discovery of gold has so much rain fallen in the month of October.

By this morning's mail, there go by the **Overland Route** *[from San Francisco]* to St. Louis: E. J. Bacon J. W. Thomas, Hiram Sparlin, and J. M. Woodworth, For Memphis: – Ed S. Mowry, and two from San Jose, For Los Angelos – C. B. Roundtree.

November 20, 1858
Celebration at Fort Smith
When the 2nd Overland Stage Arrived

November 20, 1858
Des Arc Citizen, Des Arc, Arkansas

From the Fort Smith Herald, 13th inst – Arrival of the ***Overland Mail*** *from San Francisco* – The **Overland Mail** from San Francisco arrived here on Wednesday morning last, having been out 22 days and some hours, with six passengers. this is the 9th through stage from California having had no detention from the Indians, but there is no dependence to be placed in the wild Indians, and U. S. troops are to be placed along the entire route.

We received two copies of the *Daily San Francisco Bulletin* of the 15th and 16th Oct., from which we extract the following:

Arrival and Reception of the Second **Overland Mail** Coach – The second **Overland Mail Coach** arrived in this city yesterday afternoon shortly after 4 o'clock, (having left St. Louis on the 20th September) and was received by the citizens with enthusiasm. The news of the arrival of the mail at San Jose was telegraphed at about 11 o'clock in the morning, and as it spread among the citizens, public expectation was aroused, and the most lively interest was excited. It was understood that the coach would arrive about half past 4 o'clock. Long before that hour the streets were thronged by thousands of people, congregated to welcome it. A number of persons also mounted fast horses and rode out to meet it.

At a quarter after 4 o'clock the coach turned from Market into Montgomery street. The driver blew his horn and

G. N. ELDRED'S

GREAT ROTUNDA

Southern Menagerie and Circus.

FIRST appearance in LITTLE ROCK, on *Monday* and *Tuesday*, 25th and 26th October, 1858.

Complete New Outfit.

Just received from *New York*, at *Little Rock*—new and splendid water proof Pavilion, Seats, and all the appurtenances necessary to give splendor and effect to the performances of this wonderful and popular troupe. This mammoth Pavilion is capable of seating 2,500 persons comfortably, and was constructed for Mr. G. N. Eldred, by *the most celebrated Pavilion Maker in New York*.

Horses, Ponies, Educated Mules,

WILD ANIMALS, among which are Lions, Tigers, Leopards, Lama, Zebras, Black Tigers, California Tiger Cats, Monkeys, Birds, &c., together with the greatest curiosity now shown in any exhibition, being a *Baby Monkey*, the offspring of one of the Marmosets, which nurses and tends it with all the care and affection of maternal solicitude.

The Troupe of Equestrians,

Clowns, Acrobats, Men of strength and agility, grace and athletic power, is unequalled by any that ever before travelled in the South, North, East or West, and challenges any company travelling, to contest with them the palm of superiority and excellence.

The Clowns.

JIMMY REYNOLDS, *the Jester of the Poets*, whose world-wide reputation causes thousands daily to flock and hear his laughable witticisms and well turned epigrams and repartees, assures the inhabitants of Little Rock, that his emporium of speeches, jests, jokes, hits at the times, and fancy lucubrations, shall be forthcoming, for their amusement and especial edification, on the 25th and 26th.

MIKE LIPMAN, the singing Buffo and Joker, will dance, talk, tumble, say good things, and make unusual sport and merriment.

MISS ALBERTINE E. ROBERTS,

The young, fascinating, and beautiful Equestrienne, Danseuse and Vocalist, will appear in her novel and graceful act, entitled

THE AERIAL NYMPH

Or, the Fairy Triumph.

Miss Roberts will also execute some of the favorite dances which have rendered her so popular, as well as sing many of the popular burlesque songs of the day.

THE TROUPE OF EQUESTRIANS

comprises gentlemen of unrivalled talent, in every grade of the Profession, making such a combination of Acrobatic and Equestrian ability, as always insures the satisfaction and delight of the immense audiences that daily and nightly, crowd the Rotunda Pavilion, of the

GREAT SOUTHERN CIRCUS.

Among the most distinguished members of the Troupe, may be found

MONS. LA THORNE, the Man of prodigious strength—*the Great Iron Globe Hurler*—Puller against Horses, &c.

Mr. THOMAS WYETH, *the Great Seminole Rider*.

MASTER SAUNDERS, the Equestrian prodigy, whose wonderful act upon a bareback horse, astonishes every beholder.

The extraordinary Patagonian brothers, Jonson and Lowrow, in their startling feats upon a chair, on the top of a pole, 60 feet high.

Masters EUGENE and DE LORME, in their graceful and startling performances upon the *corde de la [illegible]*.

Mr. MOSE LIPMAN, the great Vaulter and 2 Horse Rider.

Mr. G. N. ELDRED, in his flying 4 horse act.

MASTER LA ROIX, the Infant Equestrian and Acrobatic Prodigy.

LITTLE HARRY, the infant Tumbler, Vaulter, &c.

Wonderful Performing Horse Champion, instructed and performed by Mr G. N. ELDRED. The United States is challenged to produce his equal, for beauty, intelligence and training.

Educated Performing Fighting Ponies, Monkeys and the Bucking Bee. *Comic Mules*.

BAND led by DICK WEBBER and comprising musicians of well known merit.

☞ Admission only 50 cents—children and servants 25 cents.

☞ It will be remembered that the price of admission is only that charged for a Circus alone, the Animals may therefore be considered a FREE EXHIBITION!

Company will exhibit at

CLARKSVILLE, MONDAY, OCT. 18.
DOVER, TUESDAY, OCT. 19.
POTTS', WEDNESDAY, OCT. 20.
LEWISBURG, THURSDAY, OCT. 21.
White's, Mouth of Cadron, Friday, Oct. 22.
BENEDICTS, SATURDAY, OCT. 23.

Circus Performs at Butterfield's Potts Station
Source: October 16, 1858 Weekly Arkansas Gazette

G. N. ELDRED'S
GREAT ROTUNDA
SOUTHERN MENAGERIE AND CIRCUS.

FIRST appearance in LITTLE ROCK, on *Monday* and *Tuesday*, 25th and 26th of October, 1858.

Complete New Outfit,

Just received from *New York*, at *Little Rock*—new and splendid water-proof Pavilion, Seats, and all the appurtenances necessary to give splendor and effect to the performances of this wonderful and popular troupe. This mammoth Pavilion is capable of seating 2,000 persons comfortably, and was constructed for Mr. G. N. ELDRED, by *the most celebrated Pavilion Maker in New York*.

Horses, Ponies, Educated Mules,

WILD ANIMALS, among which are Lions, Tigers, Leopards, Lama, Zebras, Black Tigers, California Tiger Cats, Monkeys, Birds, etc., together with the greatest curiosity now shown in any exhibition, being a *Baby Monkey*, the offspring of one of the Mamozets, which nurses and tends to it with all the care and affection of maternal solicitude.

The Troup of Equestrians,

Clowns, Acrobats, Men of strength and agility, grace and athletic power, is unequalled by any that ever before traveled in the South, North, East or West, and challenges any company traveling, to contest with them the palm of superiority and excellence.

THE CLOWNS.

JIMMY REYNOLDS, *the Jester of the Poets*, whose world-wide reputation causes thousands daily to flock and hear his laughable witticisms and well-turned epigrams and repartees, assures the inhabitants of Little Rock, that his emporium of speeches, jests, jokes, hits at the times, and fancy funniments, shall be forthcoming, for their amusement and especial edification, on the 25th and 26th.

MIKE LIPMAN, the singing Buffo and Joker, will dance, talk, tumble, say good things, and make unusual sport and merriment.

MISS ALBERTINE E. ROBERTS,

The young, fascinating, and beautiful Equestrienne, Danseuse and Vocalist, will appear in her novel and graceful act, entitled

THE ÆRIAL NYMPH,
Or, the Fairy Triumph.

Miss Roberts will also execute some of the favorite dances which have rendered her so popular, as well as sing many of the popular burlesque songs of the day.

THE ÆRIAL NYMPH,
Or, the Fairy Triumph.

Miss Roberts will also execute some of the favorite dances which have rendered her so popular, as well as sing many of the popular burlesque songs of the day.

THE TROUPE OF EQUESTRIANS

comprises gentlemen of unrivalled talent, in every grade of the Profession, making such a combination of Acrobatic and Equestrian ability, as always insures the satisfaction and delight of the immense audiences, that daily and nightly, crowd the Rotunda Pavilion, of the

Great Southern Circus.

Among the more distinguished members of the Troupe may be found

MONS. LA THORNE, the Man of prodigious strength—*the Great Iron Globe Hurler*—Puller against Horses, etc.

Mr. THOMAS WYETH, the Great Seminole Rider.

MASTER SAUNDERS, the Equestrian prodigy, whose wonderful act upon a bareback horse, astonishes every beholder.

The extraordinary Patagonian brothers, JOHNSON and LOWLOW, in their startling feats upon a chair, on the top of a pole, 60 feet high.

Masters EUGENE and DE LORME, in their graceful and startling performances upon the corde de la trappeze.

Mr. MOSE LIPMAN, the great Vaulter and 2-Horse Rider.

MASTER LA ROIX, the Infant Equestrian and Acrobatic Prodigy.

LITTLE HARRY, the infant Tumbler, Vaulter, etc.

Wonderful Performing Horse Champion, instructed and performed by G. N. ELDRED. The United States is challenged to produce his equal, for beauty, intelligence and training.

Educated Performing Fighting Ponies, MORRISSEY and the BENICIA BOY. *Comic Mules.*

BAND led by DICK WEBBER, and comprising musicians of well known merit.

☞ Admission only 50 cents—children and servants 25 cents.

☞ It will be remember that the price of admission is only that charged for a Circus alone, the Animals may therefore be considered a FREE EXHIBITION!

Company will exhibit at LEWISBURG, 21st Oct.
MOUTH CADRON, 22d October.
BENEDICT'S, 23d "
Oct. 20, 1858.

LIST OF LETTERS remaining in the Post-

Circus performs at three Butterfield Overland Mail Co. points in Ark.: the mouth of the Cadron on Oct. 22, 1858; Lewisburg on Oct. 21, 1858; and Little Rock on Oct. 25 & 26, 1858 cracked his whip; at which the horses, four in number, almost seemed to partake of his enthusiasm, and dashed ahead at a clattering pace; and the dust flew from the glowing wheels. At the same time a shout was raised, that ran with the rapidity of an electric flash along Montgomery street, which throughout its length was crowded by an excited populace. As the coach dashed along through the crowds, the hats of the spectators were whirled in the air and the hurrah was repeated from a thousand throats, responsive to which the driver, the lion of the occasion, doffed his weather-beaten old slouch, and in uncovered dignity, like the victor of an Olympic race, guided his foaming team towards the post office.

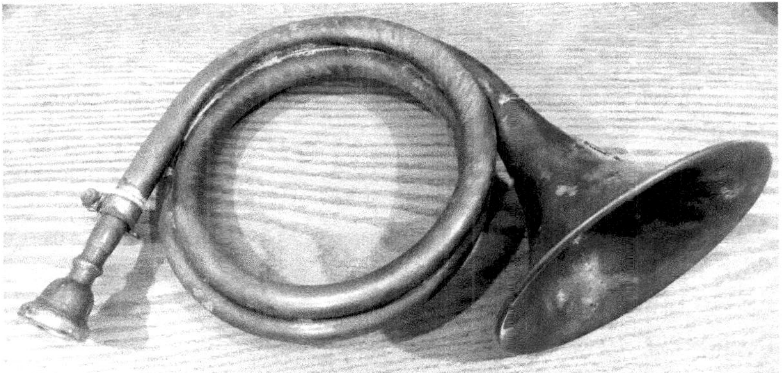

This replica of an 1831 ***post horn*** *is in the possession of the author. The POST HORN (also posthorn, post-horn, or coach horn) was a valveless cylindrical brass or copper instrument with cupped mouthpiece. The instrument commonly had a circular or coiled shape with three turns of the tubing, though sometimes it was straight. The cornet was developed from the post horn by adding valves. The instrument was used to signal the arrival or departure of a mail coach used especially in the 18th and 19th centuries.*

It is safe to say that no returning conqueror, loaded with barbaric spoils ever called forth a more unanimous burst of applause than did the dust-begrimed Delos Cole, "who brought the good news."

As the coach sped along Montgomery street Monumental Engine Co., No. 6 fired a salute in honor of the event from the plaza. As it reached the post office, at the instance of

Postmaster Weller, the assembled crowd gave three cheers. After delivering the mails, the coach proceeded to the plaza where more cheers were given and more enthusiasm exhibited.

November 24, 1858
California Newspapers

November 24, 1858, page 2
Arkansas True Democrat, Little Rock, Arkansas

TOPICS OF THE WEEK – Our California exchanges are filled with exultations over the successful trips of the **Overland Mail coaches.** They had dinners, speeches, firing of cannon and other joyful demonstrations.

November 27, 1858
"Jack Ass" Mail to Transfer to Overland Stages

November, 27, 1858, Saturday, page 3
Des Arc Citizen, Des Arc, Arkansas

WASHINGTON, NOV. 23 – The Postmaster General has issued orders for weekly mail from New Orleans, to connect with the regular coaches of the San Diego and San Antonio line to El Paso, when it will then be transferred to the **Memphis Overland Mail** for San Francisco.

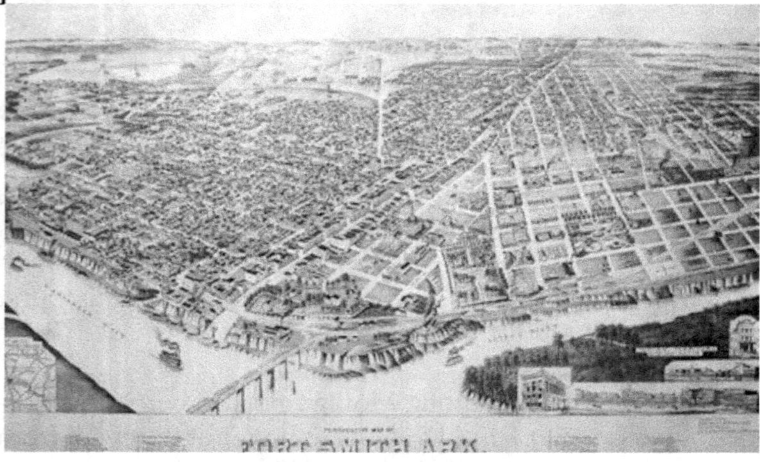

1887 Perspective Map of Fort Smith

November 27, 1858
Future Railroad May Follow Overland Route

November, 27, 1858, Saturday, page 3
Des Arc Citizen, Des Arc, Arkansas

WASHINGTON, NOV. 17 – It is understood that the president will, in his message, recommend congress to provide for the construction of a railroad through the territories, to connect California with the Atlantic States, leaving it to the States on either side to make the connection entirely across the continent. The practicability of the El Paso route having been demonstrated by the successful operations of the **Overland Mail Company.** Texas has already provided for a road to El Paso, and will do more if necessary. California would doubtless make provision to connect at its southern limits. Such views, and others considered as pertinent, will doubtless be submitted in the president's message. The president has no preference of route beyond what facts demonstrate as the one most practicable. – *Correspondent New York Herald*

FORT SMITH, ARKANSAS, RECENTLY CAPTURED FROM THE UNITED STATES BY THE SECESSIONISTS.

"Fort Smith, Arkansas,
Recently Captured From the United States Secessionists,"
Source: Illustrated London News, May 20, 1861, page 499.

November 27, 1858
Description of Fort Smith
Merger Point of the Overland Stagecoaches

November 27, 1858

Arkansas State Gazette and Democrat, Little Rock, Ark.

OUR CITY AND COUNTY – Fort Smith is situated on an eminence at the junction of and below the mouth of the Poteau River where it flows into the Arkansas, and is immediately adjoining the country belonging to the Choctaws, while on the opposite side of the Arkansas River, is the Cherokee country.

The Fort from which the city derives its name, is on a reserve of that part of the Choctaw land lying on the east side of the Poteau and a portion of the lands in the State of Arkansas, bought of private individuals; so that the Fort grounds are partly in the Choctaw Nations and partly in the State of Arkansas. The city is laid off at right angles, the streets one way, being parallel with the river. The streets are 50 feet wide and alleys 20, and the lots 50 by 140 feet. The main street, called Garrison Avenue and lying between the Fort and city is 120 feet wide. The site of the city is one of the most beautiful in the western country, gradually rising from the river until it attains an elevation of about 100 feet and is then gently undulating. The view from the river is the most picturesque in the State. The population is about 3,000 and increasing very rapidly.

One thing that astonishes the stranger, here is the diversity of languages, nearly every foreign language of note and many different Indian languages being spoken. Most of the merchants have an Interpreter who speaks several Indian languages.

This city carries on an extensive trade with the Choctaw, Cherokee, Creek, Chickasaw and Seminole Indians. There are some 25 or 30 mercantile establishments, some of which sell over 100,000 dollars worth annually.

The country back of the city is variegated with gently swelling hills, and with lowlands good for meadow, and woodland and prairie, and is as fertile as most of the uplands in the west, but being located by speculators, some 20 years ago, has been a serious drawback to settlement. These men are however, within a year or two, selling at reasonable prices and their lands are being fast disposed of to actual settlers. Four or five miles out, improved land can now be purchased at $5 to $7 per acre: at 10 or 15 miles some lands may be found unlocated and from 10 to 20 miles they may yet be located by actual settlers at 12 1/2 to 25 cents per acre.

Fort Smith, ca. 1870

Sebastian county is 50 miles in length on an air line and some 23 miles in breadth and lies lengthwise along the Choctaw line. Some of the graduated lands at 15 to 25 miles are worth as high as 75 cents and $1 to actual settlers and $1.25 to all other persons. An actual settler, who can always take 320 acres if he likes, is doing very well when he can get land at 12 1/2 or 25 cents per acre, that is superior to the uplands in Alabama and Georgia, now rated at $25 to $50 per acre. Again large quantities of swamp land can yet be bought in this country at 50 per acre.

November 27, 1858
Little Rock Should Not Be On The Route and a Letter from John Butterfield

November, 27, 1858, Saturday,page 2
Des Arc Citizen, Des Arc, Arkansas

THE **OVERLAND MAIL** – THE MEMPHIS ROUTE – We find the Memphis papers the following extract of a letter from **COL. BUTTERFIELD**, addressed to COL. CARROLL, Post-Master at Memphis, bearing date New York, November 3.

Whoever led **Col. Butterfield** to believe that he could carry the **Overland Mail** from Little Rock to Fort Smith by steam was either a knave or a fool. The "sudden falling of the water" spoken of by the Colonel, happens so often with that stream, that it is rendered unnavigable below Little Rock, as well as above that point.

The recommendation of COL. HUTTON, a Civil Engineer in the employ of government, has more good senses and correct judgement in it than all the advice **Col. Butterfield** has received from all the wiseacres who have spared neither falsehood or fiction to divert the **Overland Mail** Route from the 35th parallel. Col. Hutton examined the route under the auspices of the secretary of the interior, and in a communication to that department recommended that this Mail be conveyed from Memphis to Des Arc by steamboats, thence westward by coaches.

This mail should never have been carried *via* Little Rock. That point *[Little Rock]* is twenty-seven miles South of the direct route to Fort Smith, and the mail matter for California could be forwarded to Fort Smith, thus saving the elbow-route to Little Rock.

We call upon the delegation in congress to do government justice in this matter, and remember that *it is an outrage to cause the **Overland Mail** to be carried via Little Rock,* instead of going direct to Fort Smith.

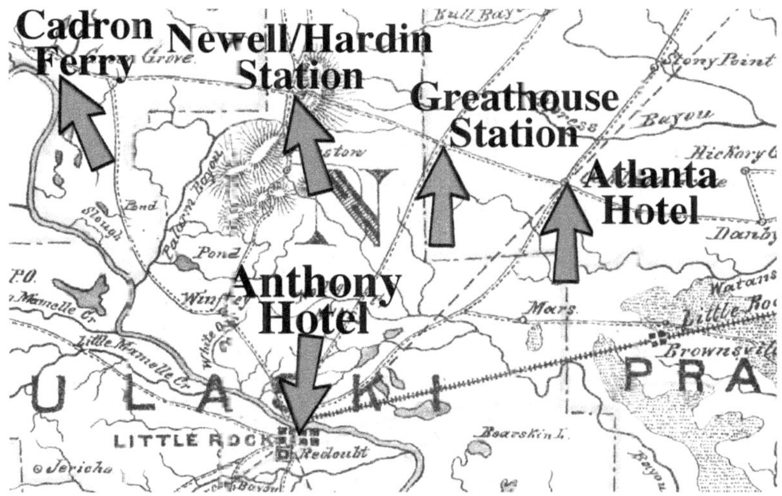

1864 Map of Arkansas

Arrows have been added to indicate location of Overland Mail Co. stations. Originally stagecoaches went direct from the Atlanta Hotel due west to the Cadron Ferry, bypassing the state capital of Little Rock. By the end of 1858, a Little Rock Home Station at the Anthony House was added to the official route (see Anthony House photo below).

The three story Anthony House was a famous landmark in Little Rock.

Following a fire in 1840, the three story hotel was rebuilt with red brick.

Source: The Arkansas State Archives (Image #ASA 5300.36)

[The above Nov. 27, 1858 article from the *Des Arc Citizen* inserted the following letter from **John Butterfield**, President, **Overland Mail Co**.:]

My present object is to call to your attention a few facts in connection with the **Overland Mail** *service to your office. When the contract was made, and always subsequently till just previous to September 16th, it was my expectation and intention to have given the Memphis portion of the route to the* BEST OR SUPERIOR *service, as it is styled by the department. That is, by steam from Little Rock to Fort Smith.*

I had obtained the consent of the department, selected and partially negotiated for the necessary boats. But a sudden falling of the water prevented me carrying out my intentions. It was too late then to stock the route, and start it in No 1 shape. My only (as I supposed at the time) available method left of performing the service agreeable to contract was to arrange with Reeside & Co., which was done by Mr. Crocker, one of our superintendents, with the understanding that the service was to be performed according to contract. From the reputation that Reeside & Co., has as good stage men, together with the fact that they already had an excellent contract with the superintendent, I felt positive that they would give good satisfaction to yourself and the people in your section of the country. In this I regret to say that I am entirely disappointed – the more so, as it has transpired since that the service on this portion of the route has been the only drawback to the complete success of the entire service on the largest mail contract ever made in any country.

At an interview with the postmaster general, I stated the case fully and fairly to him, and informed him, as I now do to you, that as soon as it is possible for me, without too great personal sacrifice, to get to your section of country, I shall have the route stocked with as good stock as is on any line in the United States, and in such a manner perform the service that neither department or the public shall have any cause to complain.

You, of course, are aware that it will take a little time

for me to get matters arranged and the stock on the ground, explore the routes to select the best in order to make time, etc., etc.

I hope soon to see you and consult with you as regards the best and most proper method to expedite the mails and satisfy the Department, yourself and the public.

Many important matters in connection with the service here – financial matters, supplies, etc. detain me here at present. As soon as these are properly in trim, I will visit you.

I trust you will tender us your influence in staying any unfavorable current of public opinion, until we can have time to redeem the promises I have here made to you

I am, dear sir, very respectfully yours,

John Butterfield,

President ***Overland Mail Company***

November 27, 1858

Butterfield Route Clear of Indian Hostilities

November, 27, 1858, Saturday,page 2

Des Arc Citizen, Des Arc, Arkansas

Overland Mail – Mr. J. B. Nichols, of the **O. M. Co.** arrived in our city on Sunday last, from El Paso, having left there on the 3rd inst. He reports the line clear through, from this place *[Fort Smith]* to San Francisco, in perfect order. Mails to and from making time at all the Stations.

Mr. N. reports late sign of hostile Indians, but met none on the trip in, and found no difficulty whatever on the route, no depredations having been committed on any of the ***[Butterfield Overland Mail]*** **Company's** property, save the stealing of some 6 mules from the Station at Grape Creek about the 1st inst.

Fears are now entertained as winter approaches, that the Indians will be quite troublesome.

The health of all the men in employ of the ***[Butterfield Overland Mail]*** **Company,** is generally, very good, and all being in good spirits, enjoying themselves 'between times' being in good spirits, enjoying themselves 'between times' hunting, as the country abounds in game, such as Deer, Elk, Antelope, Turkeys, Prairie Hens & c.

The road from Red River out is in fine order, the road cleared and streams bridged from Red River. Here the road is not so good, those being improved some, and in places are well worked. One the whole, he says, that the ***[Butterfield Overland Mail]*** **Company** do not *[does not]* anticipate difficulty, sufficiently great to prevent them from making contract time throughout the year. – *Fort Smith Times, 24th inst.*

November 27, 1858
Jack Ass Mail Transfers to Butterfield at El Paso Instead of Continuing on to San Diego

November, 27, 1858, Saturday,page 3
Des Arc Citizen, Des Arc, Arkansas

WASHINGTON, NOV. 24 – The Postmaster General has issued orders for the weekly mail from New Orleans, to connect with the regular coaches of the San Diego and San Antonio line *['Jack Ass Line']* to El Paso when it will then be transferred to the **Memphis Overland Mail** for San Francisco.

Anthony House *(LITTLE ROCK'S BUTTERFIELD STATION)* ***Original Owners***
Major James C. Anthony (left) founder of the Anthony House, and his son, Phillip Lee Anthony (right), who succeeded his father in 1842 as proprietor of the Anthony House until it was sold in 1858.
Images compliments of Reflections - A Pictorial History of Pulaski County.

December 4, 1858
Anthony House Butterfield Station Sold

ANTHONY HOUSE,

LITTLE ROCK, ARKANSAS.

THE above Hotel, having been purchased by Messrs. PETER HANGER and WM. E. ASHLEY, is now kept by the undersigned, who are ready to accommodate travelers and sojourners.

Their Table will be well supplied with the substantials and delicacies of both the foreign and the home markets.

Their servants are of the best that can be procured, and as good as those of the best Hotels in the country.

Speedy preparations are making for a thorough refitting and repairing of the House; and so soon as necessary, arrangements can be effected, extensive additions and improvements will be made to the buildings.

The offices for all the Stage lines coming to Little Rock, are kept at the Anthony House.

JOSEPH O. ASHLEY.

Little Rock, June 4, 1858. 48—

The Anthony House Livery Stable.

THIS fine Stable is kept by the undersigned, who is ready to give attention to all business in his line with promptness. His long experience in the Stable business, he hopes, will enable him to give satisfaction to all. SAML. E. FOUST.

Little Rock, June 5, 1858. 48—

Weekly Arkansas Gazette, Dec. 4, 1858, page 1

December 4, 1858

Why is the Mail Delayed on Memphis Route?

December 4, 1858, page 2
Des Arc Citizen, Des Arc, Arkansas

OVERLAND MAIL – Mr. Walton, agent of the California **Overland Mail Company**, informs the editors of the *Memphis Enquirer* that he has just returned from a visit to ascertain the cause why the route from Fort Smith to Memphis was not as well filled as that to St. Louis. He finds that owning to other contracts of the sub-contractors, the mail is laid over about 48 hours at Fort Smith, and about 24 at Des Arc. At present this cannot be remedied; but arrangements are in progress for putting stock on the line under the direct supervision of the contractors, **Messrs. Butterfield & Co.** As soon as these arrangements are completed, the same grade of work will be done between Memphis and Fort Smith, as between the latter place and St. Louis. *[This article was reprinted in the December 11, 1858 issue of the Weekly Arkansas Gazette on page 3.]*

December 4, 1858

Additional Stations Are Being Added Along Overland Mail Route

December 4, 1858, page 3
Des Arc Citizen, Des Arc, Arkansas

Stations are said to be fast springing up on the great **Overland California Route**, and the accommodations are rapidly increasing.

December 4, 1858

Overland Passenger's Story

December 4, 1858, page 3
Des Arc Citizen, Des Arc, Arkansas

We were pleased to meet with WARREN BAER, ESQ., who came passenger by the **Overland Stage** from Tucson. Mr. B., has spent several days here, and left on the steamer Return on Wednesday for Memphis. We present the following from his pen as an inkling of the various scenes on the route:

A Beautiful Scene – Death of a Wolf on the Plains – During the late snow storm on the Plains through which the ***Overland stage route*** *passes, the stage with passengers for the East passed over the rolling prairie, about twenty-five miles from Fort Chadbourne. The sun rose from his frozen bed with more than usual splendor – sending his brilliant beams across an almost illimitable field of sleet. The Musquite* [Mesquite] *bushes were encased in ice of half inch thickness, while every blade of grass was varnished with the dazzling frost. On this frozen field of ice the deer stood huddled together in shivering groups, while the wolves ran howling on the frosty earth in search of warmth and shelter. One very large red wolf approached the stage, and squatting near the road, gave utterance to the most mournful howls, and commenced licking his stiffened chops, while gazing at the passengers. Three revolvers were instantly brought to bear upon this stranger on the road, when he fell wounded at the first fire, biting and snapping at the side on which the ball had entered. The passengers then dismounted and fired two shots at his skull, but the balls glanced from his cranium, and he was only dispatched by the knife. He was dragged with great difficulty from the road by two of the passengers, and they represent his weight at over one hundred and fifty pounds. He died, snapping at his slayers till the last gasp. The stage had scarcely started on its journey before the icy plain was alive with the howling wolves hasting to feast upon their unfortunate companion.*

December 11, 1858

Overland Stage Arrives, Mowry as Passenger

December 11, 1858, Saturday

*Arkansas State Gazette a*nd Democrat, Little Rock, Ark.

Telegraphed to the Memphis Bulletin – St. Louis, Dec. 3 – The great **Overland Mail** has arrived. Lieut. Mowry, who came as a passenger, says that the gold mines near Gila

City are represented by old and experienced miners as being equal to any in California.

The Atlanta Hotel was the Butterfield Home Station in Oakland Grove (Austin), Arkansas

ATLANTA HOTEL,

BY J. J. PEEBLES,

Atlanta, Prairie Co., Ark.,

HAVING leased this finely located Public House, and re-fitted it entire, I am prepared to accommodate the traveling public.

☞ The stage office of Messrs. Chidester, Reeside & Co's., U. S. Mail Line from Des Arc to Fort Smith is kept at this house. Also, passengers from Des Arc to Little Rock, will be forwarded by Hanger's Stage Line from Batesville to Little Rock. [dec11-3m.

Source: Dec. 11, 1858, Des Arc Citizen, Des Arc, Arkansas

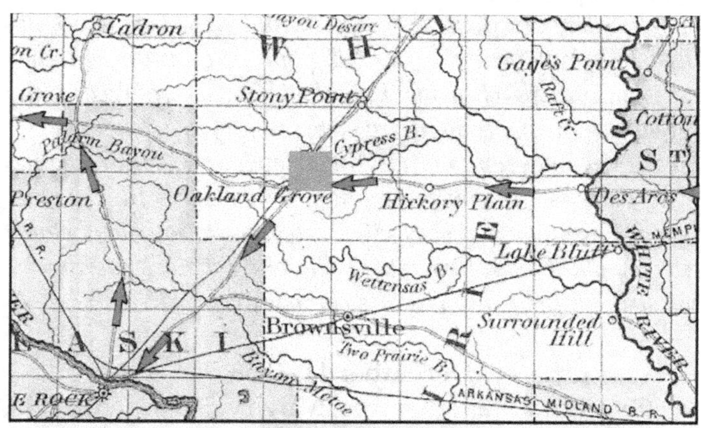

1855 Map of Arkansas by J. H. Colton
Red arrows added to highlight the Butterfield Historic Trail.
Green box highlights the location of the Oakland Grove Post Office where this cover was postmarked, and where cover was transferred to the Overland Mail stagecoach.,
The southern dip to Little Rock was added to the route in Oct. 1858, to appease residents of the state capital.

The Jackson House was the Overland Mail Home Station in Des Arc, Arkansas - weekly guest listed below.

Arrivals at the Jackson House.

UP TO FRIDAY EVENING DEC. 3, '58.

Lewis Robinson, Ark; Mrs High and son, Augusta; James Hart, do; G R Quarles and lady, country; R M Duff, Tenn; W A Cordan, Ky; Jerry Tomlinson, Ark; Willy Tomlinson, do; Mr Barks, do; D F Reinhart, country; W Bair, San Francisco; S Mosley, Ala; J G Mays, Searcy; W E Finkley, N O; A Eldridge, Ten; W J Benson, ark; John S Mathis, Darceneile; Miss Lucy Caviness, do; F M Yarbrough, ark; Rus Evans, co; R M Brimer, S J Payne and lady, Searcy; Harvey Bell, mail agent; J T Parham, Tenn.; T E Ellison, Atlanta; T J Alison, do; J A Moon, city; Turner Millium, Jos Guir, W Stewart, J S Knight, J L Ragan, Ten; Thos English, sr, Thos English, jr, W H Carrington, W Carrington, J M R Carrington, J S Freeland and family, Miss; Robt Brainbridge, N O; J R Docking, country; W J Rucker, do; J W Martin, Des Arc; W W Williamson, A B Hope, do; B S Steed, Ga; G W Burger, Tenn; Jacob Pilman, J J Pulbs, W M Harrison, ark; W W Kirkpatrick, Ga; F M Woods, Tenn.

Source: December 4, 1858, page 3 Des Arc Citizen, Des Arc, Arkansas

Jackson House Home Station for Overland Mail Put Up for Sale

Jackson House for Sale.

THE undersigned is desirous to sell the above House, which is situated in Des Arc. The house is a brick building containing twelve rooms—connected therewith is a frame dining room, 45 feet long, 16 feet wide. Also, connected is an office with a good Bar and a back room—each 18 feet square. There is, also, another tenement disconnected from the main building, suitable for a Barber Shop—it is now occupied as a Silver-smith Shop. There is in all sixteen rooms. There is a good Livery Stable within 30 yards of the premises.

I am not anxious to sell because the business will not pay, but on account of my health being bad, I cannot give my personal attention to the House. I venture the assertion that this tavern has cleared more money for the amount invested than any other business in the State. It is situated within 100 yards of the Steamboat Landing, immediately on the main street. The U. S. Mail Stage Office is kept at this House.

TERMS.—One-third cash; balance in one and two years, with a lien on the property until the last payment is made.

☞ If not sold by the 1st day of January next, this property will be for rent or lease.

☞ For further information address me at Des Arc. M. M. ERWIN.

nov. 13, 1858–t.1.j.

Source: Dec. 11, 1858, Des Arc Weekly Citizen, Des Arc, Arkansas
This ad ran weekly from Nov. 13 to Dec. 25, 1858

December 15, 1858
President Buchanan's Support

December 15, 1858, page 3
Arkansas True Democrat, Little Rock, Arkansas

A CHARGE REFUTED – It having been stated by the opposition that President Buchanan was at one time opposed to the establishment of the **Overland Mail** route to California, it may be well enough to publish the following from a Washington correspondent of the *St. Louis Republican.* No one acquainted with that sheet could reasonably accuse of partiality to the administration. The letter-writer says:

> *"I have ascertained that Mr. Buchanan was, from the beginning, favorable to the establishment of the great* ***Overland Route*** *now in charge of* ***Messrs. Butterfield & Co.****, and consistently backed Postmaster General Brown in all his efforts to put the route into prompt and successful operation. It was in the establishment of the other* ***overland mails*** *that Mr. Buchanan halted and hesitated, inconsequence of the depressed and crippled condition of the treasury."*

President James Buchannan, (1791-1868)

December 15, 1858
Mules Stolen • High Water Delays Mail

December 15, 1858, page 3
Arkansas True Democrat, Little Rock, Arkansas

The Comanches had driven off six mules from one of the stations on the **Overland Mail Route**.... The California mail had not arrived, though due two or three days at Fort Smith. High water was the supposed cause of the detention.

In the 18th and 19th centuries, Comanche
lived in most of present-day northwestern Texas and adjacent areas in eastern New Mexico, and southeastern Colorado.

December 15, 1858
Red River Navigation

December 15, 1858, page 3
Arkansas True Democrat, Little Rock, Arkansas

...and as the **Overland Mail to California** has been put in operation, crossing Red River at Preston, thence to the Rio Grande, passing through a fertile and healthy country, which is now almost an entire wilderness; but the well-known characteristics of the Anglo-Saxon race, love of adventure, a desire to emigrate and explore unknown regions will soon cause this section of country to be densely populated; and it is nothing more than our just rights, that Congress should grant us aid and assistance in improving and completing the navigation of Upper Red River. The interests and welfare of her citizens demand it.

Mules were used, instead of horses, to pull the stagecoach when the roads were rough or mountainous.

December 18, 1858
Memphis Route Complaints

December 18, 1858, page 2
Des Arc Citizen, Little Rock, Arkansas

THE **OVERLAND MAIL** TO THE PACIFIC – J. T. Trezevant, Esq., in a communication published in the Memphis Appeal, shows conclusively that great injustice has been done the Memphis end of the **"Overland Pacific Mail Line,"** in the non-reception of mails and passengers, while the St. Louis end of the same line has been regularly supplied by the contractors. Mr. Trezevant says:

> *"But the liberal ideas of the Postmaster General about making Memphis one of the Mississippi valley termini of this enterprise, are rendered really futile by the conduct and management of* **Butterfield & Co.**, *the contractors.*
>
> *It surely was as practicable to stock the line from Fort Smith to Memphis, as from Fort Smith to St. Louis, for it*

> *is nearer from that diverging point to Memphis than to St. Louis. There was no more necessity for subletting the Memphis line than was for subletting the St. Louis line. Yet is was done; and when remonstrance was made, and orders issued from the Post Office Department,* ***Butterfield's*** *reply was a long plausible explanation, and an earnest* PROMISE *to correct the gross injustice done to this end of the service. Yet, in the face of all this, the telegraph still continues to make the regular announcement to the citizens of Memphis, that the "***Overland Mail*** *has arrived at St. Louis;" when it is known to all that this mail ought to reach Memphis at least a day earlier than St. Louis. What is the consequence? Why, no traveler going or coming to, or from California by the* ***overland*** *route, will think of coming by Memphis, for the chances of making the connections at Fort Smith are all against him.*
>
> *All this outrage to our rights will continue with renewed protests, apologies and promises until* ***Butterfield*** *will so manage matters as to get Congress to do away with the Memphis connection entirely, and let him confine his contract to the St. Louis line. Last winter and spring this course was apprehended, and the indications are that it will yet be done, despite the liberal wishes and remonstrances of the Post Office Department."*

Mr. Trezevant suggests a public meeting of the citizens of Memphis, to protest against this palpable evasion of the duty imposed upon the contractors by the Postmaster General. So far, so good. But there are some other facts in connection with this matter which we will briefly state.

The distance from Memphis to Fort Smith is 300 miles direct, by land, *via* Des Arc. The **Overland Mail** has been carried through several times in less than 70 hours, *via* Little Rock, which is 27 miles from the 35th parallel or direct route to Fort Smith. But this was at a season of the year when the roads were good. The contractors, **Messrs. Butterfield & Co.,** can never succeed in delivering their mails promptly the year round, unless they procure a good steamboat to run from Memphis to Des Arc, for at least six months in the year. This boat can make the run in 35 hours, and connect here with their stages for Fort Smith. The carrying of the **Overland Mail** *via* Little Rock is 54 miles out of the way, and is an outrage that the General Government should no longer countenance. We have no fears of the route being changed from Des Arc, for every exertion has been made to accomplish it that was in the power of those who are afraid of the future prospects of our town.

We *[Des Arc]* are on the direct line to the Pacific – the route that all men of mature judgment define as the only feasible one for the erection of the Pacific Railroad upon. The sub-contractors under **Butterfield & Co.,** promptly selected the 35th parallel as *the route* upon which to carry the **Overland Mail,** and should they see fit to displace them, there is no alternative left but to continue the mail over the same route, with the exception of the 54 miles to Little Rock and back, and the running of a steamer six months in the year from Memphis to Des Arc.

December 18, 1858

Four Postal Routes to the Pacific Established

December 18, 1858, page 2

Des Arc Citizen, Little Rock, Arkansas

FOUR **OVERLAND ROUTES** TO THE PACIFIC – One feature of Mr. *[President]* Buchannan's policy is of unimpeachable popularity. This is the establishment of a set of continental mail routes – not a single one, but several of them – through our own territory to the Pacific. Each of these lines is not only a happy and enduring band of inter-state harmony, but it is the cheapest, and surest means of Indian repression. Every regularly traveled route is equal to a series of forts, and are ten times as valuable, and may be had at a twentieth the outlay of a regular military post.

Of the four **overland** routes now settled upon, the *St. Louis Republican* says the Southern one will be open all the year, and the other three for summer travel. These routes

Map of Mail Routes

The source of the three maps below: "Mails of the Westward Expansion, 1803 to 1861" by Steven C. Walske and Richard C. Frajola, Western Cover Society, 2015

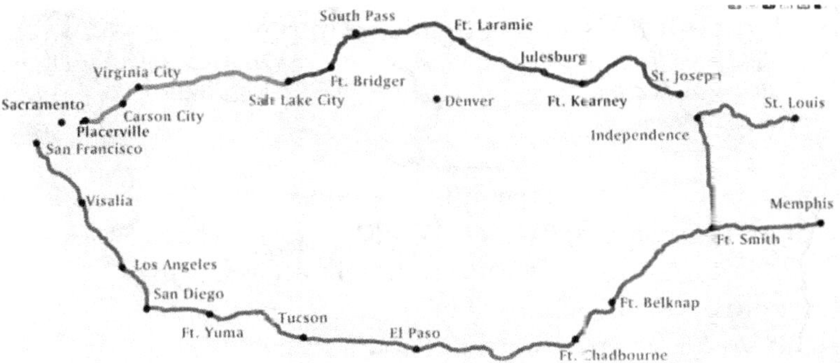

Map of Butterfield's Overland Mail Route, 1858-1861 (lower)
Map of Pony Express Route , 1860-1861 (upper)

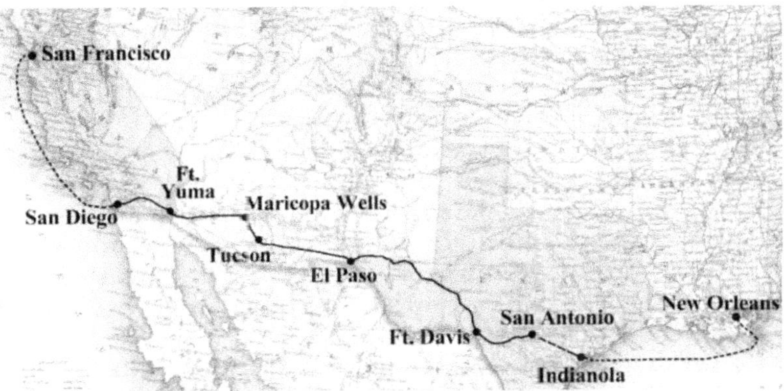

Map of San Diego to San Antonio "Jackass" Route , 1857-1860

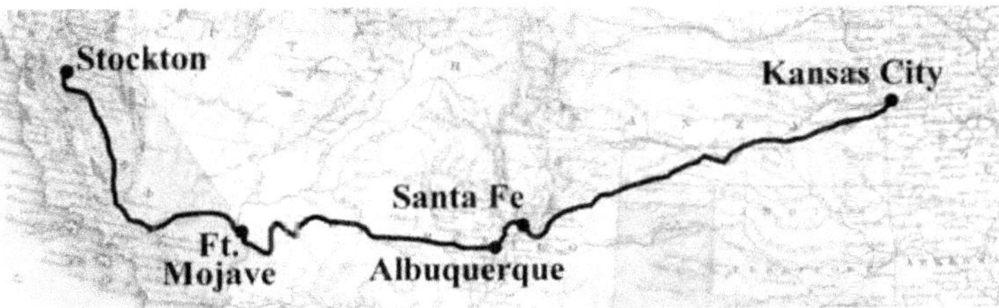

Map of contract Mail between Kansas City and Stockton, 1858-1859

belt the continent in parallels so judiciously distributed by the care of Postmaster General Brown that each great division of the Union is now brought into stage and railroad connection with all the others. Nations have sung "Te Deums" for infinitely less valuable triumphs. – *Washington*

[Note: Te Deum laudamus, {Latin: "God, We Praise You"} also called Te Deum, Latin hymn to God the Father and Christ the Son, traditionally sung on occasions of public rejoicing.]

December 18, 1858
The Cadron Ferry, Used Weekly by Overland Stages is Put Up for Sale

December 18, 1858, Saturday

Arkansas State Gazette and Democrat, Little Rock, Ark.

For Sale.

THE Cadron property, thirty-six miles above Little Rock, fronts the Arkansas river two miles in a compact body, and can be divided into three or four farms, giving to each a desirable *River* or *Hill residence.*

This tract includes the Cadron Mills and Ferry —160 acres cleared and in cultivation, from five to six hundred deadened, spring, well and cistern water, with buildings sufficient to accommodate from 50 to 100 hands. Title unquestionable. If desired, I will sell with the place 100 head of cattle and as many hogs.

For richness of soil and convenience to market this place is unsurpassed by any lands in this country.

I will also sell *a magnificent tract of river land,* fifty miles above Little Rock, fronting the river ¾ of a mile, containing 600 acres—125 in cultivation—150 deadened. For further particulars apply to the undersigued, at Lewisburg, Ark.

W. L. MENEFEE.

Oct. 23, 1858. 16—tf.

Source: Dec. 18, 1858, Sat.
Arkansas State Gazette and Democrat, Little Rock, Ark.

We have no description of the Cadron Ferry, but this South Dakota image is typical of a simple flat bottom ferry of the 1850's in common use across Arkansas.

December 22, 1858
Presidents' Address to the Senate & House

December 22, 1858, page 2
Arkansas True Democrat, Little Rock, Arkansas

Fellow Citizens of the Senate and House of Representatives: ...The post office department occupies a position very different from that of the other departments. For many years it was the policy of the government to render this a self-sustaining department; and if this cannot now be accomplished, in the present condition of the country, we ought to make as near an approach to is as may be practicable.

The Post Master General is placed in a most embarrassing position by the existing laws. He is obliged to carry these into effect. He has no other alternative. He finds, however, that this cannot be done without heavy demands upon the treasury over and above what is received for postage; and these have been progressively increasing from year to year until they amounted, for the last fiscal year, until they amounted for the last fiscal year ending on the 30th of June, 1858, to more than four millions and a half of dollars; whilst it is estimated that for the present fiscal year they will amount to $6,290,000. These sums are exclusive of the annual appropriation of $790,000 for *"compensation for the mail service performed for the two houses of Congress and other departments and officers of the government in the transportation of free matter."*

The cause of these large deficits is mainly attributable to the increased expense of transporting the mails.

In 1852, the sum paid for this service was but a fraction above four millions and a quarter. Since that year, it has annually increased until in 1858, it has reached more than eight millions and a quarter; and for the service of 1859, it is estimated that it will amount to more than ten millions of dollars.

The receipts of the Post Office Department can be made to approach to equal its expenditure, only by means of the legislation of Congress.

In applying any remedy, care should be taken that the people shall not be deprived of the advantages which they are fairly entitled to enjoy from the Post Office Department.

The principal remedies recommended to the consideration of Congress by the Postmaster General, are to restore the former rate of postage upon single letters to five cents; to substitute for the franking privilege the delivery to those now entitled to enjoy it, of post office stamps for their correspondence, and to direct the department, in making contracts for the transportation of the mail, to confine itself to the payment of the sum necessary for this single purpose, without requiring it to be transported in post coaches or carriages of any particular description.

Under the present system, the expense to the government is greatly increased, by requiring that the mail shall be carried in such vehicles as will accommodate passengers. This will be done without pay from the department over all roads where the travel will remunerate the contractors.

The recommendations deserve the grave consideration of Congress.

December 22, 1858
Arkansas General Assembly Resolution

December 22, 1858, page 2

Arkansas True Democrat, Little Rock, Arkansas

In the Senate last week, Mr. Floyd offered the following important resolutions:

Whereas, the Postmaster General of the United States, under and by the provision of an act of Congress, let to contract the great **Overland Pacific Mail** from two points on the Mississippi River to make a junction at some point west of Arkansas In pursuance of said act of Congress, the Post Master General let said mail service to contract, fixing one point or terminus at St. Louis, thence via Jefferson City, Springfield and Fayetteville to Fort Smith, and the other at the city of Memphis, thence to the city of Little Rock, and from thence to form the said junction at the city of Fort Smith, and that **Messers. Butterfield & Co.**, became the contractors. The said contractors are now in the pursuance of the stipulations, of their contract, performing good service on the northern terminus from St. Louis to Fort Smith, and regularly carrying the great Pacific mail on that route with full and complete grade of service to the entire satisfaction of all who are concerned in the northern interest, while said contractors at the same time in violation of the plain letter and condition of their obligation made with the government of the United States have wholly and totally failed to make provisions to put stock and coaches on the line from the terminus at the city of Memphis on the Mississippi River by the city of Little Rock, to the western junction at the city of Fort Smith

And further, we regard such failure on the part of the contractors, **Messrs. Butterfield & Co.,** to perform the conditions of their contract as an injury and an outrage on the rights of the people of the State of Arkansas, that should not for a moment longer be tolerated – when they are at the same time receiving full pay form the United States government for carrying the great **Overland Mail** to San Francisco in California.

And, it is understood, that said contractors in violation of the liberal provisions made by the Post Master General to give the people of Arkansas a full grade of mail service, will endeavor to have their contract so modified by an act of Congress as to permit them to make St. Louis the sole terminus of the great Pacific mail route.

Therefore be it resolved by the General Assembly of the State of Arkansas, That we here enter our protest against any modification of the contract made with **Butterfield & Co.**, in relation to the Pacific mail contract service by the Congress of the United States or by the Post Master General, and that the authorities of the United States should by all possible means within their power require a faithful performance of the contract for carrying the great **overland mail** to the Pacific Ocean.

Be it further resolved, That our senators in Congress are hereby instructed and our representatives are requested to use all their influence to see that **Messrs. Butterfield & Co.**, be required to perform their contract to the very letter of their obligations, that the preamble and resolutions be immediately forwarded by the Governor of this State to our members of Congress.

December 25, 1858
Butterfield's Steamboat Jennie Whipple Carrying Overland

December 25, 1858, Saturday

Arkansas State Gazette and Democrat, Little Rock, Ark.

ARRIVALS Dec. 20 –

Jennie Whipple at Little Rock from St. Louis

DEPARTURES Dec. 20 –

Jennie Whipple from Little Rock to Ft Smith

The Jennie Whipple

John Butterfield purchased The Jennie Whipple in St. Louis and it arrived in Little Rock on December 20, 1858. To date, no image of the Jennie Whipple has been found, however it would be similar to the steamboat Eagle - the first steamboat to every reach the port of Little Rock (1822). The Jennie Whipple was a sternwheel packet with a wood hull, built in 1857 at Brownsville, Pennsylvania. She was 138 tons, 135 feet long, and 30 feet wide. The engines were 15 $^{1}/_{2}$'s 3 $^{1}/_{2}$ ft, with three boilers.

The Jennie Whipple was built for the Chippewa River with Capt. Charles C. Gary, but soon went to the Arkansas River from 1858 to 1859 with Capt. Charlie Gray and Capt. A. D. Storm running to Memphis.

On only eight occasions, John Butterfield's steamboat, Jennie Whipple, was able to fulfill his original plan of carrying Overland passengers and mail between Memphis and Fort Smith. On 73 additional occasions Jennie Whipple was able to complete the Little Rock to Memphis leg of the route.

On four additional occasions the Jennie Whipple made a run between Little Rock and Fort Smith, with stagecoaches completing the Little Rock to Memphis portion of the Overland Mail route.

In 1860 and 1861, the Jennie Whipple was stranded for more than a year in Indian Territory (Oklahoma) because of record low water levels in the Arkansas River.

During the Civil War, the Jennie Whipple transported Union troops and arms on numerous occasions.

For more information on the Jennie Whipple, see Bob Crossman's book: "Butterfield's Overland Mail Co. Use of STEAMBOATS to Deliver Mail and Passengers Across Arkansas 1858-1861."

Image source: Sketch by DeSpain, 1975,
from the collection of Bob Crossman

December 25, 1858
Report of Two Overland Passengers
Road Conditions – The Gold Mines – Murder

December 25, 1858, Saturday, page 3
Arkansas State Gazette and Democrat, Little Rock, Ark.

Later Dates from California – Two passengers came through from San Francisco, D. Jones and Christian Krause. They left that place *[San Francisco]* early on the morning of the 22d of last month, and have made the trip within twenty-five days, being some twelve hours ahead of the regular time. Four of the passengers who started in the same mail came on as far as the new gold diggings in Arizona.

In 1858, Arizona's first gold rush began when Jacob Snively led an expedition that discovered a deposit of gold on the Gila River about 19 miles east of Yuma. This postcard from around 1909 shows an unidentified gold mine near Phoenix, Arizona.

Mr. Jones reports the road along the entire distance is in admirable condition for travel. No unnecessary detentions occurred to the mail, during the journey, which fact is highly commendatory of the well systematized plan under which affairs of the road are conducted, and the invariable efficiency of its operation.

In reference to the Gila River gold miles, our informant states that comparatively little excitement exists in San Francisco concerning them, although from along the road for hundreds of miles, on both sides of the mines, there is an immense emigration pouring into them, and the emigrants are eager to test their productiveness. This gave ample evidences of the interest which rumors from the auriferous *[rocks containing gold]* region had excited throughout the country. There is much excitement at Los Angelos about the mines, and many people are leaving for them. The statement of our informant is corroborative of previous accounts concerning the extent and richness of the diggings. He said, however, in addition, that later prospects made 150 miles up the Gila River, on both sides of that stream, have revealed new deposits.

Panning for gold on the Mokelumne River in California.

Provisions at the regular diggings are scarce, but large supplies are being brought in from various directions. The greatest difficulty arises from an inadequate supply of water for mining operations. Many miners are compelled to carry the dirt on their backs a distance of a mile and a half to the river. Proper mining implements are also difficult to be obtained in sufficient quantities to meet the increasing demand.

None of the regular employees of the **Overland Company** have deserted the stations for the mines, but some of them are very sick with the gold fever. Quite a number of the supernumeraries, such as grooms and side-drivers, have left for the diggings.

It will be recollected that sometime in September last, a party of men were attacked at Dragoon Springs by Mexicans and all killed, with the exception of Charles Jones, who escaped badly wounded by a stab in the side, and a shot in the shoulder. He was met a short distance west of the Colorado District, on his way to San Francisco. He was in a fair way to recover from his wounds. Five hundred dollars reward has been offered by the **Overland Mail Company** for the apprehension of the Mexican murderers.

December 29, 1858
Memphis Route Complaints

December 29, 1858, page 3
Arkansas True Democrat, Little Rock, Arkansas

The **Overland Mail** – Mr. Editor, The subject referred to in the caption of this article, is one that vitally affects the interests of the State of Arkansas.

But the point to which I wish to direct your attention, is the failure on the part of **Messrs. Butterfield & Co.**, to put the route from Memphis to Fort Smith, into operation in accordance with the terms of their contract. This is the part of the route which most concerns us, as it is essentially the Arkansas part of it.

My attention has been attracted to this delinquency on

the part of the contractors, by an article in a New York paper, which alleges that the mail cannot be carried from Memphis to Fort Smith in time to connect with the mail from St. Louis. This statement is untrue and unfounded, and if the Memphis mail has not reached Fort Smith in time, it is the fault of the contractors.

It is well known that they never have put the route in operation themselves, but have underlet it. The distance from St. Louis to Fort Smith is 468 miles, one hundred and sixty miles of which is by railroad; over the balance of the distance 308 miles, the mail is carried in stages. The distance from Fort Smith to Memphis is not exceeding 320 miles, over forty miles of which, a railroad is now in full operation, leaving 280 miles for staging.

Now sir, it is perfectly apparent to those who are acquainted with the route, that it is possible to run stages from Madison to Fort Smith in as short a time, as from Tipton in Missouri, to Fort Smith. In other words, it is as easy to make 280 miles in Arkansas, as 308 in Missouri and Arkansas.

I am informed that a responsible and reliable company has already submitted a proposition to carry the **overland mail** from Memphis to Fort Smith in as short time as it is carried from St. Louis, and I am satisfied that if the contract be awarded to them they will carry the mail through in less than forty-eight hours.

The Postmaster General should require **Messrs. Butterfield & Co.**, to put this route in operation, and when the facts are brought before him, no doubt that he will insist upon a full performance of the conditions of the contract, or give it to those who will do so.

The large portion of Arkansas is directly interested in the Memphis branch of this mail, and it is unjust to the whole State *[Arkansas]* to permit these contractors to give undue prominence to the St. Louis branch.

It is already mentioned by northern papers that this branch must be abandoned, and hence it is proper to call the attention of the public to the injustice likely to be perpetrated by which we will lose the advantages to be derived from the successful transportation of the mail through our State – *B. T. Duval*

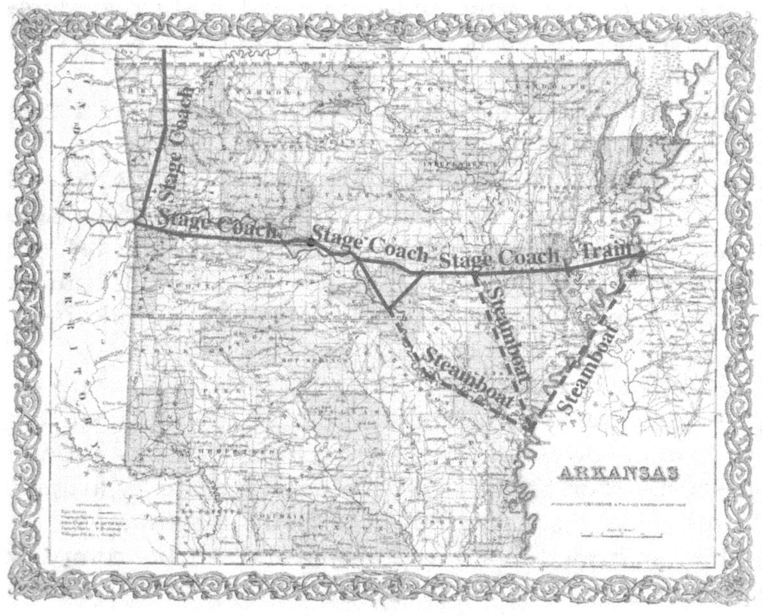

1855 Map of Arkansas
Published by J. H. Colton & Co., New York
Lines have been added to show the approximate route of ***Butterfield's Overland*** *stage and steamboat.*

December 29, 1858
Postmaster General Praised

December 29, 1858, page 1
Arkansas True Democrat, Little Rock, Arkansas

THE POSTMASTER GENERAL – ... His recent establishment of a set of continental mail routes, not one, singly, but a number of them, to the Pacific, through our own territory, is a master-stroke of national policy...

Postmaster General Aaron Brown

Of the four **overland** routes now settled upon, the St. Louis *Republican* says the southern one will be open all the year, and the other three for summer travel...

...from the *Erie Observer*... "We think one of the greatest and most beneficial enterprises that has yet been planned and executed by our government, is the establishment of an **overland mail** route to California... First and foremost will be the speedy growth of a line of settlements from the now western borders of civilization to California, thus securing a safe, cheap, and always open avenue from our Atlantic to our Pacific possessions through our own territory. This must soon be followed by the construction of a railroad – for how long will the "universal Yankee nation" *[Term introduced by wealthy New Englanders to proselytize their hopes for national and global influence.]* be satisfied with a stage route, consuming 20 or 23 days, when a railroad can be constructed, and the distance *[2,700 miles]* done in three or four? ...

December 29, 1858
Debate on Relocating Overland Route

December 29, 1858, page 2
Arkansas True Democrat, Little Rock, Arkansas

OVERLAND MAILS – It appears that there are three routes now in active operation, but the preference is universally given to **Butterfield's** route. The Missourians, although they are prosecuting a northern route by way of Salt Lake with vigor, evidently believe that a more southern route is the only practicable one and will endeavor to divert the line to St. Louis and intersect it so far west of as to have no terminus in this State *[Arkansas]*. Mr. Phelps is a man of acknowledged ability and we rather doubted that he would ignore the interests of his own State *[Missouri]* to build up any place in Arkansas or Tennessee. Knowing that the route on the 35th parallel would meet with supporters and could be established, he was content to have a terminus at St. Louis and one at Memphis, and afterwards to discontinue the part of the line through Arkansas – Mr. Phelps is a Missourian, and naturally had the welfare of his State *[Missouri]* at heart. In all this thing, so far as he did not deal double, and we do not know that he did, his acts were commendable.

But it appeared to us at the time, and does yet, that instead of playing into the hands of Missouri, it was the policy of western Arkansas to encourage a line of roads, railroads if possible, up the valley of the Arkansas River. It is evident that, unless regular and speedy communication can be had with Memphis, that the line of travel will tend to St. Louis. This, once established and the detour to Van Buren and Fort

Smith, will be sought to be avoided and no part of the route will pass through our State *[Arkansas]*.

Congressman Phelps of Missouri served 1845 – 1863
as the United States Congressman from Missouri. On numerous occasions he attempted to introduce legislation that would close the Memphis route, leaving St. Louis as the only eastern terminus.

That part of the route from Memphis to Fort Smith, should be insisted upon and the contractors not permitted to discontinue service on any portion of it.

In connection with this subject, we give the following from the *San Francisco National* of late date:

*"The arrivals of the **overland mails** within the past fortnight have closely approached scheduled time, and created very general confidence in the operations of the mail service by the **Butterfield route.** We are informed that the contractors are entirely satisfied that the route chosen is best suited for the service they have undertaken. The latest **Overland Mail** from St. Louis and Memphis is now arrived, bringing dates to October 11th. Although we*

*cannot look for as great punctuality during the entire wet season, yet we may safely expect that the steamer mails will be often anticipated by the reception, **overland**, of dates comprising one-half the interval between their semi-monthly departures.* [Ocean mail steamships ran twice monthly, Butterfield mail stages ran twice weekly] *The principal impediments in winter trips, by the now established southern line, will be found within the limits of California. Portions of the road in this State will be rendered difficult of travel by the rains, but the more serious obstacle of snow is entirely avoided.*

The latest news from Utah announce that snow had already fallen on the mountains east of Salt Lake, rendering it necessary for the merchants of that city to dispatch one hundred head of oxen to aid trains [wagon trains] *in crossing. Dr. Chorpening, the mail contractor by this route, had however reached Salt Lake on the 18th October. The period for testing the relative advantages of the several lines of **overland** communication is near at hand, and congress will at its approaching session be in possession of that positive knowledge relating thereto, which is necessary to the attainment of prompt and united action upon the great measure of a continental railroad.*

*The dream of a **transcontinental railroad** did not become a reality until May 10, 1869. Known originally as the "Pacific Railroad" the 1,911 mile continuous railroad line connected the existing eastern U.S. rail network at Council Bluffs,*

Iowa with the Pacific coast at the Oakland Long Wharf on San Francisco Bay. The transcontinental railroad provided fast, safe, and cheap travel. The fare for a one-week trip from Omaha to San Francisco on an emigrant sleeping car was about $65 for an adult. It replaced most of the far slower and more expensive stagecoach $200 ticket.

December 29, 1858
President & Postmaster Praised

December 29, 1858, page 3

Arkansas True Democrat, Little Rock, Arkansas

From the Philadelphia Argus – The Postmaster General – In no one thing as the far-reaching sagacity and profound judgment of Mr. *[President]* Buchanan been more conspicuously demonstrated, than in his selection of Gov. A. V. Brown to fill the important position of postmaster general. He is admitted on all hands to be the most able, enterprising and energetic head which that department of the government has ever had. He is winning an enviable renown for the wonderful achievements he has already so successfully consummated, as well as those which are still in progress of development.

We have watched the public career of this prominent American statesman, for many years, with peculiar interest. He is one of the few men now living who belong to the primitive school of American Democracy; to an age of republican simplicity and republican purity in morals and politics. Stern, unbending, unwavering in his devotion to the great principles enunciated by Thomas Jefferson, partaking in an uncommon degree of that indomitable firmness and inflexible adherence to justice, which so eminently characterized the immortal hero of the Hermitage, General Andrew Jackson, he has always received the homage and respect of his party at home and the people abroad – Few statesmen living have warmer or more enthusiastic personal and political friends, than has Gov. A. V. Brown, and few deserve to have them more justly than he.

His recent establishment of a set of continental mail routes, not one, singly, but a number of them, to the Pacific, through our own territory, is a master stroke of national policy, and will give him even a prouder position in the estimation of the American people than he has hitherto occupied. A contemporary *[Dec. 18, 1858 issue of Des Arc Citizen]* says, very forcibly and justly, that:

> *"Each of these lines is not only a happy and enduring bond of interstate harmony, but it is the cheapest and surest means of Indian repression. Every regularly traveled route is equal to a series of forts, and are ten times as valuable, and may be had at a twentieth the outlay of a regular military post.*
>
> *Of the four* ***overland*** *routes now settled upon, the* St. Louis Republican *says the Southern one will be open all the year, and the other three for summer travel. These routes belt the continent in parallels so judiciously distributed by the care of Postmaster General Brown that each great division of the Union is now brought into stage and railroad connection with all the others. Nations have sung "Te Deums" for infinitely less valuable triumphs."*

We are glad to see that the leading journals of the country are disposed to do full justice to the sterling merits of the Postmaster General. The moderate and candid portion of the opposition press does not hesitate to award him a high meed of praise. The democratic papers of this state are enthusiastic in their approbation of his policy, and their eulogies are warm and glowing in the extreme. From among many we select the following from the *Erie Observer,* commending it to the careful attention of our numerous readers:

> *Eire, Ohio – A Great and Beneficial Enterprise – We think one of the greatest and most beneficial enterprises that has yet been planned and executed by our government, is the establishment of an* ***Overland Mail Route*** *to California. It has attracted very little attention – indeed, many thought the idea chimerical* [chimerical: a mythical animal formed from parts of various animals]– *but the results to flow from it, who can estimate them?*
>
> *First and foremost will be the speedy growth of a line*

of settlements from the now western borders of civilization to California, thus securing a safe, cheap, and always open avenue from our Atlantic to our Pacific possessions through our own territory.

This must soon be followed by the construction of a railroad – for how long will the "universal Yankee nation" be satisfied with a stage route, consuming 20 or 23 days, when a railroad can be constructed and the distance done in three or four? But we have not time to enumerate the results to flow from the successful issue of this project; we merely designed to call attention to the fact that, while but little has been said on the Atlantic side of the continent, the people of the Pacific side fully appreciate the benefits to flow from it, and are ready to render to the head of the post office department, Governor Brown, the praise he is so justly entitled to in bringing this matter to such a successful issue. [Also quoted in the Dec. 29, 1858 Arkansas True Democrat.]

SANTA CLARA, CALIFORNIA – As for instance, we notice that the citizens of Santa Clara, California, met on the 14th of October, for the purpose of giving expression to the views entertained by the people of that town, of the great benefits to be derived from the successful establishment of the **Overland Route.** The following resolutions were adopted on the occasion:

Resolved, That the people of Santa Clara view with pride, the successful establishment of the **Overland Mail Routes**, *and hail the event as one calculated to give impulse to a speedy immigration to the Pacific shores.*

Resolved, That the establishment of the various routes now in successful operation, will have a tendency to encourage the speedy projection of the Pacific railroad, the consummation of which will serve to connect more closely the cherished homes of our "fatherland," with the sons and daughters of the Pacific coast.

Resolved, That the Hon. A. V. Brown, Postmaster General, in his wise policy in the management of the department under his charge, and for his untiring efforts to give the people of California a speedy communication across our continent, deserves our heartfelt gratitude.

SAN FRANCISCO – A large and enthusiastic meeting of the citizens of San Francisco was held on the 10th inst., to give expression to the sense entertained by the people of that city of the great benefits they are to receive from the establishment of the **Overland Mail Route.** The annexed resolutions were adopted:

Resolved, That the people of San Francisco, in mass meeting assembled, esteem the successful establishment of the most important work hitherto attempted for the developing of the wealth and permanent prosperity of our possessions on the Pacific coast.

Resolved, That the emancipation of the people of California from the thraldom [thraldom: the state of being in slavery or bondage to ocean steamships bound for California] *of the only speedy routes hitherto available, the necessity of whose use has subjected our citizens to the dangers and privations of sea travel and oft repeated indignities and wrongs from semi-civilized foreign governments, is hailed with sentiments of joy and of gratitude to those by whose energy and indomitable perseverance so glorious a result has been achieved.*

Resolved, That the Hon. A. V. Brown, Postmaster General, in his official acts, presents claims to our consideration of no ordinary character, in the successful result we now celebrate, in the establishment of the various lines of communication across our continent.

BUFFALO – The *Buffalo Commercial,* always a fair and honorable opposition journal, in remarking upon this subject, says that whatever faults and extravagances may be charged upon the general management of the federal government, the post office department deserves the approval of the public. Since Postmaster General Brown went into office he has completed and perfected a thorough system of trans-Atlantic mail transportation, connecting this country with all the more important portions of Europe by distinct lines; has secured a triumphant success of the great **Overland Mail Route**, and now looks to a more regular and reliable communication with both the eastern and western shores of South America.

WASHINGTON CITY – The Washington correspondent of the *New York Times*, in commenting on these achievements, calls attention to another great and feasible scheme in the following language:

> *"But will Gov. Brown stop here, and rest upon his laurels? He is not the man to stop half way or leave his work unfinished. I then draw the fair conclusion from the established premises that the report of the Postmaster General Brown will urge upon Congress the necessity for a line of mail steamers between San Francisco and some of the ports of China.*
>
> *Such a line of steamers is not only called for to complete the great mail line now almost belting the globe, but it would be a great stroke of national policy. It would at once attract the entire European mails for the east, all of which would pass over this line, and by the amount of postage received would not only pay the expenses of the Pacific steamers but would relieve the treasury from the burden of supporting the Atlantic lines."*

The arguments here advanced are weighty, and the probability that such a trans-Pacific line would support itself is well maintained.

December 29, 1858
One Hundred Tickets Sold

December 29, 1858, page 2

Arkansas True Democrat, Little Rock, Arkansas

NEWS ITEMS – One hundred passengers were booked for seats in the stage at St. Louis, for California, by **Butterfield's Line.** One hundred dollars premium was offered for seats.

1859

January 1, 1859
Butterfield's Steamboat Carrying Overland

January 1, 1859, Saturday
Arkansas State Gazette and Democrat, Little Rock, Ark.

ARRIVALS – Dec. 28

Jennie Whipple at Little Rock from Fort Smith

DEPARTURES – Dec. 29

Jennie Whipple from Little Rock to Fort Smith

[*Note: These same arrivals and departures were also reported in the Arkansas True Democrat, January 5, 1859, page 3.*]

January 1, 1859
Summary of Postmaster General's Report

January 1, 1859, Saturday, page 1
Arkansas State Gazette and Democrat, Little Rock, Ark.

POSTMASTER GENERAL'S REPORT – Our summary of the Postmaster General's report... we now give this most interesting points of the document...

He strongly favors the service in relation to this remote territory *[Panama Isthmus]*, and says:

> *"The route by Panama has never repaid in postage half its expense; yet the nation has been, in her trade and commerce, remunerated a thousand fold. So of the great* **Overland Routes**, *the main one* [Butterfield's] *of which has been established by the express enactment of Congress. None of the latter can ever make postal at all proportionate to their cost; but through their agency nearly one-half of our republic will be developed in its agricultural and mineral resources.*
>
> *And, therefore, while in the 'ordinary business' of transmitting correspondence, the department should be thrown entirely on its own revenues, the cost for 'any service on sea or on their land, namely, if not exclusively for*

national objects – such as the extension of our commerce, the spread of our population, and the development of the various resources of the country' the cost ought to be borne by the national treasury."
[The postmaster believed the cost of the transcontinental routes should not come out of his budget.]

January 5, 1859
Letter from John Butterfield

January 5, 1859, page 2
Arkansas True Democrat, Little Rock, Arkansas

LETTER FROM **COL. BUTTERFIELD** – NEW YORK, DEC. 2, 1858 – DEAR SIR – You are aware that it was my intention to put steamboat packets on the Arkansas River last summer, but was thwarted by the lowness of the water. You are also aware that the impossibility of using the river was apparent to me at too late a period to allow of my stocking the line between Memphis, Little Rock and Fort Smith in time to commence mail service on the 16th September, and was therefore compelled to make arrangements to have that service performed by others.

The service, thus unintentionally confided to others, has not been of a grade nor of a speed satisfactory to me, nor to the post office department, and is entirely below the just expectations of the people of Arkansas, Texas and of the Indian country, as well as of the traveling community generally.

That route from Memphis through Little Rock to Fort Smith, and then to northeast Texas direct, is exceedingly important. I intend to put on to it fine stock and first class coaches and spring wagons without delay; I intend the route shall be as well stocked as any route in the United States.

Then if the good people of Arkansas will do their duty manfully, that route, through the centre of the state, will be one of the greatest thoroughfares in the southwest. It will be not only important to Arkansas, but to all the citizens of the south who have business in Arkansas, and the Indian country or Texas. That duty is to build a good turnpike road from Memphis to Little Rock, and then to Fort Smith. Not a railroad, which, at $30,000 per mile, would cost nine millions of dollars in money and ten years in time, but an old fashioned, well drained dirt road costing at $300 per mile, only $90,000 in money, and 60 or 90 days in time.

It was in this way that New York, Pennsylvania, Maryland, Virginia, and other states opened up to market the interior settlements – afterwards followed by canals and railroads.

So in Arkansas, let the legislature pass a law, ordering turnpike road, appropriating $90,000 or $100,000 to pay for it. If the appropriation does not hold out, I doubt not, the planters, farmers, counties, villages, and merchants along the route will gladly contribute to its completion. I have seen a good many of your people, and I am not mistaken. To a practical scheme, they are as ready to contribute as any people in the world – at any rate, I intend to visit Little Rock and ask the attention of the legislature to the subject. I have no fears from what I have seen of the people of Arkansas, that their legislature will fail to give a candid hearing to a plain old-fashioned man of business, when pleading the necessity of a state thoroughfare, if, Arkansas would secure a fair portion of the trade, emigration and travel which Missouri will otherwise engross.

The distance from Fort Smith to Memphis through Little Rock ought not to exceed 300 miles, whilst the distance actually traversed by the **Overland Mail Company**, between Fort Smith and St. Louis, is 483 miles, and with full loads, in from one to two days quicker time. With a good turnpike and using 40 miles of railroad running west out from Memphis, we could travel the whole line in two days. When this is done, no state north or south can direct business from Arkansas, for the establishment of trade, emigration, and travel will promptly settle the country, increase values, and cause the railroad to be built at an early day.

Will you, sir, lend your influence and your aid to this

enterprise? Will you explain to the people the importance of constructing a good road through the center of the state, which everybody may travel free of charge for its use, if they would promote settlements, multiply villages, increase trade and hasten the construction of a rail road?

Will you tell them through your journal, that Missouri has built 162 miles of road which will increase by Christmas to 168 miles over which her people expect, as a just reward for their enterprise, to attract the whole of the business of western Arkansas, the Indian country lying to the west of it, and of Upper Texas, until the Central Road of Arkansas is opened?

But do not misapprehend me. I do not desire to build up one state at the expense of the other. I wish to see them both prosper. If both rapidly fill up with people, our interests are promoted; if either remains stationary, we are injured, inasmuch as our stages for the long period of six years are to run entirely across both of these. Good roads, connecting our St. Louis route with the railroads north of the Ohio and our Memphis route with the railroads of the entire southern states and with Washington City, are indispensable to the attainment of the object of the government in establishing the **Overland Mail** stages, viz: the extension, and easy communication with settlements between the Mississippi and California.

Missouri is earnestly engaged on one route – will not Arkansas as earnestly labor, in order to develop its own great resources to perfect the other? If the subject is thoroughly considered, I have no doubt but wise and energetic action will follow.

A great central road will be created before the end of June next. I feel satisfied that I can so employ and direct the necessary labor as to secure the building of a good turnpike road across Arkansas as to keep the cost within the sum of $300 per mile, including the bridging of all streams not navigable, which would establish and maintain a mail stage communication across the State, which shall please your people and satisfy the government of my country. And this with God's blessing, I intent to do.

From this purpose, I shall allow nothing to direct my attention, to carry it out; I find good roads wanting, and to obtain good roads, I appeal to the good sense, to the interests, and to the public spirit of the people of Arkansas.

With the aid of the public press, to clearly explain what will be the effect upon Arkansas, if she does nothing, when Missouri is doing so much, I shall be disappointed if I am not able to drive four horse stages of the first class through central Arkansas, upon a good turnpike road within the year of 1859. I shall be disappointed if our horses and stages are left another year to slowly wallow and flounder in the oceans of mud in the alluvial bottoms of eastern Arkansas.

Most respectfully,***John Butterfield***
President, **Overland Mail Company**

P. S. Since writing the above, I have purchased a boat, the Jennie Whipple, with which I shall leave in the early part of the week to establish and start the route, and hope, yet to satisfy the people that, if they will lend their aid to improve the roads, that they will reap the benefits that they desire. J. B.

John T. "Chit" Chidester, primary owner of Chidester, Reeside & Co.

A word of appreciation for Chit, is found in a letter to the editor of the

Memphis Avalanche, Feb. 21, 1859: *"I understand that you have been coming down upon Messrs. Chidester, Rapley & Co., the mail contractors from Madison to Little Rock, for failures in the mail connections. How this may be I know not, but I can say that I have been familiar with stage lines all my life, and that I have never seen such time made under such circumstances, nor a more thorough-going, energetic set of men than their drivers. Our way lay for miles and miles through a country flooded with water by the most tremendous rain storm in the memory of man, yet not one of the drivers ever said stop. Without waiting to consider whether the water was shallow or deep, they plunged in, and frequently swimming their horses for yards, still got through, and over twenty-six miles of such country, only came into Madison about two hours behind time."*

January 5, 1859
John T. Chidester - Butterfield's Sub-Contractor

January 5, 1859, page 2

Arkansas True Democrat, Little Rock, Arkansas

QUICK WORK – Our enterprising fellow townsman, C. A. Rapley of the firm of Hanger, Rapley & Co., who is associated with John T. Chidester, the well known mail contractor, in the contract to carry the mail from Madison, the terminus of the Memphis and Little Rock railroad, to this place *[Little Rock]*, handed us on last Sunday the Memphis papers of Saturday.

This is unprecedented in the history of mail facilities in this State *[Arkansas]*. And, what is more, the contractors say that they intend to keep it up. If so, we will be able to furnish the latest news, and if they crowd us much will set us to thinking about issuing a tri-weekly if not a daily.

January 5, 1859
John T. Chidester - Butterfield's Sub-Contractor

January 5, 1859, page 2

Arkansas True Democrat, Little Rock, Arkansas

TRAVEL BY **OVERLAND MAIL** COACHES – Speaking of the arrival of the eighteenth **Overland Mail** from San Francisco, the St. Louis *Republican* says:

Since the Overland Mail has indubitably proven itself a cheap, speedy, and secure means of travel, the rush at San Francisco, Los

Angeles and other places, to obtain seats in the coaches has become tremendous.

When our informant left San Francisco no less than one hundred persons had made application at the office of Mr. McLean, the agent there, for passage. So eager and importunate were they to secure passage that they had adopted the course of deciding by lot who has to stay over. To facilitate this, and be as impartial as possible, the agent would not accept engagements for seats more than two stages ahead. Every few days, therefore, there were places in a third [stage] *to be drawn.*

About half way over the route a passenger was found at a way station, where he had stopped to lay over for a few days nearly a month previously. As all the succeeding stages came by so filled with passengers he had been unable to get on again to complete his journey on to St. Louis. At the time the late mail arrived there he was so well worn out with his long resting spell that he offered a large bonus for his seat, but failed to get it.

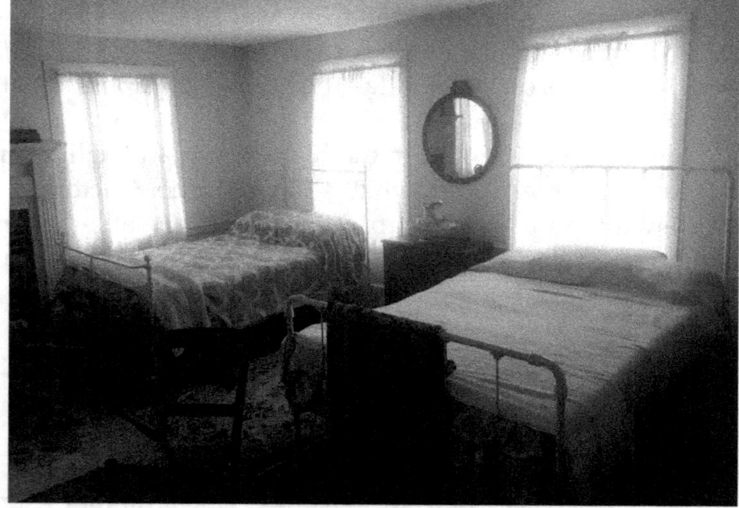

2nd Floor Bedroom, Potts Inn

Kirkbride Potts, station agent for Butterfield's Potts Station, provided, at his beautiful home, an upstairs bedroom with four beds for passengers who wanted to disembark for a couple days rest before attempting to board the next stagecoach to complete their journey. The beautifully restored Potts Station is open for tours and houses the Pope County Museum in Pottsville, Arkansas.

January 5, 1859
John T. Chidester - Butterfield's Sub-Contractor

January 5, 1859, page 3
Arkansas True Democrat, Little Rock, Arkansas

From the Memphis Avalanche – **Overland Mail Route** – Glorious News for Memphis! J. T. Chidester the universally known mail contractor in the south, with his associates, has taken a contract to carry the mail six times per week from Madison, the terminus of our Arkansas railroad, to Little Rock, and tri-weekly from Little Rock to Fort Smith.

Chidester & Co., have now in Arkansas about four hundred head of horses and a full supply of stage coaches. Every one is satisfied now that passengers and mails to and from Memphis and Fort Smith will hereafter be taken through in less time than **Butterfield & Co.** will be enabled to come through from St. Louis.

In one month from today all Southern and Northwestern travel to California by the **overland route** will be confided to Chidester's line. The road is infinitely better than that from St. Louis, and more than 90 miles shorter, if a branch route were established from Des Arc to Little Rock, by which 40 miles of the distance to Fort Smith would be saved. The distance from Memphis to Fort Smith, on a direct line, is only about 260 miles; from St. Louis it is not less than 350 miles.

We have never believed it possible that **Butterfield and Co.** could have carried the mails to St. Louis in the time represented by the telegraph reports – **Butterfield & Co.** are St. Louis men, and there is no one in that city who does not desire the suppression of the Memphis branch route, which, from the necessity of nature of things, must finally break down the more northern line, or at least materially injure its business.

It will soon become a fixed universally conceded fact, that the great highway to the Pacific cannot be north of the thirty-fifth parallel of latitude, and even St. Louis and **Butterfield & Co.** must come down to this.

To show our readers what is thought of Chidester by those who know him best, we clip the following from the Washington correspondence of the *Tuscumbia Enquirer:*

> "Your townsman, John T. Chidester, esq., seems to possess more of the *hic et ubique [Latin –here and everywhere]* characteristics than falls to the common lot of men – in Alabama today, away in Arkansas tomorrow; in a few days more in the federal metropolis, busy in the P. O. D., *[Post Office Department]* where, for the last few days, he might have been seen, at one moment in earnest conversation with some M. C., *[Member of Congress]* at another, waiting an audience with the Postmaster General, with whom, I learn, he has contracted to carry the U. S. mails on the route from Memphis to Little Rock, connecting with Memphis and Little Rock Railroad at Madison, Arkansas. "Chit" is certainly 'some' in the transaction of business – be that in the post-office department or in connection with the supervision of the Bazaar, in your town."

The editors of the *Enquirer*, after endorsing the above, say of Mr. Chidester:

> "Today he is rich – independent in means of the word's gear, and possessed of a mature energy which is better than the mines of California. Go it Chidester! Open up the far west by your stage coaches. Bring California to our doors. If not the projector, you will be recorded as the agent in unfolding new fields of civilization, of agriculture and commerce. Gov. Brown has done well in accepting you as one of the pioneers to open the great Pacific route."

In this connection we may instance, as an evidence of "Chits" energy and resolve, but yesterday he arrived here from a visit to Washington, and already has been on the way to Memphis obtaining the necessary stock of horses for the western lines of mail and stage coaches. Tuscumbia *[Alabama]* may well be proud of her citizen."

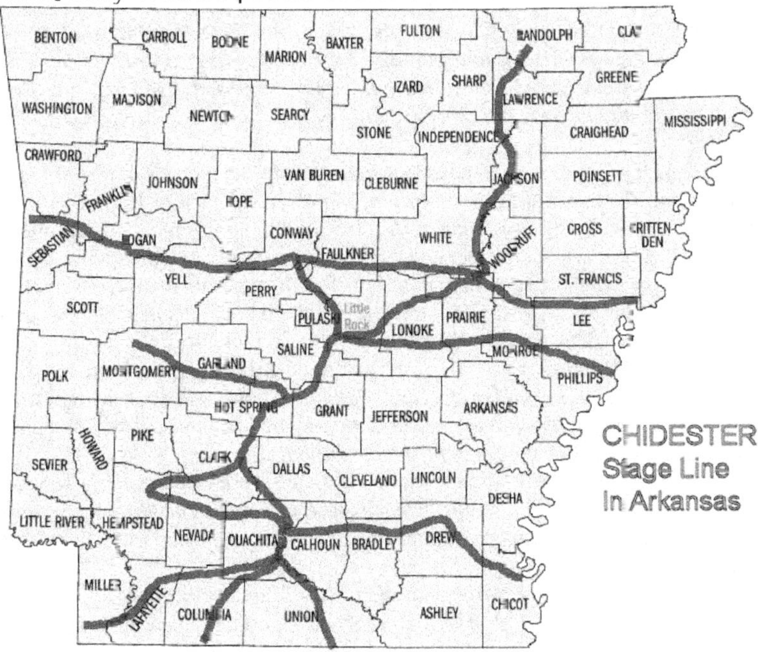

Stage Routes of John T. Chidester
Map provided by the McCollum-Chidester Museum

The map above shows the various stage routes that Chidester established - most of them before John Butterfield received the Overland Mail Co. contract. While we usually credit John Butterfield for establishing the central Arkansas route, it may be more correct to credit John Chidester for setting the initial land stage route of home and swing stations between Memphis and Fort Smith in April of 1858.

In April of 1858, Brimmer, Chidester, Reeside & Co. received a contract from the U.S. Post Office contract to provide mail service from Des Arc, Arkansas to Ft. Smith, three times a week (Route 7831) – bidding against 14 others for the contract.

Five months later, in September of 1858 Butterfield's Overland Mail subcontracted with Chidester, Reeside & Co. to carry mail and passengers from Memphis to Fort Smith over the same route.

There were problems during the first four months. Memphis was learning by telegraph that the stages were arriving in St. Louis a day or so ahead of the stage bound for Memphis. Investigating the reason for the delays, Butterfield

Agent, Walton, on Dec. 4, 1858, reported: "owing to other contracts of the sub-contractors, the mail is laid over about 48 hours at Fort Smith, and about 24 at Des Arc. At present this can not be remedied."

In Feb. 9, 1859, James Glover wrote, concerning these problems, that mostly due to poor road conditions and fulfilling their overlapping contract to carry the regular mail from Fort Smith to Memphis "their route was so circuitous, and they had to stop at so many offices, that they were unable to comply with this contract."

Therefore, a new sub-contract was made between Butterfield and Chidester. *The new sub-contract, beginning about the first of February, 1859, allowed Chidester 45 hours to carry the Overland from Memphis to Dardanelle, where Overland Mail and passengers were transferred to Butterfield owned stages and horses for a 15 hour trip to Fort Smith, stopping at Butterfield operated swing stations between Dardanelle and Fort Smith. This new 60 hour plan would be 24 hours faster than the Fort Smith to St. Louis stage.*

Apparently this new sub-contract was only in effect between Feb. and May of 1859. *In the Jan. 5, 1859, Arkansas True Democrat, John Butterfield writes, "Memphis through Little Rock... I intend to put on to it fine stock and first class coaches and spring wagons without delay."*

In the May 4, 1859 issue of the Arkansas True Democrat, it is reported that James Glover told the editor: "He tells us that they intend stocking the road from Dardanelle to Memphis and carrying their own mails, and to make this, the superior arm of the service."

On May 28th Glover writes that they are still procuring stock.

On August 13th, Butterfield Agent Nichols reports that they are "now stocked with excellent teams, first class coaches, and reliable drivers, for the purpose of carrying on the route - either way or through passengers."

In mid August, 1859 Butterfield Overland Mail ended the sub-contract with John T. Chidester. *From Aug. 1859 to March 1861 all of the stations, stages and horses on the Memphis to Fort Smith Route were the property of the Overland Mail Co.*

(Source: February 9 and May 28 articles reprinting letters from James Glover, O. M. Superintendent and the August 13, 1859 Weekly Gazette article quoting Agent Nichols.)

January 8, 1859

River is Not Reliable from Little Rock to Fort Smith

January 8, 1859, Saturday

Arkansas State Gazette and Democrat, Little Rock, Ark.

Honor to Whom Honor is Due – In alluding to the mail facilities, and service, in Arkansas, we have had frequent occasion to condemn the policy of Postmaster General Brown.

We are delighted to record one set of his which is worthy of the highest commendation – that is, the establishment of the daily mail from this place to Memphis, to run in connection with the rail road. By this line the stages and rail road make the trip from here to Memphis in a little over twenty-four hours; and this is the only line, coming into this State from the eastern or Southern border, which makes regular connections with the mails outside of the State.

The **Overland California Mail** comes to this place by this route, in due time; and if the line be continued it can reach Fort Smith far in advance of the St. Louis branch. But to do this, and do it with certainty, the ***[Butterfield Overland]*** mail must be carried by land from here to Fort Smith. The river is not reliable; and, if it could be relied upon, the boats in the service cannot make the time.

But we commenced to speak of Postmaster General Brown; he deserves all the praise for sending stages through Memphis to this place *[Little Rock]* in the time he sends them; but his work is not complete until he makes the Postmaster at Memphis send all our *mail matter* in the stages, aforesaid.

January 8, 1859
Butterfield's Steamboat Jennie Whipple Carrying Overland Mail

January 8, 1859, Saturday
Arkansas State Gazette and Democrat, Little Rock, Ark.

ARRIVALS JAN. 3 –

Jennie Whipple at Little Rock from Fort Smith

DEPARTURES JAN. 4 –

Jennie Whipple from Little Rock to Fort Smith

Butterfield Station on Concha River

January 8, 1859
Overland Stage Arrives

January 8, 1859, Wednesday, page 2
Des Arc Citizen, Des Arc, Arkansas

NEWS BY THE **OVERLAND MAIL** – *St. Louis, Jan. 3* – The **Overland Mail** of the 6th inst. arrived on Saturday. Major Mory, passenger, confirms the previous accounts about the Gila River gold mines. There was considerable emigration to Sonora. The California mail station on Concha River had been attacked by the Comanches, and thirty-one mules stolen.

UTAH – ... Major Crossman had not left for the States. Snow in the mountains was very deep, which caused great suffering to men and animals. *[Note: This article was also reprinted in the January 9, 1859 issue of the Weekly Arkansas Gazette, page 2.]*

January 8, 1859
Overland Stage Arrives with News

January 8, 1859, Saturday
Arkansas State Gazette and Democrat, Little Rock, Ark.

ST. LOUIS, DEC. 31 – The **Overland Mail** of the 3d has arrived here. The news from the Gila mines is very favorable. The road from San Francisco to Red River is very good, but is very bad from thence to Tipton. The Indians had robbed one of the stations of the entire stock of mules.

January 12, 1859
Butterfield's Steamboat Jennie Whipple Carrying Overland Mail

January 12, 1859, Wednesday
Arkansas True Democrat, Little Rock, Arkansas

ARRIVALS – Jan. 9 Jennie Whipple, from Fort Smith

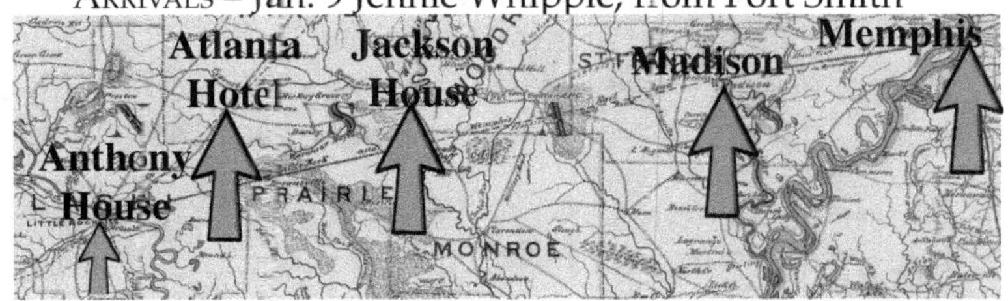

1864 Arkansas Map with arrows added to show Butterfield Overland Home stations between Memphis and Little Rock.

January 12, 1859
Letter from a Butterfield's Overland Passenger Written from the Little Rock Home Station

January 12, 1859, page 2
Arkansas True Democrat, Little Rock, Arkansas

ANTHONY HOUSE, LITTLE ROCK, JANUARY 8TH, 1859

MR. EDITOR: Having business in your town we availed ourselves of the facilities offered to us by the new line of ***[Butterfield Overland]* mail coaches** just put into operation between Madison, the termination of the Memphis and Little Rock railroad, and this place by those enterprising and energetic men, Chidester, Rapley & Co., and although owing to the heavy rains which has just fallen, the roads were in the worst possible condition, we with the mail, were safely landed at our destination *[Little Rock]* yesterday afternoon, making the time from Madison, our starting point, in about twenty-seven hours, and the connection between

Memphis and this place in about thirty hours.

After the journey was safely accomplished we could not refrain from contrasting our speedy trip in comfortable coaches with the slow, wearisome tugging and plodding through mud and mire we have heretofore endured in passing over the same on horseback. When first informed of the great enterprise of making the mail connection between Memphis and this place in but little more than one day's time by means of coaches, we were inclined to doubt the possibility of effecting so desirable an object; but now we know that in the worst of weather and most unfavorable condition of the road, there has not, since the line went into operation, been a single failure to deliver the mails in due time, and to carry passengers with safety and comparative comfort.

Indeed, those who know Mr. Chidester well, also know that there is no such word as "fail" in his vocabulary. From an acquaintance with him, and from witnessing the energy which has been infused into all the employees connected with this line we are fully assured that the contractors will not only be successful in carrying the mail in schedule time, but that they will also be able to transport any number of passengers in comfortable coaches, drawn by fleet horses, and driven by experienced, careful and accommodating drivers.

We feel no hesitation in saying that the citizens of the state ought to consider themselves fortunate, that this and all the other lines of coach mail transportation in their midst have fallen into the hands of such a company of enterprising and thorough-going men as Chidester, Rapley & Co.

The line from Memphis to this place is more important than any other in the state because it is the pioneer which marks out a route to be followed by the great Pacific railroad, which must sooner or later be built by the general government or by private enterprise. The protection of immense territory and the urgent demands of the commerce of the world require it, and render it a work of necessity. Its construction is sure, being now only a question of time. In this point of view the immense importance of this line to the state, to the south and to the whole Union is too apparent to need comment.

Now it may be safely said that the days of old fogyism *[fogyism: an adherence to old-fashioned or conservative ideas and intolerance of change, often coupled with dullness or slowness of personality]* are waning, and days of advancement and improvement are beginning to dawn even upon Arkansas which has hitherto made so little progress in developing the might resources of wealth and greatness, so long concealed and unknown within her borders. And may we not hope that the citizens will arouse to press forward every movement which will promote our progress and improvement.

It is understood that **Col. Butterfield**, who is now here, is engaged in supervising the transportation of the **Overland Mail** to California, thus showing that at least one arm of the great Pacific railroad must pass through our midst.

In wishing success to Chidester, Rapley & Co., we cannot refrain from congratulating our most excellent Post Master General, Aaron V. Brown, for his success in establishing and putting in operation by means of such active and go ahead agents the important mail connection by **Overland** with California, thus binding with another cord the golden state of the Pacific coast with her older sisters of the east.

Yours Truly,

J. P. Graves, R. Mallory, C. W. Blazley

January 15, 1859
Butterfield's Steamboat Jennie Whipple Carrying Overland Mail

January 15, 1859, Saturday
Arkansas State Gazette and Democrat, Little Rock, Ark.

ARRIVALS JAN. 9 –

Jennie Whipple at Little Rock from Fort Smith

ARRIVALS JAN. 11 –

Jennie Whipple from Little Rock to Memphis

"The Jennie Whipple" *painted by Ralph Law.*

Butterfield's steamboat Jennie Whipple traveling from Memphis directly to Fort Smith

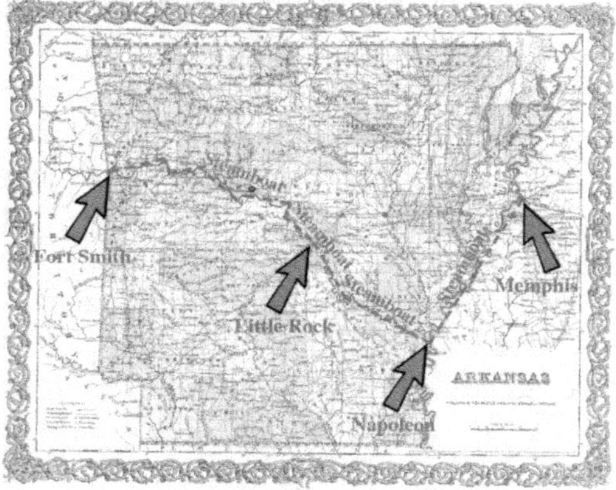

1855 Map of Arkansas
Published by J.H. Colton & Co., 112 Williams St., New York
The dotted red lines show the approximate route of the steamboat Jennie Whipple.

REGULAR U. S. MAIL PASSENGER PACKET.
MERCHANTS' AND PLANTERS' LINE.
JENNIE WHIPPLE,
C. C. GRAY, *Master*....G. W. HYSSON, *Clerk.*

THIS splendid, swift running passenger steamer will run regularly between Little Rock and Memphis, leaving Little Rock weekly for Memphis. Passengers ticketed through to Louisville, St. Louis or Cincinnati, by this boat.

For freight or passage, apply to
MERRICK & WASSELL, *Agents*,
Or on board.

April 2, 1859. 38—3m.

This advertisement began to be printed in the Weekly Arkansas Gazette, Little Rock, Arkansas, starting on Saturday, Apr 2, 1859.

Port of Little Rock, 1859
Source: Arkansas River Historical Society

January 22, 1859
Complaint that the Overland Doesn't Provide Passenger Service to Memphis

January 22, 1859
Arkansas State Gazette and Democrat, Little Rock, Ark.

THE MAILS – The new daily line continues to arrive from Memphis, with great regularity; and, though passengers come through, in good time, and report this as good as the other stage lines in the State *[of Arkansas]*, yet we regret that this route is almost, if not entirely, valueless for the transportation of the mails. Col. Harley, the mail agent, has taken the matter in hand, and if he does not make all right we shall allude to it again.

The Memphis branch of the **Overland Pacific Mail** does not come through from Fort Smith to this place as it ought to come. Within the past week we have heard of complaints from passengers who come by this line as far as Fort Smith *[from San Francisco]*, and found no mode of conveyance to Memphis – and the report goes that the company not only failed to forward its passengers, but refused to refund to them any part of their passage money.

The St. Louis branch, though, is reported to go through with the greatest possible regularity and dispatch.

If we find that Messrs. **Butterfield & Co.** are attempting to throw Arkansas and Memphis off, and favor a more Northern route, we shall feel it to be our duty to hold them up in their true colors before our people.

January 26, 1859
Butterfield's Steamboat Jennie Whipple
Carrying Overland Mail

January 26, 1859, Wednesday
Arkansas True Democrat, Little Rock, Arkansas

ARRIVALS – Jan. 23 Jennie Whipple from Memphis
DEPARTURES – Jan. 24 Jennie Whipple for Memphis

January 26, 1859
Memphis Route to Be Improved

January 26, 1859, Wednesday
Arkansas True Democrat, Little Rock, Arkansas

...The postmaster general has for a long time been determined to make the Memphis and Fort Smith branch of the **Overland Mail** equal in all respects, so far as the service is concerned, to those of St. Louis, and sometime since so informed the contractor, and that unless he did so at an early day, he would annul his contract. He now has assurance that all will be working well within a short time so that the people of Arkansas may rest easy on that score.

In this matter of the **overland mail**, as well as in all their mail arrangements they own much to Gov. Brown. He has done more for the state than could be expected, so much in fact, that he has spoiled the people, as every neighborhood have asked, or are on the eve of asking, that they be supplied through four horse daily or tri-weekly post-coach lines. The same localities, heretofore, were contented with semi-weekly horse mails. But if Gov. Brown can do nothing more for Arkansas, they have no reason to complain of him.

Port of Memphis, 1850, Where the Jennie Whipple Picked up Butterfield's Overland Passengers and Mail

January 29, 1859
Butterfield's Steamboat Jennie Whipple Carrying Overland Mail

January 29, 1859, Saturday
Arkansas State Gazette and Democrat, Little Rock, Ark.

ARRIVALS JAN. 22 –
Jennie Whipple at Little Rock from Memphis

DEPARTURES JAN. 22 –
Jennie Whipple from Little Rock for Memphis

February 4, 1859
Negative Response to Glover's Explanation for Memphis Route Shortcomings

February 4, 1859, Friday, page 3
Des Arc Citizen, Des Arc, Arkansas

OVERLAND CALIFORNIA MAIL – James Glover, Superintendent of the **Overland Mail Company**, makes a fruitless attempt in the columns of the *Memphis Appeal* to apologize for the failure in delivering this mail promptly at Memphis. Mr. Glover, like many others who have been essentially humbugged, adheres to the idea that this mail can be carried by light draught steamboats from Little Rock to Fort Smith. There is not a little negro on that stream *[Arkansas River]* but would laugh at the idea.

The route from Little Rock to Madison has been imposed upon the department at Washington, as suitable for conveying the U. S. Mail in four-horse post coaches, the year round. This is as great a mistake as the idea of navigating Arkansas River from Little Rock to Fort Smith the year round. We admit that through the summer months the route from Little Rock to Madison is over a passable road, but at that season of the year the Arkansas River is "dead low." It is therefore plain that one portion of this route will always defeat the other.

The Memphis branch of this road should be discontinued unless **Col. Butterfield** and his agents stop being led by the nose, and influenced by a set of men who use their exertions for the benefit of certain locations, regardless of the best and shortest route.

The route from Des Arc to Fort Smith is the shortest, and ever the best road. Six months in the year the mail should be brought from Memphis to Des Arc, overland, and the other six months by steamboat. This would ensure promptness in its delivery at Memphis, and until it is changed from the elbow route to Little Rock, failures will continue to be announced, and finally the Memphis route will be discontinued.

February 9, 1859
Senate Resolution No. 24 Concurred In

February 9, 1859, Wednesday, page 4
Arkansas True Democrat, Little Rock, Arkansas

Senate joint resolution No. 24, relative to the **overland mail** to the Pacific, etc., was taken up, and read three times and concurred in.

February 9, 1859
Butterfield's Steamboat Jennie Whipple Carrying Overland Mail

February 9, 1859, Wednesday
Arkansas True Democrat, Little Rock, Arkansas

ARRIVALS – Feb. 5, Jennie Whipple from Memphis
DEPARTURES – Feb. 6, Jennie Whipple for Memphis

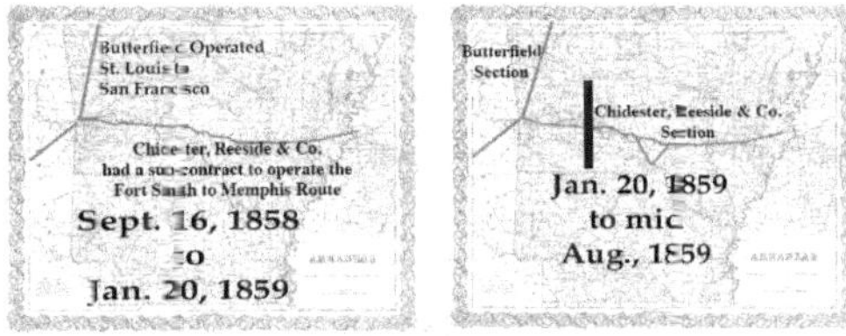

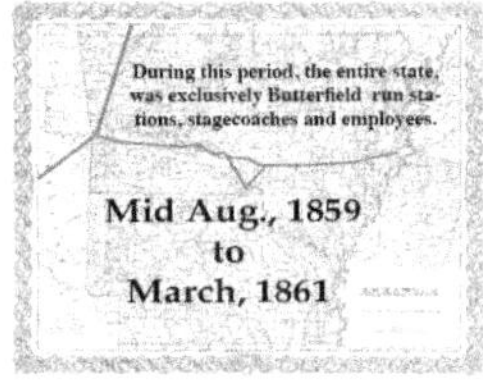

In mid August, 1859 Butterfield Overland Mail ended the sub-contract with John T. Chidester. From Aug. 1859 to March 1861 all of the stations, stages and horses on the Memphis to Fort Smith Route were the property of the Overland Mail Co. Source: February 9 and May 28 articles reprinting letters from James Glover, O. M. Superintendent and the August 13, 1859 Weekly Gazette article quoting Agent Nichols

February 9, 1859
Official Response to Memphis Route Complaints

February 9, 1859, page 2
Arkansas True Democrat, Little Rock, Arkansas

From the Memphis Appeal – THE **OVERLAND MAIL**

Gayoso House. Memphis, Jan. 28, 1859

MESSRS. EDITORS: I regret to learn that the citizens of Memphis and surrounding country, are very much dissatisfied with the failure of **Messrs. Butterfield & Co.**, to deliver the California mails here as early as at St. Louis.

Some explanation of the causes of their failures may tend to satisfy the public that the company are not so much to blame as has been generally thought.

You are no doubt aware that the *[Overland Mail]* company, believing that they could run light draught boats the year round on the Arkansas River, obtained the consent of the post master general to run boats between Little Rock and Fort Smith; this change was ordered too late for the company to have the class of boats which were necessary to run in low water with; they sent to almost every boat-yard and city in the south and west, hoping to find some already built, but failed in finding any of light enough draught.

They continued this fruitless search until very near the time for the mails to commence running – too late for them to put stock and coaches on this arm of the route – and they were forced to make a contract with Messrs. Chidester, Rapley & Co., who were carrying tri-weekly mails from this place to Fort Smith, to carry their mails for them; these gentlemen did all they could to put their mails through in schedule time, but their route was so circuitous, and they had to stop at so many offices, that they were unable to comply with this contract.

Failing in this they *[the Overland Mail Co.]* bought the contract from Dardanelle to Fort Smith, and put on their own stock, and made a contract with Chidester, Rapley & Co., to take their mails from Memphis to Dardanelle – the time allowed them being forty-five hours; from Dardanelle the company to carry them in their own stages to Fort Smith in fifteen hours; thus making the trip between Memphis and Fort Smith in sixty-hours – twenty-four hours less than that from St. Louis.

There have been but four mails since this arrangement was made, and the road between Memphis and Little Rock has been in such wretched condition that Messrs. Chidester, Rapley & Co., have not been able to go through in the time they had contracted to do, but think that when the roads become good they will be able to run it very regularly, and you will then get the mails from California at least one day in advance of St. Louis.

I am quite certain that the company intends to act in good faith with the post master general, who would never have consented to change the connecting point of the two branches from Little Rock to Fort Smith if he had thought that St. Louis would get the mails in advance of Memphis, and if Messrs. Chidester, Rapley & Co. do not comply with their contract, **Messrs. Butterfield & Co** will stock the road themselves and carry their own mails, and they have already proven to the country that where ever they use their own stock they invariable make good time.

I hope the public will not be too severe in their censure until the company have had time to try the new arrangement made with Chidester, Rapley & Co.

Very Respectfully, James Glover
Superintendent **Overland Mail Company**

Grayoso Hotel, Memphis

James Glover wrote the above letter from the Gayoso House, the first luxury hotel in Memphis. The hotel was built in 1842, when the city was barely twenty years old. It cost $144,000, an exorbitant amount at the time, and it was "The Place" to stay in Memphis.

Muddy Roads Across Arkansas Often Caused Delays

Passengers were required to assist in getting the stagecoach out of mud holes or deep sand so the stage could remain on schedule.

February 12, 1859
Butterfield's Steamboat Jennie Whipple Carrying Overland Mail

February 12, 1859, Saturday
Arkansas State Gazette and Democrat, Little Rock, Ark.

ARRIVALS FEB. 5 –
Jennie Whipple at Little Rock from Memphis
DEPARTURES FEB. 6 –
Jennie Whipple from Little Rock for Memphis

February 12, 1859
Memphis Route Complaints

February 12, 1859, Saturday
Arkansas State Gazette and Democrat, Little Rock, Ark.

FOR THE STATE GAZETTE AND DEMOCRAT – The establishment, by the government, of the Memphis branch of the **California Overland Mail**, was hailed by our citizens, as a matter of great interest to the whole State: feeling assured as they did that the successful performance of the contract would not only test the practicability of building the Pacific Rail Road, through our State *[of Arkansas]*, and over this route, but would result in many other advantages to our people. And this would be the case, but the contractors on this route have humbugged the government and the people ever since the contract was put in operation

They first brought the mail from White River to Little Rock by stages; and then carried it back to Atlanta on horseback, and from thence by stages by Dardanelle to Fort Smith thereby avoiding Little Rock in a great manner.

The Post Master at Little Rock very properly objected to this procedure and represented the facts to the Post Office Department. The Postmaster General then addressed **Mr. Butterfield**, one of the contractors, a note, which was published in the papers, stating that he would be required to carry the mail, in four horse coaches; by Little Rock, and from thence direct to Fort Smith, as contemplated by the contract; **Mr. Butterfield** then promised to "do better," by a strict performance of the contract, and it was believed and hoped, for a while, that the contract would be faithfully carried out; as he made new arrangements and sub let the contract to Fort Smith, to gentlemen of known responsibility, energy, and industry.

Now these latter sub-contractors, are carrying the mail again, on horseback to Norristown, where they put it in their Des Arc and Fort Smith stage. These sub contractors first bought out the state route to Fort Smith, on the north side of the river, as far as Norristown; but finding they could not make the connection with their Des Arc and Fort Smith route at Dardanelle, they have abandoned trying to carry the mail in stages; and instead of four horses, they have three horses, to two horse hacks, which as before stated do not make the connection at Dardanelle – another serious objection to the manner of performing this contract is, that these contractors carry two mails, that belong to separate and distinct contracts, all the way through the same stage, which is not only a gross violation of law, but in many cases would greatly discommode *[inconvenience]* passengers. Contractors have no more right to violate a contract with the Government, than they would have in like manner to impose on an individual. The writer has no objection, and would like to see these gentlemen make their pockets full of money; but it is to be hoped for the sake of the great interest the State of Arkansas, and our whole people have in the matter, that they will be held by the proper authorities to a strict performance of this contract. It is too glaring an outrage to be longer tolerated. In order therefore that public attention may be directed to it, I hope you will give place in your columns for this short communication. Respectfully, &c., yours,

An Old Settler on the Route

Commercial Hotel

According to the April 6, 1860 issue of the Memphis Daily Appeal, page 2, the Commercial Hotel housed Butterfield's Overland Mail offices in Memphis. The hotel was built in 1848 and survived until about 1891.

February 19, 1859
Memphis Route Complaints

February 19, 1859, Saturday, page 2
Arkansas State Gazette and Democrat, Little Rock, Ark.

THE **OVERLAND CALIFORNIA MAIL** – *The South Sold* – Some weeks since we expressed the belief that it was the purpose of **Butterfield & Co.** to throw Arkansas and Memphis off, and favor St. Louis, and a more Northern terminus of the **California overland mail**. We had, last Sunday, the pleasure of meeting Major BEN MCCULLOUGH, of Texas, who came a passenger, by this route, from the Plains, and from a conversation with him, we regret to say that our previous fears were confirmed, and we have now so doubt of the fact that it is the deliberate intention of **Butterfield & Co.** to divert the travel from the Arkansas route and turn it to St. Louis, the distance to which point is greater, and the road rougher, than by the Arkansas and Memphis route.

Major McCullough says that the agents and strikers over the whole line west of Fort Smith, speak of St. Louis as *the* route for travelers – no allusion is made to the Arkansas *[Memphis]* route, and if passengers persist in making enquiries as to it, they speak of it only as a branch, and as subordinate and inferior, in every respect, to the St. Louis route.

Major McCullough informs us, further, that instead of being forwarded by the stages of **Butterfield & Co.** immediately, as were the St. Louis passengers, the Arkansas and Memphis passengers were detained at Fort Smith from twelve till half past three o'clock; and on the route, that they were detained at Dardanelle from eight o'clock in the forenoon until one o'clock in the afternoon.

Plummer Station ca. 1950
The home and adjoining leather shop of Samuel Plummer still stands, but they are in great disrepair.

That they were detained at Mr. Plummer's in Conway County, from ten o'clock at night until five o'clock next morning; that it took the stages from five o'clock in the morning until six o'clock in the evening to reach Little Rock – a distance of only forty-three miles; and they were detained at Little Rock from six o'clock Saturday evening until the next Monday at four o'clock in the morning – making, in all a detention of more than forty-eight hours from the time of the arrival of the stages at Fort Smith, until their departure from Little Rock for Memphis.

It is true that the contractors in this route forward the mails which are sent by it, so as to reach Little Rock and Memphis within or perhaps, before, the schedule time; and in response to our enquiry why the mail was not forwarded in four-horse stages as **Butterfield & Co.** have contracted to do, we have been answered – because there were no passengers to make stages necessary. It does not matter whether there are passengers or not, the contract required that the service should be done – and the contract should be complied with. But has it not occurred to those apologists why no passengers come by this route! The reason is plain: it is because there are not stage facilities on it to convey them to Memphis as soon as **Butterfield & Co.** convey them to St. Louis on the other route. The grade of service is below that required by the contract, and the detention, on this route, enables passengers to get through sooner by taking the St. Louis branch. It is but fair to presume, if things continue as they are now, that passengers *never will* come by way of the Memphis and Arkansas route. This too in the face of the known fact that it is the nearest route, that the road is not so rough, and that the climate is milder, than on the St. Louis route.

Messers. Butterfield & Co. have sub-let their line from Fort Smith to Memphis, to a company of very worthy gentlemen residing at this place; and we are informed and believe that they comply with their contract with **Butterfield & Co.** to the letter; We say this in justice to them, because they are men who are in the habit of making no contracts which they do not comply with. We wish them the greatest amount of pecuniary *[financial]* success in their contract, to which we have but a single objection: which is, that they are not the principals instead of sub-contractors. As principals, they would comply faithfully with their contract with the government; as sub-contractors, they only have to comply with their contract with **Butterfield & co.**, which may be a very different thing from a contract with the government.

There is also an objection to sub-letting a mail contract, to contractors who already have a contract to carry another mail over the same route. It is that their duties, on their own contract, are paramount to, and must take precedence of, all other duties – and it might frequently happen that the faithful discharge of those duties would occupy all of their time and means, and prevent them from doing duty at all as sub-contractors.

If we intended that this line should be the fore-runner of the Pacific rail road, and mark out its way. Hence the Northern contractors, with their Northern interests and feelings, favor a Northern route. Hence **Butterfield & Co.**, Northern men, prefer the Northern route and throw obstacles in the way of the Southern, which they know to be the nearest, best, and most practicable.

Hence they sub-let their contract from Fort Smith to Memphis, and make special drummers of all their agents for the St. Louis route – thus paying the contractors pecuniarily *[financially]* as well as politically.

We are in the minority, and speak only for ourself – and we can stand the oppression and injustice of the government, and the bad acts of **Butterfield & Co.**, as well, and as long, as any one. But we are anxious to see the majority, for once unite with the minority, on a question which all admit to be right and contend for their right as Southern men, all of which are embraced in the simple word – *justice.*

Gov. Brown, the Post Master General, is a Southern man, and his letting of the **overland mail** was heralded as a great measure for the benefit of the South. Now that the South is about to have its benefits wrested from her, will he do her justice, by compelling **Butterfield & co.** to do their duty, or procure some contractor who will comply faithfully with his contract! Or, as the Governor is said to have cast a longing eye towards the White House, will he desert the South and "crook the pregnant hinges of the knee" *[quote from Hamlet, Act 3, scene 2]* to the North, the seat of power and of votes! *"We shall see what we shall see."*

Early Memphis to Hopefield Ferry, perhaps the ferry "Nashoba"
*When steamboats were not available, the **Overland Mail** crossed from Memphis to Hopefield, Arkansas by ferry, then boarded the train for a short 24 mile trip, where stagecoaches carried the mail and passengers the next 2,700 miles to San Francisco. Image compliments of Gene Gill, www.historic-memphis.com*

February 19, 1859
Butterfield Overland Passenger

February 19, 1859, Saturday, page 2
Arkansas State Gazette and Democrat, Little Rock, Ark.

Among the distinguished arrivals of the week, we note that Major BEN McCULLOUGH, of Texas. We have known Major McCullough for several years, and in many respects, he is a man of decided mark. His participation in the frontier scenes of Texas, and his long service, and many daring deeds, as a Texas Ranger, are matters belonging to the history of the times; and, if future historians do him justice, he will rank among the first, and most prominent, of the early

Texans. He came to this place from Sonora, Mexico, a great part of the way by the **overland California stages**. From him we received much valuable information in regard to the route, and the manner in which it is conducted; and on him we place great reliance, in having many of the abuses of the contractors remedied or abated – for he promised to see the Postmaster General, and confer with him fully on the subject.

Major Ben McCullough, of Texas

Brigadier-General Benjamin McCulloch (November 11, 1811 – March 7, 1862) was a soldier in the Texas Revolution, a Texas Ranger, a major-general in the Texas militia and thereafter a major in the United States Army (United States Volunteers) during the Mexican–American War, sheriff of Sacramento County, a U.S. marshal, and a brigadier-general in the army of the Confederate States during the American Civil War.

February 19, 1859
Butterfield's Steamboat Jennie Whipple Carrying Overland Mail

February 19, 1859, Saturday
Arkansas State Gazette and Democrat, Little Rock, Ark.

ARRIVALS FEB. 17 –

Jennie Whipple at Little Rock from Memphis

DEPARTURES FEB. 18 –

Jennie Whipple from Little Rock for Memphis

February 23, 1859
Butterfield's Steamboat Jennie Whipple Carrying Overland Mail

February 23, 1859, Wednesday
Arkansas True Democrat, Little Rock, Arkansas

ARRIVALS – Feb. 18 Jennie Whipple from Memphis
DEPARTURES – Feb. 18 Jennie Whipple for Memphis

February 26, 1859
Overland Stagecoaches in Peril from Indians

February 26, 1859, Saturday, page 3
Arkansas State Gazette and Democrat, Little Rock, Ark.

The most important article of news received by the **Overland Mail**, arrived last night, is that a company of men of the First Dragoons, under the command of Col. Hoffman, had been compelled to retire after a sharp conflict before an allied force of eight hundred Indian warriors.

It seems that a grand alliance has been formed between several of the most important Indian tribes on the Colorado, and will probably extend to the Yumas, who are known to be on friendly relations with the Mojaves. If so, it will place the **Butterfield Overland Route** at a great peril as it has the Salt Lake Route, which traverses the country of the Paiuteutah on the projected route from Albuquerque, which passes through the country of the Mojaves.

Our Indian wars are assuming an aspect of grave importance when we reflect that the Oregon war alone cost the country over five millions of dollars, and that all the expenses and costs proceeding therefrom within the past twelve months, will probably reach ten millions of dollars. General Clark, with his well known promptitude and energy, will doubtless take immediate steps to reinforce the threatened portion of our State *[of Arkansas]*, and reduce the wretched savages to obedience in as summary a manner as he taught the warlike tribes of Oregon the necessity of maintaining peaceful relations with our people.

Mojave Indians
Mohave or Mojave (Mojave: 'Aha Makhav) are a Native American people indigenous to the Colorado River in the Mojave Desert.
Image published by U.S. Government. ca. 1860

March 2, 1859
Butterfield's Steamboat Jennie Whipple
Carrying Overland Mail

March 2, 1859, Wednesday
Arkansas True Democrat, Little Rock, Arkansas

ARRIVALS – Feb. 28 Jennie Whipple from Memphis
DEPARTURES – March 1 Jennie Whipple for Memphis

March 5, 1859
Praise for the Overland Mail Co.

March 5, 1859
The Arkansian, Fayetteville, Arkansas

The **Overland Mail** continues to meet the most sanguine expectation, of every body, it is almost universally in advance of schedule time.

March 5, 1859
Butterfield's Steamboat Jennie Whipple Carrying Overland Mail

March 5, 1859, Saturday
Arkansas State Gazette and Democrat, Little Rock, Ark.

ARRIVALS FEB. 28 –
Jennie Whipple at Little Rock from Memphis

DEPARTURES MARCH 1 –
Jennie Whipple from Little Rock for Memphis

March 5, 1859
Debate in Congress

March 5, 1859
Weekly Arkansas Gazette, Little Rock Arkansas

Telegraphed to the Memphis Bulletin – WASHINGTON FEB. 23RD P. M . – HOUSE – In the evening session a long debate ensued on the subject of the **Butterfield Overland California Mail** contract. It was contended on the one hand, that the selection of the route was left to the contractors, but the Administration had violated the law by compelling them to go nine hundred miles out of the way. Others argued that this attack was intended to break down the Southern branch of the **Overland route** and that the parties had mutually agreed to the present arrangement.

ST. LOUIS, *FEBRUARY 24* – The **Overland Mail** of the 31st has arrived.

March 12, 1859
Bill in Senate Proposes Reduction to Weekly Service

March 12, 1859, Saturday, page 2

Weekly Arkansas Gazette, Little Rock Arkansas

Washington, March 2 – Senate – The amendment reducing **Butterfield's** mail contracts and establishing a weekly mail from St. Josephs to Placerville; also from Kansas City to Stockton; raising the rates of postage and abolishing the franking privilege *[the ability of congress to send mail by one's signature rather than by postage]* – adopted.

Mr. Stewart, of Michigan, moved to amend the post office appropriation bill so that the **Butterfield Overland** contract be reduced to a weekly service at $450,000 instead of $600,000 per annum – agreed to.

[Reprinted in Washington Telegraph, March 16, 1859.]

March 12 1859
Stagecoach Manufactured in Fayetteville
Sound of the Conductor's Horn

March 12 1859

The Arkansian, Fayetteville, Arkansas

The Mails – The mails both North and South, arrive and leave this place, with accommodations regularity. It ought to be generally known that the neat, comfortable, strong and commodious stage coaches upon the Southern line, are the handiwork of a citizen of this town *[of Fayetteville]* – Mr. John R. Cato. They have been pronounced by connoisseurs, to be every way equal in finish and appearance to the California stage. Mr. Cato has ... clearly demonstrated the folly of sending to eastern cities for Stage Coaches.

Fayetteville A City – ...Already visions of future splendor and magnificence begin to crowd our fancies, when the clash and rattle of the **Overland** coaches is heard in our streets, and the toot of the driver's "tin horn" is borne to our ears from the distant environs; we fancy it to be the rush and whistle of the locomotive, and we find ourselves involuntarily, starting, for the depot.

March 12, 1859
Apache Engagement

March 12, 1859, Saturday, page 2
Arkansas State Gazette and Democrat, Little Rock, Ark.

Telegraphed to the N. O. Picayune – St. Louis, March 2

LETTER FROM THE INDIAN WARS – The **Overland California Mail**, from San Francisco the 7th ult. – two days later – has arrived.

It brings most exciting and important news from New Mexico, and all along the route and Indian frontier.

Another engagement has taken place with the Apaches, in which our troops were finally compelled to retire.

It appears that, a few weeks since, a band of these Indians made a descent upon several haciendas in the southern part of the Territory, where the inhabitants are by no means well protected, and stole a number of horses and mules.

News of this had soon reached Fort Bliss, when Lieut. Lazella, of the eighth Infantry, was at once despatched to chastise the Indians.

Lieut. Lazella took with him a detachment of mounted riflemen, (number of men not stated). He was also seconded by several volunteers from San Eleazario.

With these men he pursued the Indians to Dog Canyon, in the mountains, where coming up with them, he at once assaulted them, but after a severe contest was finally compelled to retire, himself mortally wounded.

He lost also one sergeant and two privates killed on the spot. Six others were severely wounded.

The Apaches lost not less than twenty killed on the spot.

The United States troops engaged in the assault numbered but twenty-two men, all told.

The Apaches numbered from a hundred and fifty to two hundred warriors.

Lieut. Lazella was in a dying state when they reached Fort Bliss.

In addition to this battle, the mail courier reports that the Comanches are very troublesome along the whole northern border of Texas.

The inhabitants are exposed to daily attacks, in one of which, just before the courier passed, a boy had been murdered near Gainesville.

The excitement all along the line was intense.

The courier also brings intelligence that Gen. Clarke's expedition against the Mohaves was fully organized, and would soon begin its march.

The people living in the bans of the Colorado had chartered a steamer to take up five or six hundred men to the seat of war.

The **overland mail** also brings four days later news from the capital and the interior of the State. It is important.

A resolution had been introduced into the legislature recommending that a new territory, to be called "the Territory of Colorado," be formed in the southern part of the state.

The territory is the same as that now infested by the Mohave Indians, against whom Gen. Clarke's expedition is, directed, and comprises all that region lying south of the parallel of Monte Diablo and between that and the Mexican line.

A resolution has also been introduced into the Senate, and by that body adopted, requesting the California delegation in Congress to urge upon the Federal Government the demand of reparation against Mexico for the massacre of Crabb *[battle between Mexico and U.S. April 1857]* and his party in the State of Sonora, something over a year ago.

March 12, 1859
Butterfield's Steamboat Jennie Whipple
Carrying Overland Mail

March 12, 1859, Saturday
Arkansas State Gazette and Democrat. Little Rock, Ark.

ARRIVALS MARCH 10 –

Jennie Whipple at Little Rock from Memphis

DEPARTURES MARCH 11 –

Jennie Whipple from Little Rock for Memphis

March 16, 1859
Post Office Appropriation Bill in Congress

March 16, 1859, Wednesday, page 3

Arkansas True Democrat, Little Rock, Arkansas

We copy the following proceedings in Congress in relation to the **Overland Mail Route**, and ask where was Mr. Phelps of Missouri?

> *"In the committee of the whole on the post-office appropriation bill, Mr. Blair offered an amendment authorizing the* ***Butterfield Company*** *to carry mails by any route they chose to, and charged the postmaster general with being interested in Arkansas lands as being the cause and reason of establishing the present route, besides several other personal and political considerations, having reference to the Pacific railway.*
>
> *Mr. Reagan, of Texas, opposed the amendment, and defended the postmaster general. The amendment was, however, adopted.*
>
> *Several amendments respecting the advertising and the printing of blanks, were adopted."*

March 16, 1859
Postage Rates Adjusted

March 16, 1859, Wednesday, page 3

Arkansas True Democrat, Little Rock, Arkansas

THE NEW POSTAGE LAW – We give below the principal features of the law lately passed...

The following rates of postage are established: For every single letter, in manuscript, or paper of any kind, in which information shall be asked or communicated in writing, or by marks or signs, conveyed in the mail for any distance between places in the United States, not exceeding 3,000 miles, five cents and for any distance over 3,000 miles, ten cents; and for a double letter there shall be charged double these rates; and every letter or parcel not exceeding half an ounce in weight shall be deemed a single letter, and every additional weight of half an ounce, or additional weight of less than half an ounce, shall be charged with an additional single rate of postage.

Apr 1, 1855	to 3,000 miles	3 cents	prepayment compulsory
	over 3,000 miles	10 cents	
Feb 27, 1861	over the Rockies	10 cents	1855 Act modified to require 10 cent prepaid postal rate on letters from any point east of the Rocky Mountains to any point on the Pacific side and vice versa **Ship rate:** 2 cent fee added to inland postage if transmitted by mail; 5 cents due if delivered at port of entry (any weight)

Source: Mails of the Westward Expansion, 1803 - 1861
by Steve Walske and Richard Frajola, Appendix G: Postal Rates

*The postal rate to send a letter during the **Butterfield's Overland Mail Co.** time was 10¢ for any distance over 3,000 miles, and only 3¢ for any distance less than 3,000 miles. During the last month of Butterfield's ox bow southern route operation, starting February 27, 1861 the rates changed to require 10¢ prepaid postal rate on letters from any point east of the Rocky Mountains to any point on the Pacific side of the Rocky Mountains and vice versa.*

Six examples from Bob Crossman's Stamp Collection:

1859 Memphis Route - Butterfield's Overland Mail to East Tennessee

This is one of just a handful of Memphis route covers that have survived. This cover was mailed from Iowa City, California, postmarked July 14, 1859. The Iowa City postmaster stamped a circular "PAID 10" to indicate the sender paid the 10¢ postage due for letters traveling 3,000 miles or more.

Leaving Iowa City, California and traveling about 140 miles south to San Francisco this cover boarded **Butterfield's Overland Mail Co.** stagecoach to Fort Smith, then on to Little Rock. Arriving in Little Rock, Arkansas about August 1 or 2, 1859, this letter departed on John Butterfield's Arkansas River steamboat ***"Jennie Whipple,"*** arriving at Memphis August 5, 1859. From Memphis this cover travelled another 400 miles due east to Philadelphia, Monroe County, Tennessee.

1859 St. Louis Route - Butterfield's Overland Mail to Massachusetts

This letter was mailed from San Francisco, California on May 22, 1859, addressed to Framingham, Massachusetts - a distance of over 3,000 miles requiring postage of 10¢. The original stamp that was affixed to this envelope either fell off in transit, or was removed at some point by a postage stamp collector. Shown here in its place is a 10¢ Scott #33 postage stamp, that has been attached to this cover to give the reader a better idea of what the cover once looked like.

1860 St. Louis Route - Butterfield's Overland Mail to Texas

Since this letter was traveling less than 3,000 miles, only 3¢ postage was required. This letter was mailed from St. Louis, Missouri on March 7, 1860 to Jacksboro in north central Texas. Jacksboro was located on the route of the Butterfield Overland Mail. The sender used a Lynde Bushnell Bookseller and Stationer advertizing cover.

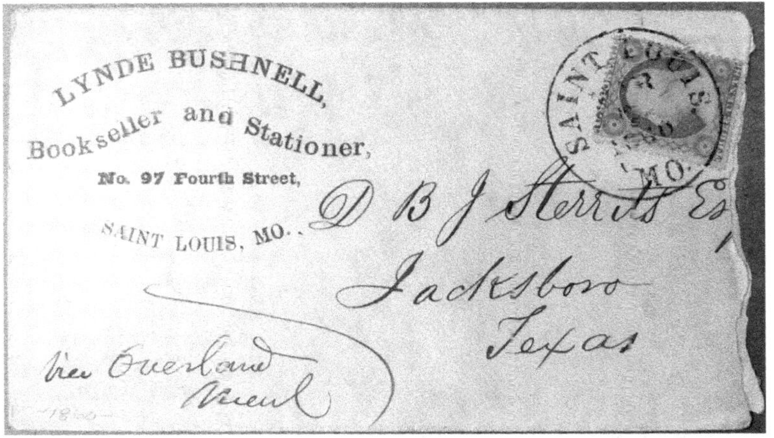

1860 Hawaii to Boston via Butterfield's Overland Mail

This letter was postmarked on Monday, November 26, 1860 in Honolulu, Hawaii, and was carried by ship to the USA, arriving at San Francisco on Friday, December 21, 1860.

Following the December 17, 1859 order of the Postmaster General that the default carrier of transcontinental mail would be **Butterfield's Overland Mail Co.** (instead of by Ocean Steamer), this letter would have been held at the San Francisco Post Office over the weekend, and placed in a mailbag departing on **Butterfield's Overland Mail** stage Christmas Day, Monday, December 24, 1860 for a 24 day trip to St. Louis, scheduled to arrive on Thursday, January 17, 1861.

This letter would have continued eastbound on a train for delivery to the Boston, Massachusetts post office to await for Judson Shute to call for his mail.

1860 Westbound Butterfield's Overland Mail Cover to California

The distance from Rome, NY to San Jose, CA was over 3,000 miles and required ten cents postage, paid here with three 3¢ and one 1¢ stamp.

1858 Eastbound Butterfield's Overland Mail Cover to California

This letter was mailed Nov. 19, 1858 in San Francisco. The Overland Mail Co. stagecoaches carried it to Tipton, Missouri where it transferred to a train to complete the journey to reach Miss Hallie L. Wales in Dorchester, Massachusetts.

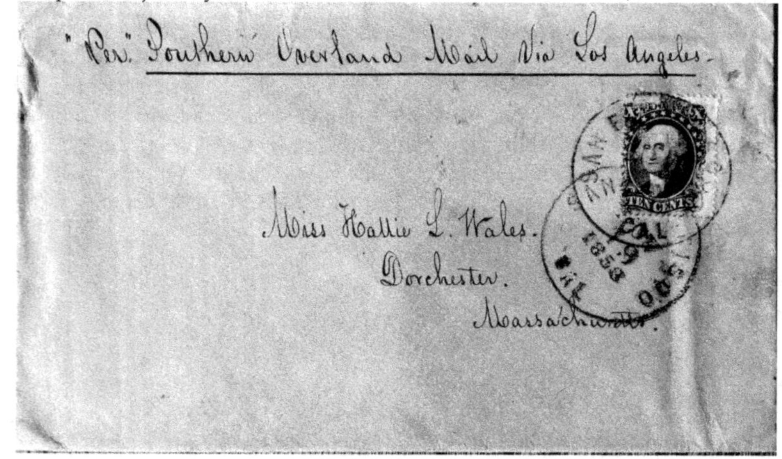

March 16, 1859
Memphis Route Complaints

March 16, 1859, Wednesday, page 3

Arkansas True Democrat, Little Rock, Arkansas

From Memphis paper – Major Ben McCullough and the **Overland Mail** – We had the pleasure of a visit yesterday from Major Ben McCullough, of Texas, who was *en route* for Washington City, from Sonora, and who came through Arizona on the **Overland Mail** coaches. Major Mc C. states that the branch of the **Overland Mail** from this city *[Memphis]* to Fort Smith is most shamefully managed, so as to detain passengers at least twenty-four hours behind the mail, which is pressed forward on horseback, leaving the passengers behind.

There can be no doubt, from the statement of Major Mc C., that the branch from here *[Memphis]* to Fort Smith is a complete sham and imposition upon the people of this section, and that the favoritism of **Butterfield & Co.**, has been carried just far enough. We now call upon the postmaster general to hold **Butterfield & Co.** to a strict compliance with their contract, or enforce upon them the penalties which the law and contract empower him to do. We have relied upon their promises long enough, and it would be a criminal connivance in this wrong longer to indulge their impositions upon this section.

March 16, 1859

Overland Hay Burned in Transit on Steamboat

March 16, 1859, Wednesday

Arkansas True Democrat, Little Rock, Arkansas

STEAMER U.S. BURNT – The steamer United States was destroyed by fire, on the 11th inst., about fifty miles above this city. The cargo was composed entirely of hay, for the government, and **Overland Mail company.** The boat was the property of the United States.

Owing to the fact that no passengers were carried on the boat, no lives were lost, but so rapid was the fire that nothing was saved; the captain informs us that he had merely time to save himself and crew. This steamer was from St. Louis, and bound for Fort Smith.

March 16, 1859
Postal Agents Responds to Mail Failures
Creeks Must be Bridged

March 16, 1859, Wednesday, page 3
Arkansas True Democrat, Little Rock, Arkansas

MAILS IN ARKANSAS – It will be seen by the following letter from the special mail agent for this State *[of Arkansas],* that the subject of mail failures has engaged his attention, and there are more reasons than one why they occur...

PRINCETON, ARK., *7TH MARCH, 1859* – Editors True Democrat – ... There are several small streams... that could be bridged with but little trouble or expense, and yet they rise so rapidly and so high, as to endanger the safety of the mails, and the drivers and horses to attempt to cross them. In many instances, therefore, the failure is not the fault of the contractor, or the "agent."

I have made it a rule to which I shall adhere, to report to the Postmaster General, *every case* of neglect of duty on the part of post masters, or contractors that may come to my knowledge. And while it becomes my duty frequently to make such reports, yet the citizens of the State *[of Arkansas]* have a duty on their part to perform before they can expect regularity in the transportation of the mails, to-wit: They must bridge the small streams, and otherwise make the public or stage roads better.

... there will be mail failures as long as rain falls and creeks are not bridged...

Your obedient servant, B. C. Harley
Special Agent, Post Office Dep't for Ark.

March 16, 1859
Postmaster General Dies

March 16, 1859, Wednesday
Arkansas True Democrat, Little Rock, Arkansas

DEATH OF THE POSTMASTER GENERAL – Gov. A. V. Brown,

postmaster general of the United States dies at Washington City, on the 8th inst.

Joseph Holt
Postmaster General 1859-1860
Upon Aaron Brown's death, Joseph Holt was appointed Postmaster General, serving 1859-1860. Joseph Holt was an American lawyer, soldier, and politician. As a leading member of the Buchanan administration, he succeeded in convincing Buchanan to oppose the secession of the South. He returned to Kentucky and successfully battled the secessionist element thereby helping to keep Kentucky in the Union.

March 16, 1859
Butterfield's Steamboat Jennie Whipple Carrying Overland Mail

March 16, 1859, Wednesday
Arkansas True Democrat, Little Rock, Arkansas

ARRIVALS – March 10 Jennie Whipple from Memphis

March 18, 1859
Overland Was Critical Part of Communication Infrastructure Across the Nation

March 18, 1859, page 3
Des Arc Citizen, Des Ark, Arkansas

We are permitted to make the following extract of a letter, received on Sunday morning, by the **Overland Mail** from Fort Arbuckle, dated February 28, 1859. The account may be relied on as authentic.

"Hurrah for the command at Fort Arbuckle! The first Coman-

ches who made their appearance were caught and killed. Lieut. Powell, while on scout with a detachment of the 1st Calvary and 1st Infantry, encountered a band of these fellows en route for Texas, and after a sharp conflict, killed five and chased the remainder until further pursuit was useless. One calvary soldier was killed and two wounded; also two or three horses.

Last night, Muncrief's were attacked by a small party on foot, and today one half of the command have gone in pursuit in different directions. Excitement runs high, and families on the Reserve are coming to the post for protection."

The fight took place on Thursday, February 24th.

March 19, 1859
Post Office Census

March 19, 1859

The Arkansian, Fayetteville, Arkansas

Number of Post Offices – The whole number of post offices in the United states on the 30th of June last was 29,977, of which 400 are of the class denominated presidential. The number established during the last fiscal year was 2,121, and the number discontinued 730, being an increase of 1,391. The number of postmasters appointed during the year was 8,284. Of these, 4,595 were to fill vacancies occasioned by resignations, 998 by removals, 278 by deaths, 292 by change of names and sites and 2,121 on establishment of new offices, The whole number of offices on the first of December 1858, was 38,573.

March 19, 1859
Letter from California Resident

March 19, 1859

The Arkansan, Fayetteville, Arkansas

Letter From California – The following extracts are from a letter written by a gentleman in California, to Capt. G. C. North of this city *[of Fayetteville]* ; dated 14th of February, 1859:

"We have had the coldest winter that I have ever experienced in this country *[of California]*, and we have had a tremendous fall of snow this month, with plenty of rain, and it bids fair to be the best water-season that we have ever had. The deep *[gold mine]* diggings are improving every year, and are only beginning to be fairly worked. I think mining is almost in its infancy in California. There are many mountains that will not be worked out for centuries.

Taking into consideration the **Over-Land Mail** route securing safe transportation by land, which we look upon as vastly more important to California than all the Steam Boat lines, together with the recent treaties with China and Japan, and the newly discovered mines, we look for a large immigration the coming season, and a bright future for California.

Stock ranges very nearly the same *[price]* as when you left – particularly beef cattle and oxen, which have changed but little in price for the last five or seven years. Cows have come down a little every year; they can be bought in lots at about $50 per head. If I were driving stock to California, I would prefer, either the route by Salt Lake or the new route from Sweet Water to City Rock, and thence to Honey Lake. If you should be late on that route, you could winter your stock at Honey Lake.

If you bring cattle, I would advise you to bring mostly beef cattle or oxen. There is no danger of bringing too many. Beef if worth from 18 to 25 cents per pound, owning to the locality – 20 cents per pound is the usual price." *R. R.*

March 23, 1859
Butterfield's Steamboat Jennie Whipple
Carrying Overland Mail

March 23, 1859, Wednesday
Arkansas True Democrat, Little Rock, Arkansas

ARRIVALS – March 21

Jennie Whipple from Memphis

DEPARTURES – March 22

Jennie Whipple for Memphis

March 23, 1859
Overland Mail Arrives

March 23, 1859, Wednesday, page 1
Washington Telegraph, Washington, Arkansas

The **Overland California Mail**, from San Francisco on the 7th ult. arrived at St. Louis, on the 2d inst. It brings most exciting and important news from New Mexico, and all along the route and Indian frontier.

March 25, 1859
High Water Washes Away Train Trestle

March 25, 1859
Des Arc Citizen, Des Arc, Arkansas

The contractors for carrying the **California Overland Mail**, have been compelled to abandon the route from White River, thence to Memphis, via Madison, owing to the high water having washed away some of the trestle work on the railroad. Most of the road is said to be under water, and the cars *[train cars]* cannot get from Memphis to Madison. The **Overland Mail** is now carried to Helena, thence to Memphis. The Helena *Southron* says:

> *"This very act of these contractors goes to conclusively establish the fact that the Rail Road to Little Rock should have been built from Helena, where it would have been free from overflow, and where nature intended to make the connection sure and safe. If Helena and the people on the line will yet build a road from this city to intercept the Memphis and Little Rock road, this will become the trunk, and the road between the Mississippi and St. Francis Rivers will be a tributary."*

March 26, 1859
Butterfield's Steamboat Jennie Whipple
Carrying Overland Mail

March 26, 1859, Saturday

Arkansas State Gazette and Democrat, Little Rock, Ark.

ARRIVALS MARCH 21 –

Jennie Whipple at Little Rock from Memphis

DEPARTURES MARCH 22 –

Jennie Whipple from Little Rock for Memphis

March 30, 1859

Depredations by the Comanches

March 30, 1859, Wednesday, page 2

Washington Telegraph, Washington, Arkansas

THE OVERLAND MAIL – The San Francisco *Alta California,* of the 19th ult., says:

Mr. S. West arrived yesterday by **Overland Mail** coach from St. Louis. He reports depredations by the Comanches, all the way from Clear Fork of Brazos to the Delaware Spring, a distance of nearly four hundred miles. Several of the stations have been visited by the savages, and all the best stock run off or stampeded. Some of the stations are left nearly destitute, and it is feared, without *[unless]* immediate protection is rendered, the mail will be without the means of carriage. The hostility of the Indians is becoming daily more manifest. They even go so far as to declare their intention of breaking up the line all through their country.

The employees and drivers are kept in constant dread of their lives, although as yet no one has been killed. Mr. West says that it was with much difficulty they got along in some parts of the Comanche ter-ritory – the few mules which the Indians have left being almost too poor and weak to draw the coach. In some places Mr. West and the drivers were obliged to help the animals by pushing the coach. At Horsehead Crossing, on the Pecos river, the stage was surrounded by some sixty Indians, who, however, doing no harm, they remained about an hour, frightened the passengers very much, and retired.

Emigrants bound for California crossing the Pecos River at Horsehead Crossing, west Texas, circa 1850.

March 30, 1859
Overland Station Food Shortage

March 30, 1859, Wednesday, page 2
Washington Telegraph, Washington, Arkansas

The Overland Mail – The passengers by the last **Overland Mail** from California, complain of a great want of the commonest articles of food at several of the stations. For some 400 miles they report that a pound of flour cannot be obtained, and at many of the stations corn laid in for the mules was the only article of food they could obtain. This they pounded into meal, and with such provender were made to satisfy the appetite rendered, keener by travel. Persons going to California by land, we doubt not, would find it more agreeable and safer to go by the San Antonio and San Diego route. The mail is now carried in good coaches from San Antonio to San Diego in fifteen days, and there is a direct line of stages from this place, via Austin, to San Antonio.

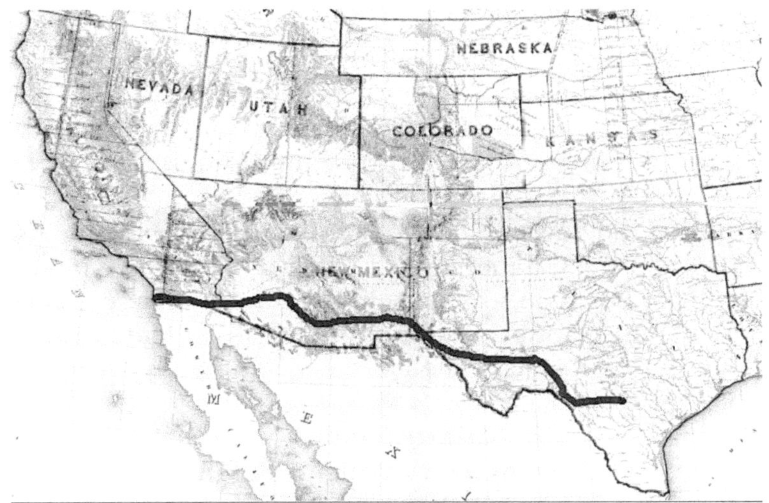

San Antonio to San Diego Route
San Antonio to San Diego, June 1857 to September 1858 (modern depiction, on 1858 War Department map in the collection of the Library of Congress.

March 30, 1859
Government Behind on Payments

March 30, 1859, Wednesday, page 2
Washington Telegraph, Washington, Arkansas

THE POST OFFICE APPROPRIATION BILL – The *Baltimore Sun*, of the 5th, says of the failure of this bill:

It is to be observed that the mail service is quarterly. The first quarter of the next fiscal year will end the 13th of September next, and as by the terms of all contracts the department renews the privilege of paying upon the second month succeeding, or on the month ending the 30th day of November, it will be seen that demands for the second quarter's service cannot be made until some weeks after Congress shall assemble at its regular session. Add to this the other fact that contractors collect generally half their pay on an average from postmasters on their respective routes in advance of settlements, it is reasoned that this amount of funds in hand, they will not suffer much from delay in payments subsequently required, provided that Congress, at its next meeting, promptly provides for their cases. Thus, things might get on tolerably, if it were not for a deficit for the present fiscal year of raising three millions, as well as the fact that as things are, there are not appropriations for **Overland** and Pacific steamship service. (The steamship service is alleged, however, to be provided for in part.) It may also be held by the Cabinet *[U S Congress]* that postage money accruing after June 13th is so in the treasury that it cannot drawn out except by authority of law, as contemplated by the act which had just failed.

March 30, 1859
Government Payments Behind

March 30, 1859, Wednesday, page 2
Washington Telegraph, Washington, Arkansas

It is said that there are now a large number of mail contractors in Washington endeavoring to settle with the Government. They have been carrying the mails since October 1st at their own expense, and cannot collect a dollar of the Government. **Butterfield & Co.**, the **Overland Mail** contractors, are among this class. On April 1st, the Government will owe them $300,000. Those now in Washington say they cannot go on longer on credit.

March 30, 1859
Memphis Route is a Failure

March 30, 1859, Wednesday page 3
Arkansas True Democrat, Little Rock Arkansas

Dear Editor: ...When financiering *[financial risk-taking]* politicians from Missouri came, and by giving a branch line down the Arkansas valley, succeeded in getting the **Overland Mail** route from St. Louis by way of Fort Smith, they were lauded and invidious *resentful]* comparisons instituted between the delegation in Congress from this State, and that from Missouri.

The branch to Memphis is a failure and a bad one, because it was so intended. The people of Sebastian county were deluded with the idea that Fort Smith was included, and the line of railroad would follow. But no reasonable man supposes that **Butterfield & Co.**, will travel on two sides of a triangle when they can reach the same point by going on the other side.

A motion was made in Congress to let the contractors fix the route, and when that is done the stages will leave the Missouri line and intersect the parallel in the Indian country. But for the sake of political effect at home, a temporary advantage offered by shrewd men was taken, a certain amount of political capital was made and true interests were lost sight of.

Whatever may be the comparative merits of the 32rd and 35th parallel routes is immaterial, but unfortunately a hungry politician seized upon one of these as a hobby whereon to ride to Congress. All through the canvass they sung and shouted "35th parallel." He came down here and sung the changes on it, till every page of the journals *[newspaper]* contains a mention of it. Admitting it to be all that is claimed for it, yet it was evident that it was used by men who cared nothing about the road to the Pacific, but who were extremely anxious concerning the road to Washington City.

One thing our Fort Smith friends may depend upon: if the initial point of the Pacific road is at St. Louis, it will never touch Arkansas. If the people of western Arkansas want the road to pass through their region of the country, they must encourage the building of the road from Memphis up the Arkansas Valley. And they must do more. Whenever these busy politicians for the sake of making political capital out of it, endeavor to make it a party question of a means of popularity, they should choke them down.

It is a misfortune that great enterprises like these should be thwarted by the maneuvers of men who would sell their souls to gain office; fellows who take hold of it because it may contribute to their popularity, and let it go when help is most needed. To build a road or roads in Arkansas we must act in concert, discard the rivalry of localities and sections, keep the question clear of polities and work for the general good.

April 1, 1859
Description of Apache Pass Station's Landscape

April 1, 1859, Wednesday, page 1
Des Arc Citizen, Des Arc, Arkansas

THE APACHE PASS – The wonders of nature in the neighborhood of the great ranges of mountains that divide the water entering the Atlantic from those running to the Pacific are as novel as they are sublime. The Apache Pass, one of these, is described as follows by one who has just passed through it.

The Pass is approached through a deep canyon, flanked on either hand by lofty mountains, bare of vegetation, presenting many singular and rare formations of rock. At the Pass proper the huge ledges suddenly close down to within thirty feet of each other, forming a perfect gateway the spurs of the ledges being thrust out in one place so as to leave barely room enough for the passage of a wagon. Beyond the Pass the canyon expands, forming a magnificent circle, in the center of which stands one of the stations of the **Overland Mail Company.** It is a singularly romantic spot shut out from the desert country, and always a favorite

Apache Pass and Fort Bowie

April 2, 1859
Support for Overland Mail Co.

April 2, 1859, Saturday, page 2
The Arkansian, Fayetteville, Arkansas

BUTTERFIELD'S OVERLAND MAIL – We notice, with regret, that some of our Missouri contemporaries complain of the **Overland Mail**; not only complain, but go so far as to ask how *"carrying the mail, will in any way pay for benefit the Government"* – that is, the People: still farther they think the **Overland Mail** *"had better be done away with."*

We are surprised, completely taken aback at such assertions and complaints. They betray either lamentable ignorance or willful and woeful prejudice. It is hard to believe that any one can be so blind to the advantages the **Overland Mail** has already conferred upon even those places through which it runs. Listen a moment. From far-off California, the grateful plaudits *[praise]* of her people come over to us acknowledging the benefits great, manifold and invaluable attending the success of this Mail. Many and many a heart has been gladdened by the messages borne across the Plains and Deserts, and through rugged mountain defiles. Many a *"business man"* has cheerfully accorded the **Overland Mail** the praise to which it is entitled, in hearing from the far East to the West, intelligence that materially affected his prosperity.

Never was punctuality more fully perfected. It is almost absolutely incredible to witness the regular, constant and repeated celerity and care with which this Mail is carried across a Continent: the half of it being a savage wilderness peopled by bloody barbarians and chequed with vast deserts and rough huge mountains. *Not a failure* has **Butterfield** made! Though his carriages are the first which ever rolled over these pathless deserts, or threaded the devious passes of these mountains - unknown before to the white man – though they have been watched with no friendly eye by the vengeful Comanche, or cruel Apache, who are ready at any time to light upon them with death; yet in the face of all these other innumerable dangers of the two thousand miles of untamed wilderness, **Butterfield's Mail** has never failed! Regularly is the Mail transported from the Pacific to the Atlantic, binding with hooks of intelligence ocean shores, whose people rejoice there at.

The success of the **Butterfield** enterprise is unequaled by the couriers of the Russian Czar, whose mail must traverse Asiatic Steppes and Siberian deserts, with a penalty of death for failure! Yet the **Overland Mail** is maligned. But no enterprise, however lofty, exists unopposed; but will be the comment of fault-finders.

So far as Arkansas and Missouri are concerned the mail facilities along the lines of the **Overland Mail** are this hour superior to those of a twelve month part a hundred fold. We, of this town *[Fayetteville]*, now enjoy as good mail privileges as any place on earth, outside of the railways. We have great reason to be thankful. Because the blessing has now become common we should not cease to prize it. Abolish or remove the **Overland Mail,** and in the hue and clamor then raised the voices of those now animadverting *[criticizing]* would be loudest for its restoration. We say three-times-three for **Butterfield**! We intend to pray that he and his compeers *[compeers: a person of equal status]* may be supported in their magnificent and portentous enterprise.

There are other and vast advantages to flow form the successful, complete and *permanent* operation of this **Overland Mail**; advantages aside from the mere transportation of mail. To these advantages, as well as mail, did the originators of this scheme look. These are the opening and settling our immense territory west; the elaboration of its incalculable resources; the protection of our States on the Pacific seaboard in case of foreign invasion; and last, but not least, the **Overland Mail** is the *sure* forerunner of that greatest design of the day, the Pacific Rail Road, over whose rails are yet to fly the wealth and power of East Indian Commerce. There are a thousand benefits yet to accrue from the **Overland Mail**. It will prove to our country an Aladdin's Lamp, lighting us to future greatness and prosperity.

One word more: Our people ought to go to work and *steadily* improve the roads – they need it. The contractors have done their duty, our people ought to do ours. Especially ought work to be continued upon the road between this and Van Buren. Put on your work, then, people, or perchance you may suddenly find yourselves not on the road. The **Overland Mail** may *find* a better route. If this work is not done, well and constantly done, the **Overland Mail** will leave us and *will* find that other and better route. A hint to the wise is sufficient. If you don't take it, people, don't blame us, we have warned you. And should the **Overland Mail** find, and run over that better route, it will be to the everlasting shame of our people. We shall even be compelled to blush in the present of the poor Choctaw – for in their country the roads are *worked* and the streams bridged.

We hope we have said enough. We hope that our people may so act that the **Overland Mail** may run through Fayetteville till the iron horse supplants it. Again we say three times three for **Butterfield**!

April 2, 1859
Butterfield's Steamboat Jennie Whipple Carrying Overland Mail

April 2, 1859, Saturday
Arkansas State Gazette and Democrat, Little Rock, Ark.

ARRIVALS MARCH 29 –

Jennie Whipple at Little Rock from Memphis

DEPARTURES MARCH 29 –

Jennie Whipple from Little Rock for Memphis

Regular U. S. Mail Passenger Packet.
MERCHANTS' AND PLANTERS' LINE.
JENNIE WHIPPLE,
C. C. GRAY, *Master*......G. W. HYNSON, *Clerk.*

THIS splendid, swift running passenger steamer will run regularly between Little Rock and Memphis, leaving Little Rock weekly for Memphis.—Passengers ticketed through to Louisville, St. Louis or Cincinnati, by this boat.

For freight or passage, apply to
MERRICK & WASSELL, *Agents,*
April 6, 1859. 3m *Or on Board.*

Source: April 6, 1859, Wednesday
Arkansas True Democrat, Little Rock, Arkansas

April 6, 1859
Butterfield's Steamboat Jennie Whipple
Carrying Overland Mail
Stops as port of Pine Bluff, Arkansas

April 6, 1859, Wednesday, page 3
Arkansas True Democrat, Little Rock, Arkansas

ARRIVALS – March 29 Jennie Whipple from Memphis
DEPARTURES – March 29 Jennie Whipple for Memphis
NOTES BY THE WAY – PINE BLUFF, MARCH 26, 1859

"MR. EDITOR: Your readers who have honored my notes with a purusal, will, I am thinking, conclude that I lead a rambling life – since no two numbers have hailed from the same locality. One week ago, I left Memphis for Monticello, per steamer **'Jennie Whipple,'** and ascended the Arkansas River to this place *[Pine Bluff]*, and made the residue of the way in a hack chartered especially for the trip.

And here, let me remark by the way, that the **Jennie Whipple** is a beautiful little craft, with a gentlemanly captain and an obliging clerk, whose endeavors to render their passengers safe and satisfied, were unremitting. Speed, comfort, and safety seem to be their watch-words.

"Pine Bluff Ferry, 1879

In 1879 H. J. Lewis drew this sketch of the little Pine Bluff sidewheel steam ferry. The foredeck was crowded with passengers, with the livestock on the aft part of the vessel. Source: "Pine Bluff and Jefferson County: A Pictorial History" 1981

Pine Bluff has improved very much since your correspondent was first here, twenty-seven years ago. It was then a very small place. Now, it ranks among the best towns in Arkansas, with an intelligent and enterprising population. I notice several churches, an elegant court house, and there is here, as I am told, one of the best schools, both male and female, to be found in this latitude. It is under the charge of Geo. D. Alexander, A. M., assisted by a corps of able teachers. Mr. Alexander's name is sufficient guaranty that the school ranks the best in the State *[of Arkansas]*. I hear it spoken in terms of great commendation...

April 9, 1859
Butterfield's Steamboat Jennie Whipple Carrying Overland Mail

April 9, 1859, Saturday

Arkansas State Gazette and Democrat, Little Rock, Ark.

ARRIVALS APRIL 8 –

Jennie Whipple at Little Rock from Memphis

"Memphis Wharf"

*The Jennie Whipple would have docked here to receive **Overland Mail** and passengers bound for San Francisco. Traveling south on the Mississippi to Napoleon, then up the Arkansas River. At Little Rock or Fort Smith, the mail and passengers transferred to stagecoaches for the balance of the 2,700 mile trip to San Francisco, California.*

*Due to low water, on only eight occasions, **John Butterfield's** steamboat, Jennie Whipple, was able to fulfill his original plan of carrying **Overland Mail** between Memphis and Fort Smith. On 73 additional occasions she was able to carry the **Overland Mail** between Memphis and Little Rock, where it transferred to stagecoaches for the balance of the trip to Fort Smith and beyond.*

Image from Gene Gill, www.historic-memphis.com

April 13, 1859
Butterfield's Steamboat Jennie Whipple Carrying Overland Mail

April 13, 1859, Wednesday

Arkansas True Democrat, Little Rock, Arkansas

ARRIVALS – April 8 Jennie Whipple from Memphis

DEPARTURES – April 9 Jennie Whipple for Fort Smith

"RIVER, ETC. – The river has reached what may be termed low water mark, with little prospects of a rise. The mail steamers to Napoleon, make their regular trips in good time. From this point *[Little Rock]* to Fort Smith, navigation is suspended except to boats of very low draught. ...**Jennie Whipple**, however, may make the trip."

"Just received per steamer **Jennie Whipple**, 10 kegs best rifle powder; 2 cases best canister powder; 500 lbs. bar lead. Apply to A. J. Hutt, April 13, 1859."

April 16, 1859
Overland Stage Passengers

April 16, 1859, Saturday, page 2
The Arkansian, Fayetteville, Arkansas

Cols. J. L Dickson and J. H. VanHoose, merchants reached home Wednesday from the East, by the "**Overland.**"

We are obliged to them for very late New York, Philadelphia, Cincinnati and St. Louis papers.

Col. Bioff and Mr. Duke have also returned; each looking - fat, full and pleasantly.

April 16, 1859
Butterfield & Co., Deserve Great Credit

April 16, 1859, Saturday, page 2
The Arkansian, Fayetteville, Arkansas

BENTONVILLE, ARK., APRIL 7TH, – EDITORS ARKANSIAN: ...**Butterfield & Co.**, deserve great credit for the untiring energy with which they transport the **Overland Mail**, for I perceive by your paper their stages continue to run within schedule time, notwithstanding the serious damage the roads must have sustained by the "ground and lofty tumbling of the aforesaid Bluffs." Yours. A.

April 16, 1859
Butterfield Horse Missing

April 16, 1859, Saturday
The Arkansian, Fayetteville, Arkansas

Strayed From the subscriber on the 6th inst., one Iron-Gray Mare; five years old this spring, about 14 and a half hands high, and has a large bunch on the left fore knee. Whoever will return said mare, or give any information where she may be found, will be liberally rewarded.

C. E. BUTTERFIELD.

April 9, 1859. 6 tf

Source: April 16, 1859, Saturday
The Arkansian, Fayetteville, Arkansas

April 16, 1859
Accident at Charles Butterfield's Fayetteville Home

April 16, 1859, Saturday, page 2
The Arkansian, Fayetteville, Arkansas

SAD ACCIDENt – While engaged, Wednesday evening, in putting up a lightning rod against the house of **Mr. Butterfield** in this city, a brick, loosened from the chimney top by an assistant, fell upon, and partly crushed the head of the operator, a Mr. Maxwell. He was not killed but his recovery is doubtful. Mr. M. is an estimable *[worthy of great respect]* citizen of Benton Co.

April 16, 1859
Butterfield Overland Mail Passenger's Story

April 16, 1859, Saturday, page 2
The Arkansian, Fayetteville, Arkansas

PHILADELPHJIA, MARCH 23, 1859 –

Dear Boudinot: – This is the first opportunity I have had of writing you since my departure from home, and now have nothing that will be of interest to our readers to communicate; however, if for nothing more that we may have some "editorial correspondence" I write and will give a hasty account of our trip to this city and of some of the things of interest I have seen.

After staying at Van Buren four days we took passage on the steamer Mary Cook for Napoleon. The accommodating Captain concluded that he would go no further than Little Rock, where we remained one day and shipped on the **Overland Mail steamer, Jennie Whipple** for Napoleon, thence on the fine passenger mail packet Kate Frisbee for Memphis. The Mississippi river at Napoleon was very high, only lacked seven inches of being to the high water mark of last spring.

Memphis is beautifully situated, entirely above overflow and seems to be rapidly improving, and will - doubtless, ere many years – be one of the most important cities in the Southwest, on account of its situation, commerce and manufactures, and being accessible from all parts of the United States by the Mississippi river and tributaries and numerous railroads converging from every direction. It is to be hoped that the citizens of Arkansas will awake to their interest, and particularly those immediately interested in the Memphis and Little Rock railroad, and second the generous efforts of Memphis in their behalf and complete, this road to Little Rock. That done, and half the battle is won. Such an impetus will then be given to internal improvement as will make Arkansas what nature designed her to be, the garden spot of the Union.

At Memphis we took the cars *[train cars]* at 7 o'clock in the evening, breakfasted next morning in Huntsville, Alabama...

April 16, 1859
Butterfield's Steamboat Jennie Whipple Carrying Overland Mail

April 16, 1859, Saturday

Arkansas State Gazette and Democrat, Little Rock, Ark.

DEPARTURES APRIL 9 –

Jennie Whipple from Little Rock for Memphis

April 20, 1859
Butterfield's Steamboat Jennie Whipple
Carrying Overland Mail

April 20, 1859, Wednesday

Arkansas True Democrat, Little Rock, Arkansas

ARRIVALS – April 15 Jennie Whipple from Fort Smith

DEPARTURES – April 15 Jennie Whipple for Memphis

April 23, 1859
Butterfield's Steamboat Jennie Whipple
Carrying Overland Mail

April 23, 1859, Saturday

Arkansas State Gazette and Democrat, Little Rock, Ark.

ARRIVALS APRIL 15 –

Jennie Whipple at Little Rock from Fort Smith

DEPARTURES APRIL 15 –

Jennie Whipple from Little Rock for Fort Smith

April 23, 1859
Conductor of Overland Stage Praised

April 23, 1859

The Arkansian, Fayetteville, Arkansas

The *Arkansian* thanks J. H. Reed, the newly installed Conductor of the **"Overland"** from Fort Smith to Springfield, for a copy of the *Fort Smith Times* of Thursday.

W. A. Watson, returned from St. Louis by **Overland** ***[Mail Co. stagecoach]*** on Tuesday.

Mississippi River Levee from the Custom House Memphis, Tennessee, circa 1900

The Jennie Whipple docked at the Memphis port to receive ***Overland Mail Co.*** *passengers and mail. She then travelled to Little Rock's port. At the Butterfield Home Station at Little Rock's Anthony House, transfer was made to stagecoaches for the balance of the 2,700 mile journey to San Francisco.*

April 27, 1859
Butterfield's Steamboat Jennie Whipple Carrying Overland Mail

April 27, 1859, Wednesday
Arkansas True Democrat, Little Rock, Arkansas

ARRIVALS – April 24 Jennie Whipple from Memphis
DEPARTURES – April 26 Jennie Whipple for Memphis

April 27, 1859
Praise for Overland Mail

April 27, 1859, page 3
Arkansas True Democrat, Little Rock, Arkansas

We take pleasure in copying the following article from the *Arkansian*, published at Fayetteville, in this state:

Our postal privileges are very great, equal to any country where there are neither railroads nor telegraphs. Daily lines of four horse stages from through Fayetteville, from Little Rock, Ark. to Tipton, Mo., the present terminus of the Missouri Central Railroad. The **California Overland Mail** passes through our town *[Fayetteville]* twice a week each way – with a post office and depot here. This mail has reached this place from San Francisco in 19 days. Passengers have been 'put through' from St. Louis to Fayetteville in 48 hours. These mails are permanent and were called forth by the wants and demands of the people.

April 30, 1859
Accident at Charles Butterfield's Home

April 30, 1859, Saturday, page 2
The Arkansian, Fayetteville, Arkansas

Mr. Maxwell who was seriously injured by the falling of a brick, while engaged in putting up a lightning rod for **Mr.**

Butterfield, has so far recovered as to be able to go to his home in Benton county.

Col. John W. Garretson and lady, and J. R. Pettigrew, of this paper arrived in our city, on the **Overland**, Wednesday.

April 30, 1859
Butterfield's Steamboat Jennie Whipple Carrying Overland Mail

April 30, 1859, Saturday
Arkansas State Gazette and Democrat, Little Rock, Ark.

ARRIVALS APRIL 25 –
Jennie Whipple at Little Rock from Memphis

DEPARTURES APRIL 25 –
Jennie Whipple from Little Rock for Memphis

April 30, 1859
Overland Stage Arrives

April 30, 1859, Saturday
Arkansas State Gazette and Democrat, Little Rock, Ark.

ST. LOUIS, APRIL 20, – The **Overland Mail** arrived here today with San Francisco dates of the 28th ult.

May 4, 1859
Mrs. Charles Butterfield has Mail

May 4, 1859, Wednesday, page 3
Arkansas True Democrat, Little Rock, Arkansas

LIST OF LETTERS remaining in the post office at Little Rock, Ark., on the 30th of April, 1859, which if not taken out will be sent to the dead letter office at Washington City.

[Among a list of 186 names:]

Butterfield, Mrs. Charles

May 4, 1859
James Glover, Superintendent, Interviewed

May 4, 1859, Wednesday
Arkansas True Democrat, Little Rock, Arkansas

PERSONAL – We had the pleasure of a short interview

with James Glover, Esq., Superintendent of the **Overland Mail Company**. He tells us that they intend stocking the road from Dardanelle to Memphis and carrying their own mails, and to make this, the superior arm of the service. The last three mails from San Francisco arrived at Memphis in 22 days.

Mr. Glover is an energetic man and there is a prospect of his settling in our city. We have great faith in his ability and go-aheaditiveness.

May 7, 1859
Butterfield's Steamboat Jennie Whipple Carrying Overland Mail

May 7, 1859, Saturday
Arkansas State Gazette and Democrat, Little Rock, Ark.

ARRIVALS MAY 5 –
Jennie Whipple at Little Rock from Memphis

DEPARTURES MAY 5 –
Jennie Whipple from Little Rock for Fort Smith

May 7, 1859
Support for Route Not to Change

May 7, 1859, Saturday, page 2
Arkansas State Gazette and Democrat, Little Rock, Ark.

From the Memphis Avalanche – We publish in another column of our pages a letter from a citizen of Arkansas in regards that stupendous fraud upon Memphis and the South generally – The **Overland Mail**. We have before stated we cared not what means the citizens of St. Louis adopted to build up their city, provided they did not result to the prejudices of our own. That **Butterfield & Co.** are resorting to most unfair expedients as regards the branch leading to Memphis can not be denied, and it is for the people of the South to demand that they shall derive a share of the advantages accruing from a direct communication with the Pacific coast. We command the perusal of the letter to our readers. It is well written, and will be found to contain facts which throw new light upon the subject.

THE **OVERLAND MAIL** A HUMBUG – *Little Rock, Ark., April 21, 1859* – Messrs. Editor: Having observed and admired the true Southern tone of your paper, as well as the frank and manly manner in which you speak out in favor of whatever you think to be right. I have thought *[it]* proper to address you upon a subject in which all the Southern States are interested, and which, now needs "aid and comfort" from every Southern man; not that it is not right – for it is so perfectly right that no one can mistake it in that aspect – but to prevent the clamor, and the bad faith of Northern men from robbing us of what we are justly entitled to. I mean the Memphis branch of the **California Overland mail**, which might be made of great advantage to the country, but which, now, is little, if any better than the merest false pretence of a service to the South.

It will be remembered by you, that, when the contract for this mail was first let to **Messrs. Butterfield & Co.**, they obligated themselves to carry the mail from Memphis and St. Louis to Little Rock, thence by the route to Preston, (Texas,) El Paso, ending at San Francisco. You will also remember, that on the petition of **Messers. Butterfield** and others, the intersection of this route was changed from Little Rock to Fort Smith; thus sending the mail at least fifty miles out of the way between Memphis and Preston. And this change was made, too, after the road from Little Rock to Preston, Texas, had been surveyed and made, and ascertained to be a better road, and through a better country for staging, than the route adopted either between Little Rock and Fort Smith, or between Fort Smith and Preston.

That you may understand this subject at a glance. I send you, herewith, a map of the two routes, and the country over which they both run. On an examination. of that I think you will come to the conclusion with me that the junction of the Eastern termini of the **Overland mail** should be at Preston, Texas, and not at Little Rock or Fort Smith. The line from St. Louis to Preston, via Fort Smith, is almost direct. So, too, is the line from Memphis, via Little Rock, Hot Springs and Caddo Cove, to Preston almost direct. The distance from St. Louis to Preston, as measured by the scale laid down on the map, is 490 miles. The distance from Memphis to Preston, according to the same scale, is 385 miles, making a difference in favor of the Memphis route of 105 miles. The distance from Memphis to Preston, as now traveled by the Fort Smith route, is to Little Rock 120 miles, to Fort Smith, 150 miles, and to Preston. –165 miles total – from Memphis to Preston. 435 miles, or, 55 miles less than the St. Louis route, and 50 miles farther than the direct route via Hot Springs and Caddo Cove.

There is another thing to be considered in this connection; which is, that the present route from Fort Smith to Preston is all through the Indian country; whereas, the proposed route (or rather, the route that was first contracted for) is, besides being by far the best route, mostly within the bounds of the State of Arkansas, and the part going through the Indian country is up the Red River valley – the most wealthy and civilised portion of the Indian country.

When these routes are examined, and the fact ascertained that the route of the original contract, from Memphis to Preston, is over a better country, and one hundred and five miles shorter than the present route from St. Louis to Preston, the fact is so glaring that we are led to inquire into the *motives* which induce the contractors to abandon a better and a shorter one, adhere to a worse and a longer route. The only answer which has suggested itself is the fact that the contractors are Northern men, and anxious to favor the Northern branch of this route, notwithstanding it is over a worse country and more than one hundred miles the farthest. And this supposition is the more plausible, from the fact that the contractors have sub let the Memphis branch of their contract, and bound their sub-contractors only to take the mail through in time – not compelling them to put passenger through in mail time, and by the additional fact that the agents, from San Francisco to Fort Smith, are all drummers for the St. Louis terminus, and the contractors, by sub letting it have made it to their own interest to come in competition with it, and divert travel from the Memphis to the St. Louis terminus. Add to these facts the further one that the contractors have been trying to get Congress to release them from their obligation to carry the mail over the Memphis branch of the route; and it requires a greater amount of charity than most Christians are possessed of to think that there is not a settled purpose on their part, to deprive the South of her just share of the advantages accruing from the **Overland mail**.

But my object was only to call your attention to the matter, so that you might take such steps as seemed right – that done, my work is also done.

May 7, 1859
Support for Route Not to Change

May 7, 1859, Saturday, page 2
Arkansas State Gazette and Democrat, Little Rock, Ark.

THE MEMPHIS BRANCH OF THE **OVERLAND MAIL** AND OTHER MATTERS – In another part of today's paper, we publish an article, and a communication, from the Memphis *Avalanche*, on the subject of the Memphis branch of the **Overland Mail**, which are worthy the consideration of our readers. We have long alone said - and have saw no reason to change our opinion - that we thought it was the deliberate intention of **Butterfield & Co**. to divert the whole of the benefits of this line to the St. Louis termination, and finally, to remove the line entirely beyond the limits of the State of Arkansas. And, the resolutions offered by Mr. Blair, the Republican member of Congress from Missouri (which we are informed **Butterfield & Co.** tried to lobby through) promising to give the contractors authority to omit the intermediate points mentioned in the contract (such as Fort Smith, Preston, El Paso, &c for example) was a covert attempt, by the company, to carry their mail to California without coming through, or even touching the State of Arkansas. Fortunately, however, this resolution was defeated.

To place the pretense of the necessity of their action, and particularly the abandonment of the Memphis route, upon a plausible footing, the contractors have done all in their power to decry and throw obstacles in the way of the Memphis route. While they have stocked the line, and advanced, freely and promptly, all the capital and labor necessary to put the St. Louis branch of their contrast into operatives, they have never stocked the Memphis branch at all, and have depended upon such arrangements as they could make, in the way of sub-letting their contract to mail contractors already on this route, whose duties, under their own contracts are paramount in, and must take precedence of all other duties and services. And these sub-contractors, as has been truly stated, have only been obliged to carry the mails through in schedule time, and if a single passenger has been put through, in that time, it has never been our good fortune to hear of the fact. The contractors having sub-let the Memphis branch, thereby putting their own (the St. Louis branch) in completion with it, can well afford to make special drummers of all their own agents, beyond Fort Smith, to induce all the travel to go to St. Louis, and thus avoid the Memphis branch. Hence few travelers from California come through by the Memphis branch of the **Overland Route**. Our authority for this charge is Maj. Ben McCullough, of Texas, who came a passenger in the **Overland** stages, and could not be scared off from the Southern branch to Memphis; and our proof is in the fact that, while many passengers go by the St. Louis branch, those coming by Memphis are few and far between – albeit the latter is much the shorter route.

In view then of this studied and deliberate attempt, on the part of **Butterfield & Co.**, to deprive the State of Arkansas of all benefit accruing from the **Overland California Mail**, and in view of the further wrong of depriving the Southern States of the benefit of a terminus of this route, and of the further and greater outrage to the traveling public and the whole country, of robbing them of the shortest and best route for the **Overland Mail**, we think it behooves the citizens of Arkansas and the South, and of right-minded and patriotic men in every part of the country, to take this matter in hand, and not rest until justice is done. It is not a question as to whether this mail shall go by Fort Smith or Des Arc, or by Little Rock or Washington, but whether it shall go through, or touch, the State of Arkansas - nor is it a question for the State of Arkansas alone; for our State has as little interest in it as many other of the States - the only question being which is the shortest and best route for this great mail, and nature and the geographical and physical conformations of the country place this route through the State of Arkansas.

The contractors being Northern men, their conduct is consistent and natural, because they serve their own North and put money in their own pockets at the same time; for their pay for the mail services, which they receive from the government, as well as that they receive for the carrying of passengers, is *by the mile,* and both are alike increased by every additional mile they travel; Hence the paying inducement to take passengers to St. Louis for that is the longest route; and, as shown, the longer the route the greater the pay from both the government and passengers. The sub-letting of the contract on the Memphis route, which is next to no service at all, also pays the contractors well for the government pays them the highest kind of prices *by the mile,* for first rate four horse service, with simple provisions for the conveyance of passengers, and they sub-let it, for an inferior grade of service, and of course, for a far less price, than they receive for the same work. so it may be seen, that, while the contractors make money by doing good services on the Northern branch of their contract, they also make money by failing and neglecting to do service on the Southern branch.

Taking the view of the writer of the communication, we submit that the Memphis branch of the **Overland Mail** is no great advantage to Fort Smith nor to the country between this place and that; for the same contractors who perform regular mail services between the two places are required to do that service, and paid for doing it, independent of the **Overland Contract** – the passengers amount to comparatively nothing. And lest the whole service be lost to the country we are of opinion that the better plan will be, in the future lettings of that contract, to let the service be done in conformity with the plan laid down by the correspondent of the *[Memphis] Avalanche* - that is, to make Preston (Texas) the connecting point, and let the branches go from that place to St. Louis, via Fort Smith; and to Memphis via Little Rock. No disinterested man can examine these routes and fail to see this justice - nay the necessity of this proposition. And we contend that it is better for the citizens of the region of Fort Smith to join in the demand for this act of justice in the whole country than to lose, as they undoubtedly will, the whole service if continued as is present carried on.

There is a mail route now advertised, and we hope some of our Arkansas bidders may get it, to carry the United States Mail from Fort Smith to Albuquerque, in New Mexico. This route, indicates and following, as it does, the line of **overland** emigration to the Pacific, and trade in the direction of New Mexico, will, if let, be of infinitely greater advantage to the West, and to the whole state, than the **Overland Mail,** as it presently carried, can ever be. Emigrants to California, or traders in the direction of New Mexico, never think of following the present route of the **Overland Mail**, but the proposed route from Fort Smith to Albuquerque is precisely the one they must travel, if they go from the Arkansas frontier; and we content that it is alone the best route for trade and travel across this part of the continent.

Let this mail route from Fort Smith to Albuquerque be established, and there is no doubt to the fact that it will soon be continued to California. But, whether that is done or not, the government will, of necessity, be compelled to put a sufficient number of troops along the line to protect the mails from depredations of the Indians. These will protect the emigrants and traders, who can go by this route, nearer, and six weeks earlier, than they can go by the Missouri route. These facts known to the world, and thousands upon thousands of emigrants, who would otherwise go to the Missouri route, would annually gather at Fort Smith, and there purchase their outfits and supplies for their journey across the plains; Thus would one great source of the wealth of Missouri, which Arkansas is entitled to, be transferred to our frontier where it naturally belongs, and where it should long alone have been.

But besides this, and of far greater advantage to the West and to the whole State *[of Arkansas]* , would be the trade which would spring up, immediately upon putting this line in operation, which, where ____ opened, would always _____. With the advantages of a _____ ____, and starting their ____ six weeks earlier than the cold weather of Missouri will permit __ could and ___ ___ New Mexico, Chihuahua and that whole country now supplied by Missouri, in time to arrive six weeks in advance and supply that country, and its _____ now furnished by the Missouri merchants and traders. This done, and we have transferred to our frontier, where it, naturally belongs, the ____ trade of New Mexico, Chihuahua, & c. with the wealth which would accompany it. The Western portion of the State of Missouri, and the city of St. Louis have been built up, and made great by this trade. The ___ merchant trains to our frontier from this trade would come richly laden with the gold and silver, and the valuable products of that vast new country. The avenue of wealth then opened upon us, would be from a new but a reliable - never failing source. And what that country has been to Missouri in point of wealth in its infancy, is but a faint foreshadowing of what it will be to Arkansas when it reaches the full grown manhood of its future development - that is, if the People of Arkansas are true to themselves.

What citizens of Arkansas would not be proud to see a city of great wealth as our frontier and the country improved and developed, and this trade would certainly improve and develop it. And there are few intelligent citizens in the State *[of Arkansas]* who are not perfectly convinced that *"all of these things shall be added unto" [Matthew 6:33]* us, if we do our duty and are but true to ourselves. How long, then, shall it be before our people move in this great matter? We think the time for action has arrived.

May 11, 1859

Overland Arrives With News of Indian Attack

May 11, 1859, Wednesday

Des Arc Citizen, Des Arc, Arkansas

THE **OVERLAND MAIL** – *ST. LOUIS, MAY 4* – The **Overland Mail** arrived here today, with San Francisco dates of the 11th inst.

Mr. Bishop, with forty men, who left Fort Tejon some time since, to co-operate with Lieut. Beale, was attached at Colorado crossing, by from six to seven hundred Mohaves, Pantahs and Tremus. The engagement lasted three hours, and a large number of Indians were killed. This occurred after Mr. Bishop had given them presents and permission to pass through the country. Mr. Bishop retreated, and sent to Col. Hoffman for assistance, who was expected to arrive and attack the Mohave villages about the 15th of April.

May 11, 1859

Butterfield's Steamboat Jennie Whipple Carrying Overland Mail

May 11, 1859, Wednesday

Arkansas True Democrat, Little Rock, Arkansas

ARRIVALS – May 5 Jennie Whipple from Memphis

May 14, 1859

Travel Time: Fayetteville to Springfield

May 14, 1859

The Arkansian, Fayetteville, Arkansas

SOUTHWEST BRANCH PACIFIC RAILROAD – ...Springfield is one hundred and ten miles from this place *[Fayetteville]*, accessible in from twelve to sixteen hours by **Overland Mail Stages**. Then when the rail road is complete to Springfield, we will be within four days of New York...

May 18, 1859
Butterfield's Steamboat Jennie Whipple
Carrying Overland Mail

May 18, 1859, Wednesday
Arkansas True Democrat, Little Rock, Arkansas

We make our lowest bow to Messrs. Gray and Parker, the gentlemanly clerks of the steamer **Jennie Whipple**, for a bundle of late Memphis and New York papers.

[NOTE: It was required that mail packets deliver and exchange newspapers up and down their routes between editors free of charge. This free postal service was based on Congressional act of 1825 that allowed "every printer of newspapers to send one paper to each and every other printer of newspapers within the United States free of postage..."]

May 18, 1859
Butterfield's Steamboat Jennie Whipple
Carrying Overland Mail

May 18, 1859, Wednesday
Arkansas True Democrat, Little Rock, Arkansas

ARRIVALS – May 15 Jennie Whipple from Memphis

DEPARTURES – May 15 Jennie Whipple for Memphis

NEWS ITEMS – Greeley, of the *N. Y. Tribune,* is going to California by the **Overland Mail Route.**

May 18, 1859
Death Occurs Aboard
Butterfield's Steamboat Jennie Whipple

May 18, 1859, Wednesday, page 2
Des Arc Citizen, Des Arc, Arkansas

"From the *Memphis Appeal,* 10th inst. MELANCHOLY DEATH – About two weeks since Walter R. Leake, Esq., the worthy President of the Bank of Waydesborough, N.C., embarked on the steamer **Jennie Whipple**, in the enjoyment of health, on a business visit to Terry's Landing, Arkansas. He sickened on the way and died, and his dead body was brought to this city *[Memphis]* yesterday by the same boat that bore him away a fortnight ago, when he was in the vigor of health and manhood."

May 21, 1859
Butterfield's Steamboat Jennie Whipple Carrying Overland Mail

May 21, 1859, Saturday
Arkansas State Gazette and Democrat, Little Rock, Ark.

ARRIVALS MAY 15 –
Jennie Whipple at Little Rock from Memphis
DEPARTURES MAY 15 –
Jennie Whipple from Little Rock for Memphis

May 25, 1859
Butterfield's Steamboat Jennie Whipple Carrying Overland Mail

May 25, 1859, Wednesday page 3
Arkansas True Democrat, Little Rock, Arkansas

ARRIVALS – May 22 Jennie Whipple from Memphis
DEPARTURES – May 23 Jennie Whipple for Memphis

NEWS ITEMS – We notice in the northern papers a debate as to whether the **Overland Mai Route** be discontinued. It would appear from this that the question of discontinuing it has been mooted. Should it be done, it will create a great deal of dissatisfaction.

May 25, 1859
Mistaken Suggestion that the Arkansas River Navigable into the Western USA

May 25, 1859, Wednesday page 3
Arkansas True Democrat, Little Rock, Arkansas

MR. EDITOR – ...The Arkansas is a long and noble steam boat river, extending far into 'the big west,' and embracing the most direct, safe, quick, cheap and practicable line of international transportation through a hospitable climate and latitude...

The Arkansas steam navigation part of the route into 'the big west' is already in the right line for cooperation; and which would answer all the commercial purposes, and, also, for travel and the **California Mail,** perhaps, better than a railroad from any point on the Mississippi, for the same parallel distance west, towards California, and save the money and apply it at once from the western head of steam navigation of the Arkansas *[River]*, to the Rocky Mountains, until the country may get rich enough to substitute a parallel railroad for the river navigation...

May 28, 1859
Butterfield's Steamboat Jennie Whipple

May 28, 1859, Saturday

Arkansas State Gazette and Democrat, Little Rock, Ark.

ARRIVALS MAY 22 –

Jennie Whipple at Little Rock from Memphis

DEPARTURES MAY 23 –

Jennie Whipple from Little Rock for Memphis

May 28, 1859
James Glover Responds to B.O.M Criticism

May 28, 1859

The Arkansian, Fayetteville, Arkansas

From the Memphis Avalanche – THE **OVERLAND MAIL** NO HUMBUG – *Grayso House, April 28, 1859 – EDITORS AVALANCHE* – SIRS: In your paper of this morning is a communication headed, *"The **Overland Mail** a Humbug,"* which contains so many errors, that I cannot permit it to pass without correction.

In the first place, I will notice his statement that *all* of the agents of the Company do all they can to induce passengers to take the St. Louis in preference to the Memphis branch. Permit me to say to your correspondent, that I am one of the Superintendents of the Company, and that I was born and raised in Tennessee, and that my residence is still in this State *[of Tennessee]*, and that I feel a deep interest in her welfare, and have on every occasion done all that I could to promote her interests.

Your correspondent's figures relative to the amount of staging to be done to reach Fort Smith as a junction are incorrect. *Miles*

Distance from Memphis to Little Rock	120
From Little Rock to Preston	325
From St. Louis to Preston	500
Amount of staging, if Preston is made the junction	945
Distance from Memphis via Little Rock to Fort Smith	270
From St. Louis to Fort Smith	320
From Fort Smith to Preston	180
	770

Thus showing that the ***[Overland Mail]* Company** saves one hundred and seventy-five miles of staging by connecting at Fort Smith instead of Preston.

Your correspondent is also mistaken in saying that the country had been explored and the road from Little Rock to Preston found to be a better road. I explored the country myself and I was satisfied that the ***[Overland Mail]* Company** could make better time by connecting at Fort Smith, than they could by connecting the two at either at Little Rock or Preston.

He is equally at fault in saying that they have much farther to pass through the Indian Territory, as they now run, than they would if Preston was the point of connection.

Let us see – The Little Rock branch, from McKean's to Preston, is 100 miles; on the St. Louis arm they would not touch Arkansas at all, but would enter Indian Territory near Neosho, MO., and pass thru it the entire distance to Preston *[Texas]* – 220 miles, making altogether 320 miles through the Indian country; while on their present route, only 160 miles of it is through their country.

Each of the mails that arrived there this week came in inside of twenty-three days, while their contract gives the company twenty-five days. Permit me to say to your many readers, and the community generally, that the ***[Overland Mail]* Company** have become satisfied that they cannot depend on other contractors to carry their mails and passengers and have notified them that they will put on their stock as soon as they can procure enough to stock the road.

Your readers should remember that the Mississippi bottom has been overflowed for two months, and the ***[Overland Mail]* company** have had to send their mails by boats, at heavy expense to Helena and from there to Little Rock, on horse's back, or wagons, or any other way they could to get through.

You have had as regular mail in your State *[of Arkansas]*. Your mails fail oftener on your railroads than they do by this route. Such staging has never been done on this, or any other continent, as is being done by **Butterfield & Co.**

Yours respectfully, James Glover
Superintendent of **Overland Mail Co.**

June 1, 1859
Butterfield's Steamboat Jennie Whipple Carrying Overland Mail

June 1, 1859, Wednesday
Arkansas True Democrat, Little Rock, Arkansas

ARRIVALS – May 30 Jennie Whipple from Memphis
DEPARTURES – May 31 Jennie Whipple for Memphis

"We are indebted to the gentlemanly officers of the Jennie Whipple for late papers."

June 4, 1859
Overland Stage Arrives with News

June 4, 1859, Saturday
Arkansas State Gazette and Democrat, Little Rock, Ark.

ST. LOUIS, MAY 25 – The **Overland Mail** from San Francisco the 2d inst., has arrived here. The news brought by the conductor from the Mexican and Indian border, however, is interesting and important.

In their treaty with Col. Hoffman, the Mojaves surrendered almost unconditionally. It is believed the war is now over for good.

St. Louis, May 30 – The **Overland Mail** arrived here today with dates of the 6th inst. A fight occurred between Major Van Dorn and a party of Northern Comanches at the fort of the Arkansas River on the 16th inst. Forty-six Indians were killed and thirty-six were taken prisoners. Two soldiers were killed and several wounded. Among the latter were Lieut. Lee and Capt. Smith. There was much excitement among the Brazos reserve Indians on account of their being five hundred Texans encamped twenty miles below, and were threatening an attack.

June 4, 1859
Overland Passenger

June 4, 1859
The Arkansian, Fayetteville, Arkansas

George C. Cove of the house of Benedict, Hall & Co., New York, arrived in the "**Overland**" on Wednesday last, on his way to Fort Smith.

June 4, 1859
Butterfield's Steamboat Jennie Whipple
Carrying Overland Mail

June 4, 1859, Saturday
Arkansas State Gazette and Democrat, Little Rock, Ark.

Arrivals May 31 –
Jennie Whipple at Little Rock from Memphis

Departures May 31 –
Jennie Whipple from Little Rock for Memphis

June 8, 1859
Butterfield's Steamboat Jennie Whipple Carrying Overland Mail

June 8, 1859, Wednesday
Arkansas True Democrat, Little Rock, Arkansas

ARRIVALS – June 7 Jennie Whipple from Memphis

MEMPHIS PACKETS – The steamer S. H. Tucker, will hereafter make weekly trips between Memphis and this point *[Little Rock]*. ... The **Jennie Whipple** is also in the same trade. So that we now have two regular Memphis and Little Rock packets.

Flour! Flour! Just received per **Jennie Whipple**, 50 barrels of St. Louis extra flour; 50 barrels of Illinois extra flour; and for sale low by John Collins & Co., June 8, 1859.

June 8, 1859
Support for Southern Route

June 8, 1859, page 2
Arkansas True Democrat, Little Rock, Arkansas

THE **OVERLAND MAIL** – The **Butterfield** route will be kept up. If any of the routes are discontinued or number of trips curtailed, it will be the northern routes. Last winter the route by Salt Lake was impassible for weeks on account of snows.

Drivers and even the mules were frozen to death and once or twice the mail bags were abandoned. On the routes still further north matters were much worse. The Indians several times attacked the persons or trains.

The routes on the 35th parallel and through Texas can be carried throughout the year, and are free from the severe wintry storms, and very little trouble by Indians.

Several of the Missouri members of Congress went to Washington to remonstrate against a discontinuance of the routes leaving the western confines of that State, with what success we do not yet know.

June 11, 1859
Census Count of Letters
Carried on Overland Stagecoaches

June 11, 1859, Saturday

The Arkansian, Fayetteville, Arkansas

OVER-LAND MAIL TO THE PACIFIC – Our readers will be pleased to learn from the following extract from the *Missouri Republican* that it is not probable that the **'Over-Land Mail'** will be changed or abrogated and that such is the decision of the Attorney General of the United States. Read the subjoined extracts.

We take it for granted, not that the Attorney General of the United States has decided that the Contract with the **BUTTERFIELD Company** cannot be abrogated or changed, that the **Overland Mail** to the Pacific may be regarded as a settled thing, and that hereafter it will grow in the public favor. The derangement and uncertainty of the Ocean lines will almost compel the employment of the **Overland Mail**, and as the Contractors have already satisfied the public of the regularity with which it may be carried, this fact ought to recommend it to general favor. In this connection, a few facts may not be without interest.

The first mail **overland** for California left this city on the 16th February, 1858, and the first mail arrived here, in return, on the 9th of October following. The first mail from St. Louis carried out about fifty letters. The mail which arrived from San Francisco on the 31st ult., brought nineteen hundred and eighty-seven letters, and that which was dispatched from this city yesterday morning carried out one thousand seven hundred and forty letters. The rate of increase, we have good reason to believe, will be much greater hereafter, as there is no longer any doubt of the security of transportation on this route. The number of letters sent from Memphis and all of the towns on the route, cannot be known to us, but they probably equal the number made up at St. Louis. When the mail was first started, the through matter was sent in the smallest sized leathern pouches used by the Department. It is now sent in the largest size, and the way mail is put in a second size bag.

The public will, we doubt not, be surprised to hear, that a sealed letter bag is made up in London for San Francisco, to go by this route in the intermediate time of the departure of the California steamer from New York three of these bags have been received here, and sent off in one mail.

In point of regularity, no mail in the world can equal this between St. Louis and San Francisco, since it was first started, it has failed to arrive in contract time only twice, and then the difficulty and delay was caused by the extreme badness of the roads between Tipton, in this State *[Missouri]*, and Fort Smith. For the last two months the trips have been made within twenty-three days, being at the rate of about one hundred miles per day. If proper instructions were given to the officers in the Post Office Department in California and the other States of the Union, the mail matter sent **overland** would soon be as much as the coaches could carry. These instructions should at once be issued. There is no propriety in keeping letters in the various offices a week or two, for no other reason than that they may be sent by the Ocean route, now rendered more uncertain than ever by the disorganized state of the companies proffering to do the service. Mails can be, and are dispatched twice a week from St. Louis, and this route ought to be adopted, throughout the country, as the best and most expeditious means of communication with California.

June 11, 1859
Postmaster Seeks to Abolish Overland

June 11, 1859, Saturday

The Arkansian, Fayetteville, Arkansas

The OVER-LAND MAIL THREATENED – A dispatch from Washington states that the Postmaster General desires to abolish the **Butterfield Overland Mail** contract, for the purpose of saving the expense it costs, and has asked the opinion of the Attorney General as to the legality of rescinding the bargain, and suspend the mail The other members of the Cabinet are said to be opposed to the proposition.

Three Railroad Workers Standing on Crank Handcar

In the above article, the Little Rock and Memphis Railroad offered to carry the Overland Mail from Hopefield to Madison by handcar, since the regular trains have not returned into service after the tracks were flooded. Source: DAG no. 1187. Daguerreotype collection, Library of Congress Prints and Photographs Division Washington, D.C.

June 11, 1859
Heavy Rain and Floods on Memphis Route

June 11, 1859, page 2

Des Arc Citizen, Des Arc, Arkansas

From the Memphis Appeal, 10th inst – The California Mails – Mr. J. N. Nichols, the popular agent at this city of the **Overland Mail Company** to California, shipped twenty-five horses for Helena yesterday, by the steamer J. C. Swon, for the **Overland Mail** service. The service in the State of Arkansas has been greatly embarrassed by the prevailing floods, but the waters have receded sufficiently, it is thought, to render it practicable to transport the mails again over the Memphis and Little Rock railroad, the superintendent having signified to the agent here his willingness to receive the mails at Hopefield *[Arkansas]* in future. The regular trains have not yet commenced running upon the road, but the mails will be transmitted through hand-cars. The labor will be tedious, but the route, even in its present precarious condition, is more practicable one, perhaps than that by way of Helena.

June 11, 1859
Butterfield's Steamboat Jennie Whipple Carrying Overland Mail

June 11, 1859, Saturday
Arkansas State Gazette and Democrat, Little Rock, Ark.

ARRIVALS JUNE 7 –

Jennie Whipple at Little Rock from Memphis

DEPARTURES JUNE 7 –

Jennie Whipple from Little Rock for Memphis

June 15, 1859
Butterfield's Steamboat Jennie Whipple Carrying Overland Mail

June 15, 1859, Wednesday
Arkansas True Democrat, Little Rock, Arkansas

ARRIVALS – June 7 Jennie Whipple from Memphis
ARRIVALS – June 13 Jennie Whipple from Memphis
DEPARTURES – June 7 Jennie Whipple for Memphis

The steamers S. H. Tucker and Jennie Whipple kindly furnished us with late papers.

From the *Pine Bluff Independent* we learn... The last trip of that star little boat, Jennie Whipple, is the quickest on record, from Memphis to this place *[Pine Bluff]*. The Jennie is a nice boat. Captain A. D. Storm commending and J. A. Gray in the office is a sufficient recommendation. Thanks for late favors.

June 18, 1859
Butterfield's Steamboat Jennie Whipple Carrying Overland Mail

June 18, 1859. Saturday
Arkansas State Gazette and Democrat, Little Rock, Ark.

Arrivals June 16 – Jennie Whipple from Memphis

DEPARTURES JUNE 14 –
Jennie Whipple from Little Rock for Memphis

June 22, 1859
Route to be Unchanged

June 22, 1859
Arkansas True Democrat, Little Rock, Arkansas

From the *Fort Smith Times* we learn the **Butterfield Overland Mail** route is to remain unaltered.

June 22, 1859
Butterfield's Steamboat Jennie Whipple Carrying Overland Mail

June 22, 1859, Wednesday
Arkansas True Democrat, Little Rock, Arkansas

DEPARTURES June 14 – Jennie Whipple for Memphis
ARRIVALS June 20 – Jennie Whipple from Memphis
DEPARTURES June 21 – Jennie Whipple for Memphis

New Flour.

50 SACKS of extra new Flour;
50 Bbls. " " " " just rec'd,
per steamer Jennie Whipple, and for sale by
June 22, '59. JOHN COLLINS & CO.

Collins & Co. ad for Flour Delivered by the *Jennie Whipple*
Source: June 22, 1859, Arkansas True Democrat

June 22, 1859
Butterfield's Steamboat Jennie Whipple
Carrying Overland Mail

June 22, 1859, Saturday
Arkansas State Gazette and Democrat, Little Rock, Ark.
Arrivals June 21 –
Jennie Whipple at Little Rock from Memphis

June 25, 1859
Butterfield's Steamboat Jennie Whipple
Carrying Overland Mail

June 25, 1859, Saturday
Arkansas State Gazette and Democrat, Little Rock, Ark.

St. Louis, June 20 – The **Overland Mail** arrived here today with San Francisco dates of the 27th ult. The news by this arrival... the reported attack on the Mohave Indians by Leut. Beale's party has proved to be incorrect. The Indians are reported as being peaceable disposed.

Departures June 20 –
Jennie Whipple from Little Rock for Memphis

June 25, 1859
Butterfield Overland Discontinued?

June 25, 1859
The Arkansian, Fayetteville, Arkansas

Reduction of Mail Service – ...We little thought, while reading the following paragraph from the *Washington Star,* that the mail route, which immediately concerns ourselves, and the majority of our readers, would be the next one attacked.

Discontinuance of the **Overland Mail** – Congress having failed at its last session to make the usual appropriations for the Post Office Department, the Postmaster General has been induced to closely examine the service for the purpose of discontinuing all that may be dispensed with without material injury to the public service. The territorial routes between Neosho, Missouri, and Albuquerque, New Mexico, and between Kansas, Missouri and Stockton, California, which were let to contract last year, have accordingly been discontinued – the discontinuance to take effect from the 1st day of July next...

June 29, 1859

Indians Hold Stagecoach Six Hours

June 29, 1859, page 2

Arkansas True Democrat, Little Rock, Arkansas

INDIANS EXAMINING THE "SWIFT WAGON" – A correspondent who has recently crossed. The Indians of the Cherokee nation are very anxious to have the route through their territory. They call the mail coaches the "swift wagon." A deputation from the heads of the nation have waited upon the **"Great Chief Butterfield of the swift wagon,"** as they call him, and ask him to run the wagon through their country. They are rich, and great slaveholders, owning more nig___s than their neighbors in Arkansas. Their country is a beautiful one. They are jealous of the whites, fearing – it is propable *[provable: evidence strong enough to establish presumption]* – that they will be driven from their homes.

The Comanches and interior Indians look upon the "swift wagon" with great curiosity and wonder. They have shown no malice or ill-will as yet. Some six hundred of them stopped the mail coach and surrounded it. They wished to see the "swift wagon" and what was in it. They detained it five or six hours, until each one had inspected it – looked under the seats – turned over the mail bags – felt of them – looked at the wheels, poles, harness and trappings, to their satisfaction, with many an interjection, "Ugh! Ugh!" They told the conductor to "go quick with the swift wagon" – (here many an, "Ugh" was grunted with satisfaction) but, "Ugh! No Railroad – No Railroad– and all grunted a hearty "Ugh!" of approbation and comment.

Young Comanche Warrior, Oklahoma Territory, 1895

July 2, 1859
Butterfield's Steamboat Jennie Whipple
Carrying Overland Mail

July 2, 1859, Saturday
Arkansas State Gazette and Democrat, Little Rock, Ark.

ARRIVALS JUNE 28 –

Jennie Whipple at Little Rock from Memphis

DEPARTURES JUNE 28 –
Jennie Whipple from Little Rock for Memphis

July 6, 1859
Butterfield's Steamboat Jennie Whipple
Carrying Overland Mail

July 6, 1859, Wednesday
Arkansas True Democrat, Little Rock, Arkansas

ARRIVALS June 28 – Jennie Whipple from Memphis
DEPARTURES June 28 – Jennie Whipple for Fort Smith
ARRIVALS July 4 – Jennie Whipple from Memphis
DEPARTURES July 5 – Jennie Whipple for Memphis

July 9, 1859
Butterfield's Steamboat Jennie Whipple
Carrying Overland Mail

July 9, 1859, Saturday
Arkansas State Gazette, Little Rock, Arkansas

ARRIVALS JULY 5 –
Jennie Whipple at Little Rock from Memphis
DEPARTURES JULY 5 –
Jennie Whipple from Little Rock for Memphis

July 13, 1859
Running Smoothly

July 13, 1859
Van Buren Press, Van Buren, Arkansas

CALIFORNIA OVERLAND MAIL – We notice the stages of the **Overland Mail Company** both going to and returning from San Francisco, pass through this city filled with passengers. The trips are made with great regularity, almost always ahead of schedule time.

July 13, 1859
Butterfield's Steamboat Carrying Overland

July 13, 1859, Wednesday
Arkansas True Democrat, Little Rock, Arkansas

ARRIVALS July 10 – Jennie Whipple from Memphis
DEPARTURES July 11 – Jennie Whipple for Memphis

July 16, 1859
Sad News • Indian War
Jennie Whipple Carrying Overland Mail

July 16, 1859, Saturday
Arkansas State Gazette, Little Rock, Arkansas

SAD NEWS – We stop the press to say that Major Gaines, just in by **Overland Mail,** from Arbuckle, brings the sad news that Frank and Joe Rector were both stabbed by Maj. Hurst just before he left. Joe was dead, and but little hopes of Frank. - *Fort Smith Herald, 9th*

AN INDIAN WAR IN SONORA – *St. Louis, July 5* – The **Overland California Mail** has arrived with dates from San Francisco to the 10th ult. The Indians had defeated the Government troops in four engagements, and were victoriously marching on Guayams, the population being compelled to take refuge on board the vessels in port.

ARRIVALS JULY 12 –
Jennie Whipple at Little Rock from Memphis
DEPARTURES JULY 12 –
Jennie Whipple from Little Rock for Memphis

July 16, 1859
Butterfield & Son Visit Fayetteville

July 16, 1859, Saturday, page 3
The Arkansian, Fayetteville, Arkansas

Col. John Butterfield Sr., President of the **Overland Mail Company**, and **Mr. John Butterfield Jr.** arrived at our City this week.

July 16, 1859
Butterfield Obtains Fayetteville to Fort Smith
Route to Carry Regular Mail

July 16, 1859, Saturday, page 2
The Arkansian, Fayetteville, Arkansas

TRI-WEEKLY MAIL TO FORT SMITH: CHANGE OF CONTRACTORS – We understand that **Col. John Butterfield**, of the **Overland Mail**, has purchased from Mr. Thomas Waldron his contract with the Government for carrying the mail tri-weekly from this place to Fort Smith.

Although Messrs. Waldron and Pollards have been very punctual during the time they have been engaged in carrying the mail over this route, we have every reason to believe and confidently expect, that there will be no falling off while under control of the present contractor. The well known energy and enterprise of **Col. Butterfield** is a sufficient guarantee to the public that on this part, every thing pertaining to the faithful, and rapid transportation of the mail will be complied with. If the road overseers and those interested will but do their duty, towards keeping in good repair the road over which the stages run, we may now gain, by the rapid transportations of the mails, in time, what we have lost because of the reduction of the service.

This then, at the present time, is the best we can wish for, and we trust that we will not be mistaken in our conjectures; for nothing tends so much to develop the resources of a country and bring in a thrifty and enterprising population, as the regular and speedy transportation of the mails. It is then a matter of interest to us all, that our means of intercourse with the outer world be increased.

Col. B. intends also running an extra coach, in connection with the **Overland Mail** from this place to Springfield, for the convenience of passengers; the tri-weekly stages will connect with the **Overland Mail** coaches and extras at this place, so that passengers can go through without delay and "double quick time."

Success, we say, to the new enterprise.

John Butterfield Jr., son of John Butterfield

John Butterfield Jr., along with Marquis L. Kenyon of Rome, NY, (one of the major stock-holders and directors) started in January 1858 by mule back to select the trail through the Southern Overland Corridor, as well as the sites for the stage stations on the 2,700 mile Butterfield Trail from Tipton, Missouri, to San Francisco, California.

The stage stations had to be stocked with horses, mules, harnesses, food, supplies, wagons, and other equipment. John Butterfield Jr. was the Superintendent at the Fayetteville, Arkansas office. He served as driver on the first ***Overland Mail Co.*** *stagecoach out of Tipton, Missouri to Fort Smith, Arkansas. Image from Frank Leslie's Illustrated Newspaper, November 27, 1858.*

July 20, 1859
Butterfield Home Station - Jackson House Leased

July 20, 1859
Des Arc citizen, Des Arc, Arkansas

DES ARC HOTEL.—Messrs. J. F. & W. R. Welch have leased the Jackson House for a term of years, and will change the name, in a few days, to that of the "Des Arc Hotel." These gentlemen have the reputation of being well suited to the position they have assumed. The hotel is being put in good order, and we have no hesitancy in recommending the proprietors to the patronage of the public. A No. 1 Hotel will pay well, in Des Arc, and we are assured that no trouble or expense will be spared by the new proprietors in making the "Des Arc Hotel" all that can be desired by travelers and all others who may tender them their patronage.

Source: Des Arc Citizen, July 20, 1859

July 20, 1859
Eastern Texas Beginning to Use the Butterfield

July 20, 1859, page 2
Van Buren Press, Van Buren, Arkansas

THE TRAVEL FROM TEXAS. -- We begin to discover that the people of Eastern Texas are acting wise for once. The merchants and traders, who buy their goods in the east, have quit the long route by the way of Jefferson and Shreveport; and now take the **Overland Mail** at Sherman, Texas, and come through to this place in two and a half or three days -- and from here to St. Louis in three days -- or to New York in *five days* from this place.

Among the throng of people that were crowding around on Saturday morning last, we spied Mr. C. C. Alexander, of Bonham, Fannin County, Texas, who was on his way to the east. If we knew how, we would induce Alex, to ship to this point instead of Shreveport, as the road is just as good; and the insurance on this river not as much as it is on Red River.

We hope the people of Texas will try the experiment -- it will pay, and then, we want to form an alliance with you any how -- we want a Railroad.

Mr. Alexander informed us that there were four other gentlemen with him from that country -- and he remarked in our presence that he felt very well considering the fast travelling -- and thought he could stand the trip through finely. --*Fort Smith Herald*

July 20, 1859
Butterfield Also Obtains Regular Mail Contract Between Fayetteville & Fort Smith

July 20, 1859
Van Buren Press, Van Buren, Arkansas

Thomas Walden, Esq. of this city has sold out his mail line from Fayetteville to Fort Smith to **Col. John Butterfield**, of the **California Overland Mail Company. Col. Butterfield** we believe now owns the whole line from Tipton to Fort Smith and the mails under his administration will put through with speed and regularity.

July 23, 1859
Butterfield's Steamboat Jennie Whipple Carrying Overland Mail

July 23, 1859, Saturday
Arkansas State Gazette, Little Rock, Arkansas

ARRIVALS JULY 20 –
Jennie Whipple at Little Rock from Memphis

DEPARTURES JULY 21 –
Jennie Whipple from Little Rock for Memphis

July 27, 1859
Butterfield's Steamboat Jennie Whipple Carrying Overland Mail

July 27, 1859, Wednesday
Arkansas True Democrat, Little Rock, Arkansas

ARRIVALS – July 20 Jennie Whipple from Memphis

DEPARTURES – July 21 Jennie Whipple for Memphis

"New Flour. 50 sacks of extra new flour; 50 bbls. of extra new flour just received; per steamer Jennie Whipple and for sale by John Collins & Co. June 22, 1859."

July 27, 1859
Stagecoach Driver Suddenly Dies

July 27, 1859, Wednesday
Des Arc Citizen, Des Arc, Arkansas

SUDDEN DEATH – MR. HENRY MYERS, who had been driving stage for Messrs. Chidester, Rapley & Co., on the Des Arc and Fort Smith line, during the past twelve months died suddenly at the Des Arc Hotel, in Des Arc, on Wednesday evening last.

Mr. Myers had complained of being unwell during the forenoon, and soon after took his bed. A physician had visited him, when he was seized with an apoplectic fit and died in a short time. His age was about 42 years.

We learn that the deceased was formerly of Staunton, Augusta County, Virginia, near which place he has two daughters and other relatives. At one time he was in the employ of Edwin Porter & Co., and drove teams out of Stauton and Warm Springs. Mr. Myers was highly esteemed as a trustworthy and industrious gentleman. At the time of his death, he was within a few days of leaving for Virginia, had settled up his business, and made all necessary preparations for his departure. His effects are in the hands of gentlemen who will take care of them until his relatives send for them. For any information in reference to the deceased, his relatives or friends are requested to address the editor of this paper.

July 27, 1859

Expense Report from Post Office

July 27, 1859, Wednesday, page 4
Des Arc Citizen, Des Arc, Arkansas

It is stated that the account between the **Overland Mail Company** and the post office department will stand thus, at the close of the six month's account: Expenditure by the department, $3,600,000; receipts, $90,000; showing a clear loss from the route of $3,510,000.

August 3, 1859

Road South of Fayetteville Surprisingly Passable

August 3, 1859, **page 2**
The Van Buren Press Van Buren, Arkansas

We have been for some years a close reader of the Arkansas Papers, and distinctly recollect reading a letter of the Editor of the *Times,* published in that paper, a short time before the California **Overland Mail** line went into operation, in which he said that it would be utterly impracticable for the mail stages to run over the road from Van Buren to Fayetteville across Boston Mountain, and gave such a vivid description of the obstacles incident to the route, that has he stated, the only route that the **Overland Mail** could be conveyed upon from Fayetteville to Fort Smith would be via Evansville, and thence through the Cherokee Nation to Fort Smith, cutting off Van Buren entirely.

Now, to show how liable the Editor is to err in judgment, we are reliably informed that he came through on the first trip of the California stage that was made, and over the very same route that he had but a month or two before said was so utterly impracticable; and the stages have continued to run on that very route from Fayetteville to Van Buren from that day to this, making good time, and so far as we are advised, without accident.

In conclusion we hope that in our efforts to promote the interests of Western Arkansas that hereafter we may not often run in counter interest to the efforts of the Times, and that in any efforts of the **Times**, and that in any efforts we may make, where the Editor of the *Times* cannot agree with us, if he *"will only lay low, then we will show him sights."*

August 3, 1859
Butterfield Stage Arrives Without Mail

August 3, 1859
The Van Buren Press Van Buren, Arkansas

The mail from St. Louis failed on Saturday, and also on yesterday; the stage arrived in due time on both trips; but failed to bring a through mail. Our latest St. Louis dates are to the 23rd ult.

The Steamboat Landing at Van Buren, Arkansas
Source: History Makers of Arkansas, 1918, by John Hugh Reynolds

August 3, 1859
Great Fire in San Francisco

August 3, 1859, page 3
Des Arc Citizen, Des Arc, Arkansas

Arrival of the **Overland Mail** – Great Fire in San Francisco – St. Louis, July 27 – The Overland Mail from California arrived today, with San Francisco dates of the 4th inst.

A destructive fire has occurred in San Francisco, destroying nearly all the buildings situated on Davis street, between Broadway and Vallejo streets; also, the buildings on the wharf, fronting on Davis Street.

1859 Fire in San Francisco, Albert Pike Temple, 1859 Geary Street

1859 San Francisco Fire
Photograph by Padre Art

August 10, 1859
Robbery of Trunk from Overland Stage

August 10, 1859
The Van Buren Press, Van Buren, Arkansas

HIGHWAY ROBBERY - We learn from a private letter from Fayetteville, that the **Overland Mail Stage** which passed through here on Monday last, was robbed of a valuable trunk while near Fayetteville.

The trunk was the property of W. W. Southgate, and contained mostly ladies' and children's apparel, gold lockets, breast pins, tea spoons,silver pitcher, with the name of W. W. Southgate marked on it, and jewelry of various kinds, to the amount of over three hundred dollars. It was a tan colored, medium size trunk and Mr. Southgate's name was painted in white letters on he end thereof. A reward of $25 is offered for its recovery.

August 13, 1859
Butterfield's Steamboat Carrying Overland

August 13, 1859, Saturday
Arkansas State Gazette, Little Rock, Arkansas

THE RIVER – low water – The mail route from this place *[Little Rock]* to Napoleon has been stocked with stages all the way through.

MR. NICHOLS, the accommodating Agent of the **Overland Mail Company**, handed us yesterday morning, San Francisco papers of the 23d ult., for which he will accept our thanks.

Mr. Nichols informs us that the **Overland Mail** is now stocked with excellent teams, first class coaches, and reliable drivers, for the purpose of carrying, on the route – either *way or through* passengers.

ST. LOUIS, AUG. 8 – The **Overland Mail** arrived in this city today with San Francisco dates of the 13th ult. The Indians were committing depredations in Humboldt Country. The Mormons were implicated in these lawless proceedings.

August 17, 1859
Butterfield's Steamboat Arrives in Van Buren

August 17, 1859
The Van Buren Press Van Buren, Arkansas

The steamer Jennie Whipple arrived from the Arkansas River last evening, with a fair trip, including a large number of passengers. Her officers report only sixteen inches of water to Little Rock. The Whipple went within twenty miles of that point, and fount it impossible to go higher. The Jennie Whipple will not return to the Arkansas River during the present season but will take advantage of the low water and go to Cincinnati for repairs.

August 17, 1859
Butterfield's Overland Home Station in Des Arc was at the Des Arc Hotel

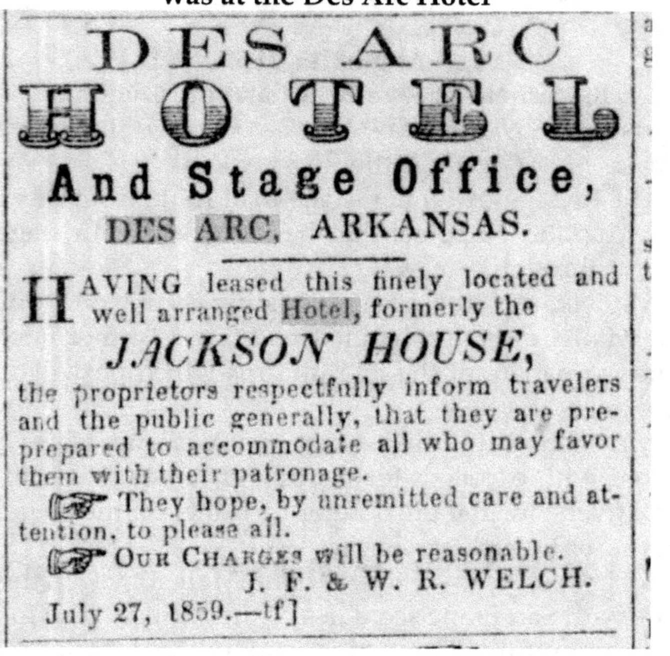
DES ARC
HOTEL
And Stage Office,
DES ARC, ARKANSAS.

HAVING leased this finely located and well arranged Hotel, formerly the
JACKSON HOUSE,
the proprietors respectfully inform travelers and the public generally, that they are pre-prepared to accommodate all who may favor them with their patronage.

☞ They hope, by unremitted care and attention, to please all.

☞ OUR CHARGES will be reasonable.

J. F. & W. R. WELCH.

July 27, 1859.—tf]

Source: Des Arc Citizen, August 17, 1859, page 3

August 24, 1859
Suggestion to Drop Little Rock from the Route

August 24, 1859
Des Arc Citizen, Des Arc, Arkansas

New Mail Route – Des Arc Within Fourteen Hours Travel of Memphis – We are pleased to learn from our worthy Postmaster, D. P. Black, Esq., that the Postmaster General has ordered that one of the weekly trips on Route No. 7831, from Des Arc to Fort Smith, be discontinued, and that the semi-weekly four horse coach service be extended from Des Arc to Madison, the end of the railroad; to go into operation on the 1st of October next. This will make a complete semi-weekly stage line from Madison to Fort Smith – over the nearest and best route from Memphis to Fort Smith.

There are several bridges needed on this route, between Des Arc and Cache River. The contract for their immediate erection was let out to Wm. Creel, Esq., on Monday last, Mr. Creel has had extensive experience in bridge building, and we are assured that no pains or expense will be spared in making them substantial and durable.

Col. R. M. Brimmer, one of the firm of Rapley, Hanger & Co., contractors on the above routes, suggested, more than a year since, the extension of the stage line from Des Arc to Madison, and there is no doubt that his exertions and representations to the department have accomplished this much desired extension of mail facilities.

The route from Fort Smith to Memphis via Des Arc is the nearest and most feasible for conveying the **Overland Mail**, both summer and winter. A great outrage has been perpetrated upon the Department, in compelling this mail to be carried via Little Rock. If **Col. Butterfield**, or some of the **Overland Mail** agents, will take a look at this route, they will be convinced that all we say is true. If Little Rock has any matter to be carried by the **Overland Route** they could send it to Fort Smith – thus saving the elbow route via Little Rock.

August 26, 1859
Charles Butterfield Praised

August 26, 1859, Friday, page 3
The Arkansian, Fayetteville, Arkansas

See "Arrivals and Departures" of the **Over-Land Mail** at this place. **Col. C.E. Butterfiel**d, Assistant Superintendent, can always be found at his post, ready to attend to passengers and other matters connected with the **Over-Land Mail** service.

August 26, 1859
Overland Mail Advertisement

August 26, 1859, Friday, page 3
The Arkansian, Fayetteville, Arkansas

OVER-LAND MAIL.

The Over Land Mail Stage arrives regularly at Fayetteville, from St. Louis & San Francisco.

(GOING NORTH.)

Monday, Wednesday and Saturday, 5 30 p. m.

(GOING SOUTH.)

Monday, Wednesday and Saturday, 3 00 p. m.

There is also an Express connected with each Stage, in charge of a special Messenger.

For particulars, enquire of

C. E. BUTTERFIELD,
Assistant Superintendent, Fayetteville.

Aug. 26, 1859. 26tf

This advertisement was printed numerous times including August 26, September 9, 16, 24, October 7, November 11, 1859 and February 17, April 6, and May 4, 1860.

August 27, 1859
Butterfield's Overland Home Station in Little Rock was at the Anthony House

ANTHONY HOUSE,
LITTLE ROCK, ARKANSAS.

THE above Hotel, having been purchased by Messrs. PETER HANGER and WM. E. ASHLEY, has been leased by the undersigned, who are ready to accommodate travelers and sojourners.

Their Table

will be well supplied with the substantials and delicacies of both the foreign and the home markets.

Their Servants

are of the best that can be procured, and as good as those of the best Hotels of the country.

The Hotel has been thoroughly refitted and furnished; and so soon as necessary arrangements can be effected, extensive additions and improvements will be made to the buildings.

The offices of all the Stage lines coming to Little Rock, are kept at the Anthony House.

STIDHAM & EDMUNDS.

Little Rock, Feb. 1, 1859. 31—tf.

Source: Weekly Arkansas Gazette, Aug. 27, 1859

August 31, 1859
Butterfield's Steamboat in for Repairs

August 31, 1859, Wednesday
The Van Buren Press, Van Buren, Arkansas

RIVER NEWS – The **Jennie Whipple** has arrived at Louisville. It was Capt. Gray's intention to go in the canal dock at

Louisville for repairs, after reshipping his Cincinnati freight and passengers. After repairing the Whipple will go to Cincinnati for a cargo for Arkansas River. – *Memphis Appeal*

September 2, 1859
Charles Butterfield Praised

September 2, 1859, Friday, page 3
The Arkansian, Fayetteville, Arkansas

We are under obligations to **Col. Charles E. Butterfield** of the **Overland Mail Company** for files of San Francisco papers, nineteen days after date. Think of it, only nineteen days from San Francisco. The **Overland Mail Company** deserve all praise for carrying regularly and successfully the mail over the longest and most difficult stage route in the world.

September 7, 1859
Regular Mail Route Difficulties

September 7, 1859
The Van Buren Press, Van Buren, Arkansas

THE MAILS – The contractors for carrying the mail on the route from this place *[Van Buren]* to Little Rock have given up their contract, and declined longer to carry the mail, although they still continue to make trips for the transportation of passengers. We have therefore, to depend upon the northern route to St. Louis ***[Overland Mail]*** exclusively for news.

We hope, and indeed expect, that this state of affairs will not long continue; the postmasters at Little Rock undoubtedly make some arrangement for the transportation of the mails between that place, Van Buren and Fort Smith. We have not received a mail from the east since last Friday. Our subscribers on the route to Little Rock will receive this as an explanation for the non-reception of their papers.

Van Buren, Arkansas ca. 1910

Van Buren, Arkansas ca. 1880

September 14, 1859
The Various Overland Routes to California
Contracts Cannot Be Cancelled

September 14, 1859, Wednesday, page 2
Des Arc Citizen, Des Arc, Arkansas

THE OVERLAND MAIL ROUTES – We deem it proper to state, s there is such a strong prejudice against the continuance of the **Overland Routes**, costing a million of dollars annually, with scarcely any return, that is is the desire of the Postmaster General to have them abolished, and that he would long since have applied the principle of retrenchment in this particular, had he not been prevented by a decision of the Attorney General. this decision was, that as the contracts for that specific object was for four years, and did not contain the usual clause empowering the Postmaster General to change the service, the routes in question could not be interfered with. Should Congress abolish them, a claim for damages would arise. – *Washington Star*

September 14, 1859
Butterfield's Steamboat Carrying Overland

September 14, 1859, Wednesday
Arkansas True Democrat

The river is still falling, with about three and a half feet in the channel from this point *[Little Rock]* to Napoleon. The navigation from here to Fort Smith is about closed. The steamers Red Wing and Jennie Whipple, both arrived last week in a slightly damaged condition, and enters protested. We learn that the goods on the latter boat *[Jennie Whipple]* are very much depreciated in value, owing to the water rising over a portion of them before the damage could be repaired.

September 14, 1859
Butterfield Overland Stage Arrives

September 14, 1859
The Van Buren Press, Van Buren, Arkansas

COL. HUGH CROCKER, of the **California Overland Mail Co.**, passed through our city on the state last Sunday, on a flying visit to New York.

September 14, 1859
Butterfield Overland Stage Arrives

September 14, 1859
The Van Buren Press, Van Buren, Arkansas

LATEST FROM CALIFORNIA BY **OVERLAND MAIL** – By the **Overland Mail** from California, which arrived here on Monday morning, we have received full files of San Francisco papers, to the date of August 20th, and Los Angeles Vineyard of the 23rd August, from which we extract.

CALIFORNIA OVERLAND MAIL – The stages of the California **Overland Mail Company** have been some little behind time for the last two trips. This is set to be wondered at, when the great quantity of rain that has recently fallen, is taken into consideration, rendering many of the streams impassible. No other company in the world, in our opinion, would have come so near up to time, when so many obstacles have to be overcome. The Fort Smith *Herald* says that the delay has been occasioned by Indian depredations along the route, all the stock at the stations east of El Paso having been run off. If this is the case, troops should immediately be sent off along the mail route.

LITTLE ROCK MAIL – The Postmaster at Little Rock has made an arrangement for transporting the *[regular non **Overland**]* mails between Little Rock, Van Buren and Fort Smith, once a week. We have received a mail on Saturday last, six days out from Little Rock – only think of it – **SIX DAYS TO TRANSPORT THE MAILS ONE HUNDRED AND EIGHTY MILES!**

September 14, 1859
Butterfield Overland Stage Arrives

September 14, 1859, page 2
The Van Buren Press, Van Buren, Arkansas

THE OVERLAND MAIL. -The whole number of the letters sent East yesterday, by the great **Overland Mail,** was 1,624, of which 1,427 were fore the States. To-day being steamer day, it is probable that the old established custom of our people prevailed to the visible diminution of the number send via the **Butterfield route** - *San Francisco News,* Aug. 20th.

September 17, 1859
Butterfield's Steamboat Jennie Whipple Carrying Overland Mail

September 17, 1859, Saturday
Arkansas State Gazette, Little Rock, Arkansas

The Jennie Whipple came in from Memphis on Saturday last.

September 21, 1859
Greeley Rides the Overland Stage

September 21, 1859
Arkansas True Democrat, Little Rock, Arkansas

Several of our exchanges in noticing the fact of Greeley's visit to California seem to think it is meant to influence the coming elections in that State...

It is said that Greeley will come home by the **Butterfield route**. If so, he will pass through a portion of Arkansas.

September 21, 1859
Overland Mail is More Popular than Ocean Route

September 21, 1859
The Van Buren Press, Van Buren, Arkansas

THE OVERLAND MAIL. - The number of letters sent East by

the **Overland Mail** which left yesterday was 3,836, of which 3,714 were dispatched through to the end of the line, thence to be circulated generally.

As compared to the number sent on Friday last, the day before the steamer sailed, (only 1,624) the increase observable is a gratifying evidence of the estimation in which the services of this great institution is held by out people. They can, by a systematic and continued use of the privileges which the **Overland Mail** affords them, exert a powerful influence toward its continuance.

We have prepared an article upon this subject based upon recent reliable intelligence concerning the options and probable movements of the powers that be at Washington, in regard to this matter, which we shall endeavor to find room for tomorrow.

September 21, 1859
Butterfield Overland Stage Arrives

September 21, 1859
The Van Buren Press, Van Buren, Arkansas

The stages of the **Overland Mail Company**, we notice continue to be filled with passengers. Most of the way passengers now take the company's coaches, being certain of making their destination without delay or detention.

September 21, 1859
Stages Delayed by Rain
Rafts Constructed to Cross Streams

September 21, 1859
The Van Buren Press, Van Buren, Arkansas

CALIFORNIA OVERLAND MAIL. - We learn from Mr. Edward Hines, who was a passenger in the last **Overland Stage** from California, that the stages have been delayed, in some degree, by the great amount of rains that have fallen between here and California.

Mr. Hinds informs us that they had, in several instances, to construct rafts for the transportation of the mails and passengers across the streams; and that nothing but the great energy displayed by the employees of the company could have gotten them through in the time they have been in making the trip from California. Notwithstanding the delay, they would arrive at St. Louis in schedule time.

September 21, 1859
Butterfield's Overland Mail Stages Crossed the Arkansas River on the Ferry at Van Buren

September 21, 1859, page 2
The Press Argus, Van Buren, Arkansas

Captain W. F. England has recently given his Horse Ferry Boat a complete overhauling and repairing, and has her in complete running order. Movers, drovers, and all others may be assured that they will meet with no detention at the Ferry and that a safe and speedy transit across the Arkansas River is assured them." (page two) "... good banks on both sides for landing and careful attentive ferrymen in attendance. The stages of the **Overland Mail Company** cross the Arkansas River at this ferry."

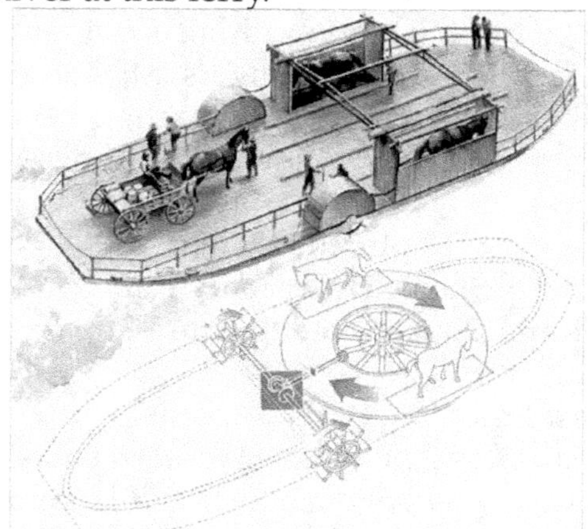

Captain W. F. England's Horse Ferry at Van Buren

[In July, 1860 passenger William Tallack describes the new 'high tech' Van Buren / Fort Smith ferry: "In the evening we crossed the Arkansas River, on a ferry propelled by two horses walking round a sort of treadmill, or nearly horizontal wheel, communicating motion to the paddles. This kind of locomo-

tive power we had not previously met with, nor did we see any recurrence of it subsequently.

William Tallack seems to be describing a ferry similar to the 63' length x 18' beam 'Superior Horse Boat Eagle' that was operating in 1841 out of Westport, New York seen in the above sketch. This New York ferry was featured in the October 1989 issue of The National Geographic. According to reports by Van Buren's The Press Argus, this ferry was seized and burned by General Blunt when he marched his troops into Van Buren after the Battle of Prairie Grove in December of 1862.

September 21, 1859
Butterfield's Overland Mail Stages Crossed the Arkansas River on the Ferry at Van Buren

September 21, 1859, page 3

The Press Argus, Van Buren, Arkansas

W. F. England. Superior Horse Ferry. Good banks on both sides for landing and careful attentive ferrymen in attendance. The stages of the **Overland Mail Company** cross the Arkansas River at this ferry. – W. F. England.

[Ad on page 3, same issue] Ferry Boat for Sale – I have for sale a new ferry flat, length about sixty feet, has been in use only one month and will be sold cheap. W. F. England.

Brig. Gen. James G. Blunt

According to reports by Van Buren's The Press Argus, the Van Buren ferry was seized and burned by General Blunt when he marched his troops into Van Buren after the Battle of Prairie Grove in December of 1862.

No photo exist of W. F. england's early ferry, but we do know it was similar to the ferry above on Arkansas' St. Francis River.

September 21, 1859

Lake Discovered on Butterfield Route East of El Paso

September 21, 1859, Wednesday, page 4
Des Arc Citizen, Des Arc, Arkansas

There is, on the route of the **Overland Mail**, about two hundred and eighty miles east of El Paso, a spring said to be one hundred and fifty feet in diameter, which has been sounded to the depth of eight thousand feet without finding bottom. The surface is as smooth as that of a mountain lake. It is slightly impregnated with alkali, and contains five varieties of fish. It is called Leon Hole.

September 21, 1859

Overland Crossed Arkansas River at Van Buren Ferry

Old Ferry for Sale – New Ferry in Place

September 21, 1859
The Van Buren Press, Van Buren, Arkansas

Van Buren Ferry – Large and Excellent Horse Boat – The subscriber has recently repaired, and has now in excellent running order his superior HORSE FERRY BOAT at the

Van Buren Ferry Travelers, Drovers, and all other may rest assured that they will meet with no detention at this ferry. Good banks on both sides for landing and careful, attentive, Ferryman in attendance. The stages of the **California Overland Mail Company** cross the Arkansas River at this Ferry...

Sept. 21, 1859 W. F. England

"Down Main Street to the Van Buren Ferry" (circa 1981)
by Marjorie Reed (1915-1997)
Oil on canvas, 24 × 36 inches, signed lower right.
Sold at Auction: $5,750 at the 2009 Coeur d'Alene Art Auction.

September 21, 1859
Overland Mail Arrives at Van Buren

September 21, 1859

The Van Buren Press, Van Buren, Arkansas

LATEST NEWS FROM CALIFORNIA BY **OVERLAND MAIL – The California Overland Mail**, which left Fan Francisco, August 26th, arrived here last Saturday noon; the stage full of passengers. The news by this arrival is generally unimportant; the papers mostly filled with political matter... The mail which left San Francisco 29th August, arrived here yesterday, there is no news of importance by it. Our dates are from San Francisco to the 29th ult., and from Los Angeles to the

30th of August.

September 21, 1859
Overland Stage Full

September 21, 1859
The Van Buren Press, Van Buren, Arkansas

The stages of the **Overland Mail Company**, we notice continue to be filled with passengers. Most of the way passengers now take the company's coaches, being certain of making their destination without delay or detention.

General A. G. Mayers, Postmaster at Fort Smith, was in our city on Friday last. Our merchants and we especially are under obligations to him for the mail matter coming by the **Overland stage**. The General improves every opportunity to forward the mail matter destined for this place at the earliest possible time.

September 24, 1859
Butterfield's Steamboat Carrying Overland

September 24, 1859, Saturday
Arkansas State Gazette, Little Rock, Arkansas

Jennie Whipple arrived from Memphis on Wed. morning.

September 28, 1859
Dardanelle Proposed Route Change to Overland

September 28, 1859, Wednesday, page 3
Arkansas True Democrat, Little Rock, Arkansas

We clip the following from the *Times*: We learn from Captain Fox, Superintendent of the **Overland Mail**, that the citizens of Dardanelle are cutting out a new road on the south side of the Arkansas River to intersect the Little Rock road at Perryville. It is thought that as soon as the road is opened, the stages of the **Overland Mail Company** will run to Little Rock all the way on this side of the river. We understand that the work on the road is well done. The people of Dardanelle are enterprising and liberal, and what they undertake they will go through with. Success to the enterprise.

September 28, 1859
Telegraph Faster Than Overland

September 28, 1859, Wednesday, page 3
Arkansas True Democrat, Little Rock, Arkansas

TELEGRAPH – ... By the southern telegraph route, through Fort Smith, we will receive the California news here three or four days in advance of its arrival at St Louis by the **Overland Mail.** The importance of this, in a financial and commercial point of view, will be considerable.

MAJOR NABORS KILLED – We learn from Mr. Sawyer, **Overland Mail**, that on Tuesday, the 13th, at Fort Belknap, that Major Nabors, and a man by the name of Murphy, had some words, relative to some horses belonging to the reserve Indians, and while engaged in the dispute a man by the name of McKnett, shot Major Nabors in the back with a double barrel shot gun, killing him instantly.

Major Nabors is extensively known as an Indian Agent on the frontier of Texas. – *Fort Smith Times*

September 30, 1859
Murder at the Mohawk Station

September 21, 1859, page 2
The Van Buren Press, Van Buren, Arkansas

HORRID MURDER ON THE OVERLAND ROUTE. - We find the following in the Visalia *Record Extra:*

The following was communicated to us by an old and reliable friend resident in the vicinity:

FORT YUMA, August 29, 1859. - Editors *Tulare Record* -- The **Overland Mail** station, known as mohawk, was attacked on last Saturday, at 4 p.m., by two Mexicans. The station keeper, Mr. Phelps was left for dead. Six stage horses were stolen. Mr. Phelps, I believe, is a native of New York. It is thought he cannot survive, as he has not spoken since he was found. SANTIAGO

P. S. -- They attacked him when he was reading a newspaper with the butt of their pistols. I understand that his skull is broken The doctor from Fort Yuma left last evening to see him. -- *Times*, Sept. 9th.

September 30, 1859
Overland Passenger

September 30, 1859
The Arkansian, Fayetteville, Arkansas

Lieutenant Brooks U.S.A. left on the last **Overland Stage** for St. Louis. Also, Sheriff Jones of Kansas notoriety came as passenger on the **Overland** from Arizonia.

The Notorious Sheriff Samuel J. Jones

In 1856, Douglas County, Kansas Sheriff Samuel J. Jones, along with a posse of some 800 pro-slavery settlers, sacked the town of Lawrence, Kansas. He confiscated weapons from the city, had his men demolish the printing presses of the town, and torch the Free State Hotel.

September 30, 1859
Butterfield Overland Stage Arrives

September 30, 1859

The Van Buren Press, Van Buren, Arkansas

Mr. William Graham, formerly of this county and for many years a resident of California, arrived on the **Overland Stage** yesterday morning, direct from San Francisco, having left there at noon on the 9th inst.

September 30, 1859
Overland Stage Arrives

September 30, 1859

The Van Buren Press, Van Buren, Arkansas

Latest News from California by **Overland Mail** – The mail which left San Francisco at noon on the 2nd inst., arrived here on the 22nd at noon being just twenty days out, and would arrive at St. Louis short of schedule time. Politics engross the attention of the papers to the exclusion of general news; it appears that the opposition to the democracy cannot succeed to any considerable degree in effecting a fusion: the Republican press speak rather despondingly of their success.

The mail which left San Francisco on the 5th inst., reached here Thursday morning last, being less than nineteen days out. By this arrival we have San Francisco dates to the 5th inst. inclusive; news generally unimportant.

The mail which left San Francisco on the 9th inst, arrived here yesterday morning - less than nineteen days out. By this arrival we have dates to the 9th inst. Sufficient election news had been received at San Francisco to render it certain that the entire Democratic ticket has been elected in California.

September 30, 1859
Current Prices in Van Buren

September 30, 1859
The Van Buren Press, Van Buren, Arkansas

PRICES CURRENT – Bacon 10¢ to 12¢; Lard 10¢; Butter 15¢; Eggs 15¢ per dozen; Flour 83¢ to $3.25 per hundred; Corn Meal 87$^1/_2$¢ per bushel; Chickens 81$^1/_2$¢ per dozen; Oats per 100 bundles 82¢; Hay $10 per ton; Irish Potatoes 50¢ per bushel. The above are prices from wagons. Wheat 85¢ per bushel delivered at the Steam Mill.

Groceries at Wholesale - Coffee 15¢; Sugar 10¢; Molasses in barrels 50¢, in half barrels 55¢; Salt $2.25; and Whisky 35¢.

September 30, 1859
Butterfield's Sub Contractor Also Carries Regular Contract Mail

September 30, 1859
The Van Buren Press, Van Buren, Arkansas

LITTLE ROCK MAIL – We understand that Col. John E. Reeside has taken the contract to transport the mail, tri-weekly between Little Rock, Van Buren and Fort Smith, on a star bid – amount of compensation we have not learnt. From the known energy and capacity of Col. Reeside, the public have assurance that the mails under his administration will be faithfully and promptly transported and delivered at their destinations. Service under Col. Reeside's contract will commence on the 10th October

October 5, 1859
Anniversary of the Overland Mail Co.

October 5, 1859, page 2
Arkansas True Democrat, Little Rock, Arkansas

WHAT ARKANSAS PAPERS SAY – The *Fort Smith Times* notices the close of the first year of the **Overland Mail** service.

The route is 2,600 miles long.

October 7, 1859
Overland Passenger

October 7, 1859
The Arkansian, Fayetteville, Arkansas

MARRIED – On Thursday the 29th of September, at Trinity Church, Utica, N. Y. by Rev. Dr. Cox. Mr. C. S. Hauptman of this city, to Miss A. Watts, of the former city. The happy couple arrived in this city by the **Over-Land** Wednesday last.

October 7, 1859
Overland Stage Arrives

October 7, 1859
The Van Buren Press Van Buren, Arkansas

REV. WM. BINET, pastor of the Episcopal church at Van Buren, arrived home on Sunday last by **Overland Stage**, in fine health. Mr. Binet preached on Sunday night, and on Wednesday night last, gave the first of a course of lectures.

FAST TIME – MR. JESSE L. HOWELL, formerly of this city, arrived here early on Sunday morning last, in the **Overland Stage**, having left Philadelphia on the Tuesday morning previous, making the trip from Philadelphia to this place *[Van Buren]* in less than five days; quicker time than the mail is, in coming from Little Rock here.

October 7, 1859
Overland Stage Arrives

October 7, 1859
The Van Buren Press Van Buren, Arkansas

LATEST NEWS FROM CALIFORNIA BY **OVERLAND MAIL** – The mail which left San Francisco on the 12th inst., reached here on the 1st inst, by which we have received files of California papers to the 12th inst. inclusive. The democratic majority will be much larger than was expected from the accounts received by the previous mail.

The **California Overland Mail** which left San Francisco on the 16th ult., arrived here at an early hour on Wednesday morning last. By this arrival we have files of papers to the 16th inclusive from which we gather full particulars of the duel between Senator Boderick and Judge Terry, which took place on the morning of the 13th ult., and resulted in Terry shooting Broderick fatally. Terry was unharmed.

R. D. Crocker, Esq., of the **California Overland Mail Co.,** will accept our thanks for the latest California papers, containing full accounts of the Broderick and Terry duel, as well as the later telegraphic dispatch to Gilry, giving an account of the unfortunate termination of the duel in the death of Senator Broderick. Particulars of which will be found in another column.

*U. S. Senator from California, **David Broderick** died of a wound received in a duel with Judge Terry three days earlier over the issue of slavery.*
Image Source: 1859's "McClees' Gallery of Photographic Portraits of the Senators, Representatives & Delegates of the Thirty-Fifth Congress"

October 12, 1859
For a Short Time, Butterfield's Sub-Contrator Used a Steamboat, the Charm, to Carry the U.S. Mail on the White River

☞ The Charm, Messrs. Chidester, Rapley & Co.'s., new boat for the mail line between Des Arc and Clarendon, arrived here with the mail yesterday noon. She will hereafter leave Des Arc every Monday and Wednesday at 12 o'clock, M. The Charm is one of the prettiest little steamers afloat. Her length is 83 feet; depth of hold 3 feet; has two seven inch cylinders of 15 inches stroke; one twelve foot boiler and measures eighty-three tons.

Source: October 12, 1859, Des Arc Citizen. page 3

October 12, 1859
Overland Stock Stolen

October 12, 1859
Arkansas Banner, Little Rock, Arkansas

The *Fort Smith Times* tells us that the Indians are robbing and murdering on the plains. Lately the stock of the **Overland Mail Company** was stolen from one of the stations, and more lately the Indians came into the neighborhood of Gainesville, Texas, killed a negro woman and ran off a hundred head of cattle.

October 12, 1859
Arrival of Overland Stage

October 12, 1859, page 2
Des Arc Citizen, Des Arc, Arkansas

Arrival of the **Overland Mail** – The **California Overland Mail** arrived last night... direct from Arizona. Capt. Henry Smith, Superintendent of Division No. 3 of the **Overland Mail Line,** also arrived in the same stage from El Paso, *en route* for New York.

October 12, 1859
One of 15 Times Chidester used His Steamboat, the Charm, to Carry U.S. Mail

[NOTE: Chidester's sub-contract with Butterfield's Overland Mail ended about August 13, 1859. However, he still had numerous contracts to carry mail on various route across Arkansas. In a May 4, 1859 Arkansas True Democrat article, James Glover told the editor: "He tells us that they intend stocking the road from Dardanelle to Memphis and carrying their own mails, and to make this, the superior arm of the service." On August 13, 1859, the Weekly Arkansas Gazette reported, "Mr. Nichols informs us that the Overland Mail is now stocked with excellent teams, first class coaches, and reliable drivers, for the purpose of carrying, on the route – either way or through passengers."]

October 12, 1859, page 3

Des Arc Citizen, Des Arc, Arkansas

The Charm, Messrs. Chidester, Rapley & Co., new boat for the mail line between Des Ace and Clarendon, arrived here with the mail yesterday noon. She will hereafter leave Des Arc every Monday and Wednesday at 12 o'clock, p.m. The Charm is one of the prettiest little steamers afloat. Her length is 83 feet' depth of hold 3 feet; has two seven inch cylinders of 15 inches stroke; one twelve foot boiler and measures eighty-three tones.

October 14, 1859
Overland Stage Arrives

October 14, 1859

The Van Buren Press Van Buren, Arkansas

LATEST NEWS FROM CALIFORNIA BY **OVERLAND MAIL** – The California **Overland Mail** which left San Francisco at noon on the 19th ult., arrived here at eight o'clock on Friday night last, bringing dates to the 19th inclusive. The funeral solemnities of the Honorable David C. Broderick took place on Sunday the 18th ult., on the Plaza at San Francisco.

The coinage at the Branch Mint at San Francisco for the week ending on the 17th ult. was $105,000 in double eagles, and $10,000 in half eagles.

October 14, 1859
Overland Stage Doesn't Stop at Van Buren

October 14, 1859
The Van Buren Press, Van Buren, Arkansas

THE MAILS – Why are we deprived of the conveniences of the **Overland Mail**? The coaches with the mail passes through our city *[Van Buren]*, taking along with it our letters from the east and west, without the privilege being allowed to our postmaster, to take them out. This inconvenience and grievance, we may add, has lasted over a year, and either the proper efforts of our citizens, or our delegation in Congress, have not been made to remove it. Ours is a heavy commercial community, and important monied interests have suffered thereby.

It seems that, if our Congressional Delegation will make the effort; this much desired object can be effected. The delay that will be occasioned by the opening of the mail in this place would be trifling, while the convenience and advantage to our citizens will be important. Senators Johnson and Sebastian, and our Representative Col. Hindman, who are over watchful and jealous of the rights and interests of their constituents, will, we have no doubt, attend to this matter, if our citizens, will only take the trouble of properly presenting it before them. If we expect our Delegation to represent our interests in Washington, we must make them known by a frank statement of what our wants and wishes are, that action can be had in the promises. After than, if nothing is done for us, then and not until then will we have any right to complain.

October 14, 1859
Overland Letter Reveals Price of Slaves

[This is a repugnant, cringe worthy, intolerable thought - that peo-

ple could be sold like horses and mules. Many of Butterfield's employees were abolitionist and got into trouble for inciting enslaved persons to seek freedom. See Arkansas Banner article of April 21, 1860.]

October 14, 1859

The Van Buren Press Van Buren, Arkansas

The following is an extract from a private letter received by a citizen of this place from Charlotte, Virginia dated Sept. 23rd, 1859 – Times in Virginia are prosperous, property of every description very high. No. 1 fellows, field hands from $1,500 to $1,700. Nice house girls from $1,450 to $1,750. No. 1 field girls from $1,200 to $1,450. Plow boys, from $1,000 to $1,500. Small girls 10 to 12 years old, from $900 to $1,200. All classes are high and the supply not equal to the demand. Horses that sold for from $125 to $160 when you lived here four years since, now command $175 to $300. Mules sold here are of a small size - sell from $125 to $175. Land has advanced in proportion.

October 15, 1859
One of 15 Times Chidester used His Steamboat, the Charm, to Carry U.S. Mail

[NOTE: Chidester's sub-contract with Butterfield's Overland Mail ended about August 13, 1859. However, he still had numerous contracts to carry mail on various route across Arkansas.]

October 15, 1859, Saturday

Des Arc Citizen, Des Arc, Arkansas

The new steamer Charm got aground ten miles below DuVall's Bluff, in White River, a few days ago, and broke her rudder in the effort to get off.

October 19, 1859
One of 15 Times Chidester used His Steamboat, the Charm, to Carry U.S. Mail

[NOTE: Chidester's sub-contract with Butterfield's Overland Mail ended about August 13, 1859. However, he still had numerous contracts to carry mail on various route across Arkansas.]

October 19, 1859, page 3
Des Arc Citizen, Des Arc, Arkansas

The Des Arc and Clarendon U.S. Mail packet Charm, Captain H. B. Hendrix, will hereafter leave Des Arc for Clarendon every Sunday and Thursday, at noon.

October 19, 1859
For a Short Time, Butterfield's Sub-Contractor Used a Steamboat, the Charm, to Carry U.S. Mail on the White River

October 19, 1859
Des Arc Citizen, Des Ark, Arkansas

NEW

ARRANGEMENT!

FROM FORT SMITH TO MEMPHIS VIA. DES ARC IN THREE DAYS.
FROM DES ARC TO MEMPHIS IN 24 HOURS.

By Stage Steamboat and Railroad!

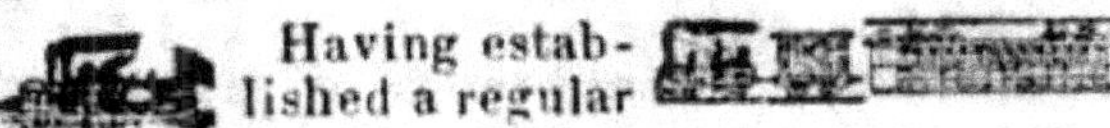

Having established a regular Semi-Weekly line of U. S. Mail Stages from Fort Smith to Des Arc—thence to Clarendon by Steamboat—thence to Madison by Stage—thence to Memphis by Railroad, the proprietors flatter themselves that they will receive a liberal patronage.

The U. S. Mail steamer CHARM, Capt. Hendrix, will leave Des Arc for Clarendon every Sunday and Thursday at 12 o'clock, M., and make regular connections through to Memphis, by Steamboat, Stage and Railroad, carrying passengers through in twenty-four hours. Extra coaches are in readiness to carry passengers from Clarendon to Madison, there connecting with the cars for Memphis.

☞ Fare from Des Arc to Memphis, $8.

oct19-tf] CHIDESTER, RAPLEY & CO.

Source: Des Arc Citizen, October 19, 1859

October 19, 1859
Proposal to Merge All Overland Mail Routes

October 19, 1859

Arkansas True Democrat, Little Rock, Arkansas

CALIFORNIA MAIL ROUTE AND RAILROAD – A few weeks ago, we took occasion to state our opinion as to the real objects of the visit of Greeley to California...

To confirm the opinion we then expressed, that the object of Greely was not to influence the election in California, as some supposed, but for those before mentioned, we find upon his arrival home, he begins to abuse the **Butterfield route**, saying, *"It is at least five hundred miles longer than it need or should be,"* urges the consolidation of all the routes in one and insists that it should go north of us. The conclusion of an article in the *Tribune* is as follows:

> *"We urge Congress to make early provision for the merging of all our California mails in a single daily* ***Overland Mail****, to be run on the most direct and expeditious route, and to carry everything offered that pays the legal rates of postage. This mail should run from the Missouri River by the Kansas Gold Mines to Salt Lake City (or Camp Floyd) and thence by the new road opened by Capt. Simpson to Carson Valley and Placerville, making the distance from Atchison or Leavenworth to San Francisco less than two thousand miles, which may be easily traversed in sixteen days, and after the first year, in fourteen. We are confident this mail can be contracted for less than $1,000,000 per annum, and that the postage created by it will soon double and ultimately treble, that derived from our present California mails. Such a mail*

would have a telegraph working by its side throughout within the next two years.

Why not have it authorized next winter?"

This then is the route selected both as combining the most influence in its behalf and strengthening the cause of the opposition. In view of this fact the people of the south should unite on one route. If the 35th or 32nd, or any other parallel be the proper one, let us insist on this, make its advantages manifest and unite the congressional representation from the south in its favor, Unless this is done as soon as **Butterfield's** contract expires we will find the route changed so as to go by Salt Lake City, a telegraph carried along the stage road, and in a few years the railroad route fixed. The route proposed by Greeley will be advocated by all the northwesten and eastern States, though a more southern route can be built more cheaply and possesses the most decided advantages.

October 21, 1859
Overland Stage Arrives

October 21, 1859
The Van Buren Press Van Buren, Arkansas

Latest News from **California by Overland Mail** – The **California Overland Mail** which left San Francisco on the 30th ult., at noon, arrived here at an early hour Wednesday morning.

Through the politeness of R. D. Crocker Esq., we are placed in possession by this arrival, of full files of California papers to the 30th ult., inclusive...

October 21, 1859
Chidester, Reeside & Co. Not Fulfilling Separate Contract to Carry Regular Mail

October 21, 1859

The Van Buren Press Van Buren, Arkansas

The Mails Again – The people of Western Arkansas have just cause of complaint, in the manner in which their mail matter is transmitted. For some time back, we have had but one mail a week from Little Rock, and that being about five and a half days on the way. We had understood that a new contract was to have gone into operation on the 10th inst., by which the mail was to be transported from Little Rock to this place and Fort Smith tri-weekly – but so far it has failed to arrive here. We have had but one mail since the 10th viz., on last Saturday, and we are informed that a portion only of that one here then, arrived at this place, the balance having been left behind to accommodate passengers. The postmaster at Little Rock can say whether this is true or not. Our citizens are forbearing people, but they are getting tired of the manner in which their mail matters are managed, and we think justly so. As it is now, we get our mail matter from New York via St Louis in about the same time that we do letters mailed at Little Rock.

October 22, 1859
Butterfield's Sub-Contractor Bought a Steamboat, the Charm, to Carry the U.S. Mail

We are pleased to learn that Messrs. Chidester, Rapley & Co., have secured the service of Capt. Hendrix, to take charge of their mail boat "*Charm*," which runs daily between Clarendon and Devall's Bluff. If the rest of their employees be as faithful and reliable, our Memphis mail matter will surely get through in time; *provided* always it is furnished them by the agents of the Post Office department.

Chidester buys the Charm

Source: Arkansas State Gazette, Little Rock, Arkansas, 22 Oct 1859, Sat

October 26, 1859
One of 15 Times Chidester used His Steamboat, the Charm, to Carry U.S. Mail

[NOTE: Chidester's sub-contract with Butterfield's Overland Mail ended about August 13, 1859. However, he still had numerous contracts to carry mail on various route across Arkansas.]

October 26, 1859, page 3

Des Arc Citizen, Des Arc, Arkansas

The Des Arc and Clarendon U.S.M. packet Charm, Captain H. B. Hendrix, arrived Sunday, and left on Monday. Captain Hendrix furnished us with Memphis papers of Saturday morning. Des Arc is now within one days travel of Memphis by this line. The Charm is due from Clarendon tomorrow noon, and will leave immediately on her return trip.

October 28, 1859
Passenger John Melvin

October 28, 1859

The Van Buren Press, Van Buren, Arkansas

John Melvin, Esq., of Fort Smith, direct from Pike's Peak, passed through here yesterday morning in the Overland Mail Coach, for his home. Mr. Melvin has been absent some six months, and intends to soon return to the gold region.

October 28, 1859
Butterfield Stage Arrives at Van Buren from San Francisco in Only 19 Days

October 28, 1859

The Van Buren Press Van Buren, Arkansas

The **Overland Mail** which left San Francisco at noon on the 7th inst., arrived here at an early hour on Wednesday morning last, less than nineteen days out. By this arrival we have dates of the 7th inst., inclusive. The news is generally unimportant. The shock of an earthquake was experienced in San Francisco on the 5th inst.

November 2, 1859
One of 15 Times Chidester used His Steamboat, the Charm, to Carry U.S. Mail

[NOTE: Chidester's sub-contract with Butterfield's Overland Mail ended about August 13, 1859. However, he still had numerous contracts to carry mail on various route across Arkansas.]

November 2, 1859, page 3
Des Arc Citizen, Des Arc, Arkansas

The Des Arc and Clarendon U.S.M. packet Charm, Captain H. B. Hendrix, arrived Sunday, and left on Monday. Captain Hendrix furnished us with Memphis papers of Saturday morning. The Charm is due from Clarendon tomorrow noon, and will leave immediately on her return trip.

November 4, 1859
Telegraph Lines Proposed Alongside Butterfield Route to California

November 4, 1859
The Van Buren Press Van Buren, Arkansas

The completion of the Telegraph along the line of road travelled by the **Overland Mail Company**, will draw us closer to that City, whilst the facilities of travel afforded by the commodious coaches of the **O.L.M. Co.,** makes it the nearest point for our trade. Goods can be transported from St. Louis at as low rates, as any point on the Ohio, and we know of no good reason why they cannot offer such inducements in *"trade and traffic"* that will cause relations between us to spring up, develop and grow to our mutual advantage and profit.

We will watch with considerable interest, the result of this new enterprise, and invite the attention of the people to a consideration of its importance. We have glanced hastily at this matter but in some of our future numbers will refer to some of the peculiar advantage arising from this connection.

November 9, 1859
Butterfield's Steamboat Struck a Snag

November 9, 1959, Wednesday

Des Arc Citizen, Des Arc, Arkansas

The steamer Jennie Whipple struck a snag and sunk near White River cut-off, in the Arkansas River, on the 1st inst.

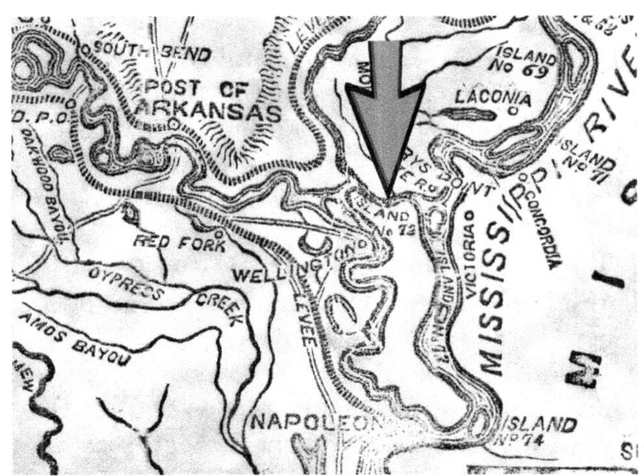

Map showing the White River cut off.

A short cut connection between the Mississippi, the White River and the Arkansas River, allowing steamboats to shorten their trip, and avoid Napoleon, Arkansas. The Jennie Whipple sunk here after striking a snag in the river. The damage was minor enough that the Whipple was raised and put back into service.

November 9, 1859
One of 15 Times Chidester used His Steamboat, the Charm, to Carry U.S. Mail

[NOTE: Chidester's sub-contract with Butterfield's Overland Mail ended about August 13, 1859. However, he still had numerous contracts to carry mail on various route across Arkansas.]

November 9, 1859, page 3

Des Arc Citizen, Des Arc, Arkansas

The Des Arc and Clarendon U.S.M. packet Charm.

Captain H. B. Hendrix, arrived Sunday, and left on Monday. Captain Hendrix furnished us with Memphis papers on Saturday morning. The Charm is due from Clarendon tomorrow noon, and will leave immediately on her return trip.

November 9, 1859

November 9, 1859, Wednesday, page 2
Des Arc Citizen, Des Arc, Arkansas

St. Louis, Oct. 31 – The **Overland Mail** from San Francisco, with California advices of the 10th instant, arrived in this city today. Business at San Francisco was extremely dull. Two hundred Indians of a hostile tribe have been captured at the head waters of the Feather River.

November 11, 1859

Latest News from California by Overland Mail

November 11, 1859
The Van Buren Press Van Buren, Arkansas

Latest News from California by **Overland Mail** – Papers of the 14th ult., say that General Scott was hourly expected to arrive at San Francisco on the steamer Golden Age. A monster fish has been caught in San Francisco Bay. The *Bulletin* describes it as follows: *"It is of the species known as black bass, about six times as large as this species of fish. It weighs 360 lbs., is seven feet and one inch in length, and five feet and two inches round the thickest portion of the body."*

November 16, 1859

One of 15 Times Chidester used His Steamboat, the Charm, to Carry U.S. Mail

[NOTE: Chidester's sub-contract with Butterfield's Overland Mail ended about August 13, 1859. However, he still had numerous contracts to carry mail on various route across Arkansas.]

November 16, 1859, page 3
Des Arc Citizen, Des Arc, Arkansas

The Des Arc and Clarendon U.S.M. packet Charm,

Captain H. B. Hendrix, arrived Sunday, and left on Monday. Captain Hendrix furnished us with Memphis papers on Saturday morning. The Charm is due from Clarendon tomorrow noon, and will leave immediately on her return trip.

November 18, 1859

Calls for Regular Steamship Routes to China and Japan

November 18, 1859

The Van Buren Press Van Buren, Arkansas

Latest News from **California by Overland Mail** – By the politeness of R. D. Crocker, Esq., of the California **Overland Mail Co.**, we are placed in possession of San Francisco papers to the 28th ult. inclusive. The papers were agitating *[debating]* the subject of establishing a regular line of Steam Packets between San Francisco and Japan and China, by such an arrangement the Pacific coast would be brought into direct communication with China in less than twenty days – such an arrangement would be of immense benefit to the whole country as well as to California.

November 18, 1859

Overland Passenger

November 18, 1859

The Arkansian, Fayetteville, Arkansas

Mr. Frank G. Watson, of St. Louis who came passenger on the **Overland** from that city Wednesday evening last, presented us with St. Louis papers of the 15 inst.

November 25, 1859

Overland Arrives in Van Buren -

San Francisco Papers Desire Overland to be Daily

November 25, 1859

The Van Buren Press Van Buren, Arkansas

Latest News from California by **Overland Mail** – The mail which left San Francisco on the 4th inst., arrived here on the morning of the 22nd, a little less than eighteen days out. By this arrival, the **Overland Mail Company** have placed us in possession of full files of California papers to the 4th instant, inclusive.

The San Francisco papers are arguing the necessity of a daily **Overland Mail**. The *Times* of the 4th inst. says:

> *"The **Overland Mail** goes out again at 8 o'clock this morning via St. Louis, and we take advantage of the occasion to say to our friends across the country, that we desire its continuance and perpetuity not only semi-weekly but daily. It is safe and reliable. For more than a year past **Butterfield & Co.**, have performed their trips with speed and regularity unparalleled, averaging some two of three days less than contract rime, with scarce a single failure out of over one hundred and twenty round trips What our citizens now require is a daily mail so that we can transport therein, not only our letter, but also our newspapers."*

November 26, 1859
Overland Arrives

November 26, 1859
Arkansas State Gazette, Little Rock, Arkansas

JEFFERSON CITY, NOV. 21 – The **Overland Mail** from San Francisco, with California advices of the 31st ult., arrived today. the business portion of the town of Valcanoville, Amadar County, was entirely destroyed by fire on the 5th ult, the loss is upward of $50,000.

FROM ARIZONA AND THE BORDER – By the San Antonio and San Diego **overland mail**, arrived yesterday, we have advices from Arizona and the Indian border to the 27th ult. The *Arizonian* of that date furnishes the following items: SHEEP FOR CALIFORNIA – Large droves of sheep have been passing through Tucson in the past few days for California: one flock alone numbering some forty-six thousand sheep. they were mostly from the Rio Grande, in New Mexico. APACHE INDIAN SCALPS.

The happiness of the Pimo Indians generally reaches its

peak whenever they are successful in killing a few Apaches, or succeed in taking a number of them prisoners. It results usually in a glorification, and dancing and drinking are kept up for days. Such celebration was observed, some days since, at their villages, upon the return of a party of their warriors with the scalps of six or more Apaches who they had succeeded in killing near the Gila River. The Pimos, in their incursions, generally go in considerable numbers, and unfortunate indeed is it for the poor Apaches if they are found in numbers too weak to resist their enemies.

November 30, 1859
One of 15 Times Chidester used His Steamboat, the Charm, to Carry U.S. Mail

[NOTE: Chidester's sub-contract with Butterfield's Overland Mail ended about August 13, 1859. However, he still had numerous contracts to carry mail on various route across Arkansas.]

November 30, 1859, page 3
Des Arc Citizen, Des Arc, Arkansas

The Des Arc and Clarendon U.S.M. packet Charm, Captain H. B. Hendrix, arrived Sunday, and left Monday. Captain Hendrix furnished us with Memphis papers of Thursday morning. The Charm is due from Clarendon tomorrow noon, and will leave immediately on her return trip.

December 2, 1859
Bag Lost or Mislaid on the Road

December 2, 1859, page 2
The Van Buren Press, Van Buren, Arkansas

The Mails – The Northern Mail, yesterday, brought nothing beyond Fayetteville: we are therefore deprived of the St. Louis papers which we usually receive by the Thursday's mail, and from which we are in the habit of making up our latest news.

We are also without any late California papers.

Mr. R. D. Crocker informs us that the **Overland Mail Company's** bag was not received, having been lost or mislaid on the road.

Our Little Rock mail remains as heretofore, there being no improvements of the mail facilities on that route.

Unless there is shortly, we would prefer that our Little Rock mail, and that of all below on the river, should be sent via St. Louis, we would get it less than than we now do.

December 3, 1859
Complaints about Mail Service To Van Buren & Overland Mail Should Stop at Van Buren

December 3, 1859

Arkansas State Gazette, Little Rock, Arkansas

From the Van Buren Press – Public Meeting – At a meeting of the citizens of Crawford county held at the Court House on Monday, the 14th inst., the following proceedings were had. Doctor J. A. Dihbrell was called to the chair, and G. Wilcox appointed Secretary. The object of the meeting being stated to be that of taking some measures in regard to the present deranged and unsatisfactory state of present mail arrangements, a committee was appointed to draft suitable resolutions expressive of the sense of the meeting. The committee reported the following Preamble and Resolutions which were adopted:

Your committee to whom was referred the grievances of the people of Western Arkansas – growing out of the deranged condition of the mails – having had the same under consideration beg leave to report briefly these facts; that at the general mail-letting in 1858, route No. 7812 was let to Charles C. Heard, for daily service in two-horse post coaches. That said daily service on said route was continued from about the first of July 1858 to about the first of August, 1859, at which time it was reduced to tri-weekly trips thereby reducing it four trips per week; that said tri-weekly service was continued until the 1st of September last, when the contractor, having first given notice to the proper Department discontinued further service thereon, and abandoned the contract so improperly rescinded by the government.

That after the service was so continued, one mail was conveyed over said route at the end of two weeks – *and only one* – from which time henceforth one mail a week has been conveyed over said route, by what is called "trip service" at most exorbitant rates, more extravagant in proportion to the service rendered than those paid for the daily service, which was the sum of $15,775, which required about 22 teams and ten stages to perform it, while this trip service required but two teams and a like number of post coaches.

That said route is one of vital importance, and that the mail conveyed over the same supplies and accommodates about 100 way offices, and tens of thousands of persons with all their mail.

That consequently weekly service is entirely insufficient and cannot, under the best possible management, supply the wants and demands of people on this route, but much more inadequate to the satisfaction of those wants and demands under the present arrangements by which it sometimes occurs that mail matter is either left at Little Rock or thrown out at the offices of the route to make room for passengers.

That owing to the present deranged state of mail facilities, growing out of the curtailment of service on this route, the letters, documents, & c., received through the mail on the same are usually so stale and uninteresting as to be wholly useless.

That the extent of country supplied with mail matter by this route, its constantly increasing population and wealth, and its great amount of business which is rapidly augmenting as the country improves and its resources become developed – the mercantile business of Van Buren alone amounting to more than $1,000,000 annually – require the facilities of a daily mail; and having enjoyed the benefits and advantages of one, it is unjust and unfair, to force us to take a step backward in this age of progress, and when our necessities demand increased facilities.

That upon other routes in this State *[of Arkansas]* the

service has not been curtailed to the same extent as upon this No. 7812, to one of which your committee beg leave to refer, viz: that from Des Arc via Dardanelle to Fort Smith, which as the general letting in '58 was let for tri-weekly service, with four horse post chaises, for the sum of $12,550 and when curtailed then of only trip per week, while service upon route No. 7812 was curtailed first of four and afterwards of six trips per week, though the former is comparatively of much less importance than the latter, conveying less mail matter, and supplying less way offices and people. Yet we do not complain of the liberality of the government in granting to the Des Arc and Fort Smith route good and sufficient mail facilities, but merely of the inequality and unfairness practised by the government toward said route, No. 7812.

That the curtailment of service upon the important routes in this State *[of Arkansas]* is to some extent attributable to the failure of the last Congress to make suitable appropriations for carrying on the same, which action of Congress is highly censurable and deserving of unqualified condemnation: but though Congress is thus censurable, your committee is not of opinion that the Post Office Department was warranted or justified in reducing the mail service in such manner as to deprive a large district of country, and hundreds of thousands of people of mail facilities, and while we concede to the Department patriotic and praiseworthy motives in thus seeming to economize the public expenditures, we beg leave to dissent from the expediency and wisdom of a policy that saves to the government a few thousand dollars at the expense of a speedy, constant and reliable dissemination of intelligence through the instrumentality of the public mails.

And further state that the greater part of our letter mail which is large, from the north and east is carried through the **Overland Mail** by way of St. Louis, first passing through Van Buren to Fort Smith whence it is returned to Van Buren, after a delay of about thirty hours; that this can be remedied by opening the **Overland Mail** at this point which your committee think ought to be done. In view of all of which your committee respectfully report the following resolutions:

Resolved, That the Post Office Department be respectfully requested to reestablish daily service on route 7812, at the earliest day possible, and thus, in some measure remove the grievances of which we complain.

Resolved, That the case of the Post Office Department, not regarding our wishes, concluded not to restore service upon said route sufficient to supply the necessities of our people, then that it may immediately stop all service on said route, which had better be blotted from existence than remain in name – a mere mockery.

Resolved, That the Post Office Department be requested to order and direct the **Overland Mail** to be opened at Van Buren, so that we may get our mail matter without the delay incident to its being carried to and returned from Fort Smith to Van Buren.

Resolved, That our delegation in Congress be requested to exert their untiring influence to accomplish all of these most desirable objects.

Resolved, That the people of Western Arkansas, particularly those living on No. 1822 be requested to hold meetings to aid us in accomplishing these most worthy objects by unmistakable expressions of public opinion.

Resolved, That copies of these proceedings be forwarded to the *Constitution* and *National Intelligencer,* and they be respectfully requested to publish the same. That all papers in Arkansas friendly to an increasing of mail facilities, and of quality and fairness in the dissemination of public benefits be requested to publish these resolutions. – *J. A. Dibbrell, Chairman*

December 7, 1859
One of 15 Times Chidester used His Steamboat, the Charm, to Carry U.S. Mail

[NOTE: Chidester's sub-contract with Butterfield's Overland Mail ended about August 13, 1859. However, he still had numerous contracts to carry mail on various route across Arkansas.]

December 7, 1859, page 3

Des Arc Citizen, Des Arc, Arkansas

The Des Arc and Clarendon U.S.M. packet Charm, Captain H. B. Hendrix, is due from Clarendon tomorrow noon, and will leave immediately on her return trip.

ARRIVAL OF THE **OVERLAND MAIL** – *ST. LOUIS, DEC. 2* – The **Overland Mail** from San Francisco, with California advices of the 14th ult., passed Warsaw, Mo. today

December 7, 1859
Butterfield's Home Station - New Owners

Based on the date of the advertisement below, the Des Arc Butterfield Home Station, the Jackson House, was purchased about July 27, 1859 by J. F. and W. R. Welch. They renamed it Des Arc Hotel and Stage Office.

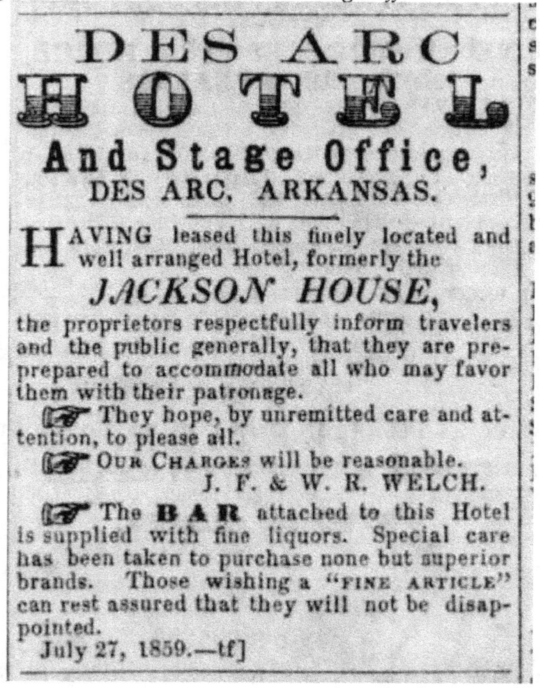

DES ARC
HOTEL
And Stage Office,
DES ARC, ARKANSAS.

HAVING leased this finely located and well arranged Hotel, formerly the

JACKSON HOUSE,

the proprietors respectfully inform travelers and the public generally, that they are pre-prepared to accommodate all who may favor them with their patronage.

☞ They hope, by unremitted care and attention, to please all.

☞ OUR CHARGES will be reasonable.

J. F. & W. R. WELCH.

☞ The **BAR** attached to this Hotel is supplied with fine liquors. Special care has been taken to purchase none but superior brands. Those wishing a "FINE ARTICLE" can rest assured that they will not be disappointed.

July 27, 1859.—tf]

Source: Des Arc Citizen, Dec. 7, 1859

December 9, 1859
Telegraph Lines

December 9, 1859
The Van Buren Press Van Buren, Arkansas

The **overland** telegraph is in operation to within 20 miles north of Springfield, and we can now get news from Washington in 24 hours, by the **Overland Mail**. We have received information by a passenger in the stage, via Springfield from Washington, to the 8th at 6 o'clock yesterday evening. Nothing going on in Congress, except balloting in the House for speaker without success.

December 10, 1859
Overland Mail Arrives

December 10, 1859, Saturday
Arkansas State Gazette, Little Rock, Arkansas

JEFFERSON CITY, MO., DECEMBER 2 – The **Overland Mail** from San Francisco, with California advices of the 11th inst., arrived in this city today.

ST. LOUIS, DEC. 2 – The **Overland Mail** from San Francisco, with California advices of the 14th ult., passed Warsaw, Mo. today. The new tubular bridge across the Yuba River has been swept away by the high water.

December 14, 1859
One of 15 Times Chidester used His Steamboat, the Charm, to Carry U.S. Mail

[NOTE: Chidester's sub-contract with Butterfield's Overland Mail ended about August 13, 1859. However, he still had numerous contracts to carry mail on various route across Arkansas.]

December 14, 1859, page 3
Des Arc Citizen, Des Arc, Arkansas

The Des Arc and Clarendon U.S.M. packet Charm, Captain H. B. Hendrix, is due from Clarendon tomorrow noon, and will leave immediately on her return trip.

December 21, 1859
One of 15 Times Chidester used His Steamboat, the Charm, to Carry U.S. Mail

[NOTE: Chidester's sub-contract with Butterfield's Overland Mail ended about August 13, 1859. However, he still had numerous contracts to carry mail on various route across Arkansas.]

December 21, 1859, page 3

Des Arc Citizen, Des Arc, Arkansas

The Des Arc and Clarendon U.S.M. packet Charm, Captain H. B. Hendrix, is due from Clarendon tomorrow noon, and will leave immediately on her return trip.

December 21, 1859
Butterfield's Steamboat Jennie Whipple Carrying Overland Mail

December 21, 1859, Wednesday

Arkansas True Democrat, Little Rock, Arkansas

There is a new line to be formed for the Memphis and Arkansas River trade. It will consist of the **Jennie Whipple**, Captain Gray; the Lake City, Captain H. Blake; and the Northerner, Captain P. A. Alford. The **Whipple** will leave this evening, and the Lake City on Wednesday. Each boat will make weekly trips, forming a tri-weekly line. We are glad to note the fact as an indication of the increase of trade between our city *[Memphis]* and one of the most fertile regions in the south. Messrs. B. E. Dill & Co., will be the agents of the line – *Avalanche*

December 21, 1859
Request of Overland Mail to be Opened at Van Buren

December 21, 1859, Wednesday

Arkansas True Democrat, Little Rock, Arkansas

Public Meeting – At a meeting of the citizens of Crawford County, held at the court house on Monday the 14th inst., the following proceedings were had...

... the greater part of our letter mail, which is large, from the north and east is carried through the **Overland Mail** by way of St. Lewis *[Louis]*, first passing through Van Buren, after a delay of about thirty hours; that this can be remedied by opening the **Overland Mail** at this point which your committee think ought to be done. In view, of all of which your committee respectfully report the following resolutions:

...*Resolved*, That the post office department be requested to order and direct the **Overland Mail** to be opened at Van Buren, so that we would get our mail matter without the delay incident to its being carried to and returned from Fort Smith to Van Buren.

Resolved, That our delegation in Congress be requested to exert their untiring influence to accomplish all of these most desirable objects...

[This article was also printed in the December 3, 1859 issue of Little Rock's Weekly Arkansas Gazette.]

December 23, 1859
Overland Agent Offers to Carry Regular Mail from Springfield to Fayetteville

December 23, 1859

The Arkansian, Fayetteville, Arkansas

SPRINGFIELD MAIL – We understand that Mr. Peck, the agent for the **Overland Mail Company** at Springfield, has generously proffered to bring the Northern mail for this city twice a week from Springfield, provided the Post Master at that office will sort the mail for this office and put it in a separate bag.

We sincerely trust the postmaster at Springfield will confer so great a favor upon the citizens of this place *[Fayetteville, Ark.]* by acquiescing in the proposition of Mr. Peck. In the present wretched condition of our mail facilities, such a favor would be duly appreciated and not soon forgotten.

December 30, 1859
Ocean Steam Ship Line Lobby for Overland Route Cancellation

December 30, 1859, Friday
The Arkansian, Fayetteville, Arkansas

...Every body and his wife are preparing for Christmas and we anticipate much fun.

I hear it rumored that the Government intend to discontinue the service on the **California Overland Mail Route**. Can you inform your readers as to the truth or falsity of the report?

The understanding is that the Mail Steamers have hired men in Washington who will strain every nerve to accomplish the discontinuance. The land route is interfering seriously with the ocean route in a pecuniary *[financial]* point of view.

I trust this will not be done, for now that **Col. Butterfield** has succeeded in the experiment, a few years ago deemed a chimera, it is unjust to cut him short in the meridian of his glory and further, if there is any desire on the part of the Government to construct a Pacific Rail Road, a mail line is the very thing to pioneer the way.

Health quite good in "these parts." All grumbling about the mails particularly, the one between your city and Springfield. Can't you do something in the way of jogging Mr. Springfield P. M.'s memory on the score of his duly?

December 31, 1859
Overland Mail Faster than Regular Mails

December 31, 1859, Saturday
Arkansas State Gazette, Little Rock, Arkansas

The Mails – As usual, the mails are a failure. But there in one thing which we can't see into. That is, how the **Overland Mail** makes regular trips, in quick time, and the other mails on the same routes make failures. The **Overland Mail** passes regularly over the route between here and Memphis – yet there is scarcely such a thing as receiving mails by the regular, direct line to Memphis. Letters are received from Fayetteville, by the **Overland Mail**, in less than three days; while the ordinary mails, on the same route, require from ten days to two weeks to make the same trip. This matter should be looked into by the mail agent. As things are now, the ordinary mail facilities for Arkansas are a decided failure.

St. Louis, Dec. 23 – A telegraphic dispatch from Malloy's Station announces that the **Overland Mail** from San Francisco, with California advices of the 2d inst., passed that place today on its way to this city. *[St. Louis]*

1860

January 4, 1860
One of 15 Times Chidester used His Steamboat, the Charm, to Carry U.S. Mail

[NOTE: Chidester's sub-contract with Butterfield's Overland Mail ended about August 13, 1859. However, he still had numerous contracts to carry mail on various route across Arkansas.]

January 4, 1860, page 3

The Des Arc and Clarendon U.S.M. packet Charm, Captain H. B. Hendrix, is due from Clarendon tomorrow noon, and will leave immediately on her return trip.

January 5, 1859
Overland Stage Arrives

January 5, 1859

The Van Buren Press Van Buren, Arkansas

The Presidents Message – A horse express with the President's Message, passed through here last Saturday evening for California – sent by **Butterfield Overland Mail Company.** It would reach San Francisco the 10th or 12th this month, so that the message will be received in California at least a week earlier than we shall receive it by the regular mail from Little Rock. What a commentary upon our mail arrangements.

We were in hopes to have received the Message in time to have a synopsis of it, in the press this week – but have not been able to obtain a copy up to the hour of go-to-press.

January 5, 1859
The importance of the Overland California Mail, is daily increasing.

January 5, 1859
The Van Buren Press Van Buren, Arkansas

The Postmaster General, has ordered the mail, made up for California at Cincinnati *[Ohio]*, to be sent by the **Overland Route**. The importance of the **Overland California Mail**, is daily increasing.

January 6, 1860
Twelve Miles an Hour!

January 6, 1860
The Arkansian, Fayetteville, Arkansas

QUICK TIME! The **Overland Mail** which conveyed the President's Message from this city to Fort Smith, made the trip IN FIVE HOURS being at the rate of ore than twelve miles per hour!! The Message was received at Fort Smith 24 hours after it was delivered at the Capitol.

January 11, 1860
Butterfield's Steamboat Jennie Whipple Carrying Overland Mail

January 11, 1860, Wednesday
Arkansas True Democrat, Little Rock, Arkansas

ARRIVALS – Jan. 2
Jennie Whipple, Capt. Gray, from Memphis

DEPARTURES – Jan. 2
Jennie Whipple for Memphis

January 11, 1860
New Postmaster General Opposes Overland

January 11, 1860, Wednesday

Arkansas Banner, Little Rock, Arkansas

It is well known that P. M. G. Brown was emphatically a western man and disposed to increase our mail facilities. *[After Postmaster Brown died and was replaced with Mr Holt..]* Mr. Holt has adopted a different line of policy. He opposes the **Overland Mail** route and tried to cut it down from weekly to semi-monthly, and now recommends that Congress should abolish it, if it can be done.

[Note: The Wednesday, January 11, 1860 issue of the Arkansas True Democrat reprinted this article and added the following:]

The Kansas and Stockton mail was discontinued. It was in operation nine months. It did a smashing business according to the report; made four trips, took one letter to California, and brought from thence two letters and twenty-six newspapers. the Independence, Salt Lake and Placerville mail was cut down to semi-monthly.

The following table from the report shows the operations of the different **overland mail routes**:

	Cost.	Receipts.	Loss to the Department.
Semi-weekly mail from St. Louis and Memphis, via El Paso, to San Francisco....	$600,000 00	$27,229 94	$572,770 06
Weekly mail from St. Joseph, Mo., to Salt Lake City..........................	190,000 00	4,210 00	185,790 00
Monthly mail from Neosho, Mo., to Albuquerque..........................	17,000 00	320 00	16,680 00
Monthly mail from Kansas, Mo., to Stockton, Cal..........................	79,999 00	1,255 00	78,744 00
Weekly mail from San Antonio, Texas, to San Deigo, Cal..........................	196,448 00	601 00	195,847 00
Weekly mail from Salt Lake City to Placerville..........................	130,000 00	1,202 03	128,797 97

January 11, 1860
One of 15 Times Chidester used His Steamboat, the Charm, to Carry U.S. Mail

[NOTE: Chidester's sub-contract with Butterfield's Overland Mail ended about August 13, 1859. However, he still had numerous contracts to carry mail on various route across Arkansas.]

January 11, 1860, page 3

Des Arc Citizen, Des Arc, Arkansas

The Des Arc and Clarendon U.S.M. packet Charm, Captain H. B. Hendrix, arrived Sunday, and departed at noon on Monday. She is due again from Clarendon tomorrow noon, and will leave immediately on her return trip.

January 14, 1860
Overland Stage Arrives

January 14, 1860, Saturday, page 2

Weekly Arkansas Gazette, Little Rock Arkansas

JEFFERSON CITY, MO., JAN. 6 – The **Overland Mail** from San Francisco, with California advices of the 16th ult., arrived in this city today.

January 18, 1860
Butterfield's Steamboat Jennie Whipple
Carrying the Overland Mail

January 18, 1860, Wednesday

Arkansas True Democrat, Little Rock, Arkansas

ARRIVALS – Jan. 14

Jennie Whipple, Capt. Gray, from Memphis

DEPARTURES – Jan. 14

Jennie Whipple for Memphis

January 21, 1860
Overland Mail Better Than Regular Route Mail

January 21, 1860, Saturday

Weekly Arkansas Gazette, Little Rock Arkansas

THE MAILS – As usual, the mails are a failure and a humbug. The Memphis mails come by the Napoleon mail boats, which now make through trips to Memphis; and it is a remarkable fact that these boats, as a general thing, bring about two days later dates from Memphis, outside of the mail, than they bring in it.

The daily mail, between here and Memphis, does not come through at all, of if it does, brings no mail matter. Last year this failure was charged to the account of the railroad: – now the cars *[train cars]* make regular daily trips on that road. The remarkable feature in regard to the Memphis mail is that, while the daily mail can not come, or does not come, the **Overland Mail** makes regular trips over the same route, and has not made a single failure, so far as we know.

We charge the whole of these mail failures where they justly belong, to the Postmaster General and his agents and employees: for if they did their duty, they would compel the contractors to do theirs.

To add to the neglect of our State *[of Arkansas]* by Post Office officials, we are informed that the contractors of the **Overland Mail** volunteered to carry a package of Memphis papers every trip between Memphis and Little Rock, and that the Post Master at Memphis refuses or fails to make up such package and put it in that mail for this place. This is outrageous.

We shall have more to say of the mails.

January 25, 1860
Butterfield's Steamboat Jennie Whipple Carrying the Overland Mail

January 25, 1860, Wednesday
Arkansas True Democrat, Little Rock, Arkansas

ARRIVALS – Jan. 21

Jennie Whipple, Capt. Parker, from Memphis

DEPARTURES – Jan. 21

Jennie Whipple for Memphis

January 27, 1860

January 27, 1860, page 3
The Arkansian, Fayetteville, Arkansas

The mails still struggle through with difficulty. The roads are reported in wretched condition.

January 27, 1860
Butterfield Stage Arrives at Van Buren from San Francisco in Only 18 Days

January 27, 1860
The Van Buren Press Van Buren, Arkansas

LATEST NEWS FROM **CALIFORNIA BY OVERLAND MAIL** – The **California Overland Mail** which left San Francisco at noon on the 6th inst., arrived here at an early hour on Wednesday morning, being less than eighteen days out.

January 28, 1860
Criticism of Postmaster General's Report

January 28, 1860, Saturday
Weekly Arkansas Gazette, Little Rock Arkansas

ABSTRACT OF THE POSTMASTER GENERAL'S REPORT – ...The $600,000 paid annually for carrying a few sacks of letters from the valley of the Mississippi to San Francisco, via El Paso, through a waste and uninhabited country, would defray the aggregate cost for mail transportation, including route agents, local agents, and messengers, in the states of Kentucky, Tennessee, and North Carolina...

January 28, 1860
Fire at Memphis Post Office

January 28, 1860, Saturday
Southern Shield, Helena, Arkansas

DESTRUCTIVE FIRE IN MEMPHIS – *LOSS OF LIFE* – About 3 a.m. yesterday a fire broke out in Woodward's Livery Stable, on Second, near Main and Jefferson Streets, in Memphis, and before the flames could be stayed the Post Office block of buildings and Gaiety Stables were destroyed. It was thought that four persons were buried in the ruins of falling buildings. Forty-one horses were burned to death. Total loss of about $70,000.

The mail matter was all rescued from the Post Office, without serious loss or damage. We have no time to give further particulars this morning.

1879 Woodcut of Memphis Waterfront

January 28, 1860
Rain Delays Overland Stage

January 28, 1860, Saturday, page 3
Southern Shield, Helena, Arkansas

The heavy trains *[obvious typo: rains]* have caused the **Overland** from San Francisco to lose thirty-six hours, and a prospect of many more between here and your city.

February 1, 1860
One of 15 Times Chidester used His Steamboat, the Charm, to Carry U.S. Mail

[NOTE: Chidester's sub-contract with Butterfield's Overland Mail ended about August 13, 1859. However, he still had numerous contracts to carry mail on various route across Arkansas.]
February 1, 1860, page 3

The Des Arc and Clarendon U.S. Mail packet Charm, has broken her machinery, but will resume her trips as soon as the necessary repairs can be made.

Arrival of the **Overland Mail** – St. Louis, January 27 – The **Overland Mail** from San Francisco with California advices of the 6th ult., arrived at Malloy's Station today.

Washington, Jan. 27 – Senate – In the Senate yesterday,

Hon. Henry M. Rice, of Minnesota, introduced a bill for the relief of mail contractors.

February 1, 1860
Butterfield's Steamboat Jennie Whipple Carrying Overland Mail

February 1, 1860, Wednesday
Arkansas True Democrat, Little Rock, Arkansas

ARRIVALS – Jan. 28 Jennie Whipple, Capt. Gray, from Memphis
DEPARTURES – Jan. 28 Jennie Whipple for Memphis

February 3, 1860
Praise for Overland Mail Co.

February 3, 1860, Friday, page 2
The Arkansian, Fayetteville, Arkansas

... We have now, however, running through our midst that triumph of swtaging the **Overland Mail**. If all the word's a stage, surely these **Overland** Stages are the only ones that run the world...

February 4, 1860
Overland Stage Arrival

February 4, 1860, Saturday, page 2
Weekly Arkansas Gazette, Little Rock Arkansas

ST. LOUIS, JAN. 27 – The **Overland Mail** from San Francisco, with advices of the 6th inst., arrived at Molloy's station today.

February 11, 1860
Butterfield's Steamboat Jennie Whipple Stuck Aground

February 11, 1860, Saturday
Weekly Arkansas Gazette, Little Rock Arkansas

We regret to learn that the independent Memphis packet Jennie Whipple, was blown so far out of the channel in the storm of the 31st ult., about 40 miles below Memphis, that she now lies in a critical condition, high and dry, some distance from the water's edge.

St. Louis, Feb 2 – The **Overland Mail** from San Francisco, with California advices of the 9th ult. reached this city today. A new gold mile had been discovered in the Pa Utah Mountains; also a silver mine in the vicinity of St. Helena Mountain. These discoveries occasioned considerable excitement; four hundred persons had gone on a prospecting tour.

February 22, 1860
New Route Across Arkansas Proposed

February 22, 1860

Des Arc Citizen, Des Arc, Arkansas

Mail Facilities – The Route from Madison to Little Rock – Superiority of the Route via Des Arc – **Overland Mail**, etc. - Mail facilities in Arkansas are acknowledgedly the most uncertain in the Union. Contractors, no doubt, do all in their power to comply with the law, make schedule time, & c.

But impossibilities are not required even of those who 'work by contract' for Uncle Sam. The mail route from Madison to Little Rock, via Carendon, Devall's Bluff, & c., as now 'occasionally traveled' by mail coaches, mud wagons, mule and ox teams, is one of the veriest humbugs ever imposed upon the General Post Office Department.

The distance from Madison to Little Rock by the above mentioned route is 141 miles, and over a country that can only be traveled occasionally during the winter and spring, and but three or four post offices can be supplied.

The route from Madison to Little Rock via Des Arc is 105 miles, over an infinitely better route, and upon which there is now eight post offices, and the number could be doubled in three months from the time the route could be stocked. The only difficulty on this route is the overflow in Cache bottom, a distance of some seven miles, and this has been recently overcome, and a safe and speedy transit can be made through what is termed Snake Bayou.

Plenty of men are ready to take the contract of conveying the mail and passengers through in a few hours.

The **California Overland Mail Company** can save thousands of dollars each year, and from one to two days time every trip, by adopting this route.

Mail contractors should not listen to the 'yarns and fabrications' of those who oppose the route from Madison to Des Arc, but they should go over the route themselves. This route is settled by an industrious and wealthy population, who in truth, are entitled to mail facilities, while the route via Clarendon and Devall's Bluff is comparatively but sparsely settled.

Will our delegation in Congress look into this matter, and see that those who are entitled to mail facilities over the nearest and most feasible route from Madison westward, are accommodated? Will Col. B. C. Harley, the U. S. Mail Agent, look into the partiality that has been extended to an unsettled portion of the State *[of Arkansas]*, while the settled and improved portion has been neglected?

THE FEW, apparently, have controlled the establishment of mail routes in Arkansas, to the serious detriment and injury of THE MANY.

March 3, 1860
Apaches Stop Stagecoach

March 3, 1860, Saturday
Weekly Arkansas Gazette, Little Rock Arkansas

FROM ARIZONA – The following items are from the *Arizonian* of the 2d: WAGON TRAIL STOPPED BY APACHES – The Apaches prowling in the vicinity of Apache Pass, a station on the **Overland Mail Route**, from accounts, are becoming more than usually troublesome.

On the 28th of January, in their efforts to steal the stock from the corral of the ***[Butterfield's Overland Mail]*** company, they fired five shots from a revolver at the hostler, who in return fired three among them, killing one. the Indians exasperated at the loss of their companion, assembled in large numbers, and showed a disposition to make a further attack.

Their attention, however, was drawn off by a train of wagons, the property of Charles Hayden, Esq., passing at the time with supplies for the Sonora and Mining Company, which they immediately surrounded. Before they were repulsed, the succeeded in killing one yoke of fine cattle, and lancing three others, besides upsetting one of the wagons.

March 3, 1860
New Postal Arrangement Proposed to be Entirely by Ocean Steam Ship Instead of Stagecoach

March 3, 1860, Saturday
Weekly Arkansas Gazette, Little Rock Arkansas

The Post Office Committee of the House of Representatives will report a bill authorizing the Postmaster General to advertise for proposals to carry the entire **Overland Mail** to San Francisco, the letter mail to go through in twenty days with a semi-weekly service, and the newspaper mail in thirty days, with a weekly service. The contracts are to run three years from the first of July next. Bids will be received for the carrying of the entire mail by the water route either from New York or New Orleans, semi-weekly or weekly. Bids for a more or less frequent service will also be received.
[NOTE: This article was also printed in the March 21, 1860 issue of the Arkansas Banner, Little Rock, Arkansas, on page 1; and on that same day in the Arkansas True Democrat, page 2.]

March 7, 1860
Additional Stage Line Proposed to Intersect Overland

March 7, 1860
Arkansas True Democrat, Little Rock, Arkansas

LETTER FROM AUSTIN, TEXAS, FEB. 17TH, 1860 – GENTLEMEN: After a long silence, I will give you a brief outline of matters and things in this portion of Texas...

...Our legislature has also memorialized Congress for a stage line to intercept the **Butterfield Overland Route** on the Concho, two hundred miles from this city and on a direct line to El Paso. Winter has passed off to the north, and our prairies are looking green...

March 14, 1860

Butterfield's Steamboat Carrying Overland Mail

March 14, 1860, Wednesday

Arkansas True Democrat, Little Rock, Arkansas

Arrivals – March 8 Jennie Whipple from Memphis

Departures – March 9 Jennie Whipple for Memphis

March 14, 1860

One of 15 Times Chidester used His Steamboat, the Charm, to Carry U.S. Mail

[NOTE: Chidester's sub-contract with Butterfield's Overland Mail ended about August 13, 1859. However, he still had numerous contracts to carry mail on various route across Arkansas.]

March 14, 1860, page 3

The Charm, Captain Hendrix, arrived from Clarendon on Sunday evening, and left Monday noon.

March 17, 1860

One Overland Mail Stage Carried 8,203 Letters

March 17, 1860, Saturday

Weekly Arkansas Gazette, Little Rock Arkansas

From the St. Louis Republican, 8th – ARRIVAL OF THE **OVERLAND MAIL** – The California **Overland Mail** arrived last night, with San Francisco dates to the 13th ult.

The number of letters dispatched in the mail of the 10th from San Francisco was 8,203, of which 303 were way letters.

March 21, 1860

One of 15 Times Chidester used His Steamboat, the Charm, to Carry U.S. Mail

[NOTE: Chidester's sub-contract with Butterfield's Overland Mail ended about August 13, 1859. However, he still had numerous contracts to carry mail on various route across Arkansas.]

March 21, 1860, page 3

The Charm, Captain Hendrix, arrived from Clarendon

on Sunday evening, and left Monday noon.

March 23, 1860
Senate Considers New Postal Routes That Would End Ocean Route to Panama

March 23, 1860, page 2
The Van Buren Press, Van Buren, Arkansas

BY STEBBIN'S LINE TO MALOY'S - THENCE BY OVERLAND MAIL. - WASHINGTON D. C., MARCH 14 - The Senate committee on Post Offices agreed at their meeting, this morning, to unanimously recommend an entirely new system of postal service between the Atlantic and Pacific States, and will authorize the Post Master General to advertise for proposals for carrying the mail twice a week, between St. Paul, Minnesota, on a line running between the 46th and 48th degrees of North latitude, and Olympia, Washington Territory, and Fort Vancouver, Oregon, in 20 days.

Also, twice a week, from St. Joseph, Missouri, on a line between the 40th and 43rd degrees of North latitude, to San Francisco, in 20 days.

Also, twice a week, form St. Louis, by the present **Overland Mail Route**, via Fort Comanche, to San Diego and San Francisco, in 20 days.

Also, from New Orleans, to San Antonia, thence to Fort Comanche, where it will intercept the present **Overland Route**, thence to San Francisco, in 20 days.

This will give Overland service 4 times a week, and abrogates the present Isthmus mail service.

March 24, 1860
Butterfield's Steamboat Jennie Whipple Carrying the Overland Mail

March 24, 1860, Saturday
Arkansas True Democrat, Little Rock, Arkansas

ARRIVALS – March 18 Jennie Whipple from Memphis
DEPARTURES – March 18 Jennie Whipple for Memphis

March 30, 1860
Overland Stage Brings Election Results

March 30, 1860, Friday, page 1
The Arkansian, Fayetteville, Arkansas

MILTON S. LATHAM – **The Overland Mail,** which arrived on Monday from California, informs us that the Legislature of that State, after an exciting contest, had elected Milton S. Latham to fill the vacancy in the United States Senate, occasioned by the death of D. C. Broderick.

April 7, 1860
Molloy's Station via Overland Mail

April 7, 1860, Saturday
Weekly Arkansas Gazette, Little Rock Arkansas

ST. LOUIS, APRIL 3 – The following is in addition to the summary of news received from Molloy's Station yesterday, via the **Overland Mail:** SAN FRANCISCO, MARCH 13 – The advices received from the Isk mines are very encouraging. The yield is very rich, averaging twenty thousand dollars to a ton of quartz. One of the owners has refused eighty thousand dollars for a fifth interest.

April 7, 1860
California Telegraph Line Coming

April 7, 1860, Saturday
Weekly Arkansas Gazette, Little Rock Arkansas

The estimated cost of the California telegraph line is $750 per mile. The capital required is $1,500,000. Government is asked for $500,000 or $50,000 a year for five years. Line to commence west of the Mississippi and end at San Francisco. Committee of both Houses of Congress have reported in its favor.

As you might expect, building the telegraph lines between Missouri and California was not the easiest job in the world. It all began in earnest with the passage of the Pacific Telegraph Act by Congress in 1860. On October 24, 1861, the first transcontinental telegraph system was completed by Western Union.

April 13, 1860
Overland Stage Passenger

April 13, 1860, Friday, page 2
The Arkansian, Fayetteville, Arkansas

James S. Dean M.D. arrived in the **Overland** last Saturday from Philadelphia, where for a long time he was been attending lectures and qualifying himself for the practice of medicine. We welcome our young friend, as does every one else that knows him, to his native land and to a life of successful practice and to the speedy making of a fortune. Let him marry and begin practicing right away.

James H. Van Hoose, and Stephen K. Stone returned home by the **Overland**, Wednesday. To the former we are under obligation for files of late Eastern papers.

April 13, 1860
C. E. Butterfield Praised

April 13, 1860, Friday, page 2
The Arkansian, Fayetteville, Arkansas

Last week we received late advices from the east through

the kindness of our fried **Mr. C. E. Butterfield.** Our readers were indebted to him for many items of interest, and we hope they will take measures for expressing their gratitude. The most appropriate way of doing so would be for them to pay their subscriptions to the *Arkansian.*

The **Overland** is running far ahead of schedule, time indeed the coaches are are plying across the continent like electric motors.

April 13. 1860
Passengers Relay News

April 13. 1860
The Van Buren Press Van Buren, Arkansas

By a passenger on the **Overland Stage** we learn that the steamer *Kate May* was burnt at Louisville, on her return trip for this river, proving a total loss. Mr. H G. Hickey and Lady of Fort Smith, were on board and barely escaped with their lives. Mr. H.'s loss is some two or three thousand dollars in money.

April 14, 1860
Postal Bill at Congress
Butterfield Cannot be Cancelled
John Butterfield Disposed to Cancel Route Anyway

April 14, 1860, page 2
Arkansas True Democrat, Little Rock, Arkansas

THE **OVERLAND MAIL ROUTE** THROUGH LITTLE ROCK BILL BEFORE CONGRESS TO CHANGE IT. –Our latest advices from Washington indicate that the Senate bill for the establishment of the **overland** communication, between the Atlantic and Pacific States, which was reported as a substitute for the House bill, which invites proposals for carrying the entire mail, will be passed.

The **Butterfield Overland Mail** contract, however, which passes through Little Rock, according to the opinion of the attorney general, cannot be got rid of; but it is understood that **Mr. Butterfield**, who is now at Washington, is disposed to cancel the contract under certain arrangements with the government.

The new bill provides for two routes, north and south – the latter to go by the way of New Orleans and Texas, discontinuing the present one from Memphis, through Little Rock to Fort Smith. The northern route to go by way of Salt Lake. This presents a suggestion to our citizens, whether they will be content to lay still and even without an expression on the part of our real estate owners, merchants and hotel keepers, railroad stock holders, and business men of every class, to the present and prospective advantage of the present route. Ought not our citizens generally in public meeting convened, and our city council as a municipal body, to forward at once a memorial to Congress protesting against any change in the Pacific mail arrangement, that takes from us our present advantages, of being on an average, only twenty days from San Francisco. *[NOTE: The Van Buren Press also printed this article on April 20, 1860, also the Arkansas Banner in its April 14, 1860 issue on page 2.]*

April 14, 1860
Overland Mail is running faster and more efficient than traditional mail from Memphis to Little Rock

April 14, 1860, Saturday
Weekly Arkansas Gazette, Little Rock Arkansas

The Mails. — Since last November the mail matter from Memphis, which should have been sent by the direct rail road and stage route, has been brought by the river line, *via* Napoleon — thus making our Memphis exchanges from four to six days old when we receive them, instead of one day, to a day and a half, as should be the case.

Now the river is so low that the mail boats can not make time; it is sometimes a week between the receipts of Eastern mails; the stages, from the rail road line across the country arrive with punctual regularity, and bring passengers through in good time ; and yet we receive no mails by them.

On Sunday we received Saturday's Memphis papers by a gentleman who came as a passenger in the stage; but never a letter or a paper in the mail.

There was probably a fault in the letting of the contract from this place to Madison. The contract should probably have been let for the carrying of the mail alone, not requiring the contractors at all times to perform what is at some times impossible — that is, to carry the mail in post coaches. But now the road is in good condition; the post coaches arrive regularly in time, and bring loads of passengers; the contractors say that they are ready and anxious to carry the mail; and if they do not carry it the Post office officials are to blame. The responsibility of our not receiving mails by the Memphis line, in the proper time, is with the Postmaster at Memphis; and if the mails from this place to Memphis are not received in due time the responsibility is with the Postmaster at Little Rock.

The stages can, and do, get through in time; if the Postmasters deliver the mails properly they must be brought through in like good time; and if the mails are properly delivered to the contractors, and do not arrive in due time, there is a Mail agent whose duty it is to go over the line, see where the abuse exists, and compel the contractors and Postmasters to do their duty.

Some twenty-five years ago, or more, Sampson Gray was the contractor, and carried a tri-weekly mail, between Memphis and Little Rock, on horse-back. Much of the country was then a wilderness; the road across the Mississippi swamp was not then thrown up as it afterwards was. Clarendon and DeValls Bluff were not points then, and there were no steam-boat facilities for avoiding the overflows on White river, by transporting the mails from one bluff, up or down the river, to another; yet we are informed that Sampson Gray carried his tri-weekly mail between Memphis and Little Rock at that early day, on horse-back, for four years without making a failure!

And, not withstanding, there is now a rail road, making

regular trips across the Mississippi swamp between Memphis and the St. Francis river, and steam boat facilities for transportation of mail matter between Clarendon and DeVall's Bluff, or between other bluffs on the White river, so that the overflows there may be avoided, yet, for nearly half the year, we get no direct mails from Memphis because, forsooth, the road is reported as impassable!

Thus the people of Little Rock, with all of the improvements of the day, are worse off for mail facilities to Memphis than they were a quarter of a century ago, when the country was a comparative wilderness.

We address ourselves to Post-Masters, Mail-agents and other Post-office officials; and now, and in future, shall hold them responsible for the failures of the mails; for, if they do their duty, they can compel the mail contractors to do theirs. If any of those officials, though, having done his own duty, will point out a case of mail contractors failing in theirs, we shall present the matter to the public, in its proper light.

That no one may be mistaken as to the intent of this article, we will say that it is intended for delinquents generally, but aimed, especially, at the Postmaster at Memphis, and Col. Harley, the mail agent.

To Mr. Rapley, of the firm of **Chidester, Rapley & Co.**, we tender thanks for his offer to carry, outside: of the mail, a package of our papers to our contemporaries with whom we exchange in Memphis, and also a package of their papers in return. So that, in future, we shall have an 'opportunity of getting our Memphis daily exchanges despite the neglect of the Post-office officials. And while upon that subject. we tender thanks to the **Overland Mail Company** for their good intentions — they having proposed to bring us our daily exchanges from Memphis the whole winter, but not being able to carry their good intention into effect, because, as we understand, the Postmaster at Memphis would not put them in the mail.

We have borne with these Post-office abuses too long already, in the vain hope that the Government officials might some time awaken to a sense of their duty. In future we shall give these gentry somewhat more of our attention; and if, like the boy up the apple tree, they will not obey the gentle suggestion of a ball of grass, we shall not despair, but resort to missiles which we hope may be more effectual in bringing about a good result.

April 14, 1860
Overland Driver, George Crull, Accused of Arson & Abolitionist Activities

April 14, 1860

Arkansas True Democrat, Little Rock, Arkansas

Fire in Lewisburg, Arkansas, April 9, 1860 – Messrs. Johnson & Yerkes – Gents: I hasten to drop you a few lines of my own and other's misfortune: on yesterday morning (Sunday) about about 8 o'clock by the gin house in this town, containing some 50 or 60 bales of cotton was discovered to be on fire. As soon as the alarm was given, the citizens and some of the neighbors responded very promptly, and rendered active and valuable service.

Soon afterwards the gin house of M. T. T. Henry, successor to Henry & Co., of this place, containing some 15 bales of cotton, was discovered to be on fire. Between these gins stood my large warehouse, which contained a large amount of cotton, beet hides, poultry and firs, together with a large amount of groceries and other goods – very soon it took fire from my gin, when all three of the buildings with nearly all of their contents were destroyed.

The work was undoubtedly from an incendiary; and I think one George Crull, an **Overland Stage Driver** did it, or knew who did – *we drove him off.* It seems that the fire was by a slow match to each of the lint rooms of the gins, as they were both found to be on fire *near the same time.* By hard word we prevented the fire from extending to any other house.

My individual loss will be about$5,000.00

Myself and R. B. Griffin " 5,000.00

Dr. F. W. Adams	"	2,500.00
T. T. Henry	"	1,200.00
R. Welborn	"	300.00
T. W. Barber	"	500.00
Jno. Breedon	"	300.00
R. Simpson	"	150.00
N. S. Williams	"	100.00
Sundry other persons	"	250.00
Total loss		$15,300.00

There was no insurance on any of the loss unless it was on Mr. T. W. Barber's which was in transportation. There was some 10 or 12 hundred dollars worth of cotton and other goods saved for various persons in a damaged condition. The citizens and friends – one and all – will please accept my most heartfelt thanks for their very extraordinary efforts to save the property. – *Your Friend, Anderson Gordon* [NOTE: *This article was also printed in the Arkansas Banner in its April 14, 1860 issue.*]

April 16, 1860
Butterfield Sub-Contractor Improves Stage line Service on his separate tri-weekly postal contract

April 16, 1860

The Van Buren Press Van Buren, Arkansas

STAGE ROUTE TO LITTLE ROCK – Mr. Reeside, who has the contract for carrying the mail between Little Rock and Fort Smith, has put the line in complete order, taking the mail and passengers through in *thirty-eight* hours. For the last week, the stage has been crowded on account of the boats not being able to make trips above the Rock [*city of Little Rock*].

April 20, 1860
Robinson replaces Crocker as Fort Smith Superintendent

April 20, 1860, Friday

The Van Buren Press Van Buren, Arkansas

HUGH CROCKER, ESQ., late Superintendent of the **Overland Mail Company,** at Fort Smith, has resigned his charge and passed through our city on Monday, on his way to New York. Mr. Robinson, of Cincinnati, Ohio takes his place.

Rumor has been floating about town for two or three days, to the effect that the **Overland Mail** is to be withdrawn from this route. If this is so, shall we, the citizens of Van Buren, sit quietly down and let it be done, without remonstrance?

April 21, 1860
Overland Drivers Accused of: Encouraging Slaves to Revolt, Attempting to Steal Slaves, and *after a mob whipped a Butterfield driver* Setting a Fire to Several Buildings near the Lewisburg Butterfield Station

April 21, 1860, Saturday, page 3
Arkansas Banner, Little Rock Arkansas

Abolition Emissaries Amongst Us – Destructive Fire

Lewisburg, Ark., April 13, 1860 – Mr. Editor: I write this for the purpose of putting our people, if possible, on the alert – it really seems as if a lethargy had seized them that could not be thrown off.

On Saturday the 7th of April, the Democrats held a township meeting in Lewisburg, and then we learned for the first time the concerted operations of the **Overland Mail Stage Employees** in our midst.

They had persuaded Dr. Menefee's negros to revolt, and the project was nearly ripe for execution, when he affair was divulged to him by a trusty old negro woman.

One of the *[**Butterfield**]* drivers acknowledged the facts as related to Menefee by the negro; and the Doctor, I suppose, in his anger and surprise forgot that the statute of our State *[of Arkansas]* would have *dealt* with him very severely. He told him *[the **Butterfield** driver]* to leave and he did so.

A citizen of our town overheard one of these men *[**Butterfield** drivers]* tell a negro that if he would wait until he made money enough stage driving, he would take him off *[help him escape slavery]* where a negro is a good as a white man. *[Perhaps referring to New York, the home of many of the **Butterfield** employees.]*

He *[apparently referring to a **Butterfield** driver]* was whipped and told to leave, and he did not wait for a second warning. *[NOTE: An April 14th article, reproduced above, gives the driver's name as George Crull.]*

So, hearing that there were two others left of the same sort *[apparently referring to two additional **Butterfield** employees - perhaps from the **Butterfield** swing station there in Lewisburg.]* a committee of citizens was appointed to wait on them and ascertain the facts. We were not disposed to punish innocent men, and having nothing tangible to operate on, we merely read them the *"riot act."*

In consequence of these proceedings, these men *[**Butterfield** drivers]* either in person or by proxy fired by slow matches the gin houses of A. Gordon and T. T. Henry, esq., which also consumed the warehouse of the first named gentlemen, situated between the two gins. The loss to these gentlemen is very large, besides many others; back country merchants who had large freights stored in the warehouse. Estimated loss $20,000, and no insurance. We have heard of several other buildings being tried around the neighborhood; but believe the damage was inconsiderable compared with the above. *[NOTE: Apparently the **Butterfield** employees are accused of unsuccessfully attempting to set fire to additional buildings.]*

These men *[**Butterfield** employees]* are still running at large and the public should use caution against all suspicious characters lurking in their midst.

We have determined if we cannot get our mail matter without having it brought by gin burners and negro stealers that we will dispense with it entirely.

signed, Vigilence

[NOTE: This letter to the Editor also printed in the Arkansas True Democrat, in the April 21, 1860 issue on page 3.[

[NOTE: An image of the historical marker at Lewisburg is reproduced in my earlier book, "Butterfield's Overland Mail Co. STAGECOACH Trail Across Arkansas." It reads in part: "A Freedmen's Bureau office opened in June 1866 to

aid freed people with labor contracts and to run a school. In 1868 the town was embroiled in conflict between the Ku Klux Klan and the Republican Militia during voter registration. Parts of Lewisburg were burned twice during December, and Gov. Powell Clayton declared Martial Law in Conway County on Dec. 8, 1868."]

At the time, the public whipping of a ***Butterfield driver*** *George Crull, echoed national tensions. This 1856 image depicts U.S. Senator Charles Sumner being beaten thirty times by Congressmen Preston Brooks in the Senate chambers. Sumner, of Massachusetts was accused of being an anti-slavery abolitionists by Congressman Preston Brooks from South Carolina.*

This modern painting depicting *"The City of Lewisburg 1852"* is displayed at the Morrilton Railroad Station Museum

This modern painting depicting "The City of Lewisburg 1852" is displayed at the Morrilton Railroad Station Museum in downtown Morrilton.

April 21, 1860
Lewisburg Slavery Story Continues
John Butterfield Asked to Only Hire "Southern Men"

April 21, 1860, Saturday, page 3
Arkansas True Democrat, Little Rock Arkansas

FROM CONWAY COUNTY – *LEWISBURG, CONWAY COUNTY, ARKANSAS – MR. EDITOR* – The citizens of this county held a meeting in Lewisburg, on Saturday April 7, and passed the following resolution:

WHEREAS, there has been an effort made in this county by certain transient persons *[**Butterfield** drivers]*, whom we have good reason to believe are abolition emissaries, to interfere with our slaves, and persuade them to assume an attitude of hostility to their masters; and whereas, we are determined to take action against all such, both vigorous and effective.

RESOLVED, That we hereby advise all suspicious men having no employment amongst us, and who are drifting about for the purpose of injuring us in the possession of our property *[slaves]*, to cease from this day any intermeddling in our domestic institutions, else we pledge them and ourselves, that we will deal with them *[more whippings]* with the utmost rigor.

RESOLVED, That the chair appoint a committee of seven to wait on the agents of the **Overland** and Fort Smith and Little Rock mail lines, and request the removal of all employees, except such as are known to be good southern men, and to engage no others. *[**Butterfield** should only hire southern men who support slavery.]*

RESOLVED, That the persons subscribing hereto shall constitute a vigilance committee, any five of whom shall have power to carry out these resolutions in spirit and effect. *[The forty signers of this resolution will serve as a vigilante mob to whip and run off any anti-slavery men.]*

RESOLVED, That the Little Rock papers be requested to

publish these proceedings.

The chair appointed as the committee Messrs. S. H. Nieman, R. Welborn, L. O. Breeden, A. Gordon, R. T. Markham, W. L. Menefee and R. W. Harper.

S. J. Stallings, Chairman
and forty others.

April 21, 1860
Overland Stages Carry 63,036 Letters

April 21, 1860, Saturday, page 2
Arkansas Banner, Little Rock Arkansas

During the month of February the **Overland Mail** carried 38,674 letters to, and 63,036 letters from California. On a late trip it brought nearly 11,000 letters from San Francisco.

April 21, 1860
Memphis Postmaster and the Overland Stage
He continues to use regular mail via Napoleon instead of Overland Mail to send newspapers.

April 21, 1860, Saturday, page 2
Arkansas Banner, Little Rock Arkansas

Why it is that the postmaster at Memphis continued to send mail matter for this place via Napoleon, instead of Madison, is a mystery to us. When the mail is forwarded by railroad and stages, we get our exchanges four days sooner than when forwarded by Napoleon. We hope the postmaster at Memphis will have some compassion on our people, and do his duty better hereafter.

April 21, 1860
Newspaper Editor Rides Memphis Overland Stage

April 21, 1860, Saturday
Weekly Arkansas Gazette, Little Rock Arkansas

The editor of this paper left for the Eastern States by the **Overland Memphis route** on Wednesday morning last. He will probably be absent a month.

April 27, 1860
Passenger Rides in Boot All The Way

April 27, 1860, Friday, page 3
The Arkansian, Fayetteville Arkansas

We learn that a passenger recently arrived in Fort Smith from California, who made the entire journey in the boot of the ***[Butterfield's Overland]*** stage coach; the stage was crowded with passengers, without trunks, and the enterprising traveler, rather than wait, took passage in the boot. "He'll do to travel."

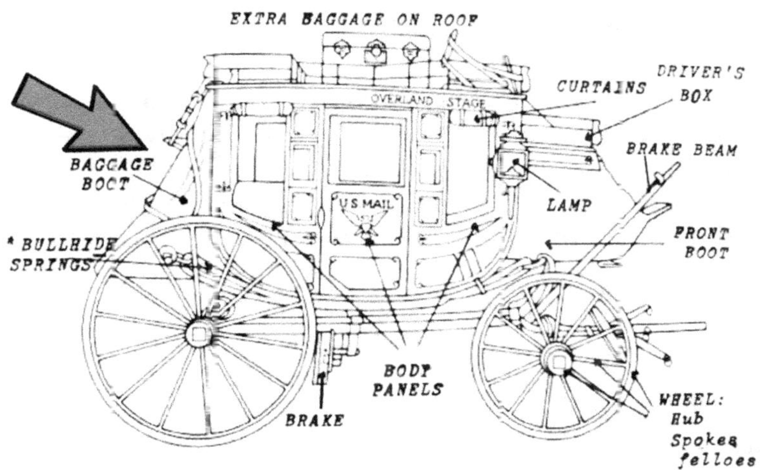

Passenger rode in the rear baggage boot the entire trip.

April 27, 1860
Congress Considers Route Change

April 27, 1860, Friday, page 3
The Arkansian, Fayetteville Arkansas

An effort is being made in Congress to change the route of the **Overland Mail**; this is an important movement, and, should it succeed, the interests of Little Rock, Fort Smith, Fayetteville and other places on the line of the present route would be materially effected.

We sincerely hope that this project will be defeated, and we heartily join with the *True Democrat, Van Buren Press,* and other papers in urging a direct, specific, and unqualified expression of remonstrance against the adoption of the proposed change.

The expense of such an important maneuver, would be equipoised by the advantages which would advance to the country, and they can; and should be shown in the most effective way.

April 27, 1860
Comanche Trouble

April 27, 1860, Friday, page 3
The Arkansian, Fayetteville Arkansas

TROUBLE IN THE **OVERLAND MAIL** – Passengers on the **Overland Mail** route report considerable trouble with the Comanches on the line of late; about one week ago the Indians made a descent upon a station, killed three of the employees and drove off the stock. This is the report and we have no doubt of its correctness.

April 27, 1860
– Butterfield's Steamboat In Trouble –

[NOTE: Jennie Whipple departs for Fort Gibson in Indian Territory. This was the fateful trip that resulted in ***Butterfield's*** *steamboat, Jennie Whipple, being stuck hard aground for fourteen month.*

This was, most likely, the last trip under ***John Butterfield's*** *ownership, and the mail delivered at Fort Smith on April 27 was the last* ***Overland Mail*** *delivery by the Jennie Whipple.]*

April 27, 1860
The Van Buren Press Van Buren, Arkansas

THE RIVER - WEATHER - STEAMBOATS - The River since our last, rose 10 feet and upwards - making a full river from bank to bank - but is now falling slowly, and up to going to press, there is plenty of water for the largest boats, and the prospect now is of a good river for some time to come.

The *Julia Roane*, from New Orleans, arrived on Saturday morning and departed on the same afternoon.

The **Jennie Whipple**, from Memphis, arrived Sunday morning, discharged her freight, and took a load for Fort Gibson and departed Tuesday morning.

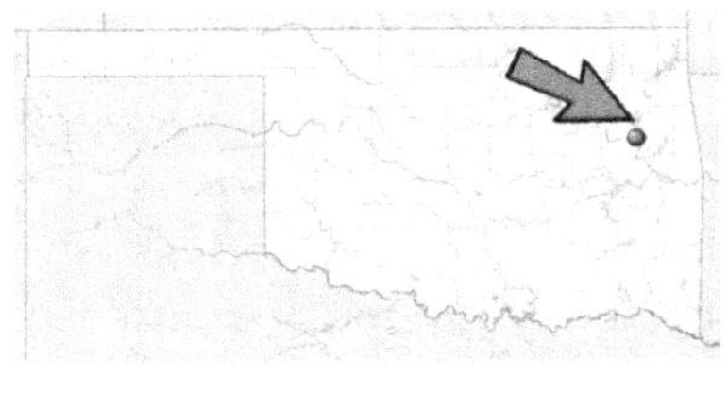

Butterfield's Steamboat, Jennie Whipple was hard aground near Fort Gibson for almost 14 months due to low water. The building above is the original Fort Gibson barracks as it appeared in 1930.

April 27, 1860
Butterfield Deposed at President of Board

April 27, 1860

The Van Buren Press Van Buren, Arkansas

WASHINGTON, APRIL 16. - The *Herald's* Washington correspondence, says the **Butterfield Overland Mail Co.**, is now under the control of Wells Fargo & Co., of New York. Mr. Butterfield has been deposed from the Presidency and replaced by Wm. B. Dinsmore, of the Adams Express Co.

Mr. Gardner has also resigned the Superintendency of the route, and Cal. Alvord, of Indiana has been appointed to fill the vacancy.

William B. Dinsmore, President of the Overland Mail Co. from March 20, 1860 to September 1864.
He was vice-president when John Butterfield was voted out of office March 20, 1860. John Butterfield remained a director of the Overland. Dinsmore remained presieent until the end of the six-year contract.

April 28, 1860
Killed – Driver & Station Agent

April 28, 1860
Des Arc Citizen, Des Arc, Arkansas

Overland Mail Station Attacked by Comanches – Three Killed – Mules Stolen – We learn from the *Fort Smith Times* of the 19th, that on the Tuesday pervious, fourteen mounted Comanches, armed with rifles, attacked the station, killed three men and run off five mules. Wm. Lambshead, station keeper, James Handy, driver, and a boy names Stier, are the names of the persons killed.

May 4, 1860
Jennie Whipple Stuck Aground

May 4, 1860
The Van Buren Press Van Buren, Arkansas

The **Jennie Whipple**, is stuck fast above with a load for Fort Gibson.

May 4, 1860
Passenger on Overland Stagecoach

May 4, 1860
The Van Buren Press Van Buren, Arkansas

A. J. Ward, of the House of Ward & Southmayd, arrived home from the East on the **Overland Stage**, on Sunday morning, 4 days from Cincinnati. He will accept our thanks for files of late papers. They are now receiving and opening a large stock of goods for wholesale and retail. The ladies will take notice of the fact, and we can assure them they will find John the very best of humor, ready to take down and put up again – in a word to turn the store upside down to please them and show the "putties." *[humorous version of "pretty things']*

John Butterfield's home in Utica, New York.

May 18, 1860
John Butterfield Visits Arkansas

May 18, 1860

The Van Buren Press Van Buren, Arkansas

PERSONAL – We were pleased to meet on Thursday last, in our city, **Col. John Butterfield**, looking in his usual robust health. **Col. Butterfield** made the trip from Utica, New York to Little Rock in three days.

May 18, 1860
Praise for Overland Mail Co.

May 18, 1860, Friday

The Arkansian, Fayetteville Arkansas

Our postal privileges are very great, equal to any country where there are neither rail roads nor telegraphs.

Daily lines of four horse stages run through Fayetteville, from Little Rock, Arks., to Tipton Mo., the present terminus of the Missouri Central Rail Road.

The **California Overland Mail** passes through our town twice a week each way -- with a post office and depot here — this mail has reached this place from San Francisco in 19 days.

Passengers have been "put through" from St. Louis to Fayetteville in 48 hours.

These mails are permanent and were called forth by the wants and demands of the people.

May 26, 1860
Republican Party Resolves Butterfield to Be Daily Instead of Bi-Weekly

May 26, 1860

Des Arc Citizen, Des Arc, Arkansas

The REPUBLICAN CHICAGO CONVENTION – *CHICAGO, MAY 17* – ... Resolutions were passed... in favor of... a daily mail to the Pacific.

June 1, 1860
Charles E. Butterfield, Superintendent Resident of Fayetteville, Departing to Visit Creek Nation

June 1, 1860, Friday, page 3

The Arkansian, Fayetteville, Arkansas

Mr. C. E. Butterfield is off on a visit to the Creek Nation.

June 2, 1860
Pony Express Rider Killed

June 2, 1860

Des Arc Citizen, Des Arc, Arkansas

ST. JOSEPH, MAY 21 – The central Pony Express arrived this afternoon at half past four... A rider was killed by Indians on the California end; mail and dispatches saved. The express was detained a day and a half by this misfortune.

The Overland Mail Company

HAVE opened an office at the "Anthony House," where seats can be procured at all times on the Overland Mail to the following and all intermediate points, viz:

Fort Smith;	**Fort Yuma;**
Sherman;	**Staked Plains;**
Fort Belknap;	**Los Angelos;**
Fort Chadbourn;	**Fort Tyson;**
El Paso;	**San Francisco;**

Also, to Madison on the arrival of the Overland Mail from San Francisco.

Extras furnished on the shortest notice to Fort Smith, *to run through in 36 hours.*

W. M. CRAIN, *Agent.*

LITTLE ROCK, June 2, 1860. 3m.

This advertisement was printed numerous times, including on June 2, 9, 16, 23, July 7, 14, 21, 1860.

June 2, 1860
Overland Mail Co. Advertizement

June 2, 1860

Arkansas State Gazette, Little Rock, Arkansas

[Note: ***Butterfields*** *steamboat, the* **Jennie Whipple,** *was hard aground upstream in Indian Territory for 14 months. The* **Overland Mail** *continued by stagecoach as advertised below. The ad features the* **Butterfield** *Home Station, The Anthony House, in Little Rock.]*

June 9, 1860
Overland Stage Passenger

June 2, 1860, page 2

Arkansas State Gazette, Little Rock, Arkansas

Hon. B. T. DuVal, who has been North and East for several weeks, departed for his home at Fort Smith on Thursday's **Overland** stage.

June 22, 1860
Stagecoaches are Full of Passengers

June 22, 1860
The Van Buren Press Van Buren, Arkansas

The stages of the **California Overland Mail Company,** we notice, are universally filled with passengers, going both East and West.

June 23, 1860

June 23, 1860, Saturday, page 2
Arkansas State Gazette, Little Rock, Arkansas

WASHINGTON, JUNE 19 – The **Overland Mail** bill has been postponed.

"An Overland Station: Indians Coming in with the Stage"
by Frederic Remington

June 23, 1860
Overland Stations Without Military Protection in Rio Mesilla Valley, Arizona Territory

June 23, 1860, Saturday
Arkansas State Gazette, Little Rock, Arkansas

CORRESPONDENCE OF THE ST. LOUIS *REPUBLICAN.* MESILLA,

A.T., May 31, 1860 – Desperate Fight with the apaches – Eighteen Americans Killed and Eight Badly Wounded – Mr. Sherrod Hunter, residing upon the Mimbres, sent an express in this morning with the news that a part of 400 Apache warriors had attacked the settlement upon the stream on the morning of the 22th.

There were mustered some thirty Americans and Mexicans who defended the settlement as well as might be. The fight was a desperate one, six Americans and five Mexicans being killed, besides eight being badly wounded.

It is impossible to tell the number of killed and wounded among the Indians; it is supposed to be from twenty to thirty. These Indians are mostly well armed with rifles, and many of them have Colt's army revolvers, besides being well mounted.

Fortunately all the American women and children had arrived in Mesilla two days before this fight came off. Upon the express reporting of this news, Gov. Owings immediately communicated the facts to Lieut. Lazelle, commanding Fort Fillmore, who sent word over that he was powerless there being but ten men on duty in the fort, and not a single animal.

Immediately upon receipt of this answer, fifteen of our most prominent citizens (all that could procure horses) volunteered to go to the assistance of the persons upon the Mimbres. They started this morning, under command of Col. S. J. Jones (ex-sheriff Jones, of Kansas). They will probably reach the Mimbres tomorrow morning when we may expect to hear more news.

The expressmen who started with the intelligence was attacked near Cook's Springs by the Indians and badly wounded with two arrows, but succeeded in reaching the **mail station** at the spring, when one of the employees of the company started with the despatch, and succeeded in safely bringing it in.

The copper mines are fast being abandoned, also the gold diggings. It seems as though the Indians had determined to wreak their long delayed vengeance at once; they are continually stealing stock from the valley, and have left our "rancheros" nearly destitute of cattle and mules.

The **Overland Company** are doubling their men at the stations, and fortifying themselves as best they can. This disturbance, it is feared will, end in eventually breaking up the line.

All this might have been in a measure averted had our Government, instead of breaking up our only military post in the valley (and, in fact, in this part of the Territory), placed more men there, better prepared to pursue and punish those Indians. Had this been done, much property, now lost, would have been rescued.

Our usually quiet town seems almost deserted, as all those who could procure horses have left for the scene of the difficulties.

What the final result will be, God only knows. It is generally feared; however, that the settlements upon the Mimbres, and around the copper mines, will be broken up. This will throw many hundred hands out of employment, and bring us "hard times" with a vengeance.

A proper military force stationed in this valley, and in the valley of the Rio Mimbres would do much towards holding these wild savages in check; but as it is now, they can roam from the Rio Bonito to the Colorado without meeting a single "regular."

The **Overland Line** is entirely without protection in a right Arizona, not having a single military post nearer than sixty miles, in the whole Territory and then but one, and that not yet erected.

Yes, we are American citizens, and have, to that protection which we were led to expect that we should receive when we settled upon Uncle Sam's domain. Shall we receive it or not? *Will Mr. Secretary Floyd answer this question?*

July 7, 1860
Overland Stage Passenger

July 7, 1860, page 3
The Arkansian, Fayetteville Arkansas

REV. ROBERT GRAHAM arrived home last Saturday by **Overland** and was welcomed by his family and numerous friends. He has been absent some ten months.

July 7, 1860
Vice President Campaigns from Overland Stage

July 7, 1860
The Arkansian, Fayetteville Arkansas

Vice President John C. Breckenridge

COME AND SEE – Hon. John C. Breckenridge, Vice-President of the United States, and candidate for President, will pass through Fayetteville on Saturday the 14th inst., by **Overland Mail**. Come and see.

July 21, 1860

July 21, 1860
Arkansas Banner, Little Rock,Arkansas

FAYETTEVILLE, ARK. JULY 8 – The **Overland Mail** coach, with San Francisco dates to the 18th ult., arrived here at 9 o'clock this morning.

BYRNSIDE HOUSE:

FAYETTEVILLE—ARKANSAS:

ISAAC TAYLOR,::::::::::Proprietor.

The Overland Mail Stage Office is kept here.

THIS well-known house, formerly occupied by Mr. Onstott, and situated on the South-west corner of the Public Square, is now under the supervision of Isaac Taylor: It having been thoroughly repaired and refurnished, is now open; and the proprietor will spare no effort nor expense on his part, to accommodate all who may favor him with a call. The table will be furnished with the best the country affords; and the stables will be well supplied with provinder, and good and faithful hostlers and servants to wait on all. Call and see for yourselves.

April 2,.1860 6'4m

This advertisement was printed numerous times including April 2, 1860, July 7, 14, 21, and Aug. 17
November 9, 17, 24, 1860 and January 5, 1861

July 14, 1860
Fayetteville's Overland Mail Office began running advertisements in the paper about meals, rooms, and its stables.

July 14, 1860, Saturday
The Arkansian, Fayetteville, Arkansas

July 14, 1860
Overland Stage Arrives in Fayetteville

July 14, 1860
Arkansas State Gazette, Little Rock, Arkansas

FAYETTEVILLE, ARK. JULY 8 – The **Overland Mail** with San Francisco dates to the 15th ult., arrived at this point today.

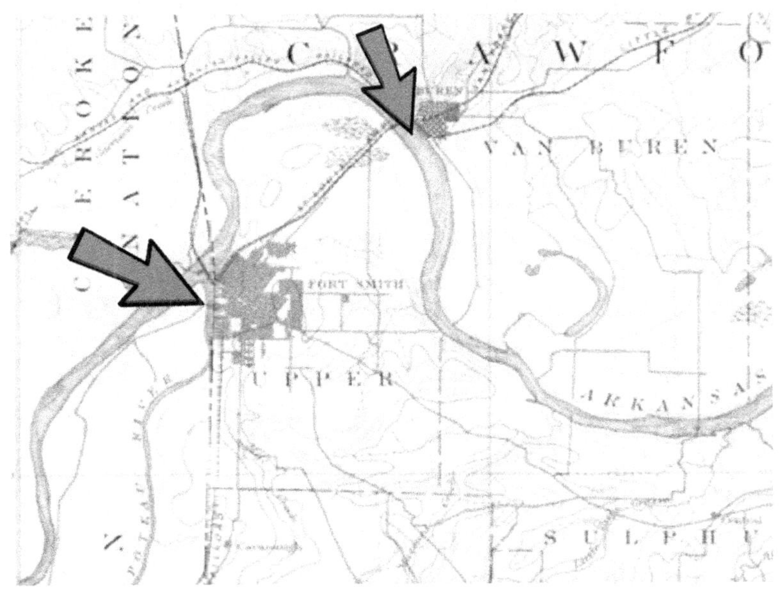

Ferry Crossings Near Fort Smith
The Overland Mail stagecoaches from St. Louis, headed south, crossed the Arkansas River by ferry from Van Buren to Fort Smith. To depart Fort Smith for Indian Territory, the merged stagecoach crossed the Poteau River, headed south to Skullyville's Watson Station.

NEW ROPE FERRY.

H. KAYSER,

TAKES this method of informing the public that he has moved his Ferry to its former location at the mouth of Poteau, where he is prepared with good and substantial boats and experienced ferrymen to wait on the public. The road to Skullyville is decidedly better than any other road leading from Fort Smith. This is also the mail route between Fort Smith, Texas and California.

This route is the shortest and best—being on a a direct line from Missouri to Texas, and offers greater inducements to the traveling public than any other Ferry on Poteau river.

Charges moderate—Ferrymen always at their post. oct. 11 '59.

Ferry Ad, West Side of Fort Smith on Road to Skullyville Swing Station
Source: July 24, 1860, *Thirty-Fifth Parallel,* Fort Smith, Arkansas

JOSEPH R. HALL,

AT the "Ring Place," lately known as the Warren place, 10 miles west of Fort Smith, on the overland mail route, in the Choctaw Nation, will provide the travelling public with the best accommodations. His House is large; for his table, there is an abundance, and his Stables are the best in the Nation. Terms moderate..

Corn for sale by the bushel.

Skullyville County, April 10, 1860. 1y

Ad for Hall House on Butterfield Route in Indian Territory
Source: July 24, 1860, Thirty-Fifth Parallel, Fort Smith, Arkansas

July 27, 1860
Passenger Killed in Accident – Runaway Horses

July 27, 1860
Van Buren Press, Van Buren, Arkansas

ACCIDENT – The California **Overland stage** met with an accident last week on Thursday night about seventy miles from Fort Smith in the Choctaw nation. On leaving what is called Mountain Station, the horses commenced running, and from some defect in the brake became unmanageable and after running nearly a half mile, dashed the stage against a tree, breaking it entirely up. One passenger whose name we understand was McKay, and who lived in Missouri, was killed, and some four or five others were seriously injured, as were also the conductor and driver. This is the first and only serious accident that within our knowledge has ever before happened to the **Overland** stage in this part of the country.

July 28, 1860
Overland Stage Arrived

July 28, 1860
Arkansas Banner, Little Rock, Arkansas

ARRIVAL OF THE **OVERLAND MAIL** – VAN BUREN, ARK. JULY 10 – The **Overland Mail**, with San Francisco advices to the 29th ult. arrived at this point today.

August 3, 1860
Proposed Route Change for Arkansas

August 3, 1860
Van Buren Press, Van Buren, Arkansas

THE **OVERLAND CALIFORNIA MAIL** – The stages of the **California Overland Mail Company** now carry the Memphis mail on the north side of the Arkansas River from this place – thereby making the actual connection from Memphis and Saint Louis at this city *[Van Buren]*. Van Buren is now the actual center between the states east of us and the states on the Pacific.

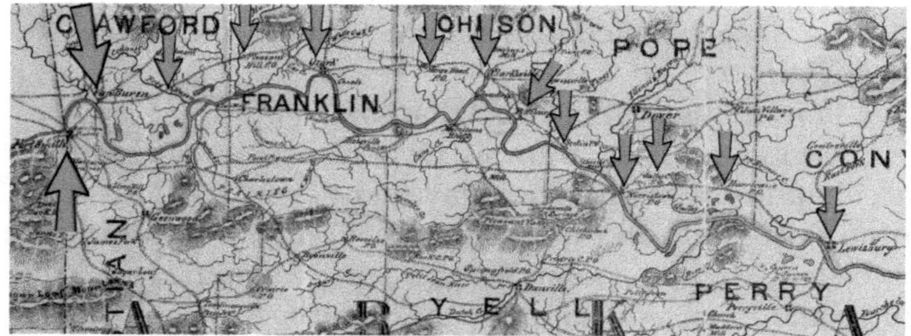

***IF** the above article is accurate, for the last 8 months of operation, **Butterfield's Overland stagecoaches** would have traveled on the north side of the Arkansas River, all the way from Memphis to Fort Smith, stopping at the original stations of Lewisburg, Hurricane, Galley Creek (Potts Station), and Norristown. Then, instead of crossing the Arkansas River, the stages would have stopped at new stations at (all these new locations had a Post Office as this 1864 Wm Hoelcke map indicates): Scotia, Pittsburg, Clarksville, Horse Head, Ozark, Pleasant Hill, crossing Frog Bayou, then crossing on the Van Buren ferry to reach the **Butterfield Home Station** at Fort Smith.*

August 3, 1860

August 3, 1860
Van Buren Press, Van Buren, Arkansas

ACCIDENT – The **California Overland Stage** upset on Boston Mountain about twenty miles north of this place on Sunday morning last. Nobody was hurt and the only damage done, that of breaking off the top of the stage. For a stage running day and night, and compelled to make by schedule the closest time, there have been the fewest accidents on this line than on any other in this country.

August 4, 1860
Overland Stage Arrives

August 4, 1860
Arkansas State Gazette, Little Rock, Arkansas

INDEPENDENCE, JULY 31 – The **Overland Mail** from San Francisco, with advices to the 9th inst., arrived at this place today.

August 17, 1860

August 17, 1860, Friday, page 4
The Arkansian, Fayetteville, Arkansas
[NOTE: It was not unusual for businesses to refer to the location of the ***Overland*** *Offices in giving directions to their business.]*

WAGONS, PLOWS,
—AND—
Blacksmithing.

J. H. CATO has now on hand, a number of Two-horse Wagons (iron and wood axels,) well finished, and a good supply of

TURNING PLOWS,

of best pattern adapted to the use of farmers in this region, made of good materials, and will be furnished at reasonable prices. He keeps a good supply of them on hand, at his

Wagon and Blacksmith Shop

east of Overland Mail station, Fayetteville.
☞Orders from a distance promptly filled.
August 4, 1860. 23tf

Source: August 17, 1860, Friday, page 4
The Arkansian, Fayetteville, Arkansas

August 24, 1860
Passenger on Overland Stagecoach

August 24, 1860
The Van Buren Press Van Buren, Arkansas

We are pleased to announce the safe arrival home, in fine health, on the **Overland Stage**, Sunday morning, of

Col. Wm. Whitfield, of our city. Colonel Whitfield has just returned by the steamer Asia, from a trip to Europe.

August 25, 1860
Immigrant Following the Route of the Overland Finding Help From O.M. Stations Along the Route

August 25, 1860
Arkansas True Democrat, Little Rock, Arkansas

In Camp Lion Holes, 20th July, 1860

Friend M – In compliance with my promise on leaving Little Rock, I now write, being the first letter written by me since our departure. We are not in camp, resting our stock at this place, which you will find by consulting your map, is about 900 miles west of Fort Smith, and about 200 east of the Rio Grande. We have been out fifty-five days, and traveled about 1,100 miles, in the heat of summer, and yet we are yet between 600 and 700 miles short of our destination...

We have now passed, entirely, the Comanche country, and although during our passage we were continually reminded by the **Overland Mail** station keepers of the hazard and extreme danger of so small a party as ours attempting to cross the plains, yet we have made the trip without seeing an isolated Indian...

We are now in the Apache country, and have been, since we crossed the Pecos River... Apaches... being totally different in this respect from their more brave and magnanimous neighbors, the Comanches, who when they attack you, always give you at least daylight and an open field.

We are full of untried courage, willing, if needs be, to measure arms with any number of savages that may wish to try our nerve; yet our courage may, when the time comes for its display (if it does come) prove no better material than old Jack's, of sack drinking celebrity, for no man, I am convinced, knows what would be his conduct in the face of extreme danger, who has never been in that situation.

That there is great danger to any number of white men

encountering a body of Comanches at all superior in number to their own, all experience abundantly shows; for while they are probably the best equestrians in the world, and always fight on horseback, they are much better armed than persons in the States generally suppose; great numbers of them being armed with rifles and six-shooters in addition to their inseparable companion, the bow and arrow, which, of itself, is no contemptible weapon in the hands of an Indian; being of as much efficiency as the six-shooter, because they can do execution with it at as great a distance as the majority of men can shoot a pistol with accuracy.

We have almost universally received at the hands of the employees of the **Overland Mail Company**, kind treatment, and gentlemanly consideration; in fact, we have met with but one exception, which was at the hands of the station keeper at the crossing of the Colorado, who refused some of our party a drink of water, which so enraged some of our number, that had it not been for the interference of cooler heads, he would undoubtedly have received rough treatment.

This, I am pleased to say, was the only exception, which speaks well for the mail company and those employed by it. No one who has not traveled over the **Overland Mail Line** can form any just idea of the magnitude of this successful enterprise, and the complete system necessary to its permanent establishment as a means of communication between the Eastern States and the Pacific. Indeed, I am convinced that is is one of the greatest achievements, as a coach mail line, that the world has ever seen, considering the extreme length of the line (2,700 miles), the character of the country through which it passes, and the immense distance necessary to transport provender *[feed and hay]* for stock, and the additional fact that during the whole time of its existence, but three mail failures have occurred on this line, and they were produced by high water. There are several "dry stations" on the line, to which water has to be hauled, in some instances, the distance of 25 miles.

August 31, 1860
Passenger on Overland Mail Stagecoach

August 31, 1860
The Van Buren Press Van Buren, Arkansas

The Rev. W. Binet, returned from the East on last Sunday's **California Stage** – and will preach in the Episcopal Church on Sunday, at the usual hour.

September 7, 1860
Passenger on Overland Writes Editor

September 7, 1860, page two
Van Buren Press, Van Buren, Arkansas\\][

FOR THE VAN BUREN PRESS - BY THE WAY: [after expressing negative opinions about remarks about train travel, he writes:]

Venerable stage: memento of other days. So full of respect for persons and monuments! Silently moving near some sacred spot; sometimes halting near some national monument. Venerable stage of olden times, with all the faults and virtues of man's home:

As long as you are outside of the stage, an unknown pilgrim, the passengers already ensconced in their narrow places, would be glad if you would not encroach on their little domain; but boldly step in, be seated, look round, meet the glances of all, and soon you are one of the happy family!

Once, as I went sight-seeing, I was shown a very large cage; within were all manner of unfortunate animals, living and traveling together; they came from different climes; birds, cats, dogs, rats, foxes - a curious assortment having nothing in common, but some native instincts which undoubtedly made them wish for the end of their journey!

We were a kind of happy family in the **Overland Mail Stage.**

There was a miner, fresh from the lower stratifications of mother earth.

There was a stage conductor from the vast plains stretching to our west; accustomed to the air of the plain, he longed for the open air, as yonder bird, in yonder "happy family" longs for the tree in the illimitable forest of his first home.

There was another man -- a type of the unknown; whence he came and wither he went, was a mystery to me and oftentimes I would have wished to trace a few pathways of his life, for, no doubt, his human heart had been attuned to sorrow's sad notes and to joy's lofty songs, thus we were a happy family.

A female traveler from California's gold diggings completed the picture; a string of gold plates surrounded an ample neck, and testified of those belts of gold which loving nature has placed upon our earth.

There were brilliant drops of perspiration produced by a hot July sun, and gathering into substantial soil the loose clouds of dust which every movement of the lumbering stage threw up, contrived to make of that neck a kind of stratified specimen of geology.

However, kind hearts were there - noble thoughts dwelt there - and a noble helping hand could have been found there!

Oh! The magnificent evil!

Nine persons in the stage, with the sun in 120 degrees hot, pouring its overflowing tide of warmth upon us.

No doubt Dante who has so graphically portrayed to man the abodes of the wicked, had he known something of modern travelling, would have placed in his "purgatorio" and underland mail especially at night, dashing and clashing amidst the rocks, ravines and dry rivers, of the Ozark Mountains, where every body's head, searching for a pillow, at least, for some immovable position, and finding none, clashed against another cranium or awoke in alarm the unsuspecting neighbor.

However, onward we went.

North of us, the sugar cane seemed to be largely cultivated.

In Missouri, the hungarian grass waved coolly to the breeze.

Whilst in the northern States timothy grass and clover prevail everywhere...

[the poem then describes traveling by sail, and life in Washington DC...]

September 14, 1860
Pony Express Arrivals Publicized

September 14, 1860

The Van Buren Press Van Buren, Arkansas

St. Joseph, Missouri, September 3 – LATER FROM CALIFORNIA – ARRIVAL OF THE PONY EXPRESS – The Pony Express, with dates to the 22nd of August, arrived last evening on time. Notwithstanding some trouble is still existing from the Indians in Carson Valley, the Express comes through in nearly, schedule time.

September 14, 1860
Passenger on Overland Stagecoach
Famous Abolitionist Arrested

September 14, 1860

The Van Buren Press Van Buren, Arkansas

Bailey, the Texas Abolitionist, who was arrested by the citizens of Washington County, passed through here in the **Overland Stage** last Sunday, in charge of men from Texas, who will take him to Fort Worth, where he will, no doubt, have justice meted to him.

September 21, 1860
Fire Destroys Fort Smith Home Station

September 21, 1860

The Van Buren Press Van Buren, Arkansas

DESTRUCTIVE FIRE AT FORT SMITH – THE BEST PART OF THE CITY IN RUINS – *FORT SMITH TIMES OFFICE – MCKENZIE'S CITY HOTEL – POST OFFICE TOTALLY DESTROYED – LOSS ESTIMATED AT $250,000* –

We learn that a very destructive fire occurred in Fort

Smith, at an early hour yesterday morning, thought to be the work of incendiary. The damages resulting therefrom are supposed to be about $250,000.

Among the houses burned are McKencie's City Hotel, the large brick house occupied by Cline as a Drug Store, by Gridley as a Billiard Saloon, the Fort Smith *Times* office, the Post Office, the stores of Satton, Spring & Co , Benton & Walton, and Bennett and Foss, and the law office of Clark & Spring, the whole amount of loss being estimated at two hundred and fifty thousand dollars, and upon which there is supposed to be only partial insurance. The fire is the most destructive one that ever occurred in western Arkansas, and the houses burnt are probably the finest ones in the State - the store house of Sutton, Spring & Co., and other having cost about forty thousand dollars. The **St. Louis California and Memphis Stage** offices which were kept in the City Hotel, were of course burned, as was the Post Office kept in Cline's Drug Store. A large number of our citizens left this morning for Fort Smith to give such aid as might be in their power to the suffers.

LATER – By Mr. L. C. Southmayd who visited Fort Smith yesterday we have the following particulars:

Fire at Fort Smith, broke out in a billiard saloon over Cline's Drug Store, about 4 o'clock, A. M. – no one about and water scarce – progressed too rapid to be subdued. Loss estimated as follows:

- City Hotel owned by John Rogers – loss $10,000, insured for $500 – $3,500 in AEtna and $1,500 in Phoenix.
- J. R. McKenzie, proprietor City Hotel, partial loss $3,000 – no insurance.
- Wm. Bennett & Co., store, loss $10,000 – insurance $5,000 in Phoenix.
- Bennett & Foss, merchandise, mostly saved – loss about $2,000.
- Walton & Courne, loss on stock, merchandise and storehouse, about $18,000 – insured $5,000 on building in AEtna.

- Wheeler & Sparks, *Times* office, total loss of everything – loss $5,000, no insurance.
- J. N. Spring law office and library, total loss about $3,000 – no insurance.
- J. B. Grilley, billiard saloon, estimated $2,000 loss – insured $1,200 in Phoenix.
- Dr. N. P. Spring, storehouse, loss $12,000 – no insurance.
- Sutton & Spring, storehouse and merchandise – merchandise partially saved estimated loss $10,000 – no insurance.
- Sisson daguerrean artist, loss $700 – no insurance. *[Note: A daguaerrean, was an early photographer using the daguerreotype method.]*
- Cline's City Drug Store, loss about $7,000 – no insurance.
- Post Office destroyed and the Memphis mail to California.
- A. G. ______, loss $300 – no insurance.

  Fire is generally supposed to have been accidental.

The City Hotel, which housed the Overland Offices was lost to fire September 28, 1860.

St. Charles Hotel about 1870.
Photo courtesy Fort Smith Public Library.

Hiram Rumfield's letters report that when a major fire occurred at the City Hotel, the Butterfield Home Station moved across the street to the Saint Charles Hotel.

September 28 1860
Wreck of Overland Stagecoach

September 28, 1860
The Van Buren Press Van Buren, Arkansas

The **California Overland Stage** from St. Louis, upset last Sunday, about fifteen miles north of this city. There were nine passengers on the stage at the time, who escaped with slight bruises. The horses, after the upset, ran away with the four wheels attached, and two of them were so seriously injured that they had to be killed.

September 28, 1860
Butterfield's Sub-Contractor Had Extensive Stage Coach Coverage of Arkansas

September 28, 1860. page 2

Thirty-fifth Parallel, Fort Smith, Arkansas

THE "ARKANSAS STAGE COMPANY"

HAVE opened an office at St. Charles Hotel, Fort Smith, Ark., where seats may be secured to

Van Buren,	Brownsville,	Pine Bluff,
Ozark,	Clarendon,	Richland,
Clarksville,	Madison,	Kapetrau,
Norristown,	Memphis,	Hot Springs,
Dardanelle,	Searcy,	Arkadelphia,
Lewisburg,	Batesville,	Washington,
Little Rock,	Helena;	

And all important points in the State. The Company have spared no expense in procuring fine stock and comfortable coaches, and have employed the most careful and experienced drivers.

☞ Conductors, leaving with every coach, will make it their special duty to give all possible attention to the comfort and welfare of the passengers.

☞ Stages leave Fort Smith every *Sunday, Tuesday* and *Thursday morning.*

For passage, or information, apply to

JOS. REESIDE, *St. Charles Hotel.*

August 31st, '60—1y.

Source: 35th Parallel, Fort Smith, Sept 28, 1860 and April 6, 1861

September 28, 1860
Butterfield's Sub-Contractor Advertises Overland Mail Route to Memphis

September 28, 1860. page 4
Thirty-fifth Parallel, Fort Smith, Arkansas

UNITED STATES TRI-WEEKLY MAIL
Line from Fort Smith to Little Rock.
LEAVES Fort Smith every Monday, Wednesday and Friday, at 8 A. M. Through to Little Rock in sixty hours.
For further information, or passage, apply at the office City Hotel.
JOS. T. REESIDE.
Fort Smith, April 26, 1860.

Source: Thirty fifth Parallel, Fort Smith, Sept. 28, 1860
Also printed April 6, 1361

September 28, 1860
Butterfield Home Station Burned to Ground in City Hotel at Fort Smith, Arkansas

September 28, 1860. page 2
Thirty fifth Parallel, Fort Smith, Arkansas

John Roger's City Hotel, and in less than two hours the whole of these buildings were in ruins; a portion of the goods were saved, in a damaged condition. Cline's Drug Store was entirely consumed; the Post Office, in Cline's Store, was consumed and not one article of the contents of the office saved, nor one dollar's worth of goods out of the Drug Store - no insurance. The loss cannot be much less than one hundred and fifty thousand dollars; about twenty thousand dollars were insured on the stock and houses. The buildings burnt were the best in the State *[of Arkansas]*. The loss, outside of the interruption of business, will be felt for a long time. Judge Wheeler (of the *Times*) lost his printing office and material, worth five thousand dollars; no insurance.

It happened to be a calm morning, or the largest portion of Fort Smith would now be in ruins; as it is the loss is very heavy, and it will be a long time before it can be repaired. Sutton & Spring are the greatest suffers – their loss must be forty or fifty thousand dollars; no insurance. Walton & Rouche, about twenty thousand; ten thousand insurance. William Bennett, building, ten thousand; stock $25,000, insurance $5,000. City Hotel, ten thousand dollars; $5,000 insured. Cline had no insurance. Gridley two thousand dollars; insured $1,250.

It is supposed the fire was caused by a foul fiend. In a word, the best part of our city is in ruins. We are sorry to say, that some unkind words were spoken about this sad affair. Let those who sneer, look to their own acts, All such epithets as we heard on the 20th of September, will do no one any injury.

...Mr. Whitmore and Mr. Dary, who were every where doing all they could to prevent the loss of property. A report that two or three men lost their lives seems to be contradicted. The ruins have not been removed, and we hope when they are, that the report that lives have been lost will prove incorrect. Many uncalled for aspersions have been made, and we hope after calmer reflections of those who made them, they will regret their ill feelings particularly so when they wish to injure innocent persons by their foul remarks. we leave all such to their own reflections, Curses like chickens come home to roost.

October 3, 1860
Overland Passengers Reports the Hanging of a Methodist Preacher in Texas

October 3, 1860
Des Arc Citizen, Des Arc, Arkansas

The *Fort Smith Herald* learns from a passenger on the **Overland Stage,** direct from Texas, that Rev. Wm. Buly of the M.E. Church *[Methodist Episcopal Church]*, was hung on the 13th ult., for being implicated in the late burning in Texas, and inciting insurrection among the negroes.

FORT SMITH, ARK., SEPT. 28 – the **Overland Mail** from San Francisco with dates to the 7th inst, passed here today, in route for St. Louis.

October 3, 1860
Fort Smith Home Station Burned

October 3, 1860, page 3
Des Arc Citizen, Des Arc, Arkansas

THE CONFLAGRATION AT FORT SMITH – It is estimated that the value of the buildings destroyed at Fort Smith on the 22th ult., was about $113,000, and in addition to which the following losses were sustained on merchandize, furniture, etc:

Sutton & Spring, dealers in dry goods, groceries, etc., loss $35,000, no insurance; Walton & Bourne, dry goods, $15,000, insured for $10,000; A. Hamilton Cline, drugs, $20,000, no insurance; Bennett & Foss, dry goods, etc., $15,000, insured $5,000; *Times* printing office, $5,000, no insurance; G. W. Sisson, $2,000, no insurance; J. B. Gridley, $1,500, insured $1,200; Col. Spring's law office, $1,500. no insurance.

Also the post office including 4,000 letters and the last ***[Butterfield Overland]*** **California Mail** for Memphis. The entire loss by this disastrous conflagration is fully $200,000. The origin of the fire is unknown, but supposed to be the work of an incendiary.

f

October 5, 1860
Daily Overland Mail Proposed

October 5, 1860, Friday, page 4
The Arkansian, Fayetteville, Arkansas

BLACK-REPUBLICAN PLATFORM – LINCOLN AND HAMLIN

Resolved, That we, the delegated representatives of the Republican Electors of the United States, in Convention, assembled in the discharge of the duty owe to our constituents and our country, unite in the following declarations:

... *16th* ...and as preliminary thereto a **Daily Overland Mail** should be promptly established.

October 6, 1860
Overland Stage Arrived

October 6, 1860
Arkansas State Gazette, Little Rock, Arkansas

FORT SMITH, OCTOBER 1 – The **Overland Mail** from San Francisco, with California advices to the 10th ult., passed here today, en route for St. Louis.

Captain John Rogers, Founder of Fort Smith
Owner of Butterfield's City Hotel Home Station

October 12, 1860
Died - Owner of the City Hotel that housed the Fort Smith offices of the Overland Mail. It's Interesting that He Died Just Two Weeks After His Hotel Burned to the Ground

October 12, 1860
The Van Buren Press Van Buren, Arkansas

ANOTHER OLD SETTLER DEAD – Capt. John Rogers, of Fort Smith, died on Monday last, at his residence in that City, a the ripe old age of 81 years. Capt. Rogers was one of the early settlers in Arkansas, and laid out the town of Fort Smith, of which he was the proprietor *[of the City Hotel that housed the offices of the* ***Overland Mail.****]* His funeral was attended by all the old settlers in this City *[of fort Smith]*, also, by the Masonic Lodge; and is said to have been the largest funeral ever attended in Western Arkansas.

October 13, 1860
Passenger on the Overland Stage

October 13, 1860
Arkansas True Democrat, Little Rock, Arkansas

Senator Latham and family were to leave San Francisco on the 15th inst., for Washington, by the **Overland Route.**

October 13, 1860
Murder South of Fayetteville Station

October 13, 1860, page 3
Arkansas True Democrat, Little Rock, Arkansas

THE MURDERER ARRESTED - *FROM THE VAN BUREN PRESS, OCT. 5, 1860* – ...Robert Davis, is from Green County, Texas, and was on his way to Ozark, Mo., his native place... In the night he got up without the knowledge of his wife, and took a stick of wood about four feet long, and as large as his leg. First struck the old man with one lick, which broke his skull, killing him instantly. Then struck the boy two licks, killing him. Took the stick, it being very bloody, and put it into the fire and burnt it up... took the **Overland Mail Road,** following it to Bryant's, then took the Spencer road, and followed that four miles into Washington county, and dark having overtaken him, he took the bodies out of the wagon, packed them down the hill, seventy-five or eighty yards from the road and there threw them down...

Yesterday, Davis, in charge of several officers, was brought to Van Buren, the murder having been committed in this county, and lodged in jail to await the sitting of the court in February next.

October 19, 1860
Road Is In Good Order

October 19, 1860, Friday, page 3
The Arkansian, Fayetteville, Arkansas

By Telegraph – Fort Smith; 17th – The **Overland Mail** brings news up to the 2nd Oct., from California. Lieut. Beale accompanied by Fred Keiden, were at Fort Mojave on the Colorado. Fifty days were spent in reaching that point from Westport, Mo. All along the route after the first 170 miles, the Indians were hostile. The road is in good order, but until protection is given it will be dangerous for emigrants to go that way, with protection they can travel the route with advantage. A report prevailed at Los Angeles, that the Indians had attacked Fort Defiance and held possession of the Sutelr's post for six hours in spite of 4 companies of U.S. troops.

Two young men late of Fort Smith, known as Frank Rivers and Bob Montgomery, were hung near San Antonio, Texas, for horse stealing.

October 26, 1860
Passenger on the Overland Stage

October 26, 1860
The Van Buren Press Van Buren, Arkansas

Jesse Howell, from the Hardware establishment of Martin and Smith, Philadelphia, arrived here in the **California**

Overland Stage, Sunday morning, direct. All wanting anything in the line of this House, will do well to give Jesse their orders. He will please to accept our thanks for late New York and Philadelphia papers.

October 26, 1860
Bridge Added on Indian Territory Route

October 26, 1860, page 4
Thirty-Fifth Parallel, Fort Smith, Arkansas

BRIDGE OVER BRAZEALE CREEK, CHOCTAW NATION –

The undersigned, respectfully inform the traveling public that they have completed their bridge over Brazeale Creek, twelve miles west of Skullyville, Choctaw Nation, on the route travelled by the stages of the **Overland Mail Company** from Fort Smith, Ark., to Sherman, Texas, intersecting the several routes leading to Forts Washita, Arbuckle and Cobb, and shall at all times keep the bridge in perfect repair, charging but the most reasonable rates of toll.

Brazeale Creek has always caused delays to the traveller when in high stage of water, but the public are assured that there will no longer be cause of detention on that stream – *McDaniel & James*

November 24, 1860
Overland Carried Freight of Cigars

November 24, 1860, Saturday
The Arkansian, Fayetteville, Arkansas

CIGARS – Paddock received by the last **Overland Mail** a lot of the finest cigars ever brought to this place. Those who indulge in this pass-off-time pleasure will not fail to prefer Paddock's cigars to any other.

December 14, 1860
Post Office Bill Debated

December 14, 1860
The Van Buren Press, Van Buren, Arkansas

WASHINGTON, DEC. 11TH. - ... The Post Office committee

met this morning to consider an **Overland Mail** bill.

After consultation, they unanimously adopted the bill, the details of which are as follows: that the postmaster general advertise for proposals for carrying the entire mail, overland daily, between St. Joe. and San Francisco, by the Central Route, from July 1861, to July 1865. Denver City and Salt Lake City, to be supplied weekly, without extra charge. The amount not to exceed $800,000 per annum -- letters and papers to be carried.

December 21, 1860
Gallant Stage Driver

December 21, 1860
The Constitutional Union, Des Arc, Arkansas

GALLANT STAGE DRIVER – A male passenger, by the California's company stage, up the other evening, says *The San Juan Press,* insulted a female passenger. The driver stopped his team, took the passenger out, "whaled" him soundly, and left him on the road. *[NOTE: This was a driver for the California Stage Company, not* ***Butterfield's Overland Mail Co.]***

December 21, 1860
Overland Conductor
Relays Weather and River Reports

December 21, 1860
The Van Buren Press Van Buren, Arkansas

We learn from the conductor of the **Overland Mail stage** that yesterday morning there was a rise of six feet *[in Arkansas River level]* at Ozark, and that heavy rains fell at Little Rock on Monday and Tuesday. He reports that most of the steamers below here are full. The reports from above are not favorable for a further rise at present.

1861

January 5, 1861
Butterfield's Steamboat Was Still Hard Aground up in Indian Territory

January 5, 1861, Saturday, page 2
Arkansas True Democrat, Little Rock, Arkansas

The **Jennie Whipple** yet tarries among the Cherokees.

January 5, 1861
Wm. Christopher is an Overland Conductor

January 5, 1861
Arkansas State Gazette, Little Rock, Arkansas

Late Papers – We are indebted to Mr. Wm. Christopher, the accommodating conductor on the **Overland Mail**, for late papers.

January 11, 1861
First Shots of the Civil War

January 11, 1861
The Van Buren Press Van Buren, Arkansas

Civil War – Hostilities Commenced between South Carolina and the Federal Government – Perhaps already a bloody and distressing civil war has commenced. The first gun has been fired. "Madness rules the hour;" the times are troublous; events are being rapidly precipitated; and no man knows what may be the result. That the horrors of civil war may be averted from our country is our sincere prayer, but at the same time let us prepare for what is to follow – for war with all its attendant evils, if it must come.

January 18, 1861
Southern States Begin to Secede

January 18, 1861
The Van Buren Press Van Buren, Arkansas

In addition to South Carolina, the states that have already seceded are, Mississippi, Alabama and Florida.

January 19, 1861
Secessionists to Seize Overland Mail

January 19, 1861, page 4
Arkansas State Gazette, Little Rock, Arkansas

New York, Jan. 14. – The Washington correspondent of the New York *Tribune* says: It is currently reported that an expedition is being fitted out for the purpose of seizing the United States mail line to California.

January 26, 1861
Wm. Christopher is an Overland Conductor

January 26, 1861, Saturday, page 2
Arkansas State Gazette, Little Rock, Arkansas

CHARLEY WILLIAMS, who always keeps a supply of the latest papers at the Anthony House, and WM. CHRISTOPHER, conductor on the Overland Mail line, have again placed under obligations by furnishing files of the latest papers.

February 1, 1861
$30,000 Breach of Agreement

February 1, 1861
The Arkansian, Fayetteville, Arkansas

George W. Swon has recovered a verdict of $30,000 for breach of agreement by Geo. Chorpenning, in an **overland mail** contract.

February 1, 1861
Ending Mail Service to Southern States

February 1, 1861, page 2
The Constitutional Union, Des Arc, Arkansas

WASHINGTON, JANUARY 24. – House – Mr. Hamilton, of Texas, desired to offer an amendment to the Post Route bill.

Mr. Colfax, before accepting the amendment, wished to know whether Texas was going to remain in the Union.

Mr. Hamilton said he could only say, as one of its citizens, that he trusted she would not withdraw. He believed that if Congress would treat her fairly as a member of the Confederacy, that it would have the effect of keeping her in; and such treatment as had been recently according in voting for the support of a mounted regiment, etc., would make it to her advantage to remain in the Union. If she withdraws, she would have no right to enjoy **mail facilities** as the expense of the government.

The offered amendment which Mr. Colfax accepted and reported, extends the existing contracts for Texas, so as to connect with the **Butterfield Route**, provided that it can be done for $800,000, and a semi-weekly connection with New Orleans.

The article below mentions the capture of the Little Rock Arsenal. This lithograph, is entitled, "United States Arsenal at Little Rock, Arkansas, Surrendered to the State Troops, February, 1861.
Source: Harper's Weekly, March 2, 1861

February 8, 1861
Arsenal at Little Rock Taken Possession

February 8, 1861, page 2
The Arkansian, Fayetteville, Arkansas

FORT SMITH – The **Overland Mail** Conductor says, the U. S. Arsenal at Little Rock was taken possession of by the State troops on Saturday evening last.

February 15, 1861
Murder at Fort Smith

February 15, 1861
The Van Buren Press, Van Buren, Arkansas

SHOCKING MURDER AT FORT SMITH - TWO MEN SHOT AND KILLED. -- A most horrid murder was committed at Fort Smith, on Monday night last. The particulars of which, as we learn from a friend residing there, are as follows:

At about 11 o'clock on Monday night, some employees of the **Overland Mail Company,** entered the Grocery of Mr. John P. Hagg, evidently with the intention of having a quarrel, which ended in Hagg and his barkeeper named Burch being shot. Burch in the heart, dying almost instantly, and Hagg between the temples, who lived until about 11 o'clock Tuesday morning.

Two of the supposed murderers have been arrested, and at our latest advices, were undergoing an examination.

Two others implicated, it is supposed, have fled south, as two men were seen about day-light on Tuesday morning, some sixteen miles north of here on the Fayetteville road, engaged at that time in cutting the Telegraph wire.

They took horses belonging to the **O.M. Company**, and it is hoped they may be arrested and brought to the punishment that they so richly deserve.

Mr. Hagg was a quiet, inoffensive and much respected citizen of Fort Smith, where he has long resided, and his untimely death has cast a gloom over that community. He leaves a wife and several children to mourn his sudden death.

February 23, 1861
Texans Seize Overland Stagecoaches

February 23, 1861, page 2
Arkansas State Gazette, Little Rock, Arkansas

FORT SMITH, ARK., FEB. 20. – Extra **Overland Mail** coach from Sherman, Texas reports the Texans had seized the **Overland** coach with the mail. They also seized the company's property and imprisoned its agents and other employees.

It was reported Forts Chadbourne and Belknap had been captured.

February 23, 1861
Mail Service Discontinued in Seceding States

February 23, 1861, page 2
Arkansas State Gazette, Little Rock, Arkansas

WASHINGTON, FEB. 10. SENATE. – The committee on post offices reported without amendment the House bill discontinuing the mail service in seceding States.

March 1, 1861
Hoax – Overland Mail Seized by Texans

March 1, 1861
The Arkansian, Fayetteville, Arkansas

THE **OVERLAND MAIL**. – The report that the **Overland Mail** etc., had been seized by the citizens of Texas turned out like many of the rumors of the times, to be a hoax, gotten up perhaps for electioneering purposes: while upon this subject and to show the position taken by the civilized Indian tribes, through whose territory the **Overland Mail** passes, in relation to the federal Government and the southern Confederacy, we learn from reliable authority, that at Greenwood during the sitting of the Circuit Court at that place on the 20th inst., Mr. Neil an intelligent gentleman of the Chocktaw Nation, in a public speech announced that it was the intention of the Chocktaws to follow the destinies of the southern Confederacy, and to that end they had appointed Commissioners to the Convention of this State as also the Confederated Congress. In addition to this below will be found a paragraph from the *Dallas Herald,* clearly showing to our submission friends that the Indian tribes adjoining Texas are up with the times and are determined not "to eat dirt," or buy a peace at the expense of personal honor. Read the extract:

The *Dallas Herald* is informed by a gentleman from the Red River tier of counties, that the Indian Tribes immediately adjoining Texas are wholly in favor of uniting with the South and utterly hostile to abolitionism. The intelligent portion of these Indians are well posted in regard to the questions that now distract the country and have made up their minds to cast their lots with the section that is identified with them in interest.

They are represented as bitterly opposed to Forts Cobb and Washita falling completely into the hands of the Federal forces and their northern allies. – We should not be astonished to hear of some demonstration against those places at an early day.

March 8, 1861
The House Votes on Overland Mail

March 8, 1861, page 2
The Van Buren Press, Van Buren, Arkansas

St. Louis, March 3rd. -- In the House, yesterday, (2d) the Senate amendments to the Post Office bill was taken up and concurred in by 117 to 43.

It was presented in the Senate by Wilson and the annual present **Butterfield Mail Route** to California by El Paso, which now cost $600,000 for semi-weekly letter source, but during the remainder of their contract time 3 1/2 years, gives them the Central Overland Route in lieu of the other. They are to carry it daily at $1,000,000 and deliver the mails at Denver and Salt Lake tri-weekly, and run a pony express, semi-weekly carrying 5 bags each trip for Government free of charge, and reducing costs of letters by said express $1.50 an ounce.

If **Butterfield & Co.**, fail to accept this before the 25th of March, the present contract be absolutely annulled, and central route contract to be let to the lowest bidder not to exceed one million, entire.

Letter mail to be carried through in 20 days, and the residue, in 35 days, with privilege of sending letter by steamer in 25 days at contractor's expense, and the latter to receive two month's pay for change of service from southern to central route

But the **Butterfield company** were required by Mr. Colfax and Sherman's amendments to enter into a written agreement to be filed in Post Office Department, and to be incorporated into their contract, agreeing to carry 600 pounds mail matter per trip, which would take all the daily papers, besides letters and likewise relinquishing all claims for damages, provided in Senate's amendments. After debate was concurred in exactly as it came from the Senate. So it is now a law.

It reduces the cost of mail service to California from $1,437,000 to $1,000,000; increases service to daily; concentrated mail-carrying on one line and abrogates the **Butterfield Company's** contract, without incurring any claims for damages.

March 8, 1861
Will Mail Contractors in Seceding States be Paid?

March 8, 1861

The Arkansian, Fayetteville, Arkansas

WASHINGTON, FEB. 19 – The mail contractors in the seceding States are continually asking whether they will be paid as heretofore, to which the Post Office Department responds affirmatively, stating that drafts will be issued to them on the Post Masters, to be paid from the postal revenue collected within the State. The Postmaster General has removed the route agent between Grafton and Parkersburg, Virginia, on the ground that he left his business, without permission, to engage in the secession movements in that State. Several Postmasters have been removed for a similar cause.

Mr. Brown, late editor of the *Constitution* has been deputized by the seceding States to inform the Federal Government of the election of Jefferson Davis; he will not be recognized.

Mr. Lincoln will occupy, temporarily, the dwelling on Franklin Square, lately occupied by the South Caroline commissioners.

March 8, 1861
The End of Butterfield's Overland Mail
Southern Ox Bow Route

March 8, 1861

The Van Buren Press Van Buren, Arkansas

STOPPAGE OF THE **OVERLAND MAIL** TO CALIFORNIA. – We learn, by telegraph, that the contract for the transportation of the **Overland Mail** on the **Butterfield** route, is to be abrogated. We are sorry to learn this, for no mail over so lengthy a route has ever before been transported with such celerity and certainty as this had, and we are sure that on a more northern route when it is hereafter ordered to be carried, that failure must and necessarily will be of common occurrence, especially in the winter season, when snows are certain to be an obstruction.

The California mail through this section of country had become to be considered as a fixed fact, and was an regularly looked for on time as any of the local mails, and we cannot see any good grounds for its abrogation.

The mail has been carried to California by **Butterfield & Co.**, under the present contract, and over the present route with more efficiency than it is possible to make over any more northern route, except it be the 35th parallel, and its abolishment seems to us, must be taken as a sectional movement on the part of the Black Republicans in Congress. The mail on this route, we are informed, will stop on the 25th inst.

March 9, 1861
Mail Service to Continue in Northern States

March 9, 1861, page 2

Arkansas State Gazette, Little Rock, Arkansas

WASHINGTON, MARCH 5. – The mails, unless repelled, will continue to be furnished in all parts of the Union, as far as possible. The people everywhere shall have that sense of perfect security which is most favorable to calm thought and reflection.

March 12, 1861
Butterfield's Southern Route Ends

March 12, 1861, page 3

The Daily True Democrat, Little Rock, Arkansas

WASHINGTON, MARCH 12. – A contract has been signed for daily mail to California over central route, and a tri-weekly by pony express; time of the former sixteen days, and latter eight days. *[This article was also printed in the March 15, 1861 issue of The Constitutional Union, Des Arc, Arkansas.]*

March 14, 1861
Butterfield's Steamboat No Longer Stuck in Indian Territory

March 14, 1861, Thursday

The Daily True Democrat, Little Rock, Arkansas

ARRIVALS - March 8 Jennie Whipple from Memphis

DEPARTURES - March 9 Jennie Whipple for Fort Smith

March 14, 1861
Contract to Replace Butterfield's Southern Route has Been Signed

March 14, 1861, Thursday, page 3

The Daily True Democrat, Little Rock, Arkansas

WASHINGTON, MARCH 12 – A contract has been signed for daily mail to California over central route, and a tri-weekly by pony express; time of the former sixteen days, and latter eight days.

[Note: This article was repeated the following day in the same newspaper.]

March 29, 1861
Butterfield Company to Move to Central Route

March 20, 1861

The Van Buren Press, Van Buren, Arkansas

ST. LOUIS, MARCH 15. -- Senator Latham has succeeded in getting a tri-weekly mail-service from St. Francis to Los Angelos with the weekly service to San Diego.

A contract was closed for the movement of the **Butterfield Company** to the central route with service from St. Louis to Placerville, California, in 16 days, daily, Sundays included. Also a pony express three times a week in eight days.

The service to commence the 15th of June. The contract was signed in Washington, today, and the **Overland** is continued till the establishment of the central service as above.

April 6, 1861
Ad Directed Toward The Overland Mail Co.

April 6, 1861, page 4
Thirty-Fifth Parallel, Fort Smith, Arkansas

OVERLAND MAIL COMPANY,
ATTENTION.

WHIP STOCKS, LASHES, &C., for sale low at M. MAYERS & BRO.
Nov. 29, '59. No. 1, Com. Row.

BUGGY and Stage Whips, Stalks, Spurs, fine English Bridles, and Sadler's material at
Oct. 18, '59. M. MAYERS & BRO.

Source: April 6, 1861, Thirty-Fifth Parallel, Fort Smith

April 6, 1861

April 6, 1861, Saturday
Thirty-Fifth Parallel, Fort Smith, Arkansas

...arrived *[at Fort Smith]* ...the **Jennie Whipple**... on the 4th, each boat brought large lots of freight for our merchants.

April 11, 1861
Last Trip of Jennie Whipple
Under Butterfield's Ownership

April 11, 1861, Thursday
Arkansas True Democrat, Little Rock, Arkansas

ARRIVALS – April 7 Jennie Whipple from Fort Smith

DEPARTURES – APRIL 7 Jennie Whipple for parts unknown

April 25, 1861

Jennie Whipple Carrying Arms for Union Army

April 25, 1861, Thursday

Arkansas True Democrat, Little Rock, Arkansas

TELEGRAPHIC – Des Arc, April 16 – To Gov. RECTOR:

It is reported here by the officers of the Golden State, just from Memphis, that the **Jennie Whipple** passed Memphis on her way to the Arkansas River with United States government arms and ammunitions of war. Her name is rubbed out.

[Note: This is the last mention of the Jennie Whipple in any Arkansas newspaper. *In the late summer of 1861, the* **Jennie Whipple** *began to be used frequently for the transportation of Union troops. The Memphis Daily Avalanche reports on December 25th that the "United States government has a line of packet running between this point and Cairo. The boats are the* **Jennie Whipple**, *and..."*

However, before and after this date, the **Jennie Whipple** *continued to advertise for passengers and freight. The Union government requisitioned into service the* **Jennie Whipple** *as the newspaper implies. However, General Grant permitted the* ***Jennie Whipple*** *to also continue its normal route.*

William J. Peterson, in his book, Steamboating on the Upper Mississippi, writes: *"Upper Mississippi steamboats did heroic work during the Civil War. Many of the boats were requisitioned into service by the government. In this group were such well known steamboats as the Kate Cassel, the* ***Jennie Whipple****, and the Ad Hine. In this way transportation was often crippled – at least temporarily. There was general rejoicing when General Grant permitted the* ***Jennie Whipple*** *to continue plying between Fort Madison and Rock Island."*

May 30, 1861
Butterfield is Closed, But the Mail Still Ran on Portions of the Route by Other Stage Lines

May 30, 1861
The Fayetteville Democrat, Fayetteville, Arkansas

ARRIVAL AND DEPARTURE – THE MAILS; FAYETTEVILLE, ARKS.

OVERLAND MAIL

Going South, arrives Wednesdays and Saturdays, at 6 P.M.; leaves 1/2 past 6

Going North, arrives Wednesdays and Saturdays, 7 P. M.; leaves 1/2 past 7.

June 29, 1861
Overland Stages Captured

June 29, 1861, page 3
Arkansas State Gazette, Little Rock, Arkansas

Syracuse, Mo., June 17. – Jackson is reported at Pomme-de-etterre with 1,200 men! **Overland Mail** coaches and teams are in Jackson's possession.

[NOTE: Pomme de Terre Lake is located in southwest Missouri at the confluence of Lindley Creek and the Pomme de Terre River. The lake is located in southern Hickory and northern Polk Counties, about 50 miles north of Springfield. Its name is the French language word for potato.]

1869

[NOTE: I have included the following newspaper clipping because it reveals that even 8 years after the end of the Butterfield Overland, the road conditions in Arkansas were still causing delays of the stage coaches of John T. Chidester. This round trip between Little Rock to Memphis includes stagecoaches, steamboats, and trains.

September 18, 1869
Chidester Stage Line Praised
Horrible Road Conditions Persist

September 18, 1869, Saturday, page 4
Daily Arkansas Gazette, Little Rock, Arkansas

Availing himself of the invitation of Chidester, Searle & Co., to accompany them on the first trip overland to Memphis of their stages, the city editor of this paper, in company with the *Republican* local, left for Memphis on Monday last, by the renovated route. What he saw and heard on the Memphis road, the new route, and many other things, can be gathered from the following:

Little Rock to Devalls Bluff –

We left Huntersville at 7:30 a. m., and arrived at the Bluff, a short time after one o'clock p. m. This was nearly a six hours run, which was occasioned by a lack of water and a large amount of hay scattered over the rails, in transportation, compelling the train to run slow. Usually this trip is made in from three to four hours, and sometimes in two hours and a half. The distance is about 45 miles. When we left the rain descended in torrents, and continued to fall at intervals during the whole of the day and night. Devalls Bluff presented rather an uninviting appearance at this time. To say it was muddy would convey but a faint idea of the truth – it was disgustingly muddy and disagreeable, and we left as soon as possible.

Devalls Bluff to Clarendon –

We took passage on the *Fairy Queen*, a beautiful little steamer of the new line, which makes daily trips between the above points. She is neat and comfortable, and is properly named – her officers are cleaver gentlemen, and did everything in their power to make us comfortable. We took dinner on this boat, and were pleased with the variety, style and general appearance of everything connected with her. After a three hours run we arrived at Clarendon, and were immediately transferred to the stage.

Clarendon to L'Anguille –

Our experiences were those usually consequent upon staging. The road at present is in excellent condition. We travelled the military road fifteen miles, to where the line of the Memphis railroad crosses it. Thence, we took the new route, just chopped out, and over which no vehicle had yet passed. It was quite dark, which added to the falling rain and the new road compelled us to go slowly. Two or three times we got out of the road, but nothing serious was the result.

About one o'clock we met Chidester *[John T. Chidester of Camden]* with two stages crowded with passengers coming this way. Chit was walking in front holding a lantern, giving orders, and reminding one very much of the commander of a small army.

After stopping a few moments, and exchanging drivers, both parties were off. Our next stoppage was at the L'Anguille River, where passengers dismounted and walked down the bank to the ferry boat. Several got mired up, and had to call for lights to see their way out. It was still raining when we arrived and the banks of course were slippery, and the mud almost equal to Devall's Bluff. All got over safe, however, and after a ride of about a mile we reached the present terminus of the Memphis and Little Rock Railroad. This was a little after four o'clock in the morning.

Here we met Col. R. D. Williams, the gentlemanly superintendent of the road. After we had breakfasted, the rain ceased, and the sun rose in a cloudless sky. At six o'clock, the whistle of the locomotive announced that it was time to leave.

L'ANGUILLE FOR MEMPHIS.

All aboard, and a run of seven miles brought us to Forrest City, a village that has sprung up since April last, and now boasts its 150 inhabitants, has six business houses, including all branches of trade, including two churches and a hotel, and is becoming a very formidable rival of Madison. One firm at this place, Messrs. Izard, Bro. & Prewitt, told us their sales would reach one hundred thousand dollars during the year. It is situated on the western slope of Crowley's Ridge. The buildings are all substantial, and present a handsome appearance. The country surrounding this new candidate for public favor, is as good as any in the state and those who live there are confident a second Omaha is born.

From Forrest City we proceeded to Madison, a distance of five miles. The deepest cut to be found on the road, is through the Ridge at this place. For a distance of probably a half mile the cut is about sixty feet. Madison is situated on the west bank of the St. Francis River. We observed no new improvements going on. The railroad bridge across the river at this point is a substantial structure. It is a Howe truss bridge. The abutments and piers are built of brick, and it is 665 feet long, including a pivit drawbridge 200 feet long.

From this point we proceeded to Hopefield, stopping occasionally to take on and discharge freight and passengers. Gangs of hands are scattered over the road from Madison to Hopefield, repairing the road, replacing old cross ties with new ones, ballasting the road bed, and making such additions and repairs as are necessary.

A great deal of the iron on this section is bent, and the rocking of the cars is a natural consequence in passing over it. This will also be remedied soon. That portion of the road which has been built this year is very good, equally as smooth as any portion of the road on the western division.

We arrived at Hopefield at 10:30, and thence were transferred to the Bluff City, by the company's ferry boat, Nevada.

Of course we registered at the Peabody Hotel, and take this occasion to thank Colonel Cockrell, and his son for agreeable treatment during our stay. The rooms of this house are elegantly furnished. In fact, everything is carried on in magnificent style. Col. C. remarked that he intended to keep a *good* house, whether he made anything or not. Success to the Peabody.

To the Memphis press gang we are indebted for many courtesies. Also to Col. B. D. Williams, superintendent, R. C. Brinkley, president, and Messrs. H. B. Edmondson and Miles Owen, of the Board of Directors, of the Memphis road, for much valuable information in reference to the prospects of the road, which we will lay before our readers in another article.

Our trip in returning, was mixed with varied experiences. At Edmondson station, fifteen miles out from Hopefield, our engine broke down on the return, and we were compelled to wait about six hours before another could be sent for and obtained. We left that point at 11 o'clock on Wednesday night, and arrived at Huntersville at 6 o'clock Thursday evening. We made this trip really in 19 hours, and believe it can be made in less time. For a quick trip we recommend this route to passengers.

We understand arrangements are now in progress by which the staging will be done in the day time, and the time for reaching Memphis reduced to 20 hours. – when the railroad is completed to the military road, it is the intention to run the Fairy Queen some eight or ten miles up the Cache River from Clarendon, to a point within eight miles of the road. This will leave so little staging that no one would object to the route on that account.

1928

July 3, 1938
Summary of the Butterfield in Fayetteville

July 3, 1938
The Fayetteville Democrat, Fayetteville, Arkansas

The famous **Butterfield** stage ran from St. Louis to San Francisco by way of Fayetteville and Fort Smith. Charles Butterfield, who with his father, owned and managed it, resided in Fayetteville in a two-story brick building located where the Democrat Building now is. This was burned by West Forkers, presumably by the famous Reed Brothers and their gang, after the Civil War. But from 1857 to 1871, it served not only as a dwelling for stage owners, but its upper story was used for a town club.

Barns for the stage line first stood on College Avenue where the Waymon Brown barn later was located and where Heerwagen Brothers garage now is. At another time they were located on West Mountain Street where Harris and Son are in business.

Eugene Fisher, who recently passed away here and whose wife, Mrs. Fisher-Vaughan lives here still, was one of the local stage drivers.

Al Horaman, still living near Fayetteville, was a branch-line stage driver.

One of the Fisher-driven coaches is in existence and until the Vaughan Livery barn was torn down a few months ago, was stored in that building.

Four coaches and 18 horses of the **Butterfield Stage Line** were kept in Fayetteville. *"When the stage horn sounded at the Gunter place,"* relates Mrs. Margaret Blakemore Taylor, *"negroes at my grandfather's tavern, the Byrnside, would put the meal on the table and the stable boys would have fresh horses ready for the coach.*

Charles Butterfield and family came here from Utica, New York, before 1858 when the line was in operation. It ceased running when the Civil War opened.

The Byrnside Tavern, located across from the Washington Hotel, on the southwest corner of the public square, was my grandfather's home. It was burned by Federals during the War. My grandfather left me his property and after an absence from Fayetteville, I returned here a bride in 1856, and to live in 1859, after my grandfather's death. We often entertained at the Tavern, guests from California and even New York. Coming of the stage was the greatest daily event. Mail and all luggage was carried by stage. It also brought students to the Arkansas College on College Avenue."

1958

On September 19, 1958 Van Buren's The Press-Argus (Arkansas' oldest weekly newspaper) issued volume 100 of it's paper - a 64 page special "Centennial Edition issued to commemorate the 100th anniversary of the Butterfield Overland Mail." The issue included a reprinting of the lengthy first person articles by Waterman Ormsby in the New York Herald issues starting September 26, 1858; and a reprint of the lengthy 1858 articles by the special overland correspondent of the San Francisco Evening Bulletin. This special edition also includes a reprint of the Bailey Report, letter from Ormsby's grandson, letter from John Butterfield's greatgrandson, Hiram S. Rumfield letters, passenger William Tallack's articles, photographs and additional articles written for the centennial celebration. This special edition also reprinted a few brief articles from the Van Buren Press of 1858-1861. Several articles from this Centennial Edition are reprinted below.

September 19, 1958
The Van Buren Ferry

September 19, 1958, Section B, page 1

The Press Argus, Centennial Edition, Van Buren, Arkansas

MID-NITE RIDE ON FLAT BOAT ACROSS RIVER, BY RUIE ANN PARK. -- The first **Butterfield** stage of the **Overland Mail Company** to cross the Arkansas River at Van Buren just before midnight on Sept. 18, 1858, just 100 years ago, performed that difficult crossing on a flat-boat ferry.

If the river was low that night, there was one man with a pole to propel the ferry; if the river happened to be a bit high from recent rains up on Lee Creek in Crawford County, Arkansas, or Poteau River in the Indian Territory, then more than one man,with sweeps, propelled the boat. On nights following regular "gully washers" up on Fall Creek, Cove Creek, Mountain Ford, Webber, Foster Branch, Blackburn and Lee Creek, then the stages halted on the Van Buren side of the river and the passengers and horses were forced to "put up" at the Hanger House, a hospitable house with good stables, located on the banks.

Many were the tales that were swapped by the old-timers of Van Buren, in the twilight of their lives, as they gathered down at the river to watch the ferrymen load the stages and to learn the news of the outside world: of what was going on up in 'Old Missoury' or over at Skullyville. My own grandfather and grandmother re-told those tales like other grandmothers and grandfathers did. The Confederate veterans on the shady side of Main Street exchanged stories of that by-gone time, while the knot of Federal veterans on the sunny side of the street reminisced on the situation down at the ferry landing when the town was sacked by their forces.

The names of the Phillips, Drennen, England, Hayman and Scott families, in that order, denote that within these early-day families of Van Buren the ferry held a place of prominence and often a means of livelihood, but it was only the Englands and the Haymans who actually performed the task of ferrying the **Butterfield** stages.

Thomas Phillips had the first ferry at Phillips Landing, the village in the canebrakes that was named Van Buren in 1831, when the post office was established.

When John Drennen arrived in 1828 at Columbus, a small town one mile below Phillips Landing and on the same side of the river, Thomas Phillips was the ferryman at Phillips Point, as it was sometimes called, and at other times Phillips Landing, and the ferry was a flat boat. It was a link in the highway to the west and the Pacific coast on what was later known as the "35th Parallel Trail."

John Drennen bought out Thomas Phillips' right to the town of Van Buren in 1836, and as previously stated, the original ferry was a flat boat, and a flat boat it continued to be until the latter part of 1850, so states a yellowed newspaper clipping from a history scrapbook belonging to Mary Glen Scott Bullock of Van Buren, the great, great grand daughter of John Drennen.

When Mary Glen's great grandfather Col. J. S. Dunham established this newspaper on July 6, 1859, it carried news of the **Butterfield Stages** and on September 21, 1859 the *Van Buren Press* reported on page two that: *"Captain W. F. Eng-*

land has recently given his Horse Ferry Boat a Complete overhaulling and repairing, and has her in complete running order. Movers, drovers, and all others may be assured that they will meet with no detention at the Ferry and that a safe and speedy transit across the Arkansas River is assured them."

On page three, of the same issue, another item stated: *"Ad, by W. F. England His superior Horse Ferry. Good banks on both sides for landing and fl careful attentive ferrymen in attendance. The stages of the* ***Overland Mail Company*** *cross the Arkansas River at this ferry. - W. F. England."*

On the same page three, the following ad appeared: *"Ferry Boat for Sale -- I have for sale a new Ferry flat, length about sixty feet, has been in use only one month and will be sold cheap. W. F. England."*

And so we know without question from the facts given and other sources that W. F. England was operating the ferry when the first **Butterfield Stage** crossed the Arkansas River, and we know from the old files of this newspaper, as quoted above, that England had installed the "Horse Ferry" by September 21, 1859, a year later.

When Waterman Ormsby, reported for the *New York Herald,* only through passenger on the first west bound **Butterfield Stage**, crossed the Arkansas River at Van Buren on the night of September 18 a century ago he wrote that, *"We crossed the Arkansas, in a flatboat much resembling a raft, at Van Buren, a flourishing little town on its banks."*

He also mentions the soft bed of the flats on the other side owning to the low state of the river, so we know the faithful one man and his pole took the first ferry over the water and landed it safely on the Fort Smith side.

In the late '50's, (1858 to be exact) H. C. Hayman came to Van Buren for the second time on persuasion of the famous steamboat captain and river man, Captain Phillip Pennywitt. He built a mill for Captain Pennywitt after his arrival and sometime later he built the first power ferry boat, a rotary tread that had two blind horses operating it. It was this style of boat that was in use in the very early days of the Civil War when General Blount with his Federal forces captured Van Buren, according to Mary Glen Bullock's scrapbook, which her distant and aged relative, the late Crawford County Historian Miss Clara Eno assisted her in collecting.

But we have another source of information about Hayman's ferry and it is this reference from the series of articles written by Tallack, an English traveler who was a passenger on a **Butterfield Stage** in late summer of 1860, that has caused confusion and has made historians report that the first **Butterfield Stages** crossed on a hooded-log raft and other contraptions. They quote Tallack without stopping to explain that Tallack, himself, says, *"This line of stages had been established two years previously, for the by-weekly conveyance of a portion of the California mails eastward, and with permission to take four 'through passengers...'"* Tallack was returning to Europe from a trip to Australia and had calculated on taking the usual route form California to New York via Panama and then to return to England on a regular steamer, when he changed his mind and decided to take the adventure of riding this new **stage line** that had the world talking. That is how he happened to be going through Van Buren.

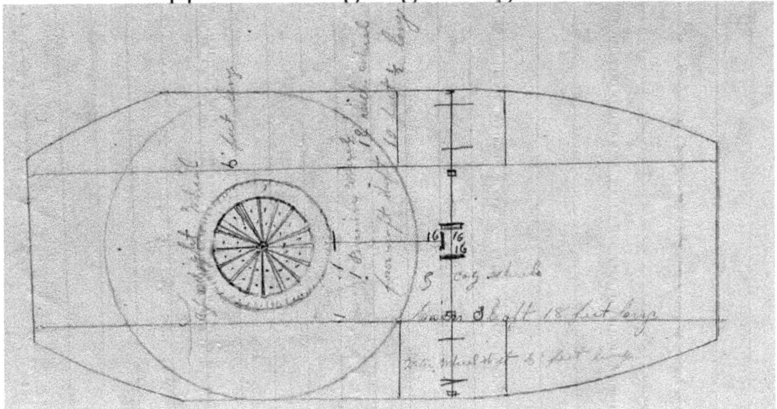

Van Buren's Treadmill Ferry

Published here for the first time, this 1861 hand drawing was discovered in 2025 by Tom Wing in the papers of the Scott Drenen House.

He wrote articles to the *"Leisure Hour"* magazine in London, the articles published in their entirety in this edition. He reports on this section of the route by writing, *"In the evening we crossed the Arkansas River on a ferry propelled by two horses walking around a sort of treadmill, or nearly horizontal wheel, communicating motion to the paddles This kind of locomotive power we had not previously met with, nor did we see any recurrence of it subsequently."*

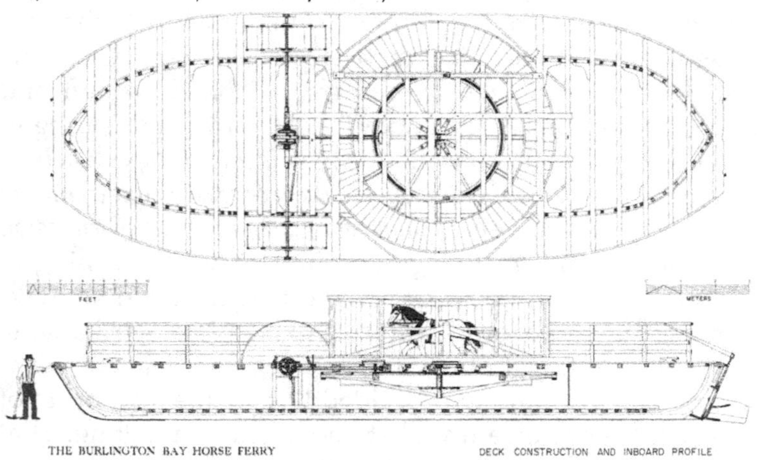

Figure 63. Horse ferry interior profile and deck construction. Drawing by Kevin Crisman.

Sketch Found on the Internet, Similar to Van Buren Ferry

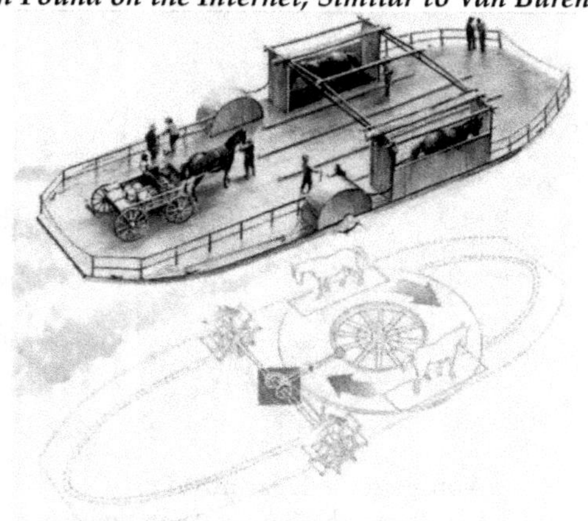

Sketch Found in the 1989 National Geographic of Similar Ferry

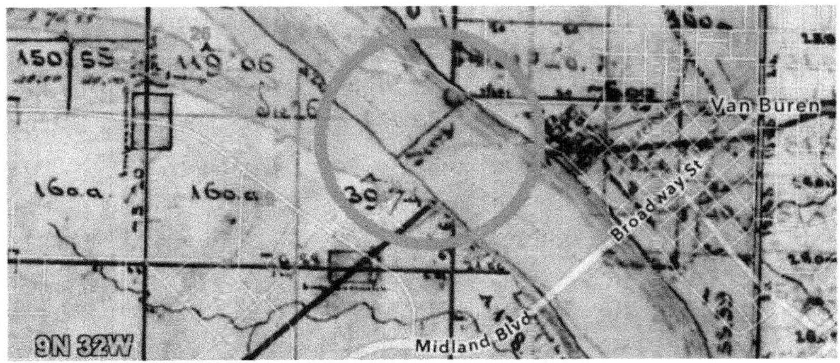

Van Buren Ferry Site from 1850's Survey

Henry Clay Hayman was an expert in power machinery. He was so understanding in his special field that he was induced to come out from Ohio by the famous Captain Pennywitt and Hayman, then built a ferry, so fine that the like of it had never been seen before by the English world-traveler, Tallack.

Hayman was born in Brown County, Ohio, in 1827, the son of Sampson and Elizabeth Reeder Hayman...

September 19, 1958
The Brodie Station

September 19, 1958, Section B, page 2
The Press Argus, Centennial Edition, Van Buren, Arkansas

HIRAM BRODIE OPERATED STAGE STATION IN LEE CREEK VALLEY. -- Hiram Brodie's **Butterfield State Station** at Lee Creek post office was situated in one of the most picturesque valleys in the Boston range of the Ozark Mountains, in a secluded spot where the drafts of winter winds did not reach it with a full onslaught, and where the fertile soil of the valley provided well for Hiram's family and stock.

Hiram was in the valley as early as 1840 for he is found there in the federal census of that year. It lists him as "Hiram Brawder" but that was a mistake of the assistant census marshal, or 'taker' as he was called in the hills, and not the fault of Mr. Brodie. He was there in the federal census of 1850, and in March of 1854 he was listed as the postmaster at Lee Creek post office, a thriving little village on a frontier wilderness trail *"that is nobody knows how old."*

Brodie's advent into the valley must have closely coincided with the arrival of the Mobley brothers, of whom at least two were soldiers of the Revolutionary War.

For all the proof, that Hiram must have been a prosperous farmer, there is evidence, also, that he was adept with horses, and that he provided well for them, and knew the trade of making harness, a trade followed in Van Buren years later by his descendants. Looking to the west from the front porch of the old double log Brodie-home-station, one could see far across the creek bottom farm land that sloped down to Lee C:reek and enclosed the acres in a semi-circle.

It was this stream that made his mountain valley property so valuable and his soil so rich, but it also was this stream that became so very, very treacherous when swollen by its many swift mountain tributaries.

There is Cove Creek, Fall Creek, and Elmore Creek, besides many smaller streams, that rush down the steep hills and gorges with a demon-like swiftness after torrential rams. A story goes that on one of these occasions, an entire family, that of Old Man Marty Farmer, was drowned and their bodies and home washed a way by the on rush of Fall Creek.

Coming down from Fayetteville up north, the Hiram Brodie stage stand, the **Butterfield Coaches** passed Hog Eye and Park's station and Strickler on their way to the Lee Creek crossing, just one mile north of the Brodie home. The conductor forded the stage across the stream just south of the old Bryant cemetery and somewhat east of the present bridge.

Old timers have passed the word down that the horses "hit the creek" ford at an angle, headed across the stream in a southwesterly direction and come out on the south side near the large rock boulders placed there in eons past by nature. The horses climbed the bank and headed toward Hiram Brodie's station through what is now the picnic grounds on the bank of the stream. Here it was that the conductors sounded his horn because the signal always was given upon approaching a station and from about a mile away.

Just before the outbreak of the Civil War in April of 1861, Hiram Brodie moved his family to Van Buren. This is known because he was living in Van Buren on Jan. 5, 1861, when a mass meeting was held at the courthouse in that town.

Hiram Brodie was a citizen of the place and was a member of the committee on resolutions *"to maintain and defend the rights and institutions of the slave-holding States at every hazard and to the last extremity,"* according to a news story in the *Van Buren Press* at that time. He was living at Lee Creek in the late summer of 1860 because he is listed there in the federal census of that decade.

When Col. J. S. Dunham started the *Van Buren Press* on July 6, 1859, he began copying his accounts in an old ledger book This ledger is among valued historical collections belonging to the newspaper and Editor and Mrs. Hugh Park. The accounts give many gleanings of Hiram Brodie's nature and business activities in those years. At the outbreak of the war and those immediately following.

According to the ledger, Hiram, on Jan. 25, 1861, was charged with ads in Col Dunham's paper to the sum of $20 for advertising the Planters' Hotel which Brodie had opened in this town. On Sept. 12 of that same year, Hiram was listed· in the accounts as having had two copies of the Press sent by mail for three months. The cost of the subscriptions being $1.25. On May 2 of 1861, Hiram spent $3.00 with Col. Durham for hand bills for the hotel...

In the old Brodie family Bible, the possession of Hiram's great, granddaughter, Miss Margaret Brodie, of Van Buren, the death of Hiram is recorded. He died Feb. 9, 1875, and was buried In Fairview cemetery. By his side is buried his wife, Matilda Brodie...

To get a picture of the Hiram Brodie family, when the

Butterfield stages were stopping at his home, partaking of meals at his table, changing the stage horses in his stables. and evidently changing drivers according to old records, it is necessary to draw a few conclusions and go to the federal census records of 1860, those reliable recordings that never fail the researcher when all else is past and gone.

Hiram Brodie would have been a very substantial citizen of Lee Creek post office, and would have been a good provider, would have been a trusted person, and one who could be depended on in all circumstances to fill his contract with **John Butterfield Sr.** and his **Overland Mail Company**. For **Butterfield** was particular whom he chose to run his stations and the stations, themselves must be the very best the section afforded. The horses must be good, their care must be excellent, the rations for the animals of a good quality, and the meals for the stage passengers substantial and as well cooked and served as was possible.

Gathered around at the Brodie homestead on the 4th day of August 1860, when D. Dickson, Assistant Census Marshal, quite a prominent person from down at the county seat of Van Buren came up on the Hiram Brodie porch and invited himself in to list every head in the household for the United States government up in Washington City, was, perhaps, the entire family and others.

The family was among the inhabitants of Lees Creek (Dickson put the 's' on Lee in that order) post office in Lees Creek Township. He turned to page 126 in his book and listed Hiram's dwelling in the order of his visitations as No. 846, and the Brodie family as being the 318th family to record.

Hiram, no doubt, gave the important information. which was copied exactly as recorded from the sheet in the National Archives:

Hiram H. Brodie, 47, farmer, real estate $5,450, value of personal estate, $1,1551 place of birth, Tenn.
Matilda, 40, place of birth, Tenn.
David W., 17, farm laborer, place of birth, Ark.
Josephine, 14, attended school within the year, place of birth, Ark.

James, 11, attended school within the year, place of birth, Ark.
Charles S., 9, attended school within the year, place of birth. Ark.
William, 5, attended school within the year, place of birth, Ark.
Annie H. Masse, 18, $1,400 personal property, born in Mo., attended school within the year.
George W. Evans. 25, stage driver, born in Pennsylvania

It is this last named inhabitant of the household who holds a special significance in the **Butterfield** story, for it is known that drivers for the **Overland Mail** did live in Crawford county. We find one at Brodie's station, and on own the old route south toward Van Buren at the next **Butterfield station** in Crawford county. Woosley's station stand, two miles south of Cedarville, two other drivers were living.

What ever became of these drivers is not known...

(page 3) It does not take too vivid imagination to visual the double log house that stood originally...

September 19, 1958
The Woosley Station

September 19, 1958, Section B, page 3

The Press Argus, Centennial Edition, Van Buren, Arkansas

SECOND STATION IN COUNTY WAS LOCATED SOUTH OF CEDARVILLE. - For a mother and a father to lose their only child is a grief that surpasses human understanding and consolation but oo.. cause this happened to the family of George Woosley· (most often pronounced Oosley) who operated the second **Butterfield scheduled stage station** in Crawford county.

Coming toward Van Buren from the north, there is a touch of historic sentiment attached to the site of the old stand that carries a significance all is own. "When the federal census was taken in 1860 in Jasper township in the county. George Woosley, age 25, and his wife, Sarah E., age 28, were the parents of a little daughter, age 7, Sarah Woosley, named for her mother.

By the time the Civil War broke upon the family, who operated the **Butterfield stand** two miles south of Cedarville, on the old wire road, little Sarah had died. She was the first of the well to do clan of Woosleys to die, so they set aside a plot of ground a half mile east of the home station and there under the towering cedar trees they laid little Sarah to rest.

Because there were so mans beautiful trees on the spot in that early day and because their child was the first to be buried there, they named the sacred ground "'Sarah's Grove." Through the years others were buried there and then on Dec. 7, 1862, William Woosley was mortally wounded at the Battle of Prairie Grove.

The family took the ox wagon and oxen and went and brought his body home to also rest in "Sarah's Grove." He is believed, without almost a single doubt, to have been little Sarah's father's brother and was the son of James Woosley (who was listed in the federal census of 1860 as livi.ng in the same neighborhood) and his wife, Patience.

Miss Lillie Matlock of Fort Smith, who is in her '80's and is the oldest native born person of the Woosley neighborhood living today, says she remembers that when she was a little girl the grave of the child, Sarah Woosley, and that of William Woosley ware enclosed with bricks and that the whole of the Woosley lot, or section, of the cemetery was enclosed with a brick wall.

Today, there are piles of crumbled bricks scattered about where the Woosleys are buried and no definite mounds to designate one grave from the other, although Sarah Grove cemetery is well cared for and is still a popular burying ground.

In a list of the very early settlers of Crawford county, the name of James Woosley is found several times; he undoubtedly was the father of George, the **Butterfield station Master.**

In 1855, the well known Judge John B. Ogden and wife, Jane B. Ogden of Van Buren, sold a tract to James Woosley; in 1853, James Woosley and wife Patience had sold land to Alfred Parraek; James Woosley sold land in 1872; James Woosley and Hiram Brodie bought land, 1851; Nathan Woosley, old deed. The Federal census lists Nathan as James son.

According to an announcement in the *Van Buren Press* dated July 6, 1859 (the very first issue of the newspaper) James Woosley was Junior Warden of Van Buren Masonic lodge No. 6. The notice announced the monthly lodge meeting.

Listed by the federal census Assistant Marshall, D. Dickson, on Aug. 7, 1860, when he was making his rounds of the neighborhood where the Woosleys lived in Jasper township, were the following members of the household of George Woosley:

George Woosley. 25 years of age, farmer, $1,500, value of real estate $5,136,. value of personal estate, born in Missouri
Sarah E. 28, born in Arkansas.
Sarah M. 7. born in Arkansas.
Preston Irnes, 26, clerk, born in Missouri.
Michael Maney, 25, stage driver, New York.
M. Dudley, 25, stage driver, Virginia.

James Woolsey was the richest man in that part of the country and one of the wealthiest in Crawford County. According to the census for 1860, he had $50,000 in personal estate, and $1,000 real estate He was:

49 years old, was listed as a farmer and was born in Kentucky.
Patience, was 49 years old, and was born in Missouri.
Joseph P., 13. born in Missouri
Thomas K. 9, born in Arkansas
Nathan, 28, farmer, $11,000 personal estate, born in Illinois;
Elizabeth, 25, born in Arkansas;
Mary E., 1, born in Arkansas; and
Mary Baily, 45, born in Missouri.

It is deducted from experience in the interpretation of census records that Elizabeth was Nathan's wife and that Baby Mary was their child; that they were living with Nathan's parents; that Nathan already had accumulated or inherited quite a fortune himself, for that day and time. Mary Baily could have been Elizabeth's mother, but this is only conjecture.

The George **Woosley's stage stand** was located where the former home of Calvin "Cal" Bassham stands, on the right side of Highway 59 going north and just a few yards north of the Uniontown turn off road that leads toward the community of Dripping Springs.

Bassham lived on the place when the Conklins, famous husband and wife team of history writers, who traveled the original **Butterfield Trail** and studied the stage stand sites in Crawford county, made their trip through here in the late '30's...

... during the Civil War... the home burned and all the Woosley records were destroyed... where once stood the fine old double log home and barns of George **Woosley's Butterfield stage stand**... not one vestige of the old station visible save the old station well...

September 19, 1958
Woosley & Brodie Were Slave Holders

September 19, 1958, Section B, page 3

The Press Argus, Centennial Edition, Van Buren, Arkansas

Station Masters Owned Slaves - Hiram Brodie and George Woosley, the two early day Crawford County settlers who were selected by **John Butterfield Sr.** to master stations in the Boston mountain region of the Ozarks were "well off enough to own slaves, the "Slave Schedules" for 1860 show, as enumerated in mid-summer of that year for the United States government.

The schedule "'taker" visited Hiram at Lee Creak post office on August 15 and made this listing of his slaves:

Hiram H. Brodie- 5 slaves,

one 40 years old, male;
one, 27, female;
one, 10, female;
one, 7, female;
one, 3 female.

Brodie had one "slave house."

The schedule recorded George Woosley in Jasper township owned two slaves but his father. James Woosley, who lived near the stage stand operated by his son, owned nine slaves. Nathan Woosley, another son of James, owned four slaves. The younger Woosley;s slaves were:

1 male, 38'
1 male, 31

James Woosley's slaves were as follows;

1 male, 60 years old;
1 male, 26;
1 female, 23,
1 female 19;
1 male, 9;
1 female 7;
1 female, 21;
1 male. 20;
1 female 40.

George Wooolsey listed one "slave house." and his father, James, owned two "slave houses " The son, Nathan, owned one "slave house" and his slaves were as follows:

1 female, 26
1 male, 25
1 female 4
1 male 2

September 19, 1958
Butterfield Sr. Takes the Reins

September 19, 1958, Section B, page 5

The Press Argus, Centennial Edition, Van Buren, Arkansas

John Butterfield Sr. Drove The Stage Down Main Street- It is said that the only place along the **Butterfield Trail** that **John Butterfield Sr.** ever "took the reins" was at Van Buren. Arkansas.

The request was made to his son, John Jr., on the first trip west by the **Butterfield stage**, and the request being granted, the father took the driver's seat and guided the horses and stage down Main street onto the flatboat ferry landing at. the Arkansas river crossing.

John Jr. had driven all the way from Tipton, Mo., because his father felt that he was the best one for the task. Often at difficult turns or hazardous points on the journey from Tipton, it is said that **John Sr.** would call from inside the stage coach (for he was a passenger to Fort Smith) to **John Jr.**, admonishing him to *"speed up"* or· *"be careful"* as the older **Butterfield** saw the case at the moment.

September 19, 1958
Stage Drivers Overlooked

September 19, 1958, Section B, page 6
The Press Argus, Centennial Edition, Van Buren, Arkansas

DRIVERS OF STAGE GO OVERLOOKED - There has been very little of a personal nature written about the drivers of the **Butterfield Overland Mail Company**, but in Crawford county. Arkansas, at least the names of three are known and a few facts concerning them.

Michael Maney and **M. Dudley** were two stage drivers who lived at the home stage-station of George Woosley up in Jasper township two miles south of Cedarvilie.

Michael was 25 years old in 1860 and was bo:rn in New York. Dudley also was 25 years old and was born in Virginia.

It is significant to a researchers of history to note that the George and James Woosley families had a neighbor, who had a son by the name of Dudley~

This was the case over at the home of Witfield Bourne. Whether there was any relationship that might have been the reason for this coincidence is not known. It is known that the Whitfield Bourne home was a local stage line station stop.

At Hiram Brodie's home stag station at Lee Creek post office in Lee Creek township, there was a stage driver living by the name of **George Evans**. He was born in Pennsylvania. He was 25 years old in 1860. Had it not been for the 1860 census, the names of these drivers, or knowledge of them would never have been recorded in this special edition.

For although books written about the **Butterfield** story mention the drivers, yet the facts are in general terms, with little personal detail. The majority of them were picked by

John Butterfield Sr. from his drivers in the east. They were the best from the Mohawk Valley and other sections where he had run stages. They were young men, and men versed in the care and driving of horses, under the best or worse conditions.

If either of the three young men who lived in Crawford county and drove the stages remained in Arkansas their descendants have failed to rise up and call them blessed, for absolutely nothing ever "turned up" about them, after the stage quit running here.

September 19, 1958
Butterfield Employee Writes Home
Details About Missouri & Arkansas Trail

September 19, 1958, Section D, page 1
The Press Argus, Centennial Edition, Van Buren, Arkansas

THE RUMFIELD LETTERS, FORT SMITH, JUNE 22, 1860 -

As soon as Possible after my arrival here (Fort Smith) on Tuesday morning I wrote you, and wrote ..somewhat hurridly as the **Overland Mail** for Saint Louis was then about due, and I did not wish to lose the opportunity by any means. I have thought that it might be of interest to you to learn something of the character of the country through which I passed after leaving the western terminus of the Pacific Rail Road, from which place I wrote you the evening before my departure for this remote region.

From **Syracuse to Springfield**, a distance of one hundred and thirty miles. a vast stretch of prairie, interspersed with occasional patches of hazel, shumach and scrub oak, intervenes. The road is firm and smooth and but few hills are met with of sufficient height to interrupt rapid driving. The surface of the ground is somewhat undulating and the soil generally harsh and gravelly and in many places of considerable extent, absolutely barren. If brought under the influence of proper cultivation much of it would doubtless prove highly productive. But of this I cannot speak advisedly, as throughout the entire portion of the State of Missouri, lying between the points named above, few improvements, amongst the many to be met with, will compare favorably even with the worst class of farms in any of the older portions of Ohio. A general and almost unvarying aspect of indolence, ignorance and shiftlessness characterizes the country throughout. The farm houses are constructed of the rudest materials and the most barbarous styles of architecture.

Dwelling houses, out buildings and fences, that have long since reached a chronic stage of dilapidation, do not seem to suggest to their respective owners the necessity of timely repairs to save them from utter demolition. Farming implements are of the most antiquated kinds and are permitted to rust and rot at the places they were last used.

The space by the road side in front of each house is generally filled up with the ruins of old wagons, sleds and harrows scattered about in promiscuous confusion, and a profusion of empty whiskey barrels too plainly indicates the true cause of the miserable slothfulness which is everywhere so plainly apparent.

Fruit and shade trees which are reared and cherished with such tender care by the thrifty and intelligent husbandman, are but seldom met with in this region of poverty and indolence. The growing of wheat is generally neglected; whilst corn is to the lazy Missourian what the camel is to the wild Bedouin of the desert. Towns are few and far between, but whenever met with they exhibit the same indications of prevailing sloth, inactivity and negligence, which are so prominently displayed throughout the country. On every hand an indifference to personal comfort is seemingly manifest.

Streets are laid out with the least regard to regularity or convenience, and are more or less obstructed with the accumulationed filth and debris of years.

The **public houses** are execrable beyond conception. Everything in and about them is calculated to excite a feeling of unutterable disgust. A moderately good meal is not to be had at any of them; and indeed would seem beyond the resources and capacity of the country to provide. The nigger cooks are greasy and filthy in the extreme, and appear to display a diabolical ingenuity in making every dish they serve up inexpressibly distasteful to the palate of the traveller. No one not accustomed to such fare, unprovided with the stomach of a mountain trapper, or a California gold hunter, can make much progress in disposing of such unsavory viands, yet for each accommodation of the kind the victimized stranger is obliged to disburse fifty cents, whether he eats anything or not.

Along the entire route north of Springfield we found an extreme **scarcity of water**. Throughout the entire state of Missouri but little rain had fallen since the opening of spring. Creeks were almost everywhere dry, and the few wells the country affords, exhausted by the extraordinary drain upon the liquid stores. At each station where the horses were changed the thirsty passengers would sally up ahead in search of a sip of nature's beverage, but in many instances they would meet with but indifferent success. Water we seldom failed to find in these periodical rambles, but none that I could have partaken of at home.

And then the utensils we were compelled to drink it from! Frequently from a gourd, but that would do very well. Sometimes from a pan lathered over with clots of sour milk; several times from the buckets which had served to supply the horses; once from an old rusty tin wash bowl which was thus brought into double service by the frugal housewife.

On another occasion a long walk at night following a devious path that led far into the wilderness brought us to a spring of muddy water, to drink of which the only available thing at hand was a portion of an article of crockery which shall be nameless— hut which many years ago, when entire, may have occupied a place beneath the bridal bed of the obliging matron who directed us to this refreshing spot.

Some miles north of **Springfield** the road leaves the plain and winds its way along the Ozark Mountains upon the summit of which the town is situated. The location is a beautiful one and the surroundings such as are calculated to inspire the enthusiastic lover of rugged natural scenery with feelings of sublimity. But unfortunately the town adds nothing to the charm, and a breakfast at the only hotel it contains will certainly dissipate any romantic notions that may have previously found their way into the head of the joumeyist.

Pursuing our way over the mountains we found the road extremely rough and circuitous. No open plain meets the eye and a succession of steep and rocky hills render travelling dangerous and wearisome. Woods on either hand so thickly studded with vines and spread oak as to be almost impenetrable to a rabbit, imparts a gloomy aspect to the highway.

For 56 miles after leaving the last named points, no town and but few settlements are met with. The **Mail Company's stations** are built by the road side and afford accommodations alone for the drivers, station men and horses.

Springs abound in these mountains. The water boils up through a mass of broken white flint stone and is incompatibly excellent. No filtered rain water cooled with northern ice would I prefer to a draught fresh from these pure sparkling springs of the wild Ozarks, when drank beneath the impenetrable canopy of foliage that shields them from the rays of the southern sun.

Travelling along day and night through this solitary region we at length come to **Fayetteville**—a lovely town in Arkansas, 110 miles from Springfield, and 60 miles from this place. The town reposes upon the mountain tops, and is handsomely shaded by deep files of trees that line the streets on either hand.

It contains a court house, several churches and many fine private residences, and is the seat of the University of Arkansas.

From the steps of the court house I there witnessed the sale of a **slave boy** — a spectacle that was indeed grating to my feelings.

From **Fayetteville to Van Buren** the point where the Arkansas river is first reached, the road lies through high and rugged mountains, the wild scenery of which is occasionally diversified by valleys covered with corn, many of which are in the form of an oblong circle and of one or two thousand acres in extent. No one who has never passed over this road can form any idea of its bold and rugged aspect. It winds along the mountain sides over a surface covered with masses of broken rock, and frequently runs in fearful proximity to precipitous ravines of unknown depth. Over such a route as this the coaches of the mail company are driven with fearful rapidity. The horses are seldom permitted to walk even when traversing the steepest and most tortuous hills, and when drove at their utmost speed, which is generally the case, the stage reels from side to side like a storm tossed bark, and the din of the heavily ironed wheels in constant contact with the flinty rock, is truly appalling.

The man who can pass over this route a passenger in one of the **Overland Mail Coaches**, without experiencing feelings of mingled terror and astonishment, must certainly be oblivious to every consideration of personal safety.

Yet with all these indications of danger and recklessness, accidents rarely occur, and since the Mail Company has been established, not a single life has been lost on this part of the route.

The **coaches** are built expressly with reference to rough service—and none but the most reliable and experienced drivers are placed upon the mountain districts. The horses are of the most powerful description to be found, and when once thoroughly trained to the service perform the laborious run with apparent pleasure and delight.

Although my letter is already extended beyond the limits originally intended I must not conclude without saying something more in relation to this place. I must say that I have been very agreeably disappointed in whatever pertains to the town and the inhabitants thereof.

Stores well stocked with goods of every quality and

description to be found in the older towns of the northern states, are numerous. One establishment in the large three story brick block across the street contains more good than can be found at Sullivan's.

Drug stores there are two; one of which is as handsomely fitted and furnished, and contains as large a stock as any concern of the kind I have yet seen in Cleveland.

There is a **bonnet and dress making** establishment where everything in that line of business is got up agreeably to the latest eastern styles and patterns.

The general appearance of the town is rather prepossessing to the stranger, than otherwise.

There are three churches of moderate architectural pretentions, and a female seminary of fine external appearance and which is said to be well conducted and liberally sustained.

There are several **hotels** in the place (Fort Smith). That at which we board is said to be the best kept, and affords accommodations with which I am tolerably well satisfied. The only drawback consists in the fact that the rooms being large contain two or more beds each and accordingly no one can get a room for his exclusive use.

The **servants** of which there is a large number for a house no larger than the City Hotel, are all slaves. They seem to perform their respective duties with alacrity, and are not so importunate for an occasional quarter as their brothers of the north.

Slaves are numerously held in and about the town and are universally full blooded blacks. Indeed I do not remember having seen a single mulatto since I came into Arkansas. As free "niggers," are not permitted to live in this state every colored person met with is presumptively a slave.

Indians of various tribes, (or nations as they are here called) are seen in large numbers about the streets every day. They come into town from the Territory usually at an early hour in the morning, and spend the day loafing among the various whisky shops fronting on the river. At night they return home as peaceably as they came and no one but themselves seems the worse of their coming—the rum-sellers certainly not. They generally ride good horses, and many of them are men of property, and hold slaves. Every where in the Territory the sale of ardent spirits is peremptorily prohibited which accounts for the regularity of their visits to this place. All along the western border of this state the whites drive a lucrative business at the expense of the "poor indian" whose proverbial appetite for strong drink leads him into the wildest excesses.

I came into possession of the keys of the office yesterday— the duties are neither arduous nor perplexing so far as I can judge from the brief experience I have had.

A word or two in relation to the **climate**. We have had pretty warm weather since my arrival here, but it does not enervate the system to the extent that the same degree of heat in the north causes us to feel. Owing to some atmospheric peculiarity it is almost impossible to contract a cold. I have slept with the windows open in a strong current of air without experiencing the slightest ill effects therefrom. This you know I could never do in Ohio, without endangering my health.

I have heard nothing from you since I left home. I shall be grievously disappointed if I do not get a letter by Sundays mail. Do not fail to write to me as often as you can as you can readily imagine how anxious I am to hear from you. I hope that you will soon become reconciled to our brief separation and if things go on as I now have reason to expect, we will try our for time for a time at least,—if providence has so ordered—in this handsome and social little city, situated upon the border of civilization.

In the meantime be of good courage. I meant to say a word or two to the dear little children but feel much fatigued with the labor of writing this long letter. Say to Mary that I will write her a nice little letter by the next mail. Kiss the children one and all for me. My respects to Mr. & Mrs. Beilhartz and the girls; also to Mrs. Craig and all others who may inquire concerning my welfare. Remember me to Angaline and the Little Anny.

Very. truly your loving Husband,
HIRAM.

P. S. Should you have any trouble in reading this letter get Mr. Beilhartz to read it for you, but show it to no one else, that is, to no person out of his family.

September 19, 1958
Butterfield Employee Writes Home
Details About Overland Mail Co. Operations

September 19, 1958, Section D, page 2
The Press Argus, Centennial Edition, Van Buren, Arkansas

THE RUMFIELD LETTERS, FORT SMITH, AUGUST 9, 1859 -

... Robinson has gone to the Red River Valley in Texas for the same object that induced the sons of Jacob to go down into Egypt to buy corn. A supply is wanted to distribute along that portion of the route above named, a distance of about 500 miles. Such is the **scarcity of grain** that in order to obtain a supply and distribute it at the points needed it will have to be wagoned hundreds of miles at an average cost, including transportation, of at least five dollar per bushel. From this you will be able to appreciate some of the difficulties encountered in keeping the "Overland" in a state of efficiency. There is not one bushel of grain to be had on the line between this point and Fort Chadboume.

The **drought** has absolutely destroyed every-thing. The grasshoppers have even perished from want of sustenance...

Last Monday night, **Old Sol**, as we familiarly called him, my principal assistant in the office, **was shot** by a Cherokee Indian, in front of the Saint Charles Hotel. The pistol ball entered near the navel and penetrated the abdominal cavity. The unhappy affair occurred about 11 o'clock. I was asleep in bed when one of the conductors aroused me, and informed me of the melancholy event. As soon as possible I hurried to the office where I found the wounded man lying on a cot, surrounded by a crowd of sympathising friends, and a doctor engaged in probing the wound.

At first sight I was convinced that the injury was mortal, though the doctor assured him that it was not necessarily so. I had him removed to the City Hotel as soon as possible where he lingered in intense agony until Tuesday evening when death kindly interposed and his sufferings were at an end. The duty of preparing for his funeral mainly devolved upon myself. Everything was done decently and in order. The funeral was appointed to take place at 11 o'clock yesterday morning. The Rev. Mr. Sample of the Presbyterian Church who, at my request had been with Sol some hours before his death, conducted the services in the great-hall of the Hotel. He preached a short but impressive discourse, and denounced the practice of carrying fire arms in the most emphatic manner. After the services the corpse was borne to the cemetery. Four large 4 horse coaches belonging to the Mail Company were first in the procession after the hearse, and were followed by many carriages and buggies belonging to the citizens and kindly tendered for the occasion. It afforded me a melancholy pleasure to witness so numerous an attendance, and the degree of sympathy that seemed to pervade the community in behalf of the unfortunate man.

Sol was formerly from Utica, New York, and came out here with the parties by whom the **Mail Company** was established, about two years ago. He was unmarried as far as we can ascertain. He was of a wealthy family, but had long since squandered his patrimony in riotous living. We Informed his friends east of the circumstances attending his death. I have always found him a useful and reliable man, and am fearful that we will not find another soon who can discharge the duties that pertained to his position with the same degree of energy and efficiency.

I enclose you one of the notices I had prepared for the funeral. The Indian was arrested soon after the occurrence that terminated so fatally. Today I have mainly devoted in preparing for his examination which is set for tomorrow. The mail has just arrived at the door and I must stop. I will write again on Saturday.

My health continues good. You must not be alarmed on my account as it regards the "Injuns" shooting one as I have nothing to say to them and keep "o' nights" like a good boy. You know that I am afraid of nothing, but I have always thought that prudence was the better part of valor and this principal I act upon. My love to the children and yourself.

In haste Truly your affectionate husband,
HIRAM

September 19, 1958
Butterfield Employee Writes Home
Details About Overland Mail Co. Operations

September 19, 1958, Section D, page 2
The Press Argus, Centennial Edition, Van Buren, Arkansas

FORT SMITH, ARKANSAS, SEPT. 25, 1860. - MY DEAR WIFE—

... **disastrous fire** was then raging on the opposite side of the street, and the devouring element threatened aU that was valuable in the city. Fortunately— I might say providentially—the morning was calm, otherwise the scene of destruction would have been fearful to contemplate. As it was, the principal buildings destroyed were the Garrison block and **City Hotel**, the latter being the house at which we boarded.

The Garrison block was the pride and glory of the city. It was erected some years since at a cost of seventy four thousand dollars, and was exclusively devoted to business. In a room on the second story of this massive pile the fire originated and so rapid was the progress of the flames that every effort to save the building was utterly unavailing. But few goods were saved from the numerous stores the building contained.

The Cline drug stores—the owners of which are cousins to the Yerks of Tiffin—was completely destroyed. The misfortune of these worthy young men is peculiarly sad and deplorable. They were engaged in the business some seven years and at the time of the disaster their drug store was one of the largest and best arranged establishments of the kind to be met with any where.

Originating in a room immediately above, the fire soon found its way through the intervening floor, and, in an instant the entire concern was enveloped in a sheet of flame. They had no insurance whatever, and thus in the brief space of a few minutes they were reduced from comparative wealth to a state of penury.

The **post office** was in Clines store; and not a single letter out of some four thousand, exclusive of the **Overland Mail** from Memphis, was saved. Among this mass of ill fated letters was one for your own dear self, which I had written and mailed the day before in expectation of the Overland mail the ensuing night...

The furniture of the City Hotel was mostly saved. The alarm was about the hour of four in the morning. As soon as I could get down stairs, I aroused the "Overland boys" and ordered a large baggage wagon to the door with all possible expedition. Everything in and about the room I occupied, on which I had any claim, was saved—except my "night shirt" and the coat I wore away with me from Tiffin. These, owing to some cause or other—not very clear to me—could not be found. After arranging for the removal of the effects of this office, in case of necessity, I returned to the Hotel, and remained upstairs aiding in the preservation of the property of the kind hearted McKensie until the advancing flames drove us from the house. The part I performed consisted in removing the furniture, bedding, etc. from the various rooms, and depositing the same at the head of the "great stair way." In this perilous service I was mainly aided by three young ladies— of position in society—where coolness during that trying hour did not forsake them. Various theories prevail as to the origin of this disastrous fire; but the generally received opinion is, that it was the work of design, and this opinion is strengthened by the force of concurrent circumstances to which I have neither space nor time to allude at present...

I am comparatively indifferent as to whether I retain my position here or not; and certainly will have no desire to remain in the service of the Mail Company in any position whatever, unless the controlling parties in New York concede to Robinson the several reforms in management and the enlarged authority he demands... Should the Directory in New York so far ignore the true interests of the Company as to compel Robinson to give way to these insolent and bombastic interlopers, they will discover, at no very remote day, that they have committed an error fraught with incalculable damage to the prospects of this "great enterprise."

Since the fire we have moved our quarters to the Saint Charles Hotel—one square below—this office, towards the river. The fare does not come up to the standard of the late City Hotel, though it is quite passable. I have secured a very comfortable single room—nearly as large as our bedroom at home. It contains a sofa bed, mahogany bureau, and other conveniences to correspond. Take it altogether, and I am much more comfortably situated than before the fire...

I am as ever Truly your affectionate Husband, HIRAM

September 19, 1958
Passengers Account of Arkansas Trail

September 19, 1958, Section D, page 10

The Press Argus, Centennial Edition, Van Buren, Arkansas

Fort Smith, Arkansas, Nov. 25, 18580. - ... About $150 has paid or will pay the whole expenses (fare, provisions, &c.,} of travel of passengers to this place. The eating is mostly had at the stations, the fare consisting of bread, coffee, meat. and sometimes beans, for which is charged 50 cents.

Were I to travel the road again, I would take but one pair of large, warm blankets, a revolver or shot-gun, and the stoutest suit of clothes I could get, with a strong loose pair of boots, as several have had swelled feet, owing to the tightness of their boots. Some cans of preserved fruits will prove a great luxury on the route...

Fort Smith, November 26, 1858 ... This town (Fort Smith)

is located on the site occupied by the Fort, or rather the land pertaining to the fortification.

The houses are most substantial structures, being built of brick and of comfortable dimensions. The Arkansas River river flows conveniently along its suburbs; and the town being built at the head of navigation renders this point one of great importance in the eyes of traders and merchants.

It is supposed that the number of its inhabitants exceeds 2,500 with a rapid influx of emigrants. Every house is occupied that can possibly be had, and others, now used for stores, are in great demand for family residences.

This being the dividing terminus of the **Overland Stage Co's** route, has attracted the attention of land speculators and horse drovers in any quantity.

Gambling flourishes to some small extent, but the faro table is not exposed to public view. It is at this place and Van Buren that the Choctaw, Chickasaw, and other neighboring Indian tribes spend their annual receipts from Government; and it is here also that the **Overland Mail Co.** spend large sums in repairing their stages, feed for horses, and other incidental charges pertaining to the carrying on of such a gigantic line of stage travel.

The fashion of carrying revolvers is recognized here; but a more hospitable and obliging set of inhabitants I have seldom seen. Seeing brick houses, struck me with a most pleasurable relief from adobe buildings and Mexican serapes.

The stage stops at the City Hotel, where most of the persons connected with the **O. L. M. C**. board. On landing at this comfortable adobe.

I was most kindly welcomed by Mrs. J. K. McZenzie the proprietor. Californians could not well fall into better hands, enjoy more pleasant quarters, or obtain choicer fare than they will find here. Yesterday the weather was quite warm and the sun sent down cheering beams of light to gladden the hearts of all sojourners, but today it has been raining, and a gloomy mist hangs over the chimney tops.

Warren Baer, Correspondent
San Francisco *Evening Bulletin*

CITY HOTEL,

AND GENERAL STAGE OFFICE

(FORMERLY ROGERS' HOTEL.)

J. K. McKENZIE, Proprietor.

CORNER OF WASHINGTON AND WALNUT STREETS

FORT SMITH, ARKANSAS.

THE CITY HOTEL, is an old stand, and is situated in the centre of the business part of the city, and is well ventilated in every department, and no pains will be spared by the proprietor, to make those stopping at the house comfortable in every respect.

A fine large stable is attached to the Hotel, and furnished with the best of provender, and attentive ostlers.

Jan. 20th 1858—tf

Butterfield's Fort Smith Home Station, Offices & Stables

Fort Smith Times, May 5, 1858, page 1

September 19, 1958

Passengers Account of Arkansas Trail

September 19, 1958, Section D, page 10

The Press Argus, Centennial Edition, Van Buren, Arkansas

MEMPHIS, DECEMBER 6, 1858.

DELAYS AT FORT SMITH AND DES ARC

On my arrival at Fort Smith, on the 24th of last month, I then and there wrote concerning matters and things that I thought would be of interest to the readers of *The Bulletin.* After being detained there for want of conveyance, for two days, until the morning of the 27th, I started in Reesides & Co.'s tri-weekly coaches for the small town of Des Arc, situated on the White river, Arkansas, being 210 miles from Fort

Smith.

[In Sept. 1858 when the Arkansas River did not allow Butterfield to use his steamboat, The Jenny Whipple, to deliver the mail between Fort Smith & Memphis. Butterfield had to hastily engage Chidester, Reeside & Co. as subcontractors to operate the Overland between Fort Smith and Memphis for the first year.]

I reached Des Arc on the morning of the 29th, and was delayed there three days more, waiting for a steamer bound for Memphis, which I was fortunate enough to obtain on the evening of December 1st. I arrived at Memphis on the evening of the 4th.

Personal Adventure

Our Correspondent Drenched at Dardanelles

The only place of any slight importance bearing the semblance of a village, was Dardanelles, which is nearly equidistant between Fort Smith and Des Arc — located on the Arkansas river. When we reached Dardanelles, it was late at night, and raining in an old fashioned way, worthy of '49 memory.

[The University of Winnipeg's Dr. Danny Blair and Dr. W. F. Rannie, have determined that 1849 was unusually cold and wet, with heavy rainfall that summer causing unusual and protracted flooding.]

We were most unceremoniously turned out of the coach by the driver, and delivered into the charge of the ferryman, who took the mailbags on his shoulder, and, his lantern in hand, told us to follow him to his boat at the ferry landing, about one mile distant up the river. There was no remedy for this unexpected tramp; so, placing our blanket on our backs, and valise in hand, the passengers proceeded to accompany him through a torrent of rain, up the river bank, and across the stream in his small boat. It was well for the coachman that he could not be found when we started on after the ferryman; he certainly would have been roughly handled. We all got soaking wet by the time we reached the coach on the opposite bank, and three of our party were considerably used up next day from the effects of the drenching.

Nine Miles East of Dardanelle Ferry - Potts Stage Station
Kirkbride Potts, postmaster and station agent, built this home in 1858 for his family. This building also served as an official Butterfield Overland Mail Co. home station. This magnificent structure is open for tours Thus.-Sat. 10-3pm in Pottsville, Arkansas. Image: "Potts Tavern" by Gloria McHahen, 1984 Print 83 of 500 in Bob Crossman's collection.

Delay in Reaching Memphis

On arriving at Des Arc, one of the passengers — that's myself — waited for a Memphis boat, while three of them took a passing steamer for New Orleans. The mail for Memphis was sent from Des Arc for Memphis on horseback over the country — being a distance of some 80 miles — while we were left to shift for ourselves in the way of getting to Memphis. The company paid our fare through. This was all right and according to agreement, but I am certain that the department at Washington never contemplated that a delay of five days would take place owing to a want of means of conveyance — being two days at Fort Smith and three at Des Arc.

The road from Fort Smith to Des Arc passes over a very even country, and through forests of oak. The soil looks cold, and much of the country is subject to overflow. We passed many farm-houses, and many fields were under cultivation — producing corn and cotton, but not, I should think, judging from appearances, in any great quantity. At many houses where we took our meals along the route, very little inquiry was made of us as to the nature and character of the route through, but there were always plenty of men and women to inquire about some Jones, Smith, or Thompson who had — many days, or rather years, ago — proceeded to California, and been absent, *"so, so long-very long-ago, and never been heard of more."*

The fare on this portion of the road was of a very ordinary, but the sweetest dish that cheered our hearts was a roast opossum — though we saw nary coon — which I know is not the case with you San Franciscans, who, I suppose, see one daily in your walks along Montgomery Street.

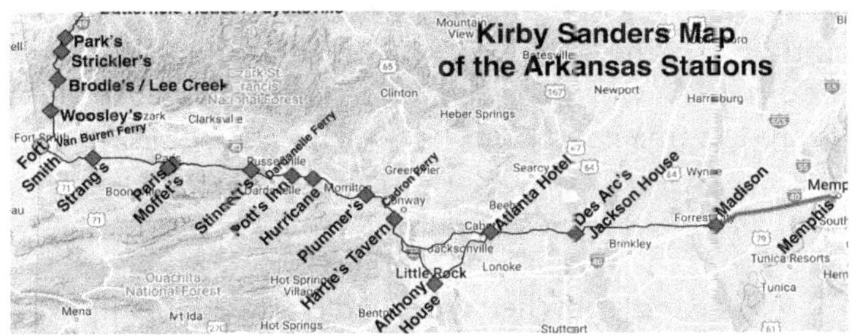

The Butterfield National Historic Trail from Fort Smith to Des Arc
Map by Kirby Sanders

The White River

It is about 300 miles from Memphis to Des Arc by water, and about 80 or 90 by land. White River is a very beautiful stream, free from snags, and resembles in size and appearance the Sacramento. I enclose a card of landings and distances. <This has not come to hand. It was probably overlooked in sealing our correspondent's package.> The stream abounds in trout, perch, and cat-fish, and the passengers amused themselves in shooting geese and ducks from the steamer's deck. It has been raining every day since we left Des Arc — sometimes nearly all day, and then a slight sprinkle the next.

Steamboats at Des Arc (Prairie County); 1860s.
Image source: Courtesy of the Arkansas State Archives

The steamer *"Return,"* on which I came, brought any quantity of game — such as deer, ducks, geese, turkeys, prairie hens*, wild pigeons*, and partridges, all of which appeared in fine condition. *[* The Greater Prairie-Chicken is now extirpated from Arkansas, and the Passenger Pigeon is now extinct.]*

Entering the Mississippi
Thoughts Suggested by It

It was near night when we entered the Mississippi River. Its muddy waters rolled quietly along as though ten thousand skeletons, the victims of steamboat accidents, lay not beneath its surface. No one, after a long absence from the shores of the Mississippi, can contemplate its mighty stream without feelings of awe, amounting almost to trepidation. On each side stand the tall, slender cottonwood trees and the buoyant willows, high up on the trunks of which are the watermarks of the late overflow. Steamers of giant proportions and costly decoration float on its muddy tide, while below the surface of its waters the alligator rattles in his toils the bones of the dead. It may be said with truth that this river has cost more lives than ever it has made fortunes. We passed the wreck of the steamer *"Pennsylvania,"* on our way up, lying between this city and the mouth of White River — in the blowing up of which 250 lives were lost I think it would take many days to make two hundred and fifty fortunes. When we take into consideration the number of steamboats constantly running up and down the Mississippi, the wonder is, not that so many lives are lost, but that more human beings are not destroyed through accident.

Nearly nine years ago, I left the mouth of this famous river, on a journey round the Horn for California, and after so long an interval of time I have returned to its banks, a wiser, I hope, if not a richer man. One knows not whether the flight of Time is the same through all space and over all lands and seas, but it seems to me that his minutes to me, since I left California, have grown into hours, and that he lags in his speed and moves not with such velocity as he was wont in the bracing air of the Pacific.

Early Memphis to Hopefield Ferry, perhaps the ferry "Nashoba"
When steamboats were not available, the Overland Mail crossed from Memphis to Hopefield, Arkansas by ferry, then boarded the train for a short 24 mile trip, where stages carried the mail and passengers the next 2,700 miles to San Francisco.
Image from Gene Gill, www.historic-memphis.com

Description of Memphis

Memphis is, as most of the readers of *The Bulletin* are doubtless aware, located on the east bank of the Mississippi River, 900 miles from the Gulf of Mexico, by the course of the river. Its population is about 30,000, with a daily floating population of some 2,500. The city is about two miles long and one mile wide, with a suburban belt quite closely settled. Besides its river commerce, it has four railroads diverging from its center to the north, south, east and west, viz: Memphis and Ohio — completed 100 miles, intended to connect Memphis and Louisville; Memphis and Charleston — completed through to Charleston, 500 miles; Mississippi and Tennessee — connecting Memphis with the Mississippi Central Railroad at Granada, Mississippi; and the Little Rock Railroad — connecting Memphis with Little Rock, Arkansas, completed to St. Francis river, 40 miles.

1872

Sketch of Memphis from the shore at Hopefield, Arkansas

Steamboat Loaded with Cotton on the Mississippi River

About 370,000 bales of cotton are shipped from this port to all other ports of the United States, being an increase of 60,000 bales over last year.

The soil in the immediate vicinity is peculiarly adapted for brick-making, being of a pure yellow clay. very sticky and tough. As a consequence of this element of city structure, the houses are mostly built of brick, being of large and capacious dimensions, and with great architectural beauty in their structure.

The city *[of Memphis]* itself is placed on a ridge of high bluffs, far above high water, and presents quite an imposing aspect from the *[Mississippi]* river. Steamers are constantly passing and stopping at the levee, which is generally covered with cotton bales and other merchandise. All night long the bells of the departing and coming steamers are sounding their approach or departure.

The greatest ornament, in the way of buildings, in the city, is the Gayoso Hotel, a very handsome edifice, standing out in bold relief, fronting the river, with a prominent portico in front. It is usually crowded with travelers, and its great hall presents a scene of constant confusion, caused by the arrival and departure of passengers.

Image Source: "Memphis Moment: The Gayoso House," by Steve Pike]

The Gayoso Hotel

The dining-room is very large, but the cooking and attendance at table is scarcely more than ordinary. The chambers are lighted with gas, and the servants are mostly slaves, very obedient but very stupid. Its floors are covered with carpet from top to bottom. The furniture is mostly of burnished mahogany. It is a most superb structure, but is only fitted to accommodate travelers whose purses are well filled with the precious dust *[gold dust]*. Liquor sells at the bar for 12½ cents per glass, but, on Sunday, all liquor must be purchased by the bottle, as it cannot be had at this hotel.

Serious Sunday Visages of the People — The Ladies

Last Sunday I walked through the city and all the people whom I met wore most sanctimonious faces, as though under the observance of the vigilant eye of the church. I always allow a certain amount of hypocrisy to all men, but really the individuals I met last Sabbath put me to blush. I should take it, that the collections taken up at the churches afford a comfortable living to the preachers. All the people here dress in black, and look as though they were going to a funeral. Probably, after all, I met nothing but cotton operators, absorbed in deep study.

The ladies here do not dress with that stylish elegance that adds so much to the superb figures of our Pacific belles The faces of the women have not that healthy glow that distinguishes the promenaders on Montgomery and Stockton streets, yet they are of robust figure and no doubt make excellent wives.

The Theaters - Miss Avonia Jones

There are two theaters here — Vy Crisp's Gaiety and the Washington Street Theatre. They are both open at the present time and doing an excellent business.

Miss Avonia Jones is performing at the Gaiety. I saw her as "Juliet" to Mrs. Jones (her mother) as "Romeo." Miss Avonia is rather handsome, with a strong, masculine voice. She has considerable grace in her carriage, and steps across the stage with some majesty; yet, I think, she would appear to better advantage in some tragic character requiring more masculine qualities than Juliet is supposed to possess. However, I saw her but for a night, and may be wrongly impressed by her acting. One of the theaters (the Gaiety) is surely the worst conductor of sound in the United States. Both these seats of the muses are much inferior to the American, in your Sansome street. Court Square, located in the center of the city, is about 450 feet square, in which a variety of trees are planted. It is quite an ornament to the city.

Approaching Home For New Orleans!

Tomorrow I take a berth in some passing steamer for New Orleans, and, I trust, may be as prosperous in the final close of my journey, as I have been favored throughout the long tramp to this place.

The river is rising, and so is my expectation and desire to reach the home of earlier days.

That some, whose faces were, once, more than familiar, and whose voices could be recognized amid the darkest hours of night, have faded from existence, is painfully true; but that many of my former friends still live in the enjoyment of health, is also true. These I trust to find as dear to me as ever; and as faithful in their friendship, kind and indulgent as they were wont to be in my youth, my wayward boyhood.

Warren Baer, Correspondent
San Francisco *Evening Bulletin*

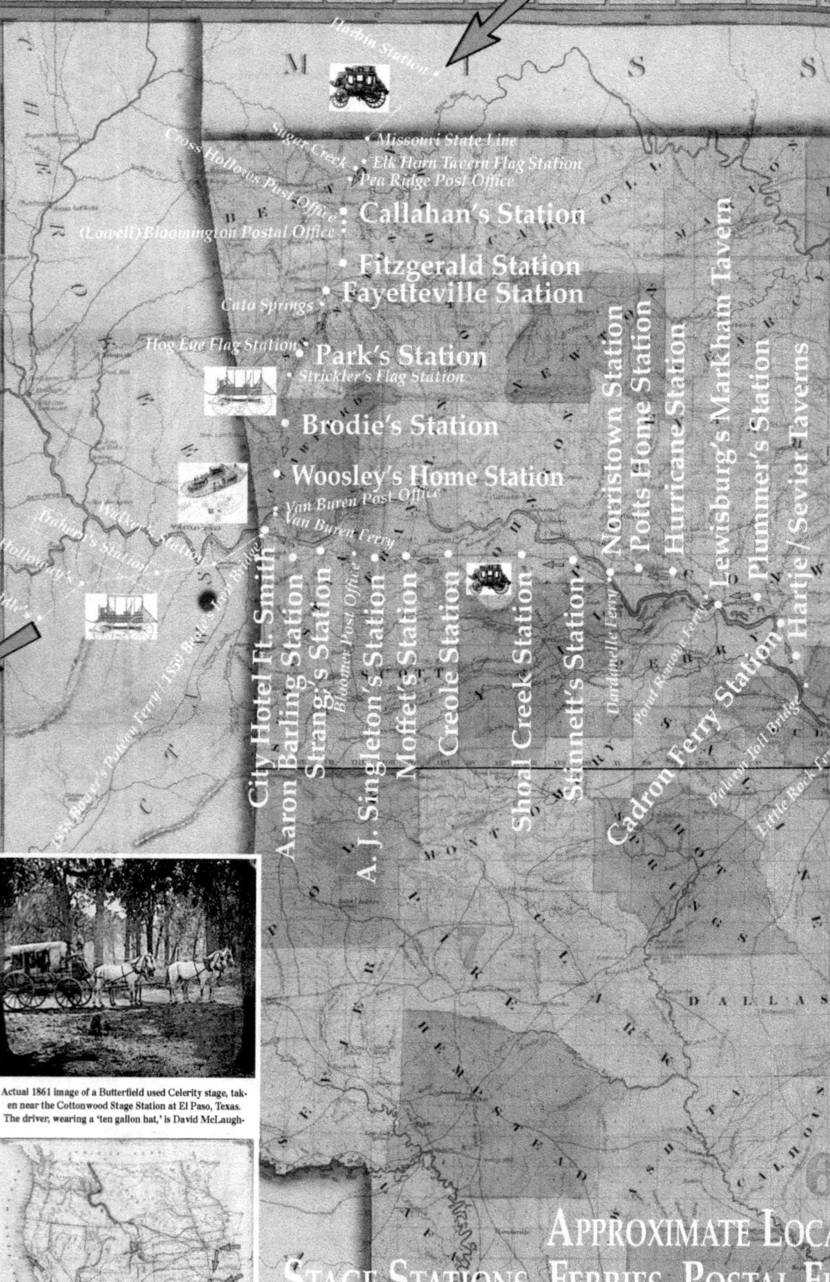

Actual 1861 image of a Butterfield used Celerity stage, taken near the Cottonwood Stage Station at El Paso, Texas. The driver, wearing a 'ten gallon hat,' is David McLaugh-

1859 Map of the United States West of the Mississippi showing the Overland Mail Route to California, by D. McGowan & G. H. Hildt

Red arrows have been added to highlight the Butterfield Overland National Trail.

Approximate Locat
Stage Stations, Ferries, Postal Fla
on the Butterfield Overland N
Across the State of Arka

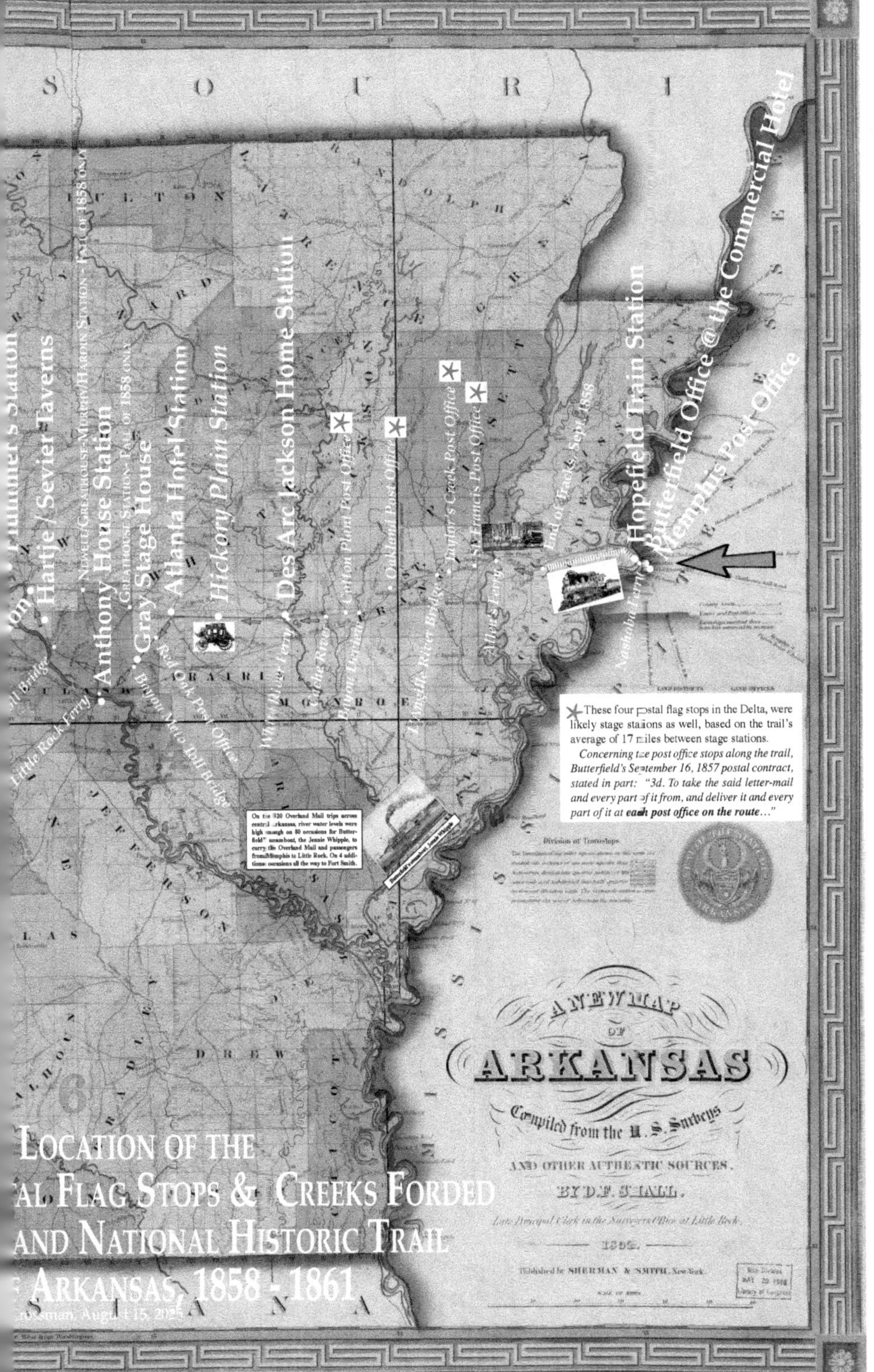

Hartje / Sevier Taverns
Newett/Greathouse-Murphy/Hardin Station - Fall of 1858 only
Anthony House Station
Greathouse Station - Fall of 1858 only
Gray Stage House
Atlanta Hotel Station
Hickory Plain Station
Des Arc Jackson Home Station
Little Rock Ferry
Bayou Meto Toll Bridge
Red Oak Post Office
White River Ferry
Cache River
Cotton Plant Post Office
Bayou Deview
Oakland Post Office
L'Anguille River Bridge
Taylor's Creek Post Office
St. Francis Post Office
Allen's Ferry
End of Tracks, Sept 1858
Nashabah Ferry
Hopefield Train Station
Butterfield Office @ the Commercial Hotel
Memphis Post Office
These four postal flag stops in the Delta, were likely stage stations as well, based on the trail's average of 17 miles between stage stations.
Concerning the post office stops along the trail, Butterfield's September 16, 1857 postal contract, stated in part: "3d. To take the said letter-mail and every part of it from, and deliver it and every part of it at **each post office on the route**…"
On the 320 Overland Mail trips across central Arkansas, river water levels were high enough on 80 occasions for Butterfield's steamboat, the Jennie Whipple, to carry the Overland Mail and passengers from Memphis to Little Rock. On 4 additional occasions all the way to Fort Smith.
Butterfield's steamboat, Jennie Whipple
MISSOURI
FULTON
RANDOLPH
GREENE
MONROE
PRAIRIE
JEFFERSON
DREW
A NEW MAP OF ARKANSAS
Compiled from the U. S. Surveys
AND OTHER AUTHENTIC SOURCES.
BY D. F. SHALL.
Late Principal Clerk in the Surveyor's Office at Little Rock.
1852.
Published by SHERMAN & SMITH, New-York.
Location of the
…al Flag Stops & Creeks Forded
…and National Historic Trail
… Arkansas, 1858 - 1861
…rossman, August 15, 2025

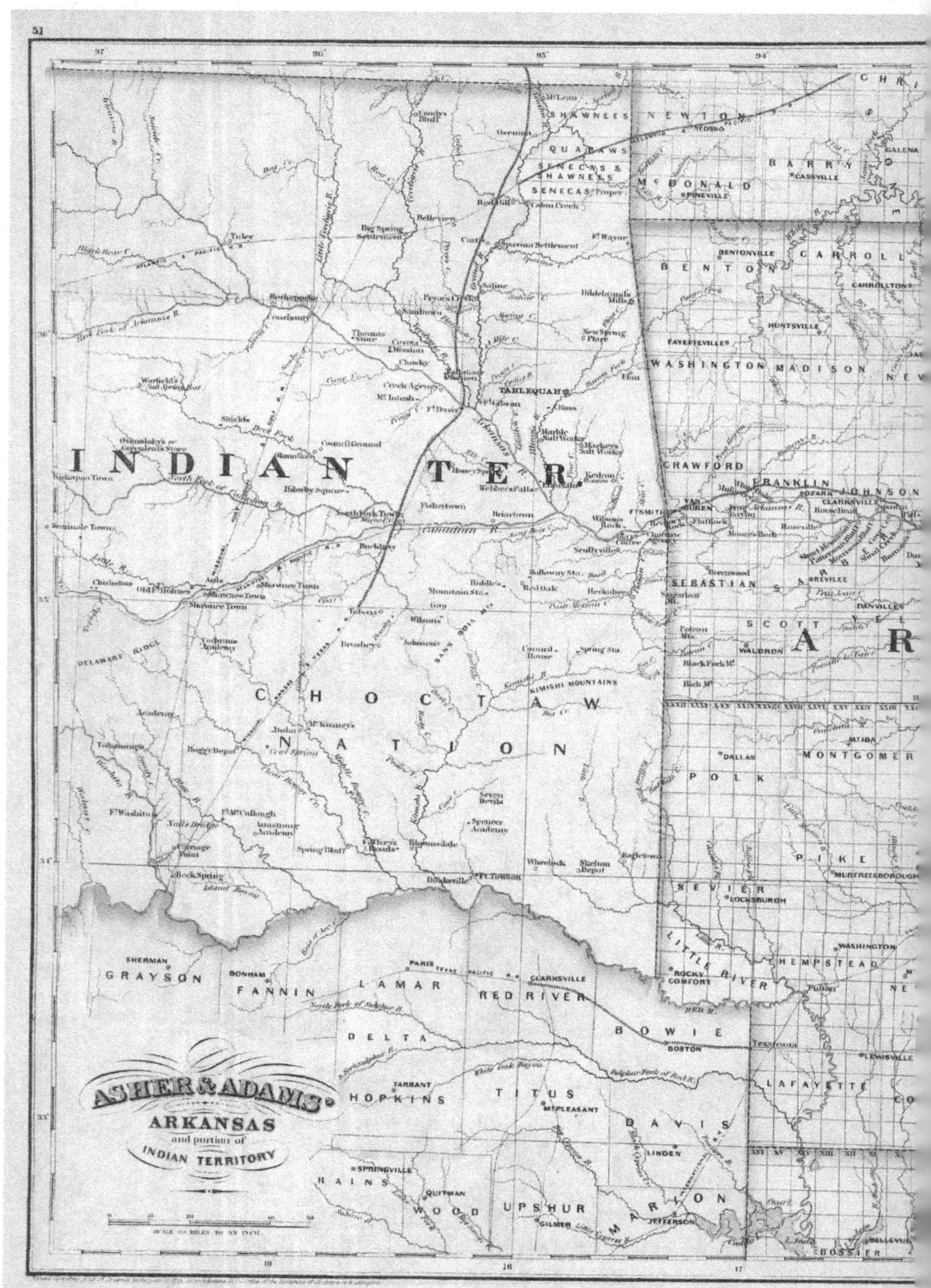
51
97°
96°
95°
94°
INDIAN TER.
CHOCTAW NATION
KIMISHI MOUNTAINS
SAN BOIS MTS.
DELAWARE RIDGE
SHAWNEES
QUAPAWS
SENECAS & SHAWNEES
SENECAS Proper
NEWTON
BARRY
CASSVILLE
GALENA
McDONALD
PINEVILLE
BENTON
BENTONVILLE
CARROLL
CARROLLTON
HUNTSVILLE
FAYETTEVILLE
WASHINGTON
MADISON
CRAWFORD
FRANKLIN
JOHNSON
OZARK
CLARKSVILLE
VAN BUREN
FT. SMITH
SEBASTIAN
SCOTT
WALDRON
DANVILLE
POLK
DALLAS
MONTGOMERY
Mt. IDA
PIKE
MURFREESBOROUGH
SEVIER
LOCKSBURGH
LITTLE RIVER
ROCKY COMFORT
HEMPSTEAD
WASHINGTON
Fulton
Texarcana
LAFAYETTE
LEWISVILLE
BOSSIER
BELLEVUE
A R
TAHLEQUAH
Ft. Gibson
Webbers Falls
Creek Agency
Boggy Depot
Ft. Washita
Skullyville
Doaksville
Ft. Towson
Wheelock
Spencer Academy
Seven Devils
Tishomingo
Seminole Town
Shawnee Town
Canadian R.
Red Fork of Arkansas R.
North Fork of Canadian R.
Arkansas R.
SHERMAN
GRAYSON
BONHAM
FANNIN
PARIS
LAMAR
CLARKSVILLE
RED RIVER
DELTA
BOWIE
BOSTON
TARRANT
HOPKINS
TITUS
Mt. PLEASANT
DAVIS
LINDEN
SPRINGVILLE
RAINS
QUITMAN
WOOD
UPSHUR
GILMER
MARION
JEFFERSON
North Fork of Sulphur R.
White Oak Bayou
Sulphur Fork of Red R.
ASHER & ADAMS
ARKANSAS
and portion of
INDIAN TERRITORY
SCALE 20 MILES TO AN INCH
19
18
17

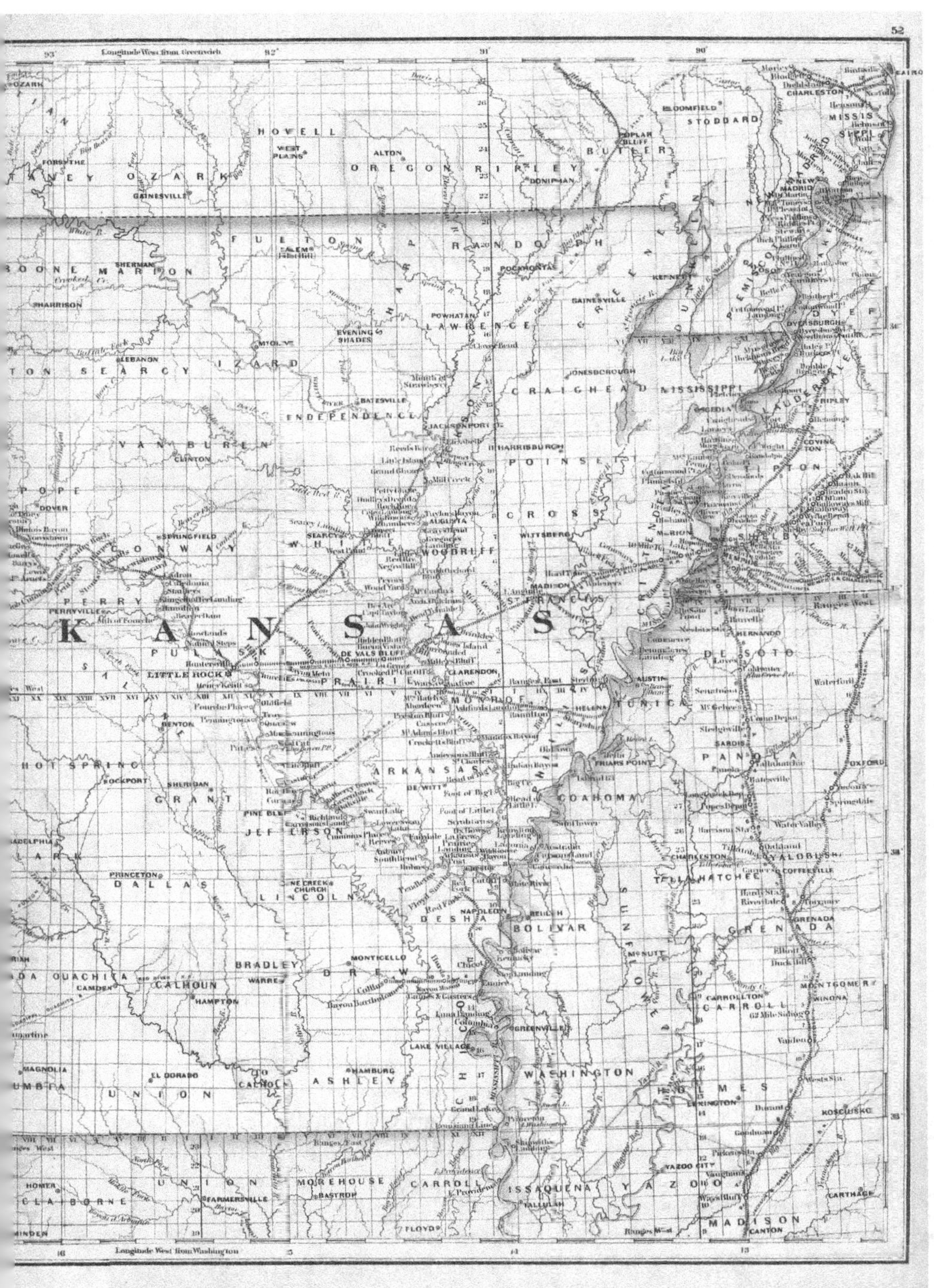
52
Longitude West from Greenwich
Longitude West from Washington
KANSAS
HOWELL
OREGON
RIPLEY
BUTLER
STODDARD
MISSISSIPPI
NEW MADRID
FULTON
RANDOLPH
SHARP
BOONE
MARION
LAWRENCE
GREENE
DUNKLIN
PEMISCOT
DYER
SEARCY
IZARD
CRAIGHEAD
MISSISSIPPI
LAUDERDALE
INDEPENDENCE
JACKSON
VAN BUREN
POINSETT
TIPTON
POPE
CROSS
CONWAY
WHITE
WOODRUFF
SHELBY
PERRY
ST. FRANCIS
CRITTENDEN
PULASKI
PRAIRIE
MONROE
DE SOTO
TUNICA
PHILLIPS
PANOLA
HOT SPRING
GRANT
ARKANSAS
COAHOMA
JEFFERSON
LINCOLN
DALLAS
DESHA
BOLIVAR
TALLAHATCHEE
YALOBUSHA
GRENADA
BRADLEY
DREW
CALHOUN
OUACHITA
CHICOT
CARROLL
MONTGOMERY
WASHINGTON
HOLMES
ASHLEY
UNION
MOREHOUSE
ISSAQUENA
YAZOO
CLAIBORNE
MADISON
CAIRO
CHARLESTON
BLOOMFIELD
POPLAR BLUFF
ALTON
WEST PLAINS
DONIPHAN
GAINESVILLE
POCAHONTAS
POWHATAN
EVENING SHADES
SHERMAN
HARRISON
LEBANON
JONESBOROUGH
BATESVILLE
JACKSONPORT
HARRISBURGH
CLINTON
DOVER
SPRINGFIELD
SEARCY
AUGUSTA
WITTSBURG
MADISON
PERRYVILLE
LITTLE ROCK
DE VALS BLUFF
CLARENDON
HELENA
AUSTIN
HERNANDO
BENTON
ROCKPORT
SHERIDAN
PINE BLUFF
DE WITT
FRIARS POINT
SARDIS
OXFORD
PRINCETON
NAPOLEON
CHARLESTON
COFFEEVILLE
GRENADA
MONTICELLO
CAMDEN
HAMPTON
CARROLLTON
WINONA
GREENVILLE
LAKE VILLAGE
HAMBURG
EL DORADO
LEXINGTON
KOSCIUSKO
YAZOO CITY
CARTHAGE
CANTON
BASTROP
FARMERSVILLE
HOMER
TALLULAH
FLOYD
Ranges West
Ranges East

John Butterfield, President, Butterfield Overland Mail Co.

Newspaper clipping from the files of the Shiloh Museum of Springdale, Arkansas, containing a first person eye witness report from 1858:

"**Mr. Butterfield**, ... a short, thick man, arrayed in a long linen duster reaching to his heels, a low flat-crowned wide brim hat, and boots was a most picturesque character. He was so greatly admired, that the store windows displayed coats, hats, shirts, cravats, and boots similar to the **'Butterfield Wardrobe'** and that no young man of any social standing whether attending church, a public function, or calling on his lady love was considered correctly attired unless he appeared clad in **Butterfield** habiliments. *[habiliments: clothing]*

Source: From the archives of the Springfield Public Library,

"Much history can be found in newspaper articles of the past, but it is a difficult time consuming task locating information about the ***Butterfield Overland Mail Route*** *across Arkansas. Bob Crossman is an excellent thorough researcher whose books are worth the effort."*
Glendle Griggs, Ouachita County Historical Society, Camden, Arkansas

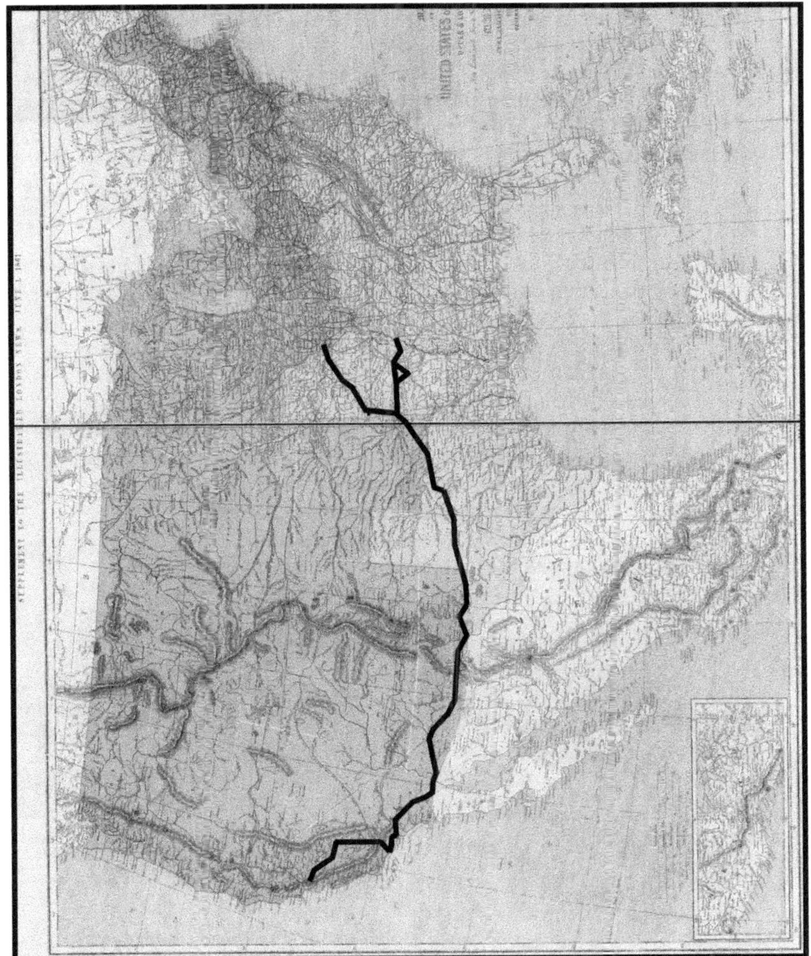

1861 Map of the United States and Mexico by Theodor Ettling
Note at the top of the map reads:
"Supplement to the Illustrated London News, June 1, 1861"
The approximate route of the Overland Mail has been added.

Bibliography of Arkansas Newspapers Quoted in this Volume

Very few issues have survived of some of these newspapers below.
*+, #, ^ or * indicate the source;   ( ) indicate dates of paper available*

+The Arkansian (1859-1861), Fayetteville
#The Arkansas Banner (1850, Oct. 1859 - Apr. 1860), Little Rock
+The Arkansas Gazette (1824 - 1835), Little Rock
+Arkansas Intelligencer (Apr. - Aug. 1858), Van Buren
Arkansas State Gazette (1836 - Dec. 20, 1849, July 9, 1859 - 1861), Little Rock
Arkansas State Gazette and Democrat (1850 - July 2, 1859), Little Rock
#*Arkansas True Democrat (1857 - 1861), Little Rock
#The Constitutional Union (Dec. 1860 - March 1861), Des Arc
#Des Arc Citizen (Nov. 1858 - Oct. 1860), Des Arc
The Press Argus (Dec. 1858 and Sept. 1859), Van Buren
+The Fayetteville Democrat (May 1861), Fayetteville
^Fort Smith Times (April 21, 1858 - Nov. 24, 1858) Fort Smith
+Fort Smith Weekly Herald (Jan. 3, Apr. 11, 1857), Fort Smith
#Southern Shield (Jan. 1860), Helena
+Thirty-Fifth Parallel (July 1860 - April. 1861), Fort Smith
*^The True Democrat (Oct., 14, 1856 - July 8, 1863), Little Rock
^The Van Buren Press (July 6, 1859 - Jan. 23, 1862), Van Buren
+*Weekly Arkansas Gazette (1850 - 1861), Little Rock
+Washington Telegraph (1850 - March 1859), Washington

+ www.newspapers.com
 # www.chroniclingamerica.loc.gov
*** www.genealogybank.com**
^ Arkansas State Archives, microfilm collection

Butterfield's stagecoaches made about 520 trips across the country from September of 1858 to April of 1861.

For more information on Butterfield's use of stagecoaches, see Bob Crossman's book: "Butterfield's Overland Mail Co. STAGECOACH TRAIL Across Arkansas 1858-1861."

Image source: Nita Stewart Haley Memorial Library at Midland, Texas.

John Butterfield purchased The Jennie Whipple in St. Louis. It arrived in Little Rock on December 20. 1858 to carry the Overland Mail.

For more information on the Jennie Whipple, see Bob Crossman's book: "Butterfield's Overland Mail Co. Use of STEAMBOATS to Deliver Mail and Passengers Across Arkansas 1858-1861."

Image source: painting by Ralph Law in the collection of Bob Crossman

About the Author

Dr. Bob Crossman is a member of the Arkansas Historical Association, Faulkner County Historical Society, and the Shiloh Museum of Ozark History.

Bob is also a member of the American Philatelic Society, Little Rock's Pinnacle Stamp Club, American Revenue Association, Carriers and Locals Society, U.S. Philatelic Classics Society, and Tucson's Postal History Foundation.

His interest in stamp collecting began with a Boy Scout stamp collecting merit badge, and later inheriting his father and grandfather's stamp collections.

Bob received a B.A. from Hendrix College in Conway, Arkansas, and received graduate and post-graduate degrees from SMU in Dallas, Texas.

He can be reached at bcrossman@arumc.org

Bob Crossman, 8 Sternwheel Drive, Conway, AR 72034-9391

†✝†

YOU WILL ENJOY ALL SEVEN OF THESE BOOKS ON THE BUTTERFIELD OVERLAND NATIONAL HISTORIC TRAIL

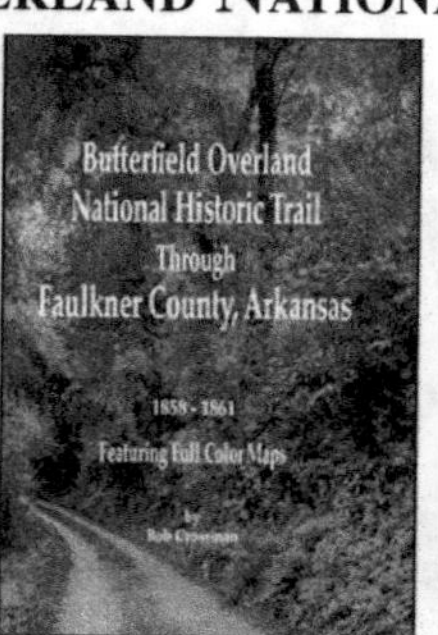

www.ingramcontent.com/pod-product-compliance
Lightning Source LLC
Chambersburg PA
CBHW070518010526
44118CB00012B/1026